D0093591

ARGUABLY

Also by Christopher Hitchens

BOOKS

Hostage to History: Cyprus from the Ottomans to Kissinger
Blood, Class and Nostalgia: Anglo-American Ironies
Imperial Spoils: The Curious Case of the Elgin Marbles
Why Orwell Matters
No One Left to Lie To: The Triangulations of William Jefferson Clinton
Letters to a Young Contrarian
The Trial of Henry Kissinger
Thomas Jefferson: Author of America
Thomas Paine's "Rights of Man": A Biography
God Is Not Great: How Religion Poisons Everything
The Portable Atheist
Hitch-22: A Memoir

PAMPHLETS

Karl Marx and the Paris Commune
The Monarchy: A Critique of Britain's Favorite Fetish
The Missionary Position: Mother Teresa in Theory and Practice
A Long Short War: The Postponed Liberation of Iraq

ESSAYS

Prepared for the Worst: Essays and Minority Reports
For the Sake of Argument
Unacknowledged Legislation: Writers in the Public Sphere
Love, Poverty and War: Journeys and Essays

COLLABORATIONS

James Callaghan: The Road to Number Ten (with Peter Kellner)
Blaming the Victims (edited with Edward Said)
When the Borders Bleed: The Struggle of the Kurds (photographs by Ed Kash)
International Territory: The United Nations (photographs by Adam Bartos)
Vanity Fair's Hollywood (with Graydon Carter and David Friend)

ARGUABLY

ESSAYS BY

Christopher Hitchens

TWELVE

NEW YORK BOSTON

The author is grateful to the following publications in which the essays of this book originally appeared, sometimes in slightly different form: *The Atlantic, City Journal, Foreign Affairs, Foreign Policy, The Guardian* (London), *Newsweek, New Statesman, The New York Times Book Review, Slate, The Wall Street Journal, The Weekly Standard, The Wilson Quarterly, Times Literary Supplement*, and *Vanity Fair.*

Twelve
Hachette Book Group
237 Park Avenue
New York, NY 10017

www.HachetteBookGroup.com

Twelve is an imprint of Grand Central Publishing.

Printed in the United States of America

First Edition: September 2011
10 9 8 7 6 5 4 3 2 1

ISBN: 9781455502776
LCCN: 2011930917

"Live all you can: It's a mistake not to."

—Lambert Strether, in *The Ambassadors*

Contents

To the memory of Mohemed Bouazizi, Abu-Abdel Monaam Hamedeh, and Ali Mehdi Zeu.

Introduction

The three names on the dedication page belonged to a Tunisian street vendor, an Egyptian restaurateur, and a Libyan husband and father. In the spring of 2011, the first of them set himself alight in the town of Sidi Bouzid, in protest at just one too many humiliations at the hands of petty officialdom. The second also took his own life as Egyptians began to rebel *en masse* at the stagnation and meaninglessness of Mubarak's Egypt. The third, it might be said, gave his life as well as took it: loading up his modest car with petrol and homemade explosives and blasting open the gate of the Katiba barracks in Benghazi—symbolic Bastille of the detested and demented Qadafi regime in Libya.

In the long human struggle, the idea of "martyrdom" presents itself with a Janus-like face. Those willing to die for a cause larger than themselves have been honored from the Periclean funeral oration to the Gettysburg Address. Viewed more skeptically, those with a zeal to die have sometimes been suspect for excessive enthusiasm and self-righteousness, even fanaticism. The anthem of my old party, the British Labour Party, speaks passionately of a flag that is deepest red, and which has "shrouded oft our martyred dead." Underneath my college windows at Oxford stood—stands—the memorial to the "Oxford Martyrs": Bishops Cranmer, Latimer, and Ridley, who were burned alive for Protestant heresies by the Catholic Queen Mary in October 1555. "The blood of the martyrs is the seed of the church," wrote the Church Father Tertullian in late first-century Carthage, and the association of the martyr with blind faith has been consistent down the centuries, with the faction being burned often waiting for its own turn to do the burning. I think the Labour Party can be acquitted on that charge. So can Jan Palach, the young Czech student who immolated himself in Wenceslas Square in January 1969 in protest against the Soviet occupation of his country. I helped organize a rally at the Oxford Memorial in his honor, and later became associated with the Palach Press: a center of exile dissent and publication which was a contributor, two decades later, to the "Velvet Revolution" of 1989. This was a completely secular and civil initiative, which never caused a drop of human blood to be spilled.

Especially over the course of the last ten years, the word "martyr" has been utterly degraded by the wolfish image of Mohammed Atta: a cold and loveless zombie—a suicide murderer—who took as many innocents with him as he could manage. The organizations that find and train men like Atta have since been responsible for unutterable crimes in many countries and societies, from England to Iraq, in their attempt to create a system where the cold and loveless zombie would be the norm, and culture would be dead. They claim that they will win because they love death more than life, and because life-lovers are feeble and corrupt degenerates. Practically every word I have written, since 2001, has been explicitly or implicitly directed at refuting and defeating those hateful, nihilistic propositions, as well as those among us who try to explain them away.

The Tunisian, Egyptian, and Libyan martyrs were thinking and acting much more like Palach than like Atta. They were not trying to take life. They desired, rather, that it be lived on a higher level than that of a serf, treated as an inconvenience by a moribund oligarchy. They did not make sordid and boastful claims, about how their homicidal actions would earn them a place in a gross fantasy of carnal afterlife. They did not wish to inspire hoarse, yelling mobs, tossing coffins on a sea of hysteria. Jan Palach told his closest comrades that the deep reason for his gesture was not just the occupation, but the awful apathy that was settling over Prague as that "spring" gave way to a frosty winter. In preferring a life-affirming death to a living death-in-life, the harbingers of the Arab spring likewise hoped to galvanize their fellow subjects and make them aspire to be citizens. Tides will ebb, waves will recede, the landscape will turn brown and dusty again, but nothing can expel from the Arab mind the example and *esprit* of Tahrir. Once again it is demonstrated that people do not love their chains or their jailers,* and that the aspiration for a civilized life—that "universal eligibility to be noble," as Saul Bellow's Augie March so imperishably phrases it—is proper and common to all.

Invited to deliver a lecture at the American University of Beirut in February 2009, with the suggested title "Who Are the Real Revolutionaries in the Middle East?" I did my best to blow on the few sparks that then seemed dimly perceptible. I instanced the burgeoning civil resistance in Iran. I cited the great Egyptian dissident and political scientist (and political prisoner) Saad-Eddin Ibrahim, now recognized as one of the intellectual fathers of the Tahrir movement. I praised the "Cedar Revolution" movement in Lebanon itself, which had brought about a season of hope and succeeded in putting an end to the long Syrian occupation of the country. I took the side of the Kurdish forces in Iraq who had helped write "finis" to the Caligula regime of Saddam Hussein, while also beginning the work of autonomy for the region's largest and most oppressed minority. I praised the work of Salim Fayyad, who was attempting to bring "transparency" to bear on the baroque corruption of the "Palestinian Authority." These were the disparate but not-unconnected strands out of which, I hoped and part believed, a new cloth could be woven.

It was clear that a good number of the audience (including, I regret to say, most of the Americans) regarded me as some kind of stooge. For them, revolutionary authenticity belonged to groups like Hamas or Hezbollah, resolute opponents of the global colossus and tireless fighters against Zionism. For me, this was yet another round in a long historic dispute. Briefly stated, this ongoing polemic takes place between the anti-imperialist Left, and the anti-totalitarian Left. In one shape or another, I have been involved—on both sides of it—all my life. And, in the case of any conflict, I have increasingly

* The best encapsulation of the disordered, sado-masochistic relationship between rulers and ruled in a closed society with a One Man regime is provided, as so often, by George Orwell, who in *Coming Up for Air* wrote of "the processions and the posters with enormous faces, and the crowds of a million people all cheering for the Leader until they deafen themselves into thinking that they really worship him, and all the time, underneath, they hate him so that they want to puke."

resolved it on the anti-totalitarian side. (This may not seem much of a claim, but some things need to be found out by experience and not merely derived from principle.) Several of these rehearsals and excursions of mine were discussed in my memoir, *Hitch-22*, and several of them are reflected here, too, again in reportage as well as argument. I affirm that the forces who regard pluralism as a virtue, "moderate" though that may make them sound, are far more profoundly revolutionary (and quite likely, over the longer term, to make better anti-imperialists as well).

Evolving or honing any of these viewpoints has necessitated constant argument about the idea of America. There is currently much easy talk about the "decline" of my adopted country, both in confidence and in resources. I don't choose to join this denigration. The secular republic with the separation of powers is still the approximate model, whether acknowledged or not, of several democratic revolutions that are in progress or impending. Sometimes the United States is worthy of the respect to which this emulation entitles it; sometimes not. Where not—as in the question of waterboarding, discussed later—I endeavor to say so. I also believe that the literature and letters of the country since the founding show forth a certain allegiance to the revolutionary and emancipating idea, and in a section on American traditions I try to breathe my best on those sparks, too.

"Barbarism," wrote Alain Finkielkraut not long ago, "is not the inheritance of our prehistory. It is the companion that dogs our every step." In writing here, quite a lot, about the examples and lessons of past totalitarianisms, I try not to banish the specter too much. And how easy it is to recognize the *revenant* shapes that the old unchanging enemies—racism, leader worship, superstition—assume when they reappear amongst us (often bodyguarded by their new apologists). I have attempted to alleviate the morbid task of combat here, by writing also about authors and artists who have contributed to culture and civilization: not words or concepts that can be defended simply in the abstract. It took me decades to dare the attempt, but finally I did write about Vladimir Nabokov. . . .

The people who must never have power are the humorless. To impossible certainties of rectitude they ally tedium and uniformity. Since an essential element of the American idea is its variety, I have tried to celebrate things that are amusing for their own sake, or ridiculous but revealing, or simply of intrinsic interest. All of the above might apply to the subject of my little essay on the art and science of the blowjob, for example, while not quite saving me from the most instantly misinterpreted of all my articles, concerning the humor deficit as registered by gender. Still, I like to believe that these small-scale ventures, too, make some contribution to a conversation without limits or proscriptions: the *sin qua non* of the sort of society that knows to keep the solemn and the pious at bay.

This book marks my fifth collection. In the preface to the first one, *Prepared for the Worst*, in 1988, I annexed a thought of Nadine Gordimer's, to the effect that a serious person should try to write posthumously. By that I took her to mean that one should compose as if the usual constraints—of fashion, commerce, self-censorship, public and perhaps especially intellectual opinion—did not operate. Impossible perhaps to live up to, this admonition and aspiration did possess some muscle, as well as some warning of how it can decay. Then, about a year ago, I was informed by a doctor that I might have as little as another year to live. In consequence, some of these articles were written with the full consciousness that they might be my very last. Sobering in one way and exhilarating in another, this practice can obviously never become perfected. But it has given me a more vivid idea of what makes life worth living, and defending, and I hope very much that some of this may infect those of you who have been generous enough to read me this far.

Christopher Hitchens
June 26, 2011

All American

Gods of Our Fathers: The United States of Enlightenment

WHY SHOULD we care what the Founding Fathers believed, or did not believe, about religion? They went to such great trouble to insulate faith from politics, and took such care to keep their own convictions private, that it would scarcely matter if it could now be proved that, say, George Washington was a secret Baptist. The ancestor of the American Revolution was the English Revolution of the 1640s, whose leaders and spokesmen were certainly Protestant fundamentalists, but that did not bind the Framers and cannot be said to bind us, either. Indeed, the established Protestant church in Britain was one of the models which we can be quite sure the signatories of 1776 were determined to avoid emulating.

Moreover, the eighteenth-century scholars and gentlemen who gave us the U.S. Constitution were in a relative state of innocence respecting knowledge of the cosmos, the Earth, and the psyche, of the sort that has revolutionized the modern argument over faith. Charles Darwin was born in Thomas Jefferson's lifetime (on the very same day as Abraham Lincoln, as it happens), but Jefferson's guesses about the fossils found in Virginia were to Darwinism what alchemy is to chemistry. And the insights of Einstein and Freud lay over a still more distant horizon. The furthest that most skeptics could go was

---

Review of *Moral Minority: Our Skeptical Founding Fathers*, by Brooke Allen.

in the direction of an indeterminate deism, which accepted that the natural order seemed to require a designer but did not necessitate the belief that the said designer actually intervened in human affairs. Invocations such as "nature's god" were partly intended to hedge this bet, while avoiding giving offense to the pious. Even Thomas Paine, the most explicitly anti-Christian of the lot, wrote *The Age of Reason* as a defense of god from those who traduced him in man-made screeds like the Bible.

Considering these limitations, it is quite astonishing how irreligious the Founders actually were. You might not easily guess, for example, who was the author of the following words:

> Oh! Lord! Do you think that a Protestant Popedom is annihilated in America? Do you recollect, or have you ever attended to the ecclesiastical Strifes in Maryland Pensilvania [sic], New York, and every part of New England? What a mercy it is that these People cannot whip and crop, and pillory and roast, as yet in the U.S.! If they could they would.... There is a germ of religion in human nature so strong that whenever an order of men can persuade the people by flattery or terror that they have salvation at their disposal, there can be no end to fraud, violence, or usurpation.

That was John Adams, in relatively mild form. He was also to point out, though without too much optimism, the secret weapon that secularists had at their disposal—namely the profusion of different religious factions:

> The multitude and diversity of them, You will say, is our Security against them all. God grant it. But if We consider that the Presbyterians and Methodists are far the most numerous and the most likely to unite; let a George Whitefield arise, with a military cast, like Mahomet, or Loyola, and what will become of all the other Sects who can never unite?

George Whitefield was the charismatic preacher who is so superbly mocked in Benjamin Franklin's *Autobiography*. Of Franklin it seems almost certainly right to say that he was an atheist (Jerry Weinberger's excellent recent study *Benjamin Franklin Unmasked* being the best reference here), but the master tacticians of church-state separation, Thomas Jefferson and James Madison, were somewhat more opaque about their beliefs. In passing the Virginia Statute for Religious Freedom—the basis of the later First Amendment—they brilliantly exploited the fear that each Christian sect had of persecution by the others. It was easier to get the squabbling factions to agree on no tithes than it would have been to get them to agree on tithes that might also benefit their doctrinal rivals. In his famous "wall of separation" letter, assuring the Baptists of Danbury, Connecticut, of their freedom from persecution, Jefferson was responding to the expressed fear of this little community that they would be oppressed by—the Congregationalists of Connecticut.

This same divide-and-rule tactic may have won him the election of 1800 that made him president in the first place. In the face of a hysterical Federalist campaign to blacken Jefferson as an infidel, the Voltaire of Monticello appealed directly to those who feared the arrogance of the Presbyterians. Adams himself thought that this had done the trick.

"With the Baptists, Quakers, Methodists, and Moravians," he wrote, "as well as the Dutch and German Lutherans and Calvinists, it had an immense effect, and turned them in such numbers as decided the election. They said, let us have an Atheist or Deist or any thing rather than an establishment of Presbyterianism."

The essential point—that a religiously neutral state is the chief guarantee of religious pluralism—is the one that some of today's would-be theocrats are determined to miss. Brooke Allen misses no chance to rub it in, sometimes rather heavily stressing contemporary "faith-based" analogies. She is especially interesting on the extent to which the Founders felt obliged to keep their doubts on religion to themselves. Madison, for example, did not find himself able, during the War of 1812, to refuse demands for a national day of prayer and fasting. But he confided his own reservations to his private papers, published as "Detached Memoranda" only in 1946. It was in those pages, too, that he expressed the view that to have chaplains opening Congress, or chaplains in the armed forces, was unconstitutional.

Of all these pen-portraits of religious reservation, the one most surprising to most readers will probably be that of George Washington. While he was president, he attended the Reverend James Abercrombie's church, but on "sacramental Sundays" left the congregation immediately before the taking of communion. When reproached for this by the good Reverend, he acknowledged the reproof—and ceased attending church at all on those

Sundays which featured "the Lord's supper." To do otherwise, as he put it, would be "an ostentatious display of religious zeal arising altogether from his elevated station."

Jefferson was content to take part in public religious observances and to reserve his scorn and contempt for Christianity for his intimate correspondents, but our first president would not give an inch to hypocrisy. In that respect, if in no other, the shady, ingratiating Parson Weems had him right.

In his 1784 book, *Reason: The Only Oracle of Man,* Ethan Allen wrote: "The doctrine of the Incarnation itself, and the Virgin mother, does not merit a serious confutation and therefore is passed in silence, except the mere mention of it." John Adams was prepared to be a little more engaged with theological subjects, in which he possessed a huge expertise, but he also reposed his real faith in the bedrock of reason. Human understanding, he wrote (seemingly following David Hume), is its own revelation, and:

> [h]as made it certain that two and one make three; and that one is not three; nor can three be one.... Miracles or Prophecies might frighten us out of our Witts; might scare us to death; might induce Us to lie; to say that We believe that 2 and 2 make 5. But we should not believe it. We should know the contrary.

From David Hume via ridicule of the Trinity to a prefiguration of Winston Smith! The connection between religious skepticism and political liberty may not be as absolute as that last allusion implies, but there is no doubt that some such connection existed very vividly in the minds of those "men of the Enlightenment" who adorned Philadelphia and Boston and New York and Washington as the eighteenth century evolved into the nineteenth.

In a first-class closing chapter on the intellectual and scientific world that shaped the Framers, Allen discusses the wide influence then exerted by great humanist thinkers like Hume, Shaftesbury, Bolingbroke, Locke, and Voltaire. It became a point of principle as well as of practice to maintain that liberty of conscience and the freedom of the individual were quite incompatible with any compulsion in religion, just as they would be incompatible with any repression of belief. (This is precisely why the French Revolution, which seemed to negate the promise of Enlightenment, was to become such a painful cause of disagreement, and worse, between Federalists and Republicans.)

In 1821 Thomas Jefferson wrote of his hope "that the human mind will some day get back to the freedom it enjoyed 2000 years ago. This country, which has given the world an example of physical liberty, owes to it that of moral emancipation also." I think that Allen is not wrong in comparing this to the finest passages in Edward Gibbon. She causes us to catch our breath at the thought that, at the birth of the United States, there were men determined to connect it to a philosophical wisdom that pre-dated the triumph of monotheism. It is the only reason for entertaining the belief that America was ever blessed by "Providence"—as Roger Williams named his open-minded settlement in Rhode Island, a refuge from the tyranny of Pilgrims and Puritans.

In a time when the chief declared enemy of the American experiment is theocratic fanaticism, we should stand together and demand, "Mr. Jefferson: Build Up That Wall!"

(*The Weekly Standard*, December 11, 2006)

The Private Jefferson

IT IS ARGUABLY A GOOD THING—and in no way detracts from Andrew Burstein's absorbing book—that *Jefferson's Secrets* does not quite live up to its title. Secrecy, death, and desire are the ingredients of the sensational, even of the violent, and they consort ill with the measure and scruple for which Thomas Jefferson is still renowned. It might be better to say that this study is an inquiry into the privacy and reticence of a very self-contained man, along with an educated speculation upon the motives and promptings for his defensive style.

Celebrated for many paradoxes, Jefferson was especially notable as a revolutionary who believed above all in order. Often ardent in his partisanship for rebellion in America and France (though somewhat less so when it came to slave revolts in Haiti and the Old South), he could seem airy and promiscuous with regard to violence. Indeed, he rather commended the Whiskey Rebellion as something desirable for its own sake—"like a storm in the atmosphere." Yet this expression in itself furnishes us with a clue. The outbreak of insurrection, like a storm, was necessary to restore normality by relieving unnatural pressure. The wisdom of nature had provided such outlets precisely in order to forestall, or to correct, what Jefferson was wont to call—always pejoratively—"convulsions."

Burstein, a professor of history at the University of Tulsa, acutely makes

Review of *Jefferson's Secrets: Death and Desire at Monticello*, by Andrew Burstein.

the connection between what men of the Enlightenment considered "the body politic" and what they thought about bodily health. Here, the maxim *Mens sana in corpore sano* was taken very seriously. Excess was to be avoided, in diet and in matters sexual, but so too was undue repression or continence. A true philosophe ought to spend as much time in exercise and labor as he did with books and papers. He should emulate the balance and symmetry of nature. He should be careful about what he put into his system, and cautious about any fluid disbursements from it.

As president, Jefferson began to suffer intermittently from diarrhea (which he at first cured by what seems the counterintuitive method of hard horseback riding), and though he was unusually hale until his eightieth year, it was diarrhea and a miserable infection of the urinary tract that eventually carried him off. In one of his few profitless speculations, Burstein quotes a letter from one of Jefferson's physicians, Dr. Thomas Watkins (whose middle name was Gassaway), in which gonorrhea is mentioned as a possible cause of the persistent dysuria. It seems plain from the context that Jefferson had not contracted gonorrhea, but rather suffered from the traditional woes of an old man's prostate; Dr. Watkins was eliminating gonorrhea as a possible cause, not diagnosing it.

However, the question of Jefferson's sex life does have to be raised at some point. Here again, we find a man who was afraid in almost equal measure of too much gratification and too little. His letters from France contain many warnings of the sexual traps set by Parisian females for unwary and innocent Americans, yet it was his own time in France that saw Jefferson at his most vulnerable and impassioned. I still remember the slight shock I experienced when I read a letter he wrote in Paris to Maria Cosway, full of rather clumsy phallic jokes borrowed from Laurence Sterne's *Tristram Shandy*. And it must have been in Paris that he first had carnal knowledge of Sally Hemings, who was his late wife's half-sister as well as his own personal property.

Burstein's chapter on this matter—which is, after all, a fairly open "secret"—is admirable. He doesn't waste time, as so many historians have, in making a mystery where none exists. It is obvious without any reference to DNA testing that Jefferson took Sally Hemings as his concubine and fathered several of her children. And, if we look at the books in Jefferson's library, and study the opinions he uttered on related matters, we can readily see how he would have justified the arrangement to himself.

First came the question of bodily integrity. The leading expert on sexual health at the time, the Swiss physician Samuel Tissot, took the view that intercourse of any kind was far less ignoble and life threatening than masturbation. Semen was provided for a purpose and should be neither squandered nor pent up. Knowing—and doubtless appreciating—this, Jefferson had nonetheless to protect the memory of his wife and avoid scandal in general. As he was well aware, the ancient Greek method of doing both these things, and of avoiding venereal disease in the bargain, was to establish a consistent relationship with a compliant member of the household. *Et voilà!* A small element of eugenics may have been involved too, since Jefferson also believed that it was necessary to people the earth and that too many men of position wasted their generative urges on alliances with unfit women. The children he had with Hemings were sturdy and smart, and they made very serviceable slaves on his near-bankrupt estate until he kept his promise to their mother to manumit them at adulthood.

Jefferson applied to himself the same method of analysis he employed for scrutinizing the universe and for anatomizing his beloved Virginia. Surely such symmetry and order implied a design, and therefore a designer? This deistic rationalism was as far as most thinking people could go in an epoch that just preceded the work of Charles Darwin (who was born on the same day as Abraham Lincoln). And Jefferson hit on the same analogy arrived at by the "natural philosopher" William Paley: the timepiece. Even a person who did not know what a clock was for would be able to tell that it was not a vegetable or a stone, that it had a maker.

Interestingly, Jefferson made more use of this example as he got older, referring to himself as "an old watch, with a pinion worn here, and a wheel there, until it can go no longer." Did he think that a creator's global creation was subject to similar laws? He appears not to have asked himself. But then, this was a man who could oppose the emancipation of slaves because he feared the "ten thousand recollections" they would retain of their hated condition, while almost in the same breath saying dismissively that "their griefs are transient."

In other words, and despite his notable modesty and decorum, Jefferson was subject to the same solipsism that encumbered all those who lived before the conclusive analysis of the fossil record and the elements of microbiology. (He could never work out, in his *Notes on the State of Virginia*, how it was that seashells could be found so high up on the local mountains.) On his Monticello mountaintop he was the center of a universe of his very own, and he was never quite able to dispense with the corollary illusions. This is what makes the account of his death so impressive. He wished to make a good and dignified end, and to be properly remembered for his proudest achievements, yet he seems to have guessed (telling John Adams that he felt neither "hope" nor "fear") that only extinction awaited him. He certainly did not request the attendance of any minister of religion.

Burstein reproduces a verse of revolting sentimentality, composed by Jefferson on his deathbed, in which he promises his surviving daughter to bear her love to the "Two Seraphs" who have gone before. The lines seem ambivalent to me, in that Jefferson speaks not so much of crossing a boundary as of coming to an impassable one: "I go to my fathers; I welcome the shore, / which crowns all my hopes, or which buries my cares." Anyway, a moment's thought will remind us that a designer who causes the deaths of infant daughters to occur so long before the death of their father has lost hold of the argument from natural order, while a moment's ordinary sympathy will excuse the dying and exhausted man this last indulgence in the lachrymose. The rest of Burstein's book has already demonstrated the main and unsurprising point, which is that the author of the Declaration of Independence was in every respect a mammal like ourselves. The only faint cause of surprise is that this can still seem controversial.

(*The Wilson Quarterly*, Spring 2005)

Jefferson Versus the Muslim Pirates

WHEN I FIRST BEGAN to plan my short biography of Thomas Jefferson, I found it difficult to research the chapter concerning the so-called Barbary Wars: an event or series of events that had seemingly receded over the lost horizon of American history. Henry Adams, in his discussion of our third president, had some boyhood reminiscences of the widespread hero-worship of naval officer Stephen Decatur, and other fragments and shards showed up in other quarries, but a sound general history of the subject was hard to come by. When I asked a professional military historian—a man with direct access to Defense Department archives—if there was any book that he could recommend, he came back with a slight shrug.

But now the curious reader may choose from a freshet of writing on the subject. Added to my own shelf in the recent past have been *The Barbary Wars: American Independence in the Atlantic World*, by Frank Lambert (2005); *Jefferson's War: America's First War on Terror 1801–1805*, by Joseph Wheelan (2003); *To the Shores of Tripoli: The Birth of the U.S. Navy and Marines,* by A. B. C. Whipple (1991, republished 2001); and *Victory in*

Review of *Power, Faith, and Fantasy: America in the Middle East, 1776 to the Present*, by Michael Oren.

Tripoli: How America's War with the Barbary Pirates Established the U.S. Navy and Shaped a Nation, by Joshua E. London (2005). Most recently, in his new general history, *Power, Faith, and Fantasy: America in the Middle East, 1776 to the Present,* the Israeli scholar Michael Oren opens with a long chapter on the Barbary conflict. As some of the subtitles—and some of the dates of publication—make plain, this new interest is largely occasioned by America's latest round of confrontation in the Middle East, or the Arab sphere or Muslim world, if you prefer those expressions.

In a way, I am glad that I did not have the initial benefit of all this research. My quest sent me to some less obvious secondary sources, in particular to Linda Colley's excellent book *Captives,* which shows the reaction of the English and American publics to a slave trade of which they were victims rather than perpetrators. How many know that perhaps 1.5 million Europeans and Americans were enslaved in Islamic North Africa between 1530 and 1780? We dimly recall that Miguel de Cervantes was briefly in the galleys. But what of the people of the town of Baltimore in Ireland, all carried off by "corsair" raiders in a single night?

Some of this activity was hostage trading and ransom-farming rather than the more labor-intensive horror of the Atlantic trade and the Middle Passage, but it exerted a huge effect on the imagination of the time—and probably on no one more than on Thomas Jefferson. Peering at the paragraph denouncing the American slave trade in his original draft of the Declaration of Independence, later excised, I noticed for the first time that it sarcastically condemned "the Christian King of Great Britain" for engaging in "this piratical warfare, the opprobrium of infidel powers." The allusion to Barbary practice seemed inescapable.

One immediate effect of the American Revolution, however, was to strengthen the hand of those very same North African potentates: roughly speaking, the Maghrebian provinces of the Ottoman Empire that conform to today's Algeria, Libya, Morocco, and Tunisia. Deprived of Royal Navy protection, American shipping became even more subject than before to the depredations of those who controlled the Strait of Gibraltar. The infant United States had therefore to decide not just upon a question of national honor but upon whether it would stand or fall by free navigation of the seas.

One of the historians of the Barbary conflict, Frank Lambert, argues that the imperative of free trade drove America much more than did any quarrel with Islam or "tyranny," let alone "terrorism." He resists any comparison with today's tormenting confrontations. "The Barbary Wars were primarily about trade, not theology," he writes. "Rather than being holy wars, they were an extension of America's War of Independence."

Let us not call this view reductionist. Jefferson would perhaps have been just as eager to send a squadron to put down any Christian piracy that was restraining commerce. But one cannot get around what Jefferson heard when he went with John Adams to wait upon Tripoli's ambassador to London in March 1785. When they inquired by what right the Barbary states preyed upon American shipping, enslaving both crews and passengers, America's two foremost envoys were informed that "it was written in the Koran, that all Nations who should not have acknowledged their authority were sinners, that it was their right and duty to make war upon whoever they could find and to make Slaves of all they could take as prisoners, and that every Mussulman who should be slain in battle was sure to go to Paradise." (It is worth noting that the United States played no part in the Crusades, or in the Catholic *reconquista* of Andalusia.)

Ambassador Abd Al-Rahman did not fail to mention the size of his own commission, if America chose to pay the protection money demanded as an alternative to piracy. So here was an early instance of the "heads I win, tails you lose" dilemma, in which the United States is faced with corrupt regimes, on the one hand, and Islamic militants, on the other—or indeed a collusion between them.

It seems likely that Jefferson decided from that moment on that he would make war upon the Barbary kingdoms as soon as he commanded American forces. His two least favorite institutions—enthroned monarchy and state-sponsored religion—were embodied in one target, and it may even be that his famous ambivalences about slavery were resolved somewhat when he saw it practiced by the Muslims.

However that may be, it is certain that the Barbary question had considerable influence on the debate that ratified the United States Constitution in the succeeding years. Many a delegate, urging his home state to endorse the new document, argued that only a strong federal union could repel the Algerian threat. In "The Federalist" No. 24, Alexander Hamilton argued that without a "federal navy... of respectable weight... the genius of American Merchants and Navigators would be stifled and lost." In No. 41, James Madison insisted that only union could guard America's maritime capacity from "the rapacious demands of pirates and barbarians." John Jay, in his letters, took a "bring-it-on" approach; he believed that "Algerian Corsairs and the Pirates of Tunis and Tripoli" would compel the feeble American states to unite, since "the more we are ill-treated abroad the more we shall unite and consolidate at home." The eventual Constitution, which provides for an army only at two-year renewable intervals, imposes no such limitation on the navy.

Thus, Lambert may be limiting himself in viewing the Barbary conflict primarily through the lens of free trade. Questions of nation-building, of regime change, of "mission creep," of congressional versus presidential authority to make war, of negotiation versus confrontation, of "entangling alliances," and of the "clash of civilizations"—all arose in the first overseas war that the United States ever fought. The "nation-building" that occurred, however, took place not overseas but in the thirteen colonies, welded by warfare into something more like a republic.

There were many Americans—John Adams among them—who made the case that it was better policy to pay the tribute. It was cheaper than the loss of trade, for one thing, and a battle against the pirates would be "too rugged for our people to bear." Putting the matter starkly, Adams said: "We ought not to fight them at all unless we determine to fight them forever."

The cruelty, exorbitance, and intransigence of the Barbary states, however, would decide things. The level of tribute demanded began to reach 10 percent of the American national budget, with no guarantee that greed would not increase that percentage, while from the dungeons of Algiers and Tripoli came appalling reports of the mistreatment of captured men and women. Gradually, and to the accompaniment of some of the worst patriotic verse ever written, public opinion began to harden in favor of war. From Jefferson's perspective, it was a good thing that this mood shift took place during the Adams administration, when he was out of office and temporarily "retired" to Monticello. He could thus criticize federal centralization of power, from a distance, even as he watched the construction of a fleet—and the forging of a permanent Marine Corps—that he could one day use for his own ends.

At one point, Jefferson hoped that John Paul Jones, naval hero of the Revolution, might assume command of a squadron that would strike fear into the Barbary pirates. While ambassador in Paris, Jefferson had secured Jones a commission with Empress Catherine of Russia, who used him in the Black Sea to harry the Ottomans, the ultimate authority over Barbary. But Jones died before realizing his dream of going to the source and attacking Constantinople. The task of ordering war fell to Jefferson.

Michael Oren thinks that he made the decision reluctantly, finally forced into it by the arrogant behavior of Tripoli, which seized two American brigs and set off a chain reaction of fresh demands from other Barbary states. I believe—because of the encounter with the insufferable Abd Al-Rahman and because of his long engagement with Jones—that Jefferson had long sought a pretext for war. His problem was his own party and the clause in the Constitution that gave Congress the power to declare war. With not atypical subtlety, Jefferson took a shortcut through this thicket in 1801 and sent the navy to North Africa on patrol, as it were, with instructions to enforce existing treaties and punish infractions of them. Our third president did not inform Congress of his authorization of this mission until the fleet was too far away to recall.

Once again, Barbary obstinacy tipped the scale. Yusuf Karamanli, the pasha of Tripoli, declared war on the United States in May 1801, in pursuit of his demand for more revenue. This earned him a heavy bombardment of Tripoli and the crippling of one of his most important ships. But the force of example was plainly not sufficient. In the altered mood that prevailed after the encouraging start in Tripoli, Congress passed an enabling act in February 1802 that, in its provision for a permanent Mediterranean presence and its language about the "Tripolitan Corsairs," amounted to a declaration of war. The Barbary regimes continued to underestimate their new enemy, with Morocco declaring war in its turn and the others increasing their blackmail.

A complete disaster—Tripoli's capture of the new U.S. frigate *Philadelphia*—became a sort of triumph, thanks to Edward Preble and Stephen Decatur, who mounted a daring raid on Tripoli's harbor and blew up the captured ship, while inflicting heavy damage on the city's defenses. Now there were names—Preble and Decatur—for newspapers back home to trumpet as heroes. Nor did their courage draw notice only in America. Admiral Lord Nelson himself called the raid "the most bold and daring act of the age," and Pope Pius VII declared that the United States "had done more for the cause of Christianity than the most powerful nations of Christendom have done for ages." (In his nostalgia for Lepanto, perhaps, His Holiness was evidently unaware that the Treaty of Tripoli, which in 1797 had attempted to formalize the dues that America would pay for access to the Mediterranean, stated in its preamble that the United States had no quarrel with the Muslim religion and was in no sense a Christian country. Of course, those secularists like myself who like to cite this treaty must concede that its conciliatory language was part of America's attempt to come to terms with Barbary demands.)

Watching all this with a jaundiced eye was the American consul in Tunis, William Eaton. For him, behavior modification was not a sufficient policy; regime change was needed. And he had a candidate. On acceding to the throne in Tripoli, Yusuf Karamanli had secured his position by murdering one brother and exiling another. Eaton befriended this exiled brother, Hamid, and argued that he should become the American nominee for Tripoli's crown. This proposal wasn't received with enthusiasm in Washington, but Eaton pursued it with commendable zeal. He exhibited the downside that often goes with such quixotic bravery: railing against Treasury Secretary Albert Gallatin as a "cowardly Jew," for example, and alluding to President Jefferson with contempt. He ended up a supporter of Aaron Burr's freebooting secessionist conspiracy.

His actions in 1805, however, belong in the annals of derring-do, almost warranting the frequent comparison made with T. E. Lawrence's exploits in Arabia. With a small detachment of marines, headed by Lieutenant Presley O'Bannon, and a force of irregulars inevitably described by historians as "motley," Eaton crossed the desert from Egypt and came at Tripoli—as Lawrence had come at Aqaba—from the land and not from the sea. The attack proved a total surprise. The city of Darna surrendered its far larger garrison, and Karamanli's forces were heavily engaged, when news came that Jefferson and Karamanli had reached an understanding that could end the war. The terms weren't too shabby, involving the release of the *Philadelphia*'s crew and a final settlement of the tribute question. And Jefferson took care to stress that Eaton had played a part in bringing it about.

This graciousness did not prevent Eaton from denouncing the deal as a sellout. The caravan moved on, though, as the other Barbary states gradually followed Tripoli's lead and came to terms. Remember, too, that this was the year of the Battle of Trafalgar. Lord Nelson was not the only European to notice that a new power had arrived in Mediterranean waters. Francis Scott Key composed a patriotic song to mark the occasion. As I learned from Joshua London's excellent book, the original verses ran (in part):

> In conflict resistless each toil they endur'd,
> Till their foes shrunk dismay'd from the war's desolation:
> And pale beamed the Crescent, its splendor obscur'd
> By the light of the star-bangled flag of our nation.
> Where each flaming star gleamed a meteor of war,
> And the turban'd head bowed to the terrible glare.
> Then mixt with the olive the laurel shall wave
> And form a bright wreath for the brow of the brave.

The song was part of the bad-verse epidemic. But brushed up and revised a little for the War of 1812, and set to the same music, it has enjoyed considerable success since. So has the Marine Corps anthem, which begins: "From the halls of Montezuma to the shores of Tripoli." It's no exaggeration to describe the psychological fallout of this first war as formative of the still-inchoate American character.

There is of course another connection between 1805 and 1812. Renewed hostilities with Britain on the high seas and on the American mainland, which did not terminate until the Battle of New Orleans, might have ended less conclusively had the United States not developed a battle-hardened naval force in the long attrition on the North African coast.

The Barbary states sought to exploit Anglo-American hostilities by resuming their depredations and renewing their demands for blood money. So in 1815, after a brief interval of recovery from the war with Britain, President Madison asked Congress for permission to dispatch Decatur once again to North Africa, seeking a permanent settling of accounts. This time, the main offender was the dey of Algiers, Omar Pasha, who saw his fleet splintered and his grand harbor filled with heavily armed American ships. Algiers had to pay compensation, release all hostages, and promise not to offend again. President Madison's words on this occasion could scarcely be bettered: "It is a settled policy of America, that as peace is better than war, war is better than tribute. The United States, while they wish for war with no nation, will buy peace with none." (The expression "the United States is" did not come into usage until after Gettysburg.)

Oren notes that the stupendous expense of this long series of wars was a partial vindication of John Adams's warning. However, there are less quantifiable factors to consider. The most obvious is commerce. American trade in the Mediterranean increased enormously in the years after the settlement with Algiers, and America's ability to extend its trade and project its forces into other areas, such as the Caribbean and South America, was greatly enhanced. Then we should attend to what Linda Colley says on the subject of slavery. Campaigns against the seizure of hostages by Muslim powers, and their exploitation as forced labor, fired up many a church congregation in Britain and America and fueled many a press campaign. But even the dullest soul could regard the continued triangular Atlantic slave trade between Africa, England, and the Americas and perceive the double standard at work. Thus, the struggle against Barbary may have helped to force some of the early shoots of abolitionism.

Perhaps above all, though, the Barbary Wars gave Americans an inkling of the fact that they were, and always would be, bound up with global affairs. Providence might have seemed to grant them a haven guarded by two oceans, but if they wanted to be anything more than the Chile of North America—a long littoral ribbon caught between the mountains and the sea—they would have to prepare for a maritime struggle as well as a campaign to redeem the unexplored landmass to their west. The U.S. Navy's Mediterranean squadron has, in one form or another, been on patrol ever since.

And then, finally, there is principle. It would be simplistic to say that something innate in America made it incompatible with slavery and tyranny. But would it be too much to claim that many Americans saw a radical incompatibility between the Barbary system and their own? And is it not pleasant when the interests of free trade and human emancipation can coincide? I would close with a few staves of Kipling, whose poem "Dane-Geld" is a finer effort than anything managed by Francis Scott Key:

> It is always a temptation to an armed and agile nation
> To call upon a neighbor and to say:—
> "We invaded you last night—
> we are quite prepared to fight,
> Unless you pay us cash to go away."
> And that is called asking for Dane-geld,
> And the people who ask it explain
> That you've only to pay 'em the Dane-geld
> And then you'll get rid of the Dane!

Kipling runs briskly through the stages of humiliation undergone by any power that falls for this appeasement, and concludes:

> It is wrong to put temptation in the path of any nation,
> For fear they should succumb and go astray;
> So when you are requested to pay up or be molested,
> You will find it better policy to say:—
> "We never pay any-one Dane-geld,
> No matter how trifling the cost;
> For the end of that game is oppression and shame,
> And the nation that plays it is lost!"

It may be fortunate that the United States had to pass this test, and imbibe this lesson, so early in its life as a nation.

(*City Journal*, Spring 2007)

Benjamin Franklin: Free and Easy

THERE CAME A TIME many years ago when I decided to agree to the baptism of my firstborn. It was a question of pleasing his mother's family. Nonetheless, I had to endure some teasing from Christian friends—how could the old atheist have sold out so easily? I decided to go deadpan and say, Well, I don't want his infant soul to go to hell or purgatory for want of some holy water. And it was often value for money: The faces of several believers took on a distinct look of discomfort at the literal rendition of their own supposed view.

Now turn, if you will, to the opening words of Benjamin Franklin's short essay "How to secure Houses, &c. from LIGHTNING": "It has pleased God in his Goodness to Mankind, at length to discover to them the Means of securing their Habitations and other Buildings from Mischief by Thunder and Lightning."

Franklin proceeds to describe the apparatus of an elementary conductor. Now, you may believe if you choose that the author of that sentence was sincerely of the opinion that God had decided to deny this blessing to his mortal creation until the middle of the eighteenth century of the Christian era. Or you may decide that an excess of humility led him to downplay or omit his

---

Review of *Benjamin Franklin Unmasked*, by Jerry Weinberger.

own seminal role in "discovering" electricity. Or you may wonder whether he was deliberately ridiculing a theistic view by setting it down so innocently, yet in such a way as to actuate a stir of unease in even the most credulous reader.

I came up with the preceding example myself, after reading Jerry Weinberger's elegant and fascinating companion to, and analysis of, the work of our cleverest Founding Father. In its title the word "unmasked" is purposely provocative and misleading, as is fitting for a book that derives from close reading and a Straussian attention to the arcane. This is not an exposé of Benjamin Franklin's *folie* in respect of the fair sex—though it doesn't suffer from lack of attention to this intriguing subject. It is an attempt to describe, rather than to remove, the disguises that he assumed in a long and sinuous life.

There are two kinds of people: those who read Franklin's celebrated *Autobiography* with a solemn expression, and those who keep laughing out loud as they go along. For centuries the book has been seriously put forward as a sort of moral manual, especially for growing boys—an ancestor of the precepts of Horatio Alger, made more lustrous by its famous provenance. But Weinberger is of the school of cackle. I deliberately postponed re-reading the *Autobiography* until I had finished his book, and then—deciding to read it in a bar in Annapolis—was continually interrupted by people asking me to share the joke. When I pointed to the cover, I met with really rewarding looks of bemusement.

The conundrum begins quite early, when Franklin refers to his habit of disputation, as acquired from his father's "Books of Dispute about Religion." He remarks that "Persons of good Sense" seldom fall into this habit, "except Lawyers, University Men, and Men of all Sorts that have been bred at Edinborough." This is dry, but with little or no edge to it. A few pages farther on we read of the tyranny exerted by his brother, who wanted both to indenture him and to beat him, "Tho' He was otherwise not an ill-natur'd Man: Perhaps I was too saucy & provoking." Surely an instance of what I call moral jujitsu (of which more later), in which pretended humility can cut like a lash. We descend into vengeful farce not long after this, when we meet the case of Mr. Keimer, Franklin's dislikable first boss in Philadelphia. Young Ben challenged this nasty Sabbatarian to keep a three-month Lenten fast, during which both would abjure all meat.

> I went on pleasantly, but Poor Keimer suffer'd grievously, tir'd of the Project, long'd for the Flesh Pots of Egypt, and order'd a roast Pig; He invited me & two Women Friends to dine with him, but it being brought too soon upon table, he could not resist the Temptation, and ate it all up before we came.

This Falstaffian scene of the hapless hypocrite demolishing an entire pig demonstrates comic genius. And only a few pages before, we met Keimer as he resented the attention paid to his young apprentice by the governor, and "star'd like a Pig poison'd." The image of porcine cannibalism makes a good counterpart to Franklin's disavowal of the vegetarian idea. Seeing large fish being gutted, and noticing smaller fish inside their bellies, he felt entitled to convince himself that there was nothing offensive in resuming his fish diet. Again, you may if you wish take this as an anecdote about nutrition, offered for the moral elevation of the young, but bear in mind the village atheist in Peter De Vries's *Slouching Towards Kalamazoo*, who could not conceive a deity that created every species as predatory and then issued a terse commandment against killing.

"Created sick, and then commanded to be well." This is one of the first, easiest, and most obvious of the satirical maxims that eventually lay waste to the illusion of faith. Franklin was well aware of this annihilating expression, which he employed in his "Dialogue Between Philocles and Horatio," written in 1730. Weinberger seizes hold of his professed and repressed attitudes to religion, and employs them as a thread of Ariadne through the labyrinth of Franklin's multifarious writings. The first and most obvious of Weinberger's targets are those who really did take the *Autobiography* at face value. It is no surprise to find D. H. Lawrence among these, because a more humorless man probably never drew mortal breath. But it is astonishing to find Mark Twain saying in effect that the book had made life harder for his Toms and Hucks, who had to bear this additional burden of schoolmarmery and moral exhortation, imposed by those determined to "improve" them at any price.

In fairness to Twain, whose fondness for imposture and joking was renowned, he may not have scanned Franklin's early and anonymous

Massachusetts journalism, in which the pen name "Silence Dogood" was an almost too obvious giveaway. To write as if in emulation of Cotton Mather's *Bonifacius*, or "Essays to Do Good," and to subvert its style and purpose so blatantly, must have repaid the tedium of many a New England Sunday. The 1747 "Speech of Miss Polly Baker," in which a common whore made a notably eloquent speech in defense of her right to bear bastard children, fooled almost everyone at the time. We may be right in speaking of an age of innocence, in which Miss Baker's apologia (she is "hard put to it" for a living, "cannot conceive" the nature of her offense, and half admits "all my Faults and Miscarriages") was received with furrowed and anxious brows. But the only wonder, once you get the trick of it, is how Franklin was able to use such broad and easy punning to lampoon the Pharisees of the day. He even tells us in the *Autobiography* how it became a delight to him to pen anonymous screeds, put them under the door of the newspaper office at night, and then watch the local worthies try to puzzle out their authorship. I always used to think when I saw the customary portraits of Franklin, with his spectacles and his Quakerish homespun garb and his bunlike hair, that there was something grannyish about him. It took me years to appreciate that in youth, at least in prose, he had been quite a good female impersonator. So that's one mask off.

In his *Persecution and the Art of Writing*, which I am assuming Professor Weinberger knows almost by heart, Leo Strauss made the surprisingly unesoteric observation that the best way to avoid the wrath of the censor is to present an apparently balanced debate in which the views of the side disliked by the censor are given a "straight" denunciation. Only a little subtlety is required to make these views slightly more attractive than the censor might wish. And many are those who have been seduced, or disillusioned, in this manner, even by debates into which no conscious "twist" has been inserted. (De Vries's novel also contains a hilarious scene in which the town atheist and the town clergyman have a public argument and succeed in completely winning each other over.)

That Franklin had the necessary cast of mind for this dialectic is not to be doubted. He even tells us himself, with an open and friendly face,

> Some Books against Deism fell into my Hands; they were said to be the Substance of Sermons preached at Boyle's Lectures. It happened that they wrought an Effect on me quite contrary to what was intended by them: For the Arguments of the Deists which were quoted to be refuted, appeared to me much Stronger than the Refutations.

But Franklin isn't done with the reader quite yet. He gives an account of a Deism in which it is quite impossible that he believed. Or is it true that he ever "from the Attributes of God, his infinite Wisdom, Goodness & Power concluded that nothing could possibly be wrong in the World, & that Vice & Virtue were empty Distinctions, no such Things existing"? Everything in his life and writing argues against this likelihood, and Weinberger wittily appends a note on how to distinguish between "dry," "wet," and "very wet" Deism. Only the ultra-dry Deists denied human beings all free will, and even then the idea that the world was as good as it possibly could be was dependent on the fatalistic and tautological conviction that it was, *ex hypothesi*, the only possible world in the first place. Franklin was never a Pangloss, and his bald statement of what such a belief would entail is the equal of Voltaire's.

He seems to have disclosed his true ambition only by appearing to disown or abandon it. At about the midpoint of the *Autobiography*, having already familiarized us with his suspicion of all established churches, he relates his intention, in 1731, of setting the world to rights by establishing a "Party for Virtue." This would form the "Virtuous and good Men of all Nations" into "a regular Body, to be govern'd by suitable good and wise Rules." This apparently platitudinous project was to involve a "creed," which would comprise "the Essentials of every known Religion" while "being free of every thing that might shock the Professors of any Religion." This was as much as to say that a frontal disagreement with the godly was not to be entertained: an unsurprising proposition in that or any other epoch. The party's manifesto included some ecumenical boilerplate about one God, divine providence, and the reward of virtue and punishment of vice "*either* here or hereafter" (my italics), but its point of distinction lay in the clause stipulating that "the most acceptable Service of God is doing Good to Man." Having laid out this essentially humanist appeal with some care over a couple of pages, Franklin writes with diffidence that the pressure of other work led him to postpone it indefinitely. Weinberger believes, to the contrary, that he made this project his unostentatious life's work, always seeking to unite men of science and reason, and even, if rather belatedly, abandoning his pro-slavery position and becoming an advocate of emancipation. There is good evidence that he is right. Franklin's decision to become a Freemason, for instance, can be interpreted first as somewhat anticlerical and second as signifying his adherence to a common brotherhood without frontiers. And there is the usual Franklin joke: With great attention to the proprieties of frugality and thrift, he still straight-facedly suggested that the "Party for Virtue" be actually named "the Society of the *Free and Easy*."

It is precisely Franklin's homespun sampler quotations about frugality and thrift that made him rich and famous through the audience of his *Almanack*. And it was these maxims, collected and distilled in the last of the Poor Richard series and later given the grand title *The Way to Wealth*, that so incensed Mark Twain as to cause him to write that they were "full of animosity toward boys" and "worked up with a great show of originality out of truisms that had become wearisome platitudes as early as the dispersion from Babel." A point, like a joke, is a terrible thing to miss. When I re-read *The Way to Wealth* from the perspective of Jerry Weinberger, I could not bring myself to believe that it had ever been taken with the least seriousness. In the old days at the *New Statesman* we once ran a celebrated weekend competition that asked readers to submit made-up gems of cretinous bucolic wisdom. Two of the winning entries, I still recall, were "He digs deepest who deepest digs" and "An owl in a sack bothers no man." Many of Poor Richard's attempts at epigram and aphorism do not even rise to this level. My favorite, " 'Tis hard for an empty Bag to stand upright," is plainly not a case in which Franklin thinks he has polished his own renowned wit to a diamond-hard edge. The whole setting of *The Way to Wealth* is a "lift," it seems to me, from Christian's encounter with Vanity Fair in *The Pilgrim's Progress*. And the heartening injunctions (of which "The Cat in Gloves catches no Mice" is another stellar example) are so foolish that it is a shock to remember that the old standby "God helps them that help themselves" comes from the same anthology of wisdom.

Franklin's moral jujitsu, in which he always seemingly deferred to his opponents in debate but left them first punching the air and then adopting his opinions as their own, is frequently and slyly boasted about in the *Autobiography*, but it cannot have afforded him as much pleasure as the applause and income he received from people who didn't know he was kidding. The tip-offs are all there once you learn to look for them, as with Franklin's friend Osborne, who died young.

> He and I had made a serious Agreement, that the one who happen'd first to die, should if possible make a friendly Visit to the other, and acquaint him how he found things in that separate State. But he never fulfill'd his Promise.

At a time when some noisy advocates are attempting to revise American history, and to represent the Founders as men who believed in a Christian nation, this book could not be more welcome. I close with what Franklin so foxily said about the Reverend Whitefield, whose oral sermons were so fine but whose habit of writing them down exposed him to fierce textual criticism: "Opinions [delivered] in Preaching might have been afterwards explain'd, or qualify'd by supposing others that might have accompany'd them; or they might have been deny'd; But *litera scripta manet*." Yes, indeed, "the written word shall remain." And the old printer left enough of it to delight subsequent generations and remind us continually of the hidden pleasures of the text.

(*The Atlantic*, November 2005)

John Brown: The Man Who Ended Slavery

WHEN ABRAHAM LINCOLN gave an audience to Harriet Beecher Stowe, he is supposed to have greeted her by saying that she was the little woman who had started this great war. That fondly related anecdote illustrates the persistent tendency to Parson Weemsishness in our culture. It was not at all the tear-jerking sentiment of *Uncle Tom's Cabin* that catalyzed the War Between the States. It was, rather, the blood-spilling intransigence of John Brown, field-tested on the pitiless Kansas prairies and later deployed at Harpers Ferry. And John Brown was a man whom Lincoln assiduously disowned, until the time came when he himself was compelled to adopt the policy of "war to the knife, and the knife to the hilt," as partisans of the slaveocracy had hitherto been too proud of saying.

David Reynolds sets himself to counter several misapprehensions about the pious old buzzard (Brown, I mean, not Lincoln). Among these are the impressions that he was a madman, that he was a homicidal type, and that his assault on a federal arsenal was foredoomed and quixotic. The critical thing here is context. And the author succeeds admirably in showing that Brown, far from being a crazed fanatic, was a serious legatee of the English and American Revolutions who anticipated the Emancipation Proclamation and all that has ensued from it.

Review of *John Brown, Abolitionist*, by David S. Reynolds.

Until 1850, perhaps, the "peculiar institution" of slavery might have had a chance of perpetuating itself indefinitely by compromise. But the exorbitance and arrogance of "the slave power" forbade this accommodation. Not content with preserving their own domain in its southeastern redoubt, the future Confederates insisted on extending their chattel system into new territories, and on implicating the entire Union in their system. The special symbol of this hubris was the Fugitive Slave Act, which legalized the recovery of human property from "free" states. The idea of secession or separation first arose among abolitionists confronted with this monstrous imposition. Men like William Lloyd Garrison took their text from the Book of Isaiah, describing the U.S. Constitution as a "covenant with death and an agreement with hell," and exhorting their supporters to "come out now and be separate." (This hermeneutic rejectionism, incidentally, is identical to that preached today by Ian Paisley and the Presbyterian hardliners of Northern Ireland.)

The proto-libertarian and anarchist Lysander Spooner argued that nowhere did the Constitution explicitly endorse slavery. It was for defenders of the values of 1776 and 1789 to help the slaves overthrow an illegitimate tyranny. In this he had the support of the Republican Frederick Douglass, who also wanted the United States to live up to its founding documents rather than to nullify or negate them. Meanwhile, the Democrats were unashamed advocates of the extension of slavery, and Lincoln was willing to submit to one humiliation after another in order, as he never tired of saying, "to preserve the Union."

John Brown could effortlessly outdo Garrison in any biblical condemnation of slavery. He could also easily surpass Lysander Spooner in his zeal to encourage and arm what the authorities called "servile insurrection." He strongly agreed with Douglass that the Union should be preserved and not dissolved. But he was incapable of drawing up any balance sheet between "preservation" and gradual emancipation, because he saw quite plainly that the balance was going the other way, and that the slave power was influencing and subordinating the North, rather than the other way about. Thus, despite his commitment to the Union, he was quite ready to regard the federal government as an enemy.

Originally a New Englander (and possibly a *Mayflower* descendant), Brown appeared to adopt and exemplify the adamant Calvinism of Jonathan Edwards, with his strict insistence on predestination and the "elect" and his vivid belief in eternal punishment for sinners. Reynolds gives some hair-raising examples of the culture of corporal punishment and cruel austerity that ruled Brown's own upbringing and the raising of his twenty children, and it is easy to see how such a combination of dogma and discipline might have given rise to the persistent rumor that he was partly unhinged (more than one of his sons became mentally disturbed). However, the story of his longer evolution makes this speculation a highly unsafe one.

For all his attachment to Calvinist orthodoxy, Brown felt himself very close to the transcendental school of Emerson and Thoreau. He formed important friendships in this circle, and relied on a "Secret Six" committee of supporters in Massachusetts, who stood ready to provide money and even weapons for his projects. He can hardly have been unaware of the religious heterodoxy of this group; and when it came to the no less critical matter of choosing his immediate entourage of radical would-be guerrillas, he readily included Jews, Indians, Paine-ite deists, and agnostics. Most of all, however, he insisted on including blacks. This at once distinguished him from most abolitionists, who preferred to act "for" the slaves rather than with them. But Brown had made a friendship with a slave boy at the age of twelve, and would appear to have undergone a Huck Finn–like experience in the recognition of a common humanity. Later he studied the life and tactics of Nat Turner, and of the rebellious Haitian Toussaint L'Ouverture, and decided that a full-scale revolt of the oppressed, rather than any emancipation from above, was the need of the hour.

I was very much interested to learn that his other great hero was Oliver Cromwell, whose "New Model Army" had swept away profane kingship in England and established a Puritan regime. The revisionist view of Cromwell as a liberator rather than a regicide was the work of Thomas Carlyle in the 1840s, and a result of Carlyle's friendship with Emerson. The American writer Joel Tyler Headley "recycled" Carlyle, as Reynolds phrases it, for the American mass market, portraying Cromwell as an ancestor of the American Revolution as well as a synthesizer of "religion, republicanism, and violence." (It seems probable that Brown got his introduction to Cromwell from Headley rather than directly from Carlyle: I cannot easily imagine him esteeming the Carlyle who apostatized from Calvinism, let alone the Carlyle who, in justifying slavery in the West Indies in 1850, published "Occasional Discourse on the Nigger Question." Reynolds does not discuss this awkward paradox.)

* * *

Reynolds focuses on the three most sanguinary and dramatic episodes in Brown's career: the engagements at Pottawatomie and Osawatomie, in Kansas, and the culminating battle at Harpers Ferry. To read this extended account is to appreciate that Brown, far from being easily incited to rage and rashness, was capable of playing a very long game. He was naturally drawn to Kansas, because it had become the battleground state in a Union that was half slave and half free. The pro-slavery settlers and infiltrators from Missouri were determined to colonize the territory and to pack its polling booths, and in this they often had the indulgence of decrepit and cowardly presidents, including Franklin Pierce. Until the appearance of Brown and his men on the scene, the slave power had had things mostly its own way, and was accustomed to using any method it saw fit. After the murder of the abolitionist editor Elijah Lovejoy, and especially after the famous assault on Senator Charles Sumner by Representative Preston Brooks, Brown decided on a reprisal raid, and slew several leading pro-slavery Kansans in the dead of night. There is no question that this represented only a small installment of payback, though Reynolds nervously characterizes it as "terrorism" and spends a great deal of time and ink in partly rationalizing the deed.

The superfluity of this is easily demonstrated. Not only had the slave-holders perpetrated the preponderance of atrocities, and with impunity at that, but they had begun to boast that northerners and New Englanders were congenitally soft and altogether lacking in "chivalric" and soldierly qualities. What could be more apt than that they should encounter John Brown, careless of his own safety and determined to fill the ungodly with the fear of the risen Christ? Every Cavalier should meet such a Roundhead. After Pottawatomie the swagger went out of the southerners, and after the more conventional fighting at Osawatomie, and Brown's cool-headed raid to liberate a group of slaves and take them all the way to Canada, they came to realize that they were in a hard fight. Furthermore, their sulfurous reaction to this discovery, and their stupid tendency to paint Brown as an agent of the Republican Party, made it harder and harder for the invertebrate Lincolnians to keep the issue of slavery under control.

In his work in Kansas, and his long toil on the Underground Railroad,

Brown was essentially mounting a feint. He knew that subscribers and supporters in New England would give him money, and even arms, for these limited and shared objectives. But he wanted to divert the money, and the arms, to the larger purpose of making any further Lincolnian retreats and compromises impossible. For years he had been studying the keystone town of Harpers Ferry, situated at the confluence of the Shenandoah and the Potomac, and handily placed for the potentially guerrilla-friendly Allegheny Mountains.

Reynolds shows that the strategic design was not as quixotic as one has often been led to believe. This northwestern portion of Virginia was generally sympathetic to abolition and to the Union (indeed, its later cleaving into the new free state of West Virginia, in 1862, is the only secession from that epoch that still survives). The fall months were the harvest season, when disaffection among overdriven slaves was more general. And the national political climate was becoming more febrile and polarized.

Brown's raid at Harpers Ferry failed badly, of course, but the courage and bearing he demonstrated after his humiliating defeat were of an order to impress his captors, who announced that far from being "mad," their prisoner was lucid and eloquent as well as brave. The slander of insanity was circulated by the weaker members of the anti-slavery camp, who cringingly sought to avoid the identification with Brown that the southern press had opportunistically made. By falling for its own propaganda, however, and in the general panic that followed the botched insurrection, the South persuaded itself that war was inevitable and that Lincoln (who had denounced Brown in his campaign against Douglas and in his famous speech at Cooper Union) was a Brown-ite at heart. The history of the six years after 1859 is the history not so much of Brown's prophecy as of the self-fulfilling prophecy of his enemies. As Reynolds hauntingly words it,

> The officer who supervised the capture of Brown was Robert E. Lee... Lee's retreat from the decisive battle of Gettysburg would pass over the same road that Brown took to Harpers Ferry on the night of his attack. The lieutenant who demanded Brown's surrender was J.E.B. Stuart, later Lee's celebrated cavalry officer. Among the officers who supervised at Brown's hanging was Thomas Jackson, soon

to become the renowned "Stonewall." Among the soldiers at Brown's execution was a dashing Southern actor, John Wilkes Booth.

If this does not vindicate Brown's view that all had been predestined by the Almighty before the world was made, it nonetheless does do something to the hair on the back of one's neck. As do the words finally uttered in Lincoln's Second Inaugural, about every drop of blood drawn by the lash being repaid by the sword, and the utter destruction of the piled-up wealth of those who live by the bondsman's toil. The final reckoning with slavery and secession was described by Lincoln himself as one great "John Brown raid" into the South, and was on a scale that would have brought a wintry smile to the stern face of Oliver Cromwell. The "Marseillaise" of that crusade ("The Battle Hymn of the Republic," which first appeared, as did many other important documents of the Brown-Emerson alliance, in the pages of this magazine) was an adaptation of the foot soldiers' song about Old Osawatomie Brown. One reserves the term "quixotic" for hopeless causes. Harpers Ferry was the first defeat, as it was also the seminal victory, of a triumphant cause, precisely because it sounded a trumpet that could never call retreat.

So much for the apocalyptic and, if you like, "transcendental" influence of Brown. Reynolds, building on the earlier work of Merrill Peterson, traces another, gentler influence that may be no less consequential. Almost all whites in that epoch feared almost all blacks. And many blacks resented the condescension of anti-slavery organizations—most especially those groups that wanted to free them and then deport them to Africa. John Brown shared his life with slaves, and re-wrote the Declaration of Independence and the Constitution so as to try to repair the hideous wrong that had been done to them. (In issuing these documents, by the way, he exculpated himself from any ahistorical charge of "terrorism," which by definition offers nothing programmatic.) The record shows that admiration for Brown was intense, widespread, and continuous, from Douglass to DuBois and beyond. Our world might be a good deal worse than it is had not numberless African-Americans, from that day to this, taken John Brown as proof that fraternity and equality, as well as liberty, were feasible things and could be exemplified by real people.

(*The Atlantic*, May 2005)

Abraham Lincoln: Misery's Child

LINCOLN'S BICENTENNIAL has permitted us to revisit and reconsider every facet of his story and personality, from the Bismarckian big-government colossus so disliked by the traditional right and the isolationists, to the "Great Emancipator" who used to figure on the posters of the American Communist Party, to the reluctant anti-slaver so plausibly caught in Gore Vidal's finest novel. Absent from much of this consideration has been the unfashionable word *destiny*: the sense conveyed by Lincoln of a man who was somehow brought forth by the hour itself, as if his entire life had been but a preparation for that moment.

We cannot get this frisson from other great American presidents. Washington, Jefferson, Madison—these were all experienced members of the existing and indeed preexisting governing class. So was Roosevelt. However exaggerated or invented some parts of the Lincoln legend may be, it is nonetheless a fact that he came from the very loam and marrow of the new country, and that—unlike the other men I have mentioned—he cannot possibly be imagined as other than an American.

No review could do complete justice to the magnificent two-volume biography that has been so well-wrought by Michael Burlingame, but one way of paying tribute to it is to say that it introduces the elusive idea of destiny from the very start, and one means of illustrating this is to show how the

Review of *Abraham Lincoln: A Life*, by Michael Burlingame.

earlier chapters continually prefigure, or body forth, the more momentous events that are to be dealt with in the later ones.

Before I try to demonstrate that, I would like to call attention to something that Professor Burlingame says in his Author's Note:

> Many educated guesses, informed by over twenty years of research on Lincoln, appear in this biography. Each such guess might well begin with a phrase like "in all probability," or "it may well be that," or "it seems likely that." Such warnings, if inserted into the text, would prove wearisome; readers are encouraged to provide such qualifiers silently whenever the narrative explores Lincoln's unconscious motivation.

It is agreeable to be informed, when embarking on such a long and demanding work, that one will be treated like a grown-up.

There is, whether intentionally or not, a sort of biblical cadence and flavor to the way in which Burlingame relates the early family history: the grandmother Bathsheba; the father's older brother Mordecai; and Mary Lincoln's half sister, who said that "the reason why Thomas Lincoln grew up unlettered was that his brother Mordecai, having all the land in his possession... turned Thomas out of the house when the latter was 12 years; so he went out among his relations." The story of Jacob and Esau, and of Naboth's vineyard, was surely known to the person who recounted that.

As for the social background, here is a sentence that conveys a great deal of misery in a very few words. It is Burlingame's summary of the area in which Sinking Spring farm, Kentucky, young Abraham's birthplace, was situated. "The neighborhood was thinly settled; the 36-square-mile tax district where the Lincoln farm was located contained 85 taxpayers, 44 slaves, and 392 horses." Lincoln himself said that his early life could be "condensed into a single sentence" from Gray's "Elegy": "The short and simple annals of the poor." But this would be to euphemize his true boyhood situation, which was much more like that of a serf or a domestic animal than of Gray's lowly but sturdy peasantry. To read of the unrelenting coarseness and brutality of the boy's father is lowering to the spirit, as is the shame he felt at his mother's reputation for unchastity. The wretchedness of these surroundings made Lincoln tell a later acquaintance in Illinois: "I have seen a good deal of the back side of this world." (Incidentally, one has to imagine this being said with some kind of wink and nudge: Burlingame is not content, as so many historians are, merely to hint at Lincoln's fondness for broad humor, but furnishes us with some actual examples, which are heavy on the side of scatology and flatulence.)

Lincoln's own experience of legal bondage and hard usage is very graphically told: Not only did his father's improvidence deprive him of many necessities, but it resulted in his being hired out as a menial to be a hewer of wood and drawer of water for his father's rough and miserly neighbors. The law as it then stood made children the property of their father, so young Abraham was "hired out" only in the sense of chattel, since he was obliged to turn over his wages. From this, and from the many groans and sighs that are reported of the boy (who still struggled to keep reading, an activity feared and despised by his father, as it was by the owner of Frederick Douglass), we receive a prefiguration of the politician who declared in 1856, "I used to be a slave." In Lincoln's unconcealed resentment toward his male parent, we get an additional glimpse of the man who also declared, in 1858, "As I would not be a slave, so I would not be a master."

Yet the contours and character of the frontier region also fitted Lincoln for compromise: This was the area of the United States where the two systems were beginning their long, cruel attrition. Both as an aspiring congressman and as an ambitious lawyer, Lincoln managed on occasion to keep silent on the slavery issue and even, when appropriately briefed, to act as counsel for a slaveholder. Burlingame gives an intriguing account of the *Matson* case of 1847, in which, on technical procedural grounds and on the principle of "first come, first served," Lincoln agreed to represent a man who wanted some of his slaves back. On the other hand, he generally steered clear of fugitive-slave cases, "because of his unwillingness to be a party to a violation of the Fugitive Slave Law, arguing that the way to overcome the difficulty was to repeal the law." Here again, we can see the legalistic and sometimes pedantic mind that exhausted all the possibilities of compromise before coming up with the tortuous form of words that finally became the Emancipation Proclamation.

In rather the same way, Lincoln sought a deft means of negotiating the shoals of the religious question. Burlingame's highly diverting early pages show Lincoln being actively satirical in matters of faith, lampooning preachers, staging mock services, and praying to God "to put stockings on the chickens' feet in winter," in the words of his stepsister Matilda. Reminiscing about frontier Baptists many years later, he told an acquaintance: "I don't like to hear cut and dried sermons. No—when I hear a man preach, I like to see him act as if he were fighting bees!"

However, in his 1846 election campaign, Lincoln was cornered by the faithful and forced to deny that he was an "open scoffer at Christianity." His handbill on the subject is rightly criticized as too lawyerly by Burlingame, who elegantly points out:

> In this document Lincoln seemed to make two different claims: that he never believed in infidel doctrines, and that he never publicly espoused them. If the former were true, the latter would be superfluous; if the former were untrue, the latter would be irrelevant.

Several moments in the narrative—the bee-fighting preacher being one such—put me in mind of Mark Twain. The tall tales, the dry wit, the broad-gauge humor, the imminence of farce even in grave enterprises: Lincoln's inglorious participation in the Black Hawk War has many points of similarity with Twain's "Private History of a Campaign That Failed." Lincoln was once invited to referee a cockfight where a bird refused combat. Its enraged owner, one Babb McNabb, flung the creature onto a woodpile, whereat it spread its feathers and crowed mightily. "Yes, you little cuss," yelled McNabb, "you are great on dress parade, but you ain't worth a damn in a fight." Long afterward, confronted with the unmartial ditherings of General George B. McClellan, Lincoln would compare the chief of his army—and subsequent electoral challenger—to McNabb's pusillanimous rooster.

Mark Twain and Frederick Douglass, too, were persons who could only have been original Americans, sprung from American ground. It is engaging and affecting to read of Lincoln's lifelong troubles with spelling and pronunciation (he addressed himself to "Mr. Cheerman" in his famous Cooper Union Speech of 1860) and of his frequent appearance with as much as six inches of shin or arm protruding from his ill-made clothes: truly a Knight of the Sorrowful Countenance. Yet despite, or perhaps because of, the extreme harshness of his early life, he was innately opposed to any form of cruelty, and despite his lack of polish and refinement, he almost never stooped to crudity or vulgarity in political speech. Without overdrawing the contrast, Burlingame shows us a Judge Stephen Douglas who was a slave to every kind of anti-Negro demagogy and political mendacity. And Lincoln bested him, admittedly while hedging on the race question, by constantly stressing the need to secure "to each laborer the whole product of his labor." In more modern terms, we might say that he used the language of class to neutralize racism. (I would say that the account given here of the famous debates surpasses all its predecessors.)

It has lately become fashionable to say that Lincoln was not, or was not "really," a believer in black-white equality. A thread that runs consistently through Burlingame's narrative is that of self-education on this question, to the eventual point where Lincoln came as close to an egalitarian position as made almost no difference. Even the infamous discussion about the postwar expatriation of black Americans to "colonies" in Africa or on the American isthmus was conducted, by Burlingame's account, with very strict regard on Lincoln's side for the dignity and stature of those whose fate he was discussing. And it goes almost without saying that he had already had every opportunity to see that there was nothing very "superior" about the color white. By the end, Frederick Douglass—who had often criticized him—was able to say that Lincoln was "emphatically the black man's President." And Burlingame's survey of the life and opinions of the "mad racist" John Wilkes Booth makes it equally plain that the white supremacists felt the same way. Still, even this is to understate the universalist intransigence with which Lincoln never conceded an inch of American ground, and with which he quarreled with his generals, including McClellan, for referring to the North as "our soil," when every state was still, always, and invariably to be considered a part of the Union.

It was once said that the Civil War was the last of the old wars and the first of the new: Cavalry and infantry charges gave way to cannon and railways, and sail gave way to steam. It is of great interest to read Lincoln's meditations on the projected postwar expansion of the United States, with a strong emphasis on mining and manufacturing. He had completely shed the bucolic influence of his early career and was looking in the very last days of his life to renew industry and immigration. Before Gettysburg, people would say "the

United States are..." After Gettysburg, they began to say "the United States *is*..." That they were able to employ the first three words at all was a tribute to the man who did more than anyone to make that hard transition himself, and then to secure it for others, and for posterity.

(*The Atlantic*, July/August 2009)

Mark Twain: American Radical

THERE ARE FOUR RULES governing literary art in the domain of biography—some say five. In *The Singular Mark Twain*, Fred Kaplan violates all five of them. These five require:

1. That a biography shall cause us to wish we had known its subject in person, and inspire in us a desire to improve on such vicarious acquaintance as we possess. *The Singular Mark Twain* arouses in the reader an urgently fugitive instinct, as at the approach of an unpolished yet tenacious raconteur.
2. That the elements of biography make a distinction between the essential and the inessential, winnowing the quotidian and burnishing those moments of glory and elevation that place a human life in the first rank. *The Singular Mark Twain* puts all events and conversations on the same footing, and fails to enforce any distinction between wood and trees.
3. That a biographer furnish something by way of context, so that the place of the subject within history and society is illuminated, and his progress through life made intelligible by reference to his times. This condition is by no means met in *The Singular Mark Twain*.
4. That the private person be allowed to appear in all his idiosyncrasy, and not as a mere reflection of the correspondence or reminiscences of others,

Review of *The Singular Mark Twain*, by Fred Kaplan.

or as a subjective projection of the mind of the biographer. But this rule is flung down and danced upon in *The Singular Mark Twain*.

5. That a biographer have some conception of his subject, which he wishes to advance or defend against prevailing or even erroneous interpretations. This detail, too, has been overlooked in *The Singular Mark Twain*.

As can readily be seen from this attempt on my part at a pastiche of Twain's hatchet-wielding arraignment of James Fenimore Cooper (and of Cooper's anti-masterpiece *The Deerslayer*), the work of Samuel Langhorne Clemens is in the proper sense inimitable. But it owes this quality to certain irrepressible elements—many of them quite *noir*—in the makeup of the man himself. I reflect on Mark Twain and I see not just the man who gave us Judge Thatcher's fetching daughter but also the figure who wrote so cunningly about the charm of underage girls and so bluntly about defloration. The man who impaled the founder of Christian Science on a stake of contemptuous ridicule and who dismissed the Book of Mormon as "chloroform in print." The man who was so livid with anger at his country's arrogance abroad that he laid aside his work to inveigh against imperialism. The man who addressed an after-dinner gathering of the Stomach Club, in Paris, on the subject of masturbation, and demonstrated that he had done the hard thinking about hand jobs. Flickers of this enormous and subversive personality illumine Kaplan's narrative, but only rarely, and then in the manner of the lightning bug that Twain himself contrasted with the lightning.

Ernest Hemingway's much cited truism—to the effect that *Huckleberry Finn* hadn't been transcended by any subsequent American writer—understated, if anything, the extent to which Twain was not just a founding author but a founding American. Until his appearance, even writers as adventurous as Hawthorne and Melville would have been gratified to receive the praise of a comparison to Walter Scott. (A boat named the *Walter Scott* is sunk with some ignominy in Chapter 13 of *Huckleberry Finn*.) Twain originated in the riverine, slaveholding heartland; compromised almost as much as Missouri itself when it came to the Civil War; headed out to California ("the Lincoln of our literature" made a name in the state that Lincoln always hoped to see and never did); and conquered the eastern seaboard in his own sweet time. But though he had an unimpeachable claim to be from native ground, there was nothing provincial or crabbed about his declaration of independence for American letters. (His evisceration of Cooper can be read as an assault on any form of pseudo-native authenticity.) More than most of his countrymen, he voyaged around the world and pitted himself against non-American authors of equivalent contemporary weight.

What about his name? Kaplan's title and introduction imply a contradiction between the uniqueness of the man and the suggestion, in his selection of a nom de plume, of a divided self. When I was a lad, I am quite sure, I read of the young Clemens's listening to the incantation of a leadsman plumbing the shoals from the bow of a riverboat and calling out, "By the mark—twain!" as he indicated the deeps and shallows. This story, if true, would account for both the first and the second name, and it would also be apt in seeing both as derived from life on the Mississippi. But there's some profit (not all that much, but some) in doing as Kaplan does and speculating on other origins. In 1901 Twain told an audience at the Lotos Club, in New York, "When I was born, I was a member of a firm of twins. And one of them disappeared." This was not the case, but by 1901 Twain had been Twain for thirty-eight years (a decade longer than he had been Samuel Clemens), and had probably acquired a repertoire of means by which to answer a stale question from the audience. Twinship and impersonation come up in his stories, it is true. *Pudd'nhead Wilson* relies on the old fantasy of the changeling, and notebook scenarios for late Huck and Tom stories involve rapid switches of identity, with elements of racial as well as sexual cross-dressing. But then, how new is the discovery that Twain never lost his access to the marvels and memories of childhood?

Clearly, he meant to create a mild form of mystery if he could, because elsewhere he claimed to have annexed the name from "one Captain Isaiah Sellers who used to write river news over it for the New Orleans *Picayune*." But the *Picayune* never carried any such byline. And Twain was known all his life to be fond of hoaxes and spoofs in print, among them the "Petrified Man." So, absent any new or decisive information, this portentous search for the roots of an identity crisis may be somewhat pointless.

* * *

One of the difficulties confronting a Twain biographer is the sheer volume of ink the man expended on his own doings. One needs a persuasive reason for preferring a secondhand account of an episode that is already available in the original. Take, for instance, Twain's inglorious participation on the Confederate side in the Civil War. We already have his own hilarious but sour account of this interlude, in "The Private History of a Campaign That Failed," a sort of brief and memoiristic precursor of *The Good Soldier Schweik*. This melancholy, rueful, and slightly self-hating account of cowardice and bravado, with its awful culmination in the slaying of an innocent, clearly sets the tone for all Twain's later writings on the subject of war. Kaplan furnishes a brisk yet somehow trudging précis of the "Private History," adding that it is "undoubtedly partly fictional" but declining to say in what respect this is so or how he knows it.

It is much the same when we come to the fabled voyage of the good ship *Quaker City* to the Holy Land and back. This wickedly close observation of the habits and mentality of the common American pilgrim was a huge sensation when first published, and it is easy to see even today how scandalized the pious and the respectable must have been. But how much fun is there to be had in scanning a condensed and potted summary of *Innocents Abroad*? Moreover, and as with the Civil War passage, Kaplan almost bowdlerizes the tale by omitting much of Twain's original pungency and contempt, or by rendering it very indirectly.

One would be grateful for some idea of the root of Twain's dislike for religiosity, and especially of his revulsion from Christianity. In a somewhat oblique earlier passage Kaplan suggests that it originated in shock at the death of his brother Henry, in a ghastly steamboat explosion in 1858. The randomness and caprice of this event, we are told, persuaded Twain that there was no such thing as a merciful Providence. This seems a pardonable surmise. Similar tragic events, however, have the effect of reinforcing faith in many other people. What was it about Twain that made him not just an agnostic or an atheist but a probable sympathizer with the Devil's party? We are not enlightened.

On lesser matters Kaplan can speculate until the cows come home. What was the origin of the physical frailty that afflicted Livy Langdon, Twain's future wife?

> It may be that her condition was psychosomatic, an instance of the widespread phenomenon of Victorian young women withdrawing from the world for unspecified emotional reasons with serious physical symptoms, often referred to as neurasthenia. It may be that her illness was organic. Perhaps she was indeed ill with a disease of the spine, such as Pott's disease, which has recently been suggested: an illness in which chronic back pain and stiffness lead to partial paralysis. Perhaps she had in fact injured her spine in a fall. Without magnetic resonance imaging and CAT scans, the Victorians were even more helpless than later generations to diagnose or cure back pain.

This is padding. (The same needless verbosity occurs when Twain's daughter Jean dies in her bath, much later on: "Perhaps Jean had had an epileptic attack and blacked out. She may have drowned. Perhaps she had had a heart attack. What exactly killed her is unclear.")

Kaplan's prose is something less than an unalloyed joy to read, and its faults are such that one can sometimes not be certain when, or if, he is joking. A little after the dull passage about Livy above we learn of Langdon's regaining the ability to walk and are informed that "Livy's recovery, along with their continued prosperity, confirmed the family's strong religious faith." After reading this aloud several times, I concluded that it was meant as a plain statement of fact. Later, in retelling a story in which Finley Peter Dunne affected to think that he himself was a greater celebrity than Twain, Kaplan appears to exclude altogether the possibility that the author of the "Mr. Dooley" columns might have been joking.

Twain was often nettled by the contrary suggestion, that he was playing the comic when in fact he was attempting to be serious. This was especially the case at the turn of the century, when he became outraged by the McKinley-Roosevelt policy of expansionism in the Philippines and Cuba, and also by the sanguinary hypocrisy of America's Christian "missionaries" in China. The articles and pamphlets he wrote in that period, some of them too incendiary to see print at the time, are an imperishable part both of his own oeuvre and of the American radical journalistic tradition. I would single out in particular his essay on the massacre of the Moro Islanders—a piece of work to stand comparison with Swift's "A Modest Proposal." Nor did he confine himself to the printed word: With William Dean Howells he helped to animate the Anti-Imperialist League. This entire passage in his career is all but skipped by Kaplan, who awards it a few paragraphs, mentioning only that the New England branch of the Anti-Imperialist League reprinted one of the polemics, and confining himself to brief excerpts from a couple of the better-known articles. This scant treatment is redeemed only partially by an account of the celebrated public exchange between Twain and the young Winston Churchill in New York. Twain famously teased and chided the youthful firebrand of Britain's imperial war in South Africa. (One would like to have been present at that meeting.) Kaplan does give us a contemporary snippet from an anonymous attendee that makes those remarks appear to have been even more sulfurous than we had previously thought.

In general, though, this biography is terse when it ought to be expansive, and expansive when it could well do with being more terse. The student who will benefit from it most is that student who wishes to study the phenomenon of the author as businessman. The record of Twain's battles over copyright and royalties, and the story of his fluctuating success and failure as an investor, are told with great assiduity. Contemptuous as he may have been of the Gilded Age and the acquisitive society, Twain was ever ravenous for money, and his acumen was almost inversely proportionate to his ambition. Usually a man with a keen eye for fraud and imposture, he was lured to invest in numerous improbable schemes, and the tale of his won-and-lost fortunes is worth relating as a great American example of thwarted but unquenchable entrepreneurship. As a result of these exigencies he wrote altogether too many words, and now his biographer has cited too many of the mediocre ones and not enough of the brilliant ones. I did eventually come across a reference to the 1879 Stomach Club lecture on "the Science of Onanism." This masterly effort is only a few paragraphs long and screams aloud for quotation but does not get it. Instead Kaplan merely repeats the title of the talk and describes it thus:

> A brilliant, bawdy takeoff on the subject of masturbation, it was, like "1601," an expression of the subversive, anti-Victorian side of Twain that, perforce, found some of its best moments in private

> jokes. Stoically he accepted that he himself and everything he did was determined by forces beyond his control. Some were cultural. Some were genetic. All were implacable.

The solemnity of this is near terminal. And the stone of non sequitur is further laid upon the grave of the joke. It is altogether wrong that a book about Mark Twain should be boring.

(*The Atlantic*, November 2003)

Upton Sinclair: A Capitalist Primer

PROBABLY NO TWO WORDS in our language are now more calculated to shrivel the sensitive nostril than "socialist realism." Taken together, they evoke the tractor opera, the granite-jawed proletarian sculpture, the cultural and literary standards of Commissar Zhdanov, and the bone-deep weariness that is paradoxically produced by ceaseless uplift and exhortation. Yet these words used to have an authentic meaning, which was also directly related to "social" realism. And the most fully realized instance of the genre, more telling and more moving than even the works of Dickens and Zola, was composed in these United States.

Like Dickens and Zola, Upton Sinclair was in many ways a journalist. His greatest novel was originally commissioned as a serial, for the popular socialist paper *Appeal to Reason*, which was published (this now seems somehow improbable) in Kansas. An advance of $500 sent Sinclair to Chicago in 1904, there to make radical fiction out of brute reality. The city was then the great maw of American capitalism. That is to say, it took resources and raw materials from everywhere and converted them into money at an unprecedented rate. Hogs and steers, coal and iron, were transmuted into multifarious products by new and ruthless means. The Chicago system created almost

---

Review of *The Jungle*, by Upton Sinclair.

every imaginable kind of goods. But the main thing it consumed was people. Upton Sinclair tried to elucidate and illuminate the ways in which commodities deposed, and controlled, human beings. His novel is the most successful attempt ever made to fictionalize the central passages of Marx's *Das Kapital*.

The influence of Dickens can be felt in two ways. First, we are introduced to a family of naive but decent Lithuanian immigrants, sentimentally portrayed at a wedding feast where high hopes and good cheer provide some protection against the cruelty of quotidian life. There are lavishly spread tables, vital minor characters, and fiddle music. Second, we see these natural and spontaneous people being steadily reduced, as in *Hard Times*, by crass utilitarian calculation. They dwell in a place named Packingtown, and "steadily reduced" is a euphemism. The extended family of the stolid Jurgis is exposed to every variety of misery and exploitation, and discovers slowly—necessarily slowly—that the odds are so arranged that no honest person can ever hope to win. The landlord, the saloonkeeper, the foreman, the shopkeeper, the ward heeler, all are leagued against the gullible toiler in such a way that he can scarcely find time to imagine what his actual employer or boss might be getting away with. To this accumulation of adversity Jurgis invariably responds with the mantra "I will work harder."

This is exactly what the innocent cart horse Boxer later says as he wears out his muscles on the cynical futilities of *Animal Farm*. Orwell was an admirer of Sinclair's work, and wrote in praise of *The Jungle* in 1940, but Sinclair may have been depressed to see his main character redeployed in the service of allegory.

Sinclair's realism, indeed, got in the way of his socialism, in more than one fashion. His intention was to direct the conscience of America to the inhuman conditions in which immigrant labor was put to work. However, so graphic and detailed were his depictions of the filthy way in which food was produced that his book sparked a revolution among consumers instead (and led at some remove to the passage of the Food and Drugs Act and the Meat Inspection Act of 1906). He wryly said of this unintended consequence that he had aimed for the public's heart but had instead hit its stomach.

> There would be meat stored in great piles in rooms; and the water from leaky roofs would drip over it, and thousands of rats would race about on it. It was too dark in these storage places to see well,

> but a man could run his hand over these piles of meat and sweep off handfuls of the dried dung of rats. These rats were nuisances, and the packers would put poisoned bread out for them; they would die, and then rats, bread, and meat would go into the hoppers together. This is no fairy story and no joke; the meat would be shovelled into carts, and the man who did the shovelling would not trouble to lift out a rat even when he saw one—there were things that went into the sausage in comparison with which a poisoned rat was a tidbit.

To this Sinclair added well-researched observations about the adulteration of food with chemicals and coloring. He also spared a thought, as did many of his later readers, for the animals themselves, especially (and ironically, in view of *Animal Farm*) for the pigs:

> At the head there was a great iron wheel, about twenty feet in circumference, with rings here and there along its edge. Upon both sides of this wheel was a narrow space, into which came the hogs... [Men] had chains which they fastened about the leg of the nearest hog, and the other end of the chain they hooked into one of the rings upon the wheel. So, as the wheel turned, a hog was suddenly jerked off his feet and borne aloft.
>
> At the same instant the ear was assailed by a most terrifying shriek... And meantime another [hog] was swung up, and then another, and another, until there was a double line of them, each dangling by a foot and kicking in frenzy—and squealing... It was too much for some of the visitors—the men would look at each other, laughing nervously, and the women would stand with hands clenched, and the blood rushing to their faces, and the tears starting in their eyes.
>
> Meantime, heedless of all these things, the men upon the floor were going about their work. Neither squeals of hogs nor tears of visitors made any difference to them; one by one they hooked up the hogs, and one by one with a swift stroke they slit their throats.

Again, the demands of verisimilitude have a tendency to work against the recruitment of any sympathy for the calloused and even brutalized laborer. Sinclair's title, *The Jungle*, along with indirectly evoking the ideology of Thomas Hobbes, inverts anthropomorphism by making men into brutes. In her rather deft introduction Jane Jacobs dwells on the passage above and on the sinister implications of machine civilization without registering what to me seems an obvious point: Sinclair was unconsciously prefiguring the industrialization of the mass slaughter of *human beings*—the principle of the abattoir applied to politics and society by the degraded experimenters of the assembly line.

Eugene Debs, the great Socialist Party leader and orator of that period, announced that his ambition was to be "the John Brown of the wage slaves." This noble hyperbole was not all that much of an exaggeration: The lower orders in Chicago may have come voluntarily, to escape a Russian or a Polish house of bondage, rather than being brought by force from Africa *to* a house of bondage; but once here they were given only enough to keep them alive until their bodies wore out. Their children were exploited too, and their womenfolk were sexually vulnerable to the overseers. Indeed, the most wrenching section of the book comes in the middle, when Jurgis discovers that his wife has been preyed upon, under threat of dismissal, by a foreman. Not following the socialist script in the least, he sacrifices self-interest for pride and pounds the foreman to a pulp. By this means he swiftly discovers what side the courts and the cops and the laws are on, and is made to plumb new depths of degradation in prison. Among other humiliations, he stinks incurably from the materials of the plant, and offends even his fellow inmates. (We are not spared another Dickensian moment when he realizes that he has been jailed for the Christmas holidays and is overwhelmed by childhood memories.) Sinclair interrupts himself at this point to quote without attribution from *The Ballad of Reading Gaol* (Oscar Wilde was not long dead in 1905), and it seems a sure thing that Sinclair would have read *The Soul of Man Under Socialism*, the most brilliant line of which says that it is *capitalism* that lays upon men "the sordid necessity of living for others."

Robert Tressell's novel *The Ragged Trousered Philanthropists* (1914) is the only rival to *The Jungle* in its combination of realism with didacticism and its willingness to impose a bit of theory on the readership. In both "proletarian" novels the weapon often deployed is satire: the workers are too dumb, and too grateful for their jobs, to consider the notions that might emancipate them.

> Jurgis had no sympathy with such ideas as this—he could do the work himself, and so could the rest of them, he declared, if they were

> good for anything. If they couldn't do it, let them go somewhere else. Jurgis had not studied the books, and he would not have known how to pronounce "laissez-faire"; but he had been round the world enough to know that a man has to shift for himself in it, and that if he gets the worst of it, there is nobody to listen to him holler.

But gradually, after being for so long the anvil and not the hammer, he awakes from his bovine stupor and comes to understand that he has striven only to enrich others. The book ends with the soaring notes of a socialist tribune of the people, and the triumphant yell—thrice repeated—"*Chicago will be ours.*"

Before this happy ending, however, there is a passage that I am surprised Jane Jacobs does not discuss. A bitter strike is in progress in the stockyards, and gangs of scabs are being mobilized. They are from the South, and they are different. Indeed, the reader is introduced to "young white girls from the country rubbing elbows with big buck negroes with daggers in their boots, while rows of woolly heads peered down from every window of the surrounding factories."

> The ancestors of these black people had been savages in Africa; and since then they had been chattel slaves, or had been held down by a community ruled by the traditions of slavery. Now for the first time they were free, free to gratify every passion, free to wreck themselves...

This is no slip of the pen on Sinclair's part. He elsewhere refers to "a throng of stupid black negroes," a phrasing that convicts him of pleonasm as well as of racism. It is often forgotten that the early American labor movement preached a sort of "white socialism" and—though Debs himself didn't subscribe to it—that this sadly qualified its larger claim to be the liberator of the wage slaves.

The final way in which Sinclair's realism got the better of his socialism is this: Like Karl Marx in *The Communist Manifesto*, he couldn't help being exceedingly impressed by the dynamic, innovative, and productive energy of capitalism:

> No tiniest particle of organic matter was wasted in Durham's. Out of the horns of the cattle they made combs, buttons, hair-pins, and imitation ivory; out of the shin bones and other big bones they cut knife and tooth-brush handles, and mouthpieces for pipes; out of

> the hoofs they cut hair-pins and buttons, before they made the rest into glue. From such things as feet, knuckles, hide clippings, and sinews came such strange and unlikely products as gelatin, isinglass, and phosphorus, bone-black, shoe-blacking, and bone oil. They had curled-hair works for the cattle-tails, and a "wool-pullery" for the sheep-skins; they made pepsin from the stomachs of the pigs, and albumen from the blood, and violin strings from the ill-smelling entrails. When there was nothing else to be done with a thing, they first put it into a tank and got out of it all the tallow and grease, and then they made it into fertilizer.

This account of the magnificent profusion that results from the assembly line and the division of labor is so awe-inspiring that Sinclair seems impelled to follow it almost at once with a correct and ironic discourse on the nature of monopoly and oligopoly: "So guileless was he, and ignorant of the nature of business, that he did not even realize that he had become an employee of Brown's, and that Brown and Durham were supposed by all the world to be deadly rivals—were even required to be deadly rivals by the law of the land, and ordered to try to ruin each other under penalty of fine and imprisonment!"

Thus, though it lives on many a veteran's bookshelf as a stirring monument to the grandeur of the American socialist and labor movements, *The Jungle* may also be read today as a primer on the versatility of the capitalist system. But not all its "morals" belong to the past. The anti-*Jungle* ethos lived on, in a subterranean fashion, through the League for Industrial Democracy, founded by Sinclair and Jack London. (Its junior branch, the Student League for Industrial Democracy, survived long enough to provide the auspices for the first meeting of Students for a Democratic Society.) In Eric Schlosser's bestseller *Fast Food Nation* (2001) the values and practices of the slaughterhouse system were revisited. Most of the reviews, rather predictably, concentrated on the shock effect of Schlosser's intimate—almost intestinal—depiction of "hamburger" ingredients. But Schlosser also spent a great deal of time with those whose lives are lived at the point of production. Recruited, often illegally, from the Central American isthmus rather than the Baltic littoral, these workers are sucked into cutting machines, poisoned by chemicals, and made wretched by a pervasive stench that won't wash off. Their wages are low, their hours long, their conditions arduous, and their job security nonexistent. The many women among them are considered bounty by lascivious supervisors, who sometimes dangle the prospect of green cards or safer jobs, and sometimes don't bother even to do that. The health-and-safety inspectors are about as vigilant and incorruptible as they were a century ago. The main difference is that these plants are usually located in remote areas or rural states, so the consolations of urban and communal solidarity are less available to the atomized work force than they were to Jurgis and his peers. This nonfiction work is also a blow to the national gut; but if properly read, it might succeed where *The Jungle* failed, and bring our stomachs and our hearts—and even our brains—into a better alignment.

(*The Atlantic*, July/August 2002)

JFK: In Sickness and by Stealth

EVEN AS I WAS grazing on the easy slopes of this book, in June and July, the quotidian press brought me fairly regular updates on the doings and undoings of the "fabled Kennedy dynasty." A new volume by Ed Klein, portentously titled *The Kennedy Curse*, revealed the brief marriage of John Kennedy Jr. and Carolyn Bessette to have been a cauldron of low-level misery, infidelity, and addiction.

The political-matrimonial alliance between Andrew Cuomo and Kerry Kennedy was discovered to be in the process of acrimonious dissolution. Representative Patrick Kennedy of Rhode Island, whose ability to find his way to the House unaided has long been a source of intermittent wonder, became inflamed while making a speech at a liberal fund-raising event and yelled: "I don't need Bush's tax cut! I have never worked a fucking day in my life." The electoral career of Kathleen Kennedy Townsend, which had never achieved escape velocity from local Maryland politics, seemed to undergo a final eclipse in the last mid-term vote. Robert F. Kennedy Jr. failed to convince anyone of the innocence of his cousin Michael Skakel, convicted of beating a teenage girlfriend to death with a golf club.

Senator Edward Kennedy of Massachusetts still retains a certain grandeur, on the grounds of longevity and persistence alone, but his solidity on the landscape derives in part from his resemblance, pitilessly identified by his

---

Review of *An Unfinished Life: John F. Kennedy, 1917–1963*, by Robert Dallek.

distant kinsman Gore Vidal, to "three hundred pounds of condemned veal." And even Vidal, who first broke a lance against the Kennedy clan with his 1967 essay "The Holy Family," might be open-mouthed at the possibility of Arnold Schwarzenegger winning the upcoming race for the governorship of California and thereby making Maria Shriver, a collateral Kennedy descendant, the first lady of the nation's richest and most populous state. Such a macho Republican triumph would be a bizarre way for the family charisma to mutate. Or would it? Not if you bear in mind Vidal's phrase about the tribe's "coldblooded jauntiness." The calculated combination of sex, showbiz, money, and bravado was—as Robert Dallek unwittingly demonstrates in *An Unfinished Life*—the successful, if volatile, mixture all along.

Otherwise, one can reasonably look forward to a future where the entire meretricious Kennedy cult has staled. It is already more or less meaningless to younger Americans. And even those like myself, who are near-contemporary with all the verbiage and imagery of the "New Frontier" or—even worse—"Camelot," have had the opportunity to become bored, sated, and better informed. Pierre Salinger and Oliver Stone, votaries of the cult, have spun off into the bliss that comforts and shields the paranoid. Arthur Schlesinger Jr. and Theodore Sorenson, the officially consecrated historians, are, one feels, at last reaching an actuarial point of diminishing returns. Meanwhile, the colossal images of September 11, 2001, have easily deposed the squalid scenes in Dallas, of the murders of Kennedy and Oswald, which once supplied the bond of a common televised melodramatic "experience."

This is not to say that hair and nails do not continue to sprout on the corpse.

Professor Dallek's title, itself portentous and platitudinous at the same time, is part of the late growth. Since President Kennedy was shot dead at the age of forty-six, it is self-evidently true in one way to describe his life as "unfinished." But anyone scanning this or several other similar accounts would have to be astonished, not that the man's career was cut short, but rather that it lasted so long. In addition to being a moral defective and a political disaster, John Kennedy was a physical and probably mental also-ran for most of his presidency. Even someone impervious to his supposed charm has to feel a piercing pang of pity when reading passages such as this one:

> Despite the steroids he was apparently taking, he continued to have abdominal pain and problems gaining weight. Backaches were a constant problem.... He also had occasional burning when urinating, which was the result of a nonspecific urethritis dating from 1940 and a possible sexual encounter in college, which left untreated became a chronic condition. He was later diagnosed as having "a mild, chronic, non-specific prostatitis" that sulfa drugs temporarily suppressed.

Moreover, a strenuous daily routine intensified the symptoms—fatigue, nausea, and vomiting—of the Addison's disease that would not be diagnosed until 1947.

This was the state of affairs when the young "Jack," pressed and driven by his gruesome tyrant of a father, first ran for a seat in Congress in 1946.

Obviously, a good deal of "spin" is required to make an Achilles out of such a poxed and suppurating Philoctetes. The difference was supplied by family money in heaping measure, by the canny emphasis on a war record, and by serious attention to the flattery and suborning of the media. (As Dallek is the latest to concede, the boy-wonder later had a Pulitzer Prize procured for him, for a superficial book he had hardly read, let alone written.) One doesn't want to overstress the medical dimension, but it is the truly macabre extent of disclosure on that front that constitutes this book's only claim to originality. At the very time of the Bay of Pigs disaster, Kennedy "struggled with 'constant,' 'acute diarrhea' and a urinary tract infection. His doctors treated him with increased amounts of antispasmodics, a puree diet, and penicillin, and scheduled him for a sigmoidoscopy."

During the next crisis over Cuba—the nuclear confrontation in the autumn of 1962—we learn that the president took his usual doses of antispasmodics to control his colitis; antibiotics for a flareup of his urinary tract problem and a bout of sinusitis; and increased amounts of hydrocortisone and testosterone as well as salt tablets to control his Addison's disease.... On November 2, he took 10 additional grams of hydrocortisone and 10 grams of salt to boost him before giving a brief report to the American people on the dismantling of the Soviet missile bases in Cuba. In December, Jackie asked the president's gastroenterologist, Dr. Russell Boles, to eliminate antihistamines for food allergies. She described them as having a "depressing action" on the president and asked Boles to prescribe something that would ensure "mood elevation without irritation to the gastrointestinal tract." Boles prescribed 1 milligram twice a day of Stelazine, an anti-psychotic that was also used as an anti-anxiety medication.

Further mind-boggling revelations are given, and it becomes clearer and clearer that Dallek wants the credit for the disclosures without allowing any suggestion that they might qualify his hero-worship for the subject. Thus, and again in lacerating detail from the "previously secret medical records" of another of his numerous physicians, Dr. Janet Travell:

> During the first six months of his presidency, stomach/colon and prostate problems, high fevers, occasional dehydration, abscesses, sleeplessness and high cholesterol accompanied Kennedy's back and adrenal ailments. Medical attention was a fixed part of his routine. His physicians administered large doses of so many drugs that they kept an ongoing "Medicine Administration Record" (MAR) cataloguing injected and oral corticosteroids for his adrenal insufficiency; procaine shots to painful "trigger points," ultrasound treatments, and hot packs for his back; Lomotil, Metamucil, paregoric, Phenobarbital, testosterone, and Transentine to control his diarrhea, abdominal discomfort, and weight loss; penicillin and other antibiotics for his urinary infections and abscesses; and Tuinal to help him sleep.

To this pharmacopoeia, Dallek somewhat fatuously adds that "though the treatments occasionally made him feel groggy and tired, Kennedy did not see them as a problem." He thus perpetuates the fealty required by and of the "JFK" school, which insists that we judge Kennedy more or less as he judged himself.

Plain evidence is available on neighboring pages that this would be simplistic or foolish in the extreme. Dr. Travell and her colleagues did not know that their famous patient had a secret relationship with yet another doctor, who flew on another plane. As early as the election campaign of 1960—this revelation is not original to Dallek—Kennedy had begun seeing Dr. Max Jacobson, the New York physician who had made a reputation for treating celebrities with "pep pills," or amphetamines, that helped combat depression and fatigue.

Jacobson, whom patients termed "Dr. Feelgood," administered back injections of painkillers and amphetamines that allowed Kennedy to stay off crutches, which he believed essential to project a picture of robust good health.

The clumsy phrasing here makes it slightly obscure whether Kennedy or Jacobson was nurturing the image, but it was clearly the candidate himself.

Even on the day of his celebrated inaugural speech, he worried that his steroid-inflated face would be too fat and puffy for the cameras, and was saved by a swift Palm Beach suntan. This false projection of youthful vigor was more than narcissism. It was the essence of the presentation, and had been the backdrop to his wild accusation of a "missile gap" between the Soviet Union and the USA, neglected by the wrinkly and tired Eisenhower regime. Also, and unlike, say, Franklin Roosevelt's polio, the concealment was of a serious condition, or set of conditions, that might really affect performance in office. If Kennedy had not succumbed to his actual ill health, he might as easily have flamed out like Jimi Hendrix or Janis Joplin from the avalanche of competing uppers and downers that he was swallowing.

But the furthest that Dallek will go here is to admit—following Seymour Hersh's earlier book *The Dark Side of Camelot*—that Kennedy's back-brace held him upright in the open car in Dallas, unable to duck the second and devastating bullet from Lee Harvey Oswald. This is almost the only connection between the president's health and his fitness that is allowable in these pages, and I presume that it is its relative blamelessness which allows the concession. On other pages, Dallek flatly if unconsciously contradicts his own soothing analysis. "Judging from tape recordings of conversations made during the crisis, the medications were no impediment to long days and lucid thought; to the contrary, Kennedy would have been significantly less effective without them and might not have been able to function."

Consider for yourself: How reassuring is that? Elsewhere we learn that, during the disastrous summit with Khrushchev in Vienna, a long day under much tension certainly accounts for most of Kennedy's weariness by the early evening, but we cannot discount the impact of the Jacobson chemicals on him as well. As the day wore on and an injection Jacobson had given him just before he met Khrushchev wore off, Kennedy may have lost the emotional and physical edge initially provided by the shot.

This is no small matter, because the sense that Kennedy retained—of having been outdone by Khrushchev in their first man-to-man confrontation—decided him to show "resolve" in the worst of all possible locations, which was Vietnam.

A mere sixty-three pages later, Dallek simply states without qualification that "personal problems added to the strains of office, testing Kennedy's physical and emotional endurance. His health troubles were a constant strain on his ability to meet presidential responsibilities."

The other "personal problems," which Dallek also approaches with a combination of fawning and concession, are at least suggested by the injections of testosterone mentioned above. This was notoriously a department in which Kennedy did not require any extra boost. We learn again from this book about the way in which he regularly humiliated his wife, abused his staffers and Secret Servicemen by suborning them as procurers, and endangered the security of his administration by fornicating with a gun-moll—the property of the Mafia boss Sam Giancana—in the White House. But Dallek almost outpoints Schlesinger himself in the deployment of euphemism here:

> Did Kennedy's compulsive womanizing distract him from public business? Some historians think so, especially when it comes to Vietnam. Kennedy's reluctance, however, to focus the sort of attention on Vietnam he gave to Berlin or other foreign and domestic concerns is not evidence of a distracted president, but of a determination to keep Vietnam from becoming more important to his administration than he wished it to be.
>
> Certainly, when one reviews Kennedy's White House schedules, he does not seem to have been derelict about anything he considered a major problem.... But the supposition that he was too busy chasing women or satisfying his sexual passions to attend to important presidential business is not borne out by the record of his daily activities. And, according to Richard Reeves, another Kennedy historian, the womanizing generally "took less time than tennis."

One is forced into a bark of mirth by the way that bathos succeeds banality here.

(Forget the fact, already admitted, that some of Kennedy's health problems originated with a clinging and neglected case of VD.) A solemn review of the official appointment book is supposed to show no trace of strenuous venery and thus to rule it out as a problem, while this non-evidence is allegedly buttressed by the assertion that the tennis court was as much of an arena as the boudoir. We are not, here, really comparing like with like. And if record-keeping is to count as evidence, then what of the numerous holes and gaps in the White House taping system that Kennedy secretly installed? Dallek does his best to explain these away, admitting in the process that the excisions probably involve assassination plots against Castro, as well as involvement with Marilyn Monroe and with Judith Campbell Exner (Giancana's girlfriend). The Kennedy Library remains as hermetic as ever, withholding the transcripts of four missing tapes, "which may contain embarrassing revelations or national security secrets." Wrong-footing himself at almost every step, Dallek lamely concludes that "by and large, however, the tapes seem to provide a faithful record of some of the most important events in Kennedy's presidency. . . ." "By and large," the same could be said of the Nixon tapes too.

Like many of his fellow devotees, Dallek rests a tentative defense on what might have been: the speech at American University about ultimate disarmament, or the possibility that reason might have prevailed in Indo-China—always given the chance of a second term. Why is it not recognized, with Kennedy, that the job of the historian is to record and evaluate what actually did happen? And why is it forgotten that, had he lived, Kennedy would necessarily have been even more distressingly ill than he was already? The usual compromise is to invest with a retrospective numinousness the relative banality of what did occur. Thus Dallek relates the set-piece events with the customary awe: the brinkmanship over Cuba, the "ich bin ein Berliner" speech, the confrontations with revolution in Vietnam and the Congo. Tougher scholarship has dimmed the phony glamour of most of these recovered memories. Michael Beschloss's *Crisis Years* demonstrated in 1991 that Kennedy was for most practical purposes complicit in the erection of the Berlin Wall, played it down as an issue wherever possible, and only made his defiant public speech when he was quite sure that it could make no difference. As in the case of Cuba, he first created the conditions for a crisis by using inflamed rhetoric and tactics, then just managed to extricate himself from catastrophe, and finally agreed to a consolidation of Communist power that was much more "locked in" than it had been before.

Whether you approach matters from the standpoint of those concerned with nuclear holocaust and superpower promiscuity, or of those desiring a long-term strategy to outlast the Stalinist monolith, this record is a dismal one. It was further punctuated by episodes of more or less gangsterish conduct, most conspicuously in the coup that murdered Kennedy's South Vietnamese client Ngo Dinh Diem, but also in such vignettes as Robert Kennedy's serious proposal to blow up the American consulate in the Dominican Republic, in order to supply a pretext for a U.S. invasion. Dallek allows this latter moment all of two sentences.

Their hysterical and profitless hyperactivity on one front is in the boldest contrast to the millimetrical trudging and grudging with which the Kennedy brothers approached their genuinely urgent, and constitutionally mandated, responsibility for civil rights. Confronted with an inescapable matter, they abandoned the flamboyance of their overseas melodramas and confined themselves to the most minimal Fabian tactics. Since Robert Kennedy was at least physically robust, it may not be fair to attribute this mood-swing regime too intimately to the influence of stimulants and analgesics. But as Robert Dallek inadvertently shows, it would be highly imprudent to discard the hypothesis altogether. The reputation of the Kennedy racket is now dependent on a sobbing effort of will: an applauding chorus demanding that the flickering Tinker Bell not be allowed to expire. It is pardonable for children to yell that they believe in fairies, but it is somehow sinister when the piping note shifts from the puerile to the senile.

(*Times Literary Supplement*, August 22, 2003)

Saul Bellow: The Great Assimilator

LOOK FIRST UPON THIS PICTURE, and on this... the two photographs of Saul Bellow that adorn the initial covers of the Library of America edition of his collected works. In the first, we see a somewhat rakish fellow, sharply dressed and evidently fizzing with moxie, who meets the world with a cool and level gaze that belies the slight impression of a pool shark or racetrack con artist. In the second, and in profile, we get a survey of a sage in a more reflective pose; but this is a sage who still might utter a well-chosen wisecrack out of the side of his mouth. The antique history of the shtetl and the ghetto is inscribed in both studies of the man, but some considerable mental and physical distance has evidently been traveled in each case.

At Bellow's memorial meeting, held in the Young Men's Hebrew Association at Lexington Avenue and 92nd Street two years ago, the main speakers were Ian McEwan, Jeffrey Eugenides, Martin Amis, William Kennedy, and James Wood (now the editor of this finely produced collection). Had it not been for an especially vapid speech by some forgettable rabbi, the platform would have been exclusively composed of non-Jews, many of them non-American. How had Bellow managed to exert such an effect on writers almost half

---

Review of Saul Bellow's *Novels 1944–1953: Dangling Man, The Victim, The Adventures of Augie March*; and *Novels 1956–1964: Seize the Day, Henderson the Rain King, Herzog.*

his age, from another tradition and another continent? Putting this question to the speakers later on, I received two particularly memorable responses. Ian McEwan related his impression that Bellow, alone among American writers of his generation, had seemed to assimilate the whole European classical inheritance. And Martin Amis vividly remembered something Bellow had once said to him, which is that if you are born in the ghetto, the very conditions compel you to look skyward, and thus to hunger for the universal.

In *The Victim*, the Jewish son of an anti-gentile and ghetto-mentality storekeeper is being given a hard time by an insecure and alcoholic WASP. "I'm a fine one to be talking about tradition, you must be saying," admits the latter:

> "But still I was born into it. And try to imagine how New York affects me. Isn't it preposterous? It's really as if the children of Caliban were running everything. You go down in the subway and Caliban gives you two nickels for your dime. You go home and he has a candy store in the street where you were born. The old breeds are out. The streets are named after them. But what are they themselves? Just remnants."
>
> "I see how it is; you're actually an aristocrat," said Leventhal.
>
> "It may not strike you as it struck me," said Allbee. "But I go into the library once in a while, to look around, and last week I saw a book about Thoreau and Emerson by a man named Lipschitz..."
>
> "What of it?"
>
> "A name like that?" Allbee said this with great earnestness. "After all, it seems to me that people of such background simply couldn't understand..."

Remember that when Bellow was growing up, Lionel Trilling could be sacked from a teaching post at Columbia on the grounds that a Jew could not really appreciate English literature. Recall also the exquisite pain with which Henry James, in *The American Scene* in 1907, had registered "the whole hard glitter of Israel" on New York's Lower East Side, and especially the way in which Yiddish-speaking authors operated the "torture-rooms of the living idiom." Bellow in his time was to translate Isaac Bashevis Singer into English (and "The Love Song of J. Alfred Prufrock" into Yiddish), but it mattered to him that the ghetto be transcended and that he, too, could sing America.

The various means of this assertion included pyrotechnic versatility with English, a ferocious assimilation of learning, and an emphasis on the man of action as well as the man of reflection.

If you reread Bellow's fiction in this light, you will, I think, be sure to find these considerations recurring to you. As early as the text of *Dangling Man*, there are fairly effortless references to Goethe, Diderot, Alexander the Great; *Measure for Measure*, Machiavelli, Berkeley, Dr. Johnson, Joyce, Marx, and Baudelaire. The novel contains, in parallel, a replication of Bellow's own life experience as a slum kid, as an illegal immigrant from Quebec, and as an aspirant member of the United States armed forces. A much later short story—"Something to Remember Me By"—sees a young Jewish boy being rolled by a whore and saved by the sordid denizens of a Chicago speakeasy, but depicts the kid as distressed most of all by the loss of a torn book that he had bought for a nickel. All around him are people who have become coarsened and street-smart, but this variety of common "wisdom" is to be despised as too cheaply bought.

When I think of Bellow, I think not just of a man whose genius for the vernacular could seem to restate Athenian philosophy as if run through a Damon Runyon synthesizer, but of the author who came up with such graphic expressions for vulgarity and thuggery and stupidity—the debased currency of those too brutalized to have retained the capacity for wonder. "A goon's rodeo" is Augie March's description of a saturnalia of the mindless. "The moronic inferno"—apparently annexed from Wyndham Lewis—is the phrasing that occurs in *Humboldt's Gift*. "Moral buggery" is the crisp summary of New York values in *Dangling Man*. Best of all, in a confrontation between a thoughtful person and an uncivilized one that also occurs in *Humboldt's Gift*, is the dawning recognition that the latter belongs to the "mental rabble of the wised-up world." The narrator of *Dangling Man* states it shortly:

> Most serious matters are closed to the hard-boiled. They are unpracticed in introspection, and therefore badly equipped to deal with opponents whom they cannot shoot like big game or outdo in daring... The hard-boiled are compensated for their silence: they fly planes or fight bulls or catch tarpon, whereas I rarely leave my room.

Yet Bellow by no means dismisses the Hemingway style as easily as that. Several of his heroes and protagonists—including the thick-necked

Henderson—rise above the sickly and the merely bookish. They tackle lions and, in the case of Augie March, a truly fearsome eagle. They mix it up with revolutionaries and bandits and hard-core criminals. Commenting on Socrates's famous dictum about the worthlessness of the unexamined life, the late Kurt Vonnegut once inquired: "What if the examined life turns out to be a clunker as well?" Bellow would have seen, and indeed did see, the force of this question. Like Lambert Strether's in *The Ambassadors*, his provisional answer seems to have been: "Live all you can; it's a mistake not to." And the tough-guy Henderson, so gross and physical and intrepid (and so inarticulate when he speaks, yet so full of reflective capacity when he thinks), cannot repress his wonder when flying: He keeps pointing out that his is the first generation to have seen the clouds from above as well as below:

> What a privilege! First people dreamed upward. Now they dream both upward and downward. This is bound to change something, somewhere.

Erich Fromm once gave a course at the New School on "the struggle against pointlessness," and one wonders whether Bellow heard of, or took, this class. Pervasive in his work is a sense of the awful trap posed by aimlessness and its cousins, impotence and the death wish. In *Dangling Man*, the narrator hears of a college friend's death in the war and diagnoses it as an indirect act of will:

> I always suspected of him that he had in some fashion discovered there were some ways in which to be human was to be unutterably dismal, and that all his life was given over to avoiding those ways.

Whereas in *The Adventures of Augie March*, the hero signs up for the same combat and, reflecting on what it does for his sex life, asks, "What use was war without also love?" Yiddishism or no Yiddishism, this must count as one of the most affirmative and masculine sentences ever set down.

Against pointlessness and futility, Bellow strove to counterpose what Augie calls "the universal eligibility to be noble"—the battle to overcome not just ghetto conditions but also ghetto psychoses. Such yearning ambition, as Bellow knew, can be a torment to those who are not innately noble to begin with. Even Wilhelm, the desperate and perspiring arriviste in *Seize the Day*, has a touch of higher aspiration amid his death-of-a-salesman panics, and he finds snatches of English lyric poetry coming back to him at improbable moments. And Allbee, the drunken anti-Semite in *The Victim*, the man who says that "evil is as real as sunshine," chooses to speak loftily about his "honor" when he comes to oppress and exhaust Asa Leventhal. In all this, the great precursor is the strongly drawn King Dahfu in *Henderson the Rain King*, who makes splendid use of his secondhand English when addressing his massive and worried American guest as follows:

> Yet you are right for the long run, and good exchanged for evil truly is the answer. I also subscribe, but it appears a long way off, for the human species as a whole. Perhaps I am not the one to make a prediction, Sungo, but I think the noble will have its turn in the world.

Perhaps the best illustration of nobility that Bellow offers is Augie March's brief glimpse of Trotsky in Mexico, from which he receives a strong impression of "deepwater greatness" and an ability to steer by the brightest stars. Bellow himself had arrived in Mexico in 1940, just too late to see Trotsky, who had been murdered by a hireling assassin the morning they were meant to meet. Like Henderson, Trotsky was a man upon whom life had "decided to use strong measures." The founder of the Red Army was also the author of *Literature and Revolution* and a coauthor of *Manifesto for an Independent Revolutionary Art*. In his own person he united the Jew, the cosmopolitan, the man of ideas, and the man of action. And the speed with which Bellow learned from the experience of Trotsky's murder is a theme in several of his fictions. In *Dangling Man*, Joseph astonishes his friend Myron by the amount he can deduce from the simple fact that a former "comrade" will no longer speak to him in public. "Oh, Joseph," exclaims Myron, as if reproving exaggeration; but Joseph isn't merely piqued in the sense of personal offense:

> No, really, listen to me. Forbid one man to talk to another, forbid him to communicate with someone else, and you've forbidden him to think, because, as a great many writers will tell you, thought is a

> kind of communication. And his party doesn't want him to think, but to follow its discipline. So there you are... When a man obeys an order like that he's helping to abolish freedom and begin tyranny.

This "insolence," Joseph concluded, "figured the whole betrayal of an undertaking to which I had once devoted myself," and who is to say that Bellow selected the wrong microcosm of *trahison*? From a detail of political etiquette, he could infer the incipient mentality of the totalitarian. His life as a public intellectual is sometimes held to have followed a familiar arc or trajectory: that from quasi-Trotskyist to full-blown "neocon," and of course it is true that the earlier novels contain portraits of members of the *Partisan Review* group, from Delmore Schwartz to Dwight Macdonald, whereas the final novel, *Ravelstein*, features an affectionate portrayal of Allan Bloom (whose *Closing of the American Mind* Bellow had helped make into a bestseller), and even of Paul Wolfowitz during the intra-Washington struggle over the Gulf War, in 1991.

But Bellow's political evolution was by no means an uncomplicated or predictable one. He had been loosely associated with the dynamic ex-Trotskyist Max Schachtman (a man, incidentally, who is much more the founder of neoconservatism than Leo Strauss). Bellow's first published short story, a fiercely polemical reply to Sinclair Lewis's novel *It Can't Happen Here* that was no less polemically titled "The Hell It Can't," was obviously written under the influence of the Trotskyist youth movement. As late as the 1990s, Bellow eulogized Schachtman's widow, Yetta Barshevsky, recalling her fiery anti-Stalinism with affection. And until quite late in the day, his name appeared on the editorial masthead of Julius Jacobson's *New Politics,* an essentially post-Schachtmanite journal of democratic socialism.

Of the single occasion when I met Bellow properly, Martin Amis has given a brilliantly scandalized account in his memoir, *Experience*. Actually, the evening wasn't as rough as all that. Bellow read to us from some fascinating old correspondence with John Berryman. He recalled the occasion when he had been denied a job at *Time* magazine by no less a person than Whittaker Chambers for giving the wrong answer to a question about William Wordsworth (the episode is loosely fictionalized in *The Victim*). When asked his opinion, Bellow had said that he thought of Wordsworth as a Romantic poet, and then been rudely turned away. He wondered aloud what he ought to have said instead, and I daringly suggested that the answer was an easy one: Chambers wanted him to say that Wordsworth was a former revolutionary and republican poet who saw the error of his ways and became a counter-revolutionary and a monarchist. This seemed to satisfy and amuse Bellow, who then wondered aloud what his writing life would have been like if he had secured that safe billet at *Time*.

So all was going fairly smoothly, except that on the reading table, like a revolver in a Chekhov play, there lay a loaded copy of *Commentary*. It soon became apparent that Bellow really had moved to the right, without losing his taste for Talmudic and *trotskisant* dialectic, and that in his mind there was a strong connection between the decay of American cities and campuses, and wider questions of ideological promiscuity. I do not think I am wrong in guessing that he regarded the battle in the Middle East as something of an allegory of the distraught state of black-white (and black-Jewish) relations in his beloved Chicago. Anyone who has read his nonfiction work *To Jerusalem and Back* will be compelled to notice that the Arab inhabitants of the holy city are as nearly invisible and alien as their equivalents in Oran in Camus's *La Peste*. At any event, we ended up having a strong disagreement about the Palestinians in general, and the work of Edward Said in particular. I have several times devoutly wished that we could have had this discussion again.

The thread in the labyrinth of Bellow's politics has undoubtedly something to do with the "ghetto" also, and with a certain awkward possessiveness about the employment of that same pejorative. In a revealing moment in *Ravelstein*, the hero objects to the commonplace use of the term as customarily applied to black American life:

> "Ghetto nothing!" Ravelstein said. "Ghetto Jews had highly developed feelings, civilized nerves—thousands of years of training. They had communities and laws. 'Ghetto' is an ignorant newspaper term. It's not a ghetto that they come from, it's a noisy, pointless, nihilistic turmoil."

So, perhaps paradoxically, Bellow echoes a defensive and even admiring attitude to the very place from which he wished to escape. This is almost conservatism defined. One can locate the same trope as early as *Dangling*

Man, where the boy recalling the horrors of slum life remembers "a man rearing over someone on a bed, and, on another occasion, a Negro with a blond woman on his lap." And the underage black boy who transmits AIDS to Ravelstein (who himself is fatally attracted to the very thing that he supposedly most despises), was in early drafts given the same name as *Augie March*'s only black character. In *Mr. Sammler's Planet*, the eponymous figure is haunted by a large "Negro" who stops him in the street and flaunts a massive penis in his face. In *The Dean's December*, black crime and big-city corruption have become hard to distinguish in Bellow's mind; he was later to manifest alarm and disgust when a black demagogue in Chicago accused Jewish doctors of spreading the AIDS virus. I don't want to make any insinuation here, but it's clear that Bellow had concluded that one of the fondest hopes of the democratic left—that of a black-Jewish alliance—had become a thing of the past: another slightly sappy project of what in a more genial and witty moment he had called "the Good Intentions Paving Company."

However, he never quite succumbed to the affectless cynicism that he had always despised. His famously provocative 1988 question, "Who is the Tolstoy of the Zulus? The Proust of the Papuans?," asked in the context of a defense of Bloom, seemed to many people to contradict the generosity of what he had offered about Africa in *Henderson*, and evidently must have struck Bellow himself in the same light, since six years later he wrote a much-less-noticed essay in praise of the novel of Zululand *Chaka*, by Thomas Mofolo. Life and politics might have had souring results, and so might personal experience, but to the end, he put his money on the life-affirming and on the will to live (as Henderson's understanding of the benediction *grun-tu-molani* loosely translates), and he could never quite abandon his faith in that crucial eligibility to be noble.

(*The Atlantic*, November 2007)

Vladimir Nabokov: Hurricane Lolita

IN AZAR NAFISI'S *Reading Lolita in Tehran*, in which young female students meet in secret with Xeroxed copies of Nabokov's masterpiece on their often chaste and recently chadored laps, it is at first a surprise to discover how unscandalized the women are. Without exception, it turns out, they concur with Vera Nabokov in finding that the chief elements of the story are "its beauty and pathos." They "identify" with Lolita, because they can see that she wants above all to be a normal girl-child; they see straight through Humbert, because he is always blaming his victim and claiming that it was she who seduced *him*. And this perspective—such a bracing change from our conventional worried emphasis on pedophilia—is perhaps more easily come by in a state where virgins are raped before execution because the Koran forbids the execution of virgins; where the censor cuts Ophelia out of the Russian movie version of *Hamlet*; where any move that a woman makes can be construed as lascivious and inciting; where goatish old men can be gifted with infant brides; and where the age of "consent" is more like nine. As Nafisi phrases it,

> This was the story of a twelve-year-old girl who had nowhere to go. Humbert had tried to turn her into his fantasy, into his dead love,

---

Review of *Lolita*, by Vladimir Nabokov; and *The Annotated Lolita,* edited by Alfred Appel, Jr.

> and he had destroyed her. The desperate truth of *Lolita*'s story is *not* the rape of a twelve-year-old by a dirty old man but *the confiscation of one individual's life by another.* We don't know what Lolita would have become if Humbert had not engulfed her. Yet the novel, the finished work, is hopeful, beautiful even, a defense not just of beauty but of life... Warming up and suddenly inspired, I added that in fact Nabokov had taken revenge on our own solipsizers; he had taken revenge on the Ayatollah Khomeini...

It's extraordinary to think that the author of those anti-tyrannical classics *Bend Sinister* and *Invitation to a Beheading*, who would surely have felt extreme pleasure at this tribute, can be posthumously granted such an unexpected yet—when you reflect on it—perfectly intelligible homage. In his own essay on the fate of *Lolita*, Nabokov recalled a publisher who warned him that if he helped the author get it into print, they would both go straight to jail. And one of the many, many pleasures of Alfred Appel's masterly introduction and annotation is the discovery that Nabokov did not realize that Maurice Girodias and the Olympia Press were specialists in—well, shall we just say "erotica"?—when he let them have the manuscript. (The shock and awe surrounding its publication were later well netted by the great lepidopterist in one of John Shade's cantos in *Pale Fire*: "It was a year of tempests, Hurricane / Lolita swept from Florida to Maine.") Innocence of that kind is to be treasured.

And innocence, of course, is the problem to begin with. If Dolores Haze, whose first name means suffering and grief, that "dolorous and hazy darling," had not been an innocent, there would be nothing tragic in the tale. (Azar Nafisi is someone who, in spite of her acuity and empathy, fails what I call the Martin Amis test. Amis once admitted that he had read the novel carefully before noticing that in its "foreword"—written not by the unreliable Humbert but by "John Ray, Jr., Ph.D."—we learn that Lolita has died in childbirth. She's over before she's begun. That's where the yearning search for a normal life and a stable marriage got *her*. I fear that the young ladies of Tehran missed that crucial, callous postdate/update sentence as well.)

Then we must approach the question of how innocent *we* are in all this. Humbert writes without the smallest intention of titillating his audience. The whole narrative is, after all, his extended jailhouse/madhouse plea to an unseen jury. He has nothing but disgust for the really pornographic debauchee Quilty, for whose murder he has been confined. But he does refer to him as a "brother," and at one point addresses us, too, as "Reader! *Bruder!*," which is presumably designed to make one think of Baudelaire's address of *Les Fleurs du Mal* to "*Hypocrite lecteur,—mon semblable—mon frère!*" I once read of an interview given by Roman Polanski in which he described listening to a lurid radio account of his offense even as he was fleeing to the airport. He suddenly realized the trouble he was in, he said, when he came to appreciate that he had done something for which a lot of people would furiously envy him. Hamlet refers to Ophelia as a nymph ("Nymph, in thy orisons, be all my sins remembered"), but she is of marriageable age, whereas a nymphet is another thing altogether.

Actually, it is impossible to think of employing *Lolita* for immoral or unsavory purposes, and there is now a great general determination to approach the whole book in an unfussed, grown-up, broad-minded spirit. "Do not misunderstand me," said Amis *père* when he reviewed the first edition, "if I say that one of the troubles with *Lolita* is that, so far from being too pornographic, it is not pornographic enough." When he wrote that, his daughter, Sally, was a babe in arms, and now even those innocuous words seem fraught with implication. This doesn't necessarily alter the case, but neither can I forget Sally's older brother, who wrote,

> Parents and guardians of twelve-year-old girls will have noticed that their wards have a tendency to be difficult. They may take Humbert's word for it that things are much more difficult—are in fact entirely impossible—when your twelve-year-old girl is also your twelve-year-old girlfriend. The next time that you go out with your daughter, imagine you are *going out* with your daughter.

When I first read this novel, I had not had the experience of having a twelve-year-old daughter. I have had that experience twice since, which is many times fewer than I have read the novel. I daresay I chortled, in an outraged sort of way, when I first read, "How sweet it was to bring that coffee to her, and then deny it until she had done her morning duty." But this latest time I found myself almost congealed with shock. What about the fatherly visit to the schoolroom, for example, where Humbert is allowed the privilege of sitting near his (wife's) daughter in class:

> I unbuttoned my overcoat and for sixty-five cents plus the permission to participate in the school play, had Dolly put her inky, chalky, red-knuckled hand under the desk. Oh, stupid and reckless of me no doubt, but after the torture I had been subjected to, I simply had to take advantage of a combination that I knew would never occur again.

Or this, when the child runs a high fever: "She was shaking from head to toe. She complained of a painful stiffness in the upper vertebrae—and I thought of poliomyelitis as any American parent would. Giving up all hope of intercourse..."

Forgive me, *hypocrite lecteur*, if I say that I still laughed out loud at the deadpan way in which Nabokov exploded that land mine underneath me. And of course, as Amis *fils* half admits in his words about "parents and guardians," Lolita is *not* Humbert's daughter. If she were, the book probably would have been burned by the hangman, and its author's right hand sliced off and fed to the flames. But, just as Humbert's mind is on a permanent knife-edge of sexual mania, so his creator manages to tread the vertiginous path between incest, by which few are tempted, and engagement with pupating or nymph-like girls, which will not lose its *frisson*. (You will excuse me if, like Humbert, I dissolve into French when euphemism is required.) For me the funniest line in the book—because it is so farcical—comes in the moment after the first motel rape, when the frenzied Humbert, who has assumed at least the authority and disguise of fatherhood, is "forced to devote a dangerous amount of time (was she up to something downstairs?) to arranging the bed in such a way as to suggest the abandoned nest of a restless father and his tomboy daughter, instead of an ex-convict's saturnalia with a couple of fat old whores." None of this absurdity allows us to forget—and Humbert himself does not allow us to forget—that immediately following each and every one of the hundreds of subsequent rapes, the little girl weeps for quite a long time...

How complicit, then, is Nabokov himself? The common joking phrase among adult men, when they see nymphets on the street or in the park or, nowadays, on television and in bars, is "Don't even think about it." But it is very clear that Nabokov *did* think about it, and had thought about it a lot. An earlier novella, written in Russian and published only after his death—*The Enchanter*—centers on a jeweler who hangs around playgrounds and forces himself into gruesome sex and marriage with a *vache*-like mother, all for the sake of witnessing her death and then possessing and enjoying her twelve-year-old daughter. (I note one correspondence I had overlooked before: The hapless old bag in *The Enchanter* bears many unappetizing scars from the surgeon's knife, and when Humbert scans Lolita's statistics—height, weight, thigh measurements, IQ, and so forth—he discovers that she still has her appendix and says to himself, "Thank God." You do not want to think about *that* for very long either.) And then there is, just once, a hint of incest so elaborate and so deranged that you can read past it, as many critics have, before going back and whistling with alarm.

> ... the thought that with patience and luck I might have her produce eventually a nymphet with my blood in her exquisite veins, a Lolita the Second, who would be eight or nine around 1960, when I would still be *dans la force d'age*; indeed, the telescopy of my mind, or un-mind, was strong enough to distinguish in the remoteness of time a *vieillard encore vert*—or was it green rot?—bizarre, tender, salivating Dr. Humbert, practicing on supremely lovely Lolita the Third the art of being a granddad.

Arresting, as well as disgusting, to suddenly notice that Lolita (who died giving birth to a stillborn girl, for Christ's sake) would have been seventy this year... However, I increasingly think that Nabokov's celebrated, and tiresomely repeated, detestation of Sigmund Freud must itself be intended as some kind of acknowledgment. If he thought "the Viennese quack" and "Freudian voodooism" were so useless and banal, why couldn't he stay off the subject, or the subtext?

> I could very well do with a little rest in this subdued, frightened-to-death rocking chair, before I drove to wherever the beast's lair was—and then pulled the pistol's foreskin back, and then enjoyed the orgasm of the crushed trigger. I was always a good little follower of the Viennese medicine man...

Many a true word is spoken in jest, especially about the kinship between Eros and Thanatos. The two closest glimpses Humbert gives us of his own self-hatred are not without their death wish—made explicit in the closing paragraphs—and their excremental aspects: "I am lanky, big-boned, wooly-chested Humbert Humbert, with thick black eyebrows and a queer accent, and a cesspoolful of rotting monsters behind his slow boyish smile." Two hundred pages later: "The turquoise blue swimming pool some distance behind the lawn was no longer behind that lawn, but within my thorax, and my organs swam in it like excrements in the blue sea water in Nice." And then there's the offhand aside "Since (as the psychotherapist, as well as the rapist, will tell you) the limits and rules of such girlish games are fluid..." in which it takes a moment to notice that "therapist" and "the rapist" are in direct apposition.

Once you start to take a shy hand in the endless game of decoding the puns and allusions and multiple entendres (the Umberto echoes, if I may be allowed) that give this novel its place next to *Ulysses*, you are almost compelled to agree with Freud that the unconscious never lies. Swinburne's poem *Dolores* sees a young lady ("Our Lady of Pain") put through rather more than young Miss Haze. Lord Byron's many lubricities are never far away; in the initial stages of his demented scheme Humbert quotes from *Childe Harold's Pilgrimage*: "To hold thee lightly on a gentle knee and print on thine soft cheek a parent's kiss," and when we look up the lines we find they are addressed to Harold's absent daughter (who, like Byron's child and Nabokov's longest fiction, is named Ada). Humbert's first, lost girlfriend, Annabel, is perhaps not unrelated to Byron's first wife, Anne Isabella, who was known as "Annabella," and she has parents named Leigh, just like Byron's ravished half-sister Augusta. The Haze family physician, who gives Humbert the sleeping pills with which he drugs Lolita preparatory to the first rape at the Enchanted Hunters Hotel, is named Dr. Byron. And while we are on the subject of physicians, remember how Humbert is recommended to "an excellent dentist":

> Our neighbor, in fact. Dr. Quilty. Uncle or cousin, I think, of the playwright. Think it will pass? Well, just as you wish. In the fall I shall have him "brace" her, as my mother used to say. It may curb Lo a little.

Another Quilty, with his own distinctive hint of sadism. "Sade's Justine was twelve at the start," as Humbert reflects, those three so ordinary words "at the start" packing a huge, even gross, potential weight... These clues are offset by more innocuous puns ("We had breakfast in the township of Soda, pop 1001") and by dress rehearsals for puns, as when Humbert decides to decline a possible joke about the Mann Act, which forbids the interstate transport of girls for immoral purposes. (Alexander Dolinin has recently produced a fascinating article on the contemporaneous abduction of a girl named Sally Horner, traces of the reportage of which are to be found throughout *Lolita*.)

All is apparently redeemed, of course, by the atrocious punishment that Nabokov inflicts for this most heinous of humanity's offenses. The molester in *The Enchanter* was hit by a truck, and Humbert dies so many little deaths—eroding his heart muscles most pitifully—that in some well-wrought passages we almost catch ourselves feeling sorry for him. But the urge to punish a crime ("Why dost thou lash that whore?" Shakespeare makes us ask ourselves in *King Lear*) is sometimes connected to the urge to commit it. Naming a girls' school for Beardsley must have taken a good deal of reflection, with more Sade than Lewis Carroll in it, but perhaps there is an almost inaudible note of redemption at Humbert and Lolita's last meeting (the only time, as he ruefully minutes, that she ever calls him "honey"), when "I looked and looked at her, and knew as clearly as I know I am to die, that I loved her more than anything I had ever seen or imagined on earth, or hoped for anywhere else."

The most unsettling suggestion of all must be the latent idea that nymphetomania is, as well as a form of sex, a form of love.

Alfred Appel's most sage advice is to make yourself slow down when reading *Lolita*, not be too swiftly ravished and caught up. Follow this counsel and you will find that—more than almost any other novel of our time—it keeps the promise of genius and never presents itself as the same story twice. I mentioned the relatively obvious way in which it strikes one differently according to one's age; and if aging isn't a theme here, with its connotation of death and extinction, then I don't know what is. But there are other ways in which *Lolita* is, to annex Nabokov's word, "telescopic." Looking back on it, he cited a critic who "suggested that *Lolita* was the record of my love affair with the romantic novel," and continued, "The substitution 'English language' for 'romantic novel' would make this elegant formula more correct." That's profoundly true, and constitutes the most strenuous test of the romantic idea that worshipful time will forgive all those who love, and who live by, language. After half a century this work's "transgressiveness" makes every usage of that term in our etiolated English departments seem stale, pallid, and domesticated.

(*The Atlantic*, December 2005)

John Updike, Part One: No Way

IN 1978, just as I was beginning to become intrigued by the nascent menace of Islamist fanaticism, I read John Updike's novel *The Coup*. Set in the fictional African state of Kush, a Chad-like vastness dominated by a demagogue named Hakim Ellelloû, it took its author far from the Pennsylvania suburbs and car lots, and indeed offered, through the hoarse voice of Ellelloû, a highly dystopian view of them. "What does the capitalist infidel make, you may ask, of the priceless black blood of Kush?" Ellelloû asks, and then answers his own question:

> He extracts from it, of course, a fuel that propels him and his overweight, quarrelsome family—so full of sugar and starch their faces fester—back and forth on purposeless errands and ungratefully received visits. Rather than live as we do in the same village with our kin and our labor, the Americans have flung themselves wide across the land, which they have buried under tar and stone. They consume our blood also in their factories and skyscrapers, which are ablaze with light throughout the night... I have visited this country of devils and can report that they make from your sacred blood slippery green bags in which they place their garbage and even the leaves that fall from their trees! They make of petroleum toys that break in their children's hands, and hair curlers in which their obese brides fatuously think to beautify themselves while they parade in

Review of *Terrorist,* by John Updike.

> supermarkets buying food wrapped in transparent petroleum and grown from fertilizers based upon your blood! Of your blood they make deodorants to mask their God-given body scents and wax for the matches to ignite their death-dealing cigarettes and more wax to shine their shoes while the people of Kush tread upon the burning sands barefoot!

I marked this passage at the time, thinking that I might one day want to refer to it. The two elements that it contains—apart from the actual commingling of oil and blood—are of some interest. The first is a sort of ventriloquization of Muslim rage, with care taken to give this an element of "social gospel" as well as Koranic puritanism. The second is an intellectual and aesthetic disgust—somewhat reminiscent of the more literary passages of John Kenneth Galbraith's *Affluent Society*—with the grossness and banality of much of American life.

This was quite prescient, and it anticipated some of the rhetorical tropes of Muslim self-pity with which we have since become so familiar. Only Monica Ali, in *Brick Lane*, has caught the same tone of pseudo-socialist populism, and in her novel the crucial speech is delivered after the aggression of September 11, 2001. On that day Updike happened to be looking at Manhattan from just across the river, in Brooklyn Heights, and later described what he saw in a "Talk of the Town" essay in the *New Yorker*, in which he wrote, inter alia:

> Determined men who have transposed their own lives to a martyr's afterlife can still inflict an amount of destruction that defies belief. War is conducted with a fury that requires abstraction—that turns a planeful of peaceful passengers, children included, into a missile the faceless enemy deserves. The other side has the abstractions; we have only the mundane duties of survivors.

Perhaps feeling that this was somewhat inert, not to say pathetic, Updike then inserted a rather unconvincing note of stoicism, urging his readers to "fly again" on planes, since (guess what?) "risk is a price of freedom," and issuing what was by comparison a bugle call: "Walking around Brooklyn Heights that afternoon, as ash drifted in the air and cars were few and open-air lunches continued as usual on Montague Street, renewed the impression that, with all its failings, this is a country worth fighting for." Understatement could do no more: Was it the ash or the absence of cars—or maybe those tempting alfresco snacks—that (America's manifold failings notwithstanding) straightened the Updike spine?

Taking time to let his manly reflections mature and ripen in the cask, Updike has now given us *Terrorist*, another vantage point from which to view Manhattan from across the water. His "terrorist" is a boy named Ahmad living in today's New Prospect, New Jersey, for whom the immolation of 3,000 of his fellow citizens is by no means enough. For him, only a huge detonation inside the Lincoln Tunnel will do. Let's grant Updike credit for casting his main character against type: Ahmad is not only the nicest person in the book but is as engaging a young man as you could meet in a day's march. Tenderly, almost lovingly, Updike feels and feels, like a family doctor, until he can detect the flickering pulse of principle that animates the would-be martyr.

Once again, obesity and consumerism and urban sprawl are the *radix malorum*. At the seaside:

> *Devils.* The guts of the men sag hugely and the monstrous buttocks of the women seesaw painfully as they tread the boardwalk in swollen sneakers. A few steps from death, these American elders defy decorum and dress as toddlers.

Whereas in the schools:

> They think they're doing pretty good, with some flashy-trashy new outfit they've bought at half-price, or the latest hyper-violent new computer game, or some hot new CD everyone has to have, or some ridiculous new religion when you've drugged your brain back into the Stone Age. It makes you wonder if people deserve to live seriously—if the massacre masterminds in Rwanda and Sudan and Iraq didn't have the right idea.

The speaker in this latter instance is Jack Levy, a burned-out little Jewish man with a wife named Beth ("a whale of a woman giving off too much heat through her blubber"). He has ended up as the guidance counselor at uninspired New Prospect Central High, while his missus piles on the fat in front of the TV. Fortunately, though, she has a sister who works for the secretary of Homeland Security and who, though she rightly regards her corpulent New Jersey sibling as a moron, keeps calling her up to tell her *absolutely everything* about the nation's anti-terrorist secrets. This, too, is fortunate, because although he doesn't yet know it (the irony!), Jack Levy has a "massacre mastermind" in his own school, right under his nose. (I have just flipped through the book again to be quite certain that I did not make any of this up.)

Young Ahmad, who has an absent Muslim father and a ditsy and whorish Irish mother (who probably has red hair and freckles and green eyes; I honestly couldn't be bothered to go back and double-check *that*), is quite a study. With such a start in life, who wouldn't start hanging around the mosque and dreaming of a high-octane ticket to Paradise? Rejecting Jack Levy's rather diffident offers of help with further education and a career, the bright lad puts all his energies into qualifying to drive a truck. The sort of truck that can carry hazardous materials. In immediate post-9/11 New Jersey, this innocent ploy by a green young Islamist sets off no alarm bells at all.

Ordinary life still manages to go on, as it must. At the high school's commencement festivities, Jack finds himself in the procession just behind a West Indian teacher (who really does address him as "mon"), who says:

"Jack, tell me. There is something I am embarrassed to ask anyone. Who is this J. Lo? My students keep mentioning him."

"A her. Singer. Actress," Jack calls ahead. "Hispanic. Very well turned out. Great ass, apparently..."

Yes, that's right: Updike has given us a black high-school teacher who, in the early years of this very century, thinks that J. Lo is a guy. And who is embarrassed to ask more about the subject. And who therefore raises his voice, at commencement, and seeks enlightenment from a sixty-three-year-old Jewish washout. Could anything be more hip and up-to-the-minute? When this Updike feels for a pulse—know what I'm saying?—he really, really, like, *feels*. Some pages later we find Jack exclaiming, "No way," and the daring idiomatic usage is explained by his "having picked up this much slang from his students." The expression was universal long before any of these students was born.

Indeed, Updike continues to offer us, as we have come to expect of him, his grueling homework. The sinuous imam of the local mosque (Shaikh

Rashid) does not try to impress the half-educated and credulous Ahmad with the duty to fight the enemies of the Prophet. Far from it. He prepares him for stone-faced single-mindedness with some intricate Koranic hermeneutics, designed to shake his faith. And guess which example is adduced? The theory of the German Orientalist Christoph Luxenberg, who has argued that the "virgins" promised to martyrs in Paradise are actually a mistranslation for "white raisins." Bet you never heard that! My feeling—call it a guess or an intuition—is that this is not how madrassas train their suicide bombers. My other feeling is that Updike could have placed this rather secondhand show of his recent learning in some other part of the novel.

But where would that be? Almost immediately after Ahmad's graduation, he is in the throes of a conspiracy that is too ingenious for words. While delivering furniture one day, he drops off an ottoman (get it?) that, when cut open in a sinister Muslim home tenanted only by men, proves to be stuffed with "quantities of green American currency." The young inductee to terrorism cannot make out the denominations of these non-blue and non-brown notes, but "to judge by the reverence with which the men are counting and arranging the bills on the tile-top table, the denominations are high." No bill is higher than a hundred, which doesn't buy you much high explosive these days, but one imagines—if one absolutely must—that a whole ottoman can also hold a goodly number of ones and fives. This novel and risky and cumbersome way of delivering cash only whets Ahmad's appetite for the more intoxicating suras of the Koran. Before we can catch our breath, he is at the wheel of his jam-packed juggernaut of annihilation (and still registering strip malls and other urban deformities), and is pressing ahead with his desperate plan. Never mind that the plot has been exposed by a cunning last-minute call from the frumpy Washington bureaucrat sister to the impossibly bulbous homebound New Jersey sister. And never mind that this exposure has *not* led the forces of Homeland Security to close the Lincoln Tunnel. No, stopping Ahmad comes down to the crushed, demoralized Jack Levy, who manages, with exquisite timing, to flag down Ahmad's truck and climb aboard and talk him out of it at the very last available cinematic second.

After I had sent *Terrorist* windmilling across the room in a spasm of boredom and annoyance, I retrieved it to check my notes in its margins. In *Roger's Version*, I remembered, Updike had described blacks and Jews as the only "magical" people in America. In this sloppy latest effort he becomes more inclusive. Here's Jack rhapsodizing about Ahmad's sluttish mama, with whom he has a torrid moment in which this constant reader could not suspend disbelief:

> *The Irish in her*, he thinks. That's what he loves, that's what he can't do without. The moxie, the defiant spark of craziness people get if they're sat on long enough—the Irish have it, the blacks and Jews have it, but it's died in him.

This is a fair-enough attempt to push all the clichés about Irish-Americans into one brief statement, and I can only think that it's put in as some kind of oblique tribute to the New York Fire Department on 9/11. Not for them the fate of the flabby, torpid average Americans, thoughtlessly reaping by their very herdlike existence the whirlwind of *jihad*-ist revenge.

When writing *In the Beauty of the Lilies*, which also opened its action in New Jersey, Updike gave us considerable insight into the Reverend Clarence Wilmot as he endured a full-dress crisis of Calvinist conscience. There was knowledge to be won from the portrayal, and some dry humor, and some imaginative sympathy. A good deal of work on the Presbyterian texts had been performed and was lightly but learnedly deployed. With *The Coup*, also, Updike had been somewhat in advance of the tremors that he was sensing. But he is now some considerable distance behind the story, giving the impression of someone who has been keeping up with the "Inside Radical Islam" features in something like *Newsweek*. It could be, I suppose, that he might write better about "exotic religions" if he kept his characters overseas, in their "exotic settings," and tried to make sense of them there. He includes one more religious set piece in *Terrorist*, of a charismatic black preacher jiving away at his congregation. Irrelevant to the "plot," this is justified by the black girl in whom Ahmad is briefly interested. As if to confirm his loathing for American sexual degeneracy, she has a boyfriend-pimp named Tylenol Jones—the sort of name that Tom Wolfe might come up with on a bad day.

The novel's conclusion is much the same as that of Updike's *New Yorker* essay. He looks at the quotidian crowd in Manhattan, "scuttling, hurrying, intent in the milky morning sun upon some plan or scheme or hope they are hugging to themselves, their reason for living another day, each impaled live upon the pin of consciousness, fixed upon self-advancement and self-preservation. That and only that." Insects, in fact. Ahmad resents them for taking away his God, and, really, one is hard put not to empathize with the poor boy. Given some admittedly stiff competition, Updike has produced one of the worst pieces of writing from any grown-up source since the events he has so unwisely tried to draw upon.

(*The Atlantic*, June 2006)

John Updike, Part Two: Mr. Geniality

THE ELEMENTS OF THIS COLLECTION fully justify the rather modest promise offered by the title. All things are indeed considered, and they are mostly considered in a highly considerate manner. As to the "due" part, John Updike himself informs us: "Bills come due; dues must be paid. After eight years, I was due for another collection of nonfictional prose." To which one might add that he seems determined to give everyone his or her due. Indeed, in a highly affable preface he wonders if his only fault might be a tendency to be critical—in the ordinary sense of the term—at all. Rereading his book reviews, he wonders aloud "if their customary geniality, almost effusive in the presence of a foreign writer or a factual topic, didn't somewhat sour when faced with a novel by a fellow-countryman." Should he perhaps have been a little kinder to E. L. Doctorow, Don DeLillo, and Norman Rush or (by implication) a fraction more harsh with Ngugi wa Thiong'o and Haruki Murakami? Such scruple no doubt does its author credit, and yet "Customary Genialities" would surely have been a rather insipid title.

In fact, on the sole occasion where Updike does display a hint of fang, it is in his treatment of Michel Houellebecq, whose novel *The Possibility of*

Review of *Due Considerations: Essays and Criticism*, by John Updike.

an Island he is determined not to allow to shock him. Nonetheless, after giving a few graphic staves of Houellebecq's not always bracing combo of obscenity and nihilism, he comments mildly that a microcosm that excludes such things as parenting and compassion is wanting in verisimilitude, and concludes that "the sensations Houellebecq gives us are not nutritive." By Updikean standards, this counts as a pretty stern condemnation. In partial contrast, when one consults the generous review of DeLillo's *Cosmopolis*, a notice that now causes its author such misgiving, we find the worst he can say is that "the trouble with a tale where anything can happen is that somehow nothing happens." I can't see DeLillo exactly biting through his umbrella handle with rage on reading that lenient verdict.

In a culture more and more dominated by dunces and frauds, it might be salutary if one of our senior critics laid about himself with a bit more brio. But Updike does not so much avoid this task as rise above it. He chooses to review classical authors, from Emerson to Proust, or, among the living or contemporary, only those who meet some kind of gold standard. And he regards the responsibility of the reviewer to be the rendering of a fair précis of the work under consideration, where the word "fair" has inescapable consequences of its own. The nearest we get to a review of the "popular" is a treatment of George MacDonald Fraser's "Flashman" series, and again, amid the punctilious summary of the subject's many admirable points, the few cautious reproaches tend to stand out. Which admirer of Fraser's "cheerful potboilers" would not concede that his historical endnotes are "distractingly informative" or ruefully agree that "to keep his pot boiling, Fraser keeps tossing fresh female bodies into it"?

I am myself familiar with the reviewing cliché, from both ends of the business, so I say deliberately that Updike's scope is rather breathtaking (from Isaac Babel straight to James Thurber on successive pages), and I add that he seems almost incapable of writing badly. When I do not know the subject well—as in his finely illustrated art reviews of Bruegel, Dürer, and Goya—I learn much from what Updike has to impart. When he considers an author I love, like Proust or Czeslaw Milosz, I often find myself appreciating familiar things in a new way. I enjoy the little feuilletons he appends, for example on the ten greatest moments of the American libido. And I admire the way he can construct a classical sentence that makes an abrupt, useful turn to the American demotic: "Having patiently read both versions" of Philip Larkin's *Collected Poems*, "this reviewer believes that the second, chastened version, confining itself to the four trade volumes Larkin supervised and the uncollected poems 'published in other places,' does give the verse itself a better shake."

This appears in one of the best long treatments of Larkin's poetry I have ever read. Those of us who adore this work have a tendency to feel personally addressed by it and to resent any other commentators as interlopers. Updike seems almost to know what we are thinking. It's of interest, also, that his own vestigial Christianity—or do I mean surviving attachment to Christianity?—proves on other pages to be not dissimilar to Larkin's own synthesis, in "Aubade" and in "Church Going," of a bleak materialism fused with an admiration for the liturgy and the architecture.

I wrote "yuck" in the margin only twice, first when Updike describes Kierkegaard (in an otherwise very penetrating essay) as "the great Dane," and second when, summarizing Peter Carey's *Theft: A Love Story*, he writes that someone turns up "strangled in a Nice (not nice) hotel." One is much more inclined to make approving ticks, as when Updike notices the prehistory of Doctorow's *Ragtime* character Coalhouse Walker in *The March*, or when he spots Tulla Pokriefke, a minor Danzig character from *Cat and Mouse* and *Dog Years*, turning up again in Günter Grass's *Crabwalk*.

Yet it was in a paragraph of the *Crabwalk* review that I began to realize what was irritating me. Discussing Grass's rather recent discovery that Germans had also been the victims of atrocities, Updike asks:

> Can a nation war against a regime without warring against the people the regime rules? Is the very concept "war crime" tautological, given the context of determined violence? As Kofi Annan, the United Nations secretary general, said a few weeks ago, "War is always a catastrophe." Are discriminations possible between appropriate and excessive bombing, between legitimate and atrocious ship-sinkings, between proper combat of armed soldiers and such tactics as using civilians, including children, as human shields or disguising an ambush as a surrender? An American soldier recently wounded in

> such an ambush, when interviewed on television, shrugged and, with striking dispassion, conceded that, given the great imbalance of firepower between the Coalition and Saddam Hussein's Iraq, he could hardly blame his attackers for their murderous ruse.

This is evenhandedness taken almost to the point of masochism. (What of the "imbalance" between the *jihad*-ists and the girls' schools they blow up?) And Updike doesn't choose to answer any of the questions—familiar enough at a sophomore level, as is Annan's affectless remark—that he poses. I have the suspicion that he is overcompensating for the rather lame defense of the war in Vietnam that he mounted in his memoir *Self-Consciousness*. The same thought recurred to me in a rereading of his offhand "Talk of the Town" report, written for the *New Yorker* after he watched the collapse of the twin towers from across the river in Brooklyn Heights:

> War is conducted with a fury that requires abstraction—that turns a planeful of peaceful passengers, children included, into a missile the faceless enemy deserves. The other side has the abstractions; we have only the mundane duties of survivors—to pick up the pieces, to bury the dead, to take more precautions, to go on living.

Really? Fair-mindedness here threatens to decline into something completely passive, neutral and inert. Come to think of it, what is the most celebrated statement about giving someone his due?

(*The New York Times Book Review*, November 4, 2007)

Vidal Loco

MORE THAN A DECADE AGO, I sat on a panel in New York to review the life and work of Oscar Wilde. My fellow panelist was that heroic old queen Quentin Crisp, perhaps the only man ever to have made a success of the part of Lady Bracknell in *The Importance of Being Earnest*. Inevitably there arose the question: Is there an Oscar Wilde for our own day? The moderator proposed Gore Vidal, and, really, once that name had been mentioned, there didn't seem to be any obvious rival.

Like Wilde, Gore Vidal combined tough-mindedness with subversive wit (*The Importance of Being Earnest* is actually a very mordant satire on Victorian England) and had the rare gift of being amusing about serious things as well as serious about amusing ones. Like Wilde, he was able to combine radical political opinions with a lifestyle that was anything but solemn. And also like Wilde, he was almost never "off": His private talk was as entertaining and shocking as his more prepared public appearances. Admirers of both men, and of their polymorphous perversity, could happily debate whether either of them was better at fiction or in the essay form.

I was fortunate enough to know Gore a bit in those days. The price of knowing him was exposure to some of his less adorable traits, which included his pachydermatous memory for the least slight or grudge and a very, very minor tendency to bring up the Jewish question in contexts where it didn't quite belong. One was made aware, too, that he suspected Franklin Roosevelt of playing a dark hand in bringing on Pearl Harbor and still nurtured an admiration in his breast for the dashing Charles Lindbergh, leader of the American isolationist right in the 1930s. But these tics and eccentricities, which I did criticize in print, seemed more or less under control, and meanwhile he kept on saying things one wished one had said oneself. Of a certain mushy spiritual writer named Idries Shah: "These books are a great deal harder to read than they were to write." Of a paragraph by Herman Wouk: "This is not at all bad, except as prose." He once said to me of the late Teddy Kennedy, who was then in his low period of red-faced, engorged, and abandoned boyo-hood, that he exhibited "all the charm of three hundred pounds of condemned veal." Who but Gore could begin a discussion by saying that the three most dispiriting words in the English language were "Joyce Carol Oates"? In an interview, he told me that his life's work was "making sentences." It would have been more acute to say that he made a career out of pronouncing them.

However, if it's true even to any degree that we were all changed by September 11, 2001, it's probably truer of Vidal that it made him more the way he already was, and accentuated a crackpot strain that gradually asserted itself as dominant. If you look at his writings from that time, thrown together in a couple of cheap paperbacks titled *Dreaming War* and *Perpetual War for Perpetual Peace*, you will find the more crass notions of Michael Moore or Oliver Stone being expressed in language that falls some distance short of the Wildean ideal. "Meanwhile, Media was assigned its familiar task of inciting public opinion against Osama bin Laden, still not the proven mastermind." To that "sentence," abysmal as it is in so many ways, Vidal put his name in November 2002. A small anthology of half-argued and half-written shock pieces either insinuated or asserted that the administration had known in advance of the attacks on New York and Washington and was seeking a pretext to build a long-desired pipeline across Afghanistan. (Not much sign of that, incidentally, not that the luckless Afghans mightn't welcome it.) For academic authority in this Grassy Knoll enterprise, Vidal relied heavily on the man he thought had produced "the best, most balanced report" on 9/11, a certain Nafeez Mosaddeq Ahmed, of the Institute for Policy Research & Development, whose book *The War on Freedom* had been brought to us by what Vidal called "a small but reputable homeland publisher." Mr. Ahmed on inspection proved to be a risible individual wedded to half-baked conspiracy-mongering, his "Institute" a one-room sideshow in the English seaside town of Brighton, and his publisher an outfit called "Media Monitors Network" in association with "Tree of Life," whose now-deceased Web site used to offer advice on the ever awkward question of self-publishing. And to think that there was once a time when Gore Vidal could summon Lincoln to the pages of a novel or dispute points of strategy with Henry Cabot Lodge.

It became more and more difficult to speak to Vidal after this (and less fun too), but then I noticed something about his last volume of memoirs, *Point to Point Navigation*, which brought his life story up to 2006. Though it contained a good ration of abuse directed at Bush and Cheney, it didn't make even a gesture to the wild-eyed and croaking stuff that Mr. Ahmed had been purveying. This meant one of two things: Either Vidal didn't believe it any longer or he wasn't prepared to put such sorry, silly, sinister stuff in a volume published by Doubleday, read by his literary and intellectual peers, and dedicated to the late Barbara Epstein. The second interpretation, while slightly contemptible, would be better than nothing and certainly a good deal better than the first.

But I have now just finished reading a long interview conducted by Johann Hari of the London *Independent* (Hari being a fairly consecrated admirer of his) in which Vidal decides to go slumming again and to indulge the lowest in himself and in his followers. He openly says that the Bush administration was "probably" in on the 9/11 attacks, a criminal complicity that would "certainly fit them to a T"; that Timothy McVeigh was "a noble boy," no more murderous than Generals Patton and Eisenhower; and that "Roosevelt saw to it that we got that war" by inciting the Japanese to attack Pearl Harbor. Coming a bit more up-to-date, Vidal says that the whole American experiment can now be described as "a failure"; the country will soon take its place "somewhere between Brazil and Argentina, where it belongs"; President Obama will be buried in the wreckage—broken by "the madhouse"—after the United States has been humiliated in Afghanistan and the Chinese emerge supreme. We shall then be "the Yellow Man's burden," and Beijing will "have us running the coolie cars, or whatever it is they have in the way of transport." Asian subjects never seem to bring out the finest in Vidal: He used to say it was Japan that was dominating the world economy, and that in the face of that other peril "there is now only one way out. The time has come for the United States to make common cause with the Soviet Union." That was in 1986—not perhaps the ideal year to have proposed an embrace of Moscow, and certainly not as good a year as 1942, when Franklin Roosevelt *did* join forces with the USSR, against Japan and Nazi Germany, in a war that Vidal never ceases to say was (a) America's fault and (b) not worth fighting.

Rounding off his interview, an obviously shocked Mr. Hari tried for a change of pace and asked Vidal if he felt like saying anything about his recently deceased rivals, John Updike, William F. Buckley Jr., and Norman Mailer. He didn't manage to complete his question before being interrupted. "Updike was nothing. Buckley was nothing with a flair for publicity. Mailer was a flawed publicist, too, but at least there were signs every now and then of a working brain." One sadly notices, as with the foregoing barking and effusions, the utter want of any grace or generosity, as well as the entire absence of any wit or profundity. Sarcastic, tired flippancy has stolen the place of the first, and lugubrious resentment has deposed the second. Oh, just in closing, then, since Vidal was in London, did he have a word to say about England? "This isn't a country, it's an American aircraft carrier." Good grief.

For some years now, the old boy's stock-in-trade has been that of the last Roman: the stoic eminence who with unclouded eyes foresees the coming end of the noble republic. Such an act doesn't require a toga, but it does demand a bit of dignity. Vidal's phrasings sometimes used to have a certain rotundity and extravagance, but now he has descended straight to the cheap, and even to the counterfeit. What business does this patrician have in the gutter markets, where paranoids jabber and the coinage is debased by every sort of vulgarity?

If Vidal ever reads this, I suppose I know what he will say. Asked about our differences a short while ago at a public meeting in New York, he replied, "You know, he identified himself for many years as the heir to me. And unfortunately for him, I didn't die. I just kept going on and on and on." (One report of the event said that this not-so-rapier-like reply had the audience in "stitches": Vidal in his decline has fans like David Letterman's, who laugh in all the wrong places lest they suspect themselves of not having a good time.) But his first sentence precisely inverts the truth. Many years ago he wrote to me unprompted—I have the correspondence—and freely offered to nominate me as his living successor, *dauphin*, or, as the Italians put it, *delfino.* He very kindly inscribed a number of his own books to me in this way, and I asked him for permission to use his original letter on the jacket of one of mine. I stopped making use of the endorsement after 9/11, as he well knows. I have no wish to commit literary patricide, or to assassinate Vidal's character—a character which appears, in any case, to have committed suicide.

I don't in the least mind his clumsy and nasty attempt to re-write his history with me, but I find I do object to the crank-revisionist and denialist history he is now peddling about everything else, as well as to the awful, spiteful, miserable way—"going on and on and on," indeed—in which he has finished up by doing it. Oscar Wilde was never mean-spirited, and never became an Ancient Mariner, either.

(*Vanity Fair*, February 2010)

America the Banana Republic

IN A STATEMENT on the huge state-sponsored salvage of private bankruptcy that was first proposed last September, a group of Republican lawmakers, employing one of the very rudest words in their party's thesaurus, described the proposed rescue of the busted finance and discredited credit sectors as "socialistic." There was a sort of half-truth to what they said. But they would have been very much nearer the mark—and rather more ironic and revealing at their own expense—if they had completed the sentence and described the actual situation as what it is: "socialism for the rich and free enterprise for the rest."

I have heard arguments about whether it was Milton Friedman or Gore Vidal who first came up with this apt summary of a collusion between the overweening state and certain favored monopolistic concerns, whereby the profits can be privatized and the debts conveniently socialized, but another term for the same system would be "banana republic."

What are the main principles of a banana republic? A very salient one might be that it has a paper currency which is an international laughingstock: a definition that would immediately qualify today's United States of America. We may snicker at the thriller from Wasilla, who got her first passport only last year, yet millions of once well-traveled Americans are now forced to ask if they can afford even the simplest overseas trip when their folding money is apparently issued by the Boardwalk press of Atlantic City. But still, the chief principle of banana-ism is that of kleptocracy, whereby those in positions of influence use their time in office to maximize their own gains, always ensuring that any shortfall is made up by those unfortunates whose daily life involves earning money rather than making it. At all costs, therefore, the one principle that must *not* operate is the principle of accountability. In fact, if possible, even the similar-sounding term (deriving from the same root) of *accountancy* must be jettisoned as well. Just listen to Christopher Cox, chairman of the Securities and Exchange Commission, as he explained how the legal guardians of fair and honest play had made those principles go away. On September 26, he announced that "the last six months have made it abundantly clear that voluntary regulation does not work." Now listen to how he enlarges on this somewhat lame statement. It seems to him on reflection that "voluntary regulation"

> was fundamentally flawed from the beginning, because investment banks could opt in or out of supervision voluntarily. The fact that investment bank holding companies could withdraw from this voluntary supervision at their discretion diminished the perceived mandate of the program and weakened its effectiveness.

Yes, I think one might say that. Indeed, the "perceived mandate" of a parole program that allowed those enrolled in it to take off their ankle bracelets at any time they chose to leave the house might also have been open to the charge that it was self-contradictory and wired for its own self-destruction. But in banana-republicland, like Alice's Wonderland, words tend to lose their meaning and to dissolve into the neutral, responsibility-free verbiage of a Cox.

And still, in so many words in the phrasing of the first bailout request to be placed before Congress, there appeared the brazen demand that, once passed, the "package" be subject to virtually no more congressional supervision or oversight. This extraordinary proposal shows the utter contempt in which the deliberative bodies on Capitol Hill are held by the unelected and inscrutable financial panjandrums. But welcome to another aspect of banana-republicdom. In a banana republic, the members of the national legislature will be (a) largely for sale and (b) consulted only for ceremonial and rubber-stamp purposes some time after all the truly important decisions have already been made elsewhere.

I was very struck, as the liquefaction of a fantasy-based system proceeded, to read an observation by Professor Jeffrey A. Sonnenfeld, of the Yale School of Management. Referring to those who had demanded—successfully—to be indemnified by the customers and clients whose trust they had betrayed, the professor phrased it like this:

> These are people who want to be rewarded as if they were entrepreneurs. But they aren't. They didn't have anything at risk.

That's almost exactly right, except that they *did* have something at risk. What they put at risk, though, was other people's money and other people's property. How very agreeable it must be to sit at a table in a casino where nobody seems to lose, and to play with a big stack of chips furnished to you by other people, and to have the further assurance that, if anything should ever chance to go wrong, you yourself are guaranteed by the tax dollars of those whose money you are throwing about in the first place! It's enough to make a cat laugh. These members of the "business community" are indeed not buccaneering and risk-taking innovators. They are instead, to quote my old friend Nicholas von Hoffman about another era, those who were standing around with tubas in their arms on the day it began to rain money. And then, when the rain of gold stopped and the wind changed, they were the only ones who didn't feel the blast. Daniel Mudd and Richard Syron, the former bosses of Fannie Mae and Freddie Mac, have departed with $9.43 million in retirement benefits. I append no comment.

Another feature of a banana republic is the tendency for tribal and cultish elements to flourish at the expense of reason and good order. Did it not seem quite bizarre, as the first vote on the rescue of private greed by public money was being taken, that Congress should adjourn for a religious holiday—*Rosh Hashanah*—in a country where the majority of Jews are secular? What does this say, incidentally, about the separation of religion and government? And am I the only one who finds it distinctly weird to reflect that the last head of the Federal Reserve and the current head of the Treasury, Alan Greenspan and Hank "The Hammer" Paulson, should be respectively the votaries of the cults of Ayn Rand and Mary Baker Eddy, two of the battiest females ever to have infested the American scene? That Paulson should have gone down on one knee to Speaker Nancy Pelosi, as if prayer and beseechment might get the job done, strikes me as further evidence that sheer superstition and incantation have played their part in all this. Remember the scene at the end of *Peter Pan*, where the children are told that, if they don't shout out aloud that they all believe in fairies, then Tinker Bell's gonna fucking *die?* That's what the fall of 2008 was like, and quite a fall it was, at that.

And before we leave the theme of falls and collapses, I hope you read the findings of the Department of Transportation and the Federal Highway Administration that followed the plunge of Interstate 35W in Minneapolis into the Mississippi River last August. Sixteen states, after inspecting their own bridges, were compelled to close some, lower the weight limits of others, and make emergency repairs. Of the nation's 600,000 bridges, 12 percent were found to be structurally deficient. This is an almost perfect metaphor for Third World conditions: A money class fleeces the banking system while the very trunk of the national tree is permitted to rot and crash.

At a dinner party in New York during the Wall Street meltdown, where the citizens were still serious enough to do what they are supposed to do—break off the chat and tune in to the speech of the President of the United States and Leader of the Free World—the same impression of living in a surreal country that was a basket-case pensioner of the international monetary system was hugely reinforced. The staring eyes (close enough together for their owner to use a monocle) and the robotic delivery were a fine accompaniment to the already sweaty "Don't panic. Don't whatever you do panic!" injunction that was being so hastily improvised. At a White House meeting with his financial wizards—and I mean the term in its literal sense—the same chief executive is reported to have whimpered, "This sucker could go down," or words to that effect. It's not difficult to imagine the scene. So add one more banana-republic feature to the profile: a president who is a figurehead one day and a despot the next, and who goes all wide-eyed and calls on witch doctors when the portents don't seem altogether reassuring.

Now ask yourself another question. Has anybody resigned, from either the public or the private sectors (overlapping so lavishly as they now do)? Has anybody even *offered* to resign? Have you heard anybody in authority apologize, as in: "So very sorry about your savings and pensions and homes and college funds, and I feel personally rotten about it"? Have you even heard the question being posed? Okay, then, has anybody been fired? Any regulator, any supervisor, any runaway would-be golden-parachute artist? Anyone responsible for smugly putting the word "derivative" like a virus into the system? To ask the question is to answer it. The most you can say is that some people have had to take a slightly early retirement, but a retirement very much sweetened by the wherewithal on which to retire. That doesn't quite count. These are the rules that apply in Zimbabwe or Equatorial Guinea or Venezuela, where the political big boys mimic what is said about our hedge funds and investment banks: the stupid mantra about being "too big to fail."

In a recent posting on the *New York Times* Web site, Paul Krugman said that the United States was now reduced to the status of a banana republic with nuclear weapons. This is a variation on the old joke about the former Soviet Union ("Burkina Faso with rockets"). It's also wrong: In fact, it's the reverse of the truth. In banana republics, admittedly, very often the only efficient behavior is displayed by the army (and the secret police). But our case is rather different. In addition to exhibiting extraordinary efficiency and, most especially under the generalship of David Petraeus, performing some great feats of arms and ingenuity, the American armed forces manifest all the professionalism and integrity that our rulers and oligarchs lack. Who was it who the stricken inhabitants of New Orleans and later of the Texas coastline yearned to see? Who was it who informed the blithering and dithering idiots at FEMA that they could have as many troops as they could remember to ask for, even as volunteers were embarking for Afghanistan and Iraq? What is one of the main engines of integration for blacks and immigrants, as well as one of the finest providers of education and training for those whom the system had previously failed? It may be true that the government has succeeded in degrading our armed forces as well—tasking them with absurdities and atrocities like Guantánamo and Abu Ghraib—but this only makes the banana-republic point in an even more emphatic way.

(*Vanity Fair* online, October 9, 2008)

An Anglosphere Future

HAVING DEVOURED the Sherlock Holmes stories as a boy, I did what their author hoped and graduated to his much finer historical novels. The best of these, *The White Company*, appeared in 1890; it describes the recruitment and deployment of a detachment of Hampshire archers during the reign of King Edward III, a period that, as Arthur Conan Doyle phrased it, "constituted the greatest epoch in English History—an epoch when both the French and the Scottish kings were prisoners in London."

This book, it's of interest to note, also influenced Dwight Eisenhower's boyhood (I owe this information to the extraordinary *Arthur Conan Doyle: A Life in Letters,* edited by Jon Lellenberg, Daniel Stashower, and Charles Foley). For there came a time when this child of German-American parents also had to muster a considerable force from Hampshire headquarters, and launch them across the Channel in one of the greatest military interventions in history. Of course, on D-Day, Eisenhower took care to have a French leader on his side (admittedly a turbulent and mutinous one), and Scottish regiments were as usual to the fore in the storming of the Atlantic Wall. But it's funny how one somehow can thrill to the same tradition, whether it's the medieval yeomen and bowmen of Anglo-Saxondom or the modern, mechanized, multinational coalition against fascism.

Doyle was only a few years from his first trip to the United States when

---

Review of *A History of the English-Speaking Peoples Since 1900*, by Andrew Roberts.

he published *The White Company*, which he dedicated as follows: "To the hope of the future, the reunion of the English-speaking races, this little chronicle of our common ancestry is inscribed." Around the same time, two other renowned figures—Cecil Rhodes and Rudyard Kipling—made similar pitches. Two monuments, the Rhodes scholarships and the poem "The White Man's Burden," still survive in American life. The purpose of the scholarships was to proselytize for the return of the U.S. to the British imperial fold. The poem, written for Theodore Roosevelt, who passed it to Senator Henry Cabot Lodge, sought to influence the vote of the U.S. Senate on the annexation of the Philippines. (The poem's subtitle was "The United States and the Philippine Islands.") In urging the U.S. to pick up the scepter of empire, Kipling had one hope and one fear: hope of Anglo-American solidarity against rising German power; and fear of a revival of the demagogic atmosphere of 1894 and 1895, in which America and Britain almost went to war after the United States, citing the Monroe Doctrine, intervened in a border dispute between Britain and Venezuela.

Doyle's visit coincided with the height of this anti-British feeling, and at a dinner in his honor in Detroit he had this to say:

> You Americans have lived up to now within your own palings, and know nothing of the real world outside. But now your land is filled up, and you will be compelled to mix more with the other nations. When you do so you will find that there is only one which can at all understand your ways and your aspirations, or will have the least sympathy. That is the mother country which you are now so fond of insulting. She is an Empire, and you will soon be an Empire also, and only then will you understand each other, and you will realize that you have only one real friend in the world.

After Detroit, Doyle spent Thanksgiving with Kipling and his American wife, Carrie, in Brattleboro, Vermont. It is of unquantifiable elements such as this that the Anglo-American story, or the English-speaking story, is composed.

To a remarkable extent, Americans continue to assume a deep understanding with the English—one that, in their view, reflects a common heritage much more than it does anything as mundane as a common interest.

This assumption, at least as exemplified in the Bush-Blair alliance that sent expeditionary forces to Afghanistan and Mesopotamia, has recently taken a severe bruising on both sides of the Atlantic, as well as north of the U.S. border and in the countries of the antipodes: the historical homelands of the "English-speaking" adventure. The conservative British historian Andrew Roberts, author of the important new book *A History of the English-Speaking Peoples Since 1900*, regards this as a matter of regret, as do I, though for different reasons. For no less different reasons, he and I believe that the "Anglosphere," to give it a recently updated name, may have a future as well as a past.

The idea is certainly in the air. Earlier this year, President Bush hosted a lunch for Roberts in the Oval Office, with senior advisers Karl Rove, Stephen Hadley, and Josh Bolten in attendance, and Dick Cheney was seen holding Roberts's book on a trip to Afghanistan. Other writers, including John O'Sullivan, have recently written about the unique virtues of Anglo-Americanism.

Roberts's book, though, exhibits some of the potential problems that can befall a defense of the Anglosphere. One shows up in its title. You will notice that Arthur Conan Doyle referred to the English speaking "races." On the model of Winston Churchill's famous book of almost the same name, Roberts prefers the term "peoples." But this is to make a distinction without much difference. No such thing as an Australian or a Canadian "race" exists, so one either means to describe people of originally Anglo-Saxon "stock" (as we used to say) or one doesn't. It hasn't been very long since Lionel Trilling was denied tenure on the grounds, frankly stated, that a Jew could not understand English literature. Without an appreciation of the ways in which the language and ethnicity are quite distinct, a kind of imperialist nostalgia is likely.

Regrettably, Roberts doesn't always avoid such nostalgia, devoting a major portion of his book to vindicating episodes in the British colonial past that most Tories long ago ceased to defend. He represents General Reginald Dyer's massacre of protesters in the Indian city of Amritsar in 1919, for example, as a necessary law-and-order measure. He defends the catastrophic Anglo-French-Israeli invasion of Egypt in 1956: a folly that Eisenhower had to terminate. He writes leniently about the white settler regimes in southern

Africa. And he never misses an opportunity to insult Irish nationalism, while whitewashing the Tory and Orange policies that led first to rebellion and second to bloody partition.

Determined to shoehorn everything into one grand theory, Roberts also flirts with tautology. For example, he mentions the opening of the Hoover Dam at Boulder City and comments: "The English-speaking peoples had long excelled at creating the wonders of the modern industrial world: the *Great Eastern*, the Brooklyn Bridge, the Sydney Bridge, the American, Canadian and Australian transcontinental railroads, the Panama Canal among them." A theory that tries to explain everything explains nothing: We can all think of other countries that have accomplished industrial and engineering marvels.

Further, the many advances in physics and medicine attributed to Jewish refugees in America (especially, for some reason, from Hungary) are slighted if credited to the genius of Englishness. Roberts describes radar as "another vital invention of the English-speaking peoples"—an insult to international scientific cooperation. One might add that Ferdinand de Lesseps did not shout orders in English when he organized the building of the Suez Canal. And the Magna Carta wasn't written in English.

Nonetheless, properly circumscribed, the idea of an "Anglosphere" can constitute something meaningful. We should not commit the mistake of "thinking with the blood," as D. H. Lawrence once put it, however, but instead emphasize a certain shared tradition, capacious enough to include a variety of peoples and ethnicities and expressed in a language—perhaps here I do betray a bias—uniquely hostile to euphemisms for tyranny. In his postwar essay "Towards European Unity," George Orwell raised the possibility that the ideas of democracy and liberty might face extinction in a world polarized between superpowers but that they also might hope to survive in some form in "the English-speaking parts of it." English is, of course, the language of the English and American Revolutions, whose ideas and values continue to live after those of more recent revolutions have been discredited and died.

Consider in this light one of Nelson Mandela's first acts as elected president of South Africa: applying to rejoin the British Commonwealth, from which South Africa had found itself expelled in the 1960s (by a British Tory government, incidentally) because of its odious racism. Many people forget that the Soweto revolt in the 1980s, which ultimately spelled apartheid's downfall, exploded after the Nationalist regime made the medium of school instruction exclusively Afrikaans, banning the classroom use of English, along with Xhosa and Zulu.

More recently, in July 2005, Indian prime minister Manmohan Singh came to Oxford University to receive an honorary degree and delivered a speech, not uncontroversial in India itself, in which he observed that many of India's splendors as a rising twenty-first-century superpower—from railroads to democracy to a law-bound civil service—were the result of its connection with England. "If there is one phenomenon on which the sun cannot set," Singh observed, "it is the world of the English-speaking peoples, in which the people of Indian origin are the single largest component." He added that the English language was a key element in the flourishing of India's high-tech sector. Few would have wanted to point this out, but it was Karl Marx who argued that India might benefit in this way from being colonized by England and not (and he spelled out the alternatives) Russia or Persia or Turkey.

We owe the term "Anglosphere" in large part to the historian and poet Robert Conquest, who this summer celebrated his ninetieth year of invincible common sense and courage in the fight against totalitarian thinking. In an appendix to his marvelous 2005 book *The Dragons of Expectation: Reality and Delusion in the Course of History*, he offers a detailed proposal for a broad Anglosphere alliance among the United States, the United Kingdom, Ireland, Canada, Australia, New Zealand, the Pacific Islands, and the Caribbean, with the multiethnic English-speaking island of Bermuda as the enterprise's headquarters. Though he unfortunately does not include India, he does find it "perfectly conceivable that other countries particularly close to our condition might also accede—for example Norway and Gambia, in each of which English is widely understood and in each of which the political and civic structure is close to that of the rest of the states." Quixotic as all this may sound, it probably understates the growing influence of English as a world language—the language of business and the Internet and air-traffic control, as well as of literature (or of literatures, given the emergence, first predicted by Orwell, of a distinct English written by Indians).

The shape of the world since September 11 has, in fact, shown the outline of such an alliance in practice. Everybody knows of Tony Blair's solidarity with the United States, but when the chips were down, Australian forces also went to Iraq. Attacked domestically for being "all the way with the USA," Australian prime minister John Howard made the imperishable observation that in times of crisis, there wasn't much point in being 75 percent a friend. Howard won reelection in 2004. Even in relatively neutralist Canada, an openly pro-U.S. government headed by Stephen Harper was elected in 2006, surprising pundits who predicted that a tide of anti-Americanism made such an outcome impossible.

Howard's statement has a great deal of history behind it. Roberts defines that history as an intimate alliance that defeated German Wilhelmine imperialism in 1918, the Nazi-Fascist Axis in 1945, and international Communism in 1989. This long arc of cooperation means that a young officer in, say, a Scottish regiment has a good chance of having two or even three ancestors who fought in the same trenches as did Americans and New Zealanders. No military force evolved by NATO, let alone the European Union, can hope to begin with such a natural commonality, the lack of which was painfully evident in Europe's post-1989 Balkan bungling (from which a largely Anglo-American initiative had to rescue it).

The world now faces a challenge from a barbarism that is no less menacing than its three predecessors—and may even be more so. And in this new struggle, a post-9/11 America came—not a moment too soon—to appreciate the vital fact that India had been fighting bin-Ladenism (and had been its target) far longer than we had. That fact alone should have mandated a change of alignment away from the chronically unreliable Pakistani regime that had used the Taliban as its colonial proxy in Afghanistan. But it helped that India was also a polyethnic secular democracy with a largely English-speaking military, political, and commercial leadership. We're only in the earliest stages of this new relationship, which so far depends largely on a nuclear agreement with New Delhi, and with the exception of Silicon Valley, the U.S. does not yet boast a politically active Indian population. But the future of American-Indian relations is crucial to our struggle against *jihad*-ism, as well as to our management of the balance of power with China.

In considering the future of the broader Anglosphere tradition, especially in the context of anti-*jihad*-ism, it may help to contrast it with the available alternatives. As a supranational body, the United Nations has obviously passed the point of diminishing returns. Inaugurated as an Anglo-American "coalition of the willing" against Hitler and his allies, the UN—in its failure to confront the genocides in Bosnia, Rwanda, and Darfur and in its abject refusal to enforce its own resolutions in the case of Iraq—is a prisoner of the "unilateralism" of France, Russia, and, to a lesser extent, China. NATO may have been somewhat serviceable in Kosovo (the first engagement in which it ever actually fought as an alliance), but it has performed raggedly in Afghanistan. The European Union has worked as an economic solvent on redundant dictatorships in Spain, Portugal, and Greece, and also on old irredentist squabbles in Ireland, Cyprus, and Eastern Europe. But it is about to reach, if it has not already, a membership saturation point that will disable any effective decision-making capacity. A glaring example of this disability is the EU's utter failure to compose a viable constitution. Roberts correctly notes that "along with over two centuries of amendments the entire (readable and easily intelligible) U.S. Constitution can be printed out onto twelve pages of A4-sized paper; the (unreadable and impenetrably complicated) proposed European Constitution ran to 265." (Roberts doesn't mention the lucidity and brevity of the British constitution, perhaps because the motherland of the English-speaking peoples has absentmindedly failed to evolve one in written form, and thus will, on the demise of the present queen, have as head of state a strange middle-aged man with a soft spot for Islam and bizarre taste in wives.)

But the temptation to construe the Anglosphere too narrowly persists. Another recent book, *The Anglosphere Challenge*, by James C. Bennett, expresses astonishment at the low price that the British establishment has put on its old Commonwealth and Dominion ties, and some hostility to the way in which European connections now take precedence. But viewed historically, it is surely neither surprising nor alarming that the British decided to reverse Winston Churchill's greatest mistake—abstaining from original membership in the European Common Market—and to associate more closely with the neighboring landmass. As Roberts himself concedes, Britain now enjoys a unique Atlanticist partnership along with full and energetic participation in the councils of the European Union.

For most of my adult life, British prime ministers were classifiable as either

Atlanticist or European in orientation. Thus, the conservative Edward Heath fixated on Brussels and distrusted Washington, while the Labour leaders Harold Wilson and James Callaghan were Euro-isolationists and little better than dittos to presidents Lyndon Johnson and Richard Nixon, respectively. In fact, with the notable exception of Margaret Thatcher, the Anglo-American relationship has fared rather better under the British center-Left. Perhaps this has something to do with the old devotion of the British Left, from Thomas Paine onward, to the ideals of the American Revolution. Of the defenders of the liberation of Iraq in the British media and political spheres, for example, most of the best-known spokesmen—Nick Cohen of the *Observer*, the *Financial Times*'s John Lloyd, and parliamentarians Denis MacShane, Peter Hain, and John Reid—belonged to the traditional Left. And it is many senior Conservatives who have recently gone the furthest in exploiting vulgar anti-American feeling among British voters. These are the ironies of history that Roberts's instinctive Toryism often prevents him from seeing.

An important thing to recognize about Tony Blair is that he was as much at home with American style and popular culture as he was when vacationing in France or Tuscany: that for the first time, the British had a prime minister who regarded the Atlanticist/European dichotomy as a false one. Nor did it hurt that on one day he could give a decent public speech in French and then on the next rally his party to identify its historical internationalism with the cause of the United States. He could even visit Dublin and claim some Irish descent, while offering a few conciliatory words about the wrongs of British policy since the Famine. And—not forgetting the Commonwealth and the Third World—he committed British forces to uphold a treaty with Sierra Leone and drove out the child-mutilating warlords who had invaded from Liberia.

This is quite a lot to set against the old Commonwealth tradition of Australian prime minister Sir Robert Menzies, who in the 1950s objected to being in the same "club" as newly independent African states and who forbade "colored" immigration to Australia itself. One of Roberts's Tory heroes, the late Enoch Powell, opposed emigration from nonwhite former colonies with the same fervor that he had once shown in opposing Indian independence. If he had stressed religion rather than race, he might have been seen as prescient; as it was, the majority of the British Right always openly favored Islamic Pakistan.

Today, the experience of true multicultural tolerance is something that needs defending, in Australia and Canada as much as in the U.K., against Islamist sectarianism and violence directed most virulently against Hindus and Jews. There is no way to fight this critical ideological battle on the imperial terrain of Kipling and Rhodes.

In late 1967, Britain's rule in Yemen ended, bringing an end to its centuries of presence "East of Suez." On the very last evening, the Labour defense minister Denis Healey shared a nostalgic sundowner with the British governor. As the shadows lengthened over the great harbor at Aden, the governor said that he thought the British Empire would be remembered for only two things: "the game of soccer and the expression 'fuck off.'" Who can doubt that these phenomena have endured and become part of the landscape of globalization? But the masochistic British attitude to inevitable decline seems to have reversed itself, at least to some extent. And the recent election of fresh governments in France and Germany shows that other Europeans—increasingly English-speaking—would rush to embrace the special American connection if, by any short-term miscalculation, the British might look to discard or vacate it.

Roberts's closing passage is his strongest. He gives a first-rate summary of the case for intransigent opposition to Islamist theocracy and to its cruel and violent epigones (as well as to its shady and illiterate apologists). He establishes all the essentials of the case for declaring our survival incompatible with totalitarianism and makes a crisp presentation of the urgency, necessity, and justice of the removal of Saddam Hussein. Along with William Shawcross's book *Allies*, his pages on this theme will find themselves consulted long after the ephemeral and half-baked anti-war texts are discredited and forgotten.

I myself doubt that a council of the Anglosphere will ever convene in the agreeable purlieus of postcolonial Bermuda, and the prospect of a formal reunion does not entice me in any case. It seems too close to the model on which France gravely convenes its own former possessions under the narrow banner of La Francophonie. It may not be too much to hope, though, that, along with soccer and a famously pungent injunction, some of the better ideas of 1649 and 1776 will continue to spread in diffuse, and ironic, ways.

(*City Journal*, Fall 2007)

Political Animals

THERE IS A CERTAIN CULTURE of humor in the speechwriting division of the Bush administration—a culture that involves a mild form of hazing. For example, David Frum, the Canadian Jewish neoconservative who helped to originate the phrase "axis of evil," was tasked with writing the welcoming address for the first White House Ramadan dinner. And last Thanksgiving, when the jokey annual ritual of the presidential turkey pardon came rolling around with the same mirthless inevitability as Groundhog Day, the job of penning the words of executive clemency on the eve of mass turkey slaughter was given to Matthew Scully, the only principled vegetarian on the team. Scully is a Roman Catholic, a former editor at *National Review*, and, I should add, a friendly Washington acquaintance of mine. He left his job in the executive mansion to forward this passionate piece of advocacy. Who can speak for the dumb? A man who has had to answer this question on behalf of the president himself is now stepping forward on behalf of the truly voiceless.

As the title suggests, Scully takes Genesis 1:24-26 as his point of departure. In that celebrated passage God awards "dominion" to man over all the fish, fowl, and beasts. As if to show that human beings are not, after all, much more reflective than brutes, Scully adopts the tone of a biblical

---

Review of *Dominion: The Power of Man, the Suffering of Animals, and the Call to Mercy*, by Matthew Scully.

literalist and wastes great swaths of paper in wrestling with the hermeneutics of this. A moment's thought will suffice to show that any pleader for animals who adopts such a line has made a rod for his own back. First, the words of Genesis are unambiguous in placing lesser creatures at our mercy and at our disposal. Second, the crucial verses do not mention the marvelous creation of dinosaurs and pterodactyls, either because the semi-literate scribes who gathered the story together were unaware of these prodigies of design or because (shall I hint?) the Creator was unaware of having made them. The magnificence of the marsupials is likewise omitted. Even more to the point, although "everything creeping that creepeth upon the earth" is cited in general, God does not explicitly seek the credit for rats, flies, cockroaches, and mosquitoes. Most important of all, there is no mention of the mind-warping variety and beauty and complexity of the microorganisms. Again, either the scribes didn't know about viruses and bacteria, or the Creator didn't appreciate with how lavish a hand he had unleashed life on the only planet in his solar system that can manage to support it.

The latter point is, I think, a telling one for another reason, which is that for many generations the human species did not at all have "dominion" over other life forms. The germs had dominion over us. And so, until the advantage was slowly wrested from them, did creatures such as locusts. Today ticks still rule over immense tracts of the terrestrial globe, and microbes rule absolutely. Even the Christian image of the shepherd, which reduces the believer to a member of a flock, conveys the idea of guarding a human-organized and quasi-domesticated system from animal predators. And that, in turn, reminds us that the shepherd protects the sheep and the lambs not for their own good but the better to fleece and then to slay them.

The only reason I can imagine for Scully's risking damage to his own argument in this way is that he feels a need to challenge the chilly eminence of Peter Singer in the field of animal rights. Professor Singer was the intellectual pioneer here, and receives generous if awkward notice in these pages, yet he is a strict materialist and regards human life as essentially, and without differentiation, mammalian. His views on the unborn—and, indeed, the born—must cause infinite distress to a man of Catholic sensibility. I can imagine that Singer would agree with me on a second-order point, which is that concern with the suffering and exploitation of animals can be expected to arise only in a fairly advanced and complex society where human beings are thoroughly in charge, and where they no longer need fear daily challenges from other species. (Or in societies under the sway of a greatly simplified unworld view like that of the Jains or some Hindus, in which it is prohibited for spiritual reasons to separate the body and soul of an ant or a flea.)

Our near absolute dominion over nature has, however, confronted us with one brilliant and ironic and inescapable insight. The decryption of DNA is not only useful in putting a merciful but overdue end to theories of creationism and racism but also enlightening in instructing us that we are ourselves animals. We share chromosomal material, often to a striking degree of overlap, not just with the higher primates but with quite humble life forms. Among those scholars who ridicule the claim of "animal rights," the irreplaceable propaganda keyword is "anthropomorphism"—that laughable combination of heresy and fallacy that uses human structure and human response for analogy. In fact the laugh is at the expense of those who deploy the word. The morphology of the anthropos is itself animalistic. This is a much better starting point than the burblings of Bronze Age Palestine and Mesopotamia, because it permits us to see fellow creatures as just that, and because it allows us to trace our filiations and solidarities with them, as well as our conflicts of interest.

When we look more closely, we see that cats do not in fact torture their mice (only an "anthropomorphist" could make such a self-incriminating transference) but, rather, are fascinated by rapid movement and lose interest only when it ceases. We observe that animals, although they may respect one another's territory, do not at all respect one another's "rights"—unless those other animals happen to be human, in which case mutual-interest bargains can often be struck, and both sides can be brought to an agreement that neither will eat the other. We notice that creationism often entails "dispensationalism"—the demented belief that there is no point in preserving nature, because the Deity will soon replace it with a perfected form. This popular teleology does not just dispense with creatures and plants: It condemns human beings to an eternity of either torment or—what may well be worse—praise and jubilation.

The three critical areas of real-world debate are the human uses of animals for food, for sport, and for experiment. All these uses have now reached the point where they would be bound to arouse alarm even in a meat-eating, sport-loving person who was hoping for a particular medicine or organ graft that required extensive laboratory testing. I said earlier that such alarm could arise only when society had reached a certain plane of detachment from raw "nature." But even in times when the idea of "rights" for beasts would have been inexpressible, many people had a conscience about the mistreatment of animals, a reverence for their dignity and sometimes their majesty, and a decent respect for the reciprocal value of good relations with them. No body of human mythology or folklore is without this element, even if it is only the ballad or epic of an exceptional war-horse or hunting dog. The prophet Muhammad cut away the sleeve of his robe rather than disturb a slumbering cat (and how Scully, who does not mention this episode, wishes that Jesus of Nazareth had by word or gesture admonished his followers to respect animals). William Blake could experience the agonies of animals almost as if they were his own. Saint Francis of Assisi may have been something of a freak, but those who heard him knew that he was employing one of the registers of human sensitivity. Animals, to make an obvious point, have been given names for at least as long as we have records. Even when this relationship was sinister or excessive or hysterical, as in ancient cults that worshipped crocodiles or bears, it shows that human awareness of a certain kinship predates our genetic mapping of it. If we call this "instinct" it is only a further acknowledgment of the same thing.

Thus when I read of the possible annihilation of the elephant or the whale, or the pouring of oven cleaner or cosmetics into the eyes of live kittens, or the close confinement of pigs and calves in lightless pens, I feel myself confronted by human stupidity, which I recognize as an enemy. This would be so even if I didn't much care about the subjective experience of the animals themselves. For example, although I find that I can't read Peter Singer for long without becoming dulled by his robotic utilitarianism, the parts of his famous book *Animal Liberation* that I find most impressive are the deadpan reprints of animal-experiment "reports," written by white-coated dolts or possibly white-coated sadists. (The connection between stupidity and cruelty is a close one.) If you subject this chimp or this dog to these given experiences, of shock or mutilation or sensory deprivation, it will exhibit just the responses any fool could have predicted. No claim of usefulness or human application is made;

only requests for further funding. Such awful pointlessness and callousness had, I thought, been set back a bit by Singer and others—and so it has. But *Dominion* is replete with examples of pseudo-scientists who still maintain that animals cannot feel pain, let alone agony. (By "agony" I mean pain accompanied by fear-protracted, repeated anguish and misery.)

The dumb academics who mouth this stuff are legatees, whether they know it or not, of René Descartes, who held that animals were machines and that their yelps or cries were the noises emitted by broken machinery. One doesn't require much conceptual apparatus to refute this, and Scully is, I think, taking its current advocates too seriously. The morons who torture animals would obviously not get the same thrill from battering a toaster. Children, who are almost always *en rapport* with animals, do not treat them as toys. (And maltreatment of animals by a child is a famously strong indicator, as our investigators of psychopathology have found, of hideous future conduct. Hogarth intuited this centuries ago, in his sequence of illustrations *The Four Stages of Cruelty*.) The many old or lonely or infirm people who find therapeutic value in animal companionship do not get the same result even from a semi-animate object such as a TV.

Sentimental stuff may have been written about animals' having personalities, but it can easily be shown that they are able to distinguish human individuals almost as readily as human beings can distinguish one another. And great repertoires of learned or taught behavior among animals are only renamed if we decide to be minimalist and call them "conditioned reflexes." Finally, and to deploy an inelegant piece of evidence that is not even hinted at by Scully, who, unlike Singer, entirely shirks the subject of interspecies intimacy, I would point out that many human beings have found consolation in sexual intercourse with animals (for instance, the prototype of Robinson Crusoe)—and who will say that this cannot lead to the sort of love that would be wasted on a car, or a lawn mower?

This would leave us and the "machinists" with only the problem of language and cognition. The whale, we are in effect informed, has its cortex but is too non-sentient to know, say, that it is an endangered species. The great apes who learn to sign whole phrases to their human friends are just improving their food-acquisition skills. Dolphins can at best (at best!) talk only to one another. To all such assertions the correct response requires no strong proof of language or logic in nonhuman brains. It is enough to know that we do not know enough. All the advances in the study of animal sentience have been made extremely recently, and some of these findings are fascinating and promising. If you insist, these same studies may even have benefits for human beings. Ordinary prudence, or straight utilitarianism, would therefore suggest that this is a bad time for us to be destroying whales for their blubber, or elephants for their tusks (or for mere "recreation"), or Rwandan gorillas in order to make their prehensile paws into ashtrays. "The end of natural history" was the arresting phrase used by Douglas Chadwick to describe this bleak state of affairs; one might suggest to the debased Cartesians that they conduct a thought experiment involving likely human response to a planet populated only by other human beings and their pets and farm animals, plus the lesser birds, reptiles, and insects. Oh, dear—I said "populated."

Opponents of the careful attitude toward animals also have their "extreme scenario" tactics. Probably no group except the pacifists is the butt of as much taunting about inconsistency as the pro-animal faction. You don't eat meat but—aha!—you do wear leather shoes. Scully shows a martyrlike patience in the face of this, as befits a man who's had to hear innumerable jests about veal and spotted owls at carnivorous Republican fundraisers. Joy Williams, in *Ill Nature*, has a more mordant reply: "The animal people are vegetarians. They'd better be if they don't want to be accused of being hypocritical. Of course, by being unhypocritical, they can be accused of being self-righteous." But it must be noted that there are so-called "deep ecologists," who materialize all the expectations of the cynics and who stoutly hold that there is no ethical difference between a human baby and a gerbil. Why must it be noted? First, because it is not the only symptom of a reactionary Malthusianism on the green fringe, and second, because arguments like this are taken up by defenders of the status quo and mobilized for dialectical purposes. The gerbil-baby equivalence is one of the very few human delusions for which there is no scriptural warrant; and for all I know, in the context of interstellar time and galactic indifference, it may be valid. There are sound reasons for concluding that all life is ultimately random. But there is no way of living and acting as if this is true; and if it is true, human beings cannot very well be condemned for making the best of things by taking advantage of other animals.

Like all casuistry and all dogmatism, this sort of stuff contains its own negation. But more interesting, and perhaps more encouraging, it also contains the germ of a complement. Just as those who experiment on animals are eager to deny that they are cruel (why, in point of their own theory, do they bother?), and just as the proprietors of factory farms maintain that the beasts are better off than they would be on the hillside, and just as some particularly fatuous Englishmen assert that the fox "really" enjoys being hunted, so the animal liberation fanatics use human life and human rights as their benchmark. What the Skinnerian behaviorists say about animals would, if true, largely hold good for people, and those who endow fleas with human rights are halfway toward ridiculing their own definition of human beings as a "plague species." Loud, overconfident dismissals of obvious qualms betray the stirrings of an uneasy conscience. Neither side can break free of an inchoate but essential notion of our interdependence.

Scully is at his best when he stops wrangling with Aquinas and other Church fathers (I notice that if he wonders about animal souls, he keeps his concern to himself) and goes out into the field. With an almost masochistic resolve, he exposes himself to the theory and practice of exploitation as it is found among the exponents of commercial hunting and industrial farming. The arguments he hears, about gutsy individualism in the first case and rationalized profit maximization in the second, are the disconcerting sounds of his own politics being played back to him. Making the finest use of this tension, he produces two marvelous passages of reporting. Without condescension but with a fine contempt he introduces us to "canned hunting": the can't-miss virtual safaris that charge a fortune to fly bored and overweight Americans to Africa and "big game" destinations on other continents for an air-conditioned trophy trip and the chance to butcher a charismatic animal in conditions of guaranteed safety. Those who can't offord the whole package can sometimes shell out to shoot a rare wild creature that would otherwise be pensioned off from an American zoo.

Millions of animals, either semi-wild or semi-domestic, would never have been born if not for human design. Pheasants and deer are bred or preserved in profusion for sport and for food, and the famous British fox is, or was until recent parliamentary challenges, protected by horse-borne huntsmen from those who would otherwise have shot or poisoned it out of hand.

Traditional farming, for which Scully evinces much nostalgia, is a logical extension of this—and factory farming seems to most people no more than a further extension and modernization of the idea that civilization and animal husbandry are inextricable. However, Scully's second graphic account, of his visit to a pig plant in North Carolina, is a frontal challenge to such facile progressivism. In page after relentless page he shows that the horrible confinement of these smart and resourceful creatures, and the endless attempt to fatten and pacify them with hormones, laxatives, antibiotics, and swirls of rendered pigs recycled into their own swill (and then to use other treatments to counterweigh the unintended consequences of the original ones), is far worse than we had suspected. A sort of Gresham's law means that more equals worse. The pigs develop hideous tumors and lesions; their litters are prone to stillbirths and malformations; their "stress levels" (another accidental revelation of the despised "anthropomorphic") are bewildering and annoying even to their keepers. Hardened migrant laborers who really need the work are frequently revolted by the slaughtering process. And, perhaps direst of all from the corporate viewpoint, the resulting meat is rank. "Pink," "spongy," and "exudative" are among the tasty terms used in internal company documents to describe the "pork" that is being prepared for our delectation. When was the last time you peeled open a deli ham sandwich, or a BLT, to take a look at the color, let alone the consistency, of what you were being sold and were about to ingest? The ham doesn't taste of anything, but upon reflection this comes as a distinct relief.

Thus in the three arenas—food, sport, and experiment—Scully asks the right questions even if he doesn't canvass all the possible answers. When he is on form, he does this in beautiful and witty prose. I think he falls down on the optional fourth issue, the question of whether we lower our own moral threshold by deafening ourselves to animal bleats and roars and trumpetings. It is obviously tempting to think so, and the example of disturbed, animal-torturing children is a powerful one; but both he and Singer are unpersuasive on this point. (Perhaps Singer has a folk memory of his fellow Australians' being forcibly employed in a historic theater of generalized cruelty.) Farmers, despite the rough jobs they have to perform with beasts, have not been more brutal, or brutalized, than those who work only with—or for—machines. The National Socialists in Germany enacted thoroughgoing legislation for the protection of animals and affected to regard Jewish ritual slaughter with abhorrence, meanwhile being enthusiastic about the ritual slaughter of Jews. Hindu nationalists are infinitely more tender toward cows than toward Muslims. As a species we can evidently live with a good deal of contradiction in this sphere. Conversely, one of the most idiotic jeers against animal lovers is the one about their preferring critters to people. As a matter of observation, it will be found that people who "care"—about rain forests or animals, miscarriages of justice or dictatorships—are, though frequently irritating, very often the same people. Whereas those who love hamburgers and riskless hunting and mink coats are not in the front ranks of Amnesty International. Like the quality of mercy, the prompting of compassion is not finite, and can be self-replenishing.

Taking myself as averagely cynical, I came to discern while reading *Dominion* that in all the cases where animal suffering disturbed me, it was largely because of rationalist humanism. When my turn comes to get a heart valve or a kidney from a pig (and how is that for anthropomorphism, by the by?), I don't want the pig to have been rotting and wretched, let alone cannibalistic or subjected to promiscuous mutations, while it was alive. Much animal experimentation is a wasteful perversion of science (Jonas Salk's vaccine seemed useless when tested on anything but a human being). The elimination of elephants and whales and tigers and other highly evolved animals would be impoverishing for us, and the disappearance of apes would be something like fratricide. The feeding of animal matter to protein-producing herds has been a catastrophe, resulting not only in ghastly pyres but in repulsive and sometimes lethally tainted food. The self-evidence of much of this has been obscured more than clarified by talk of "rights," which in the case of non-bipeds does seem to meet Bentham's definition of "nonsense upon stilts." Rights have to be asserted. Animals cannot make such assertions. We have to make representations to ourselves on their behalf. To the extent that we see our own interest in doing so, we unpick both the tautology that hobbles the utilitarian and the idealist delusion that surrounds the religious, and may simply become more "humane"—a word that seems to require its final vowel as never before.

(*The Atlantic*, November 2002)

Old Enough to Die

THE UNITED STATES OF AMERICA executes its own children. What is wrong with that sentence? Well, nothing factual. We may differ about whether the formative years are an age of innocence or experience, but a whole body of law establishes and defends certain age limits, below which one is considered a child. And seventy-three such children have been growing old under sentence of death in American prisons as I write. William Blake, who perhaps excelled all other authors in his rage against cruelty to the young, put his "Little Boy Lost" in the "Experience" section of his *Songs of Innocence and of Experience*:

> The weeping child could not be heard,
> The weeping parents wept in vain;
> They strip'd him to his little shirt,
> And bound him in an iron chain.
>
> And burn'd him in a holy place,
> Where many had been burn'd before:
> The weeping parents wept in vain.
> Are such things done on Albion's shore.

Albion's shore—an antique name for England—was, in the eighteenth and nineteenth centuries, famous for two things: intense sentimentality about images of innocent children, and extreme ruthlessness in the sexual and commercial and penal treatment of the very young. We shake our heads, now, at the obviousness of this hypocrisy. But here's what happened to George Stinney, in Clarendon County, South Carolina, on June 16, 1944. At the age of 14, weighing 95 pounds and standing five feet and one inch, he was lashed into an electric chair and a mask was put over his face. He was then given a hit of 2,400 volts. The mask, which was perhaps too big for him, thereupon slipped off. The witnesses saw his wide-open and weeping eyes, and his dribbling mouth, before another two jolts ended the business and fried him for good. They may not have "burn'd him in a holy place," but it was a reverent state occasion and you can bet there was a minister on hand to see fair play done.

But, you say, this kind of thing doesn't go on anymore. That's true up to a point. On Albion's shore, it certainly doesn't. Nor are juveniles sentenced to death in any other European nation. Since 1990, indeed, only six countries have executed juvenile offenders: Iran, Yemen, Pakistan, Saudi Arabia, Nigeria, and the United States of America. The United States has, you may be interested to hear, left the silver and bronze medals to be divided among these other fine contenders, keeping the gold for itself both by conducting the most executions and by having the largest number of juveniles awaiting extinction on death row.

Now, exactly what kind of village does this take? I can scarcely scan the press without learning that "our kids" are in need of more protection. In their name, I am supposed to have my Internet access and my cable TV more closely supervised. It will be years until I can send my teenage son out to buy my whisky and my tobacco supplies, and years until he can buy his own. You can't vote or be impaneled on a jury or sign up to be all you can be in Kosovo until you are at least eighteen. But if you step far enough out of line, the protections that safeguard the minor are abruptly withdrawn, and the state will snuff you like an old sow that eats her farrow. On the whole, and in most states of the union that rely on the death penalty, you need to be at least sixteen to hear a judge instruct the proper authorities to take your life. But Governor Gary Johnson of New Mexico and former governor Pete Wilson of California are impatient with this "kid-glove" leniency. They have toyed with the idea that eighth-graders be brought within the tough-love embrace of the gas chamber and the lethal injection, Johnson by calling for the execution of thirteen-year-olds, and Wilson (influenced no doubt by California's laid-back style) by suggesting that the authorities wait only until the perp is fourteen.

Let's try not to be sentimental, or, rather, let us see what happens if we are not. Teenagers can be hell, and they have attained the age of reason if not responsibility. Most adults, reviewing the molten years of their own puberty, can think of at least one occasion where they really, really needed a break or a second chance, and where their lives and careers might have been literally as well as figuratively over if they hadn't had one. ("Get me out of this and I swear...") But then, most people manage to get by without turning a .44 on their folks and without—as young Master George Stinney was said to have done—murdering an eleven-year-old girl. Sean Sellers, the condemned American youth most recently executed, for crimes committed when he was sixteen, was a bad poster boy for any cause. The state of Oklahoma killed him last February 4, for the casual murder of a store clerk and the deliberate slaying of his mother and stepfather. He never seriously pretended to be innocent; indeed, he was engaged at the time in a supposedly satanic effort to violate all of the Ten Commandments. While on death row, he additionally failed to get my personal vote by professing ostentatious reborn Christian evangelism, and by featuring on a Web site devoted to redemption through fundamentalist writings and a comic book. However, you do not lose any, let alone all, of your civil rights by opting for either yucky cults or sickly religiosity. (Where would we be if you did?) And the question for me became, as I went into the case: Was this boy gravely sick or not? There is, after all, a legal and moral presumption against executing even adults who are insane.

Anyone who has been involved with a death-row prisoner knows the piercing yet dull sense of pity and shame that descends. It's always the same: the family background that makes you want to weep; the home usually festooned (as in the Sellers case) with deadly weapons; the educational and cultural level that would raise eyebrows in Calcutta or Bogotá; the overworked public defender who had two dimes and two days to make his case; the absence of any useful teacher or priest or shrink or "counselor" until it was too damned late; the occasional thoughtful relative who puts up some dough; the endless hearings and rehearings and then the long, dreary wait for a "stay" of execution that becomes a torture if it comes at all. Sometimes, at the last minute, an intercession from a celebrity or a certified moral authority. And then the tawdry ritual with the needles or the gas or the electric current, and then on to the next.

Often abandoned as an infant by his truck-driving mother and stepfather (his maternal grandfather took his side at trial) and introduced to Satanism by one of his many baby-sitters, Sean Sellers seems to have suffered from a childhood brain lesion and from multiple-personality disorder. Bob Ravitz, the public defender who represented him, was allowed by the state $750 to pay for an expert witness but, on this princely scale, wasn't able to afford a proper psychiatric evaluation. The extent of the boy's disorder—several different styles of handwriting, several different names for himself, various delusions, even the ability to switch from left- to right-handedness—was not discovered until he had been on death row for an awfully long time. But the whole point of the appeals procedure, and the whole justification for the grisly business of warehousing condemned people, is to avoid a miscarriage of justice.

In 1992, six years after his trial, a panel of three physicians administered a quantitative electroencephalograph test to the boy, who had become a legal adult while in prison. They discovered the traces of the childhood brain injury, the presence of several "alter" personalities, and the strong likelihood, therefore, that Sean Sellers had not in any sense attained a condition of criminal responsibility when he was tried and convicted.

Here comes the part that causes me to make a low and growling noise, even as I reread it for the dozenth time. In February 1998 the United States Court of Appeals Tenth Circuit finally heard the medical and psychiatric evidence that had gone undiscovered at the initial arraignment. The three judges wrote the following opinion:

> Although troubled by the extent of uncontroverted clinical evidence proving Petitioner suffers from Multiple Personality Disorder, now and at the time of the offenses of conviction, and that the offenses were committed by an "alter" personality, we are constrained to hold Petitioner has failed to establish grounds for federal habeas corpus relief. *Even though his illness is such that he may be able to prove his factual innocence of those crimes, we believe that he must be left to the avenue of executive clemency to pursue that claim.* [My italics.]

So a sober panel of robed figures, calmly reviewing the life-and-death case of a disturbed child, determines in writing that said child may be "factually" or technically innocent, but further determines that this is not really any of its business. A federal district court in Oklahoma had briefly considered Sean Sellers's case in light of Clinton's newly minted Antiterrorism and Effective Death Penalty Act (A.E.D.P.A.). This brave new law says that if you don't present your exculpatory evidence by a given date, then you are too late, mate. However, it wasn't this provision that doomed the appeal or its successor pleas in higher courts. The "controlling legal authority" here is the decision of the Rehnquist Supreme Court in 1993, known as *Herrera* v. *Collins*, where it was baldly stated that the execution of an innocent person is not necessarily a violation of federal constitutional protections. This February, Sellers was led out of his cell and put down like a diseased animal.

Article 6(5) of the International Covenant on Civil and Political Rights states that the "sentence of death shall not be imposed for crimes committed by persons below eighteen years of age." The United Nations Convention on the Rights of the Child makes the same stipulation. So does the American Convention on Human Rights. The United States has signed the first and third of these treaties, while reserving the right to execute any person except a pregnant woman (presumably out of deference to the natural right of children rather than mothers). It is one of only two nations that have yet to ratify the U.N. Convention on the Rights of the Child. The other nonsignatory is Somalia, for reasons you probably don't want to think about. Even Iran and Saudi Arabia have ratified the U.N. Convention. So astoundingly at variance with the international community is the position of the American state that in 1997 the U.N. Commission on Human Rights asked its special rapporteur to visit this country, to seek meetings with high officials, and to report back. At once, there was a titanic outcry from Senator Jesse Helms and others. What is this? We monitor other people's violations. How dare you ask to inspect *ours*?

Adults sentenced to death in this country are almost always vicious creeps, pitiable failures, or innocent losers. (Recall the instance of Anthony Porter, freed from seventeen years on death row this February after a Northwestern

University journalism class did a project on his case by pure chance and discovered what the prosecutors and the judges had not: that he could not possibly have committed the double murder. For one thing, the more plausible suspect confessed to the crime, the sort of fact a good prosecutor is trained never to overlook. Mr. Porter has an I.Q. of 51 and is, in his way, a child also.) But the children condemned to death are losers in a category all their own. A decade ago, *The American Journal of Psychiatry* published an investigation, using a sample of four states, that covered juveniles on hold for execution. There were fourteen of them. Only two of these had I.Q. scores higher than 90.

Every one of them had suffered severe head trauma during childhood. All had deep psychiatric problems; only two had managed to grow up without extreme physical or sexual abuse, and five of them had undergone this at the hands of family members. Only five of them had been evaluated by psychiatrists before standing trial. (In case you wonder, yes, a disproportionate number of them were African-American. I don't think that Master George Stinney—see above—would have been roasted by the state of South Carolina even in 1944 if the same hadn't been as true of him as it was untrue of his victim.)

Very often, in fact, these minors are in trouble—real bad trouble—because they were the ones too slow or too panicked to flee the scene, or because they were used by cynical older criminals as patsies or decoys. Joseph John Cannon, executed in Texas in April of last year, was illiterate, brain-damaged, sexually scarred, and heavily addicted when they caught him, at the age of seventeen. He had attempted suicide at age fifteen, and told his interviewers that he could not remember anything good that had ever happened to him. Well, it was apparently the job of the state of Texas to make sure that this unbroken record was maintained. (During his execution by lethal injection, which took place over the objections of His Holiness the Pope, who was overruled by Governor George W. Bush, the needle "blew out" of Cannon's arm and the witnesses had to wait while a drape was brought in and a "new" vein was found.)

And the irony was not at Joseph John Cannon's expense. It may seem odd, to some people reading this column, that the United States joins Yemen and Pakistan in putting down its troublesome young, and that it reads lectures on human rights to other countries while refusing to ratify treaties which most civilized societies regard as the ABCs of law. But I doubt Joseph John Cannon would have seen the joke. He probably never realized that he was living in the land of the free and the home of the brave to begin with. And soon he wasn't. And a country with a positive glut of lawyers and grief counselors and spiritual-awareness artists and fancy shrinks will continue to wonder what is wrong with kids these days.

(*Vanity Fair*, June 1999)

In Defense of Foxhole Atheists

ONE MONDAY IN MAY, I was setting off from Washington to Colorado Springs, home of the United States Air Force Academy. I had kindly been invited by the academy's "freethinkers association," a loose-knit group of cadets and instructors who are without religious affiliation. As I was making ready to depart, and checking my e-mail, I found I had been sent a near-incredible video clip from the Al Jazeera network. It had been shot at Bagram Air Force Base last year, and it showed a borderline-hysterical address by one Lieutenant Colonel Gary Hensley, chief of the United States military chaplains in Afghanistan. He was telling his evangelical audience, all of them wearing uniforms supplied by the taxpayer, that as followers of Jesus Christ they had a collective responsibility "to be witnesses for him." Heating up this theme, Lieutenant Colonel Hensley went on: "The Special Forces guys, they hunt men, basically. We do the same things, as Christians. We hunt people for Jesus. We do, we hunt them down. Get the hound of heaven after them, so we get them in the kingdom. Right? That's what we do, that's our business."

The comparison to the Special Forces would seem to suggest that the objects of this hunting and hounding are Afghans rather than Americans. But it's difficult to be certain, and indeed I am invited to Colorado Springs partly because chaplains there have been known to employ taxpayer dollars to turn the hounds of heaven loose on their own students and fellow citizens. As the Bagram tape goes on, however, it becomes obvious that Afghans are the targets in this case. Stacks of Bibles are on display, in the Dari and Pashto tongues that are the main languages in Afghanistan. A certain Sergeant James Watt, a candidate for a military chaplaincy, is shown giving thanks for the work of his back-home church, which subscribed the dough. "I also want to praise God because my church collected some money to get Bibles for Afghanistan. They came and sent the money out," he beamingly tells his Bible-study class. In another segment, those present show quite clearly that they understand they are in danger of violating General Order Number One of the U.S. Central Command, which explicitly prohibits "proselytizing of any religion, faith, or practice." A gathering of chaplains, all of them fed from the public trough, is addressed by Captain Emmit Furner, a military cleric who seems half in love with his own light-footed moral dexterity. "Do we know what it means to proselytize?" he asks his audience. A voice from the audience is heard to say, "It is General Order Number One." To this Sergeant Watt replies: "You can't proselytize but you can give gifts.... I bought a carpet and then I gave the guy a Bible after I conducted my business." So where's the harm in a man who is paid by the United States government to be a Christian chaplain strolling condescendingly through the *souk* and handing out religious propaganda as if it were a handful of small change or *backsheesh?* Probably not much more damaging to the war effort, or insulting to Afghan sensibilities, than the activities of the anonymous torturers who have been found operating elsewhere on the Bagram base. But it is taking the ax to the root of the United States Constitution, never mind General Order Number One. (Neither of these seems to be in force locally: No action against the uniformed missionaries has been taken.)

The film was originally shot by Brian Hughes, a maker of documentaries and a former member of the United States military who had fought in the Gulf War. It was made available to James Bays, one of Al Jazeera's more experienced Afghan reporters. By the time I had landed in Colorado Springs, later that day, I expected that the thing would have become a national story and that the cadets, perhaps most especially the freethinkers club, would be talking about it. But I was mistaken twice. Only a few fringe anti-war malcontents had made anything of this outrageous clip, and there was a general shrug when I mentioned it. "That sort of thing happened to me a lot in Afghanistan," I was told by Carlos Bertha, a veteran of the war who now teaches philosophy to cadets and who helped organize my talk. "I used to complain and sometimes the word would come down to lay off, but it was always ready to start up again."

He was talking, however, about in-your-face Christian-fundamentalist displays at the entrance to the chow hall. Perhaps local Afghan hired helpers would have to see these, too, but the propaganda wasn't being inflicted directly on them. So the question becomes two related questions: Is there a clique within the United States military that is seeking to use the wars in Iraq and Afghanistan as an opportunity to mount a new crusade and to Christianize the "heathen"? And does this clique also attempt to impose its beliefs on young Americans in uniform, many of whom may even be Christian already? If the answer to either question is "yes," then we are directly financing the subversion of our own Constitution and inviting a "holy war" where we will not be able to say that only the other side is dogmatic and fanatical.

To take the questions in reverse: A few years ago I wrote a book that mentioned an astonishing state of affairs at the Air Force Academy. But don't take my word for it. An official USAF panel of inquiry, reporting in 2005, admitted that the commandant of cadets, Brigadier General Johnny A. Weida, had sent out an academy-wide e-mail reminding all hands of the upcoming and exclusively Protestant National Day of Prayer. He had further informed cadets that they were "accountable to their God" and came up with an ingenious call-and-response chant that went like this: "Jesus... *Rocks!*" Evidently quite a warrior. The head football coach, Fisher DeBerry, had improved on this only slightly by staging locker-room prayer-pleas to "The Master Coach" and hanging out a banner that read, "Team Jesus." A screening of Mel Gibson's incendiary, Jew-baiting homoerotic extravaganza, *The Passion of the Christ*, had flyers in its favor placed on every seat in the Air Force Academy dining hall. A Pentecostal chaplain warned cadets that they should accept Christ or "burn in hell." About the latter incident, the Air Force investigative panel decided to be lenient, on the perfectly good grounds that such language is "not uncommon" in this denomination. And that, I suspect, is part of the problem to begin with: Unexamined extremist Christian conservatism is the cultural norm in many military circles. One Lutheran chaplain at the academy, Captain Melinda Morton, resigned from the service after being transferred for protesting that the evangelical pressure was "systematic." And, despite the tolerance for Pentecostal hellfire rants, by no means all forms of expression could be indulged; a nonbelieving cadet was forbidden to organize a club for "freethinkers."

That has now changed as a result of the indoctrination scandal, which is why I was able to be at the Springs. The academy's chaplains still would not allow our meeting to take place on the base, but that was fine by me, as it meant we could all meet out of uniform at the Old Chicago pub downtown. The last survey of student opinion found that of the 4,400 cadets, 85 percent were Christian of one kind or another, 2 percent were declared atheists, 1.5 percent were Jewish, 0.4 percent Muslim, 0.3 percent Hindu, and—note this—9.3 percent either indicated no allegiance or identified themselves as "other." According to all measurements of opinion, the latter is the fastest-growing minority in the United States, and only slightly under-represented at the Air Force Academy. (The Pew report on the subject says that unbelievers in the armed services overall represent a *higher* percentage than that of the general population: This would track with my experience and disprove that silly old line about there being no atheists in foxholes.)

I am still not going to give any real names of cadets attending my little event: There were about twenty of them, mostly males. Two of the group, one Baptist and one Mormon, had given up their faith since enlisting at the academy. The others fluctuated between doubt and agnosticism and straight-out unbelief. They were good-humored, outspoken, and tough-minded: the sort of people who make you proud of being defended by a volunteer military. According to most of them, the situation had improved since the last scandal, or rather because of it. In an acronym-dominated world, the school's SPIRE (Special Programs in Religious Education) could now include meetings for unbelievers, but even so an S.C.A. (Scheduling Committee Action) had to be approved before they could be allowed to meet with your humble servant in a pub overlooked by Pikes Peak. It seemed weird to me that people willing to fight and die for the United States should be treated as if they were children (or do I mean members of a "flock"?).

They all told me that they felt quite able to stand up to peers and community members who wanted to evangelize them. (The Colorado Springs area is home to James Dobson's "Focus on the Family" campaign, as well as to the fragrant Reverend Ted Haggard, crusader and, when entwined with male hookers, meth buyer as well.) What they would object to would be evangelizing from higher up. And there is ever stronger reason to think that, at the Pentagon, the fish rots from the head. It emerges that during the invasion of Iraq, one of Donald Rumsfeld's directors of intelligence, Major General Glen Shaffer, began to attach fiery biblical excerpts to the photographs that accompanied the daily briefings. For example, on one document delivered to President Bush by Rumsfeld there was a picture of an F-14 "Tomcat" on the deck of a carrier, with the accompaniment of verses from Psalm 139: "If I rise on the wings of the dawn, if I settle on the far side of the sea, even there your hand will guide me, your right hand will hold me fast, O Lord." Over a photograph of Saddam Hussein appeared the words, from the First Epistle of Peter: "It is by God's will that by doing good you should silence the ignorant talk of foolish men." (I pause to note that this suggests that General Shaffer had no idea what hellishness Saddam Hussein had actually, apart from his inexplicable failure to accept Jesus as his personal savior, been responsible for.)

More alarming still is a book called *Under Orders: A Spiritual Handbook for Military Personnel*, by an Air Force lieutenant colonel named William McCoy, publicity for which describes the separation of church and state as a "twisted idea." Nor is this the book's only publicity: It comes—with its direct call for a religion-based military—with an endorsement from General David Petraeus.

It is outrageous that brave and intelligent young officers, seeing such theocratic absurdity rampant among the top brass, could suspect even for a second that their road to promotion was a longer one unless they acquiesced in this use of public resources for the promotion of (a single) religion. And if that thought can arise in a military academy or the corridors of the Pentagon, how much more oppressive is it when the volunteer is far from home, on the frontier, on a firebase, or aboard a submarine or a carrier, and being told that this time the objects of conversion are also the people we supposedly came to rescue from the Taliban and al-Qaeda? Captain Melinda Morton was, before quitting the Air Force Academy, a missile-launch commander. She believes that there is a fusion between the two types of proselytization. The evangelicals, she told Jeff Sharlet—whose work on this has been path-breaking—see the whole military as "a mission field. They wanted to send their missionaries to the military, and for the military itself to become missionaries to the world." If this bizarre ambition came anywhere close to being realized, it would make civilian taxpayers into mere hewers of wood and drawers of water for an armed but unelected religious elite, and it would make our soldiers into unwitting pawns in a very dangerous game where they were considered expendable cannon fodder for Christ. The only certain winners would be the death cultists of *jihad*, who are already marveling at their luck in being proved right about the Americans as "crusaders." This is as near to mutiny and treason as one could hope to sail and still wear the uniform.

And please do not think for a single second that, if proselytizing in our armed forces is permitted to extremist Christians, the precedent will not be taken up by other fanatics as well. There was a time when a man named Abdurahman Alamoudi was operating freely in this country, and even being deployed as a "moderate" Muslim spokesman by the State Department. More than once received at the White House, he also helped found an outfit with the intriguing name of the Muslim Armed Forces and Veteran Affairs Council, which was used to select Islamic chaplains in the armed services. Mr. Alamoudi's run of luck ended in 2004, when he was given a long sentence in federal prison for activities related to terrorism. Since then, serving officers like the now famous Major Nidal Malik Hasan have had to go online for their extremist spiritual advisers, such as the fugitive preacher Anwar al-Awlaki, who issued a general religious permission to shoot down U.S. servicemen only a short time before Major Hasan rose to his feet and sprayed his fellow countrymen at Fort Hood. Awlaki later praised the gallant major as "a hero." This was not the only evidence of an early-stage attempt at setting up *jihad*-ist penetration of the ranks, but, yet again, the authorities decided to treat Major Hasan's alarming statements as if they were protected religious speech rather than early warnings of the effect of a homicidal theology. A psychiatrist gives a lecture at Walter Reed Army Medical Center, on the government's dime, and exclaims proudly that Muslim fighters love death more than we love life... Not very Hippocratic.

Throughout modern American history, the armed forces have been a great engine for assimilation and integration. Segregation of blacks was abolished in the services long before it was done away with in the wider society. Hispanic soldiers who are not yet full citizens have won many awards for bravery in the field. Women—not always approved of by religious fanatics—have risen to occupy serious command posts at all levels. (Discrimination against homosexuals, another religion-based prejudice, remains official, but that is a political decision, not a military one, and even the British services now recruit gay men and women, so change is probably not far off.) It would be an unimaginable catastrophe for America if the ranks became an arena of contestation between competing religious sectarians, and the effect on morale in the field would be disastrous also. It is of high importance to stop it before it can get started, and this means applying the principle of church-state separation right across the military spectrum.

James Madison was the coauthor with Thomas Jefferson of the Virginia Statute on Religious Freedom, which became the basis of the First Amendment to the Constitution. Not accidentally the first clause of our Bill of Rights, this amendment unambiguously forbids any "establishment of religion" *in* or *by* these United States. In his "Detached Memoranda," not published until after his death, Madison even wrote that the appointment of chaplains in the armed forces, and indeed in Congress, was "inconsistent with the Constitution, and with the pure principles of religious freedom." He could never have foreseen a time when state-subsidized chaplains would be working to *subvert* the Constitution, and violating their sacred oath to uphold it. Let us be highly thankful that we have young soldiers and sailors and Air Force personnel who, busy and devoted as they already are, show themselves brave enough to fight back on this front too.

(*Vanity Fair* online, December 15, 2009)

In Search of the Washington Novel

FICTION ABOUT the nation's capital is a growth that flourishes only on the lower slopes of Parnassus. Think of the flower of our novelists—Updike, Mailer, Roth, Cheever, Bellow—and see if you can call to mind a single scene that is set on the banks of the Potomac. Mailer did a famous nonfiction account of the march on the Pentagon (*The Armies of the Night*), and Updike briefly created a lifelike President Buchanan, but that second exception proves a more general rule, exemplified by Gore Vidal's canon: Historical reconstruction is the form in which our novelists prefer to approach the matter.

Can one imagine a Dickens without London or a Zola or Flaubert without Paris? The *radix malorum* can probably be found in the famous bargain between Thomas Jefferson and Alexander Hamilton, made when New York was still the capital of these United States. In exchange for an agreement to build the constitutionally mandated new Federal City on the border of Jefferson's beloved Virginia, Hamilton could have his coveted national bank. Thus, and allowing for certain Philadelphian interludes, it was decided early on that the cultural capital of America would be separated from its political one. Other countries that have made similar two-headed arrangements include Australia, Brazil, Burma, and Canada: We yet await the Brasilia or Canberra novel.

I'm among the few who consider Mailer's *Harlot's Ghost* a triumph, but to the extent that it is a novel of Washington rather than of the Cold War, it's part of a formula on which too many authors have relied: the political thriller. As Thomas Mallon, one of the city's few resident literary novelists, once put it:

> Washington novels, such as they are, tend to be found on racks at National Airport, the raised gold letters of their titles promising a bomb on Air Force One or a terrorist kidnapping of the First Lady. There's a reason for all the goofiness. A serious novelist must take his characters seriously, regard them as three-dimensional creatures with inner lives and authentic moral crises; and that's just what, out of a certain democratic pride, Americans refuse to do with their politicians.

"Democratic pride": the original of the Washington novel is Henry Adams's *Democracy*, published in 1880 with its very title a sneer at the illusion of popular sovereignty. (It also founded the tradition that culminates with Joe Klein and *Primary Colors*: Adams published his book anonymously, hoping that readers would attribute it to his friend John Hay. Joan Didion borrowed the title, if not the practice, in her antipolitical novel of the same name, published in 1984.)

Probably without wishing to do so, Adams provided a template for later authors to use as their glass of fashion and mold of form. Essential *dramatis personae* include a president, a society hostess, a British ambassador, a lobbyist or journalist, and a senator—the last customarily outfitted with a "mane." This mixture is repeated almost pedantically as late as Allen Drury's classic *Advise and Consent*, published in 1959. I suspect that it was only with the assassination of President Kennedy that the stately Potomac-paced *roman-fleuve* began to give way to the imperatives of the anything-goes thriller and to the mounting demand for Washington stories that could easily make the transition to the big screen. I speak as one whose D.C. apartment, with its view of the presidential motorcade, was used by Clint Eastwood as the location of his character's hideout in the movie version of David Baldacci's novel *Absolute Power*. And do I not remember sneering in print at the close of one of Tom Clancy's ill-carpentered Jack Ryan hack jobs, which ended with a plane crashing into the Capitol dome during a joint session? Currently, a special bipartisan committee is working on recommendations for what to do if that ever *does* happen, as it so nearly did in 2001. That body's deliberations on the constitutional implications of such an event could form the basis for a fine novella.

But Washington, so dull to outward appearances, does have a way of outpacing the imagination of pulp writers. John F. Kennedy smuggling the Mob's molls into the White House bedroom? Nixon and Kissinger praying on the Oval Office rug? Nixon and Chuck Colson discussing a possible bombing of the Brookings Institution? Oliver North running a parallel state and a private treasury from the White House basement? Ronald Reagan musing on the biblical end times with the head of the American Israel Public Affairs Committee? Bill Clinton's furtive cigar with Monica Lewinsky, tagged and bagged by the FBI on the grounds—this actually is in a footnote of the Starr Report—that smoking materials were forbidden in the executive mansion?

Fiction somehow declines the responsibility of creating a realistic Washington in favor of various genre approaches. Of the comic one, always so tempting, my friend Christopher Buckley is the acknowledged maestro, feasting on the buffet provided by lobbyists and Hill rats and those unhinged by ambition. (I pause to acknowledge his underrated and *noir*-ish earlier novel, *Wet Work.*) Of the politico-ideological and also of the Potomosexual genre, I would nominate Mallon as the leader. How come that's two literary guys with backgrounds as conservative Catholic Republicans? Search me. Mallon's most recent novel, *Fellow Travelers,* is a splendid evocation of Washington in the McCarthy era, with two kinds of victims as the atmosphere thickens: the covert Communists and the closet gays (a faction with a foot more in the camp of the persecuting than in that of the persecuted). It also has what few District fictions possess: a sharp working knowledge of the city's neighborhoods, from northeast Capitol Hill to Foggy Bottom and the Penn Quarter. (George Pelecanos, in his novels about the city in the time before the 1968 race riots, has the same level of shoe-leather skills.)

But here again, we are on the relatively secure turf of the known past. In this dimension, Gore Vidal has no rival. I once heard Newt Gingrich rebuke someone who was bad-mouthing Vidal's politics, insisting that he wished to hear no ill of the author of the magnificent *Lincoln*. This work is indeed enormously praiseworthy, as is the larger sequence of which it forms a part. In *Burr*, for example, Vidal guessed the truth about Thomas Jefferson and Sally Hemings long before most historians grudgingly conceded the point. However, Vidal's narrative—like the rest of his career—declines as it reaches its end: The last novel of the cycle, *The Golden Age*, gave as free a rein to paranoia about FDR's supposed foreknowledge of Pearl Harbor as the old boy's public pronouncements did to the drivel about 9/11 "truth."

Here is what Mrs. Lightfoot Lee, the inquisitive widow of Adams's tale, thinks about moving to a town where she will dwell "among the illiterate swarm of ordinary people who... represented constituencies so dreary that in comparison New York was a New Jerusalem, and Broad Street a grove of academe." Perhaps there will be compensations for this exile to the provinces:

> What she wished to see, she thought, was the clash of interests, the interests of forty millions of people and a whole continent, centering at Washington; guided, restrained, controlled, or unrestrained and uncontrollable, by men of ordinary mould; the tremendous forces of government, and the machinery of society, at work. What she wanted, was POWER.

Of course, that's not exactly what she gets, what with the enervating climate and the pervasive atmosphere of corruption and cynicism. She has to be content with some unsought attentions from a too-powerful senator (the name of this odious charmer is Clinton, as it happens; there is also a character named Gore). No, the fact is that Washington is and always has been irretrievably bogged down in *process*. And process doesn't generally make for electrifying prose—unless you're a fan of the novels of C. P. Snow, which describe the intestinal workings of inner-sanctum power struggles conducted by micro-megalomaniacs.

This brings us to Ward Just, possibly chief among those who have depicted the nation's capital as the bureaucratic and constipated place that it in fact is. Perhaps by way of offsetting the innate or latent tedium of this enterprise, Just—a former reporter for the *Washington Post* and *Newsweek*, who, like Allen Drury, pulled off the journalist's dream of publishing his bottom-drawer fiction—has a flair for the arresting title. He called one of his books *Honor, Power, Riches, Fame, and the Love of Women*, which certainly outpaces *Democracy* as an eye-catching title on a bookstall, as well as outbidding it as a definition of what most of our politicians actually work for. One of his short stories—"The Congressman Who Loved Flaubert"—is my selection for the most improbable title ever evolved on the banks of the Potomac.

Like Vidal, Just anchors his narratives in history, but unlike Vidal, he often brings them into our own day. In *Echo House*, he describes three generations of a political family named Behl. Somewhat didactic, the book is full of reminders that politics is not for the idealistic and is increasingly dominated by the media-savvy and the telegenic. (For some reason, we make this simple discovery anew every decade or so.) After an early disappointment connected with his failure to secure a vice-presidential nomination, the senior Behl hands his son a signed first edition—of Adams's *Democracy*.

It must say something that the Adams mold is so hard to break. The days of the Georgetown hostess are gone; the hostesses themselves are gone, too. Their reign began to close years ago, when senators started canceling dinners to appear on shows like *Nightline*. (There's a prefiguration of this in Larry McMurtry's neglected 1982 Washington novel *Cadillac Jack*, in which a character pontificates on world-shaking matters of which he knows little.) The Washington pundit is also a thing of the past: It's been a good while since any insider columnist had the kind of access or influence that Ben Bradlee enjoyed with John F. Kennedy. And the British Embassy, while it still stages some of the best dinners, is not the brokerage of influence that it once was. Yet—if we except the intermittent efforts at describing catastrophe or conspiracy, themselves mostly falling short of observable reality—this is the sort of stereotype in which the model remains confined.

Mrs. Lightfoot Lee can say a bit more for herself than her creator, who stressed that consuming interest in POWER. She has a reflective capacity also:

> "Who, then, is right? How *can* we all be right? Half of our wise men declare that the world is going straight to perdition; the other half that it is fast becoming perfect. Both cannot be right. There is only one thing in life," she went on, laughing, "that I must and will have before I die. I must know whether America is right or wrong."

It is that question, and no matter of process or advice or consent, that transcends all the others. We still await the novelist who can address the matter of the last, best hope of earth and treat it without frivolity, without cynicism, and without embarrassment.

(*City Journal*, Autumn 2010)

Eclectic Affinities

Isaac Newton: Flaws of Gravity

WHEN I WAS A YOUNG BOY at a Methodist boarding school in Cambridge, England, I used to try to drink as much water as I possibly could. This practice was based on the false hope that I might acquire some slight knowledge of science and mathematics. In these areas I was hopelessly deficient, yet it seemed that only the water in Cambridge could explain the extraordinary profusion of mathematical genius that had flowered in this rather chilly little city on the flatlands of East Anglia.

You could take a walk in the town, for example, and pass the Cavendish Laboratory on Free School Lane. You could easily miss it: Its quaint lack of space and resources, its generally shoestring and amateur character are lovingly satirized in Penelope Fitzgerald's lovely novel *The Gate of Angels*. But a grand total of twenty-nine Nobel Prizes have been awarded for work done in this unassuming building, perhaps the best-known being to Sir John Cockcroft and Ernest Walton for the development of the first nuclear particle accelerator (which allowed them to be the first to split the atom without using radioactive material), in 1932. This was during the exceptional directorship of Professor Ernest Rutherford, under whose benign and brilliant rule work at the Cavendish also garnered Nobels for Sir James Chadwick's discovery of the neutron and Sir Edward Appleton's demonstration of the existence of a layer of the ionosphere that could reliably transmit radio waves. It's not exactly a footnote to add Sir Mark Oliphant, who pioneered the deployment of microwave radar and flew to the United States during the war to assist American scientists in their pursuit of the non-peaceful implications of Cavendish's split atom and the setup that would become the Manhattan Project. Within a very short time, Robert Oppenheimer, another of Rutherford's Cavendish protégés, was watching the first nuclear detonation, near Alamogordo, New Mexico, and murmuring to himself a line from the *Bhagavad Gita*: "I am become death: the shatterer of worlds."

As against that, and taking a break from work at the same laboratory on February 28, 1953, researchers James Watson and Francis Crick went round the corner to a pub on nearby Bene't Street. Watson recalled feeling "slightly queasy when at lunch Francis winged into the Eagle to tell everyone within hearing distance that we had found the secret of life." The structure of deoxyribonucleic acid, building block of existence itself, turned out to have the shapely form of a double helix. Humanity was well on its way to unraveling and analyzing the crucial strands that are our DNA. (It was in the Eagle, less momentously, that I later drank my first illegal beer and kicked the stupid water habit for life.)

Continuing our stroll—or pub crawl—we might pass Christ's College, alma mater of the Reverend William Paley. In the early nineteenth century, Paley's book *Natural Theology*, arguing that all of "creation" argued for the evidence of a divine designer, became the key text for those who saw the hand of god in the marvels of nature. A young student named Charles Darwin came to the same college not all that long afterward and was overcome by awe at being given the same rooms as Paley had occupied. As a naturalist and biologist, Darwin hoped to follow in the great man's path and perhaps himself become a priest. In the event, his research was to compel him to a somewhat different conclusion. Tipping our hat to this astonishing double act, we might also pause to reflect outside the gates of Trinity Hall, the college that helped produce Stephen Hawking, who is now the Lucasian Professor of Mathematics and a fellow of Gonville & Caius College as well. Until relatively recently, it was possible to spot the celebrated anatomist of time and space, born on the 300th anniversary of the death of Galileo, grinding around these medieval streets and squares in his electric chariot: as good an instance of pure brain and intellect as one could hope to meet.

Who can pass the great and spacious lawns of Trinity College without thinking of Bertrand Russell, who could have been world famous in several departments, from adultery to radicalism, but whose most imposing work is probably *Principia Mathematica*, the result of a ten-year collaboration with Alfred North Whitehead. "The manuscript became more and more vast," recalled Russell in his autobiography, and in merely writing it out, when the main labor was complete, he worked "from ten to twelve hours a day for about eight months in the year, from 1907 to 1910...and every time that I went out for a walk I used to be afraid that the house would catch fire and the manuscript get burned up. It was not, of course, the sort of manuscript that could be typed, or even copied. When we finally took it to the University Press, it was so large that we had to hire an old four-wheeler for the purpose." Reflecting on this grueling experience, he remembered that it caused him to contemplate suicide very often, and wrote that "my intellect never quite recovered from the strain. I have been ever since definitely less capable of dealing with difficult abstractions than I was before." (This, from the man who went on to produce *A History of Western Philosophy*.)

But to mention Trinity is also to summon the greatest figure of them all: the man who wrote the very first *Principia Mathematica*, who was Lucasian Professor of Mathematics more than three centuries before Hawking and who, while the rest of the country was paralyzed by fear of the Great Plague of 1665–66, "revolutionized the world of natural philosophy. He gave the first proper treatment of the calculus; he split white light into its constituent colors; he began his exploration of universal gravity. And he was only twenty-four years of age."

I am quoting from Peter Ackroyd's new biography of Sir Isaac Newton, who did not, as legend has it, find his consciousness of the implications of gravity provoked by the fall of an apple. He was rather more meticulous than that in his researches and, like Madame Curie with radium, was unafraid to experiment on himself. In his eagerness to distinguish light from color, he stared at the sun with one eye, to discover the consequences. He was reckless of his own sight in the process, and had to spend three days in a darkened room in order to recuperate from the experience. Later, to test Descartes's theory that light pulsated as a "pressure" through the ether, he slid a large needle "betwixt my eye and the bone as near to the backside of my eye as I could." Single-minded to the point of obsession, he was attempting to alter the curve of his retina so he could observe the results, even at the risk of blinding himself.

We tend to love anecdotes about apples and eurekas because they make scientific genius seem more human and more random, but that other great Cambridge denizen Sir Leslie Stephen was closer to the mark when he claimed genius was "the capacity for taking trouble." Isaac Newton was one of the great workaholics of all time, as well as one of the great insomniacs. His industry and application made Bertrand Russell look like a slacker (and, like Russell, he was morbidly afraid of fire among his papers and books—fire which did, in fact, more than once break out). When he decided that a reflecting telescope would be a better instrument than the conventional refracting model, he also decided to construct it himself. When asked where he had obtained the tools for this difficult task, he responded with a laugh that he had made the tools himself, as well. He fashioned a parabolic mirror out of an alloy of tin and copper that he had himself evolved, smoothed, and polished to a glass-like finish, and built a tube and mounting to house it. This six-inch telescope had the same effectiveness as a six-foot refracting version, because it removed the distortions of light that were caused by the use of lenses.

In contrast with this clarity and purity, however, Newton spent much of his time dwelling in a self-generated fog of superstition and crankery. He believed in the lost art of alchemy, whereby base metals can be transmuted into gold, and the surviving locks of his hair show heavy traces of lead and mercury in his system, suggesting that he experimented upon himself in this fashion, too. (That would also help explain the fires in his room, since alchemists had to keep a furnace going at all times for their mad schemes.) Not content with the narrow views of the philosopher's stone and the elixir of life, he thought that there was a kind of universal semen in the cosmos, and that the glowing tails of the comets he tracked through the sky contained replenishing matter vital for life on Earth. He was a religious crackpot who, according to Ackroyd, considered Catholics to be "offspring of the Whore of Rome." He was also consumed by arcane readings of the book of Revelation and obsessed with the actual measurements of the Temple of Solomon. Newton elected to write his already difficult *Principia Mathematica* in Latin, boasting that this would make it even less accessible to the vulgar. He is still revered in the little world of esoteric and conspiratorial mania, featuring as a member of "the Priory of Sion" in *The Da Vinci Code*. And secularists and rationalists conspire, too, in their way, to keep his mythic reputation alive. The beautiful "Mathematical Bridge," which spans the River Cam at Queen's College, is still said to have been designed by Newton to stay in place without nails or screws or joints, and to be supported by gravitational force alone. When later scientists dismantled it to discover the secret, according to legend, they could not work out how to put it back together again, and had to use crude bolts and hinges to re-erect it. Newton died in 1727, and the bridge was not built until 1749, but rumors and fantasies are much stronger than fact.

But then, so are unscientific prejudices. Francis Crick didn't believe in god at all (he proposed having a brothel at his Cambridge college instead of a chapel), but he did follow the godly Newton in speculating that life had been "seeded" on Earth by a higher civilization. His "double-helix" colleague James Watson has several times speculated, against all the evidence, that female people and people with too much melanin pigmentation are genetically programed to underperform. Perhaps we shouldn't be too surprised at this. Joseph Priestley, the great Unitarian humanist and discoverer of oxygen, was wedded to a bogus theory of the chemistry of gasses wherein they burned into "phlogiston," which he called a "principle of inflammability." Alfred Russel Wallace, Darwin's great collaborator and perhaps even intellectual inspiration, was never happier than when attending spiritualist séances and marveling at the appearance of ectoplasm. It may not be until we get to Albert Einstein that we find a true scientist who is also a sane and lucid person with a genial humanism as part of his world outlook—and even Einstein was soft on Stalin and the Soviet Union.

We are inclined to forget that the word "scientist" itself was not in common use until 1834. Before that time, the rather finer title of "natural philosopher" was the regnant one. Isaac Newton may have been a crank and a recluse and a religious bigot and (during his period as master of the Royal Mint) an enthusiast for the hanging of forgers. However, the study of ancient thinkers and antique languages was second nature to him, and when he listed the seven colors of the spectrum—having carefully separated these from their formerly all-enveloping white light—he did so by an analogy with the seven notes of the musical scale. Any other conclusion, he felt, would violate the Pythagorean principle of harmony. He was probably wrong in this glimpse of the unified field theory that was to elude even Einstein, but one has to admire someone who could dare to be wrong in such a beautiful way.

Not everything about Newton was so harmonious. He clearly hated women, may well have died a virgin, and was terrified of sex (and believed that the menstrual blood of whores possessed magical properties). Peter Ackroyd, one of England's premier writers, makes a mystery where none exists when he writes of Newton's obsession with crimson and the furnishing of his room entirely in that color, from the drapes to the cushions. "There have been many explanations for this," he writes, "including his study of optics, his preoccupation with alchemy, or his desire to assume a quasi-regal grandeur." I would have thought that an easier and more uterine explanation might present itself...

The book I have been discussing is the third volume in Ackroyd's Brief Lives series. Himself a gay son of Clare College, Cambridge, who has already "done" Chaucer and Turner, as well as longer biographies of Dickens, T. S. Eliot, Blake, and the city of London (at 800-plus pages), he may well be the most prolific English author of his generation. And, which I find encouraging, he can write movingly and revealingly about Isaac Newton while being no more of a scientist or mathematician than I am. In our young day in Cambridge, the most famous public squabble was between the "scientist" C. P. Snow and the "literary" F. R. Leavis. It eventually turned into a multivolume international tussle about "the two cultures," or the inability of physicists to understand or appreciate literature versus the refusal of the English department to acquire the smallest "scientific" literacy. Ackroyd helps to show us that this is a false distinction with a long history. Keats, for example, thought that Newton had made our world into an arid and finite and unromantic place, and that work like his could "conquer all mysteries by rule and line... Unweave a rainbow." He couldn't have been more wrong. Newton was a friend of all mysticism and a lover of the occult who desired at all costs to keep the secrets of the temple and to prevent the universe from becoming a known quantity. For all that, he did generate a great deal more light than he had intended, and the day is not far off when we will be able to contemplate physics as another department—perhaps the most dynamic department—of the humanities. I would never have believed this when I first despairingly tried to lap the water of Cambridge, but that was before Carl Sagan and Lawrence Krauss and Steven Weinberg and Stephen Hawking fused language and science (and humor) and clambered up to stand, as Newton himself once phrased it, "on the shoulders of giants."

(*Vanity Fair* online, April 14, 2008)

The Men Who Made England: Hilary Mantel's *Wolf Hall*

EARLY LAST FALL, the Vatican extended a somewhat feline paw in the direction of that rather singular group of Christians sometimes denominated as "Anglo-Catholic." If this separated flock would rejoin the fold, the word came from Rome, it could be permitted to keep its peculiar English liturgy and even retain the married status of its existing priests. The reclaimed faithful need only forgo the ordination of women and of (I think I should here add the word "avowed") homosexuals. This clever overture, evidently long meditated by Pope Benedict XVI as part of his generous approach to other conservative schismatics and former excommunicants like the ultra-right Lefebvrists, was written up mostly as a curiosity; a dawn raid on the much-beset Anglican Communion. In reality, it was another salvo discharged in one of Europe's most enduring cultural and ideological wars: the one that began when the English Reformation first defied the divine rights of the papacy. On the origins of this once-world-shaking combat, with its still-vivid acerbity and cruelty, Hilary Mantel has written a historical novel of quite astonishing power.

Three portraits by Hans Holbein have for generations dictated the imagery of the epoch. The first shows King Henry VIII in all his swollen arrogance

---

Review of *Wolf Hall*, by Hilary Mantel.

and finery. The second gives us Sir Thomas More, the ascetic scholar who seems willing to lay his life on a matter of principle. The third captures King Henry's enforcer Sir Thomas Cromwell, a sallow and saturnine fellow calloused by the exercise of worldly power. The genius of Mantel's prose lies in her reworking of this aesthetic: Look again at His Majesty and see if you do not detect something spoiled, effeminate, and insecure. Now scrutinize the face of More and notice the frigid, snobbish fanaticism that holds his dignity in place. As for Cromwell, this may be the visage of a ruthless bureaucrat, but it is the look of a man who has learned the hard way that books must be balanced, accounts settled, and zeal held firmly in check. By the end of the contest, there will be the beginnings of a serious country called England, which can debate temporal and spiritual affairs in its own language and which will vanquish Spain and give birth to Shakespeare and Marlowe and Milton.

When the action of the book opens, though, it is still a marginal nation subservient to Rome, and the penalty for rendering the Scriptures into English, or even reading them in that form, is torture and death. In Cromwell's mind, as he contemplates his antagonist More, Mantel allows us to discern the germinal idea of what we now call the Protestant ethic:

> He never sees More—a star in another firmament, who acknowledges him with a grim nod—without wanting to ask him, what's wrong with you? Or what's wrong with me? Why does everything you know, and everything you've learned, confirm you in what you believed before? Whereas in my case, what I grew up with, and what I thought I believed, is chipped away a little and a little, a fragment then a piece and then a piece more. With every month that passes, the corners are knocked off the certainties of this world: and the next world too. Show me where it says, in the Bible, "Purgatory." Show me where it says "relics, monks, nuns." Show me where it says "Pope."

Thomas More, he reflects, will burn men, while the venal Cardinal Wolsey will burn only books, in "a holocaust of the English language, and so much rag-rich paper consumed, and so much black printer's ink." Cromwell has sufficient immunity to keep his own edition of William Tyndale's forbidden English Bible, published overseas and smuggled back home, with a title page that carries the mocking words printed in utopia. Thomas More will one day see to it that Tyndale, too, burns alive for that jibe. Curtain-raised here, also, is Cromwell's eventual readiness to smash the monasteries and confiscate their revenue and property to finance the building of a modern state, so that after Wolsey there will never again be such a worldly and puissant cardinal in the island realm.

These are the heavy matters that underlie the ostensible drama of which schoolchildren know, the king's ever-more-desperate search for a male heir and for a queen (or, as it turns out, queens) who will act as his broodmare in the business. With breathtaking subtlety—one quite ceases to notice the way in which she takes on the most intimate male habits of thought and speech—Mantel gives us a Henry who is sexually pathetic, and who needs a very down-to-earth counselor. A man like Cromwell, in fact, "at home in courtroom or waterfront, bishop's palace or inn yard. He can draft a contract, train a falcon, draw a map, stop a street fight, furnish a house and fix a jury." Cromwell it is who catches the monarch's eye as it strays toward the girls of the Seymour clan, and promptly invests in a loan to their family, whose country seat is named Wolf Hall. But this is not the only clue to the novel's title: Cromwell is also acutely aware of the old saying *Homo homini lupus*. Man is wolf to man.

And so indeed he is, though in Greek-drama style, Mantel keeps most of the actual violence and slaughter offstage. Only at second hand do we hear of the terrifying carnage in the continuing war for the Papal States, and the sanguinary opportunism with which King Henry, hoping to grease the way to his first divorce, proposes to finance a French army to aid the pope. Cromwell is a practical skeptic here too, because he has spent some hard time on the Continent and knows, he says, that "the English will never be forgiven for the talent for destruction they have always displayed when they get off their own island."

Still, from these extraordinary pages you can learn that it's very bad to be burned alive on a windy day, because the breeze will keep flicking the flames away from you and thus protract the process. You come to see also how small heresies are bound to lead to bigger ones: Cromwell's origins are so plebeian that he doesn't know his own birthday. "I don't have a natal chart. So I don't have a fate." Astrologers for the wealthy are of course eager to make up the difference with their elaborate charts, but the king's chief minister is not impressed by any "hocus pocus" (the irreverent popular jeer at the *hoc est corpus* of the Latin Mass). He hears people saying the unsayable—that the sacrament of that Mass is only a scrap of bread—and is unshocked. He tracks down and exposes wonder-working nuns and other charlatans, leftovers from *The Canterbury Tales*, and instead of hanging or flogging them compels them to confess their fraudulence in public. Most of all, he understands that print is a revolution in itself, and that Thomas More will be defeated not just by William Tyndale but by William Caxton. As he tells the appalled bishop of Winchester:

> Look at any part of this kingdom, my lord bishop, and you will find dereliction, destitution. There are men and women on the roads. The sheep farmers are grown so great that the little man is knocked off his acres and the plowboy is out of house and home. In a generation these people can learn to read. The plowman can take up a book. Believe me, Gardiner, England can be otherwise.

Part of the greatness of Orwell's *Nineteen Eighty-four*, it has always seemed to me, is its conscious analogy to the English Reformation. The Inner Party is the holder of a secret book, on which profane eyes may not gaze, and the public language of the dictatorship is a jargon designed to obliterate the very possibility of free thought. Regular rituals of execration denounce the infidel and the Evil One. Over the scene rules an Eternal Father, or rather Big Brother. The struggle of the dissenter is to find a tongue in which to speak: a vernacular that is, as the Thirty-Nine Articles of the Church of England so quaintly yet memorably put it, one "understanded of the people."

Mantel contrives an unusual solution to the problem of idiom. She does not, for the most part, try to have her characters talk in sixteenth-century English. She does show Thomas More insulated in his library of Greek and Latin and Hebrew texts (and insisting that the great epistle of Saint Paul about "faith, hope, and love" should in English be "faith, hope, and charity"). She gives splendid examples of demotic blasphemy and obscenity from bargemen and publicans, one of the latter bluntly advising Cromwell not to choose a soup course that looks like what's left over after "a whore's washed her shift." And she throws in—occasionally rather jarringly—some current English and even American slang usage. "Cost it out for him," says Cromwell to Wolsey, proposing that Anne Boleyn's father be shown the credits and debits. King Henry is described as "cutting a deal" over Church property. Expressions like "payoff," "pretty much," "stuff it," and "downturn" are employed. Like sprinkles of holy water, even if these do no harm, they do no good, either.

A sequel is plainly in view, as we are given glimpses of the rival daughters who plague the ever-more-gross monarch's hectic search for male issue. The ginger-haired baby Elizabeth is mainly a squalling infant in the period of the narrative, which chiefly covers the years 1527–35, but in the figure of her sibling Mary, one is given a chilling prefiguration of the coming time when the bonfires of English heretics will really start to blaze in earnest. Mantel is herself of Catholic background and education, and evidently not sorry to be shot of it (as she might herself phrase the matter), so it is generous of her to show the many pettinesses and cruelties with which the future "Bloody Mary" was visited by the callous statecraft and churchmanship of her father's court. Cromwell is shown trying only to mitigate, not relieve, her plight. And Mary's icy religiosity he can forgive, but not More's. Anyone who has been bamboozled by the saccharine propaganda of *A Man for All Seasons* should read Mantel's rendering of the confrontation between More and his interlocutors about the Act of Succession, deposing the pope as the supreme head of the Church in England. More discloses himself as a hybrid of Savonarola and Bartleby the Scrivener:

> "Let us be clear. You will not take the oath because your conscience advises you against it?"
> "Yes."
> "Could you be a little more comprehensive in your answers?"
> "No."
> "You object but you won't say why?"
> "Yes."
> "Is it the matter of the statute you object to, or the form of the oath, or the business of oath-taking in itself?"
> "I would rather not say."

By this time, any luckless prisoner of More's would have been stretched naked on the rack, but his questioners persist courteously enough until he suddenly lashes out as the arrogant theocrat he is:

> You say you have the majority. I say I have it. You say Parliament is behind you, and I say all the angels and saints are behind me, and all the company of the Christian dead, for as many generations as there have been since the church of Christ was founded, one body, undivided—

This casuistry is too much for Cromwell, who loses his composure for the first and only time:

> "Oh, for Christ's sake!" he says. "A lie is no less a lie because it is a thousand years old. Your undivided church has liked nothing better than persecuting its own members, burning them and hacking them apart when they stood by their own conscience, slashing their bellies open and feeding their guts to dogs. You call history to your aid, but what is history to you? It is a mirror that flatters Thomas More. But I have another mirror, I hold it up and it shows a vain and dangerous man, and when I turn it about it shows a killer, for you will drag down with you God knows how many, who will have only the suffering, and not your martyr's gratification."

The splendor of this outburst may conceal from the speaker, but not from us, the realization that he, too, will succeed More on the scaffold and that generations of sentimental and clerical history will canonize More while making Cromwell's name a hissing and a byword.

The means by which Mantel grounds and anchors her action so convincingly in the time she describes, while drawing so easily upon the past and hinting so indirectly at the future, put her in the very first rank of historical novelists. I cannot be quite sure why she leaves out the premonitory stirrings of the so-called Pilgrimage of Grace, the last stand of traditional conservative Catholic England against King Henry (so well caught by John Buchan in *The Blanket of the Dark*), unless she intends a successor volume. She certainly has the depth and versatility to bring off such a feat. *Wolf Hall* is a magnificent service to the language and literature whose early emancipation it depicts and also, in its demystifying of one of history's wickedest men, a service to the justice that Josephine Tey first demanded in *Daughter of Time.*

(*The Atlantic*, March 2010)

Edmund Burke: Reactionary Prophet

IT HAS ALWAYS BEEN WITH ME," William Hazlitt wrote, "a test of the sense and candour of any one belonging to the opposite party, whether he allowed Burke to be a great man." Not all radicals have been so generous. In a footnote to Volume One of *Das Kapital*, Karl Marx wrote with contempt of Burke:

> The sycophant—who in the pay of the English oligarchy played the romantic *laudator temporis acti* against the French Revolution just as, in the pay of the North American colonies at the beginning of the American troubles, he had played the liberal against the English oligarchy—was an out-and-out vulgar bourgeois.

The old bruiser of the British Museum would not have known that he was echoing a remark by Thomas Jefferson, in a letter written to Benjamin Vaughan in May of 1791:

> The Revolution of France does not astonish me so much as the revolution of Mr. Burke. I wish I could believe the latter proceeded from

---

Review of *Reflections on the Revolution in France*, by Edmund Burke, edited by Frank W. Turner.

> as pure motives as the former... How mortifying that this evidence of the rottenness of his mind must oblige us now to ascribe to wicked motives those actions of his life which wore the mark of virtue and patriotism.

This attribution of mercenariness to Burke (who had in fact accepted a small pension from the British government for services rendered, and who had also been the London lobbyist or representative of the colony of New York during his defense of the rights of the American colonists) is also to be found in the work of Thomas Paine and Dr. Joseph Priestley. It is a frequent vice of radical polemic to assert, and even to believe, that once you have found the lowest motive for an antagonist, you have identified the correct one. And such reductionism makes a sort of rough partnership with the simplistic view that Burke was the founder or father of modern conservatism in general, and of its English Tory form in particular.

In point of fact Edmund Burke was neither an Englishman nor a Tory. He was an Irishman, probably a Catholic Irishman at that (even if perhaps a secret sympathizer), and for the greater part of his life he upheld the more liberal principles of the Whig faction. He was an advanced opponent of the slave trade, whose "Sketch of a Negro Code" was written in the early 1780s, and who before that had opposed the seating of American slaveholders at Westminster. His epic parliamentary campaign for the impeachment of Warren Hastings and the arraignment of the East India Company was the finest example in its day of a battle *against* pelf and perks and privilege. His writings on revolution and counterrevolution, and on empire, are ripe for a "Straussian" or Machiavellian reading that seeks to discover the arcane or occluded message contained within an ostensibly straightforward text.

This is most particularly true of his *Reflections on the Revolution in France*, which has seldom if ever been better analyzed and, so to speak, "decoded" than in this excellent companion edition. One might begin by giving this imperishable book its full name. The original 1790 title page read "Reflections on the Revolution in France, and on the Proceedings in Certain Societies in London Relative to That Event: In a Letter Intended to Have Been Sent to a Gentleman in Paris." The gentleman in question was Charles-Jean-François Depont, a young man of Burke's acquaintance who had become a member of the French National Assembly and had written to him in the fall of 1789. Burke owed him a reply, which turned into a very long letter indeed after its author had been further inspired to put pen to paper. The further inspiration was supplied by two meetings in London, of the Constitutional Society and of the Revolution Society, at which were passed warm resolutions welcoming the fall of the Bastille. It was, more than anything else, the alarm he felt at these latter developments that impelled Burke to his response. Please note, then, that Burke chose to stress not the French Revolution but "The Revolution in France." He seems to have intended, here, to speak of the phenomenon of revolution as it applied to French affairs, and as it might be made to apply to English ones. Hence the emphatic mention of "certain societies in London."

The Revolution Society was not as insurgent or incendiary as its name might suggest. It was a rather respectable sodality, dedicated to celebrating the "Glorious Revolution" of 1688, a relatively bloodless coup that installed William and Mary of the House of Orange on the English throne, and established Protestantism as the state religion. One of the society's leaders was the Reverend Richard Price, a great friend to the American Revolution and a staunch Unitarian clergyman. His resolution, carried by the same meeting that had forwarded a "Congratulatory Address" to the National Assembly in Paris, read in part, "This Society, sensible of the important advantages arising to this Country by its deliverance from Popery and Arbitrary Power..."

It was made immediately plain to Burke that those who had enthused over revolution across the Channel were also interested in undermining and discrediting the same Church that he—an Irishman brought up under anti-Catholic penal laws—felt so obliged to defend. (This deep connection has been established by Conor Cruise O'Brien in a masterly series of studies that began with his own edition of the *Reflections* in 1968.) But the point is not a merely sectarian one. In 1780 London had been convulsed and shamed by the hysterical anti-Papist Gordon Riots, in which a crazed aristocratic demagogue had led a mob against supposedly subversive Catholics. (The best evocation of the fury and cruelty of that episode is to be found in Dickens's *Barnaby Rudge*.) This memory was very vivid in Burke's mind, and goes far to explain his visceral detestation of crowd violence. No less to the point, some emulators of Jacobinism—the United Irishmen, with many Protestants among their leaders—were at work in Ireland trying to bring off a rebellion that would compromise all parliamentary "moderates." And several of the pro-Jacobin activists and spokesmen in England, not excluding the rather humane Price himself, had had political connections with Lord George Gordon. As between the Jacobite and the Jacobin, Burke could not be neutral for an instant; he might give up the Jacobite cause out of loyalty to the British crown, but he was profoundly stirred when he saw old-fashioned anti-Catholicism renascent under potentially republican colors. So one does well to keep *Barnaby Rudge* in mind along with *A Tale of Two Cities*.

Three questions will occur to anybody reconsidering the *Reflections* today. Was it a grand and prophetic indictment of revolutionary excess? Was it the disdainful shudder of a man who despised or feared what at one stage he described as the "swinish multitude"? And did it contain what we would now term a "hidden agenda"? The answer to all three questions, it seems to me, is a firm yes. Let us take the two most celebrated excerpts of Burke's extraordinary prose. The first is the prescient one:

> It is known; that armies have hitherto yielded a very precarious and uncertain obedience to any senate, or popular authority; and they will least of all yield it to an assembly which is only to have a continuance of two years. The officers must totally lose the characteristic disposition of military men, if they see with perfect submission and due admiration, the dominion of pleaders; especially when they find that they have a new court to pay to an endless succession of those pleaders; whose military policy, and the genius of whose command, (if they should have any,) must be as uncertain as their duration is transient. In the weakness of one kind of authority, and in the fluctuation of all, the officers of an army will remain for some time mutinous and full of faction, until some popular general, who understands the art of conciliating the soldiery, and who possesses the true spirit of command, shall draw the eyes of all men upon himself. Armies will obey him on his personal account. There is no other way of securing military obedience in this state of things. But the moment in which

> that event shall happen, the person who really commands the army is your master, the master (that is little) of your king, the master of your Assembly, the master of your whole republic.

This is almost eerily exact. Even in the solitary detail in which it does not body forth the actual coming of Napoleon Bonaparte (who did not emerge until well after the execution of King Louis), it takes care to state that the subordination of existing monarchy would be the least of it. There is only one comparably Cassandra-like prediction that I can call to mind, and that is Rosa Luxemburg's warning to Lenin that revolution can move swiftly from the dictatorship of a class to the dictatorship of a party, to be followed by the dictatorship of a committee of that party and eventually by the rule of a single man who will soon enough dispense with that committee.

Contrast this with Burke's even more famous passage about the fragrance and charisma of Marie Antoinette:

> It is now sixteen or seventeen years since I saw the queen of France, then the dauphiness, at Versailles; and surely never lighted on this orb, which she hardly seemed to touch, a more delightful vision. I saw her just above the horizon, decorating and cheering the elevated sphere she just began to move in,—glittering like the morning-star, full of life, and splendour, and joy. Oh! what a revolution! and what a heart must I have to contemplate without emotion that elevation and that fall! Little did I dream when she added titles of veneration to those of enthusiastic, distant, respectful love, that she should ever be obliged to carry the sharp antidote against disgrace concealed in that bosom; little did I dream that I should have lived to see such disasters fallen upon her in a nation of gallant men, in a nation of men of honour, and of cavaliers. I thought ten thousand swords must have leaped from their scabbards to avenge even a look that threatened her with insult. But the age of chivalry is gone. That of sophisters, economists, and calculators, has succeeded; and the glory of Europe is extinguished for ever. Never, never more shall we behold that generous loyalty to rank and sex, that proud submission, that dignified obedience, that subordination of the heart, which kept alive, even in servitude itself, the spirit of an exalted freedom. The unbought grace of life, the cheap defense of nations, the nurse of manly sentiment and heroic enterprise, is gone! It is gone, that

> sensibility of principle, that chastity of honour, which felt a stain like a wound, which inspired courage whilst it mitigated ferocity, which ennobled whatever it touched, and under which vice itself lost half its evil, by losing all its grossness.

One has read this passage very many times (I shall never forget the first time I heard it read out loud, by a Tory headmaster), and its meaning and majesty appear to alter with one's mood and evolution. "The unbought grace of life" is a most arresting phrase, however opaque, just as "the cheap defence of nations" remains unintelligible. The gallantry, and the appeal to chivalry, can sometimes seem like "the last enchantments of the Middle Age," breathing with an incomparable melancholy and resignation. Alternatively, the entire stave can be held to rank with the most preposterous and empurpled sentimentality ever committed to print—not to be rivaled until the moist, vapid effusions that greeted the death of Diana Spencer, also in Paris, in a banal traffic accident.

The latter view, or something very like it, was the one expressed by Burke's friend and confidant Philip Francis, to whom he had sent the draft and the proofs. The friendship more or less ended when Francis replied,

> In my opinion all that you say of the Queen is pure foppery. If she be a perfect female character you ought to take your ground upon her virtues. If she be the reverse it is ridiculous in any but a Lover, to place her personal charms in opposition to her crimes. Either way I know the argument must proceed upon a supposition; for neither have you said anything to establish her moral merits, nor have her accusers formally tried and convicted her of guilt.

The gash that this inflicted on Burke was not a shallow one: He had admired Philip Francis ever since the latter took an active part in the defense of the rights of India and the consequent impeachment of Warren Hastings. Francis, moreover, was one of the most feared and skillful pamphleteers of the day, writing excoriating letters under the pseudonym "Junius"—whose identity Burke was one of few to guess. (I can't resist pointing out here that Rosa Luxemburg wrote her most famous pamphlet under the same *nom de guerre*. I do so not just to make a connection that hasn't been observed before but because "Junius" is taken from Lucius Junius Brutus, not the Shakespearean regicide but the hero and founder of the Roman republic.) Not content with taunting Burke about his emotional spasm over Marie Antoinette, Francis urged him in effect to give up the whole project; and when it was finally published in spite of this advice, he wrote Burke a letter in which he coupled "the Church" with "that religion in short, which was practiced or professed, and with great Zeal too, by tyrants and villains of every denomination." This English Voltaireanism had the effect of spurring Burke to an even more heated defense of the alliance of religion with order and property. To him, the alleged "deism" of the revolutionaries was a shabby mask for iconoclastic atheism. Nor did he care much for the then fashionable chatter about liberty and "rights." As he stated early in the *Reflections*,

> Am I to congratulate an highwayman and murderer, who has broke prison, upon the recovery of his natural rights? This would be to act over again the scene of the criminals condemned to the galleys, and their heroic deliverer, the metaphysic knight of the sorrowful countenance.

In other words, Burke was quite ready to anticipate, or to meet, any charge of quixotism. This did not prevent Thomas Paine from responding that "in the rhapsody of his imagination, he has discovered a world of windmills, and his sorrows are, that there are no Quixotes to attack them."

Paine's reply, to the *Reflections* in general and to the paean to Marie Antoinette in particular, is no less celebrated. In mourning the plumage, he wrote in *Rights of Man*, Burke forgot the dying bird. It is true, as O'Brien has pointed out, that this statement has since been employed by many pitiless revolutionaries to justify their less tasteful or unscrupulous actions, and that it can be made to rank with the omelet and the eggs as a remark that is dismissive and callous when applied to a "mere" individual. Indeed, in his essay in this edition O'Brien proposes Burke as the moral ancestor of all those who have warned until the present day of the awfulness of absolutist revolutions and of the terrifying results that ensue from any scheme for human perfectibility.

However, Paine—who also disliked the "mob," and who described Lord George Gordon as a "madman"—was to take a much more considerable risk, in theory and practice, to assure humane treatment for the plumage. As a deputy in the French National Convention for the district of Pas de Calais, he spoke out strongly against the execution of King Louis. He did so first because of the way in which royalist France had come to the aid of the American Revolution. (Some historians, including Simon Schama, now maintain that the expense of this commitment led to the emptying of the French treasury, and thus to the original crisis of bankruptcy that precipitated the events of 1789.) He did so second because he could see that measures of revenge were likely to coarsen the French revolutionary regime. And he did so third because of an inborn revulsion against capital punishment, which he had seen practiced with the utmost brutality by the British authorities. The taking of these positions (and let us not forget that the vote on the execution of King Louis almost resulted in a tie) involved him in a very tough parliamentary confrontation with none other than Jean Paul Marat, who denounced Paine as a Quaker and a foreigner and ignited the train of suspicion and paranoia that would land Paine in a foul-smelling Parisian cell under sentence of death. It was in such circumstances that Paine composed *The Age of Reason*. In that book, as is often forgotten, he tried to vindicate deism against atheism, and certainly succeeded in disproving Burke's crude contention that this was a distinction without a difference. For Paine, the Robespierrean annexation of religious property was not at all a separation between Church and State but, rather, a nationalizing by the State of the Church. That may be a more radical and useful objection than Burke's furious refusal to regard the least trespass on ecclesiastical power as anything but profane or obscene.

The chief weakness of this volume is its refusal to take Paine at all seriously, or to consider whether he, too, might not have been defending one revolution in his own way in order to safeguard another. O'Brien has established to most people's satisfaction that Burke pleaded the cause of the American colonists, and indignantly denounced the French Revolution, because he hoped in this way to make the case for reform in Ireland and knew how far he could go. Paine, who had wanted the American Revolution to go further than it did (in the abolition of slavery, for example), wished to keep the French Revolution from becoming too bloody and fanatical. Like Jefferson and Lafayette, he had a not-so-hidden motive: to expand and consolidate a system that might rescue the new American republic from isolation. Along with Lafayette, he suffered considerable persecution and contumely from French hard-liners as a result.

Professor John Keane has reminded us, in his 1995 biography of Paine, that there was a time when Burke and Paine were friends. Burke accompanied Paine on some trips into the English countryside, in search of a site for Paine's newly designed iron bridge. Both were suspicious of arbitrary power ("We hunt in pairs," Burke once joked), and Paine had no reason to doubt that Burke, in his *Thoughts on the Causes of the Present Discontents* (1770), had been sincere in his liberal belief that it was corrupt authority, not protest against it, that required justification. The astonishment Paine expresses in *Rights of Man* at Burke's refusal to criticize or even to enumerate the crimes and cruelties of the *ancien régime* is clearly genuine. So is his scorn at Burke's concept of the franchise as a reward for property and piety. (Until Paine tried to salvage it the term "democracy"—like the words "Tory" and, later, "suffragette" and "impressionist"—had been deployed only as an insult.) Paine was a Newtonian and a believer in economic growth and modern technique; Burke was a prisoner of the feudal and the landed conception of society, who employed the words "innovation" and "despotism" as virtual twins. Notice, for example, how the word "economist" in the Marie Antoinette passage is used as a synonym for knavery. Paine was for a written constitution and a carefully designed welfare state (adumbrated in the second half of *Rights of Man*), whereas Burke was for the semi-mystical "unwritten constitution" of a Crowned Parliament, and spared few thoughts even for the deserving poor.

However often one awards the winning of the longer-term argument to Paine, the fact remains that he and Jefferson and Lafayette never even dreamed of the advent of Bonapartism. They all believed, at the time that the argument was actually taking place, that France would become a constitutional monarchy, or had actually become one already. It was Burke who took this romantic delusion—a delusion shared by Charles James Fox and the leaders of Burke's own Whig party, and even for a time by William Pitt and the more pragmatic Tories—and mercilessly exploded it. He also showed that the outcome of the French Revolution would be war on a continental scale. The tremendous power of the *Reflections* lies in this, the first serious argument that revolutions devour their own children and turn into their own opposites.

Indeed, Marx might have paid a little more attention to Burke in drawing his conclusion that the French events of 1789 were the harbinger chiefly of a bourgeois revolution.

Burke's attachment to the old order at least allowed him to see this with exemplary clarity. He wrote,

> If this monster of a constitution can continue, France will be wholly governed by the agitators in corporations, by societies in the towns formed of directors of assignats and trustees for the sale of church lands, attornies, agents, money-jobbers, speculators, and adventurers, composing an ignoble oligarchy, founded on the destruction of the crown, the church, the nobility, and the people. Here end all the deceitful dreams and visions of the equality and rights of men.

In a similar piece of magnificent disdain for what English aristocrats used to call "trade," he made another penetrating observation about the kinship between tradition and the social contract:

> The state ought not to be considered as nothing better than a partnership agreement in a trade of pepper and coffee, calico or tobacco, or some other such low concern . . . it becomes a partnership not only between those who are living, but between those who are living, those who are dead, and those who are to be born. Each contract of each particular state is but a clause in the great primeval contract of eternal society, linking the lower with the higher natures, connecting the visible and invisible world, according to a fixed compact sanctioned by the inviolable oath which holds all physical and all moral natures, each in their appointed place.

Again, one has to peel away the layers of holy awe with which Burke protected the idea of an ordained social and moral hierarchy, and the complacency of the hereditary principle in general. But something essential in him, not all of it attributable to his political allegiances, rebelled at the notion of a society *begun anew*—a place where humanity should begin from scratch. This is of huge importance, because Paine and Jefferson very adamantly took the view that only the living had any rights. "Man has no property in man," Paine wrote, making what could have been a very fine argument against slavery but going on to say,

> Neither has any generation a property in the generations which are to follow. The parliament or the people of 1688, or of any other period, has no more right to dispose of the people of the present day, or to bind or to control them *in any shape whatever*, than the parliament or the people of the present day have to dispose of, bind or control those who are to live a hundred or a thousand years hence. Every generation is, and must be, competent to all the purposes which its occasions require. It is the living, and not the dead, that are to be accommodated.

Thus the French calendar that began the human story over again, or that at least tried to rewind its odometer. Thus Jefferson's notorious 1793 letter to William Short, stating that he had rather "seen half the earth desolated; were there but an Adam and Eve left in every country," than see the French Revolution defeated. A little stretch is required to derive the Khmer Rouge "Year Zero" from this; but those who are willing to be millennial about origins will sometimes be millennial about consequences. Yet such hectic and short-term radical enthusiasm is distinctly odd in one way, since both Paine and Jefferson derived many of their claims of liberty from supposedly ancestral Saxon institutions that predated the Norman Conquest, and since Paine can hardly have been unaware that in challenging the 1688 revolution, he was pushing at an open door as far as Burke was concerned. Equally extraordinary is the implied lack of any duty toward future generations, which revolutionaries at all times have claimed to stand for. If modern conservatism can be held to derive from Burke, it is not just because he appealed to property owners in behalf of stability but also because he appealed to an everyday interest in the preservation of the ancestral and the immemorial. And the abolition of memory, as we have come to know in our own time, is an aspect of the totalitarian that spares neither right nor left. In the cult of "now," just as in the making of Reason into an idol, the writhings of nihilism are to be detected.

It is vastly to the credit of Conor Cruise O'Brien that he still feels it necessary to defend Burke from the charge of being a "reactionary." It may not be feasible to make this extenuation a consistent one. Burke was strongly in favor of repressive measures at home, including the silencing of all dissent. In calling for an all-out war, he outdid William Pitt himself. He died before the worst of the Bonapartist project for Europe was revealed, and it cannot easily be said that his gravest fears in this respect did not materialize. But in his discussion of the French *philosophes* he declined even to cite any of their secular and rationalist critique, because, as he put it in a footnote to *Reflections*, "I do not choose to shock the feeling of the moral reader with any quotation of their vulgar, base, and profane language." That's Tory pomposity defined. Furthermore, and as Darrin McMahon points out in his chapter of this edition, Burke in the year of his death (1797) wrote to the exiled Abbé Barruel to thank him in the most profuse terms for a copy of his *Mémoires pour servir à l'histoire du jacobinisme.* This was a work, infamous in its time, of the most depraved and retrograde Jesuitism, which purported to find a grand conspiracy of Freemasons and other subversives in the overthrow of the Bourbons. Burke's letter was no mere courtesy; it lauded the *abbé* for his justice, regularity, and exactitude. This is the only charge against Burke that I cannot find mentioned or dealt with in Conor Cruise O'Brien's tremendous biography *The Great Melody;* but as O'Brien has observed in another context, those intellectuals who will not give up "civility" and "objectivity" for the cause of revolution have sometimes been observed to sacrifice these qualities for the sake of the counterrevolution. Clearly, Burke saw himself as willing to try all means and all alliances in order to "contain" revolutionary France, lest it pose a challenge similar to that presented by the Protestant Reformation, and then as far as possible to destroy it.

By 1815 that project might have been accounted a success. But the idea of the French Revolution managed to survive the Duke of Wellington and Prince Metternich as well as the literary power of Edmund Burke. The trinity of "*liberté, egalité, fraternité*" outlived those who had butchered in its name, and was deposed from the French currency only during the time of Vichy (which replaced it with the less sonorous "*travail, famille, patrie*"). Lafayette lived long enough to take part in the anti-Bourbon Revolution of 1830. Paine died ruined and disappointed, yet his opinions resurfaced in the movement for the franchise that eventually defeated the Duke of Wellington's government. And Thomas Jefferson was able to double the land area of the United States of America. The terms of the Louisiana Purchase would not have been available had it not been for a slave revolt in Haiti, inspired by the ideals and proclamations of 1789, that annihilated Napoleon's fleet and army and put an end to French ambitions in the hemisphere. What might Burke have made of this momentous insurrection, later so brilliantly described by C. L. R. James? One recurs to Hazlitt's generous judgment when one wishes to have read Burke on what happened when Jacobinism crossed the Atlantic and became black.

(*The Atlantic*, April 2004)

Samuel Johnson: Demons and Dictionaries

HOW OFTEN OUR USAGE manages to accomplish, for a name or an expression, the precise negation of its originally intended meaning. To satirize the sycophants among his courtiers, King Canute sarcastically commanded the waves to keep their distance and allowed his own majesty to be wetted by the tides: Now we give the name Canute to anyone in authority who foolishly attempts to ward off the inevitable. For the young scion of the Veronese house of Montague, only one girl in the whole world could possibly possess meaning, or be worth possessing: Accordingly, we use the word *Romeo* to designate a tireless philanderer. In eighteenth-century England, John Wilkes was the leader of a radical political faction known as the Patriots. In Dr. Samuel Johnson's Tory view, affiliation with that subversive party was "the last refuge of a scoundrel": This now is construed as an attack on all those—most often Tories themselves—who take shelter in a too-effusive love of country.

The life and sayings of Johnson were so replete with ironies that perhaps it is no surprise to find literalness exacting its effect over the course of time. Peter Martin's outstanding new biography gives the best account I have yet read of another of its subject's celebrated observations—"Depend upon it,

---

Review of *Samuel Johnson: A Biography*, by Peter Martin.

Sir, when a man knows he is to be hanged in a fortnight, it concentrates his mind wonderfully." In 1777, a popular and fashionable clergyman named William Dodd was sentenced to death for forgery. Having read Johnson's *Rambler* essays on the vagaries of the criminal-justice system, he bethought himself of the good doctor as a man who might be persuaded to intercede for him. Johnson took up the case for clemency and wrote not only a petition to the monarch, as if penned by Dodd, but also a sermon, "The Convict's Address to His Unhappy Brethren," which the hapless reverend delivered to his fellow inmates of Newgate Prison. So affecting was this address that it helped complete the swing of public opinion in favor of a pardon for Dodd. But authority was unflinching, and the wretched cleric was duly and publicly executed. There were those who doubted that he had possessed "the force of mind" required to have written such a fine sermon himself, and those who even suspected that Johnson might have been the "ghost" writer in the case. It was to quell such speculation that Johnson made the remark, which we can therefore understand not as a cynical and clever one but as a very elegant and modest disclaimer. Having been disappointed by the failure of Walter Jackson Bate to tell this important tale aright in his immense 1978 biographical study, I was full of admiration for Peter Martin for managing to summarize it so deftly.

Not that Johnson was by any means incapable of cynicism. He made quite a little income by writing anonymous sermons for a two-guinea fee, and he assured a friend's newly ordained son:

> The composition of sermons is not very difficult. Invent first and then embellish... Set down diligently your thoughts as they rise in the first words that occur... I have begun a sermon after dinner and sent it off by the post that night.

He was quite as able to be terse and memorable when in conversation and, like Oscar Wilde (who was, like him, disconcertingly vast when seen at close quarters), seems seldom to have been off duty when it came to the epigrammatic and aphoristic. The urge felt by so many of Johnson's contemporaries—not James Boswell alone—to keep a record of his doings and utterances has placed him among the first figures in history whom we feel we "know" as a person. Indeed, so well are even his tics and mannerisms and symptoms conveyed that Martin can confidently say that Johnson more probably suffered from emphysema than asthma, and Oliver Sacks was able some years ago to make a fairly definite retrospective diagnosis of Tourette's syndrome.

And yet for all this, we know barely enough to know what we don't know. In the last days of his life, in the mean little court off Fleet Street where he made his dwelling, Johnson staged a mockery of the disclosure industry that is associated with that address, and heaped up a huge pyre of his papers, diaries, manuscripts, and letters. With his loyal black servant, Frank Barber, serving as counter-amanuensis, he spent a week at the task of self-immolation. Had it not been for Boswell's retention of some of their mutual correspondence, and Johnson's own (and presumably significant) inability to burn the letters of Mrs. Hester Thrale, we might have lost the whole trove.

But if it comes to that, we might very nearly never have heard of Samuel Johnson of Lichfield in the first place. Having almost expired in childbirth (and having thus been hastily baptized to save his immortal soul), the little boy fell victim to scrofula and was stricken partially blind and deaf. In those days the remedy for scrofula—also known as "the King's Evil"—was to be magically "touched" by the hereditary monarch. Young Samuel was taken to be touched by Queen Anne, and if the charm did not "take" in his case, well, then, it could be because there had been a disturbance in the legitimacy of the line after the Jacobite convulsions. Johnson thus operates in that extended period of English (and American) history when the divine right of kings is not yet quite exhausted or discredited but when the concept of "the rights of man" has yet to be fully born. Considering how nearly he was extinguished before he could play any part in this great argument, it is perhaps surprising how little he esteemed Thomas Gray, author of the greatest elegy for the unsung.

Martin pursues the argument, about the relationship of health to personality, beyond the physical and well into the psychological. In his view, Johnson felt permanently hag-ridden by guilt, by fear of divine punishment, by self-loathing at his own laziness and greed and inadequacy, and also (this being my own interpretation of the case as presented) by his very failure to feel that guilt and fear strongly enough. His conscious mind, in other words, was at war with his superstitious instincts. His main mental weapon in this combat was his own industry. Sometimes even this industry took its contradictory forms—the only time Johnson ever got up early to read a book, it was Burton's *Anatomy of Melancholy*—but we owe his triumphs of spoof-parliamentary reportage, his *Rasselas*, and above all his immortal dictionary to the struggle against anomie, and against the hell of despair to which anomie can be the antechamber.

This in turn means that we are very much indebted to Mrs. Thrale, who in 1766 rescued him from that pit, nursed him back from a near-complete breakdown, and for the next sixteen years gave him a refuge in south London from the quotidian melancholies of his working life. The other members of his ever-famous "Club"—Sir Joshua Reynolds, Edmund Burke, Oliver Goldsmith, Edward Gibbon, and David Garrick—also had an alternative place of resort from their customary Soho haunt. Johnson's dependence on Mrs. Thrale was in some ways so utter and complete that it has given rise to speculations about literal masochism and its sadistic counterpart. In an essay published sixty years ago, Katharine Balderston claimed to have identified a recurrent motif of manacling and beating, begged for by Johnson and duly administered by his mother substitute. Walter Jackson Bate later argued—successfully, I think—that the same letters between them could have contained their private code for the understanding and treatment of incipient madness. More recently, Jeffrey Meyers has revived the Balderston speculation (because, after all, Johnson *did* give Mrs. Thrale a padlock, which she preserved), while Peter Martin follows Bate in identifying Johnson's obsessions about enchainment with the fear of that epoch's cruel treatment of the insane. For myself, I think that the evidence most often adduced in favor of the hypothesis is the most persuasive testimony for the other side of the case. In her *Thraliana*, Mrs. Thrale recounts:

> Says Johnson a Woman has *such* power between the Ages of twenty five and forty five, that She may tye a Man to a post and whip him if She will.

It's not at all hard to imagine Johnson saying this, but when Mrs. Thrale adds her own footnote to tell us, "This he knew of him self was *literally* and *strictly* true I am sure," why, then, sir and ma'am, I think we may take it as obvious that whoever was plying the lash, if indeed a lash was ever "literally" applied, it was certainly not the respectable lady who wrote those disarmingly ingenuous words.

It was, though, some harsh breed of the "black dog" that helped condition the two constants in Johnson's life and writing: his Toryism and his religion. Martin makes some pleas in mitigation as regards the Toryism, reminding us of Johnson's sympathy for the poor and the failed and the deformed, but he cannot keep the jury out for very long. Johnson's pitiless and violent hatred of the American Revolution, and his contemptuous cruelty toward those who apostatized from the established church (even if it was to join another Christian sect) was strong and consistent. The word *established* may well be the key one here, religion for Johnson being more a matter of security and stability (public as well as private) than a matter of faith, and the episcopal system a further insurance against the fearful "sedition," which he regarded as the twin of John Wilkes's "impiety."

Just as it was a primitive fear of hell that caused his parents to baptize him at birth lest his infant soul be consigned to the fire, so it was increasingly a holy terror that came to dominate his last years. As Macaulay was later to write, about the great man's ghastly tendency to superstition: "He began to be credulous precisely at the point where the most credulous people begin to be skeptical." Again, I see no reason to attribute this fixation upon eternal torture to any masochistic tendency. Johnson felt, as many fine writers have done, that he had wasted most of his time and squandered the greater part of his gift. (Exorbitant praise from others, such as Boswell in this instance, may often have the effect only of reinforcing such a morbid conviction of failure.) Yet it is owing to Boswell's generosity and curiosity that we have, and from the very same witness, an account of the deathbeds of both David Hume and Samuel Johnson. Hume—who lay dying in the days of 1776 that launched the American Revolution so much hated by Johnson—famously told Boswell that he was no more afraid of his own extinction after death than he was of the nonexistence that had preceded his birth. Johnson, when informed of this calm attitude, declined to credit it—I am going here by Hesketh Pearson's account—and would not listen even when Boswell reminded him that many Greek and Roman heroes had faced death stoically without the benefits of Christianity. At a subsequent meeting with Adam Smith, who vouched for the truth of Boswell's story, Johnson loudly called Smith a liar, to which Smith coldly responded that Johnson was "a son of a bitch." This collision with the author of *The Theory of Moral Sentiments* seems to prepare one for Macaulay's later observation that Johnson "could discern clearly enough the folly and meanness of all bigotry but his own."

It occurs to me that both Hume and Smith were Scots (or "Scotchmen," as Johnson preferred to say) and that dislike for the North British was perhaps the one thing that Johnson had in common with his unscrupulous enemy Wilkes. Should you choose to look up any of Johnson's celebrated jokes at the expense of Scotland, whether in his dictionary or his reported speech, you will, I believe, notice that they fall short of the Wildean in being too long-winded and contrived, and too reliant for their leaden effect on mere prejudice. Teasing is very often a sign of inner misery: Johnson's grandeur is diminished the more we come to know of the well-earned honor and eminence of some of those with whom he did battle, as well as the sheer paltriness of some of the imaginary demons with which he merely fancied himself doing so.

(*The Atlantic*, March 2009)

Gustave Flaubert: I'm with *Stupide*

THE DEVOTEE of Gustave Flaubert may feel some of the same inhibition, in deciding whether to embark upon *Bouvard and Pecuchet*, as the admirer of Dickens or Schubert in contemplating *Edwin Drood* or that famously incomplete symphony. If their originators couldn't manage to finish them, then why should we? And in the case of Flaubert's last novel—initially reconstructed by his niece from some 4,000 manuscript pages after his sudden death in 1880—the word "finish" carries not just the meaning of completion but that crucial element of polish and rounding-off, so essential in the case of the man who fretted endlessly over *le mot juste*.

Economy and perfectionism in point of words would have been the last concern of the two losers featured here, whose working lives were spent as copy clerks and to whom words were mere objects or things. Drawn to each other by a common mediocrity (Flaubert's original title was *The Tale of Two Nobodies*), Bouvard and Pecuchet are liberated by an unexpected legacy to embark on a career of unfettered fatuity. Many fictions and scenarios have depended upon a male double-act, usually enriched by contrast as in the case of Holmes and Watson or Bertie and Jeeves, or of course the Knight of the

---

Review of *Bouvard and Pecuchet*, by Gustave Flaubert, translated from the French by Mark Polizzotti.

Sorrowful Countenance and his rotund and pragmatic squire. More recently, each half of the sketch has been equally hapless and pitiful, as with Laurel and Hardy, Abbott and Costello, Vladimir and Estragon, or "Withnail and I." If you stir in the rural setting, plus a shallow addiction to the mysteries of technique and innovation, you find that Flaubert's pairing has also anticipated *Dumb and Dumber*. It's often necessary to mark off two fools or jerks by discrepant heights: Bouvard is tall but pot-bellied while Pecuchet is short. A mnemonic here might be Schwarzenegger and DeVito in *Twins*.

An early disappointment for the reader of this deft and elegant new translation by Mark Polizzotti, therefore, is the way in which Flaubert's first draft so often reduces this field of alternation by telling us merely what "they" got up to. It is as if we had two Quixotes or two Sanchos. Two Quixotes would be nearer the mark, since this undynamic duo is at least fixated upon grand schemes of discovery and improvement. Together, they set out to illustrate and underline the Popean maxim that a little learning is a dangerous thing.

Flaubert is pitiless with his wretched creations, allowing them no moment of joy, or even ease. It is enough for them to turn their hands to a project for it to expire in chaos and slapstick, and after a while this, too, shows the shortcomings of the unpolished, because we can hear the sound of collapsing scenery before the stage has even been set. True bathos requires a slight interval between the sublime and the ridiculous, but no sooner have our clowns embarked on a project than we see the bucket of whitewash or the banana skin. The story is set in motion by their rash decision to quit Paris for the Norman countryside: It was a rule of fiction before Flaubert that city clerks attempting agricultural improvements would end up with smellier sewage, thinner crops, sicker animals, and more combustible hayricks than even the dullest peasant. A hinge event in Flaubert's writing is the revolution of 1848. If he ever read Marx and Engels's manifesto of that year, with its remark about "the idiocy of rural life," he evidently decided to go it one better. In his bucolic scheme, every official is a dolt, every priest a fool or knave, every milkmaid diseased and unchaste, every villager either a boozer or a chiseler. (I am influenced here, perhaps, by Polizzotti's use of American idioms like "Are you putting me on?")

If only Bouvard and Pecuchet would restrict themselves to excavating bogus fossils or to collecting unsorted specimens of archaeology, Flaubert's unforgiving attitude might appear unkind. But they insist upon inflicting themselves, as advisers and even as physicians, upon others. Impatient with the counsel of Dr. Vaucorbeil, "they began visiting patients on their own, entering people's homes on the pretext of philanthropy." Their quackery does less harm than one might expect, but then they weary of it in favor of marveling at what we might call intelligent design: "Harmonies vegetal and terrestrial, as well as aerial, aquatic, human, fraternal and even conjugal: all of these were included.... They were astounded that fish had fins, birds wings, seeds a skin—and they subscribed to the philosophy that ascribes virtuous intentions to Nature and considers it a kind of St. Vincent de Paul perpetually occupied with spreading its munificence."

Alternately eclectic and omnivorous, our heroes are like cushions that bear the impression of whoever last sat upon them. Before they are through, they have tried mesmerism and magnetism, phrenology and the spiritualist séance, as well as some experiments in cross-breeding that might have made Lysenko blush. No fad or pseudoscience is beyond their hectic enthusiasm, and Flaubert's own ruthless skepticism about the idea of "progress" is evinced, I think, in the occasional cruelty that results from seeing human and other creatures as potential subjects for experiment. The examples are given more or less deadpan: Dr. Vaucorbeil's office has "a picture of a man flayed alive"; kittens are found to die after five minutes under water; and a cat is boiled in a cauldron by one of the children the hopeless couple adopt before they become bored with the idea. Callousness itself is a child of stupidity. In *Sentimental Education* the revolution of 1848 is a Parisian fiasco with some grandeur, but in these pages it appears as a provincial circus that is all farce and no tragedy.

This novel was plainly intended to show its author's deep contempt, however comedically expressed, for all grand schemes, most especially the Rousseauean ones, to improve the human lot. Such schemes founder because the human material is simply too base to be transmuted. Even Bouvard and Pecuchet receive a glimpse of this, if only through their own solipsism: "Then their minds developed a piteous faculty, that of perceiving stupidity and being unable to tolerate it. Insignificant things saddened them: newspaper advertisements, a burgher's profile, an inane comment overheard by chance.... They felt upon their shoulders the weight of the entire world."

This anomie is the preface to a suicide pact (and they can't even get that right) and is then succeeded by a Christmas Eve reconciliation with Holy Mother Church that makes *It's a Wonderful Life* seem like an education in unsentimentality.

Jorge Luis Borges was of the opinion that Flaubert, the craftsman of the first truly realist novel with *Madame Bovary*, was also, with *Bouvard and Pecuchet*, the saboteur of his own project. And it is not difficult to trace the influence of these two men without qualities on the work of Joyce and Musil and Beckett, and on the twentieth century's evolution of the anti-hero. What is amazing is the industry with which Flaubert assimilated so many books on arcane subjects (some 1,500, according to Polizzotti), all of this knowledge acquired just so that a brace of nobodies could manage to get things not just wrong, but exactly wrong.

In one or two places in the story, most notably with his discussion of suicide and of syphilis, Flaubert makes indirect allusion to his celebrated *Dictionary of Received Ideas* (or "Accepted Ideas"). He had begun it as early as 1850, but he plainly intended to update it as a coda to *Bouvard and Pecuchet*, along with a *Catalogue of Fashionable Ideas*, which Polizzotti also includes. Flaubert's taxonomy is in fact one of expressions rather than opinions: It forms a collection of ready-made clichés for the use of the conformist or the unimaginative. Some of these make one blush ("Laurels: Keep one from resting") because one has used them oneself. Others are too self-evident ("Flagrante Delicto: Use in Latin. Is applied only to cases of adultery"). Some are outmoded ("Syphilis: Pretty much everyone has it"), or apply chiefly to Flaubert himself, who contracted syphilis enough times to cancel out many other people. Still, it is a trope to rival that of Proust's Madame Verdurin, who loved nothing better than "to frolic in her billow of stock expressions." At the close, as we know from the notes that Flaubert left behind, the two clerks would have been back at a common desk, once again copying out whatever was put in front of them. The *Dictionary* would have been part of the leaden chain that bound them to that desk.

(*The New York Times Book Review*, January 22, 2006)

The Dark Side of Dickens

IF OFFERED the onetime chance to travel back into the world of the nineteenth-century English novel, I once heard myself saying, I would brush past Messrs. Dickens and Thackeray for the opportunity to hold speech with George Eliot. I would of course be wanting to press Mary Ann Evans on her theological capacities and her labor in translating the liberal German philosophers, as well as on her near-Shakespearean gift for divining the well-springs of human motivation. When compared to *that* vista of the soul and the intellect, why trouble even with the creator of Rebecca Sharp, let alone with the man who left us the mawkish figures of Smike and Oliver and Little Nell, to say nothing of the grisly inheritance that is the modern version of Christmas? Putting it even more high-mindedly, ought one not to prefer an author like Eliot, who really did give her whole enormous mind to religious and social and colonial questions, over a vain actor-manager type who used pathetic victims as tear-jerking raw material, and who actually detested the real subjects of High Victorian power and hypocrisy when they were luckless enough to dwell overseas?

I can still think in this way if I choose, but I know I am protesting too much. The first real test is that of spending a long and arduous evening in the alehouses and outer purlieus of London, and here it has to be in the company of Dickens and nobody else. The second real test is that of passing the same

---

Review of *Charles Dickens*, by Michael Slater.

evening in company with the possessor of an anarchic sense of humor: This yields the same result. What did oyster shuckers *do*, Dickens demanded to know, when the succulent bivalves were out of season?

> Do they commit suicide in despair, or wrench open tight drawers and cupboards and hermetically-sealed bottles—for practice? Perhaps they are dentists out of the oyster season? Who knows?

This pearl was contained in a private letter not intended for publication (Dickens was almost always "on") and is somewhat more searching than the dull question—"Where do the ducks in Central Park go in winter?"—that was asked by the boy who spoke so scornfully of "all that David Copperfield kind of crap."

It would be understating matters to say that Thackeray rather looked down on Dickens, but, even as *Vanity Fair* was first being serialized in 1847, he picked up the fifth installment of *Dombey and Son* and then brought it down with a smack on the table, exclaiming the while, "There's no writing against such power as this—one has no chance! Read that chapter describing young Paul's death: It is unsurpassed—it is stupendous!"

Almost a decade later, Dickens was dispatching an admiring note to George Eliot on the publication of her very first fiction, *Scenes of Clerical Life*. He felt he had penetrated the guileless disguise of her nom de plume: "If [the sketches] originated with no woman, I believe that no man ever before had the art of making himself, mentally, so like a woman, since the world began."

So I find the plan of my original enterprise falling away from me; I must give it up; there is something *formidable* about Dickens that may not be gainsaid.

He may not have had Shakespeare's or Eliot's near omniscience about human character, but he did say, in an address on the anniversary of the Bard's birthday: "We meet on this day to celebrate the birthday of a vast army of living men and women who will live for ever with an actuality greater than that of the men and women whose external forms we see around us." As Peter Ackroyd commented in his *Dickens* (1990), he must have been "thinking here of Hamlet and Lear, of Macbeth and Prospero, but is it not also true" that in Portsmouth in February 1812 were born "Pecksniff and Scrooge, Oliver

Twist and Sairey Gamp, Samuel Pickwick and Nicholas Nickleby...the Artful Dodger and Wackford Squeers...?" I cite this occasion for a reason. In Michael Slater's volume, we learn only that on April 22, 1854, Dickens chaired "a Garrick Club dinner to celebrate Shakespeare's birthday." This is of course worth knowing in its own right, but is perhaps a little bloodless by comparison. Slater is invariably flattering toward Ackroyd's work, but could perhaps have taken a leaf or two from its emotional eloquence.

Who does not know of the formative moments in the life of Dickens the boy? The feeble male parent, the death of a sibling, the awful indenture to "the blacking factory," the pseudo-respectable school where the master slashed the boys with a cane as if to satisfy what was later identified in Mr. Creakle as "a craving appetite." The sending of the father to the Marshalsea debtors' prison, the refuge taken by a quakingly sensitive child in the consoling pages of fiction...all this we have long understood. So great was the dependence of Dickens on his own life experience that he almost resented the fact and was very guarded, even with his loyal biographer, John Forster, on the question, as if unwilling to admit such a (very non-Shakespearean) limitation. This is why it is so good to have the "autobiographical fragment" that Forster preserved and later published, which formed a sort of posthumous codicil to *David Copperfield* and still helps explain why that novel above all others was its author's favorite. Forster diagnosed in his subject a syndrome of "the attraction of repulsion," which, while simple enough in its way, goes far to explain why Dickens was at his best when evoking childhood misery, incarceration, premature mortality, hard labor, cheating and exploitation by lawyers and doctors, and the other phenomena that were the shades of his own early prison house. With these, as we now slackly say, he could "identify."

If valid, this analysis would also go some distance to explain the very severe constraints on Dickens's legendary compassion. This is the man who had a poor woman arrested for using filthy language in the street; who essentially recast his friend Thomas Carlyle's pessimistic version of the French Revolution in fictional form in *A Tale of Two Cities* (Slater is especially good on this); who dreaded the mob more than he disliked the Gradgrinds. It would also account for his weakest and most contrived novel, *Martin Chuzzlewit*, and its companion nonfiction compilation, *American Notes*.

Genuine radicals and reformers in mid-nineteenth-century England were to be defined above all as sympathizers with the American Revolution and with the cause of the Union in the Civil War. Dickens was scornful of the first and hostile to the second. His exiguous chapter on slavery in *American Notes* was lazily annexed word-for-word from a famous abolitionist pamphlet of the day, and employed chiefly to discredit the whole American idea. But when it came to a fight on the question, he was on balance sympathetic to the Confederate states, which he had never visited, and made remarks about Negroes that might have shocked even the pathologically racist Carlyle. I had not understood, before Slater's explanation, that the full title, *American Notes for General Circulation*, was a laborious pun on the supposed bankruptcy of the whole "currency" of the United States. Karl Marx, that great supporter of Lincoln and the Union, was therefore probably lapsing into a rare sentimentality when he wrote to Friedrich Engels that Dickens had "issued to the world more political and social truths than have been uttered by all the professional politicians, publicists and moralists put together." (Ackroyd mentions this letter, while Slater does not.)

Ackroyd, I find, is also more clear-eyed when it comes to Dickens and the Victorian empire. It's easy to tell, from the protractedly unfunny sarcasm about Mrs. Jellyby and the mock-African hellhole of Borrioboola-Gha in *Bleak House*, that the author did not possess the gift of imaginative sympathy when it came to those outside his immediate ken, or should I say kin.

But what is to excuse Dickens's writing to Angela Burdett-Coutts, about the 1857 Indian rebellion, that if he had the power, he would use all "merciful swiftness of execution... to exterminate [these people from] the face of the Earth"? Slater allows this an attenuated sentence, while Ackroyd quotes a fuller and even fouler version of the same letter, adding, "It is not often that a great novelist recommends genocide." Nor will it do to say that such attitudes were common in that period: When Governor Eyre put down a revolt in Jamaica with appalling cruelty in 1865, it was Dickens and Carlyle who warmly applauded his sadism, while John Stuart Mill and Thomas Huxley demanded that Eyre be brought before Parliament. Once again, Ackroyd emphasizes this while Slater speeds rapidly past it.

Finally, is there not something a trifle sinister in Dickens's letter to Lord Normanby (such a name of lofty entitlement, he himself would have been hard put to invent), written while he was struggling to finish *The Old Curiosity Shop*, offering to go to Australia on behalf of the British government and there to write a properly cautionary account of the hellish conditions in Her Majesty's penal colonies? He had worried that the deterrent effect of this horrible system had been diluted, with too many stories in circulation of ex-convicts making fortunes. Old Magwitch, evidently, should not have been let off so easily... (One of Dickens's ostensible purposes in visiting America was to study its prisons, yet Slater tells us there is no evidence that he ever troubled to read Tocqueville, who had formed and carried out the same intention in rather superior form. But what we want to understand is whether Dickens engaged in any vicarious gloating, on this and other "attraction-repulsion" forays into the lower depths.)

What is necessary, therefore, is a portrait that supplies for us what Dickens so generously served up to his hungry readers: some real villainy and cruelty to set against the angelic and the innocent. Yet somehow the same tale continues to write itself. We "know" the bewitching figure so well that speculations are possible about his suffering from obsessive-compulsive disorder and versions of the bipolar. Claire Tomalin has etched in for us the long-absent figure in the frame, Ellen Ternan, who was plainly the consolation of Dickens's distraught sexual life. We are aware that the great prose-poet of childhood was acutely conscious of having failed his own offspring. Yet we remain in much the same position as those naive Victorian readers who were so upset when John Forster told them that the respectable old entertainer was a man who had drawn his dramatis personae from wretched life itself. Always saying that he sought rest, and always exhausting himself, he may have been half in love with easeful death. The next biography should take this stark chiaroscuro as its starting point.

(*The Atlantic*, May 2010)

Marx's Journalism: The Grub Street Years

COMMENTING ACIDLY on a writer whom I perhaps too naively admired, my old classics teacher put on his best sneer to ask: "Wouldn't you say, Hitchens, that his writing was somewhat journalistic?" This lofty schoolmaster employed my name sarcastically, and stressed the last term as if he meant it to sting, and it rankled even more than he had intended. Later on in life, I found that I still used to mutter and improve my long-meditated reply. Emile Zola—a journalist. Charles Dickens—a journalist. Thomas Paine—another journalist. Mark Twain. Rudyard Kipling. George Orwell—a journalist par excellence. Somewhere in my cortex was the idea to which Orwell himself once gave explicit shape: the idea that "mere" writing of this sort could aspire to become an art, and that the word "journalist"—like the ironic modern English usage of the word "hack"—could lose its association with the trivial and the evanescent.

P. G. Wodehouse's 1915 novel, *Psmith, Journalist*, was a great prop and stay to me in this connection. The near-unchallenged master of English prose sets this adventure in New York, where Psmith pays a social visit that acquires significance when he falls in with the acting editor of the floundering journal

---

Review of *Dispatches for the New York Tribune: Selected Journalism of Karl Marx*, edited by James Ledbetter, with a foreword by Francis Wheen.

Cosy Moments. The true editor being absent on leave, Psmith beguiles the weary hours by turning the little weekly into a crusading organ that comes into conflict with a thuggish slumlord. Threats and violence from the exploiters (which at one point lead to bullets flying and require Psmith to acquire a new hat) are met with a cool insouciance. A fighting slogan is evolved. "*Cosy Moments*," announces its new proprietor, "cannot be muzzled." He addresses all his friends and staff by the staunch title of "Comrade." At the close, the corrupt city politicians and their gangland friends are put to flight, and Psmith hands back the paper to its staff. Some years ago, when I wrote a book for Verso (the publishing arm of the *New Left Review*), we were sued by some especially scabrous tycoons and our comradely informal slogan became, to the slight bewilderment of our lawyers, "*Cosy Moments* cannot be muzzled."

Wodehouse often shows a fair working knowledge of Marxist theory (the locus classicus here being the imperishable Mulliner short story "Archibald and the Masses"), and it isn't as far as you might think from *Psmith, Journalist* to Karl Marx, journalist extraordinaire. Let us begin the tale where Francis Wheen began it in his admirable Marx biography. The great Spanish republican militant Jorge Semprun is being taken by cattle truck through Germany in the early days of the Nazi conquest of Europe. His fictionalized memoir *The Long Voyage* has the death train to Buchenwald stopping at the town of Trier, in the Moselle valley. When he sees the station sign through the window, the Semprun character reacts rather as Charles Ryder does when he realizes that he's pulled to a halt at Brideshead, or as Edward Thomas does when he sees the name "Adlestrop."

A magic place-name has been pronounced, one that exorcises all the banality and evil of the surrounding circumstances. Here Karl Marx—the Jewish internationalist name that haunts the demented Nazis—was born in 1818. And here, this son of an exhausted rabbinical line abandoned all belief in religion and began a career in radical writing for marginal campaigning newspapers. His first effort, for a Dresden sheet called the *Deutsche Jahrbucher*, was a blast against the evils of censorship as practiced by the Prussian monarch Friedrich Wilhelm IV; an essay that was unsmilingly banned by those it lampooned. The closure of the *Jahrbucher* itself was not long delayed. Marx thereupon applied to the *Rheinische Zeitung*, a Cologne publication, which in May 1842 printed his very first published effort: another assault upon censorship and on those in the Prussian parliament who did not abhor it. As he phrased matters, expressing the feelings of every writer who has had to submit his prose to the sub-literate invigilations of state hirelings: "The defenders of the press in this assembly have on the whole no real relation to what they are defending. They have never come to know freedom of the press as a vital need. For them, it is a matter of the head, in which the heart plays no part."

Wheen adds: "Quoting Goethe, who had said that a painter can only succeed in depicting a type of beauty which he has loved in a real human being, Marx suggested that freedom of the press also has its beauty, which one must have loved in order to defend it."

But his attachment to the forms of free expression was something more than merely platonic. On becoming the editor of the *Rheinische Zeitung* a little while later (and how many promising writers have we lost as a result of their being promoted to the editorial chair?), he embarked on a piece of exposé journalism that connected the ideal of free inquiry to the material circumstances of the dispossessed. The inhabitants of the Rhineland had for generations been allowed to gather fallen branches for firewood, but now—in an assault on tradition that reminds one of the enclosures—they were told that this scavenging for elementary livelihood would become a crime against private property. The penalties would depend on the assessed "value" of what had been free timber, and would be determined by the putative "owners" of what nature and weather had let fall to the ground.

As with Newton's apple and Darwin's finches, Marx's early polemics on this injustice were germinal. They contain the seed of his later views on the material superstructure of society, and the distinction between use value and exchange value. Another spasm of suppression was to follow their publication. Tsar Nicholas I of Russia became annoyed at the general tone of the newspaper and asked his Prussian monarchical counterpart to silence it in early 1843. Marx was then twenty-four, and obscure. It gives one a distinct frisson to think that the tsar's later namesake and descendant Nicholas II was to lose his throne and his life to Marx's less tender-minded Bolshevik disciples, but we need not dwell upon that too much for now. The point was that the young man had declared, in his heart, that the *Rheinische Zeitung* could not be muzzled.

He was true to this promise when he moved back to Cologne after the revolutionary upsurge of 1848, after his coauthorship with Friedrich Engels of *The Communist Manifesto*, to edit the revived *Neue Rheinische Zeitung*. There he met an inquisitive and intelligent young American editor named Charles A. Dana, an energetic member of Horace Greeley's staff at the *New York Tribune* who seems to have been a talent-spotter. But this time the Prussian authorities were taking no chances and, after arresting the staff of his paper, served Marx with an order of deportation, which was arguably the biggest mistake any reactionary government made in the whole of that year. In 1850, Marx took the route that many asylum-seekers have taken before and since, and came to London. The full flourishing of his journalistic career, and of his other careers as well, begins with that enforced exile, and with the approach that the *Tribune* made to him shortly after.

I have been both a Marxist and a journalist, and in some eclectic ways still am both of these things, and I can't decide which is the most interesting fork in the road to follow at this point. Let's take journalism. It is a profession full of vagaries and insecurities, and any of its practitioners will sympathize with Marx's familiar dilemma, and to a lesser extent with Greeley's: The spirited and ambitious author is caught in a trap of potboiling and hack-work in order to pay the rent, while the proprietor is locked in a cost-cutting war with (in this case) the *New York Times*. Of the toil he had to perform to make ends meet, Marx self-hatingly wrote that it amounted to "grinding bones and making soup of them like the paupers in a workhouse." Meanwhile, Greeley is bitching about the cut-throat and race-to-the-bottom tactics of the *New York Times*: "crowding us too hard... conducted with the most policy and the least principle of any paper ever started. It is ever watching for the popular side of any question that turns up, and has made lots of friends by ultra abuse of Abolitionists, Women's Rights..." I never myself walk through midtown Manhattan, past the Greeley Square that so few now notice, and toward the headquarters of the city's now dominant flagship paper, without thinking of this old circulation war that so impoverished the future author of *Das Kapital*.

Impoverished him, in fact, to the point where he wrote to Engels that "I have written nothing for Dana because I've not had the money to buy newspapers." The sheer Grub Street indigence of this to one side, it points up something that the great Murray Kempton noticed in his brilliant essay ("K. Marx: Reporter") in a very early number of the fledgling *New York Review of Books* in 1967. Marx was not at all ashamed to derive his reportage and analysis from secondary sources. "He was," wrote Kempton, "the journalist of the most despised credentials, the one who does not have access." In a witty speech to the American Newspaper Publishers Association, again in Manhattan, at the Waldorf-Astoria hotel in April 1961 (probably suggested by the late Arthur Schlesinger Jr.), the newly inaugurated President John F. Kennedy could perhaps be forgiven for getting the significance of this point so wrong. "We are told," he said to his audience of print magnates, "that foreign correspondent Marx, stone broke, and with a family ill and undernourished, constantly appealed to Greeley and managing editor Charles Dana for an increase in his munificent salary of $5 per installment, a salary which he and Engels ungratefully labelled as the 'lousiest petty-bourgeois cheating.' But when all his financial appeals were refused, Marx looked around for other means of livelihood and fame, eventually terminating his relationship with the *Tribune* and devoting his talents full time to the cause that would bequeath to the world the seeds of Leninism, Stalinism, revolution and the Cold War. If only this capitalistic New York newspaper had treated him more kindly; if only Marx had remained a foreign correspondent, history might have been different."

A president is not on his oath when trying to amuse a publishers' convention, but this is about as far from the truth as one might easily get. Marx's family was a bit more than "ill and undernourished" (his firstborn son, Heinrich Guido, had died in the year he moved to London) but, as the record of the *Rheinische Zeitung* showed, there was no persuasion of any kind, moral or material, that could have reconciled him to social and political conditions as they actually were. And in any case, and despite the wretched pay and conditions, he continued to churn out first-rate copy for Greeley and Dana for a decade after complaining that they didn't pay enough to keep up his daily subscriptions. Yet the point that JFK missed—and that almost everyone else has gone on to miss—is that much of this journalism was devoted to upholding and defending the ideas not of the coming Russian and Chinese or (as Kennedy failed to appreciate at the time) Cuban Revolutions, but of the earlier American one.

If you are looking for an irony of history, you will find it not in the fact that Marx was underpaid by an American newspaper, but in the fact that he and Engels considered Russia the great bastion of reaction and America the great potential nurse of liberty and equality. This is not the sort of thing they teach you in school (in either country). I beseeched Wheen to make more of it in his biography, and his failure to heed my sapient advice is the sole reproach to his otherwise superb book. Now James Ledbetter, himself a radical American scribbler, has somewhat redressed the balance by reprinting some of Marx's most lucid and mordant essays on the great crisis that preoccupied Greeley and Dana: the confrontation over slavery and secession that came near to destroying the United States.

In considering this huge and multi-faceted question, Marx faced two kinds of antagonist. The first was composed of that English faction, grouped around the cotton interest and the *Times* newspaper, which hoped for the defeat of Abraham Lincoln and the wreckage of the American experiment. The second was made up of those Pharisees who denied that the Union, and its leader Lincoln, were "really" fighting a war for the abolition of slavery. Utterly impatient with casuistry, and as always convinced that people's subjective account of their own interests was often misleading, Marx denounced both tendencies. Henry Adams, the direct descendant of two presidents and at that time a witness of his father's embattled ambassadorship to London, wrote in his celebrated memoirs that Marx was almost the only friend that Lincoln had, against the cynical Tories and the hypocritical English Gladstonian liberals. Surveying the grim landscape of the English industrial revolution, he wrote, in *The Education of Henry Adams*, that it "made a boy uncomfortable, though he had no idea that Karl Marx was standing there waiting for him, and that sooner or later the process of education would have to deal with Karl Marx much more than with Professor Bowen of Harvard College or his Satanic free-trade majesty John Stuart Mill."

Marx himself, in reviewing a letter of Harriet Beecher Stowe's to Lord Shaftesbury (and how splendid to have the author of *The Eighteenth Brumaire of Louis Napoleon* seconding the author of *Uncle Tom's Cabin*), ridiculed the smarmy arguments of papers such as the *Economist*, which had written that "the assumption that the quarrel between the North and South is a quarrel between Negro Freedom on the one side and Negro Slavery on the other, is as impudent as it is untrue." The Lincolnians, it was generally asserted, were fighting only for the preservation of the Union, not for the high-sounding cause of emancipation. Not so, said the great dialectician. The Confederacy had opened hostilities on the avowed basis of upholding slavery, which meant in turn that the Union would be forced to tackle emancipation, whether its leadership wanted to or not. See how he makes the point in so few sentences, and shows that it is the apparently hard-headed and realistic who are in practice the deluded ones: "The question of the principle of the American Civil War is answered by the battle slogan with which the South broke the peace. Stephens, the Vice-President of the Southern Confederacy, declared in the Secession Congress that what essentially distinguished the Constitution hatched at Montgomery from the Constitution of the Washingtons and Jeffersons was that now for the first time slavery was recognized as an institutional good in itself, and as the foundation of the whole state edifice, whereas the revolutionary fathers, men steeped in the prejudices of the eighteenth century, had treated slavery as an evil imported from England and to be eliminated in the course of time. Another matador of the South, Mr. Spratt, cried out: 'For us, it is a question of founding a great slave republic.' If, therefore, it was indeed only in defense of the Union that the North drew the sword, had not the South already declared that the continuance of slavery was no longer compatible with the continuance of the Union?"

Written in 1861, this cut like a razor through the cant of the pseudo-realists, while not omitting a good passing slap at the luckless Mr. Spratt (remember that Marx was teaching himself English as he went along). As war progressed, Marx and Engels were to predict correctly that the North would be able to exert industrial power as against Dixie feudalism, that iron-clad ships would play an important role, that the temporizing Union generals such as George McClellan would be fired by an impatient Lincoln, and that an emancipation proclamation would be required as a war-winning measure. For good measure, Marx helped organize a boycott of southern slave-picked cotton among British workers, and wrote and signed a letter from the International Workingmen's Association in 1864, congratulating Lincoln on his re-election and his defeat of the anti-war Democrats. No other figure of the time even approached his combination of acuity and principle on this historic point, which may contain a clue as to why the American Revolution has outlasted the more ostensibly "Marxist" ones.

Marx's appreciation of the laws of unintended consequence, and his disdain for superficial moralism, also allowed him to see that there was more to the British presence in India than met the eye. No doubt the aim of the East India Company had been the subordination of Indian markets and Indian labor for selfish ends, but this did not alter the fact that capitalism was also transforming the subcontinent in what might be called a dynamic way. And he was clear-eyed about the alternatives. India, he pointed out, had always been subjugated by outsiders. "The question is not whether the English had a right to conquer India, but whether we are to prefer India conquered by the Turk, by the Persian, by the Russian, to India conquered by the Briton." If the conqueror was to be the country that pioneered the industrial revolution, he added, then India would benefit by the introduction of four new factors that would tend toward nation-building. These were the electric telegraph for communications, steamships for rapid contact with the outside world, railways for the movement of people and products, and "the free press, introduced for the first time to Asiatic society, and managed principally by the common offspring of Hindus and Europeans." His insight into the Janus-faced nature of the Anglo-Indian relationship, and of the potential this afforded for a future independence, may be one of the reasons why Marxism still remains a stronger force in India than in most other societies.

His belief that British-led "globalization" could be progressive did not blind him to the cruelties of British rule, which led him to write several impassioned attacks on torture and collective punishment, as well as a couple of bitter screeds on the way in which Indian opium was forced upon the defenseless consumers of foreign-controlled China. As he wrote, reprobating Victorian hypocrisy and religiosity and its vile drug traffic, it was the supposedly uncivilized peoples who were defending decent standards: "While the semi-barbarian stood on the principle of morality, the civilized opposed to him the principle of self."

And in writing about another irony—the fact that the Indian "mutiny" of 1857 began not among the wretched peasants, but among the sepoy soldiers whom the British had themselves trained and clothed and armed—he hit upon a powerful formulation: "There is something in human history like retribution; and it is a rule of historical retribution that its instrument be forged not by the offended but by the offender himself."

This recalls his more general proposition that, by calling into being a skilled working class concentrated in huge cities and factories, capitalism itself had given birth to its own eventual gravedigger. Of course, it goes without saying that this concept of his was in turn to fall prey to its own unintended consequences.

Like many a journalist before and since, Marx was not shy of recycling his best lines. Writing about Lord Palmerston's parliamentary effusions, he said: "He succeeds in the comic as in the heroic, in pathos as in familiarity, in tragedy as in farce, although the latter may be more congenial to his feelings."

Probably almost every literate person knows that Marx made a famous crack—derived from Hegel—about the first episode in history being tragic and the second time being farcical. (Like many of his memorable lines, it also comes from the opening of his best-ever essay, *The Eighteenth Brumaire.*) He obviously liked it enough to keep on giving it further workouts, as in the following account of still another British parliamentary occasion, this time on the opening of the Crimean War: "A singularity of English tragedy, so repulsive to French feelings that Voltaire used to call Shakespeare a drunken savage, is its peculiar mixture of the sublime and the base, the terrible and the ridiculous, the heroic and the burlesque. But nowhere does Shakespeare devolve upon the Clown the task of speaking the prologue of a heroic drama. This invention was reserved for the Coalition Ministry . . . All great historical movements appear, to the superficial observer, finally to subside into farce, or at least the common-place. But to commence with this is a feature peculiar alone to the tragedy entitled 'War With Russia.' . . ."

Again—and as sometimes with writers such as Joseph Conrad and Isaac Deutscher, who came to mastery of it late in life—one notices that Marx is only just acquiring his magnificent hold on the English tongue. ("Peculiar alone" is a tautology, or maybe a pleonasm.) This makes it the more remarkable that he was able to lay bare the awful background to the no less awful war in the Crimea; a war that was launched over a stupid quarrel about great-power stewardship in Jerusalem, and thus a war that is still, in our own day, continuing to be fought. His essay "On the History of the Eastern Question" has the same penetrating quality as some of his writings on France and Russia, combining an eerie prescience about the consequences of imperialist "holy" war with a fine contempt for all theocracies and all superstitions, whether Christian, Jewish, or Islamic. If ruling elites and powerful states only squabbled over identifiable interests and privileges, there would have been no need for Marxist analysis. The genius of the old scribbler was to see how often the sheerly irrational intruded upon the material and utilitarian world of our great-grandfathers. That he knew and loved the classical texts as much as his despised antagonists was no disadvantage to his muscular prose style. Murray Kempton, indeed, puts him second only to Edmund Burke in this and other respects.

And I think it is with Kempton's compliment that I ought to close. How can it be, he asked, that Marx knew so much about countries he had never visited and politicians he had never interviewed? How was it that we can read his scornful dismissal of the British government that was elected in 1852, and then turn to the memoirs of the statesmen who were directly involved and discover that they privately feared the very same paralysis and inanition that Marx had diagnosed?

Part of the answer involves a compliment to the Victorians, who compiled honest statistics about death rates and poverty and military spending (and even torture in India), and who published them for all to read. Like the late I. F. Stone, one of Washington's greatest muckrakers, Marx understood that a serious ruling class will not lie to itself in its own statistics. He preferred delving in the archives to scraping acquaintance with the great and the good. When it came to the ghastly twin trades of slavery and opium, he was "a moralist with every stroke of his pen," as Perry Anderson once phrased it. But he never lost his anchorage in the material world, and never ceased to understand that a purely moral onslaught on capitalism and empire would be empty sermonizing. Isaiah Berlin, contrasting the two Jewish geniuses of nineteenth-century England, preferred Benjamin Disraeli to Karl Marx because the former was a hero of assimilation and accommodation and the latter was a prickly and irreconcilable subversive. Well, you may take your pick between the Tory dandy who flattered the Queen into becoming the Queen-Empress and the heretical exile who believed that India would one day burst its boundaries and outstrip its masters. But when journalists today are feeling good about themselves, and sitting through the banquets at which they give each other prizes and awards, they sometimes like to flatter one another by describing their hasty dispatches as "the first draft of history." Next time you hear that tone of self-regard, you might like to pick up *Dispatches for the New York Tribune* and read the only reporter of whom it was ever actually true.

(*The Guardian* [London], June 16, 2007)

Rebecca West: Things Worth Fighting For

MORE THAN A DECADE AGO, at the height of the Balkan wars of the 1990s that succeeded the disintegration or "fall" or "destruction" of Yugoslavia (and so much then hung upon which of the preceding terms one chose to employ for that bloody catastrophe), I returned from a voyage to Macedonia to attend a meeting for Yugoslav democrats at the Cooper Union in New York City. Here I was, under the roof where Abraham Lincoln himself had spoken of union and of the consequences of disunion, and I remember the shiver with which I stood on the same podium to give my own little speech. At a bookstall, I picked up a copy of Ivo Andrić's classic *The Bridge on the Drina*, and a few other texts I had read or desired to reread, and then hesitated over the book that you now hold in your hands.

I know, in other words, what you may be thinking: more than eleven hundred pages of densely wrought text, concerning what Neville Chamberlain once called, in the same context but another reference, "a faraway country of which we know nothing." Not just far away in point of distance, either, but remote in point of time and period: a country that no longer exists, an Atlantis of the mind. (On page 773 of the edition I picked up, West resignedly and pessimistically alludes to "this book, which hardly anyone will read

Introduction (2007) to *Black Lamb and Grey Falcon,* by Rebecca West.

by reason of its length.") The action of buying it seemed almost antiquarian: like laying out money for the purchase of a large anachronistic device. Nevertheless, having learned from other readings to respect the mind of Rebecca West, I decided on the outlay and have been regarding it as a great bargain ever since.

Imagine that you have, in fact, purchased at least four fine books for the price of one: The first and most ostensible of these volumes is one of the great travel narratives of our time, which seeks to net and analyze one of the most gorgeous and various of ancient and modern societies. The second volume gives an account of the mentality and philosophy of a superbly intelligent woman, whose feminism was above all concerned with the respect for, and the preservation of, true masculinity. The third volume transports any thoughtful or historically minded reader into the vertiginous period between the two World Wars: a time when those with intellectual fortitude could face the fact that the next war would be even more terrible than the last, and who did not flinch from that knowledge. The fourth volume is a meditation on the never-ending strife between the secular and the numinous, the faithful and the skeptical, the sacred and the profane.

The woman who brought off this signal polymathic achievement, based on three separate but interwoven visits to the Balkans and published just as the Second World War was disclosing itself as a conflict of ultimate horror, was born Cicely Fairfield in 1892. She demonstrated early brilliance as a reviewer and journalist, soon adopting the name Rebecca West (the heroine of Henrik Ibsen's play *Rosmersholm*). Her first published book, a study of Henry James, was issued in 1916 and her first novel, *The Return of the Soldier*, in 1918. She was thus ideally positioned, in point of age and precocity, to take a hand in the journalistic and critical ferment that followed the Great War. Although inclined to experiment and to the eclectic—she published articles in Wyndham Lewis's vorticist magazine *BLAST* in addition to Ford Madox Ford's *English Review*—she was no intellectual butterfly and, after a brief flirtation with Garsington and Bloomsbury and the world of Virginia Woolf and Ottoline Morrell, found her natural intellectual home on the freethinking liberal left. She was on terms with George Bernard Shaw and Bertrand Russell while barely out of her teens and continued this pattern by conducting a long "older man" affair with H. G. Wells, by whom she soon had a son, Anthony. Her relationships with men were always to be passionate and distraught and full of misery and infidelity (and they included a fling with Lord Beaverbrook, the power-crazy newspaper tycoon who is the original of Lord Copper in Evelyn Waugh's *Scoop*). She managed a long marriage to an English banker ("my husband," otherwise never named, in *Black Lamb and Grey Falcon*), but even while in Yugoslavia with him, as her letters and diaries reveal, she was racked with anxiety about another lover. One has, from most accounts of her very long and tempestuous life, the sense of a brilliant and ambitious but unhappy woman, deeply intellectual and much preoccupied with public affairs, who had to strive extremely hard in a man's world and who found men both essential and impossible. There is an evocative description of her by Virginia Woolf, who wrote that "she has great vitality: is a broad-browed, very vigorous, distinguished woman, but a buffeter and a battler: has taken the waves, I suppose, and can talk in any language: why then this sense of her being a lit up modern block, floodlit by electricity?"

"Block," there, may be somewhat unflattering—though for Mrs. Woolf to instance "the waves" is obviously a mark of respect—but "lit up" though West may have seemed, she was also frequently plunged into darkness. Indeed, nothing better conveys her sense of mingled urgency, responsibility, and pessimism than the way in which she describes the onset of her profound engagement with Yugoslavia. Recovering from surgery in a hospital ward in England in October 1934, she hears a radio announcement of the assassination of King Alexander and appreciates at once that a grand crisis is in the making. Like any intelligent European of that date, she experiences a natural frisson at the murder of a crowned head of the Balkans, but she is also aware that the political class in her country is not much less myopic than it was at the time of Sarajevo, only twenty years earlier. She feels at once helpless and ignorant, and culpable in both these aspects. To know nothing about the Balkans is, she reflects, to "know nothing about my own destiny." At this time, Naomi Mitchison is writing about the bloody events in Vienna that will lead to the Anschluss, and others are experiencing the premonition of impending confrontation in Spain, but for West it is Yugoslavia that is the potentially seismic country.

In considering her book, then, we must try to envisage that now-obliterated nation as she did. This is to say, we must begin by looking at it through the reverse end of the telescope. The murder of King Alexander puts her in mind, successively but not in order, of the assassination of Empress Elizabeth of Austria in 1898 (which had much discomposed her own mother); of the fervor of the schismatic Donatists of the fourth century; of the cruel butchery of King Alexander Obrenović of Serbia, together with his wife, Queen Draga, in the royal palace in Belgrade in 1903; and finally of the cataclysmic shooting of the Austrian archduke Franz Ferdinand and his consort in the capital of Bosnia in June 1914. Of this event, West notes ruefully that at the time she was too much absorbed in her own private concerns to pay the necessary attention. We know that West was a strong admirer of Marcel Proust and believed him to be one of the originators of modernism; and Janet Montefiore, one of the most deft and penetrating students of her work, is surely right in describing this bedridden moment of connected recollection as a Proustian "layering."

Indeed, and without getting too much ahead of our story, the "madeleine" of June 28, 1914, in particular, prompts memories in many more minds than that of Rebecca West. It was on that same day in 1389—St. Vitus's Day—that the Serbian armies of Prince Lazar had known the bitterness of utter vanquishment at the hands of the Turks on the Field of Kosovo: a permanent wound in the national heart that was to be cynically reopened by an anniversary speech given by Slobodan Milošević on the very same date in 1989. For West in 1934, it seemed more simply that "when I came to look back upon it my life had been punctuated by the slaughter of royalties, by the shouting of newsboys who have run down the streets to tell me that someone has used a lethal weapon to turn over a new leaf in the book of history."

I shall have to do some interleaving and "layering" myself, in distinguishing and also separating these four books: Unschooled as she was, Rebecca West decided at once that the slaying of King Alexander was the work, at least by proxy, of the thuggish and covetous regime of Benito Mussolini. In the first few pages of the book, she offers an angry but mordant psychological profile of the mentality of Italian fascism, and of its Croatian and Macedonian clients:

> This cancellation of process in government leaves it an empty violence that must perpetually and at any cost outdo itself, for it has no

> alternative idea and hence no alternative activity. The long servitude in the slums has left this kind of barbarian without any knowledge of what man does when he ceases to be violent, except for a few uncomprehending glimpses of material prosperity.... This aggressiveness leads obviously to the establishment of immense armed forces, and furtively to incessant experimentation with methods of injuring the outer world other than the traditional procedure of warfare.

The above passage can be taken as representative of many others in which West combines a near-patrician contempt for the baseness of fascism with her own political radicalism and her keen insight into motive. That this latter insight is essentially feminist is proved repeatedly by her choice of words and examples. Of the martyred Empress Elizabeth, for example, she writes that she

> could not reconcile herself to a certain paradox which often appears in the lives of very feminine women. She knew that certain virtues are understood to be desirable in women: beauty, tenderness, grace, house-pride, the power to bear and rear children. She believed that she possessed some of these virtues and that her husband loved her for it. Indeed, he seemed to have given definite proof that he loved her by marrying her against the will of his mother, the Archduchess Sophie.

Against this latter woman West deploys a rhetorical skill that is perhaps too little associated with feminism: the ability to detect a pure bitch at twenty paces:

> The Archduchess Sophie is a figure of universal significance. She was the kind of woman whom men respect for no other reason than that she is lethal, whom a male committee will appoint to the post of hospital matron. She had none of the womanly virtues. Especially did she lack tenderness.... She was also a great slut.

Incautious would be the man, but still more the woman, who incurred the fine wrath of Rebecca West. Her ability to appraise historical and global figures as if she had recently been personally oppressed or insulted by them was a great assistance in driving her narrative forward.

Speaking of narrative, she tells us very early on that her preferred analogy—her chosen means of connecting the past to the present—is that of "the sexual affairs of individuals":

> As we grow older and see the ends of stories as well as their beginnings, we realize that to the people who take part in them it is almost of greater significance that they should be stories, that they should form a recognizable pattern, than that they should be happy or tragic. The men and women who are withered by their fates, who go down to death reluctantly but without noticeable regrets for life, are not those who have lost their mates prematurely or by perfidy, or who have lost battles or fallen from early promise in circumstances of public shame, but those who have been jilted or were the victims of impotent lovers, who have never been summoned to command or been given any opportunity for success or failure.

She speculates that this is "possibly true not only of individuals, but of nations," and this hypothesis becomes, in fact, the organizing principle of the book. Two other recurring notes are likewise introduced early on: West makes the first of innumerable cross-references to England (throughout her travels she compares towns, landscapes, historical events, and individuals to their English counterparts, as if to provide a familiar handhold both to her readers and to herself) and asks, immediately following the passage above: "What would England be like if it had not its immense Valhalla of kings and heroes?"

She also, in discussing Russia's influence on the region, shows a defensive but definite sympathy for the Soviet system. Having been an early critic of Bolshevism, and sympathizer of its leftist and feminist victims, she appears like many to have postponed this reckoning until the more imperative menace of fascism had been confronted. "Those who fear Bolshevist Russia because of its interventions in the affairs of other countries," she wrote, "which are so insignificant that they have never been rewarded with success, forget that Tsarist Russia carried foreign intervention to a pitch that has never been equaled by any other power, except the modern Fascist states." In this, she reflected some of the left-liberal mentality of her day, and there is no doubt that this bias inflects a good deal of her Yugoslav analysis. "There is no man in the world," she wrote, "not even Stalin, who would claim to be able to correct in our own time the insane dispensation which pays the food-producer worst of all workers." To diagnose in so few words a problem that is still with us requires skill, but to portray Joseph Stalin as a friend of the peasant would have been eyebrow-raising even in 1937. (Should we allow that, in that year, the "story" of Russian communism was after all a little nearer to its inception than its end?) At any rate, at the beginning of her journey, we can identify an ardent woman who manifested a nice paradoxical sympathy for the honor, bravery, and pageantry of the past, and for the apparently more modern ideas of socialism and self-determination. She had stepped onto the perfect soil for one so quixotic.

She never chances to employ the word, but Serbo-Croat speech has an expression that depends for its effect not on the sex lives of humans, but of animals. A *vukojebina*—employed to describe a remote or barren or arduous place—means literally a "wolf-fuck," or more exactly the sort of place where wolves retire to copulate. This combination of a noble and fearless creature with an essential activity might well have appealed to her. The term—which could have been invented to summarize Milovan Djilas's harsh and loving portrayal of his native Montenegro, *Land Without Justice*—is easily adapted to encapsulate a place that is generally, so to say, fucked up. This is the commonest impression of the Balkans now, as it was then, and West considered it her task to uncover and to praise the nobility and culture that contradicted this patronizing impression.

Assisting her in this purpose, and sometimes contradicting her as well, is the near-ubiquitous figure of "Constantine." He is supposed to speak for all those who have resisted the long, rival tyrannies of Austria-Hungary and Turkey, and who are now trying to teach the discordant peoples of Yugoslavia to speak with one voice. One's attitude to the book, and to West herself, depends to a very great extent on one's view of Constantine. A composite based on a real person named Stanislas Vinaver, he is at once a government bureaucrat and "official guide," a Serb, a Jew, a nationalist, and a cosmopolitan. To add to the jumble of this picture, he is also married to Gerda, a German woman of frightful aspect and demeanor who despises almost all foreigners—most especially Jews—and who is a clear prefiguration of a full-blown Nazi. (I happen to like Stanislas/Constantine. When dealing with an incensed young Bosnian who accused him of being a government stooge, he responds with some gravity by saying: "Yes. For the sake of my country, and perhaps a little for the sake of my soul, I have given up the deep peace of being in opposition." This is one of the more profoundly mature, and also among the most tragic, of the signals that West's ear was attuned to pick up.)

We meet Constantine early on, and we also encounter a method of Rebecca West's that has given rise to much criticism. Her nonfictional characters are conscripted more as dramatis personae—Montefiore likens her to Thucydides—and given long speeches, even soliloquies, in which to represent sets of ideas and prejudices. This is a privilege extended not only to the people she meets: Throughout the book both she and her husband make long and quite grammatical addresses that would be unthinkable in real life, if only because they would be interrupted if given in mixed company and walked out upon if they occurred at the domestic hearth. As a didactic tool, however, this has its uses in that people are permitted to be advocates and are given the room to make their case. (Paul Scott employs the same means in his historical fiction of the British Raj in India, often to great effect. The soliloquy is not to be despised as a means of elucidation.) The first use of it occurs when West and her husband are in the Croatian capital of Zagreb, and Constantine gets into fights and arguments with some local intellectuals who do not trust or respect the new national regime with its political headquarters in the Serbian capital of Belgrade. His rather emotional attempts to make them think and feel like "Slavs" are recorded sympathetically by West, but this is the stage at which we can first surmise that the Serbs will turn out to be her favorites.

Ambivalent as she was about Stalin, Rebecca West was acutely sensitive to the early warnings of fascism and very heartily repelled by all its manifestations. She identified it in the Yugoslav case with a general conspiracy by foreign powers to subvert and fragment the country (in which she was by no means mistaken), and she identified it in the Croatian case with the ambitions of the Vatican (in which she was not wrong, either). The world now knows about the Ustashe, the cruel and chauvinistic surrogate party that established a Nazi protectorate in Croatia, under military and clerical leadership, during the Second World War. West saw it coming, in the uniformed Catholic "youth movements" set up in Croatia in the 1930s, and in the persistent hostility of the Church to the Yugoslav idea in general, and to the allegiance of the Serbs to Eastern Orthodoxy in particular.

It deserves to be said that she tries to compensate for this partisanship by almost immediately writing a paean to Bishop Strossmayer, a Catholic Croatian eminence of the preceding century who had been genuinely humane and ecumenical, but it is also at this point that one can begin to notice her distaste for chiaroscuro. In describing Strossmayer's life and habits and character, she supplies an almost devotional portrait of a man about whom she could have known only by hearsay. Of his supposed hospitality she writes: "After supper, at which the food and drink were again delicious, there were hours of conversation, exquisite in manner, stirring in matter." This approaches the gushing.

A writer who falls in love with a new and strange country will always find experience heightened in this way. The dawns are more noble, the crags loftier, the people more genuine, the food and wine more luscious.... Here might be the point to try to explicate the lamb and the falcon of West's title. About halfway through the narrative she is in Belgrade, and finding, as many lovers do, that her new inamorata is beginning to remind her just a little too much of her previous ones. The men in the hotel bar, and the hotel itself, are making Yugoslavia's capital into an emulation of some imagined bourgeois ideal, replete with modern architecture and up-to-date ideas of businesslike cleverness. Soon, she begins to feel, the food will become indistinguishable as well. The hotel will "repudiate its good fat risottos, its stews would be guiltless of the spreading red oil of paprika.... I felt a sudden abatement of my infatuation for Yugoslavia.... I had perhaps come a long way to see a sunset which was fading under my eyes before a night of dirty weather." Disillusionment and banality menace her on every hand, and the false jollity at the bar is mounting to a crescendo, when

> the hotel doors [swung] open to admit, unhurried and at ease, a peasant holding a black lamb in his arms.... He was a well-built young man with straight fair hair, high cheekbones, and a look of clear sight. His suit was in the Western fashion, but he wore also a sheepskin jacket, a round black cap, and leather sandals with upturned toes, and to his ready-made shirt his mother had added some embroidery.

It is as if an Englishman, raised on the romance of the Western and pining in a phony tourist saloon in Wyoming, were to see the saloon doors swing open and hear the jingle of true cowboy spurs....

> He stood still as a Byzantine king in a fresco, while the black lamb twisted and writhed in the firm cradle of his arms, its eyes sometimes catching the light as it turned and shining like small luminous plates.

So there is still hope that traditional, genuine, rural society continues to pulse away, under the gaudy patina of commerce and affectation. However, the next time we encounter a black lamb we are in Macedonia almost four hundred pages further on, and this time West is not at all so sure that she likes what she sees. The Muslim peasants are converging on a large rock in an open field, and the rock is coated with coagulating blood and littered with animal body parts:

> I noticed that the man who had been settling the child on the rug was now walking round the rock with a black lamb struggling in his arms. He was a young gypsy, of the kind called Gunpowder gypsies, because they used to collect saltpeter for the Turkish army, who are famous for their beauty, their cleanliness, their fine clothes. This young man had the features and bearing of an Indian prince, and a dark golden skin which was dull as if it had been powdered yet exhaled a soft light. His fine linen shirt was snow-white under his close-fitting jacket, his elegant breeches ended in soft leather boots, high to the knee, and he wore a round cap of fine fur.

Again, one notices West's keen eye for the finely featured man and for his apparel. But this time, the ambience strikes her as brutish and disgusting—even alarming.

> Now the man who was holding the lamb took it to the edge of the rock and drew a knife across its throat. A jet of blood spurted out and fell red and shining on the browner blood that had been shed before. The gypsy had caught some on his fingers, and with this he made a circle on the child's forehead.... "He is doing this," a

> bearded Muslim standing by explained, "because his wife got this child by coming here and giving a lamb, and all children that are got from the rock must be brought back and marked with the sign of the rock."... Under the opening glory of the morning the stench from the rock mounted more strongly and became sickening.

Sunset in Belgrade... sunrise in Macedonia—and suddenly the evidence of "authenticity" seems to contradict itself. This is a difficulty that recurs to West throughout her explorations.

The gray falcon comes to her on another field of sacrifice: this time the plain of Kosovo on which Prince Lazar of Serbia saw his forces divided by betrayal and slaughtered by the Turks. An antique Serbian folk song, translated on the spot by Constantine, begins the story thus:

> There flies a grey bird, a falcon,
> From Jerusalem the holy,
> And in his beak he bears a swallow.
>
> That is no falcon, no grey bird,
> But it is the Saint Elijah...

This sky-borne messenger brings to Prince Lazar (or "Tsar Lazar," as the poem has him) a choice between an earthly kingdom and a heavenly one: a choice that he decides in a way that West comes to find contemptible. Her two chosen images, therefore, are neither symmetrical nor antagonistic but, rather, contain their own contradictions. It is important to know at the start what she registers throughout and at the conclusion: that feeling that some English people have always had for a patriotism other than their own. Byron in Greece had a comparable experience, of simultaneous exaltation and disillusionment, and even as West was making her way through the Balkans, English volunteers in Spain were uttering slogans about Madrid and Barcelona that they would have felt embarrassed to hear themselves echo for London or Manchester. Many of them were to return disappointed, too.

"The enormous condescension of posterity" was the magnificent phrase employed by E. P. Thompson to remind us that we must never belittle the past popular struggles and victories (as well as defeats) that we are inclined to take for granted. Two things are invariably present in Rebecca West's mind and, thanks to the lapse of time, not always available to our own. The first of these is the realization that an incident in Sarajevo in June 1914 had irrevocably splintered the comfortable and civilized English world of which she had a real memory. When she says "The Great War," she means the war of 1914–1918 because, though she can see a second war coming, there has as yet been no naming of the "First" World War. The next is her constant awareness that men decide and that women then live, or die, with the consequences of that decision making. The first assault on the Yugoslav idea had been made by the hairless demagogic Italian poet Gabriele D'Annunzio—the man who borrowed the phrase "the year of living dangerously" from Nietzsche, though West did not know this—and who had led the wresting of Trieste and Fiume from Yugoslav sovereignty in 1920. This piece of theater and bombast was the precursor to Mussolini's March on Rome, and caused West to reflect:

> All this is embittering history for a woman to contemplate. I will believe that the battle of feminism is over, and that the female has reached a position of equality with the male, when I hear that a country has allowed itself to be turned upside-down and led to the brink of war by a totally bald woman writer.

Useless for a male critic to interpose that Joan of Arc apparently had a full head of hair, or that Dolores Ibárruri ("La Pasionaria") was even then making strong men shed hot tears for the ideals of Joseph Stalin—or that neither of these ladies was a writer or poet in the accepted sense. One simply sees what she means.

And, very often, one has exactly no choice *but* to see what she means, and to respect her intuitions as well as her better-reasoned insights. Her intuitions and generalizations are offered in no niggardly spirit and make no attempt to disguise themselves as objective let alone impartial. After a sweep along the Adriatic, with some animadversions about the decay and enfeeblement of the Venetian Empire, she stops at the island of Rab and declares that

> these people of Dalmatia gave the bread out of their mouths to save us of Western Europe from Islam, and it is ironical that so successfully did they protect us that those among us who would be

> broad-minded, who will in pursuit of that end stretch their minds until they fall apart in idiocy, would blithely tell us that perhaps the Dalmatians need not have gone to that trouble, that an Islamized West could not have been worse than what we are today.... The West has done much that is ill, it is vulgar and superficial and economically sadist, but it has not known that death in life which was suffered by the Christian provinces under the Ottoman Empire.

An unintended element of posterity's condescension may be apparent at the close of this passage, where West writes, "Impotent and embarrassed, I stood on the high mountain and looked down on the terraced island where my saviors, small and black as ants, ran here and there, attempting to repair their destiny."

The difficulty, in crediting any group or state with delivering Europe from the Turks or from Islam, is that there are too many rival claimants for that honor and distinction. Austrians and Poles can boast of having defended the gates of Vienna; Venetians and Maltese to have hung on until the victory at Lepanto; Hungarians and Greeks to have fought to the last against Ottomanism. In Rebecca West's own lifetime, the Sublime Porte in Constantinople had staked everything on a declaration of *jihad* against the British Empire and on the side of the German one in 1914, and had ended up not just losing the war but its caliphate as well. She was always somewhat ambivalent about the British Empire, reserving the right both to admire it and to criticize it, but toward most of the other empires and nations I have just mentioned she was generally hostile. And this was because of her feeling that they had all, at different times, betrayed the people of the Balkans, most especially the people of Serbia.

It was not, after all, the arrogant Turks who had issued an ultimatum to Serbia in July 1914 (though Turkey was to take the side of Austria-Hungary and Germany in the ensuing combat). Yet perhaps the most sustainedly brilliant passage in the entire book is her reconstruction of the events that led up to, and away from, the assassination of the Austrian archduke Franz Ferdinand. When one scans these pages, one must continually bear in mind that for her, as for most educated English people, the events of June 28, 1914, were the moral and emotional equivalent of September 11, 2001, the terrible date on which everything had suddenly changed for the worse. I cannot possibly hope to summarize the intensity and scope of her effort in this regard. In its awareness of the grand consequences of the event, it manifests an almost vibrant sense of history and drama. In its minute attention to detail, it rivals some of the more obsessive and forensic retracings of what happened in Dealey Plaza in Dallas, Texas, on November 22, 1963 (and shares with some of those studies a subliminal but unmistakable wish that the newsreel could be run again, and one turn of the car avoided or one wretched coincidence averted, so that the fatal bullet would not meet its target after all).

A little too much time and ink, perhaps, is expended in "proving" that the Austro-Hungarian staff must have at least covertly wished for the archduke to have been shot. For these frigid and cynical men, a mild heir with an embarrassing wife was thereby removed and an ideal provocation for war simultaneously furnished. It could well have been so. Certainly, the pro-war forces in Vienna seemed a little more than ready for the excuse that was offered them, and hastened to force conditions on Serbia that they knew were both unjust and unacceptable. However, as West fails to mention, the socialist faction in the outraged Serbian Parliament, led by Dimitrije Tucovic, nonetheless refused to vote even for a war of "self-defense." This was partly because of what they had seen of Serbian atrocities against Albanians and others in the Balkan War of 1912. These men were the equivalents of Jean Jaurès and Rosa Luxemburg in their own country: How disappointing that West's evident sympathy for Marxist internationalism should have deserted her just when it might have done her some good.

There is another marvelous passage, also derived from her stay in Sarajevo, which is this time an eyewitness description, and which actually can be summarized by quotation. She chanced to be in the city on the day of a state visit from the Turkish prime minister İsmet İnönü: the first such courtesy call since the conclusion of hostilities in 1918 and the proclamation by Kemal Atatürk of a secular republic in place of the caliphate. The large Muslim middle class of the city turned out in force, the bearded men donning fezes and the women wearing veils, and some hardy souls even bearing the old green flag with the crescent emblazoned upon it. Their consternation, on seeing clean-shaven high Turkish officials wearing Western suits and bowler hats, was palpable. Even worse was the shock they endured on hearing the speeches of İnönü's delegation, as translated from Turkish by the Yugoslav minister of war. The distinguished visitors from Ankara

> stood still, their eyes set on the nearest roof, high enough to save them the sight of this monstrous retrograde profusion of fezes and veils, of red pates and black muzzles, while the General put back into Serbian their all too reasonable remarks. They had told the Muslims of Sarajevo, it seemed, that they felt the utmost enthusiasm for the Yugoslavian idea, and had pointed out that if the South Slavs did not form a unified state the will of the great powers could sweep over the Balkan peninsula as it chose. They had said not one word of the ancient tie that linked the Bosnian Muslims to the Turks, nor had they made any reference to Islam.

The crowd dispersed, West recorded: "Slowly and silently, as those who have been sent empty away. We had seen the end of a story that had taken five hundred years to tell. We had seen the final collapse of the Ottoman Empire. Under our eyes it had heeled over and fallen to the ground like a clay figure slipping off a chair." Once again, one is forced to note her innate prejudice in favor of the traditional and (somehow, therefore) the more "authentic," even if this involves a preference for the fez over the standard bowler hat and thus a slight revision of what has been said earlier about Ottoman slavery and torpor. Perhaps, as for Simone Weil, West's definition of justice was that of "a refugee from the camp of victory." If the corollary of this was to hold, and the defeated were to enjoy a closer natural relationship with justice, then much of her Serb-enthusiasm is, at least at that date, fairly easily explicable as well.

In any event, anybody with the least sympathy for the Balkan underdogs would by then have been recruited to their side, with a high degree of militancy, by the extraordinary above-mentioned figure of Gerda. It is never explained how this appalling philistine German female—a character from whom Christopher Isherwood's ghastly Berlin landlady would have been a distinct relief—can possibly have married the Jewish intellectual Constantine (their true names were actually Stanislas and Elsa Vinaver), but married they are. And their grotesque partnership provides an ideal element of the farcical and the sinister, both increasing and lightening the solemn load that

West and her husband must carry on their very serious trip. Gerda's presence is a torture to Constantine and a perpetual embarrassment to his English guests, but it affords some useful comic relief as well as a Bob Fosse–like premonition of the nature of the "new Germany." Informed at one point that the Wendish minority in Germany is in fact Slavic, she demands of West to be informed:

> "If all the Wends are Slavs, why do we not send them out of Germany into the Slav countries, and give the land that they are taking up to true Germans?" "Then the Slavs," I said, "might begin to think about sending back into Germany all the German colonists that live in places like Franzstal." "Why, so they might," said Gerda, looking miserable, since an obstacle had arisen in the way of her plan of making Europe clean and pure and Germanic by coercion and expulsion. She said in Serbian to her husband, "How this woman lacks tact." "I know, my dear," he answered gently, "but do not mind it, enjoy the scenery."

Gerda, then, as well as the gelder of her husband, is a racist both pure *and* simple, an "ethnic cleanser" *avant de la lettre*, and she is one of those Teutonic types who cannot forgive—who can in a way not even believe—the defeat and humiliation of her country in 1918. That a crew of worthless Slavs were among the apparent "victors" is to her an offense against nature. "Think of all these people dying for a lot of Slavs," as she puts it on visiting the French war cemetery. The local food disgusts her: When handed a dish at a picnic, "her face crumpled up with a hatred too irrational to find words." Most of the people West meets and likes in Sarajevo are Jewish, and she suddenly comes to understand that this is why Gerda has no time for them. Like most English liberals and radicals of that period, West was only too conscious of the injustices imposed upon Germany by the Treaty of Versailles, and at one point goes out of her way to remind us that "Gerda is, of course, not characteristically German," but her husband is less tender-minded and reduces the matter to the paradoxical statement that "nobody who is not like Gerda can imagine how bad Gerda is." (He often supplies quite shrewd and gnomic remarks: Noticing that a shrine to the Karageorgevićs dynasty is strictly Serbo-Byzantine in style and like most shrines is built "all on strictly Serb territory," he adds that "this building with its enormously costly mosaics can mean nothing whatsoever to any Croatians or Dalmatians or Slovenes. Yet it is the mausoleum of their King, and superbly appropriate to him. I see that though Yugoslavia is a necessity it is not a predestined harmony." This terse observation is worth more than many of West's own hyper-romantic excursions into the quasi-mythical history of Serbian royalty.)

A considerable and almost purple chapter of such romance and mythmaking follows almost at once, as West visits the monastery at Vrdnik, where lies the coffin of Prince Lazar, the martyr of Kosovo. "There is no need to manufacture magic here," she writes, before proceeding to do just that:

> When this man met defeat it was not only he whose will was frustrated, it was a whole people, a whole faith, a wide movement of the human spirit. This is told by the splendid rings on the Tsar Lazar's black and leathery hands; and the refinement of the pomp which presents him in his death, the beauty and gravity of the enfolding ritual, show the worth of what was destroyed with him. I put out a finger and stroked those hard dry hands, that had been nerveless for five hundred years.

To admire Rebecca West is to admire the toughness of her mind and the steadiness of her gaze: It is a little dispiriting to see her committing such an evident non sequitur between the first and second of her opening sentences, and a little more than dispiriting to see her caressing a relic like any silly old woman hoping for a cure for the scrofula.

She commits a more serious contradiction a little further along, this time after appearing to take at their face value the mad prophecies of a Serbian Nostradamus named Mata of Krema. In reprobating a later Serbian dynasty—the Obrenović line, of Miloš and Milan—she first blames King Milan for allowing the Treaty of San Stefano in 1878, which gave almost the whole of Macedonia to Bulgaria, and then denounces the later Congress of Berlin, which undid the injustice she complains of, as "called for no other reason than to frame a treaty which should deprive the democratic Slavs of their freedom and thrust them into subjection under the imperialism of Turkey and Austria-Hungary." That sequence already seems somewhat disordered, but then it is followed by this sentence:

> It is not to be wondered at that in 1881 Milan signed a secret convention with Austria which handed over his country to be an Austrian dependency.

On the contrary, if any of West's foregoing assumptions are sound, this action seems almost incomprehensible (as does her earlier use of the term "democratic"). She is beginning to regard Serbia as a country that, even if unable to do anything right, can yet never be said to be in the wrong. And again we encounter her preference, at least on first meeting, for anything that is raw and elemental over anything that is tame or domesticated:

> Men like Miyatovich [King Milan's favorite foreign minister, by the by] wanted the Serbians to lay aside this grandiose subject matter *which their destiny had given them for their genius to work upon*; and instead they offered them, as an alternative, to be clean and briskly bureaucratic and capitalist like the West. It was as if the *Mayflower* and Red Indians and George Washington and the pioneer West were taken from the United States, and there was nothing left but the Bronx and Park Avenue. [My italics.]

Before long, this admiration for the atavistic has led her to describe the vile Balkan War of 1912 as a "poem," and to write that "there has been no fighting in our time that has had the romantic quality" of that conflict. (A useful corrective to this nonsense can be found in the Carnegie Endowment's contemporary report on the war, and in Leon Trotsky's firsthand reports of Serbian atrocities as printed in liberal Russian newspapers.)

Thus, at the almost exact midpoint of the book, West has arrived at a stage where she approves of King Alexander Karageorgevićs, who had hoped at the beginning of the First World War

> not for a Yugoslavia, not for a union of all South Slavs, but for a Greater Serbia that should add to the Kingdom of Serbia all of the Austro-Hungarian territories in which the majority of the inhabitants were Serbs, that is Slavs who were members of the Orthodox Church. The school of thought to which he belonged *rightly considered* the difference between the Roman Catholic and the Orthodox

> Churches so great that it transcended racial or linguistic unity. *It cannot be doubted that this Greater Serbia would have been a far more convenient entity than Yugoslavia.* [My italics.]

Something very like the blindness of love must again be involved here: West quite fails to see that her ideal Greater Serbia program is open to precisely the same objections as Gerda's fantasy of a pure Germany that adjusts the populations of its neighbors to suit itself. Moreover, it is with a note of unmistakable rue that she notes the thwarting of King Alexander's dream, which depended for its success on the continued survival of Russian tsarism. This from the woman who credited Stalin's agricultural reforms and who has, only a few pages before this, used the term "Soviet" in a wholly positive sense.

I risk mentioning the blindness of love again because, in her assessment of Alexander's pro-tsarist policy, she makes mention of his wish to marry one of the tsar's daughters and asserts that "it is beyond doubt that this was for Alexander a real affair of the heart. He did not merely want to be the husband of one of the tsar's daughters. He wanted to have this particular daughter as his wife." Now, West does not even trouble to specify which Romanov daughter this was. (We are told only that she was a schoolgirl when Alexander met her.) And we are asked not only to overlook the self-evident interest of kingly statecraft in the matrimonial alliance, but to believe something that West cannot possibly have known herself. This is not history. It is not even journalism. It is passion.

As it happens, we know from Rebecca West's diaries of her trip (which were sequestered in the Beinecke Library at Yale, with instructions that they were not to be made available until after the death of her husband and her son) that she was highly distraught during her Balkan voyages. She had been unwell and in some pain since her operation (for a hysterectomy) in 1934, and she was also recovering from an unhappy affair with an English surgeon named Thomas Kilner, whom she describes with mingled disgust and desire as "that horrible cheating sadistic little creature." With Henry Andrews, her husband, she did have very occasional sexual relations on the journey, but these are usually written up as unsuccessful or unexciting. With Constantine (Stanislav Vinaver) she was necessarily uneasy, since on her previous solo trip he had attempted to possess her by force, if not actually to rape her. I dislike venturing even one step onto the territory of the psycho-historian, but some of her diary entries do seem to warrant a comparison with the finished book, and for one reason in particular: She tends to experience her few moments of repose or reflection when in churches or when visiting tombs, or at holy sites where the simple folk come for healing.

Thus we have a woman of powerful mind, recently sterilized at the difficult age of forty-two. It may be significant that her only allusion to her beloved Proust is to a passage where he reflects on how with age one's body ceases to be oneself and turns into an enemy. She is dissatisfied for discrepant reasons with all the men in her life. (The few references to H. G. Wells in the book proper, which usually take the form of comments on his work by Yugoslavs who do not know of her connection to him, are almost invariably of a rather belittling kind.) Nonetheless, she can be funny about men. (Macedonian Albanians have trousers that are always on the point of falling down, "and to make matters psychologically worse they are of white or biscuit homespun heavily embroidered in black wool in designs that make a stately reference to the essential points of male anatomy. The occasion could not seem more grave, especially as there is often a bunch of uncontrolled shirt bulging between the waistcoat and these trousers. Nothing, however, happens.") And though she is angry at the abysmal treatment of Balkan womanhood—in Kosovo she writes a few paragraphs of controlled rage at the sight of an old peasant walking free while his wife carries a heavy iron-bladed plow—she can be tender about the male as well. When females become emancipated:

> The young woman and the young man dash together out of adolescence into married life like a couple of colts. But presently the woman looks round and sees that the man is not with her. He is some considerable distance behind her, not feeling very well. There has been drained from him the strength which his forefathers derived from the subjection of women; and the woman is amazed, because tradition has taught her that to be a man is to be strong. There is no known remedy for this disharmony.

Perhaps suggestively, she several times resorts to the term "lechery," and the then contemporary slang "letch," to explain hidden motivations. An old abbot in Macedonia is given high marks for his "lechery for life," in view of his continued survival "in a country where death devoured that which most deserved to live," while on the aforementioned field of animal sacrifices West detects "a letch for cruelty." The dialectic between Eros and Thanatos is continuous in these pages, as it was in their author's conscious and unconscious mind. The most repeatedly pejorative word in her lexicon is "impotent," as the reader will by now have spotted. Her detestation of homosexual or effeminate men is often vented.

I do not think it is any great exaggeration to say that, by the end of her travels, West had come to identify the Serbs with the nobler element of the masculine principle: those who were the least affected by hysteria and masochism and sickly introspection, those whose tradition made the least apologetic appeal to sacrifice and the martial virtues, and those who would be least inclined to let an invader warm his hands at their hearth. This conclusion was not reached without a number of ambiguities, not to mention excursions and digressions from the main path, but it led there in the end. Given the mind-concentrating prospect of imminent war with Nazi Germany, West sometimes remembered that she was a twentieth-century socialist and feminist, who had had, probably at one point, high hopes for the League of Nations. Two hundred pages after her lucubrations about "Greater Serbia" and its dubious dynasties, and before she has quite done with a long encomium to the Serb leader Stephen Dušan, who might or might not have contrived to restore the glory of Byzantium, she turns Fabian again and makes what amounts to a straightforward policy statement:

> The Serbs are... *irritating* when they regard their Tsar Dushan not only as an inspiration but as a map-maker, for his empire had fallen to pieces in the thirty-five years between his death and the defeat at Kosovo. The only considerations which should determine the drawing of Balkan frontiers are the rights of the peoples to self-government and the modifications of that right to which they must submit in order to keep the peninsula as a whole free from the banditry of the great powers. [My italics.]

Change "self-government" to "self-determination" in the above, and it is the voice of the principled bluestocking, come back to address the girls at her old school on the need for world order and punctilious diplomacy. The word "irritating" is especially well chosen for this effect.

However, the old world of commingled chivalry and superstition still exerts its hold on her and compels her to share what she has learned with those comfortable readers at home to whom politics is still a matter of party and welfare rather than warfare and sacrifice. And this desire produces two connected set pieces of extreme power. Recall the blood of the black lamb, spurting out to create fertility for the barren and ground-down Muslim women of Macedonia. In this primitive ritual, West does not at first wish to see the parallel with Christian doctrines of the atonement, or rather, of vicarious atonement by means of which a scapegoat can be gutted or sacrificed for the greater good of the tribe. But the sense of smell is an acute prompter, and the sheer reek and stench of that Sheep's Field, clotted with drying blood and dismembered carcasses, provokes in her a profound nausea:

> The rite of the Sheep's Field was purely shameful. It was a huge and dirty lie.... Its rite, under various disguises, had been recommended to me since my infancy by various religious bodies, by Roman Catholicism, by Anglicanism, by Methodism, by the Salvation Army. Since its earliest days Christianity has been compelled to seem its opposite. This stone, the knife, the filth, the blood, is what many people desire beyond anything else, and they fight to obtain it.

If the grisly sacrifice of cocks and lambs, and the nasty blend of gore and grease, make her gag at the paganism and stupidity of millennial custom, this is nothing to the shock she experiences on the field of Kosovo, consecrated to the apparently willing and glorious *self*-sacrifice of human beings determined to uphold a great cause. As she approaches the center of the landscape, she is informed that it is often red with poppies to symbolize the fallen Serbian martyrs, and I find it odd that she does not observe any connection with the celebrated poppies of Flanders and Picardy, emblematic as these are of a slaughter on the Somme that would have been all too fresh and vivid in her own mind. It is when she arrives at the heart of the place, and has the "grey falcon" poem explained to her, that she undergoes a shock that exceeds anything that has come before.

It is characteristically preceded by another piece of paradoxical generosity. West has been brought to Kosovo—*Kosovo Polje*, or "the Field of the Blackbirds"—to see the place where Turkish imperialism crushed the Serbs, and all her sympathies have been engaged on the Serbian side, but she takes care to visit the mausoleum of Sultan Murad, one of the Turkish leaders who also lost his life there, to note the sad decrepitude of Muslim life in the Prishtina district and to set down the following:

> It is impossible to have visited Sarajevo or Bitolj or even Skoplje, without learning that the Turks were in a real sense magnificent, that there was much of that in them which brings a man off his four feet into erectness, that they knew well that running waters, the shade of trees, a white minaret the more in a town, brocade and fine manners, have a usefulness greater than use, even to the most soldierly of men.

Once again, one notes the implicit compliment to virility.

And this helps set the stage for what follows. The poem about the gray falcon, as recited and adumbrated by Constantine and his more vigorous driver, Dragutin, reveals to West that when Lazar was offered the choice between a military victory and a sacrificial but holy defeat, he chose the latter. He summoned the bishops, administered the Eucharist to his soldiers, and lost "seven and seventy thousand" of them. But nevertheless, as the poem concludes:

> All was holy, all was honorable
> And the goodness of God was fulfilled.

This immediately strikes West as even more horrible than the blood sacrifice and pseudo-atonement of the Sheep's Field. Behind its bravado there lurks an awful death wish and an equally despicable abjection and fatalism. "So that was what happened," she says abruptly when the recitation is completed. "Lazar was a member of the Peace Pledge Union."

Some context may be needed here: The Peace Pledge Union (PPU) was a British organization of the mid-1930s founded by a genial but simpleminded Anglican clergyman named Dick Sheppard. Membership involved a commitment not unlike the earlier Christian "pledge" to swear off alcohol: the signing of a statement that "I renounce all war and will never support or sanction another." Enormous numbers of people signed this pledge and did much to influence the already craven attitude of the British establishment toward the rise of fascism. And in fact, naively pacifist though the membership of the PPU was, its leadership contained several people who either sympathized with German war aims or who did not think that such aims should be opposed by force. (In the course of the eventual Second World War, it would be extensively lampooned and denounced by George Orwell, who was incidentally a great admirer of Rebecca West's writing.) Making the rather strained analogy between Kosovo in 1389 and Europe in 1938, West decides that "this poem shows that the pacifist attitude does not depend on the horrors of warfare, for it never mentions them. It goes straight to the heart of the matter and betrays that *what the pacifist really wants is to be defeated*." [My italics.]

She reflects on the "anti-war" meetings that she has attended back home and echoes Orwell's famous attack on the vegetarians, fruit-juice drinkers, sandal wearers, "escaped Quakers," and other radical cranks by remarking on the eccentric dress of the women at these events and the love of impotence that is evident there:

> The speakers use all accents of sincerity and sweetness, and they continuously praise virtue; but they never speak as if power would be theirs tomorrow and they would use it for virtuous action. And their audiences also do not seem to regard themselves as predestined to rule; they clap as if in defiance, and laugh at their enemies behind their hands, with the shrill laughter of children. *They want to be right, not to do right.* They feel no obligation to be part of the main tide of life, and if that meant any degree of pollution they would prefer to divert themselves from it and form a standing pool of purity. In fact, they want to receive the Eucharist, be beaten by the Turks, and then go to heaven. [My italics.]

Amid these mocking but stern reflections on the attitudinizing and stagnancy of "the left-wing people among whom I had lived all my life," she encounters an Albanian carrying yet another black lamb in his arms, and the threads are drawn together: "The black lamb and the grey falcon had worked together here. In this crime, as in nearly all historic crimes and most personal crimes, they had been accomplices":

> And I had sinned in the same way, I and my kind, the liberals of Western Europe. We had regarded ourselves as far holier than our Tory opponents because we had exchanged the role of priest for the role of lamb, and therefore we forgot that we were not performing the chief moral obligation of humanity, which is to protect the works of love. We have done nothing to save our people, who have some little freedom and therefore some power to make their souls, from the trampling hate of the other peoples who are without the faculty of freedom and desire to root out the soul like a weed. It is possible that we have betrayed life and love for more than five hundred years on a field wider than Kosovo, as wide as Europe.

Thus on this stricken field, far from the England that will so soon be in a death grapple with Hitler, West makes her own form of "atonement" for the "progressive" illusions that have consoled her up until then.

Only two more episodes remain before this theme—of an impending confrontation that cannot and must not be shirked—becomes dominant and then conclusive. She spends some time at a large mine run by one of those Scottish engineers who were the backbone and the vertebrae of British enterprise all over the Empire: one of those gruff and decent and honest men who make us utter expressions like "salt of the earth" (West was herself somewhat proud of her Scots-Irish provenance). Old Mac has brought efficiency and improvement to his remote part of Kosovo and has taught many of the locals to work together despite their linguistic and confessional differences. This is a sort of oasis of modernity and rationality, involving perhaps a slight nostalgia on West's part for the ordered gardens and settled routines of her homeland, before the journey is resumed. It takes her through Montenegro and then back to the coast, and is unusually full of her sprightly observations and aperçus. ("She was one of those widows whose majesty makes their husbands especially dead." . . . "Like all Montenegrin automobiles, it was a debauched piece of ironmongery.") It also features a very sobering moment at a war memorial. This is a black obelisk covered in names, and these turn out not to be the dead of an entire town, as seems probable, but only of one local clan. Moreover, the dates of the war are given as 1912–1921, which at first astonishes West until she remembers that this mountain people had been "continually under arms" for that length of time. That is a splendid microcosmic observation of Montenegrin history and character, and it is matched by a tremendous description of the *Cserna Gora*, or "Black Mountains," which give this lovely and forbidding and unique statelet its imposing name. (Montenegro may have been the setting for Ruritanian-style operettas, but there has been little of courtly polish and affectation in its grim history, unless one counts the old capital of Cetinje, still preserved as if in aspic or amber with the pre-1914 charms that an Anthony Hope or a Franz Lehár might have found diverting.)

The closing passages of the book are defiant rather than fatalistic, sketching in the background of a picture that is steadily darkening. West reflects on the virus of anti-Semitism, shrewdly locating one of its causes in the fact that "many primitive peoples must receive their first intimation of the toxic quality of thought from Jews. They know only the fortifying idea of religion; they see in Jews the effect of the tormenting and disintegrating ideas of skepticism." When her guide and friend Constantine moves from nervous illness to something more like a collapse, she records awkwardly that "I did not know how to say that he was dying of being a Jew in a world where there were certain ideas to which some new star was lending a strange strength," and we feel chilled by the shadow of the encroaching swastika. Creepy old men in monasteries tell her that they look forward to receiving visits from eminent Nazis. Back on the seacoast she and her party notice, as in an Eric Ambler novel, German and Italian agents behaving with increasing confidence and arrogance. Mussolini is about to seize power in Albania, and his fascist proxies, according to Constantine, now "control the whole country; some day they will have their army there too, and it will be as a pistol pointed at Yugoslavia." He shuddered violently and said, "*Ils avancent toujours.*" Before long, his worst anticipations are vindicated, and news is brought of a massacre of Albanian leftists that presages a full-fledged fascist coup. With this, West and her husband make ready to depart. But just before she comes to the end of her time in Yugoslavia, and is again contemplating the eclipse of the Turks while staring out of a window, she is visited by a kind of epiphany:

> I said to myself, "My civilization must not die. It need not die. My national faith is valid, as the Ottoman faith was not. I know that the English are as unhealthy as lepers compared with perfect health.

> They do not give themselves up to feeling or to work as they should, they lack readiness to sacrifice their individual rights for the corporate good, they do not bid the right welcome to the other man's soul. But they are on the side of life, they love justice, they hate violence, and they respect the truth. It is not always so when they deal with India or Burma; but that is not their fault, it is the fault of Empire, which makes a man own things outside his power to control. But among themselves, in dealing with things within their reach, they have learned some part of the Christian lesson that it is our disposition to crucify what is good, and that we must therefore circumvent our barbarity. This measure of wisdom makes it right that my civilization should not perish."

This must count as one of the most halting and apologetic proclamations of patriotism ever uttered, yet it would be foolish to miss the power of its understatement.

Her way home took her through pre-Anschluss Vienna, recently the scene of a Nazi-inspired pogrom against the left and soon to become an enthusiastic place of self-abnegation that would give up even its nationality and throw itself eagerly at Hitler's feet. This was in some sense a homecoming for the Führer: As West points out (and who was it who said that Austria's twin achievement was to have persuaded the world that Hitler was a German and Beethoven a Viennese?), the great dictator was Austrian to the core "and nothing he has brought to postwar Germany had not its existence in pre-war Austria." This could have led her into a discussion of how it is that nationalism and chauvinism are often strongest at their peripheries—Alexander the Macedonian, Bonaparte the Corsican, Stalin the Georgian—but instead it prompted her to reflect on why it was that so many "progressive" types had so little sympathy for the smaller nations that lay in Hitler's path. She concluded that "nationalism" had become a dirty word, much like "imperialism," and that the grand plans of the rational and the logical did not allow for the eccentric and the anomalous. *Black Lamb and Grey Falcon* closes with an impassioned account of the resistance to the Axis on the part of small nations like Albania, Serbia, and Greece—which actually inflicted the first military defeats on fascism—and with the hope that a similar spirit has been evinced by the British when facing the Blitz. It is dedicated "To my friends in Yugoslavia, who are now all dead or enslaved."

* * *

As I mentioned at the opening of this essay, it is impossible today to read Rebecca West's travelogue without retrospection, in the literal sense of reviewing her project through the lens or prism of the terrible events of the early 1990s. A new generation of readers hears the name "Sarajevo" and sees the pitiless Serbian bombardment of an undefended city. The stony face of Milošević in the dock is the symbol of ethnic cleansing—a term made real to us by the official Serbian propaganda that employed the word *ciste* ("clean") for one of the devastated towns along the river Drina. Another term—*Chetnik*, or Serbian "chauvinist"—derives from a Serbian militia of the Second World War, led by General Draža Mihajloviė, who at the time enjoyed Rebecca West's strong support. The expression "Greater Serbia," used by her almost as a positive, has become synonymous with the massacre at Srebrenica. The cultural treasures of Dubrovnik, on the Adriatic Coast, were shelled and looted by Montenegrin irregulars fighting on the Serbian side. (Actually, several of the most wanted war criminals from this period, from Radovan Karadžić to Ratko Mladić to Milošević himself, were Serbs of partly Montenegrin origin—which might lend point to my observation above, about nationalism being most intoxicating at its periphery.) The same, it must be said, held true of the fascists from western Herzegovina who united with some of their Croatian brothers to revive the Ustashe, who shattered and ruined the city of Mostar with its beautiful Ottoman bridge, and who made a cynical pact with Milošević and Karadžić to divide the territory of a defenseless Bosnia. About the Ustashe, West had warned us repeatedly. But she could not have pictured it acting in collusion with Serb irredentism. Milošević and his henchmen did dreadful damage to Croatia and to Bosnia, with their Gerda-like belief, much of it derived from the mythology of 1389, that all Serb populations outside Serbia proper should be united under a common flag and rhetoric. But the greatest harm was arguably inflicted upon the Serbs themselves, who eventually saw their people driven out of ancestral territory in the ancient Krajina region (more or less unmentioned by West) and in Kosovo itself. More poignant still, Serbia lost its national honor and became an international pariah, trading arms with Saddam Hussein and relying on Mafia-type militias to do its dirty work. The body of Ivan Stambolić, Milošević's "disappeared" predecessor in office, was discovered in a shallow grave just as Milošević's trial for war crimes was getting under way in The Hague. The glory had departed: Serbia stood before the world as a blood-spattered, bankrupt, quasi-fascist banana republic. By the end, even the loyal Montenegrins voted to quit the rump "federation" that was all that remained of the Yugoslav idea.

Arguments against Western intervention to end the war were often derived from an image of Serbian bravery and intransigence that drew upon West's celebrated work, while very little in *Black Lamb and Grey Falcon* would have prepared the modern reader for the emergence of a secular Bosnian nationalism or for the long struggle of the Kosovar majority population against Serbian rule. I wrote to some of my more internationalist and liberal friends in the region, asking for their opinion of West and her book, and received answers like the following, from a Croatian academic who had strongly opposed the reactionary regime of Franjo Tudjman in his own country:

> A good example is the chapter on Dubrovnik. She hated Whiggish England and "saw" her mum and dad in Dubrovnik. Hence, no sympathy for ol' Ragusa. All of this seasoned with suspect history. Pure caricature. Or, the reductionist connection of Croatia with Germany, as opposed to the Serb noble savagery, that is pro-Allied and free of awful Teutonic formalism. Or the title: the noncomprehending idiot look of the Muslim who sacrifices a lamb at the Sheep's Field vs the falcon of the Kosovo myth—Lazar's choice, which is her choice.

Or this, from a Slovenian dissident:

> Concerning the "Black Lamb" book: all of us "Slavs" are used to the double-bind situation: if you are too Westernized you are a fake: if not then you are a brute, primitive, etc. Rebecca West seems to avoid it by seeing Slavs as something special and admirable, if they remain true to themselves. So there again is the catch: somehow we keep falling out of our real selves. She has done her homework and mostly well enough. Still, almost no introspection, not much reflection on the nature of her own impact though a strong conviction of being at least a privileged observer.

Interestingly, in view of the fact that both these correspondents had themselves had somewhat "Red" pasts, neither mentions the most obvious lacuna in West's book, which is her complete failure to anticipate the rise of Yugoslav communism during the Second World War. Whenever she mentions communist activity in the country—which is extremely seldom for a book of such length—it is in order to say things like this:

> An English friend of mine once came on a tragic party of young men being sent down from a Bosnian manufacturing town to Sarajevo by a night train. All were in irons. The gendarmes told him that they were Communists. I expect that they were nothing of the sort. Real Marxian Communism is rare in Yugoslavia, for it is not attractive to a nation of peasant proprietors and the Comintern wastes little time and energy in this field.

While she was writing these words, a tough Croatian-Slovenian operator named Josip Broz Tito was rising through the apparat of the Comintern and was to go on to create a Red "partisan" army whose legend has still not quite died. Perhaps the reason for West's endorsement of the Serb Chetniks in the ensuing Second World War was connected to her feeling that chieftains and brigands are somehow more representative of local traditions.

If the book fails certain tests as a history, and even as a travelogue, and if it has little predictive value and if (as Janet Montefiore has also pointed out) it shows some "unreliable narrator" characteristics as between West's own private diary entries and the way in which the same events are set down on the page, then why does it, or why should it, remain a classic? I would tentatively offer three reasons, related to those that I gave at the outset. First, it shows the workings of a powerful and energetic mind, a mind both honed and dulled by anxieties that have only recently become intelligible to us. Second, it makes a sincere and admirable effort—often aspired to but seldom surpassed by later travel writers—to capture the texture and sinew of another civilization. (I find myself generally unmoved by religious architecture and devotional decoration, but I have made a visit to the church at Grachanitsa and found myself engrossed almost to the point of enchantment in her description of it almost six decades before. Writing on this level must be esteemed and shown to later generations, no matter what the subject.)

Finally, I believe that West was one of those people, necessary in every epoch, who understand that there are things worth fighting for, and dying for, and killing for. As a modern woman she at first felt a need almost to apologize for this old-fashioned understanding, but then she shook herself awake and especially in her ice-cold but white-hot epilogue decided to defend it and advance it instead. If you like, she knew that the facing of death could be life affirming, and also that certain kinds of life are a version of death. Has anyone ever described the spirit of Munich, and its sudden evaporation, as finely or as tersely as this?

> The instrument of our suicidal impetus, Neville Chamberlain, who had seemed as firmly entrenched in our Government as sugar in the kidneys of a diabetic patient, was gone.

Or this?

> It was good to take up one's courage again, which had been laid aside so long, and to feel how comfortably it fitted into the hand.

In any time of sniggering relativism and overbred despair, such as we have known and may know again, it is good to know that some enduring virtues can be affirmed, even if the wrong people sometimes take the right line, and even if people of education and refinement are often a little reluctant to trust their guts. Rebecca West was not at all too ladylike to emphasize the viscera and was often agreeably surprised when her stomach and her heart were (like those of her heroine Queen Elizabeth I) in agreement with her intellect. These are the elements from which greatness comes—and might even come again.

Ezra Pound: A Revolutionary Simpleton

THE IMPOSING FIRST VOLUME of A. David Moody's biography of Ezra Pound, which takes us up to the publication of "Hugh Selwyn Mauberley" and the writing of the early *Cantos*, deserves to stand in its own right as a study of Pound's germinal years. But no sooner has one written the word *germinal* than one begins to experience the desire to peep ahead at the ending or, rather, to look in the beginnings for symptoms of the terminus. I found myself doing this even with the very impressive photographs that Moody has collected. In most of them, Pound looks like a highly well-made young man, with an ironic and quizzical expression. He's especially dashing in an extraordinary group shot taken in January 1914, where he stands in a cluster of talent (which includes W. B. Yeats and Richard Aldington) around the patriarchal figure of Wilfred Scawen Blunt. There's no apparent sign of the obsessive crank of the declining years, barking obscenities and gibberish over Mussolini's radio. Yet on the cover of the book, and reproduced inside, is a 1910 study from Paris, in which Pound confronts the camera with a hunched, autistic, haunted look, with a tinge of van Gogh to it.

Pound's early life story is in some respects not unlike that of T. S. Eliot,

---

Review of *Ezra Pound: Poet, Vol. I, 1885–1920*, by A. David Moody.

the man who in his dedication to *The Waste Land* called Pound "*il miglior fabbro*" (which can mean either "the better writer" or "the better craftsman"). They shared the same desire to escape from provincial gentility in America to Europe and perhaps especially to England, the same struggle to convince parents and family that the effort was one worth endorsing and financing, the same quixotic belief that poetry could be made to yield a living and that poets were a special class, and the same register of annihilating shock when in the summer of 1914 the roof of the over-admired European civilization simply fell in.

It is always impressive to read of the sheer dedication and conviction with which Pound approached poetry, and of the immense hopes he entertained for its regenerative powers. In a single season between 1912 and 1913 in London, we find him taking up the Bengali master Rabindranath Tagore and advising the Irish genius Yeats. Moody writes:

> The measures, melodies and modulations of the songs in their original Bengali, which he had Tagore sing and explain to him, interested him as a seeker after "fundamental laws in word music," and seemed to correspond to the sort of metric he was working for in English. He went on to wax enthusiastic about the prospect of Bengali culture providing "the balance and corrective" to a Western humanism which had lost touch with "the whole and the flowing." "We have found our new Greece," he declared. "In the midst of our clangour of mechanisms."

But within a short time he had tired of all this wholeness and flowing, and suspected Tagore of being just another "theosophist," and was sitting up late with Yeats to help revise "The Two Kings" line by line. Yeats was urged to purge his verses of their "Miltonic generalizations," and he told Lady Gregory that Pound helped him

> to get back to the definite and the concrete away from modern abstractions. To talk over a poem with him is like getting yon to put a sentence into dialect. All becomes clear and natural.

It must be reckoned immensely to Pound's credit that he so early detected the vitality and importance of Eliot and of Yeats, going so far as to write that the latter "is the only living man whose work has more than a most temporary interest. I shall survive as a curiosity." That second observation has a curious prescience to it; meanwhile, one might note that he wasn't always such a sufferer from false modesty. It was at the same time that he composed his "Ballad of the Goodly Fere," telling his father that it was "probably about the strongest thing in English since 'Reading Gaol.'" In its evocation of the crucifixion (a little bizarre in view of Pound's general contempt for Christianity) the "Ballad of the Goodly Fere" is a strangely affecting and beautiful piece of work, but it doesn't place him in the same class as Wilde. It's incidentally interesting for being written in dialect and for hitting an early and clearer note of Pound's later dark obsession with usury:

> I ha' seen him drive a hundred men
> Wi' a bundle o' cords swung free
> That they took the high and holy house
> For their pawn and treasury.

Pound's mood swings, between feelings of unworthiness and grandeur, may nonetheless supply a clue. Just as he would ricochet from new enthusiasm to new influence—at different times Rudyard Kipling, James McNeill Whistler (on whose signature he modeled his own), Ernest Dowson, and Wilfred Owen—so his sail was rigged in such a way as to be swollen by any febrile gust of enthusiasm. Under the influence of T. E. Hulme and Wyndham Lewis, he made what was certainly the most extreme contribution to the inaugural issue of Lewis's Vorticist magazine, *BLAST*, published on the unintentionally momentous day of June 20, 1914, one week before the archduke's murder in Sarajevo. The same issue contained a story by Rebecca West and the first chapter of Ford Madox Ford's *The Good Soldier*, while Pound emitted a statement titled "THE TURBINE":

> The vortex is the point of maximum energy. All experience rushes into this vortex. All the energized past, all the past that is living and worthy to live. All MOMENTUM, which is the past bearing upon

> us, RACE, RACE-MEMORY, instinct charging the PLACID, NON-ENERGIZED FUTURE. The DESIGN of the future in the grip of the human vortex. All the past that is vital, all the past that is capable of living into the future, is pregnant in the vortex, NOW.

Again, one can surely be forgiven for seeing a harbinger here, and not only of eventual mental unhingement. In fact, though strictly speaking it lies outside the scope of Moody's book, let me quote from what Wyndham Lewis was later to write about experiencing the energy-loving and race-memory-oriented fascism that he had at first welcomed so warmly:

> The senseless bellicosity of the reactionary groups of the *Action Française* type may certainly result in far more violence, before long, than anyone is able to measure.

On another occasion he wrote, "Fascists have the word 'action' on their lips from morning to night." In the same book—*Time and Western Man*—he described his former *BLAST* colleague Ezra Pound as a "revolutionary simpleton." That could perhaps furnish a title for Moody's second volume.

Lewis of course turned against fascism, if only because he decided that it was ultimately just as mob-centered as democracy. Pound's contempt for democracy was of a more determinedly elevated and "artistic" type. It's rather charming to find him turning up at the United States Embassy in London in 1918, opposing the possible drafting of T. S. Eliot into the Army on the grounds that

> if it was a war for civilization (not merely for democracy) it was folly to shoot, or have shot one of the six or seven Americans capable of contributing to civilization or understanding the word.

In a letter home to his father, discussing his own prospects as a conscript, Pound stated more tersely: "It is not however the habit of democracies to use my sort of intelligence." It's difficult to gauge how much this rather airy solipsism had to do with a version of survivor guilt, or an awareness that friends like Ford and Lewis either had endured the test of wartime experience or (like Henri Gaudier-Brzeska, creator of the brilliant statue of Pound that its subject happily considered "phallic") had not survived it.

And this must bring us to the writing of "Hugh Selwyn Mauberley," which was his farewell to England and his envoy, also, to both "democracy" *and* "civilization." I have never especially admired the *bitch/botch* echo in the poem, which speaks of the huge wartime sacrifice in which Pound himself played no part and then describes it as having been made for "an old bitch gone in the teeth / for a botched civilization." The whole thing reeks of trying too hard, and it anticipates the fanatical drone of "Canto XIV" in which Londoners are described as living in a place full of "financiers / lashing them with steel wires" and:

> The slough of unamiable liars,
> bog of stupidities,
> malevolent stupidities, and stupidities,
> the soil living pus, full of vermin,
> dead maggots begetting live maggots,
> slum owners,
> usurers squeezing crab-lice...

Sometimes credited with presaging or echoing *The Waste Land*, this stuff actually bodies forth and even exceeds the lowest of Eliot, and there can be small doubt, even on a brisk review of the lines, of the sordid direction in which things are tending.

Toward the close of this dense and clever and generally sympathetic study, Moody does cite an essay by Pound on "The Tribe of Judah" and "the pawnshop" where, as he deftly points out, there is a telltale confusion between Judaism and "the Jew." This distinction would eventually become completely lost on Pound, whose eccentric article was written for A. R. Orage's *New Age*, in the offices of which (and what a life he lived for the small and obscure magazine) Pound was to meet Major C. H. Douglas, the crackpot Green-Shirt founder of the Social Credit movement. In Douglas's program, Pound had found his true muse: a blend of folkloric Celtic twilight with a paranoid hatred of the money economy and a dire suspicion about an ancient faith.

Moody supplies two very telling examples. In April 1917, Pound had written to his friend John Quinn, urging him to impress on Theodore Roosevelt, of all people, the need for "some system of *direct supply*... straight from the factory to the particular section of the front where stuff is wanted." But this amateur-planner megalomania was only a foretaste of the pathos to come. In 1921, just before his departure from England, Pound managed to corner Arthur Griffith, easily the most reactionary and ethereal of the Irish leaders, during the tortured negotiations for his nation's independence. He ranted at Griffith in an attempt to convince him to adopt Social Credit so as to use the infant Irish republic as its laboratory. According to Pound, Griffith eventually responded: "All you say is true. But I can't move 'em with a cold thing like economics."

Moody does not mention it, but this very phrase later recurs as a line in "Canto XIX," by which time Pound's poetry had become little more than a doctrinaire and propagandistic screed: a mechanical attempt to make poetry do what economics could not. That such an outcome was a tragedy no reader of this biography can doubt. If one seeks or desires to explain the tragedy, one might say that Shelley wanted poets to be "the unacknowledged legislators" of the world, while Pound sought hectically for acknowledgment, not just for poetry but for himself, and lost the sense of both in the process.

(*The Atlantic*, April 2008)

On *Animal Farm*

For all I know, by the time this book [Animal Farm] is published my view of the Soviet régime may be the generally-accepted one. But what use would that be in itself? To exchange one orthodoxy for another is not necessarily an advance.
—George Orwell, "The Freedom of the Press"

ANIMAL FARM, as its author later wrote, "was the first book in which I tried, with full consciousness of what I was doing, to fuse political purpose and artistic purpose into one whole." And indeed, its pages contain a synthesis of many of the themes that we have come to think of as "Orwellian." Among these are a hatred of tyranny, a love for animals and the English countryside, and a deep admiration for the satirical fables of Jonathan Swift. To this one might add Orwell's keen desire to see things from the viewpoint of childhood and innocence: He had long wished for fatherhood and, fearing that he was sterile, had adopted a small boy not long before the death of his first wife. The partly ironic subtitle of the novel is *A Fairy Story*, and Orwell was especially pleased when he heard from friends such as Malcolm Muggeridge and Sir Herbert Read that their own offspring had enjoyed reading the book.

Like much of his later work—most conspicuously the much grimmer

Introduction (2010) to *Animal Farm*, by George Orwell.

Nineteen Eighty-four—*Animal Farm* was the product of Orwell's engagement in the Spanish Civil War. During the course of that conflict, in which he had fought on the anti-Fascist side and been wounded and then chased out of Spain by supporters of Joseph Stalin, his experiences had persuaded him that the majority of "Left" opinion was wrong, and that the Soviet Union was a new form of hell and not an emerging utopia. He described the genesis of the idea in one of his two introductions to *Animal Farm*:

> [F]or the past ten years I have been convinced that the destruction of the Soviet myth was essential if we wanted a revival of the Socialist movement.
>
> On my return from Spain I thought of exposing the Soviet myth in a story that could be easily understood by almost anyone and which could be easily translated into other languages. However, the actual details of the story did not come to me for some time until one day (I was then living in a small village) I saw a little boy, perhaps ten years old, driving a huge cart-horse along a narrow path, whipping it whenever it tried to turn. It struck me that if only such animals became aware of their strength we should have no power over them, and that men exploit animals in much the same way as the rich exploit the proletariat.
>
> I proceeded to analyse Marx's theory from the animals' point of view.*

The apparently beautiful simplicity of this notion is in many ways deceptive. By undertaking such a task, Orwell was choosing to involve himself in an extremely complex and bitter argument about the Bolshevik Revolution in Russia: then a far more controversial issue than it is today. *Animal Farm* can be better understood if it is approached under three different headings:

---

*Orwell once wrote that all his happiest memories of boyhood were somehow connected to animals, yet his favorite word of disapproval for human behavior was "beastly." He made his name with an almost self-hating essay about shooting an elephant. As an amateur farmer he came to detest pigs. In *Nineteen Eighty-four* the most horrifying moment involves the use of rats as instruments of torture. Yet he also loved the Thames Valley and was plainly influenced by *The Wind in the Willows*. One wants to read, or perhaps write, an essay on this subtext and its implications.

its historical context, the struggle over its publication and its subsequent adoption as an important cultural weapon in the Cold War, and its enduring relevance today.

Historical Background

The book was written at the height of the Second World War, and at a time when the pact between Stalin and Hitler had been replaced abruptly by an alliance between Stalin and the British Empire. London was under Nazi bombardment, and the original manuscript of the novel had to be rescued from the wreckage of Orwell's blitzed home in North London.

The cynical way in which Stalin had switched sides had come as no surprise to Orwell, who was by then accustomed to the dishonesty and cruelty of the Soviet regime. This put him in a fairly small minority, both within official Britain and among the British Left. A considerable number of "progressive" persons still believed that Communist collectivization of Russian agriculture had benefited the peasants, and maintained that Stalin's judicial murder of his former political comrades had constituted a fair trial. Orwell had not visited the USSR but he had seen the Spanish version of Stalinism at close quarters and broadly took the side of the Left Opposition or Trotskyist forces, whose perspective is expounded by a four-legged character in this book. With a few slight alterations to the sequence of events, the action approximates to the fate of the 1917 generation in Russia. Thus the grand revolutionary scheme of the veteran boar Old Major (Karl Marx) is at first enthusiastically adopted by almost all creatures, leading to the overthrow of Farmer Jones (the Tsar), the defeat of the other farmers who come to his aid (the now-forgotten Western invasions of Russia in 1918–19), and the setting up of a new model state. In a short time, the more ruthless and intelligent creatures—naturally enough the pigs—have the other animals under their dictatorship and are living like aristocrats. Inevitably, the pigs argue among themselves. The social forces represented by different animals are easily recognizable—Boxer the noble horse as the embodiment of the working class, Moses the raven as the Russian Orthodox Church—as are the identifiable individuals played by different pigs. The rivalry between Napoleon (Stalin) and Snowball (Trotsky) ends with Snowball's exile and the subsequent attempt to erase him from the memory of the farm. Stalin had the exiled Trotsky murdered in Mexico less than three years before Orwell began work on the book.

Some of the smaller details are meticulously exact. Due to the exigencies of the war, Stalin had made various opportunistic compromises. He had recruited the Russian Orthodox Church to his side, the better to cloak himself in patriotic garb, and he was to abolish the old Socialist anthem "The Internationale" for being too provocative to his new capitalist allies in London and Washington. In *Animal Farm*, Moses the raven is allowed to come croaking back as the crisis deepens, and the poor exploited goats and horses and hens are told that their beloved song "Beasts of England" is no longer to be sung. Orwell's rendition of those yearning and touching verses was one of the many ways in which he managed to keep the essentially tragic narration relatively light. This is also one of the very few of his works to contain any jokes: After the revolution the animals discover some hams hanging in Jones's kitchen and take them outside for decent burial; the first time they take a vote on the rights of non-domestic animals the farm's cat is found to have voted on both sides.

There is, however, one very salient omission. There is a Stalin pig and a Trotsky pig, but no Lenin pig. Similarly, in *Nineteen Eighty-four* we find only a Big Brother Stalin and an Emmanuel Goldstein Trotsky. Nobody appears to have pointed this out at the time (and if I may say so, nobody but myself has done so since; it took me years to notice what was staring me in the face). In the 1930s and the 1940s, and indeed for some decades afterward, there was a very hot dispute about whether or not Stalin's terror was a direct consequence of Lenin's revolution, and also speculation concerning the likelihood or otherwise that Trotsky would have been better than Stalin. Orwell had broadly Trotskyist sympathies but did not necessarily believe that any one form of Russified Communism would have been superior to another. Uncharacteristically for him, then, and possibly for the sake of simplicity, he seems to have decided to let this evident contradiction remain unaddressed.* This didn't save him from the censure of those who could see the dangerously

*In "The Freedom of the Press" he does make an approving reference to Rosa Luxemburg, the martyred Jewish German-Polish revolutionary, murdered in 1919 by the German right-wing, who was on the extreme Left but who had prophetically warned Lenin of the danger of making a habit of "emergency measures."

subversive possibilities that were latent in his apparently innocuous version of the pastoral.

The Story of Publication

It is sobering to consider how close this novel came to remaining unpublished. Having survived Hitler's bombing, the rather battered manuscript was sent to the office of T. S. Eliot, then an important editor at the leading firm of Faber & Faber. Eliot, a friendly acquaintance of Orwell's, was a political and cultural conservative, not to say reactionary. But, perhaps influenced by Britain's alliance with Moscow, he rejected the book on the grounds that it seemed too "Trotskyite." He also told Orwell that his choice of pigs as rulers was an unfortunate one, and that readers might draw the conclusion that what was needed was "more public-spirited pigs." This was not perhaps as fatuous as the turn-down that Orwell received from The Dial Press in New York, which solemnly informed him that stories about animals found no market in the United States. And this in the land of Disney...

The wartime solidarity between British Tories and Soviet Communists found another counterpart in the work of Peter Smollett, a senior official in the Ministry of Information who was later exposed as a Soviet agent. Smollett made it his business to warn off certain publishers, as a consequence of which *Animal Farm* was further denied a home at the reputable firms of Victor Gollancz and Jonathan Cape. For a time Orwell considered producing the book privately with the help of his radical Canadian poet friend, Paul Potts, in what would have been a pioneering instance of anti-Soviet samizdat or self-publishing. He even wrote an angry essay, titled "The Freedom of the Press," to be included as an introduction: an essay which was not even unearthed and printed until 1972. Eventually the honor of the publishing business was saved by the small company Secker & Warburg, which in 1945 brought out an edition with a very limited print-run and paid Orwell forty-five pounds for it.

It is thinkable that the story could have ended in this damp-squib way, but two later developments were to give the novel its place in history. A group of Ukrainian and Polish socialists, living in refugee camps in post-war Europe, discovered a copy of the book in English and found it to be a near-perfect allegory of their own recent experience. Their self-taught English-speaking leader and translator, Ihor Ševčenko, found an address for Orwell and wrote to him asking permission to translate *Animal Farm* into Ukrainian. He told him that many of Stalin's victims nonetheless still considered themselves to be socialists, and did not trust an intellectual of the Right to voice their feelings. "They were profoundly affected by such scenes as that of animals singing 'Beasts of England' on the hill... They very vividly reacted to the 'absolute' values of the book." Orwell agreed to grant publication rights for free (he did this for subsequent editions in several other Eastern European languages) and to contribute the preface from which I quoted earlier. It is affecting to imagine battle-hardened ex-soldiers and prisoners of war, having survived all the privations of the Eastern Front, becoming stirred by the image of British farm animals singing their own version of the discarded "Internationale," but this was an early instance of the hold the book was to take on its readership. The emotions of the American military authorities in Europe were not so easily touched: They rounded up all the copies of *Animal Farm* that they could find and turned them over to the Red Army to be burned. The alliance between the farmers and the pigs, so hauntingly described in the final pages of the novel, was still in force.

But in the part-acrimonious closing scene, usually best-remembered for the way in which men and pigs have become indistinguishable, Orwell predicted, as on other occasions, that the ostensible friendship between East and West would not long outlast the defeat of Nazism. The Cold War, a phrase that Orwell himself was the first to use in print,* soon created a very different ideological atmosphere. This in turn conditioned the reception of *Animal Farm* in the United States. At first rejected at Random House by the Communist sympathizer Angus Cameron (who had been sent the book by Arthur Schlesinger Jr.) and then by a succession of lesser publishers, it was rescued from oblivion by Frank Morley of Harcourt, Brace, who while visiting England had been impressed by a chance encounter with the novel in a bookshop in Cambridge. Publication was attended by two strokes of good fortune: Edmund Wilson wrote a highly favorable review for the *New Yorker*

*In an especially acute feuilleton entitled "You and the Atomic Bomb" in *Tribune* in October 1945.

comparing Orwell's satirical talent to the work of Swift and Voltaire, and the Book-of-the-Month Club made it a main selection, which led to a printing of almost half a million copies. The stupidity of The Dial Press notwithstanding, the Walt Disney company came up with a proposal for a film version. This was never made, though the CIA did later produce and distribute an *Animal Farm* cartoon for propaganda purposes. By the time Orwell died in January 1950, having just succeeded in finishing *Nineteen Eighty-four*, he had at last achieved an international reputation and was having to issue repeated disclaimers of the use made of his work by the American right-wing.

The Afterlife of Animal Farm

Probably the best-known sentence from the novel is the negation by the pigs of the original slogan that "All Animals Are Equal" by the addition of the afterthought that "Some Animals Are More Equal Than Others." As communism in Russia and Eastern Europe took on more and more of the appearance of a "New Class" system, with grotesque privileges for the ruling elite and a grinding mediocrity of existence for the majority, the moral effect of Orwell's work—so simple to understand and to translate, precisely as he had hoped—became one of the many unquantifiable forces that eroded communism both as a system and as an ideology. Gradually, the same effect spread to Asia. I well remember a Communist friend of mine telephoning me from China when Deng Xiaoping announced the "reforms" that were ultimately to inaugurate what we now know as Chinese capitalism. "The peasants must get rich," the leader of The Party announced, "and some will get richer than others." My comrade was calling to say, with reluctance but with some generosity, that perhaps Orwell had had a point after all.

In Burma, one of the longest-lasting totalitarian systems in the world—an amalgam of military fascism, Buddhist dogma, and Communist-style rhetoric about collectivization—George Packer of the *New Yorker* not long ago heard a saying that had become popular among democratically minded Burmese. "We revere George Orwell very much," they told him, "because he wrote three books about our country: *Burmese Days, Animal Farm*, and *Nineteen Eighty-four*." Thus far, *Animal Farm* has not been legally published in China, Burma, or the moral wilderness of North Korea, but one day will see its appearance in all three societies, where it is sure to be greeted with the shock of recognition that it is still capable of inspiring.

In Zimbabwe, as the rule of Robert Mugabe's kleptocratic clique became ever more exorbitant, an opposition newspaper took the opportunity to reprint *Animal Farm* in serial form. It did so without comment, except that one of the accompanying illustrations showed Napoleon the dictator wearing the trademark black horn-rimmed spectacles of Zimbabwe's own "Dear Leader." The offices of the newspaper were soon afterward blown up by a weapons-grade bomb, but before too long Zimbabwean children, also, will be able to appreciate the book in its own right.

In the Islamic world, many countries continue to ban *Animal Farm*, ostensibly because of its emphasis on pigs. Clearly this cannot be the whole reason—if only because the porcine faction is rendered in such an unfavorable light—and under the theocratic despotism of Iran it is obviously forbidden for reasons having to do with its message of "revolution betrayed." I was recently approached by a group of Iranian exiles who are hoping to produce a pirate edition, and so one can hope for an Orwell revival in these latitudes as well.

Almost as an afterthought I will venture to predict a quite different renaissance for *Animal Farm*. Recent advances in the study of our genome have shown how much we possess in common with other primates and mammals, and perhaps especially with pigs (from whom we can receive skin and even organ transplants). In Orwell's own time the idea of "animal rights" let alone "animal liberation" would have seemed silly or fanciful, but these now form part of our ever-expanding concept of rights, and bring much thought-provoking scientific discovery to bear. We too are "animals," whose claim to the "dominion" awarded us in the Book of Genesis looks increasingly dubious. In that grand discussion, this little book will probably earn itself an allegorical niche.

All the examples I have given are specific to time and place but I believe that there is a timeless, even transcendent, quality to this little story. It is caught when Old Major tells his quiet, sad audience of over-worked beasts about a time from long ago, when creatures knew of the possibility of a world without masters, and when he recalls in a dream the words and the tune of a half-forgotten freedom-song. Orwell had a liking for the tradition of the

English Protestant revolution, and his favorite line of justification was taken from John Milton, who made his stand "by the known rules of ancient liberty."* In all minds, perhaps especially in those of children, there is a feeling that life need not always be this way, and those malnourished Ukrainian survivors, responding to the authenticity of the verses and to something "absolute" in the integrity of the book, were hearing the mighty line of Milton whether they fully understood it or not.

*This is from his Sonnet XII, in which he defends himself from various traducers. It attacks them as "owls and cuckoos, asses, apes and dogs." One wonders if Orwell was fully aware of the animal element here.

Jessica Mitford's Poison Pen

IT IS SAID THAT, just before the Sino-Soviet split, Nikita Khrushchev had a tense meeting with Zhou Enlai at which he told the latter that he now understood the problem. "I am the son of coal miners," he said. "You are the descendant of feudal mandarins. We have nothing in common." "Perhaps we do," murmured his Chinese antagonist. "What?" blustered Khrushchev. "We are," responded Zhou, "both traitors to our class."

For a true appreciation of the character and style of Jessica Mitford, it is necessary to picture Lady Bracknell not only abandoning the practice of arranging marriages for money but also aligning herself with the proletariat, while still managing to remain a character in a Wilde play. The carrying cut-glass voice; the raised eyebrow of disdain that could (like that of P. G. Wodehouse's forbidding Roderick Spode) "open an oyster at sixty paces"; the stoicism born of stern ancestral discipline yet, withal, a lethal sense of the "ridic," as Ms. Mitford was fond of putting it. Here she is, writing to her sister the Duchess of Devonshire in 1965, about a suitable present for her niece:

> People are always asking me to join committees against the wicked toys they've got here (like model H-bombs, etc) but I can't bear to join because I know I should have rather longed for a model H-bomb if they had been about when we were little. Anyway, the wickedest toy of all, and the one that has been written up and condemned

---

Review of *Decca: The Letters of Jessica Mitford*, edited by Peter Y. Sussman.

> bitterly all over the U.S., is a *real* guillotine (real model of, anyway) and a toy person with toy head that comes off when the knife drops, and a colouring set with red for blood etc. So be expecting it, but don't tell Sophy for fear that the campaign has been successful and they've stopped selling them...

Little Sophy was then about eight, but neither this consideration nor the solidity of the duchess's social position would have inhibited "Decca"—all the sisters stuck for life to their English-country-house girlhood nicknames—from proposing the perfect anti-aristo gift for all seasons.

Her many devotees will, I hope, excuse a précis here: Jessica Mitford was one of a clutch of children born to the uncontrollably eccentric Lord and Lady Redesdale and raised in an isolated mansion where neither formal education nor contact with outsiders was permitted. Only one of the sisters, Deborah, fulfilled parental expectation by marrying a duke. Of the remainder, Unity and Diana betrayed their country, if not their class, by falling in love with Adolf Hitler in the first instance and Sir Oswald Mosley—founder of the British Blackshirt movement (and the nonfiction model for Roderick Spode)—in the second. Another sister, Nancy, became a celebrated novelist and brittle social observer.

In bold contrast, so to say, Jessica eloped with a Communist nephew of Winston Churchill's named Esmond Romilly, fled to Spain to support the Republican cause, and immigrated to the United States as the Second World War was approaching. The couple had lost one child to illness, had a second one just after Romilly enlisted in the Canadian air force and returned to Europe to fight, and lost another to miscarriage just before his plane went down over the North Sea. Jessica's next child—by her second husband, Robert Treuhaft, a prominent "Red" labor lawyer in the Bay Area—was killed in a traffic accident. Her last-born child developed severe bipolar disorder. These themes—of kinship and class, flight from same, residual loyalties to same, commitment to revolution, and stiff-upper-lippery in the face of calamity—recur throughout this assemblage of Jessica's correspondence.

The best encapsulating anecdote might be this one: When Winston Churchill made his first wartime visit to Washington, D.C., only a few weeks after Pearl Harbor, he was charged by his own daughters to invite his nephew's widow to the White House. He had to tell Jessica that Romilly's plane had not been found. She, in turn, told him that he was grossly in error to have given her sister Diana Mosley, along with Diana's Fascist husband, special treatment in the prison in which they were interned. ("No!" she once told me emphatically when I asked if she had ever been in touch with Diana again. "Apart from darling Nancy's funeral, it's been absolute *nonspeakers* ever since Munich." Her second marriage, to a Communist Jew, was also emphatic, in its own way.)

Waugh-type debutante argot stayed in her speech and prose for life; it isn't difficult to master the combination of overstatement and understatement of which it consists. Anything faintly nice is "bliss"; anything vaguely clever is "brill." Anything below par is "ghastly." Work in progress is "dread" used adjectivally, as in "the dread manuscript." The absolutely worst thing to be is "boring," or "a bore." There are deliberate lapses into "common" speech, such as "me" for "my." This upper-crust style could be used to telling effect. Jessica was confronted once with a racist southern educator who, skeptical of what she told him about desegregation in Oakland schools, said, "It don't seem possible, do it?" Jessica responded icily, "To me it do," and left him shriveled like a salted snail.

She shot to fame—finally impressing her sister Nancy, in whose shadow she had always felt herself to be—with her hilarious-but-serious exposé of the funeral industry, *The American Way of Death*. Almost perfect as a subject for her macabre humor, the book was in fact a by-product of her husband's work for labor unions, whose members' "death benefit" was being eaten up by unscrupulous morticians. It was followed by equally satirical mini-masterpieces, notably the demolition of the "Famous Writers" racket, in which supposed men of letters like Bennett Cerf put their names to a rip-off writing-school scheme, and by "Checks and Balances at the Sign of the Dove," certainly the finest revenge ever taken by a customer on a pretentious restaurant. In the letters currently under review, one can follow Jessica's talent for vendetta as it evolves, and see her extraordinary tenacity and persistence. Woe to the petty official or scam artist who crossed Ms. Mitford. Writing from an absurd beauty-restoration resort in Arizona whose false promises she was exposing, she tells her husband, "Then lunch, by far the most interesting part of the day so far. We repaired to a patio for it (by the way, paper napkins which I did think squalid)." *Noblesse*, yes. *Oblige*, no.

* * *

Because of Jessica's extraordinary manner, many people deceived themselves into thinking that she regarded everything as a huge joke. Not so. Her natural tough-mindedness was schooled and tempered by a fierce devotion to the Communist Party, and in particular to its work for civil rights and civil liberty. She was bouncing through Dixie in an old car long before the Freedom Riders, and when she took up a case it got taken up properly. She even persuaded William Faulkner to sign a petition against the execution of a wrongfully condemned black man.

Pursuing another case of injustice, in Arkansas in the early 1980s, she remembered that a young Hillary Rodham had once been an intern in her husband's law firm, and so she tracked Hillary all the way to Little Rock and the governor's mansion. These particular letters make for interesting reading: In the intervening years Mrs. Clinton had evidently become a bit more of a "realist." Jessica Mitford, in contrast, was one of those who get more radical as they get older. Her lampoon of the ghastliness of party-line jargon—a clever parody of Stephen Potter titled *Life Itselfmanship*—is the forerunner of all mockeries of "politically correct" sloganeering. But when she abandoned the Communist Party she made it absolutely clear that it was because it had become too conservative for her taste.

Her seriousness on this point is illustrated by another magnificent example of upper-class insouciance, when she writes to her friend Virginia Durr, a lifelong correspondent and doyenne of the early civil-rights movement:

> I'm afraid I was a rather rotten mother to [the children], as I was totally preoccupied with CP politics when they were growing up; so while I was v.fond of them, I didn't pay too much attention to them when they were little.

The "v.fond" is nicely phrased. No doubt her own loveless childhood had something to do with it.

To her sister the duchess, she offhandedly writes to see if her own wayward son, Benjamin, has by any chance turned up at the former's mansion, adding, "Don't let him into the house if he's too filthy, he can easily sleep in the car." To the lad himself, she writes very sternly some years later, informing him that his bipolar disorder has become a bore and that he'd better buck up and pull himself together; the letter closes with an offer of maternal help "if you should ever tire of the manic condition." (It must say something that Benjamin allowed this letter to be published; and indeed, in my memory his mother was fiercely devoted to him, in that, shall I say, *understated* way that she had.)

Alarmingly severe as her tone may appear, it makes for a bracing contrast to the therapeutic self-loving culture by which she was surrounded in northern California and for which—like anything else that was bourgeois—she could find no time.

She was great chums with many great hostesses—most notably Katharine Graham, with whom she formed a wartime friendship that lasted for life—and might have been a considerable one herself if she could have been bothered. One excellent letter advises against the huge mistake she once made of inviting to dinner two grandes dames (Edna O'Brien and Lillian Hellman) on the same evening. Her gift for comradeship illustrates the old Hugh Kingsmill maxim that friends are God's apology for relations. But she was always willing to quarrel on a point of principle, nearly coming to a breach with her beloved Maya Angelou, for example, when the latter stuck up for the Supreme Court nomination of Clarence Thomas.

Covering the trial of Dr. Spock in Boston at the height of the anti-war movement in May 1968, she writes to a friend about her shortcomings as a court reporter and adds, "I even missed the riot yesterday, which was so sloppy of me." But on the whole she was on time for the riot, and well turned out for it to boot. The cult of the Mitfords, which now features a shelf of books and several TV documentaries, threatens in itself to become a bore on an almost Bloomsbury scale.

But her mad father, when making dispositions of his property, wrote in his will the words "except Jessica." And the bookstore at the Devonshire stately home in Chatsworth displays works by and about every Mitford sister but her. These paltry aristocratic gestures confirm, as do these letters, that it was Decca, exiled and intransigent, who was the exceptional one.

(*The Atlantic*, October 2006)

W. Somerset Maugham: Poor Old Willie

HERE IS THE OPENING SENTENCE of Anthony Burgess's *Earthly Powers* (1980)—incidentally, one of the most underrated English novels of the past century: "It was the afternoon of my eighty-first birthday, and I was in bed with my catamite when Ali announced that the archbishop had come to see me."

One knows at once who is the object of this pastiche. One knows it before "Geoffrey," described tersely as "my Ganymede or male lover as well as my secretary," is further described as responding to the intrusion by "pulling on his overtight summer slacks." Yet one is tempted to continue quoting, about the Mediterranean villa and the goings-on there ("I lay a little while, naked, mottled, sallow, emaciated, smoking a cigarette that should have been postcoital but was not"). This is quite simply because the parody is so much better than anything that W. Somerset Maugham ever wrote himself. Poor old "Willie" was more given to openings like this: "I have never begun a novel with more misgiving. If I call it a novel it is only because I don't know what else to call it."

Thus the deadly kickoff to *The Razor's Edge*, a story that furthermore turns out to be narrated by someone named Maugham. There was a time when many readers thought this kind of thing to be profound, and quite

---

Review of *Somerset Maugham: A Life*, by Jeffrey Meyers.

the cat's meow when it came to the delineation of searing human emotion. Even at that time, however, one shrewd writer—and also near-perfect pasticheur—saw through it without too much difficulty. "How about old S. Maugham, do you think?" P. G. Wodehouse wrote to Evelyn Waugh.

> I've been re-reading a lot of his stuff, and I'm wondering a bit about him. I mean, surely one simply can't do that stuff about the district officer hearing there's a white man dying in a Chinese slum and it turns out that it's gay lighthearted Jack Almond, who disappeared and no-one knew what had become of [him] and he went right under, poor chap, because a woman in England had let him down.

Well, it turned out that one simply could do that stuff, and go on doing it. Sometimes, for the sake of variety, it's the white woman who goes right under, or who succumbs in other ways to the lush madness of the tropics. Such is the case in "Before the Party," "P&O," and "The Force of Circumstance," though with females there is usually the redemptive possibility of a return by steamship to dear old England. The best of the sweltering colonial stories, which I can remember re-reading for the sake of atmosphere in a Malayan hotel once patronized by Maugham, is "The Outstation." Here we meet Warburton, a solitary middle-aged Englishman who is the resident administrator of a jungly area somewhere in the Malay archipelago. Rigid in respect of the upper lip, he sticks to a stern routine of exercises and always dresses in formal attire for dinner. His copy of the London *Times* arrives by sea mail six weeks late, and sometimes several successive days' editions are delivered by the same post, but he disciplines himself to open them one at a time, in strict order. The greatest test of this practice comes during the faraway Battle of the Somme, when by opening some later editions he could easily discover the outcome. But Warburton forces himself to keep his nerve, and breaks the wrappers seriatim. The effect is that of Conrad in tweeds. Maugham's overall debt to Conrad is so evident that one usually finishes by putting him down and picking up the real thing.

Just as he was a character in one of his best-known novels, so Maugham worked assiduously to create a persona for himself in life. And the life was, according to this admirable biography, a good deal more exquisite, dramatic, torrid, and tragic than any of the works. Born and brought up in France, Maugham lost his parents when quite young and from then on was farmed out to mean relatives and cruel, monastic boarding schools. The traditional ration of bullying, beating, and buggery seems to have been unusually effective in his case, leaving him with a frightful lifelong speech impediment and a staunch commitment to homosexuality. (Ashenden—the name of his secret-agent character—was also the name of a comely youth at the King's School in Canterbury, where Maugham served his term, so to speak.)

An ideal way to "lock in" homosexual disposition is probably to spend time as a gynecologist in a slum district of London—which, astonishingly enough, is what the fastidious young man did. Though he would ultimately abandon medicine, he passed considerable time delivering babies in the abysmal squalor of Lambeth, on the south bank of the River Thames. As part of his training he witnessed cesarean births in the hospital, where death was not uncommon. The experience gave him the raw material for *Liza of Lambeth*, his first novel, and also made him surprisingly radical in his infrequently expressed political views, which were strongly sympathetic to the Labour Party's social-welfare proposals. The arbitrariness of death and suffering, moreover, persuaded him that religious belief was merely fatuous.

Throughout Jeffrey Meyers's book one is reminded of the remarkable difference made to English letters by the Victorian-era law that prohibited homosexual conduct. Maugham was a young man during the Oscar Wilde scandal, and he developed all the habits of subterfuge that were necessary to his survival. It seems certain that he married Syrie Wellcome partly as "cover," and thereby doomed himself to decades of misery and litigation. But Meyers allows us to speculate that he did this, and also embarked on a dismal exercise in fatherhood, in order to satisfy himself as a writer that he had done everything at least once. (My contribution to the gay-marriage debate would be this: Remember what vast unhappiness was generated in the days when homosexuals felt obliged to marry heterosexuals.) Syrie was a greedy and impossible bitch to begin with, and did not improve upon intimate acquaintance, or want of acquaintance, of that kind. If one scans the few and cringe-making attempts to describe man-woman sex in Maugham's fiction, or if one attempts to infer anything of his conjugal relations, one is forced to picture him screwing his courage to the sticking place (or perhaps vice versa).

One of the many great appeals of war for men is that it allows and legitimizes flight from domestic entrapment. The year 1914—his own fortieth year—afforded Maugham just this chance of deliverance. He spoke French perfectly and he had a medical qualification, and before his only child, Elisabeth (naturally called "Liza" for most of her life), was born he had volunteered for the Western Front. The work of an ambulance man in wartime was the perfect counterpoint to gynecology—and has a vivid connection to gay iconography, as we know from the poetry of Walt Whitman and also the work of Wilfred Owen and Yukio Mishima. It's not by coincidence that the pierced and bleeding nudity of Saint Sebastian (whose name is shared by Waugh's epicene hero in *Brideshead Revisited*, with the addition of "Flyte" to suggest arrows) is the supreme symbol here. Not long after his arrival in the trenches Maugham met a dashing young American named Gerald Haxton, and never slept with a woman again. He had found the great entanglement of his life, and though Haxton was every bit as bitchy and greedy as Syrie, and exhibited many other vices as well, he seems never—or at any rate seldom—to have been boring. For the next several decades it was part of Maugham's job to look after the person whom he'd ostensibly hired to look after him, and to keep him out of jail.

The succeeding interlude in Maugham's life was also ready-made for his purposes as a popular novelist. He was recruited by British intelligence. For some reason they wanted to send him to Western Samoa, which had been German-occupied until 1914. This was his introduction to the Pacific. In a subsequent letter unearthed by Meyers, Maugham explained his long connection with the region thus:

> The exotic background was forced upon me accidentally by the fact that during the war I was employed in the Intelligence department, and so visited parts of the world which otherwise I might not have summoned up sufficient resolution to go to.

Note the slight clumsiness, which seems to have inflected everything Maugham ever wrote. Out of this episode, however, came *The Moon and Sixpence*, a rather prettily done fictionalization of that other great refugee from domesticity, Paul Gauguin.

The ludicrous failures of British and American intelligence during the

Russian Revolution, retold many times through the biographies of Bruce Lockhart and Sidney Reilly, can be encapsulated in the single fact that in mid-1917 Somerset Maugham was dispatched from the Pacific to Saint Petersburg as chief agent. He had never visited the country before and had only a nodding acquaintance with the language. He made the trip by railway across Siberia, and in the preface to *Ashenden* he wrote about it in this manner:

> I felt the lonely steppes and the interminable forests; the flow of the broad Russian rivers and all the toil of the countryside; the ploughing of the land and the reaping of the ripe wheat; the sighing of the wind in the birch trees; the long months of dark winter; and then the dancing of the women in the villages and the youths bathing in shallow streams on summer evenings.

Only the haunting strings of the balalaika, the warm scent of the samovar, and the glimpse of an onion dome would be required to make this the perfect summary of all clichés about Russia. Moreover, the ploughing and reaping bit was presumably "felt" secondhand, since the salient fact of the moment was that there was no bread. Indeed, the Bolshevik slogan "Peace, Bread, and Land" was enough in itself to negate the British aim of staving off revolution while continuing to insist on Russian participation in the war. It did not, to his credit, take Maugham very long to see that his task was an impossible one. He gave an account of a meeting with Kerensky, the preferred British candidate, that confirms the opinion later expressed in my hearing by Isaiah Berlin—that Kerensky was "one of the great wets of history."

A latent connection has often been supposed to exist between homosexuality and espionage. This seems to "work" in the cases of Anthony Blunt and Guy Burgess, but it emphatically does not explain the (rather superior) performances of Kim Philby and Graham Greene. Elements of secrecy and disguise and "code" may be innate in the gay makeup, but they didn't confer any advantage on Maugham when he was confronted with Lenin and Trotsky. It was simply a matter of drawing realistic conclusions, which he generally did. In any case, by that time he was leading enough of a double life already. And, as for so many of the homo duplex English literary queens of that epoch, the solution was—abroad.

Maugham's splendid exile at the Villa Mauresque, on the coast between Nice and Monte Carlo, was the centerpiece of his reputation as well as the answer to his problems. No longer would he have to fear the deportation of Gerald Haxton, who as an American was constantly running that risk in his trawlings through the bars of London. France was Maugham's birthplace, and the British tax inspectors couldn't follow him there either. He could shelter his growing literary income and his private life at the same time. The villa had been built by the odious King Leopold II of Belgium, as a place to house his personal confessor. (Not even Anthony Burgess could have made that up.) It had a Moorish style, as the name implies, with some fake-Renaissance appurtenances, but Maugham removed the vulgar cupola, built a library, and began to assemble a collection of Oriental art and classical painting.

Comparable, I suppose, to Harold Acton's celebrated retreat in Florence, and visited by critics such as Kenneth Clark and Raymond Mortimer, the villa managed to be at once a museum and a discreet place of resort for what was later to be called the Homintern. That aspect to one side, every page of description seems to contain a useful hint for one's own retirement: the Bernini fountain, for instance, and the specially planted avocado trees, with a skilled resident cook to transform the luscious green fruit into an ice cream flavored with rum. (This contrasts with the rebarbative lobster ice cream served by Ribbentrop at a dinner recorded in *"Chips": The Diaries of Sir Henry Channon.*) Quentin Crisp was entranced, and summed up Maugham as one of "the stately homos of England." Christopher Isherwood and Don Bachardy were slightly aghast when the tireless staff unpacked and laid out all their belongings, including the tubes of lubricant and the powder for warding off crab lice. Edna St. Vincent Millay, making a stop at the villa at a time when Noël Coward and Cecil Beaton were of the party, exclaimed loudly, " 'Oh Mr. Maugham, it's fairy land here!' . . . Noël and Cecil were just a bit taken aback." This is all quite good fun (Maugham to Emerald Cunard, excusing himself for leaving early: "I have to keep my youth." Cunard to Maugham: "Then why didn't you bring him with you?"), but it does begin to pall after a bit, as it must have done in fact.

Things were not all brittle and witty and artistic, in any case. The Villa Mauresque exerted a magnetic force on spongers and toadies and climbers of all sorts, and poor Maugham was always finding his bookshelves and wine cellar and bric-a-brac subjected to shameless pilfering. Gerald Haxton, caught between the twin local lures of the Monte Carlo casinos and the waterfront full of sailors, became mad, bad, and dangerous to know. Through it all, and even through the Second World War, which saw him expelled from Cap Ferrat, and during a long and more respectably senescent friendship with his contemporary Winston Churchill, Maugham kept to a rigorous regime at his desk, and turned out third-rate prose by the yard, or the furlong. If he put his genius into his life and property rather than his work, it was because the former were apter repositories for such talent as he possessed.

The main contradiction seems to be this: Maugham was gay, all right (he probably exaggerated when he said that he was one-quarter "normal"), but he wasn't especially pleased about the fact. Pursuing a pet artistic theory of his, that the paintings of El Greco were revelations of the aesthetic of a repressed homosexual, he chose to phrase it like this:

> It cannot be denied that the homosexual has a narrower outlook on the world than the normal man. In certain respects the natural responses of the species are denied him. Some at least of the broad and typical emotions he can never experience...A distinctive trait of the homosexual is a lack of deep seriousness over certain things that normal men take seriously. This ranges from an inane flippancy to a sardonic humour.

Deciding that "the homosexual can never reach the supreme heights of genius," as Maugham did, may be slightly preferable to the tiresome insistence of some gays that all great artists have been members of the club. However, if one merely keeps the name W. H. Auden in mind while reading the above passage, one sees that Maugham's difficulty was not just a tinge of self-hatred but a real inability to see literary "genius" when he encountered it. (Though Auden, by the way, rather liked his stuff.) And this was not merely a question of his particular repression or guilt. He just got things wrong. One could hardly classify Kingsley Amis's *Lucky Jim* as a gay novel, even subliminally, yet when it was published Maugham wrote a review praising Amis for his outright attack on the young barbarians ("they are scum") who were then threatening English campuses with their beery, plebeian subversiveness. As a satire on the "Angry Young Men" this would have been delicious (and in the long run rather prescient), but it became painfully apparent that Maugham was being entirely and pedantically literal.

See for yourself: Pluck down *The Razor's Edge* from the shelf. Elliot

Templeton, in lieu of characterization, is described as "well-favored, bright, a good dancer, a fair shot, and a fine tennis player." More effort is expended on describing the rugs and drawings that he owns. The sending of flowers and chocolates is alluded to as if it were a breathless social secret, and repeated in the first few pages. "Gregory Brabazon, notwithstanding his name, was not a romantic creature." Come again? A girl enters a room during dinner and asks,

> "Are we late?... I've brought Larry back. Is there anything for him to eat?"
>
> "I expect so," smiled Mrs. Bradley. "Ring the bell and tell Eugene to put another place."
>
> "He opened the door for us. I've already told him."

So that was a waste of dialogue, wasn't it? A little further on we learn of Gray Maturin that "though built on so large a scale he was finely proportioned, and stripped he must have been a fine figure of a man." Presumably this would also be true of him when unstripped.

I deliberately did not look up Edmund Wilson's once celebrated polemic against the terrifying banality of *The Razor's Edge* before revisiting the book myself, but I defy anyone to come to a different conclusion. Even Gore Vidal, himself no stranger to the Mediterranean-villa milieu, was compelled to agree that Maugham's success was, in effect, in writing for people who did not have a clue about English as a medium for either tragedy or comedy. I would add that mass wants class and always has, and that without the snobbery and the knowing references to fine chefs, splendid galleries, and refined houses, the enterprise wouldn't have stood a chance. But the old boy did show generosity and patience, and set up a prize in his name that encouraged many young writers, among them Kingsley Amis. Despite his exile and his increasingly distraught public and private life, Maugham eventually received an honor from the Crown—but it was for "services to literature," rather than for literature itself, and this distinction represents all the difference in the world.

(*The Atlantic*, May 2004)

Evelyn Waugh: The Permanent Adolescent

EVEN AS GEORGE ORWELL was dying, in 1949, he continued to wrestle with the last book review to which the life of the freelance hack had condemned him. Dogged to the final deadline, he also made some more-general notes about that novel's author. The book was *Brideshead Revisited*, and the author was Orwell's exact contemporary, whose centennial is also being observed this year. We now have Orwell's fragmented, unfinished comments on Evelyn Waugh, and they certainly infuse me with a strong wish to have been able to read the completed essay.

> Within the last few decades, in countries like Britain or the United States, the literary intelligentsia has grown large enough to constitute a world in itself. One important result of this is that the opinions which a writer feels frightened of expressing are not those which are disapproved of by society as a whole. To a great extent, what is still loosely thought of as heterodoxy has become orthodoxy. It is nonsense to pretend, for instance, that at this date there is something daring and original in proclaiming yourself an anarchist, an atheist, a pacifist, etc. The daring thing, or at any rate the unfashionable thing, is to believe in God or to approve of the capitalist system. In 1895, when Oscar Wilde was jailed, it must have needed very considerable moral courage to defend homosexuality. Today it

> would need no courage at all: today the equivalent action would be, perhaps, to defend antisemitism. But this example that I have chosen immediately reminds one of something else—namely, that one cannot judge the value of an opinion simply by the amount of courage that is required in holding it.

This manuscript peters out after a few more shrewd paragraphs, and is succeeded by some cryptic notes on *Brideshead*:

> Analyse "Brideshead Revisited." (Note faults due to being written in first person.) Studiously detached attitude. Not puritanical. Priests not superhuman... *But.* Last scene, where the unconscious man makes the sign of the Cross. Note that after all the veneer is bound to crack sooner or later. One cannot really be Catholic and grown-up.
>
> Conclude. Waugh is about as good a novelist as one can be (i.e. as novelists go today) while holding untenable opinions.

Tantalizing as this may be, in conceding that moral courage may be shown by reactionaries or good prose produced by snobs, it does not make the leap of imagination that is required to state the obvious: that Waugh wrote as brilliantly as he did precisely *because* he loathed the modern world. Orwell identified "snobbery" and "Catholicism" as Waugh's "driving forces," and so they were. But the first of his miniature masterpieces, *Decline and Fall*, was composed before Waugh joined Holy Mother Church. It contains a piece of absolutely hilarious rudeness and bad taste, directed at one of the world's most innocuous minorities—the Welsh.

> "The Welsh character is an interesting study," said Dr Fagan. "I have often considered writing a little monograph on the subject, but I was afraid it might make me unpopular in the village. The ignorant speak of them as Celts, which is of course wholly erroneous. They are of pure Iberian stock—the aboriginal inhabitants of Europe who survive only in Portugal and the Basque district Celts readily intermarry with their neighbors and absorb them. From the earliest times the Welsh have been looked upon as an unclean people. It is thus that they have preserved their racial integrity. Their sons

> and daughters rarely mate with humankind except their own blood relations. In Wales there was no need for legislation to prevent the conquering people intermarrying with the conquered..."

Much of the remainder of Waugh's iridescent first novel is imbued with the same breezy, heartless spirit, which recurs memorably in *Black Mischief, Scoop*, and *The Loved One*. And most of the delicious elements that were his hallmarks are present from the beginning. There is an innocent abroad; one might call him Candide if the Voltairean association were not obtuse. There are many ancillary characters who act without conscience and don't mind admitting it, and who don't seem to suffer in consequence. (The awful subtexts of *Decline and Fall* are pederasty and prostitution, and I remember being quite astounded when I was first introduced to the novel, at the age of twelve, by a boarding-school master who later had to be hastily taken away.) There is a fine English country house that is threatened with decay or demolition—in this instance the Tudor mansion King's Thursday, to be ravaged by a Bauhaus barbarian.

That last observation prompts another—namely, Waugh's familiarity with the outlines of the emerging modernity that he came to detest. Aesthetically he was one of the earliest to register the effect of T. S. Eliot and *The Waste Land*. In *Brideshead Revisited*, Anthony Blanche reads the Tiresias section of that poem through a megaphone; the title of *A Handful of Dust* is annexed directly from one of Eliot's more ominous stanzas (the whole stanza appears on Waugh's title page).

This brings us eventually to the matter of Roman Catholicism. In *Decline and Fall*, Waugh treated all devotional matters as the raw material of farce. But the concept of a capricious cosmos was already jostling in his mind with the notion of original sin. Thus, in that book a little boy named Lord Tangent (the son of Lord and Lady Circumference: Waugh both ridiculed and revered the nomenclature of English nobility) is grazed by a bullet during a sporting event, is reported as having had his foot turn black, and is subsequently said to have suffered first amputation and then death. All this is deadpan, callous humor, most of it offstage, as if Waugh half believed in those Fates that animated Greek drama and did not stop to explain themselves. As his work progresses, however, dreadful outcomes seem to be connected to a warped idea of divine justice. Basil Seal, in *Black Mischief*, doesn't actually *know* that he is eating his old girlfriend at a cannibal repast, but it's in the ironic nature of things that he should be dining in this way. In *Brideshead*, Sebastian Flyte squanders his beauty and charm on alcohol and indigence, and eventually in masochistic self-sacrifice, because he has been rashly fleeing the vocation for the priesthood that his elder brother would have so humbly welcomed.

Waugh was not a mere propagandist, and we would not still be reading him if he had been. The ends that he reserves for the meek and the worthy and the innocent are condemnations of the worldly and the vain, as surely as in John Bunyan's *Pilgrim's Progress*, but they are also highly diverting for their own sake. William Boot, in *Scoop*, is given a thorough drubbing by reality the moment he risks leaving the shelter of Boot Magna Hall, his bucolic den. Tony Last, in *A Handful of Dust*, is a doomed man once he agrees to give up his country seat of Hetton and embark on a venture of overseas exploration. The element of what we glibly call *noir* is a fluctuating one: Both Boot and Last (cobbler's names) are treated with extraordinary cruelty by the women they love, but the outcomes are arranged along the spectrum between pity and terror. Waugh's mastery is most often shown by the light flick with which he could switch between the funny and the sinister. And the delicacy of this touch is shown by the breathtaking deftness with which he handled profane subjects. I have already mentioned that the gross pedophilia of *Decline and Fall* is so artfully suggested that an adolescent might read it unawares. And many adult reviewers of *Brideshead* have somehow managed to describe it as a languorous evocation of the "platonic" nature of English undergraduate affection.

But toying with his innocents, and showing how cleverly and suddenly their creator could bring them low, was for Waugh part of a serious mandate. He wanted to bring the Book of Job to life for those who had never read, or who feared, it. And he chose a time—the mid-twentieth century—when the Church he had joined was very plainly marked not just with a nostalgia for the days of Thomas More or even of Thomas Aquinas but by a reactionary modernity of its own. It is for this reason, I propose, that Waugh and Eliot still seem fresh while G. K. Chesterton and Hilaire Belloc appear quaint and antique. The plain fact is that both felt and transmitted some of the mobilizing energy of fascism.

The tweedy, fogy types who make an affectation of Waugh are generally fondest of his almost camp social conservatism: his commitment to stuffy clubs, "home" rather than "abroad," old clothes, traditional manners, ear trumpets, rural hierarchy, ancient liturgy, and the rest of it. Their master ministered very exactly to this taste in the undoubted self-parody that adorns *The Ordeal of Gilbert Pinfold* and is titled "Portrait of the Artist in Middle Age."

> His strongest tastes were negative. He abhorred plastics, Picasso, sunbathing, and jazz—everything in fact that had happened in his own lifetime. The tiny kindling of charity which came to him through his religion sufficed only to temper his disgust and change it to boredom. There was a phrase in the thirties: "It is later than you think," which was designed to cause uneasiness. It was never later than Mr. Pinfold thought.

His face eventually grew to fit this mask, but Waugh had been very much "of" the Jazz Age, and brought it hectically to life, most notably in *Vile Bodies* and *Brideshead*. Sexual experiments, fast cars, modern steamships and airplanes—these, plus a touch of experience with modern warfare, gave him an edge that the simple, fusty reactionaries did not possess. Thus he celebrated Mussolini's conquest of Abyssinia as in part a victory for progress and development, defended Franco's invasion of Spain as a stand for tradition and property, and, in his travel book *Robbery Under Law*, denounced the Mexico of Cárdenas as an anti-clerical socialist kleptocracy. On some things he was conservative by instinct. (He always abominated, for example, the very idea of the United States of America.) But the dynamic element in modernism was not foreign to him, much as he later liked to pretend otherwise. And he made excellent use of this tension in his writing.

Another tension or contradiction also occurs in both the life and the work. Waugh was a celebrated misanthrope and an obvious misogynist, capable of alarming and hateful bouts of anger and cruelty toward friends, children, and colleagues. When his friend Clarissa Churchill married a divorced man, he wrote to her saying that she had deliberately intensified "the loneliness of Calvary." During his wartime service—which, it must be said, was often conspicuous for its gallantry—he almost had to be protected from assassination at the hands of the soldiers under his command. Permanently injured by the flagrant adultery of his first wife, and almost certainly a badly repressed homosexual, he made a living example of Cyril Connolly's "Theory of Permanent Adolescence," whereby Englishmen of a certain caste are doomed to re-enact their school days. The vices of the boy are notably unappealing in the grown man, and Waugh was frequently upbraided for the apparent contrast between his extreme nastiness and his ostentatious religiosity. To this he famously replied (to Nancy Mitford) that nobody could imagine how horrible he would be if he were *not* a Catholic. A nice piece of casuistry, but not one that bears much scrutiny. In at least two cases—his support for the Croatian Fascist Party during his wartime stint in the Balkans, and his animosity toward Jews—there was a direct connection between his spleen and his faith. And in at least two of the novels, *Helena* (which is based on the life of the early Christian empress of that name) and *Brideshead*, the narrative is made ridiculous by a sentimental and credulous approach to miracles or the supernatural. This is what Orwell meant by the incompatibility of faith with maturity.

A further proof of this point, from a somewhat different angle, might be Waugh's lamentable inability to write about sex, along with his insistence on trying to do so. A properly reticent traditionalist should have avoided the topic altogether, or dealt with it by the faintest possible allusion. Waugh once tried to take refuge in a Jamesian hideout, stating rather too finally that "our language took form during the centuries when the subject was not plainly handled with the result that we have no vocabulary for the sexual acts which is not quaintly antiquated, scientific or grossly colloquial." Never mind what Chaucer or Shakespeare or Swift or Burns or Byron might have made of that piece of evasion; the fact is that Waugh knew his readers and also knew that they employed pungent and emphatic and sometimes hilarious words for the obvious. Thus there is no conceivable excuse for passages like this one:

> It was no time for the sweets of luxury; they would come, in their season, with the swallow and the lime-flowers. Now on the rough water there was a formality to be observed, no more. It was as

> though a deed of conveyance of her narrow loins had been drawn and sealed.

Or this one:

> The silk rustled again as though falling to the ground. "It's best to make sure, isn't it, darling, before we decide anything? It may just be an idea of yours that you're in love with me. And you see, Paul, I like you so very much, it would be a pity to make a mistake, wouldn't it?"

Or this:

> No sign or hint betrayed their distress but when the last wheels rolled away and they mounted to their final privacy, there was a sad gap between them, made by modesty and tenderness, which neither spoke of except in prayer. Later they joined a yacht at Naples and steamed slowly up the coast, putting in at unfrequented harbors. And there, one night in their state room, all at last came right between them and their love was joyfully completed.

The writhe-making aspects of these passages (drawn, respectively, from *Brideshead Revisited, Decline and Fall,* and *Men at Arms*) are in bold contrast to the somewhat swaggering and sniggering mentions of surreptitious sex in Waugh's posthumously published *Diaries*. Evidently, he distrusted either his readers or himself, or perhaps both, when it came to the fictional crux. I admit that I found the second passage powerfully erotic when I first read it—but I was then under monastic tutelage and worse, and was, as I have said, only twelve. It's somewhat confirming to read of Waugh's rather bizarre second marriage, to an odd woman who bore him numerous children with no great evidence of relish on her part or pride on his—as if, indeed, offspring were to be regarded as random gifts, wanted or unwanted, from the divine. (By what is perhaps an unconscious inversion of the same dispensation, Waugh makes most of his protagonists into orphans or half orphans, missing at least one parent.) "Family values," too tedious for straight depiction, nonetheless had to be upheld for reasons of propriety.

There is evidence that he knew not to push this kind of religiosity too far.

In a conversation between Waugh and Graham Greene, recorded by Christopher Sykes, Greene described the plot of his then impending novel *The Quiet American*, and observed that it would be "a relief not to write about God for a change." To which Waugh rejoined, "Oh, I wouldn't drop God if I were you. Not at this stage anyway. It would be like P. G. Wodehouse dropping Jeeves halfway through the Wooster series."

It is notable, for example, that none of Waugh's fictional Catholic clergy are morally impressive. (The "priests," as Orwell pointed out, are "not superhuman.") They tend to be simple-minded or (in the case of *Men at Arms*) resentful Irishmen. In *Vile Bodies* there is a caricature of a scheming, socially smooth Jesuit, but he is given the distinctly un-Romish name of Father Rothschild. We meet him carrying a suitcase that contains a false beard and "six important new books in six languages," and we learn that he has the precious gift of recalling "everything that could possibly be learned about everyone who could possibly be of any importance." To this incarnation of venality is given an astonishingly solemn short speech as the frivolity of the 1930s dies away, and the jazz band starts to pack up, and the sounds of war begin to be heard.

> I know very few young people, but it seems to me that they are all possessed with an almost fatal hunger for permanence... We long for peace, and fill our newspapers with conferences about disarmament and arbitration, but there is a radical instability in our whole world-order, and soon we shall all be walking into the jaws of destruction again, protesting our pacific intentions.

For the generation that was young in the 1920s and 1930s, and for whom Waugh was in some ways the blithe spirit, the unresolved question was this: Were they living in a postwar world or a pre-war one? The suppressed hysteria of this time—the echo of the preceding bloodshed and the premonition of more impending—was never captured better, except perhaps by F. Scott Fitzgerald.

If one adopts Graham Greene's distinction between "novels" and "entertainments" in his own fiction, and applies it experimentally to Waugh, then the two world wars become the crucial points of reference. *Brideshead* was published toward the end of the Second World War, but it evokes almost to perfection the atmosphere of Oxford just after the First World War, populated by young men who are acutely conscious of having barely missed the great test of combat. This type or "set"—Paul Pennyfeather, Adam Fenwick-Symes, Ambrose Silk, Basil Seal—provides the figures of the "entertainments." Charles Ryder, in *Brideshead*, is no longer young and epicene when he becomes a junior officer and has to embrace responsibility. *Put Out More Flags* concludes with many callow and superficial former partygoers behaving better than might have been expected of them (if only to point up a contrast with W. H. Auden and Christopher Isherwood, "Parsnip and Pimpernell," who committed what was to Waugh a double offense by avoiding military service *and* emigrating to America). Dennis Barlow, the cynical protagonist of *The Loved One*, has learned the craft of poetry in the British Army from 1939 to 1945. (I should add that Waugh's Catholicism, however lightly or invisibly worn, was obviously a stylistic and aesthetic advantage in that novel. It enabled him to confront the sheer wasteland of a Hollywood funeral industry that idiotically, hedonistically, denied death.)

Thus, the *summa* of Waugh's effort is probably rightly held to be the wartime trilogy that he began to compose in 1951 and completed a decade later. Collectively titled *Sword of Honour*, this consists of *Men at Arms*, *Officers and Gentlemen*, and *Unconditional Surrender* or (in the U.S. edition) *The End of the Battle*. Unlike many or most of Waugh's "entertainments" (to which I would add some of the imperishable "original sin" short stories, including "Mr. Loveday's Little Outing"), this trilogy cannot be read at a sitting. Nor do very many of its passages commit themselves virtually to memory, like the descriptions of William Boot's telegraphese in *Scoop*, or the Welsh silver band in *Decline and Fall*. I postponed re-reading it with definite anticipation, which wasn't enough by itself to account for my disappointment.

Of course there is an ancient English Catholic family, with an endangered English country house. The names—Crouchback for the family and Broome for the house—are well up to Waugh's standard. War is coming, and the young Crouchback hears the call of the bugle. But—and this makes him nearly unique in modern English writing—he is not really convinced of the justice of his country's cause. Britain is potentially allied with communism against not just Nazism but Christendom. Guy Crouchback, we learn, is quite reconciled to fascism in Italy, and indifferent to the fate of Czechoslovakia. He is only momentarily cheered by the news of the Nazi-Soviet pact: "The enemy at last was plain in view, huge and hateful, all disguise cast off. It was the Modern Age in arms. Whatever the outcome there was a place for him in that battle."

With these divided loyalties he prays at the shrine of a Crusader knight and sets off to enlist. ("Sometimes he imagined himself serving the last Mass for the last Pope in a catacomb at the end of the world.") Yet, starting out in well-trodden territory, we find ourselves kept within its bounds. The image of the desolate shrine is from the closing pages of *Brideshead*. Crouchback's disastrous choice of a wife, and her subsequent desertion of him, are very like Waugh's own experience—and reminiscent of the agony faced by Tony Last in *A Handful of Dust*. Arthur Box-Bender's fatuous complacency about the Nazis is lifted straight from Rex Mottram's in *Brideshead* ("The Germans are short of almost every industrial essential. As soon as they realize that Mr. Hitler's bluff has been called, we shan't hear much more of Mr. Hitler"), and in both cases the bluster is put into the mouth of a pro-Churchill Tory politician. Having joined his regiment, Guy begins to experience "something he had missed in boyhood, a happy adolescence," which is almost precisely what Charles Ryder says of his affair with Sebastian Flyte. Guy's fellow officer Sarum-Smith makes exactly the calculation about wartime service—that it will do him good when the time comes to return to life in business—that Hooper announces in *Brideshead*. Guy compares his love for and disillusionment with the army to a marriage, exactly as Ryder does. And this is all in the first eighty pages or so of *Men at Arms*. In most of the instances I have cited, the preceding books phrased it better.

In *Brideshead*, Ryder reflects,

> Here my last love died... as I lay in that dark hour, I was aghast to realize that something within me, long sickening, had quietly died, and felt as a husband might feel, who, in the fourth year of his marriage, suddenly knew that he had no longer any desire, or tenderness, or esteem, for a once-beloved wife; no pleasure in her company, no wish to please, no curiosity about anything she might ever do or say or think; no hope of setting things right, no self-reproach for

> the disaster. I knew it all, the whole drab compass of marital disillusion; we had been through it together, the army and I, from the first importunate courtship until now, when nothing remained to us except the chill bonds of law and duty and custom.

In *Sword of Honour*, Crouchback broods,

> Those days of lameness, he realized much later, were his honeymoon, the full consummation of his love of the Royal Corps of Halberdiers. After them came domestic routine, much loyalty and affection, many good things shared, but intervening and overlaying them all the multitudinous, sad little discoveries of marriage, familiarity, annoyance, imperfections noted, discord. Meanwhile it was sweet to wake and to lie on in bed; the spirit of the Corps lay on beside him: to ring the bell; it was in the service of his unseen bride.

The first of the dawn thoughts of these two English soldiers is latently tragic, whereas the second is mostly banal (and gives rise to the suspicion that Waugh did not truly recall the first even while he was carpentering the second).

The cause of this depression in the narrator, and perhaps of the routine and repetition in the author's prose, is disclosed quite early on. Guy sits in a warm officers' mess, far, "immeasurably far, from the frontier of Christendom where the great battle had been fought and lost; from those secret forests where the trains were, even then, while the Halberdiers and their guests sat bemused by wine and harmony, rolling east and west with their doomed loads." Waugh's meaning soon becomes clear: "England had declared war to defend the independence of Poland. Now that country had quite disappeared and the two strongest states in the world guaranteed her extinction." This is Waugh the Catholic pessimist as well as (not quite the same thing) Waugh the Catholic reactionary. Note also that the existence of the United States as a great power is not acknowledged even latently. Indeed, almost the only appearance made by America in this wartime trilogy is in the absurd and irritating person of "The Loot"—an opprobrious nickname for an affected and obsequious and somewhat shady American officer named Lieutenant Padfield—and of three disgusting Stateside reporters, Scab Dunz, Bum

Schlum, and Joe Mulligan. The depiction of this vile trio is not a patch on the portrait of revolting journalists that appears in *Scoop*. And one might sadly observe that here Waugh's high facility for laughable yet plausible names seems to have deserted him in favor of rank crudity.

On re-reading, it also struck me as unwise for Waugh to include some of the same people and places and names—Julia Stitch, Marchmain House, the *Daily Beast*—that featured in his earlier, more fanciful works. *Sword of Honour* follows "real" historical events, from however idiosyncratic a perspective, and it is distracting to see stage characters winking from behind such imposing scenery. Indeed, it undermines the chief virtue of the trilogy, which is its rigorous portrayal of the splendors and miseries of the great calling of arms. Waugh's account of the battle for Crete, with its stark and humiliating depiction of the British army in shabby, demoralized, cowardly retreat, is one of the great passages of wartime prose. This, one says to oneself, is what defeat and shame must really have felt like. Many whiskered veterans have told me that the following is *exactly* how the return to barracks and the report to duty appeared to them:

> Guy saluted, turned about and departed only very slightly disconcerted. This was the classic pattern of army life as he had learned it, the vacuum, the spasm, the precipitation, and with it all the peculiar, impersonal, barely human geniality.

Nor did Waugh skimp on the farcical and capricious elements that are inseparable from warfare. Sometimes the humor is cruel; people die at random and in pointless ways. The figure of Guy's brother officer Apthorpe, at once pompous and pitiable, is beautifully drawn, even if it follows the outline of Captain Grimes (in *Decline and Fall*) a little too faithfully. Then there are serio-comic set pieces. At a critical moment one of Guy's soldiers asks for permission to go on leave, so that he can take part in a competition.

> "Competition for what, Shanks?"
>
> "The slow valse, sir. We've practiced together three years now. We won at Salford last year. We'll win at Blackpool, sir, I know we will. And I'll be back in the two days, honest, sir."
>
> "Shanks, do you realize that France has fallen? That there is

every likelihood of the invasion of England? That the whole railway system of the country is disorganized for the Dunkirk men? That our brigade is on two hours' notice for active service? Do you?"

"Yes, sir."

"Then how can you come to me with this absurd application?"

"But, sir, we've been practicing three years. We got a first at Salford last year. I can't give up now, sir."

"Request dismissed, sergeant-major."

In accordance with custom (sergeant-major) Rawkes had been waiting within view in case the applicant for a private interview attempted personal violence on his officer...And Guy remained to wonder: was this the already-advertised spirit of Dunkirk? He rather thought it was.

In the "entertainments," however often one reads them, there is always a detail that leaps out as if for the first time. (In *Decline and Fall* applicants to an agency that supplies prep-school teachers are instructed to furnish a photograph "if considered advisable." In *Scoop*, Lord Copper is searching for an example of the lowliest among his newspaper's staff, and after a pause announces that he is "accessible to the humblest...book reviewer.") With *Sword of Honour*, despite its flashes ("Guy felt no resentment; he was a good loser—at any rate an experienced one"), there are slower buildups, larger tracts, and, it must be said, many longueurs. Graham Greene once wrote that the opening pages of *Brideshead* seem lengthy in the memory but are brilliantly brief when, so to speak, revisited. The reverse is the case here, and that is because the state of Guy Crouchback's soul is insufficiently interesting to merit the introspection it receives. We may assume that he is Waugh (he is given the same day, month, and year of birth), and his sense of despair really does not take very long to elaborate. He believes that the Second World War has made his country into a corrupt, collectivized state at home and an accomplice in Bolshevism and atheism abroad. For him there has been no "Finest Hour." The very title of the trilogy is sarcastic: The only sword in the story (apart from the ancient Crusader blade next to which Guy prays) is the one made on the orders of King George VI, to be presented to Stalin in recognition of the gallantry of Soviet resistance. This, and what it represents, is to Guy a sword of dishonor. He runs into Box-Bender and is told,

> "Everything is going merrily on the eastern front."
>
> "Merrily?"
>
> "Wait for the nine o'clock news. You'll hear something then. Uncle Joe's fairly got them on the run. I shouldn't much care to be one of his prisoners."

Here Waugh condenses a vast contempt into a small space. But his revenge on Box-Bender (whose prisoner-of-war son elects to become a Catholic monk) seems all the pettier for that. The conversion to Rome of Guy's once and future wife, Virginia, is likewise mawkish and artificial, and the ludicrous character of his uncle Peregrine, obsessed with family genealogy and religious arcana, is a composite of many previous figures of fun. Only in the clever, lethal way in which he caricatured certain Anthony Blunt-like persons in the Foreign Office and the intelligence services did Waugh really succeed in landing a blow on the forces he hated.

In his private journal for February of 1944 Waugh wrote,

> The battle at Nettuno looks unpromising. It is hard to be fighting against Rome. We bombed Castel Gandolfo. The Russians now propose a partition of East Prussia. *It is a fact that the Germans now represent Europe against the world.* [Italics added]

The long and didactic closing stages of *Sword of Honour* are amazingly blatant in the utterance they give to this rather unutterable thought. Guy Crouchback regards the Yugoslav partisans as mere ciphers for Stalin, sympathizes with the local Fascists, and admires the discipline of the German occupiers. We know from many published memoirs that Waugh himself was eventually removed from this theater of operations for precisely that sort of insubordination. We also know that his first writerly trip after the German surrender was to observe the Nuremberg trials in 1946. He left the city after only two days, "finding the reality tedious," in the words of his biographer Selina Hastings. So it is slightly unsettling to find Guy Crouchback performing an act of mercy and piety, which his creator never even attempted. In a protracted and sentimental episode at the close of *Sword of Honour* he devotes himself to the rescue of a group of displaced Jews, and persists in this quixotic policy despite every variety of British official discouragement. The Jews themselves are never represented except as extras—as Guy's rather bedraggled objects of charity. There isn't any color or life or dignity to them. Is it then mistaken for one to suggest that they are included as a makeweight, or as a clumsy atonement many years later for Waugh's actual views at the time? Whatever may be the case, the passage is one of the most bogus and leaden things he ever wrote, fully materializing Orwell's earlier misgivings. And in this instance it is the suspect politics that directly occasion and condition the bad writing—which is to say, they negate the whole genius of Waugh in the first place.

Many literary careers are doomed to go on slightly longer than they should, and to outlive the author's original engrossing talent. Waugh himself lived to lament the Second Vatican Council and to deplore the abolition of the Latin Mass—which meant that he became not more Catholic than the Pope but more curmudgeonly than his own confessors and more conservative than the Church itself. This has the accidentally beautiful result of making *Sword of Honour* into a literary memorial not just for a lost world but for a lost faith. In Catholic doctrine one is supposed to hate the sin and love the sinner. This can be a distinction without a difference if the "sin" is to *be* something (a Jew, a homosexual, even a divorcée) rather than to *do* something. Non-Christian charity requires, however, that one forgive Waugh precisely because it was his innate—as well as his adopted—vices that made him a king of comedy and of tragedy for almost three decades.

(*The Atlantic*, May 2003)

P. G. Wodehouse: The Honorable Schoolboy

I DARESAY THAT ONE CAN CLAIM, without running overmuch risk of contradiction, to have been reading Frederick Taylor's recent history of the obliteration of Dresden with no intention of looking for laughs. And yet when I reached page 46, I found myself open-mouthed with joy, and eager to share my mirth. Taylor carefully sets the scene of pre-war Nazi Saxony, and devotes several paragraphs to the unpleasing figure of Martin Mutschmann, the party gauleiter. From these passages I learned that Herr Mutschmann had left school at fourteen and had taken "various management positions in lace and underwear companies." I at once laid down the book and wondered whom I should call or e-mail with this precious page reference.

Some of you who are still with me will already have caught my drift. In the climactic scene of *The Code of the Woosters*, Bertie confronts Sir Roderick Spode, the sinister bully who is "founder and head of the Saviours of Britain, a Fascist organization better known as the Black Shorts." He reduces Spode to a jelly by disclosing that he knows the would-be dictator's ghastly secret—his ownership of Eulalie Soeurs, a female underwear consortium. Devotees of this incandescently funny novel may quarrel with my brief summary here.

Review of *Wodehouse: A Life*, by Robert McCrum.

Bertie needs to fail hilariously at least once, and to enlist the help of the invaluable Jeeves before he can bring off the coup. However, I can confidently expect some fellow sufferers to write in, and to thank me in broken tones for this confirming serendipity.

Indeed, if anything could ever put one off being a Wodehouse fan, it would be the somewhat cultish element among his admirers and biographers. Such people have a tendency to allude to him as "The Master." They publish monographs about the exact geographical location of Blandings Castle, or the Drones Club. They hold dinners at which breadstuffs are thrown. Their English branch publishes the quarterly *Wooster Sauce,* and their American branch publishes the quarterly *Plum Lines*: two painfully unfunny titles. They materialize, in other words, Evelyn Waugh's view that Wodehouse created a delightful, self-contained world of his own. The only modern comparison I can think of is to the sterner "Irregulars" who have their shrine at 221b Baker Street.

Robert McCrum is by no means immune from the lure of all this, but his biography has a tendency to let in daylight upon the magic. Wodehouse was a rather beefy, hearty chap, with a lifelong interest in the sporting subculture of the English boarding school and a highly developed instinct for the main chance. He had no sex life or love life worth recording, and seemed to reserve his affections primarily for animals. He was so self-absorbed that he was duped into collaboration with the Nazis and had to plead the "bloody fool" defense. His subsequently wrecked reputation was redeemed only by an almost manic focus on work, and by an insistence on reproducing a lost and dreamy world of English innocence.

Well, to take these points in reverse order, there's no mystery about the continuing fascination of Blandings Castle and the universe of Jeeves, or their appeal for those who have never met a butler or received an invitation to an English country house. George Orwell pointed out long ago, in his penetrating essay on "Boys' Weeklies," that the children of the back streets would spend their scant pocket money in order to immerse themselves in stories about upper-crust life in ivy-covered "public" schools. And why should this astonish us, when we see today's American youngsters stating with confidence which "house" at Hogwarts School they would join if they only could?

Fantasy worlds are so-called for good reason, and richly and rightly rewarded is the author who can truly create one.

As for the bizarre moment when the creator of Jeeves and Ukridge and Psmith appeared on Nazi radio after being trapped by the fall of France, McCrum is only the latest of many biographers to acquit his subject on the main charge. Here is one of the opening paragraphs of Wodehouse's first chat, broadcast on June 28, 1941:

> Young men, starting out in life, have often asked me, "How can I become an Internee?" Well, there are several methods. My own was to buy a villa in Le Touquet on the coast of France and stay there till the Germans came along. This is probably the best and simplest system. You buy the villa and the Germans do the rest.

The genius of this, in my opinion, lies not merely in its deadpan intonation but in its essential truth. (There must have been, one likes to think, an editor in Berlin who vetted the transcript and said to himself, "That seems harmless enough.") Wodehouse and his wife, Ethel, had in fact followed exactly that "system," and had been too innocent and unworldly to try to run away until it was too late. They had also been unwilling to put their Pekingese in quarantine—which goes to show how far the stereotype of the English dog lover can be pushed. Fat-headed as he was for accepting the Germans' invitation in the first place, Wodehouse was not actually working for Joseph Goebbels and his Ministry of Propaganda. He was, as McCrum shows, being used by the more civilized elements in the German Foreign Office, who disliked Goebbels. Unlikely as it is that he would have appreciated the difference, Wodehouse responded to the baited invitation with the genial attitude of one who says "When in Rome," or "One must be civil." It's quite impossible that the man who had invented Sir Roderick Spode in 1938 was prey to any covert sympathy for fascism.

Prior to this moment of hideous embarrassment, Wodehouse had manifested the same almost childlike stoicism when deported from France and interned in a disused lunatic asylum in the town of Tost, Poland. As he was later to put it, "Tost is no beauty spot. It lies in the heart of sugar-beet country.... There is a flat dullness about the countryside which has led many a visitor to say, 'If this is Upper Silesia, what must Lower Silesia be like?' "

McCrum and his fellow Wodehousian Anthony Lane, of the *New Yorker*, have both fractionally raised their eyebrows at this levity, given that Silesia was the site of Auschwitz. (McCrum also falls into error when he says that "by association" Wodehouse had put himself into "the company of genuine traitors like William Joyce." Joyce—"Lord Haw Haw"—may have been a genuine fascist, but he was a U.S. citizen who owed no allegiance to the British crown. The British government's decision to execute him after the war was a judicial scandal.) There is absolutely no reason to think that Wodehouse knew what was afoot in the East, and in any case the Final Solution did not begin until after the Nazi invasion of the Soviet Union, which did not commence until after Wodehouse had done to Tost what Bertie did to Totleigh Towers: shaken its dust from his feet.

Innumerable English reminiscences of prison-camp life during the Second World War are devoted to making one point: It was all much easier to bear if you had the experience of an English boarding school under your belt. Nicknames for obnoxious guards, complaints about the food, jokes based on the absence of females, the lampooning of stupid routines—it was an invitation to re-create the lost world of boyhood, and Wodehouse actually finished *Money in the Bank,* to be ranked among his more amusing novels, while in the self-evidently absurd position of an internee. One might also add that during the process of deportation, a German soldier came up to shake his hand and to say "Thank you for Jeeves." This helped confirm Wodehouse in his view that people were all basically good chaps underneath, when you got to know them.

There can be little doubt that Wodehouse was a very advanced case of arrested development. Born into a family of colonial merchants and civil servants, he was abandoned by his parents for long stretches and learned to find and maintain his equilibrium in (aha!) the servants' quarters and (aha! again) the comradeship of all-male boarding schools. In the comparable cases of Kipling and Saki this entailed the early realization that childhood was a place of terror, not innocence. In the case of Pelham Grenville Wodehouse (he disliked both his given names and rather grudgingly accepted the nickname "Plum" that resulted), the resolution was more like that of young

Matzerath in *The Tin Drum*: He would simply stop growing up. McCrum takes too little account of the mumps that struck Wodehouse in adolescence. It seems fairly obvious that this early affliction had a gelding effect on him, stunting his libido and making him noticeable, even to his least curious friends, as a large, pink, plump, hairless, and somewhat neuter person for the rest of his life. This was the high price he paid for the protective Eden that he never escaped.

Two other boyhood deprivations might have become a source of resentment. Wodehouse, who had always assumed that he would "go up" to Oxford University, was abruptly told by his parents that the family funds would not run to it. He was told, further, that he would have to work in a menial position in the London branch of the Hong Kong and Shanghai Bank. Though not as demeaning as debtors' prison or an apprenticeship in a blacking factory, this combination of disappointment and tedium might have shriveled a lesser soul. Again, McCrum only skates over the evidence that Wodehouse took a keen interest in the street-corner speakers of the early British socialist movement. A number of his mature stories—most notably "Archibald and the Masses"—demonstrate that he picked up more than a passing knowledge of the leftist vernacular. In the earlier tales, most obviously *Psmith in the City*, we learn that young Psmith became a devotee of Marxist theory when he was taken away from Eton and robbed of the chance to play cricket for the most snobbish school team in the country. Writing about Henry Hyndman, the founder of the Social Democratic Federation and a contemporary of Karl Marx, Barbara Tuchman said that he "adopted socialism out of spite against the world because he was not included in the Cambridge eleven." Benny Green, an earlier Wodehouse biographer, encapsulates Psmith's ethos as "an irrefutable argument that most work is a distasteful necessity which nobody in his right mind would ever dream of performing unless he needed the money desperately." Actually, this is hardly less true of many of the later stories, wherein a shortage of ready money comes second only to blighted romance as an obstacle to felicity.

McCrum tends to stress Wodehouse's later conservatism—his aversion to the Hollywood Communists in the Screenwriters Guild, for example, and his long battle with the tax authorities in England and America. Some of the more Marxist Wodehousians, such as Alexander Cockburn and Francis

Wheen, conversely emphasize the Spode satire, or the salient point that the upper classes in Wodehouse's world are helplessly dependent on their manservants and pig keepers. The honors here can be divided more or less equally. What Wodehouse did discover, though, was that once he had cast off the shackles of the proletarian condition and become self-employed, the long day was never done. This book depicts a man who eventually managed to live in grand and comfortable circumstances, but who never for a single moment forgot that he had an infinitely demanding and ruthless taskmaster—himself. Class be damned; but he was a worker all right. His chief skill lay in making the product of his labor look easy.

He toiled in three demanding vineyards: musical comedy, screenwriting, and fiction. And he would seem to have made the decision, quite early in life, to become an American. The two determinations were obviously related, because in the early decades of the twentieth century it was evident to any aspiring Brit that New York was (a) where the action was and (b) where the money was. Still, it comes as a slight surprise to find him writing, "in a perfect agony of boredom" with London in the 1920s, that "all I want to do is get back and hear the American language again." This surprise, however, is soon overtaken by the realization that American idioms, especially the idioms of the Prohibition era—"rannygazoo," "horn-swoggle," "put on the dog," "bum's rush," "dude"—pervade the speech of his characters. Indeed, it was as an American, or at any rate as a writer with a large American audience, that he was thought useful by the Germans during the long period of U.S. neutrality. However much people like to yoke him with the phrase "quintessentially English," it was on American soil that he did much if not most of his best work. It's nice to remember that at his formative Dulwich School he was a near contemporary of Raymond Chandler's.

In Hollywood, where he didn't do much memorable work but did make a considerable amount of money, he helped found the Hollywood Cricket Club, in 1931. Its members included Boris Karloff, Errol Flynn, and David Niven (who appears in the movie version of *Thank You, Jeeves*). To this we are indebted, clearly, for the marvelous opening scene of Evelyn Waugh's *The Loved One*.

Jazz Age Wodehouse, as caught by McCrum, is out on Long Island with the Scott Fitzgeralds, staying at the Algonquin, sweeping up Broadway in triumph with Jerome Kern and Cole Porter, writing musical parts for William Randolph Hearst's future sweetie Marion Davies, hobnobbing with Flo Ziegfeld, and getting hot reviews from George S. Kaufman and Dorothy Parker. Frank Crowninshield, of *Vanity Fair*, paid him top dollar. But all the time, in this world saturated with money and glamour and sex, he remained, in McCrum's phrase, "the laureate of repression." And he was, when he got home to his desk, slowly evolving the primal innocence of Lord Emsworth and Bertie Wooster—an attainment that would bring him fame far beyond the Great White Way.

Attempting to explain this dissonance between the knowing and the guileless, and between the cynical world of gay-dominated musical comedy and the blameless universe of Bertie and the Earl, I once proposed that Wodehouse must have seen or read *The Importance of Being Earnest* and somehow sublimated it. The theory is pathetically simple once you start to test it: Oscar Wilde's play opens with some witty backchat between an idle young bachelor and his butler, proceeds to introduce a terrifying aunt in the shape of Lady Bracknell, and carries on with two intertwined and frivolous engagements, which are resolved in a country house with the help of a silly rural clergyman. With Wodehouse as with Wilde, nobody has any father or mother, only aunts and uncles. (I can go on about this at length if challenged, mentioning the dates when Wodehouse began going to the theater and not omitting the fact that his father was named Ernest.) McCrum even makes a bow in my direction, asserting that although Wodehouse undoubtedly knew of Reginald Bunthorne, the "fleshly poet" satirized by Gilbert and Sullivan in *Patience*, he never included any Wildeisms in his widely scattered literary allusions.

Nor did he—by allusion, at any rate. But I've recently been unhorsed by Mark Grueter, a brilliant graduate student of mine, who came across the following in the story "Pigs Have Wings." Set in Blandings Castle, as the title implies, it features the scapegrace Galahad Threepwood ("Gally") and the mettlesome American girl Penny Donaldson. The ambition of this dangerous young woman is to keep an appointment with her unsuitable suitor, Jerry Vail, in London. Lord Emsworth's forbidding sister Lady Constance, warns Galahad, will not hear of this.

"The expedition arrives in London tomorrow afternoon, so tomorrow night I shall be dining with my Jerry."

Gally gazed at her in amazement. Her childish optimism gave him a pang.

"With Connie keeping her fishy eye on you? Not a hope."

"Oh yes, because there's an old friend of Father's in London, and Father would never forgive me if I didn't take this opportunity of slapping her on the back and saying hello. So I shall dine with her."

"And she will bring your young man along?"

"Well, between us girls, Gally, she doesn't really exist. I'm like the poet in Shakespeare, I'm giving to airy nothing a local habitation and a name. Did you ever see *The Importance of Being Earnest*?"

"Don't wander from the point."

"I'm not wandering from the point. Do you remember Bunbury, the friend the hero invented? This is his mother, Mrs. Bunbury. You can always arrange these things with a little tact."

I devoutly wish, but not for the sake of my theory, that I had never had to read this passage. It does prove, after all, my original point that Wodehouse must have read or seen the play. But it makes the reference in such clunking, leaden tones that one would prefer to have been kept guessing. Most of Wodehouse's beautifully timed literary nudges do not give chapter and verse. (And Algernon as "the hero"?) So I sadly propose that we have here a fusion of the workaholic and the self-conscious: a grisly combination that doesn't recur until the groan-making moment, in *Aunts Aren't Gentlemen* (1974), when Bertie Wooster goes out for a stroll and runs into an anti-war demonstration. (That's what I mean by letting in daylight upon magic.)

I had once thought, rather simple-mindedly, that Wodehouse's downplaying of Wilde might have to do with a revulsion from homosexuality. And his few references to the subject in his nonfictional life—he called it "homosexualism"—are generally mildly disobliging. But I learned from McCrum that in the interwar years he used to thoroughly enjoy staying with a militantly gay cousin, usefully named Charles Le Strange, who owned an eccentric but well-appointed country house in East Anglia. The most Wodehouse could be induced to say of this relative was that he was "a weird bird." Elements of his sojourns at Hunstanton Hall were pressed into service for the innumerable country-house episodes that, Wodehouse later admitted, he relied on so greatly because any scene set under such a roof seemed somehow credible.

His staunchest admirer would be hard put to deny that Wodehouse wrote too much, but that's partly because he lived so long. And a biographer can't decently quarrel with that, even though the declining years offer less and less by way of incident and amusement, and less still by way of humorous genius. McCrum is one of those who esteem the "Uncle Fred" stories, which detail the wry adventures of Lord Ickenham. One can't quite allow this. The appeal is simply too broad; too general. If a volume of collected Wodehouse could be assembled, and could include no more than two full-length novels (*The Code of the Woosters* and *Right Ho, Jeeves*, the latter containing Gussie Fink-Nottle's prize-giving at Market Snodsbury Grammar School); perhaps a dozen of the more finished Jeeves and Bertie short stories (to include "The Great Sermon Handicap," "Jeeves and the Old School Chum," and "Jeeves and the Song of Songs"); and a selection of the Mulliner tales (both stories about the cat named Webster, the "Buck-U-Uppo" reminiscences, and the accounts of Archibald and Sacheverell), one would have a real corker that could never, ever die. As it is, one so often bumps into lost souls who claim to have "tried" Wodehouse and not got the joke. These are the unfortunates who in early and impressionable youth were handed a duff anthology by a well-meaning but mirthless aunt (or, admittedly, uncle).

Wodehouse never really went back to England after the Second World War; he had been semi-officially "cleared" of any charge of treason or collaboration, but the authorities, in a nasty bit of petty sadism, did not actually tell him they had in fact concluded that the evidence was insufficient. So he continued to churn out Edwardian-era plots from a home on Long Island, and to help set up the revoltingly named "Bide-A-Wee" home for stray and abandoned pets. This slushiness, like his sporadic interest in spiritualism and the occult, is of exactly the sort that he was best at lampooning—most especially in the Princess Diana–like person of Madeleine Bassett, a ghastly girl who thinks that the stars are God's daisy-chain. ("All rot, of course," Bertie says of this. "They're nothing of the sort.") But it may have come in useful in his frequent descriptions of an almost ectoplasmic Jeeves, as he "shimmered" into a room, or sometimes "filtered" or "floated" out.

Simile and metaphor provide so much of the energy of Wodehouse's narration: "He writhed like an electric fan"; "He wilted like a salted snail"; "Ice formed on the butler's upper slopes"; "There came a sound like that of Mr. G. K. Chesterton falling onto a sheet of tin"; "He looked like a sheep with a secret sorrow"; "A lifetime of lunches had caused his chest to slip down to the mezzanine floor"; "Aunt calling to aunt, like mastodons bellowing across the primeval swamp." I myself jumped like a pea on a hot shovel only twice during the reading of this biography: first when I read of Wodehouse's referring to his youthful case of "clap," and second when, in his letters from prison, he twice employed the word "toilet" for "lavatory." It's important that his votaries be able to think of him as virtually disembodied. In a great and noble defense of Wodehouse against the wartime calumny that was spread about him, Orwell observed that the complete omission of the sex joke was an astonishing sacrifice for a comic writer to make. But for Wodehouse it seems to have been no sacrifice at all. His marriage to Ethel, though it led to a great stepfatherly love for her daughter, was a business arrangement, with pets—preferably Pekes—standing in for offspring. The nearest approach to even an innuendo comes in *Thank You, Jeeves*, when Bertie finds his former fiancée, the American Pauline Stoker, in his bed, wearing his "heliotrope pajamas with the old gold stripe." He phrases it thus: "The attitude of fellows toward finding girls in their bedroom shortly after midnight varies. Some like it. Some don't. I didn't."

One gasps at Wodehouse for going even as far as that. And given that he mentioned his "clap" only to his much more seasoned friend Guy Bolton, and late in life too, I prefer to believe that he was just trying to keep up, to appear to be one of the boys. He never found this easy, however. One of his editors, Christopher Maclehose, told me that he had once been to visit "Plum" on Long Island, and had found him shyly reading a copy of Alec Waugh's novel *A Spy in the Family*. This little effort was an extremely mild essay in erotic comedy, but Wodehouse found it profoundly shocking and asked Maclehose if everything in England had become so filthy in his absence. If not disgruntled, as Bertie Wooster once put it in another connection, he wasn't exactly gruntled either. But this is just as one might have hoped it to be.

His admirers will desert P. G. Wodehouse for his archaic *Upstairs Downstairs* settings on the same day that people discard Oscar Wilde for being too fond of the drawing room or discover Charles Dickens to be anachronistic for writing about stagecoaches in an age of steam. His attention to language, his near faultless ability to come up with names that are at once ludicrous and credible, and the intricacy of his plotting are imperishable. Unlike Wilde, though, he put his genius into his work, not his life.

(*The Atlantic*, November 2004)

Anthony Powell: An Omnivorous Curiosity

TO GET ONE QUESTION out of the way before we begin:

> At one of these public interrogations (I am not sure which college) a professor prefixed a question by saying—rather archly—that he was uncertain how to pronounce my name. As an inspiration of the moment I replied that like the Boston family of Lowell I rhymed it with Noël rather than towel.

Here Anthony Powell was describing an incident on his tour of New England in the early 1960s, and he gave some tincture of both period and place. In Boston,

> The restaurant of our hotel...was called *The Hungry Pilgrim*. Outside stood an examplar of esurient puritanism dressed in a black-and-white Cromwellian costume with hair in a pigtail, which was a shade anachronistic and had not yet become at all chic for men. From time to time, looking as if he had just landed from *The Mayflower* and was

---

Review of *To Keep the Ball Rolling: The Memoirs of Anthony Powell.*

> in urgent need of a square meal, this gaunt figure would ring a bell. In general, however, Boston, a city of considerable charm, suggests a date later than the 17th century... Boston does not disappoint. Even on the briefest visit one can detect layer upon layer of the Bostonianism celebrated in such a long American literary tradition. When I was there in 1961 Little, Brown's, with much other entertaining, gave me luncheon at that haunt of ancient peace, shrine of Boston brahminism, the Somerset Club. The party included Edwin O'Connor, an American novelist I had already come across in England.
>
> The Somerset Club is deservedly famous. I doubt if any club in London could equal—certainly none surpass—the inspissated and enveloping club atmosphere of The Somerset. Ancient armchairs and sofas underpropped one or two equally antiquated members, ossified into states of Emersonian catalepsy in which shadow and sunlight were not only the same, but had long freed them from shame or fame. It was comforting to see so splendid a haunt from the past surviving intact in a widely disintegrating world.

And it is cheering to think of Powell, the pre-eminent novelist of English traits, discoursing there so happily with the author of *The Last Hurrah*.

Some of the supposed difficulty or intractability of Anthony Powell is on show in these passages—a slight fussiness about etiquette and detail, and an almost affected pleasure in the antique or the nearly expired. Moreover, why say "esurient" when "hungry-looking" would do, or "inspissated" instead of "stifling"? Perhaps because "esurient" may also suggest "greedy" or even "voracious," and because "inspissated" denotes an atmosphere or an element that has been thickened or congealed *by evaporation*—the perfect term for clubland's residuum. In the context of commercialized puritanism in one case and brahminism in the other, we find an author who would rather be thought puritanical—or even stuffy—than use a lazy or obvious word. Look again, and you will see an observant prefiguration of the "theme" kitsch that we now all take for granted. Look one last time, and muse on the implications of "Emersonian catalepsy." Look up the whole excerpt, and you will find that O'Connor told Powell a very amusing story about Evelyn Waugh, which story Powell subsequently tracked to its principals before finding it to be quite untrue but well worth repeating.

* * *

This is all part of the task for which I happily volunteer: recommending the reading of Anthony Powell. I say "happily" because I have never induced anyone to try him and been subsequently cursed for my pains. Indeed, I have been thanked in almost broken tones. Yet those of us who till this vineyard, on either side of the broad Atlantic, occasionally adopt a pre-emptively defensive posture all the same. When Powell died, in March of last year, at the age of ninety-four, the *New York Times Book Review* devoted a "Bookend" column to the obsequy, written by Ferdinand Mount, the editor of the *Times Literary Supplement* and Powell's nephew by marriage. (A revision of his piece serves as the foreword to this edition of the memoirs.) Not even Mount, though writing at such a moment, felt that he could avoid a long, throat-clearing refutation of charges of snobbery, elitism, and such-like. "As a matter of fact," he asserted of his uncle-in-law, "his fiction was extraordinarily democratic."

Oh, dear. I agree with this claim, but without feeling the slightest need to advance or defend it. (Can there be "undemocratic fiction"—the only discovery that would necessitate or imply its counterpoint?) Powell's fiction is "democratic" because it is realistic and humane and somewhat given to the absurd. If you like, it also shows an acute awareness of a stable and long-settled society in transition. It confronts sex and death and unfairness, and brushes against love, poverty, and war.

To Keep the Ball Rolling (which is an abridgment of *Infants of the Spring, Messengers of Day, Faces in My Time*, and *The Strangers All Are Gone*, originally published as four separate volumes) is democratic in that it shows a great and omnivorous curiosity about the lives and motives of others. And if one chooses to read these memoirs from the standpoint of the New—or, indeed, the old—Criticism, they may stand as a *Bildungs*-memoir or palimpsest of Powell's celebrated twelve-volume *A Dance to the Music of Time*. For example, as a small boy Powell was taken to watch the funeral of King Edward VII, in 1910 (an experience shared by many London children), and he knew enough about the need to please adults to claim that he had seen Caesar, the late King's dog, which had padded along behind the royal coffin and thus became, as Powell dryly recorded, "a great tear-jerker." From this distillation of childhood half memory he intuited the following:

> I must, however, have glimpsed for a moment the officer of 2nd Life Guards commanding the escort riding a short way behind the gun-carriage. This was the 5th Earl of Longford, later killed at Gallipoli; father of my future wife. We possess a photograph which includes my father-in-law, as well as my father: Lieutenant-Colonel Lord Longford on his charger just behind Caesar's kilted attendant; Captain Powell among the group of regular army adjutants standing at attention with drawn swords.

Powell's novels appear to depend much on delicate threads of coincidence, and some readers have claimed to find the coincidences too dependent on the inbreeding of class. However, probably many English people could have discovered their future fathers-in-law in an early group shot, even if that shot was not taken at a royal interment. More indicative as a childhood memory is this one. The author reckoned that he was no more than six.

> After the park and the street the interior of the building seemed very silent. A long beam of sunlight, in which small particles of dust swam about, all at once slanted through an upper window on the staircase, and struck the opaque glass panels of the door. On several occasions recently I had been conscious of approaching the brink of some discovery; an awareness that nearly became manifest, then suddenly withdrew. Now the truth came flooding in with the dust infested sunlight. The revelation of self-identity was inescapable. There was no doubt about it. I was me.

This passage helps to introduce the oft-attempted comparison between Powell and Proust. There is, first and most obviously, that ability to evoke childhood which is, alas, lost to so many of us but still, somehow, recognizable when well done. Then occurs a possibly related thought: Does this capacity, in its literary expression, bear any relation to the existence of a secure and well-ordered society—the sort of predictable structure and placement that a curious and intelligent child could begin to puzzle out for himself? And then a succeeding thought: May not a self-awareness acquired so early be invaluable in both noticing and delineating the character of others?

Powell showed great familiarity with the work of Proust while avoiding much direct reference to him. The allusions are mostly oblique, as in this very laconic reflection on the art of memoir:

> One of the most peculiar aspects of autobiography is the way in which some authors are acceptable in their sexual and suchlike intimacies (Proust masturbating in the lavatory), others are without great interest in these rôles, at worst only embarrassing. At first sight, the simple answer seems to be that some write "well," others less well; but in the field of self-revelation the altogether uninstructed can produce a masterpiece of apt expression; the seasoned writer, at times a cliché. I can find no literary explanation other than that only certain personalities are appropriate to dissection; others not.

The words "others not" are quite superfluous to that sentence, and indeed to that passage; nonetheless, they form a coda that I would not be without. Like Proust, Powell was not exactly pithy (I can't offhand recall any "quotations" from Powell, as one can from his great contemporaries Wodehouse and Waugh), but I hope I have conveyed something of the worthwhileness of hearing him out. One learns to trust certain raconteurs, even if they appear at first to be long of wind.

And Powell could be terse when he chose. During the early Nazi bombardment of Britain he was in uniform and received the news that his frail wife, after at least one miscarriage, had given birth to a son: "I found that becoming a father had a profound effect upon the manner in which one looked at the world." That's all he wrote about that. The clear implication is that those who understand will understand already, and those who do not either never will or will find out in their own good time. No waste of words.

This tone or style is often described as "typically English," and though Powell was proudly and decidedly Welsh (and stressed the Welsh pronunciation of his family name), it is no more possible to picture him as, say, Russian than it is to imagine Proust's hailing from Barcelona. Just like Nicholas Jenkins, the first-person narrator of *A Dance to the Music of Time,* Powell was born into the British military caste, educated at Eton and Oxford, "launched" in the world of literary London in the 1920s and 1930s, and gravely inconvenienced but also much matured by wartime; he attained seniority and status just as the old and solid Britain and its empire were undergoing deliquescence. Every page of both fiction and memoir bears the impress of these facts in one form or another.

The Duke of Wellington is still tirelessly quoted as having said that the Battle of Waterloo was really won "on the playing-fields of Eton"—a tribute to the values of the rigid upper lip and all that. One of the minor delights of these memoirs is that Powell, who took a particular interest in the aristocracy, met a later Duke of Wellington while serving in the British army. Among this duke's "keenest convictions was that his ancestor had never uttered the opinion... [and he offered] a standing remuneration of a hundred pounds to anyone who could prove its authenticity." Nor is this the only example of Powell's readiness to write against stereotype. In an early section on his first days at a boys' school he recorded, "Teaching was good, though not at all intensive. Mr. Gibbs, an attractive personality, showed that it was perfectly possible for a headmaster to be also a nice man." I reeled back as I read this betrayal of the canonical tradition; no self-respecting Brit can write about his early education without at least some reference to sadism and misery, and to my knowledge no author has tried it since Byron set the standard. So one is relieved to find that at his very next school Powell was starved and brow-beaten, and that by the time he was fourteen, he was able to make quite a brisk diagnosis of one of the masters, who "preferred goodlooking boys to plain ones, but not to excess, and one would suppose him a repressed bisexual." Powell continued, "A touch of kinkiness was added by a fervid preoccupation with ladies' shoes (a fancy said to presage masochism)." That's more like it.

In point of his own political outlook Powell achieved some comparable understated effects. He seems at first glance to have been an axiomatic and inflexible young Tory. He described a contemporary as "given to singing the *Internationale*, a tune for which tone-deafness presented no handicap." Visiting Spain in 1933, he recorded the impression that "administration was breaking down everywhere"—as if this were a law-and-order problem rather than the stirrings of a republic. He evinced no apparent interest either in the social questions or in those who were occupied with them; the radicals in his novels and in these pages are mainly clowns or hypocrites. Yet for several crucial years he was extremely close to George Orwell, whose flinty socialist principles—and persistence in trying to live up to them—might well have invited Powell's gentle ridicule but (perhaps because they were not bogus) instead won his respect. The pages recollecting his friend are of interest and some beauty:

> Goodness knows what Orwell would have been like in the army. I have no doubt whatever that he would have been brave, but bravery in the army is, on the whole, an ultimate rather than immediate requirement, demanded only at the end of a long and tedious apprenticeship.

Here again, reading that deceptively dense sentence, one is reminded of what it is to be molded by a very highly evolved and somewhat stratified society. In such a system courage is neither a sufficient nor even in the strict sense a necessary condition for the high calling of arms; a force that depended on mere bravery would be merely a militant rabble—subject to mood swings, perhaps, and indubitably depriving its officer corps of opportunities for understatement. Such almost invisible writing about the most palpable of questions is a continual distinction of Powell's work and an unending reward for the reading of it.

Powell chose the hymns for Orwell's funeral, in 1950:

> The Lesson was from Ecclesiastes, the grinders in the streets, the grasshopper a burden, the silver cord loosed, the wheel broken at the cistern. For some reason George Orwell's funeral service was one of the most harrowing I have ever attended.

As I say, Powell knew when and how to write sparely. He also had some sense of the gold standard as applied to people. The fact of his having helped out liturgically at the funeral of that determined atheist calls attention to what I think is the inescapable conclusion that Powell, too, had no use for religion per se. He didn't flaunt the fact, but the absence of religion as a subject—an absence also very large in his fiction—eventually obtrudes itself. Consider this statement of his cherished values:

> It is better to remain calm; try to remember that all epochs have had to suffer assaults on commonsense and common decency, art and letters, honor and wit, courage and order, good manners and free speech, privacy and scholarship; even if sworn enemies of these abstractions (quite often wearing the disguise of their friends) seem unduly numerous in contemporary society.

Hard to imagine leaving "faith" out of that taxonomy unless on purpose.

Writing of a close and admired wartime friend, Alexander Dru (a relative by marriage of Evelyn Waugh's), Powell wondered (as one so often does about newly made friends) how it was that he had never met Dru before. Later on he supplied a clue by observing in passing that Dru was "a Roman Catholic of profound—though incessantly searching—belief, he was on the whole inclined to frequent Catholic circles (no doubt one of the reasons we never met)." Something more was being said here than that Powell was not himself a Catholic. As the memoirs scrolled out in four "movements"—childhood, youth, maturity, and late middle age, mirroring the subdivision of *Dance* into the four seasons—Powell began to strike the note of "melancholy." (A word search—not that he would countenance such a thing—would disclose an increasing reliance on the term.) This is interesting in two respects: Nicholas Jenkins is represented as working on a biography of Robert Burton, the author of *The Anatomy of Melancholy*, and Powell decided to face the problem head-on in, so to speak, real life.

> Even after reaching one's early sixties letters start to arrive from insurance firms and the like opening with the words: "You will soon be sixty-five, etc., etc.," causing the recipient to reflect: "Well, it's been kind to allow me to stay so long." As the eighth decade gradually consumes itself, shadows lengthen, a masked and muffled figure loiters persistently at the back of every room as if waiting for a word at the most tactful moment; a presence more easily discernible than heretofore that exhales undoubted menace yet also extends persuasive charm of an enigmatic kind.

> Death is the mother of beauty, hence from her,
> Alone, shall come fulfilment of our dreams
> And our desires
>
> Anyway that was what Wallace Stevens thought; others too. Again—as with loudly decrying the world and its ways—a tranquil approach is probably to be preferred, rather than accept too readily either Death's attractions or repulsions... better that the dual countenances of the ubiquitous visitant should not cause too prolonged musings on either the potential relief or potential afflictions of departure. Better, certainly, not to bore other people with the subject.

Again, in this masterly harnessing of the stoic to the limpid, a brisk coda ensures against any languor or, indeed, longueur. Try reading it in combination with the arm-wavings of that other Welshman Dylan Thomas, all about rage and dying and light, and see which holds up best. And then, just as one thinks that must be the old boy's final word (the term "bore" is designedly the most annihilating in the English vernacular), there is this:

> All the same the presence in the corner—whose mask and domino never quite manage to keep out of sight the ivory glint of skull and bones beneath—seems to imply, even if silently, something of that once familiar cadence, harsh authoritarian knell of the drinker's passing day... "Last orders, please—time, gentlemen, time," in this case the unspoken sanction: "Last conclusions, please."

Such a nicely subliminal evocation of *The Waste Land* gives a polite nod, in passing, to the faithful while helping to demonstrate that Powell himself declined their invitation.

The reflections of successful writers on other writers, and on the craft of writing, can be astonishingly banal. On the whole, Powell preferred to make very vague and general and lenient remarks about his fellow authors, especially if they were contemporary. But many readers, I suspect, would be surprised by his lack of enthusiasm for P. G. Wodehouse—a lack that, although not elaborated, is explained in part by this mild but firm judgment on Evelyn Waugh.

> He really did believe in entities like a "great nobleman," "poor scholar," "literary man of modest means." Of course, in one sense, such stylized concepts may certainly exist, but at close range they usually require a good deal of modification...
>
> The "high-life" of *Decline and Fall* is mostly depicted from imagination, hearsay, newspaper gossip-columns. Later, when Waugh himself had enjoyed a certain amount of first-hand experience of such circles, he was on the whole not much interested in their contradictions and paradoxes. He wished the beau monde to remain in the image he had formed, usually showing himself unwilling to listen, if facts were offered that seemed to militate against that image.

In Powell's understated terms, this ranks quite high on the scale of condemnation. (He was elsewhere at some pains to praise Waugh as a man, to sympathize with him in his troubles, and to defend him from some accusations of rudeness.) The position he was championing, it must be emphasized, was that of realism. Waugh may have fancied himself a Tory modernist, but Powell intuitively knew that the claim was somewhat phony. He was also implicitly defending himself as the chief claimant while indirectly rebuking the critics who lazily arraigned his work for Waugh's sins of snobbery.

In his youth Powell spent some time in the Baltic and in Finland, where his father was *en poste* as a military attaché. (The experience led to one of his early experimental novels, *Venusberg*.) I do not know whether this conditioned him to an interest in Russian writing, but in a paragraph so brief that one might almost miss it he did say roundly that for him the chief author was Dostoyevsky, whose "characters and situations have one of the qualities I prize highest in a novelist, the ability to be at once grotesque yet classical, funny and at the same time terrifying."

This struck me forcibly when I read it again, because these memoirs do consent, every now and then and with a certain resignation, to identify certain minor characters in Powell's *Dance*, the detection or unmasking of whom is a long-established parlor game in English literary circles. Yet Powell never ventured the least discussion of his most finished and fearsome cast member, the Dostoyevskian Kenneth Widmerpool. There are multiple and variegated achievements in *Dance*, but this creation is Powell's certain ticket to literary immortality, an evil figure of fun whose crass, obtrusive, unstoppable visage we are all doomed to confront at some time or another. I apologize for quoting myself on Widmerpool, but the effort it cost me to summarize him when reviewing *Dance* is one I could not bear to attempt again.

> The shortest way of capturing the essence of this grotesquely fascinating and repellent figure might be to say that he is a monster of arrogance and conceit, *but entirely wanting in pride.* Bullying to those below him, servile and fawning to those set in authority, entirely without wit or introspection, he is that type of tirelessly ambitious, sexless, and charmless mediocrity that poisons institutional life, family life, and political life. He is the perfected utilitarian and philistine.

You've met him, all right. He would be recognizable in any culture. But he has never been traced to any "model," and Powell disdained to play the game anyway in this instance—for the excellent reason that Widmerpool belongs with Falstaff and Raskolnikov and Uriah Heep, and not in the pages of *Who's Who.*

American readers inclined to regard Powell as too insular might be surprised, and not unpleasantly, by his selection of Hollywood and American encounters: F. Scott Fitzgerald, Erich von Stroheim, and Paul Robeson.

"Fitzgerald," he wrote, "—that rare phenomenon, a 'bad' writer who made himself into a 'good' writer—had lost much of his former appeal simply because he had begun to produce immeasurably better novels than his early work." The two men lunched at the MGM commissary during Powell's rather disappointing stint in Hollywood in 1937. His description of the meeting contains one of the best encapsulations of character on short acquaintance that I know of. It is rounded off, from the memoir point of view, by Powell's being acute enough to notice, from later reading, that the date of the lunch (July 20, 1937) was the day on which Fitzgerald had his fateful dinner meeting with Sheilah Graham.

Powell met Stroheim more glancingly, some years later, at a festival of Stroheim's films in London. Stroheim was evidently in a "profoundly melancholy" mood, from which he was roused only by Powell's recollection of the group of military attachés on Monteblanco maneuvers in *The Merry Widow*. (During the war Powell had been a liaison officer with the exiled military staffs of Hitler's victim nations.) Stroheim kindled at this compliment to his sense of detail—or sense of realism—but lapsed back into melancholy, saying, "I no longer look like the *Oberleutnant* I once was."

As for Robeson, Powell met him during a KGB-supervised lunch for the hack Stalin-era novelist Mikhail Sholokhov. The following vignette gives one a sense of missed opportunity.

> I mentioned to Paul Robeson that I had been fortunate enough to see his Othello which he had played in London a long time before. I would have liked to discuss with him the Black WPA *Macbeth* watched in Los Angeles [in 1937], but new introductions had begun to take place. In fact, Robeson's Othello had been interesting rather than impressive. He had seemed to tackle the role with a sense of grievance alien to Shakespeare's self-confident Moor. The Black WPA players had been infinitely less tense.

Again the dry sting in the tail; it would have been something to witness the scheme of this conversation as played out in a Soviet Embassy drawing room. (Powell passed on a tip from Gore Vidal about attending workers'-paradise writers' conferences in the old days: "I always sit next to a man in a turban. You get photographed more.")

As for the writerly life itself, Powell gave occasional guidance throughout, much of it rather conversational but none of it trite, and some of it, it seems to me, positively lapidary. There is more than meets the eye in this memory of adolescent reading:

> One day in School Library I came across a magazine (I suppose *The Criterion*) which contained a long account of James Joyce's *Ulysses*. I was very interested by what was said, but this interest seemed quite separate in itself; causing, so to speak, no conversion

> or repentance as to middlebrow reading matter. Such forms of intellectual double-harness are perhaps characteristic of literary self-education.

When this boy was a bit older, he applied the same pragmatism to the design of an extraordinarily ambitious literary project:

> I had been turning over in my mind the possibility of writing a novel composed of a fairly large number of volumes, just how many could not be decided at the outset. A long sequence seemed to offer all sorts of advantages, among them release from the re-engagement every year or so of the same actors and extras hanging about for employment at the stagedoor of one's creative fantasy. Instead of sacking the lot at the end of a brief run—with the moral certainty that at least one or two of the more tenacious will be back again seeking a job, if not this year or next, then in a decade's time—the production itself might be extended, the actors made to work longer and harder for much the same creative remuneration spread over an extended period; instead of being butchered at regular intervals to make a publisher's holiday.
>
> There were many objections to setting out on such a hazardous road, chiefly the possibility of collapse, imaginatively speaking; simply dying (something bound to happen sooner or later) before completing the book.

These memoirs open with a very young man who began to frequent an antiquarian bookshop run by an indigent admirer of Oscar Wilde's. They conclude in Margaret Thatcher's Britain (the closing volume was published in 1982, when the author was indeed alive to see the vindication of his project), in a long meditation on the authenticity and the sexual character of William Shakespeare. The raw material of life interested Powell, as it had to; its slow refinement into the finished product of culture and society and language absorbed him far more. The suggestion in that last excerpt, of all the world's being a stage, contains a very bold insinuation: a parallel between this diffident and subtle novelist and that inspired, panoptic but ultra-practical Elizabethan actor-manager, who was always ready to write a new scene at need, or to raise an appreciative laugh from the cheaper seats, but who was able to capture both pity and terror in a delicate verbal noose. The implication strikes me as less profane than it might once have done. Powell (even by his choice of a Bardic title for the closing volume) wisely left it latent; but as I say, he did have a sense of the gold standard.

(*The Atlantic*, June 2001)

John Buchan: Spy Thriller's Father

THERE IS A DRY WIND blowing through the East, and the parched grasses wait the spark." I can remember the frisson I felt when I first read that line, as I can recall the faint sense of absurdity that accompanied the thrill. People don't really talk like that, as I half understood when I was twelve, but then, they don't really talk like Kipling's believable soldiers either. The words—which occur in the opening pages of John Buchan's *Greenmantle*—are uttered in a secret office near Whitehall, in London, as Sir Walter Bullivant briefs Richard Hannay on the extreme hazard and implausibility of his upcoming mission to save the empire. Even at that age I preferred Bullivant's style to the affected gruffness of "M" as he summoned Commander James Bond to a confidential session on the newest Red Menace supervillain.

In several respects Buchan is as different from Fleming as chalk is from cheese. The hero Hannay is uninterested in sex, revolted by all forms of cruelty, and ill at ease in the modern world of cleverness and greed and deceit. He is a late-Edwardian version of the strong, silent type that upheld chivalric values while playing "The Great Game," and he is doomed to see most of his friends immolated in the trenches of the Western Front. But Buchan spanned the gap between Kipling and Fleming, and his stories furnished a

---

Review of *John Buchan: The Presbyterian Cavalier*, by Andrew Lownie.

crossover point for beginning readers between the straightforward "adventure" book and something resembling the adult novel. I like to think that they still do, and this in spite of their occasional preposterousness ("There are some things," Hannay reflects near the beginning of *Mr. Standfast*, "that no one has a right to ask of any white man").

Buchan's following in America probably derives chiefly from *The Thirty-nine Steps*—the first of the Hannay tales, and the one that was famously transferred to celluloid by Alfred Hitchcock. Here one has a very well-shaped thriller, with many vertiginous shifts of plot and scene, a dastardly set of foes, and a game played for exceedingly high stakes. The reliance on coincidence or the fortuitous is often questionable, but the results at the same time are never quite incredible. And the hero is, as I hinted before, more of an innocent abroad than a calculating agent. He is actuated principally by loyalty, either to friends or to country, and when he meets sheer evil, he is often baffled as well as repelled. This innocence may or may not be the counterpart of his creator's rather alarming sense of integrity. What is a modern and wised-up reader to make, for example, of Hannay's encounter (again in *Mr. Standfast*) with the lovely Mary Lamington: "I didn't even think of her as pretty, any more than a man thinks of the good looks of the friend he worships"? Since Mary is also described as having a boylike grace of movement, even the least jaded attention is inevitably drawn to what is apparently being disowned. We do not nowadays think of the British Secret Service as a place where the polymorphously perverse was unknown.

One of the merits of Niall Ferguson's recent work on the British Empire is the reminder it provides of how Scottish that empire was. Not only did the Scots provide a vast proportion of the soldiers and miners and ship's engineers of the system (I have seen it argued that Scotty on *Star Trek* is a tribute to this grand tradition), but several colonies bore a distinctly Caledonian stamp. Even today a visitor to New Zealand or Canada is bound to notice the influence of Scottish architecture and of the Scottish educational and religious heritage; and in the Cameron Highlands of Malaysia, and the city of Blantyre, in Malawi, the imprint of Scotland is to be felt in numerous distinctive ways. The battle flag of the Confederacy, indeed, displayed the cross of Saint Andrew; and I recently read an account of the revolution in Texas in which one of the proclamations under discussion featured a stirring line from the poetry of Robert Burns—the more impressive because it was unattributed and assumed to be familiar in the context.

Scotland, Christianity, and empire were the air in which Buchan moved. Born to a struggling minister of the Free Church of Scotland (a congregation that had seceded from the established local church and stood for a flinty Calvinism), he revered the epic story of David Livingstone as a missionary in Africa, went out to serve as a member of Sir Alfred Milner's governing team during and after the Boer War, was elected to Parliament as a Scottish member (on a liberal Conservative and Ulster Unionist platform), and ended his days in 1940 with the title of Lord Tweedsmuir and the office of governor-general of Canada. In his fiction Highland and Lowland dialects are employed in almost every chapter, and there are recurrent allusions to Scottish vernacular poetry and song.

The famous contrast in the Scottish character is between the dour, stoic, and economical and the romantic, passionate, and rebellious. Buchan was a salient instance of this contradiction, which expressed itself mainly in the contrast between his life and his writing. He was continent in all matters; punctilious as to time and bookkeeping; deeply attached to his national Church; and a tightly buttoned scholar, civil servant, politician, and diplomat. His every leisure moment was devoted to writing, with an output of novels, biographies, and histories that amounted to graphomania. His chief recreational outlets were riding, climbing, and walking. An ulcerated stomach compelled a strict dietary regime. No breath of scandal touched his public or private life. His attitude to authority and empire was trustful and loyal. But his writing shows an attraction first to the exotic and the numinous, and second to the underdog, the rebel, and the outsider. In many of his novels there are mysterious and evil women with hypnotic, magical properties—including the bewitching Hilda von Einem, in *Greenmantle*, and a female in *The Three Hostages* whose hands "were laid on the arms of the chair"; "hands more delicate and shapely I have never seen, though they had also the suggestion of a furious power, like the talons of a bird of prey."

The occult, especially as it derives from the East or from Africa, provides a continual undertone of fascination, attractive and repulsive in almost equal degrees. In a remarkable short story, "The Grove of Ashtaroth," the hero finds himself obliged to destroy the gorgeous little temple of a sensual cult, because he believes that by doing so he will salvage the health and sanity of a friend. But he simultaneously believes himself to be committing an unpardonable act of desecration, and the eerie voice that beseeches him to stay his hand is unmistakably feminine.

In a not dissimilar way Buchan found himself admiring the spirit of the defeated Boers, who with their stern Calvinism and equestrian tactics may have reminded him of clan fighters on the Scottish borders. One of his best-drawn fictional heroes is the Afrikaner tracker Peter Pienaar, Richard Hannay's tough and self-sacrificing sidekick in three of the novels. Buchan wrote and rewrote a biography of the Marquis of Montrose, the seventeenth-century Scot who was perhaps best described as a Presbyterian Cavalier—the same coincidence of qualities that lends Andrew Lownie's new biography its subtitle. And when put in charge of British propaganda during the First World War, he made space for something more than a footnote in history by recommending that the American journalist Lowell Thomas go and see T. E. Lawrence. Buchan and Lawrence became close after the war; they shared an interest in the classics and an admiration for Montrose. But their concepts of asceticism and mortification were more discrepant than Buchan can possibly have guessed.

Buchan used to be far more readily acknowledged as the father of the spy thriller than he is today. Reviewing his last novel, *Sick Heart River*, in 1940, Graham Greene wrote, "What is remarkable about these adventure-stories is the completeness of the world they describe." He also pointed out that Buchan was the first to realize "the enormous dramatic value of adventure in familiar surroundings happening to unadventurous men... the death that may come to us by the railings of the Park." And the impress of Buchan on Greene's early work is plain enough. However, when Greene came to write his memoir *Ways of Escape*, forty years later, he recorded that by the time he sat down to begin *This Gun for Hire*, he "could no longer get the same pleasure from the adventures of Richard Hannay."

> More than the dialogue and the situation had dated: the moral climate was no longer that of my boyhood. Patriotism had lost its appeal, even for a schoolboy, at Passchendaele... It was no longer a Buchan world.

This is a less persuasive account of disillusionment than it appears on the surface. Buchan's most celebrated thrillers were written and published during the awfulness of the First World War and the reaction to it that set in: *The Thirty-nine Steps* in 1915, *Greenmantle* in 1916, and *Mr. Standfast* in 1919. The conflict is not presented as straightforwardly Manichaean: Gallantry is attributed to Germans and to Turks. Moreover, it was a fact of Buchan's life that he had many friends among the Red and anti-imperialist leaders on the proletarian Clydeside, and that he tried to do honor to these antagonists both in his novels and in his public speeches. Even when the spy genre itself became a near synonym for cynicism, John Le Carré had his George Smiley adopt the nom de guerre "Mr. Standfast"—and he would not, I think, take refuge in the claim that the name comes from *Pilgrim's Progress* in the first place. Buchan took Bunyan as a pattern in much of his writing and his fine autobiography, *Memory Hold-the-Door*, was published in North America under the title *Pilgrim's Way*. It has been almost forty years since the first biography, by the Scottish writer Janet Adam Smith, was published; this more recent effort, by another Scot, is intended to acquit Buchan of charges of bigotry and also of obsolescence. (Mr. Lownie is in some respects as straight-faced and innocent as his subject: He records with perfect gravity that in 1931 Buchan agreed to become president of the Federation of University Conservative and Unionist Associations, a body with initials that were not amended for some years.)

As Lownie points out, one respect in which this is more a "Buchan world" than the formerly up-to-date might be willing to credit is this: Buchan understood very early that the United States would become the decisive actor. The rather cardboard American who comes to Hannay's aid in *Greenmantle*, a fat and rich but nonetheless brave and humorous figure named John Scantlebury Blenkiron, is included for no other purpose than to make this point. As Canada's governor-general in the late 1930s, Buchan made every attempt to establish cordial relations with President Franklin Roosevelt. (It was a contradiction in this posture that he disliked Winston Churchill and tended to favor appeasement, but it's also clear that his dread of a second world war was conditioned above all by the shudder he experienced when contemplating the first one.)

* * *

Like Greene and Evelyn Waugh and many others of the period, Buchan has been accused of anti-Semitism. Two defenses have frequently been offered in these cases: that the alleged anti-Semite harbored a prejudice no greater than was commonplace at the time, and that he had many Jewish friends. A third possibility—that the offending words are uttered by fictional characters and not by the author—is sometimes canvassed. None of these will quite do in Buchan's case. It's not merely that anti-Jewish clichés occur in his books; it's that they occur so frequently. The usual form they take is a reference to Judeo-Bolshevism—the sympathy of Jews, even rich ones, for the Russian Revolution. That, however, might be described as political anti-Semitism, just as Buchan's energetic support for the early Zionist movement might be called political philo-Semitism. Paradoxically, perhaps, Buchan greatly disliked as a person the most anti-Jewish and pro-Zionist figure of his day, Arthur Balfour. Indeed, Balfour was the basis for the villain Andrew Lumley in Buchan's first thriller, *The Power House*. I mention this for two reasons. First, the book describes an invisible, string-pulling, sinister secret government, but one run by English lords and financiers rather than exotic or cosmopolitan types. Second, Buchan openly admitted that his model in the writing of it (he called the novel "a tribute at the shrine of my master in fiction") was E. Phillips Oppenheim, whom he further described—in an instance, perhaps, of trying too hard—as "the greatest Jewish writer since Isaiah." In "The Grove of Ashtaroth" the friend for whom the purgative enterprise is undertaken is a man described by the narrator as a Jew trying to "pass," who because of his ancestry is vulnerable to the delicious temptations of strange gods. This is excessive on Buchan's part, and arguably a "transferred" aspect of that very element in himself: the element of the mystical and the bizarre that the Scots call "fey."

The same ambivalence can be detected in *Greenmantle*, which is certainly his masterpiece. Here the subject is *jihad*. As a wartime propaganda officer, Buchan was fascinated by the ability of Germany to use its Turkish allies to enlist Muslim sentiment against the British Empire. The words of Sir Walter Bullivant with which I opened occur in their context thus:

> Though the Kaiser proclaims a Holy War and calls himself Hadji Mohammed Guilliamo, and says the Hohenzollerns are descended

> from the Prophet, that seems to have fallen pretty flat. The ordinary man again will answer that Islam in Turkey is becoming a back number, and that Krupp guns are the new gods. Yet—I don't know. I do not quite believe in Islam becoming a back number... The Syrian army is as fanatical as the hordes of the Mahdi. The Senussi have taken a hand in the game. The Persian Moslems are threatening trouble. There is a dry wind blowing through the East, and the parched grasses wait the spark. And that wind is blowing toward the Indian border.

Despite this Whitehall Orientalism, when Hannay gets out into the field he is astonished to find his gallant friend Sandy Arbuthnot—the ideal blend of Scots daredevil and *Gunga Din* special agent—half convinced that the Muslim zealots are in the right.

> The West knows nothing of the true Oriental. It pictures him as lapped in color and idleness and luxury and gorgeous dreams. But it is all wrong... It is the austerity of the East that is its beauty and its terror... They want to live face to face with God without a screen of ritual and images and priestcraft.

This capacity for vicarious identification—even imaginative sympathy—was Buchan's most sterling quality as a man and as an author. And it was in order to ignite the spark of Islam pre-emptively, so to speak, and to set the parched Eastern grasses afire in a way that the Ottoman Empire did not expect, that Lawrence was sent to Arabia in the first place. So we do indeed inhabit a world partly shaped by a dogged Scots puritan, and we may even discover—or rediscover—that Buchan's invocations of grit and pluck and hardihood are not as mockably retrograde as all that.

(*The Atlantic*, March 2004)

Graham Greene: I'll Be Damned

GRAHAM GREENE ONCE WROTE a celebrated essay about a *doppelgänger* who cared enough to haunt and shadow him, even to masquerade as him. This "other" Greene appeared to have anterior knowledge of the movements of his model, sometimes showing up to grant an interview or fill a seat in a restaurant, so that Greene himself, when he arrived in some old haunt or new locale, would be asked why he had returned so soon. The other man was suitably nondescript yet camera-shy. He was caught once by a society photographer, and captioned in the press into the bargain, but a combination of flash and blur allowed him to escape unmasking. So who or what was he? *Semblable*? *Frère*? Or perhaps *hypocrite lecteur*?

This mode of imitation or emulation or substitution—at once a form of flattery and a species of threat, or at any rate of challenge—was and is analogous to the role that Greene himself played and still plays in the lives of many writers and readers. A journalist, most especially an Anglo-American travel writer, will run the risk of disappointing his editor if he visits Saigon and leaves out any reference to quiet Americans, or turns in a piece from Havana that fails to mention the hapless Wormold. As for Brighton, or Vienna, or Haiti—Greene was there just before you turned up. Leaving the *Orient Express*, you will glimpse the tail of a raincoat just at the moment when that intriguing and anonymous fellow passenger vanishes discreetly at the end

---

Review of *The Life of Graham Greene, Vol. II 1955–1991*, by Norman Sherry.

of the platform. In Mexico or Sierra Leone some old veteran will mumble something about the stranger in the off-white suit who was asking the same questions only a while back. On one of my first ventures as a foreign correspondent, in 1975, I sat in the garden bar of a *taverna* in Nicosia, reading about the adventures of Dr. Saavedra in *The Honorary Consul*, visualizing what I had just seen along the haunted "Green Line" that slashed through the ruins of the city, and moaning with relief that Graham Greene had never been to Cyprus. Even so, as I crossed that same border in the broiling noon of the next day and heard only the cicadas and the click of the rifle bolts at the frontier, I was composing a letter to him in my mind.

It was a matter not just of place but of character. Disillusioned diplomat whose wife was drying up before his unseeing eyes? Snake-eyed cop? Priest to whom Eden was forever lost? Sentimental terrorist spokesman? All these went straight into the notebook. You could divide the eager freelances into roughly three types: those who had been influenced by *Scoop*, those who were stirred by *Homage to Catalonia*, and those who took their tune from *The Quiet American*. Overlap with Le Carré fans was frequent in the third instance: Their preferred quarry was the naive guy at the U.S. embassy, insufficiently comprehending of the ancient hatreds and millennial routines that had been so quickly mastered by the old/new hands.

Greene's centennial year, just now past, saw the reissue of many of his classics in beautiful new editions from Penguin Books, along with publication of the third and closing volume of Norman Sherry's biography. In an effort to isolate and identify the elusive and evasive figure who could so plausibly be impersonated—to lay his ghost, so to speak—I set myself to reading it all. I think that what surprised me the most, when I had finished, was his sheer conservatism.

Greene, after all, was nothing if not radical, even subversive, in his self-presentation. Always at odds with authority, not infrequently sued or censored or even banned, a bohemian and a truant, part exile and part émigré, a dissident Catholic and a sexual opportunist, he personified the fugitive from the public school, Foreign Office, rural and suburban British tradition in which he had been formed. By what means did this pinkish roué gradually mutate into a reactionary?

The first and easiest reply is: By means of the sameness of his plot formula. This tends to consist of a contrived dilemma, on the horns of which his characters arrange to impale themselves with near masochistic enthusiasm. Dear God, shall I give him/her up, for your sake? Or might it be more fun to wager my immortal soul? The staginess and creakiness of all this was well netted by George Orwell, himself no stranger to the sweltering locale and the agonies of moral choice, in his review of *The Heart of the Matter* for the *New Yorker* in 1948. Of the central character he asserted,

> Scobie is incredible because the two halves of him do not fit together. If he were capable of getting into the kind of mess that is described, he would have got into it years earlier. If he really felt that adultery is mortal sin, he would stop committing it; if he persisted in it, his sense of sin would weaken. If he believed in hell, he would not risk going there merely to spare the feelings of a couple of neurotic women. And one might add that if he were the kind of man we are told he is—that is, a man whose chief characteristic is a horror of causing pain—he would not be an officer in a colonial police force.

I have always found *The End of the Affair* to be a sickly business in rather the same way, in that Sarah Miles, who might have continued being a perfectly good mistress as well as a more than adequate wife, decides to spoil everything for everybody—not by any means exempting herself—on the basis of an off-the-cuff promise to God. This resolution doesn't even result from an "answered prayer," since the crucial event on which she stakes everything (the sparing of her lover, Maurice Bendrix, during a Nazi air raid on London) has actually taken place by the time she troubles deaf heaven with her bootless cries.

These and other quasi-morality tales are all informed, it is needless to say, by Greene's own Catholicism (though one notices that he never ventures far beyond adultery or murder or espionage, or confronts a really harsh topic such as abortion). There is every reason to think that he enjoyed playing a version of the game in his own life: He originally converted to the faith in order to wear down the long resistance of a woman—his first wife, Vivien—who essentially refused to sleep with him until he had been "received" into Holy Mother Church. (For some reason this reminds me of Jessica Mitford, who decided at the last minute *not* to say, when asked at her naturalization hearing why she wanted to become an American citizen, that the Communist Party of the USA would not otherwise allow her to join.) In a rather defensive manner Greene later in his life complained when reviewers laid any stress on the predominance of Catholic themes and characters in his work; any novel about English people and society that did not contain some Catholics, he wrote, would be to that extent lacking in "verisimilitude." Notice that he did not choose to say "realism"; how likely is it, after all, as J. M. Coetzee inquires in a superb new introduction to *Brighton Rock*, that the depraved and deprived "Pinkie" and his wretched, slum-bred girl would both be so intimately familiar with the Latin forms? *"Agnus Dei qui tollis peccata mundi"* ... the repetition throughout is like that other "toll," of a continuous knell. But the dramatic convenience of such characters is this: They consign themselves to an eternity of torment while being fully aware that they are doing so. When Rose says to Pinkie, "We're going to do a mortal sin," she says it "with a mixture of fear and pride." This, by the way, is how she knows that it is to be her wedding day.

For Pinkie, meanwhile (not otherwise detectable as a reflective type), the same counter-redemptive ceremony merely consummates the ephemeral matter of "his temporal safety" in return for "two immortalities of pain." "He was filled with a kind of gloomy hilarity and pride. He saw himself now as a full-grown man for whom the angels wept." But Pinkie is not left without consolation. He can take pleasure only from giving or receiving pain, and his mind constantly returns to the schoolroom dividers with which he learned, before graduating to razors at the racetrack, to be a torturer and a maimer. We know from his memoirs that Greene was lavishly and inventively bullied and tortured while he was at school, and if we did not know this we could certainly guess. In *The Heart of the Matter*, published a decade later, the comparatively conscience-stricken Major Scobie is having a bad moment with his scrawny and tedious mistress and notices that "she was like a child with a pair of dividers who knows her power to injure." But by then, in the course of an equally bitter and arid moment with his wife, he has heard himself saying (this time in English, for some reason): "O Lamb of God, who takest away the sins of the world." It must be said for Greene that he didn't trouble his non-Catholic readers with any very complex renditions of the liturgy.

On the other hand, or as against that, he did trouble such readers with reflections like this. Scobie encounters a fellow colonialist named Perrot at a disaster-stricken border station that divides British-held Sierra Leone from its neighboring Vichy colony. Perrot hands him a drink and says, in an accent that is cartoonishly Scots, "Of course ye know I find it hard to think of the French as enemies. My family came over with the Huguenots. It makes a difference, ye know." Greene continues,

> His lean long yellow face cut in two by a nose like a wound was all the time arrogantly on the defensive: the importance of Perrot was an article of faith with Perrot—doubters would be repelled, persecuted if he had the chance... the faith would never cease to be proclaimed.

So at last we meet a Graham Greene character who keeps up his faith despite a torrid Conradian setting, but he is openly jeered at—because he is of Protestant provenance. A ruined Irishman expiring among the empty flagons and exhaling an *Ave Maria* would be sympathetic. But a righteous, continent Huguenot, never. (Incidentally, since the Huguenots were driven from France to England after a shocking pogrom sponsored by both throne and clergy, the identification with France itself, let alone with Catholic vichy, seems a bit like blaming the victim.) Perrot is further scorned for speaking sarcastically about events in Freetown, the capital of humble Sierra Leone.

> The words "big city" came out with a sneer—Perrot couldn't bear the thought that there was a place where people considered themselves important and where he was not regarded. Like a Hugue not imagining Rome, he built up a picture of frivolity, viciousness and corruption.

This seems doubly ungenerous when considered in the light of the epigraph from Leon Bloy with which Greene opened *The End of the Affair*: "Man has places in his heart which do not yet exist, and into them enters suffering in order that they may have existence." Is this creative agony available only to those who believe in transubstantiation?

* * *

To be fair to Greene, whose answer to that question was fairly obviously in the affirmative, one must admit that he extended the same indulgence to one other group: the Communists. His two best-drawn heroes in this category, both noble men facing insuperable odds, are Doctor Magiot, in *The Comedians*, and Dr. Czinner, in *Orient Express*. (Here might be the place to say that I contributed an introduction to the latter for the new Penguin series.) The theme of martyrdom is constant, even with these secular materialists. "For a moment, Dr. Czinner"—confronted in a railway compartment—"flattened himself against the wall of a steep street to let the armored men, the spears and the horses pass, and the tired tortured man. He had not died to make the poor contented, to bind the chains tighter; his words had been twisted." This is the observation of what later became known as "liberation theology" (something that, incidentally, seems to have fallen from view lately), and one notes in passing that "Czinner" is a not very artful name for a fallen Everyman.

Greene had briefly been a Party member while at Oxford, and although he was too intelligent and too prudent to remain a true adherent for long, he kept up a residual form of Catholic fellow-traveling until the end of his life. In 1967 he wrote a celebrated letter to the London *Times*. Its ostensible purpose was to join the protest against the imprisonment of two Russian writers, but its main effect was to qualify that protest by stating the following: "If I had to choose between life in the Soviet Union and life in the United States of America, I would certainly choose the Soviet Union, just as I would choose life in Cuba to [sic] life in those southern American republics, like Bolivia, dominated by their northern neighbor, or life in North Vietnam to life in South Vietnam."

Greene never had to make this choice, if only because he was often refused a visa for the United States and never "chose" to spend much time in the Soviet Union. He did, however, keep up a lifelong friendship with a permanent resident of that latter state, Kim Philby. Perhaps the most ruthless and successful espionage agent of the entire Cold War, Philby had actually risen to be a senior British intelligence officer and a colleague trusted by James Angleton, of the CIA, while acting as a dedicated agent of the KGB. Greene contributed the introduction to Philby's Soviet-edited memoir, *My Silent War*, in which he wrote, "He betrayed his country—yes, perhaps he did, but who among us has not committed treason to something or someone more important than a country?" Leave aside that "perhaps." This, with its sanctimonious echo of "Let he who is without sin cast the first stone," also recalls E. M. Forster's hope that he would "have the courage" to betray his country before his friends. This itself was almost as morally slippery as the original "casting the first stone" injunction: In any case, Philby, who sold out the colleagues he had trained himself, certainly betrayed both. Norman Sherry records that Greene lost his temper only once in the course of all their interviews—when Sherry pointed this out.

If betrayal is the motif of so many Greene novels, then its cousin treason was the motif of Kim Philby's entire life. In that sense alone Philby might have made the ideal friend for Greene. But that still left open the question of whom he had betrayed. It was surely more Greene's gentle native England than the wicked, vulgar United States. But to this Greene had a sort of reply ready. In the English past it had been considered "treasonous" to be a Roman Catholic. Official persecution was the underside of Elizabethan England. Many fine men, like Father John Gerard, had been slandered and tortured for their disloyalty (which happened to take the form of working for Catholic potentates on the mainland in order to prepare for an invasion). So strongly did Greene identify with these reactionary subversives that he became a Shakespeare-hater, accusing the national bard of being an accomplice in repression, if only a silent one. In a public address in Hamburg, accepting a Shakespeare prize from some well-meaning but unknowing academics, he astonishingly referred to John of Gaunt's dying speech about "this England" as "complacent" and pointed out that it was first published in 1597: "Two years before, Shakespeare's fellow poet Southwell had died on the scaffold after three years of torture. If only Shakespeare had shared his disloyalty, we could have loved him better as a man."

That was bad history as well as bad literary criticism. If Shakespeare had become an agent of the Vatican and King Philip of Spain, he would not have been a successful playwright in a flourishing and relatively uncensored Protestant London. (The obtuseness of Greene is increased rather than diminished when we appreciate the considerable scholarship suggesting that Shakespeare probably came from a Catholic family that had decided to practice the religion in secret, and that it was this, if anything, that explained his reticence on the matter.) Greene was very fond of his own professed attachment to the underdog. In that same lecture he asserted that "[the writer] stands for the victims, and the victims change." In *Our Man in Havana* we find that "there was always another side to a joke, the side of the victim." Simplicity here demands simplicity in return. Simply put: Is someone an underdog who aligns himself with an absolutist papacy, or with the state security services of the USSR?

It was *The Quiet American*, far more than any other novel, that gave Greene his still-enduring reputation for prescience. Had he not, in the figure of Alden Pyle, encapsulated the combination of American arrogance and naiveté that eventuated in the "quagmire" of Vietnam? The novel was published in 1955, shortly after the shattering defeat of French arms at Dien Bien Phu, and this coincidence made its acuity appear almost uncanny. Yet who was it who had written this, in 1952?

> The Indo-Chinese front is only one sector of a long line which crosses Korea, touches the limits of a still-peaceful Hong Kong, cuts across Tongking, avoids—for the moment—Siam, and continues into the jungles of Malaya. If Indo-China falls, Korea will be isolated, Siam can be invaded in twenty-four hours and Malaya may have to be abandoned.

This almost absurdly crude statement of the "domino theory" was published by Graham Greene in *Paris Match*. It can be found in his *Reflections*, under what I consider to be the suggestive title "Indo-China: France's Crown of Thorns." If you re-read *The Quiet American* today, you will see that it blames the blundering Americans largely for failing to understand or to emulate the sophisticated French style of colonialism in Vietnam. For many of us the original sin—if I may annex that term—of the American intervention was precisely its inheritance of a doomed French war. For Greene, rather, it was the failure to *live up to* that legacy. Whatever this was, it was not a revolutionary or radical position. And it seems to have been content to overlook quite a few "victims."

But however frenziedly inconsistent he was on everything else, Greene was unwaveringly hostile to the United States. When, in the closing volume of his biography Norman Sherry gets to the publication of *The Comedians*, in 1966, he says of the Smith couple therein depicted: "At last, sympathetic Americans in a Greene novel." Well, that Mr. and Mrs. Smith have some sterling qualities is beyond doubt. But they are represented as culpably and laughably unworldly, obsessed with vegetarianism and abstention from alcohol. (Protestants, in fact.) They are, further, quite unable to see the horrors of the Duvalier regime, reluctant as they are to be too "judgmental" about anything for which black people can be blamed. This satire upon their innocence was rather clever of Greene, I always thought, because he was able to borrow the fatuous apologetics of the anti-American fellow-traveler and, so to speak, transfer it to an American target.

This element in Greene's prose needs no guilt-sodden, sweat-stained policeman to hunt it out. In more than one published reminiscence and interview he told of the seminal influence of *The Pirate Aeroplane*, an adventure story written by Captain Charles Gilson and read by Greene in early boyhood, in which an avaricious American airman, cheroot between his teeth, violates and plunders a lost civilization. Even in *Travels with My Aunt*, one of his lightest and wittiest books, Greene's narrator passes through Paris and achieves an understated masterpiece of condescension by saying, "I noticed a plaque which tells a visitor that here La Fayette signed some treaty or celebrated his return from the American revolution, I forget which."

Sherry's work is so replete with absurd and sinister remarks by Greene on his own un-Smith-like travels as a tourist of revolution in the Caribbean and Latin American zone that one could fill this page with balls-aching propagandistic remarks that impeached him out of his own mouth. It was unfortunate for "Papa Doc" Duvalier that he went so far as to be denounced for heresy by the Catholic Church: This licensed a full-out attack on him by Greene, even if the success or regime in Haiti, the "Baby Doc" nightmare, did receive the endorsement of the Holy See and of Mother Teresa. Of Fidel Castro, Greene would not hear an ill word spoken; he even differed with Kenneth Tynan and other sympathizers on the point and chose to celebrate (as I strongly suspect Tynan would not have) the then warm relations between Fidel and the papal nuncio. In 1987, with two years left to go in the life of Soviet communism, Greene turned up in Moscow and made the following speech at some "peace" conference or other:

> We are fighting together against the death squads in El Salvador. We are fighting together against the *Contras* in Nicaragua. We are fighting together against General Pinochet in Chile. There is no division in our thoughts between Catholics—Roman Catholics—and Communists.

That may have been during the Gorbachev period, but he had been doing this sort of thing ever since the 1950s, when he indulged the Stalinist regime in Poland because it maintained a Catholic front organization called Pax Christi. Yet if we are charitable, and admit that there was a pulse of humanism under all this piffle (who, after all, except for some very dogmatic and often Catholic conservatives, will say a good word for the *contras*, or Pinochet, or the death squads?), this still leaves us empty-handed when it comes to General Manuel Noriega, of Panama. Greene obviously liked Panama as a country, and may have had some justification for his friendship with Omar Torrijos, a mediocre personality even as depicted in *Getting to Know the General* but quite possibly a man of some charm. Noriega, however, was purely and merely a sadist and a thief. He may not have instigated the murder of Torrijos (though Norman Sherry seems to implicate him in this crime), but he most certainly arranged the kidnapping, torture, and killing of one of Panama's most distinguished dissidents, Dr. Hugo Spadafora. The good doctor might have been a Greene hero if he had occurred in a different political context, but as it was Greene took the side of the oppressor, even telling an interviewer after the dictator's deposition in 1989, "I hope General Noriega will harass the invaders from bases in the mountains." In one of his last novels, *Monsignor Quixote*, Greene has an old priest and an old Communist rambling around Spain in a beat-up car and exchanging likable platitudes about the nature of (and the similarity of) their faiths. But what is quixotic about wishing an extension of life and power to a fascistic zombie like Noriega?

The term "anti-American" is a loose one, and loosely employed. My own working definition of it, admittedly a slack one also, is that a person is anti-American if he or she is consistently contemptuous of American culture and furthermore supports any opponent of U.S. policy, whoever this may be. And if an author accuses America of being insufficiently colonial in Vietnam, and lives long enough to endorse a Noriega resistance in Panama, he meets the qualification. That such a position should also be so largely "faith-based" is not as much of an irony as it might seem—not in the age of globalized (but of course anti-"globalization" and anti-American) *jihad.*

It is an irony, however, that Greene should have spent so much of his career trying to adapt himself to that most singularly American of the arts, the cinema. The distinction he made in his fictions—between novels and "entertainments"—was one that he first evolved to excuse himself for writing an openly catchpenny movie script in the form of *Orient Express.* A few years later, in 1937, he composed an essay on the film industry in which he claimed, "The poetic cinema, it is worth remembering, can be built up on a few very simple ideas, as simple as the idea behind the poetic fictions of Conrad: the love of peace, a country, a feeling for fidelity." In the same essay he chose to laud the cinematic honesty of D. W. Griffith.

Even his rivals and critics grant him a facile "I am a camera" skill. Evelyn Waugh conceded that with Greene's prose "the affinity to the film is everywhere apparent... it is the camera's eye which moves." J. M. Coetzee adds,

> In *Brighton Rock* the influence of Howard Hawks can be felt in the handling of the violence at the racetrack; the ingenious use of the street photographer to advance the plot suggests Alfred Hitchcock. Chapters characteristically end with the focus being pulled back from human actors to the greater natural scene—the moon over city and beachfront, for instance.

These filmic qualities are, to put it not much higher, well-made clichés. So, for that matter, are the virtues "love of peace, a country, a feeling for fidelity." But Greene managed to betray all those, too. His many lost and exhausted and discredited causes need not evoke much nostalgia in us, but it is somehow fitting that his most lasting impression should be a celluloid one.

(*The Atlantic*, March 2005)

Death from a Salesman: Graham Greene's Bottled Ontology

[In Havana] where every vice was permissible and every trade possible, lay the true background for my comedy.
—Graham Greene, *Ways of Escape*, 1980

GRAHAM GREENE FAMOUSLY subdivided his fictions into "novels" and "entertainments" (this present one falling with a slightly suppressed chuckle into the second category) as if to slyly warn his audience that an element of the ludic and the flippant would sometimes be permitted to him and should be forgiven by his readers. If, in his infrequent confessions, he might have mentally reclassified some offenses as venial rather than mortal, something of the same analogy holds throughout his work.

I should like to propose a third, or subcategory: the whisky (as opposed to the nonwhisky) fictions. Alcohol is seldom far from the reach of Greene's characters, and its influence was clearly some kind of *daemon* in his work and in his life. A stanza of that witty and beautiful poem "On the Circuit," written in 1963, registers W. H. Auden's dread at the thought of lecturing on a booze-free American campus and asks, anxiously and in italics:

Introduction (2007) to *Our Man in Havana*, by Graham Greene.

Is this my milieu where I must
How grahamgreeneish! How infra dig!
Snatch from the bottle in my bag
An analeptic swig?

Describing a visit to a 1987 conference of "intellectuals" in Moscow in the early Gorbachev years, both Gore Vidal and Fay Weldon were to record Greene making exactly this dive into his bottle-crammed briefcase. "Analeptic" literally means "healing," and there was no doubt of a buried connection in Greene's mind between the restorative properties of holy water and the redeeming qualities of raw spirit. In at least three of his literary ventures Greene chose to make the subject a central one. The lost but resigned little fugitive cleric in *The Power and the Glory* (1940) is actually aching at all times for a shot of brandy, but the Mexican vernacular deems his type "the whisky priest." The burned-out figures of British intelligence in *The Human Factor* (1978) seem at times to be engaged in some sort of contest to amass the greatest number of "blend" labels, from J&B to Johnnie Walker, and even to create a new pseudo-scotch by mixing White Label and Johnnie Walker on the grounds that "they're all blends anyway."

The view that both sides in the Cold War were an admixture—at best—of each other's hangover-inducing ingredients was an abiding belief of Graham Greene and is never more on show than in this miniature drama, and drama of miniatures. The action commences in a bar, and almost every subsequent moment in the story is set in a place where alcohol is dominant. To speak generally, if not absolutely, one may say that dependence on booze is a symptom of weakness, and although Jim Wormold (not a name to inspire immediate confidence) does turn out to possess a few latent strengths, he is presented from the first as a feeble man who *is* both a hostage—to his own poverty and inanition—and who *has* a hostage: his foal-like sixteen-year-old daughter, Milly. This girl, a combination of slight tart and vague Madonna striding through the worldly and corrupt streets of Havana, makes the hapless vacuum-cleaner salesman a prisoner of her childhood, and of his own. How wrenched yet charmed he is, having lost the wife to whom he promised that Milly would be educated as a Catholic, to hear the little girl solemnly praying "Hail Mary, quite contrary." Yet how oppressed he is by the recollection of his own misery as a schoolboy:

> Childhood was the germ of all mistrust. You were cruelly joked upon and then you cruelly joked. You lost the remembrance of pain through inflicting it.

(Many is the Greene novel and reminiscence, most conspicuously *Brighton Rock*, where this trope of sadistic bullying makes its twitchy appearance. The slightly older boy who so relentlessly tortured him in his public-school days—a boy named Lionel Carter, as it happens—has put us eternally and unintentionally in his debt. And let us not forget that, as both tormentor and victim would have been taught: "In the lost boyhood of Judas, Christ was betrayed.")

Evidently resolving—for purposes of the "entertainment"—to not make all this too lugubrious, Greene introduces Milly rather as Evelyn Waugh presented the more-ominously named Cordelia in *Brideshead Revisited*. That good/bad little girl once made a novena for her pet pig, and was mentioned in her convent school report as the naughtiest girl in the memory of the oldest nun. She ended up by volunteering to be a nurse for the forces of General Franco. Milly unknowingly gratifies her father by setting fire to a teasing schoolmate named Thomas Earl Parkman, Junior; shows her class the collected postcards of great aesthetic nudes; and gives artless yet casuistic replies to direct questions from her easily-baffled and highly-impoverished single parent. She also offers novenas in the hope of acquiring a horse, and allows herself to be escorted by the saturnine Captain Segura, a man who would have seemed exceptionally sadistic even in the ranks of Franco's phalanx.

Thus it is made as clear as possible, within a few pages of the opening, that Wormold is living a life of quiet desperation. He cannot go on as he is, but he is set in his ways and wedded to mediocre respectability. This would be dire enough even if—like Henry Pulling in *Travels with My Aunt*—he was back in suburban Wimbledon. But in exotic Havana, with business going poorly and with a burgeoning daughter to boot, he is additionally expected to keep up appearances as an awkward Englishman abroad. Yet this is precisely what makes him attractive to Hawthorne, the relentlessly incompetent envoy of British Intelligence who decides to sign him up as a subagent and (within limits) "put him in the picture." To us, Hawthorne seems like yet another English *naïf* in the tropics, concerned, like any harassed salesman, with giving a pleasing impression to his ultimate boss in London, but to the hunted and needy Wormold he belongs to "the cruel and inexplicable world of childhood," and it thus feels like no more than natural justice to exploit him and fleece him to the very hilt. The two men do, however, have an initial bond. When they meet in Sloppy Joe's bar, Hawthorne surveys the range of bottles on offer and says:

> "Eighteen different kinds of Scotch... including Black Label. And I haven't counted the Bourbons. It's a wonderful sight. Wonderful," he repeated, lowering his voice with respect. "Have you ever seen so many whiskies?"
>
> "As a matter of fact I have. I collect miniatures and I have ninety-nine at home."

And this collection is about to be enhanced by the man with whom Wormold already has a bond, another lonely loser named Dr. Hasselbacher who divides his time between a few remaining patients and the rival Wonder Bar.

> "There is always time for a Scotch." It was obvious from the way he pronounced Scotch that Dr Hasselbacher had already had time for a great many.... He took from his pocket two miniature bottles of whisky: one was Lord Calvert, the other Old Taylor. "Have you got them?" he asked with anxiety.
>
> "I've got the Calvert, but not the Taylor. It was kind of you to remember my collection, Hasselbacher." It always seemed strange to Wormold that he continued to exist for others when he was not there.

This touching and abject allusion to Bishop Berkeley's famous question is followed immediately by a playful and half-drunken ontological interlude, this time in the Seville-Biltmore bar where Dr. Hasselbacher, flown with scotch, imagines that he has already won the next day's lottery and is awash in dollars. Addressing a stray American who doubts him, he says:

> "I have won them as certainly as you exist, my almost unseen friend. You would not exist if I didn't believe you existed, nor would those dollars. I believe, therefore you are."
>
> "What do you mean I wouldn't exist?"

> "You exist only in my thoughts, my friend. If I left this room..."
>
> "You're nuts."
>
> "Prove you exist, then."
>
> "What do you mean, prove? Of course I exist. I've got a first-class business in real estate: a wife and a couple of kids in Miami: I flew here this morning by Delta: I'm drinking this Scotch, aren't I?" The voice contained a hint of tears.

From Berkeley to Descartes in a few paragraphs: Greene's theological-philosophical subtext is always available to him. ("Like Milly, Dr. Hasselbacher had faith. He was controlled by numbers as she was by saints.") And interestingly, the innocent and faithful Hasselbacher offers the annoyed American the alternative existence of "a Secret Service agent"—the very career upon which Wormold is, all unaware, about to embark.

Before we leave this scene, we may notice that the American is like all the other Americans in the novel: banal and bourgeois and self-pitying. (He doesn't even consider claiming the words "I think" as proof of his existence: The real-estate business comes first.) Most of the Yanks are tourist cameos, worried about the wave of violence that is afflicting the island and tending to congregate in yet another bar at the Hotel Nacional. Their days of treating Havana as a vacation and business backyard are about to be over, "for the President's regime was creaking dangerously toward its end."

Our Man in Havana was published on October 6, 1958. On New Year's Day 1959 Fidel Castro's luxuriantly bearded guerrillas emerged from the *sierras* and the villages and captured the city. As with his setting of *The Quiet American*—in Vietnam just before the critical battle of Dien Bien Phu—or with his decision to locate *The Comedians* in the midnight of "Papa Doc" Duvalier's Haiti, Greene seemed to have an almost spooky prescience when it came to the suppurating political slums on the periphery of America's Cold War empire. In 1958—the year that *Doctor No* was first published—Ian Fleming, from his own Caribbean home, had not yet captured the world's attention with a British agent who carried a number as well as a gun (and a license to use it). Nor had humanity learned to associate Cuba with missiles, and with the possibility of thermonuclear annihilation. And Greene in any case was having fun, with his unarmed "Agent 59200/5," and his wholly invented missile sites based on vacuum-cleaner blueprints.

Moreover, the eclipse of British power after the Suez catastrophe of 1956 had not quite then become self-evident. "I think we've got the Caribbean sewn up now, sir," Hawthorne tells "The Chief" on his return to London. This black-monocled clubman and thwarted fiction writer—a distinctly non-"M"-like creation—also invents agents in his own mind, and is thus intrigued to learn more about "our man in Havana."

> "Doesn't run after women, I hope?"
>
> "Oh, nothing of that sort, sir. His wife left him. Went off with an American."
>
> "I suppose he's not anti-American? Havana's not the place for any prejudice like that. We have to work with them—only up to a point, of course."

("The Chief"—which was also the staff nickname given to Lord Copper in Evelyn Waugh's *Scoop*—is fond of this "up to a point" mantra, which he inflicts on Hawthorne rather than, as with Lord Copper's underling Salter, having it practiced on him.) His character occupies only a few brief scenes but is nonetheless one of the most finished and polished portrayals in the entire book. Like Lord Copper, he too is easy to delude or, as was said of President Coolidge, "once bamboozled, impossible to unbamboozle." Greene's own wartime relationship with British Intelligence, and his lifelong comradeship with its most famous traitor Kim Philby, evidently conditioned him to view "the Service" as a place of collapsing scenery and low comedy, populated by a cast of jaded misfits. Thus he presents Wormold's fraud and dishonesty in a sympathetic light: The mandarins of M16 are eager to deceive themselves, and to be deceived, and they get no more than what they ask for.

I forget who it was who once updated the old moral couplet: "Oh what a tangled web we weave / When first we practice to deceive" by adding the lines:

> But when we've practiced quite awhile
> How vastly we improve our style!

That later version (which was entitled "A Word of Encouragement") could have been composed with Wormold in mind. *Facilis descensus Averno!*

How easily he takes to the world of padded expenses, false reports, and fabricated salaries for non-existent staffers. But for Greene, the world of farce always has its bitter limitations. The inoffensive Dr. Hasselbacher is drawn into the net of Wormold's fantasy and suffers ruin and humiliation as a consequence. Now Wormold feels himself becoming coarsened:

> Shut in his car Wormold felt guilt nibbling around him like a mouse in a prison-cell. Perhaps soon the two of them would grow accustomed to each other and guilt would come to eat out of his hand... There was always another side to a joke, the side of the victim.

That this last insight had been dearly bought by Greene, from his boyhood onward, there can be no doubt. Its counterpart and corollary—"Sometimes it seems easier to run the risk of death than ridicule"—does not make its appearance until much nearer to the culmination of the story.

From the name of the "Atomic Pile" vacuum cleaner to the shock effect produced on "The Chief" by the outlines so deftly and falsely sketched by Wormold, Greene also indulges in the lighter side of "schoolboy" humor:

> "Vacuum cleaner again. Hawthorne, I believe we may be on to something so big that the H-bomb will become a conventional weapon."
>
> "Is that desirable, sir?"
>
> "Of course it's desirable. Nobody worries about conventional weapons."

This could almost have come from a Peter Sellers script of the same epoch, and will inevitably remind some of today's readers of more recent fiascoes associated with paranoia about weapons of mass destruction. However, there is nothing flippant or innocent about Captain Segura. In the figure of this torturer and mutilator and sex maniac, evidently appropriated from the dictator Batista's dreaded "enforcer" Captain Ventura, Greene offers a foretaste of the "death squads," with their dark glasses and special unmarked automobiles, who were to terrorize Latin America and horrify the world in the succeeding decades. Once again, this character is not on stage very often or for very long, but he furnishes another well-etched and highly memorable "miniature." It would not, perhaps, be correct to see in him an instance of the banality of evil. His evil is too overt and too ingrained for that. But he does have a way of turning up in banal or even jovial settings, reminding me of what Greene wrote about the skill of John Buchan as a thriller writer: his ability to summon the specter of death right up against the railings of the leafy and relaxing park. It is over a routine game of "checkers"—accompanied this time by daiquiris rather than scotch—that Segura casually mentions his belief in the "torturable" and "non-torturable" classes. Wormold affects shock and may even feel it: At any rate he reacts as if he were a stuffy Englishman who is quite new and unused to native customs:

> "I didn't know there were class distinctions in torture."
>
> "Dear Mr. Wormold, surely you realize there are people who expect to be tortured and others who would be outraged by the idea. One never tortures except by a kind of mutual agreement... Catholics are more torturable than Protestants, just as they are more criminal."

Greene is here showing us a third-rate Grand Inquisitor, in a church gone bad, who no longer applies the rack or the thumbscrew out of any exalted conviction. (Indeed, we later learn that Segura has been hoarding money in case he has to make a sudden opportunistic dash for Miami.) So perhaps banality and evil are not as much separated as all that...

In the novel, Greene makes his creation Wormold behave in a manner that is absurdly out of character. (It is plainly outside the bounds of credibility, given his aching feelings for his vulnerable daughter, that he would permit her to continue an association with a policeman whose cigarette case is upholstered with human skin.) However, Wormold himself proves to be a man who can confect fictional personalities more or less at will. Having initially invented them in order to bluff his superiors, he finds that they have taken on an existence of their own:

> It astonished Wormold how quickly he could reply to any questions about his characters; they seemed to live on the threshold of consciousness—he had only to turn a light on and there they were, frozen in some characteristic action.... Sometimes he was scared at the way these people grew in the dark without his knowledge.... There

were moments when Wormold thought it might have been easier if he had recruited real agents.

However, this second ontological interlude—if I may so phrase it—comes to an abrupt end when the universe of rugged reality decides to claim Wormold for its own. His flesh-and-blood assistant Beatrice is a woman of unsettlingly keen intuition. "You talk like a novelist," she observes—while still bamboozled—when he muses on the fate of one of his "agents." "You've been writing his elegy like a bad novelist preparing an effect," she adds, in a line that is altogether too improbable and self-referential. It is she, who has been cheerfully paying part of the price of Wormold's irresponsibility, who signals the very harsh new tone and turn of events at just the moment when he himself is under pressure and about to "revert" to sheer puerility and denial. (To be exact, he is playing with a children's cereal box after breakfast.) "I don't want you murdered," she sternly announces. "You see, *you are real.* You aren't *Boy's Own Paper.*" (Italics mine.) It is the palpable womanhood of Beatrice, combined with the increasing and alarming grown-upness of his beloved Milly, that compels Wormold to play the "real man" at last. In earlier and easier and happier scenes, the big weapons have been conjured from his imagination, and the small-bore weapon has been a soda siphon in a hotel garden, aimed playfully at Captain Segura but easily laughed off with the excuse that it was directed at a "Dimpled Haig" scotch. On that occasion, Captain Segura had resorted to an abrupt vernacular obscenity (all the indecent expressions in this novel are rendered in Spanish) and "squeezed out a smile. It seemed to come from the wrong place like toothpaste when the tube splits." Greene's gift for the sinister implication, and for the recurring analogy to booze, is further illustrated by the sentence: "You could not estimate his danger from his size any more than you could a hard drink." And it is clear that the silly splash from the soda siphon has by no means diluted the Captain, or his venom. But by the time Segura takes off his gun-belt and lays it to one side, in preparation for the climactic whisky-dominated game of checkers (or "droughts" if you prefer) it is as plain as the old maxim of Chekhov that a gun once displayed in plain sight will not be reholstered until it has been fired in anger. The "Wormold," in other words, has turned. The meek little shopkeeper is ready to commit murder. This is to be death *from* a salesman.

His thirst to kill is supplied by a hideous, stuttering, impotent double-agent named—like Greene's boyhood tormentor—Carter. If this odious and parodic Englishman had not offered Wormold poisoned scotch at the dreary, joyless business banquet into which he is lured and enticed (and at which different flasks and blends are continually offered and contrasted), and if the innocuous Dr. Hasselbacher had not been subsequently slain for trying to warn Wormold off, and if the whole callousness and cynicism of the spy-racket had not begun to sicken Wormold well beyond the point of disgust, I think that Greene meant us to understand that his salesman might yet have remained passive, and preferred to stay in the camp of the victim. But what Wormold is forced to realize is that he is in just as much danger from his "own" side. How quickly the tepid appeals to patriotism and Britishness and Lamb's *Tales from Shakespeare*, proffered so smoothly by Hawthorne at their first meetings, mutate into their sordid opposite. It's not unlike the blue movie that he and Beatrice find themselves viewing while sheltering in one of Havana's celebrated nightclubs:

> There was an odd intimacy between them as they watched together this blueprint of love. Similar movements of the body had once meant more to them than anything else the world had to offer. The act of lust and the act of love are the same; it cannot be falsified like a sentiment.

And so Wormold, determined to vindicate friendship and love over treachery and murder, finds it surprisingly easy to discover what he must do. In three sentences that might almost define the world we know as "Greeneland":

> He stood on the frontier of violence, a strange land he had never visited before; he had his passport in his hand. "Profession: Spy." "Characteristic Features: Friendlessness." "Purpose of Visit: Murder." No visa was required. His papers were in order.

At such a critical moment, no Greene character would refrain from at least some reflection on faith, however terse and bitter:

> Vengeance was unnecessary when you believed in a heaven. But he had no such belief. Mercy and forgiveness were scarcely virtues in a Christian; they came too easily.

Even so, when it comes to the moment of truth—or "reality"—Wormold is almost unable to destroy another human being and has to rationalize his actions even as he is undertaking them. He is thankful that the decision is taken out of his hands by Carter's vile conduct, and indeed is still rationalizing busily when the shock moment of actual crisis occurs, and the question of will or volition is snatched (unlike the fortunately purloined gun) out of his hands.

This stroke of impulsive decision does not succeed in dispelling the mist of moral ambiguity. Wormold still has to live in the world that he has—with his own lies and practical jokes—helped to make. Once again, a rationale is required of him, and he chooses (as does Beatrice) a version of E. M. Forster's celebrated moral calculus. If one had the choice of betraying one's country or one's friends, said the author of *Howards End* and of that momentous phrase "the world of telegrams and anger," one should hope for the courage to betray one's country. Wormold's confected cables to London have some of the absurdity of William Boot's telegrams to Lord Copper's *Daily Beast*, but his anger takes a Forsterian form:

> I don't give a damn about men who are loyal to the people who pay them, to organizations.... I don't think even my country means all that much. There are many countries in our blood, aren't there, but only one person. Would the world be in the mess it is if we were loyal to love and not to countries?

Many years later, in his rash introduction to Kim Philby's KGB-vetted autobiography *My Silent War*, Greene was to write, again with a question mark that asked rather a lot:

> He betrayed his country—yes, perhaps he did, but who among us has not committed treason to something or someone more important than a country?

With or without its "perhaps," this is bound to strike many readers as a bit too glib and convenient (as indeed it is). And how many times, after all, does a choice between country and friends really come up? But, safely back in

London, where admittedly there are no torturers or executioners, Wormold and Beatrice discover that their secret employers, too, are immersed in moral ambiguity and expert in the means of manipulating it. In essence, and in return for his silence about the whole fiasco, Wormold is offered a sinecure and an official decoration. In one of the weaker sections of the book, Beatrice then repeats at greater and less probable length everything that Wormold has just declaimed above. In retrospect, we can see that this Greene "entertainment" was in many ways the curtain-raiser for the bleak universe of Le Carré's George Smiley, and of the shadowland where any appeal to loyalty and the old decencies was little more than a rhetorical prelude to a stab in the back.

The conclusive end of the Cold War, and the implosion of one party to it, now makes some of Greene's own rhetoric seem even more facile. The revolution did indeed come to Cuba, and the Captain Seguras did indeed take themselves off to Miami, and for a while Greene himself was an honored guest of—and ardent apologist for—the Fidel Castro regime. (His admiring chronicler Norman Sherry gives some disquieting instances in Volume III of his immense biography.) Greene was not, in fact, neutral in the Cold War, nor a sincere practitioner of moral equivalence. He was by inclination a supporter of the "other" side and, above all culturally and politically hostile to the United States. In 1969 he delivered a lecture entitled "The Virtue of Disloyalty" in Hamburg, in which (never mind Lamb's *Tales*) he accused Shakespeare himself of having been too patriotic, and too reticent about Catholic dissidents sent to the gibbet. He was delighted when a Soviet cosmonaut took *Our Man in Havana* into outer space. But his audience and readership were in the "West," so the "shades of Greene" were adjusted accordingly. And this needful ambivalence was often useful in his novels, since it compelled him to phrase his ethical dilemmas in liberal and individual, rather than Marxist or collective, terms.

Having already touched on Greene's debt to Waugh, and most especially to *Brideshead Revisited*, I ought to try to return the compliment, even if obliquely. Writing in praise of *Brideshead* many years after its first publication, Greene said that he had remembered the novel's beautiful opening chapter as very long, and was thus astonished to find, upon rereading, that it was as brief as it was. This he certainly intended as a compliment. One should say the same for his own swiftly-drawn but contemptuous portrait of the British ambassador to Cuba, whose appearance in the novel occupies no more than a page and a half. The desiccated and frigid envoy repeatedly insists that he knows nothing of what has been going on, and wishes for nothing more than to remain in this blessed state of unawareness. It is Greene, not the provincial and suburban Wormold, who is able to assemble a whole diplomatic biography from the *objets d'art* on view while he is being kept waiting by this dignitary:

> Wormold thought he could detect a past in Tehran (an odd-shaped pipe, a tile), Athens (an icon or two), but he was momentarily puzzled by an African mask—perhaps Monrovia?

In "real" life, Greene was to greatly annoy the British Foreign Office by writing some devastating letters to the press a few weeks after the publication of *Our Man in Havana*. Announcing a post-revolution cancellation of the sale of weapons to Cuba, the Foreign Secretary Selwyn Lloyd had claimed that, when the weapons contract had been signed, there had been no evidence of strife. Greene wrote at his withering best:

> Any visitor to Cuba could have given Her Majesty's Government more information about conditions in the island than was apparently supplied by our official representatives: the mutilation and torture practiced by leading police officers... the killing of hostages.

By one of those right-place-right-time occurrences that swelled his reputation as both journalist and novelist, Greene had stumbled into contact with rebels and lawyers—Armando Hart, Haydée Santamaria, Melba Hernandez—whose names are still totemic in the Cuban Revolution and some of whom are admired even by those who later underwent a painful rupture with Castro. Whether it is deliberate or not I cannot say, but Greene's description of the Havana Seville-Biltmore's upper rooms as being "built as prison cells round a rectangular balcony" is a near-analogy to the "Panopticon" jail in which Castro was held by Batista on the Isle of Pines after his legendary attack on the Moncada barracks in 1953. Greene was well ahead of the story, before he fell well behind it. His secular and personal religion, which always stressed "the side of the victim" and which ostensibly forbade him to "see no evil," did not safeguard him from letting both his Communism and his Catholicism get in the way of truth-telling about the rebel-turned-caudillo as the years went on.

By an irony of his beloved Cuban Revolution, which has left the island stranded in time and isolated from many recent currents of history and political economy (with its still-bearded leader now paunchy and gray and the only remaining Latin American head of government always to be seen in a uniform), the city of Havana has been compelled to remain very much as Greene described it.* The more flamboyant and amoral nightclubs did undergo a period of eclipse, but the sex trade has rebounded with a vengeance as the regime has become more dependent on tourism than Batista ever was. Communism, though—"the highest stage of underdevelopment," as Hans Magnus Enzensberger once tautly summarized the case—has preserved (some might like to say "spared") the old harbor-front and its hinterland. Ernest Hemingway's old haunts at the *Floridita* and the *Bodeguita del Medio*, the Calle Obispo and the "pock-marked pillars on Avenida de Macco"; all the little landmarks of Wormold's life, are still rather seedily there. Nor is this depiction valued only by nostalgic foreigners. Pedro Juan Gutiérrez, Cuba's great chronicler of low-life and the author of *Trilogía Sucia de La Habana* (Dirty Havana Trilogy), has devoted an entire novel to the imaginative reconstruction of Greene's visit, and titled it *Nuestro GG in Havana* (Our GG in Havana). Greene's ability to evoke a sense of place and time, as in his clever mention of Havana's "blistering October" are encoded in this book as in no other, and remain redolent and real. In some ways, indeed, the existence of an antique rather than a modern Havana, until the day when the dam breaks and the full tide of Americanization flows in, is part of his literary and political bestowal. As is, of course, the silhouette of the anomic and rumpled and disillusioned Englishman in a torrid zone, nursing a bottle of scotch and musing ineptly on Pascal while caught somewhere between the status of émigré and internal exile. The human condition seen through the bottom of a glass: darkly.

---

*I completed this essay on the day before Fidel Castro fell ill and handed over power to the Cuban armed forces, in the shape of his brother Raúl, in August 2006.

Writing to his mistress Catherine Walston in 1956, Greene told her that *Our Man in Havana* was potentially a "very funny plot which if it comes off will make a footnote to history." I feel almost as if I owe an apology for having taken so long to illustrate his elementary point.

(2007)

Loving Philip Larkin

IN MAY 1941, Philip Larkin was the treasurer of the Oxford University English Club and in that capacity had to take the visiting speaker George Orwell out to dinner after he had addressed the membership on the subject of "Literature and Totalitarianism." Larkin's main recollection of the evening was that the meal was an indifferent one at a "not-so-good hotel," the club's hospitality funds having been hopelessly depleted by an incautious earlier invitation to Dylan Thomas.

Nudged and intrigued by this near-miss of a potential meeting of minds, I once attempted a comparison and contrast between Larkin and Orwell, as exemplars of a certain style of "Englishness." Both men had an abiding love for the English countryside and a haunting fear of its obliteration at the hands of "developers." (Here I would cite Larkin's poem *Going, Going* and Orwell's novel *Coming Up for Air*.) Both were openly scornful of Christianity but maintained a profound respect for the scripture and the Anglican liturgy, as well as for the masterpieces of English ecclesiastical architecture. (See Larkin's poem *Church Going* and the same Orwell novel, as well as numberless of his letters and reviews.) They each cherished the famous English affection for animals and were revolted by any instances of human cruelty to them. (Here consult Larkin's poem *Myxamatosis*, about the extirpation of the country's rabbit population, as well as at least one Orwell source that's too obvious to require mentioning.)

Review of *Letters to Monica*, by Philip Larkin, edited by Anthony Thwaite.

In somewhat different ways, Orwell and Larkin were phlegmatically pessimistic and at times almost misanthropic, not to say misogynistic. Both also originated from dire family backgrounds that inculcated prejudice against Jews, the colored subjects of the British Empire, and the working class. Orwell's detested father was a servant of the Empire who specialized in the exceptionally nasty sub-division that traded opium between India and China, and Larkin's detested father was a professional civil servant who came to admire the "New Germany" of the 1930s and supported the British Union of Fascists. But these similarities in trait and background produced radically different conclusions. Orwell educated himself, not without difficulty, out of racial prejudice and took a stalwart position on the side of the workers. Larkin energetically hated the Labour movement and was appalled at the arrival of emigrants from the Caribbean and Asia. Orwell traveled as widely as his health permitted and learned several foreign languages, while Larkin's insularity and loathing for "abroad" was almost parodic. In consequence, Orwell has left us a memory which gets English decency rated as one of humanity's versions of grace under pressure, whereas the publication of his *Selected Letters* in 1992, and a biography by Andrew Motion in 1993, posthumously drenched Larkin in a tide of cloacal filth and petty bigotry that was at least somewhat self-generated.

I now wish I had understood enough to push my earlier comparison a little further. For there is another aspect of "Englishness," netted in discrepant ways by Harold Pinter and Monty Python, in which both men had a share. This is the world of wretched, tasteless food and watery drinks, dreary and crowded lodgings, outrageous plumbing, surly cynicism, long queues, shocking hygiene and dismal, rain-lashed holidays, continually punctuated by rudeness and philistinism. Orwell's *Keep the Aspidistra Flying* is the most graphic distillation of all this in his early fiction, but it is an essential element of the texture of *Nineteen Eighty-four*, and was quarried from the "down and out" journalism of which he produced so much. A neglected aspect of the general misery, but very central once you come to notice it, is this: We are in a mean and chilly and cheerless place, where it is extraordinarily difficult to have sex, let alone to feel yourself in love. Orwell's best shorthand for it was "the WC and dirty-handkerchief side of life."

Philip Larkin's own summary was if anything even more dank: He once described the sexual act as a futile attempt to "get someone else to blow your nose for you." These collected letters reflect his contribution to a distraught and barren four-decade relationship with Monica Jones, an evidently insufferable yet gifted woman who was a constant friend and intermittent partner (one can barely rise to saying "mistress" let alone "lover") until Larkin's death in 1985. During that time, he strove to keep her to himself while denying her the marriage that she so anxiously wanted, betrayed her with other women sexually, and eagerly helped Kingsley Amis to employ her as the model for the frigid, drab and hysterical Margaret Peel in *Lucky Jim*.

On an initial scrutiny, *Letters to Monica* struck me as rather thickening the squalid atmosphere of some of the preceding accounts. But so unalleviated—I almost wrote "artless"—is its tone that the material takes on a certain integrity and consistency. Not unlike Larkin's paradoxical infatuation with jazz, also, it helps furnish a key to his muse. The key in both cases—which is why "artless" would be such a mistake—is that about suffering he was seldom wrong. The dismal paltriness of the suffering doesn't really qualify this verdict.

One of his ways of keeping Monica while keeping her at bay—they did not co-habit until very near the end, forced into mutual dependence by decrepitude on his part and dementia on hers: perhaps the least romantic story ever told—was to make an over-full confession of his own inadequacies as a male. "I'm sorry our lovemaking fizzled out," he writes after a disappointing provincial vacation in 1958. "I am *not* a highly-sexed person." This comes just after a letter in which he invites her to consider their affair in the light of "a kind of homosexual relation, disguised: it wdn't surprise me at all if someone else said so." And even earlier—it is not as if this is the record of a hot thing cooling—he writes in December 1954 that "if it were announced that all sex would cease on 31 December, my way of life wouldn't change at all." This naturally prompts one to review one of his best-known poems, *Annus Mirabilis*:

> Sexual intercourse began
> In nineteen sixty-three
> (Which was rather late for me)
> Between the end of the *Chatterley* ban,
> And the Beatles' first LP.

The lines can easily be read as a non-literal satire on the exuberant 1960s in general. The less-quoted succeeding verse is arguably more revealing:

> Up till then there'd only been
> A sort of bargaining,
> A wrangle for a ring,
> A shame that started at sixteen
> And spread to everything.

In Larkin's mind, marriage was invariably a trap set by females; a ring in exchange for some perfunctory sex and then a lifetime of domestic servitude and—even more appalling—the rearing of children. Once again the poetry is unambiguous. *The Life with a Hole in It* conveys the cringe with greater complexity, but *Self's the Man* is not unrepresentative:

> He married a woman to stop her getting away.
> Now she's here all day.
> And the money he gets for wasting his life on work
> She takes as her perk
> To pay for the kiddies' clobber and the drier....

Even *The Whitsun Weddings*, in which he manages to write with some *tendresse* about a famous northern English nuptial tradition, closes with an extremely melancholy metaphor of energy mutated into futility, or possibly potency into liquefaction: "A sense of falling, like an arrow-shower / Sent out of sight, somewhere becoming rain." And as for the thought of parenthood, not just by or from oneself, but even *of* oneself, we need look no further than the celebrated poem that probably convinced his admirer Margaret Thatcher that he wasn't the family-values type. *This Be The Verse* opens by saying "They fuck you up, your mum and dad / They may not mean to, but they do," and closes by advising "Get out as early as you can / And don't have any kids yourself." There are virtually no references to children in Larkin that are not vivid with revulsion, the word "kiddies" being the customary form which the automatic shudder took.

No keen analyst is required to unravel this. Not only did Larkin have a bombastic fascist for a father, but he also had a simpering weakling for a mother. Sydney Larkin had the grace to die early but his widow Eva lingered on, querulous, demanding and hypochondriac (as well as extremely unwell) for decades. She may not have meant to make her son's life a nightmare of guilt and annoyance, but she did. This resulted in Monica Jones winning at least one round. On no account, she told her man, should he be blackmailed into living with Eva. "Don't be robbed!" she beseeched him. "Don't be robbed of your soul." If she couldn't have him, she at least wouldn't surrender him to that form of "the other woman."

To have read Larkin's *Letters* and Motion's biography is to be "in" on a rather dirty joke that surreptitiously permeates these pages. Larkin may not have been highly-sexed in the conventional sense, but he was a heroic consumer of pornography and amateur composer of sado-masochistic reveries, which he often shared with his worldly friends Robert Conquest and Kingsley Amis. He didn't much like the capital city but would never pass through London without spending good money, or paying through the nose as one might say, on the vendors of semi-licit glossies in the Soho quarter. Why Andrew Motion maintains that he didn't have specialized tastes I cannot think: On those dark and costly visits he was in constant search of material featuring schoolgirls, flagellation, and sodomy. (In 1958 to Conquest: "I agree *Bamboo* & *Frolic* are the tops, or rather bottoms: do pass on any that have ceased to stimulate.") This celebrated fixation, too, is thought by some to be "quintessentially English." At his death, along with many other private papers, the vast library of a hectically devoted masturbator had to be hastily burned. (He obviously had not mistaken his calling as an archivist.) Once one "knows" this, many of the letters to Monica become instantly intelligible. He comments slyly but learnedly on the buggery implications of the D. H. Lawrence novel that was then on trial in the courts. "*You and your bottom*" he elsewhere writes fervently. "I lay in bed one morning last week remembering one after-breakfast time when you were looking out of my kitchen window... You were wearing the black nylon panties with the small hole in!" Or "You must look a wonderful sight in fur hat and boots—nothing else? Holding a rawhide whip? (You see how naturally my imagination composes aesthetic *montages* for you.)" On and on his plaintively suggestive appeals recur and—this is somehow impressive—*she never seems to take the hint.* What Larkin wanted was a Nora Barnicle and what he got was—Margaret Peel. The sole exception seems to prove my rule: In late 1958 he plumbs the depth of abjectness by writing to her in apology for what clearly must have been a bungled episode of anal penetration. ("I am sorry too that our encounter had such unhappy results for you! I really didn't expect such a thing, though I suppose it might have been predicted. I am sorry. It does rather spoil the incident, even at best, which was very exciting for me anyway. Let's hope all rights itself soon.")

Not since Hemingway so overdid the lapine pillow-talk in *For Whom the Bell Tolls* has any man referred to a woman as a rabbit with such regularity and intensity. Most of the letters are addressed to either "Bun" or "Bunny" and not a few are illustrated with drawings of rabbits, references to rabbits in literature, or condemnations of British government policy toward rabbits. The obsession did yield the fine poem *Myxamatosis* that I mentioned earlier, but Larkin's attempt to make a Beatrix Potter nursery story out of the stand-off is often in jarring contrast to the content. The sad grovel I quoted from above is concluded by the sentence: "You sound as if you want comforting Fat rabbit lovely pretty rabbit," which is a lot to bear for those of us who respect Larkin for his lack of sentimentality. And rabbits are above all philoprogenitive... Incidentally all resemblances to Orwell break off at this point: The author of *Animal Farm* had a tough enough time with women but was eager for marriage and anxious for children, preferring to adopt rather than go without.

This collection is an accidental success as a period piece. The Britain of the immediate postwar was in many ways even more austere and impoverished than the Britain of the Depression, with bad and scarce housing, for example, made very much worse by aerial bombardment. Larkin, who once told an interviewer that "deprivation is for me what daffodils were to Wordsworth," found his poetic promptings in the overcrowded, overworked, underfed society that he so much purported to resent. Not only that, but his chosen career as a librarian led him to live in Belfast, Britain's (and Ireland's) most immiserated and forbidding city, at the cusp of the 1940s and '50s. His political sympathies can scarcely have been Republican, but a description of an Orange Day rally is one of the best short evocations of massed boorish fanaticism I have ever read. "It was a parade of staggering dullness (every face wore the same 'taking himself seriously' expression) & stupefying hypocrisy."

Indeed, those of the Terry Eagleton crew, who have become so righteously fixated on the later "revelations" of Larkin's racism and xenophobia, might be surprised at the absence of jingoism and nastiness in these letters. He is very strict with Kipling's excesses, for example, accusing him of betraying his talent in order to be a crowd-pleaser ("hunts with the pack"). Perhaps the uneasy memory of parental Nazism is too close, even though this makes it the more eerie to notice that he never, ever alludes to the then-recent horror of the Third Reich, either in these pages or any others. Alternative diagnoses include Motion's opinion that he didn't quite surrender to reactionary impulses until he became much older, and the high likelihood that much of what he did write in that vein was designed to amuse friends in private letters, by way of outraging the new forms of correctness. A thwarted and furtive sex-life, one may speculate, would have been no obstacle in the formation of a carapace of contempt for modernity and its hedonistic outriders.

And this returns us to the luckless Monica, whose possibly Aspergerish manners he strove in vain to correct. "I *do* want to urge you, with all love and kindness, to *think* about *how much* you say & *how* you say it..." Deploying—in a different but surely conscious declension—the most deadly word in the English vernacular, he warned her that "you're getting a habit of *boring* your face up or around into the features of your listener." That was in 1952, with almost thirty years of on-again off-again stretching before the pair of them. But he must have caught something of value in her opinions, because he took seriously her part-grammatical objection to line four of the closing stanza of *Church Going*: today perhaps his best-loved poem. Ought it to have been "And so much never can be obsolete," instead of "that much"? Look and see. Even if, like me, you cannot imagine changing a word, you notice that she was a shrewd and attentive reader. (Here might be the place to say that Anthony Thwaite's meticulous footnoting and cross-referencing have made this book much more capacious and lively than it might have been, as well as affording us a unique view of some of Larkin's most lapidary poems when they were still fluid and in formation.)

Rising above the low-level rancor and tedium that can make the scrutiny of private *anomie* so lowering to the spirit, *Letters to Monica* obliquely shows the civilizing effect that even the most trying woman can exert on even the most impossible man. With the exception of the occasional rather weak joke in passing, Larkin respected Miss Jones too much, it seems, to try any of his vulgar prejudices or cheaper doggerel on her. Most impressive of all, I found, was that even his anti-libidinous propaganda could yield its warm and poetic aspect. Take this stern epistle from 1951:

> I think—though I am all for free love, advanced schools &
> so on—someone might do a little research
> on some of the *inherent qualities* of sex—its *cruelty*, its *bullyingness*,
> for instance. It seems to me
> that *bending someone else to your will* is the very stuff of sex, by force
> or neglect if you are male,
> by spitefulness or nagging or scenes if you are female. And what's
> more, both sides *would sooner*
> *have it that way than not at all.* I wouldn't.

Such an ostensibly repressive and limited view, with its unimaginative image of "both sides," had been given the most starkly beautiful expression by a poem that Larkin wrote the preceding year. *Deceptions*, suggested by a harrowing anecdote of forced prostitution from Henry Mayhew's history of the London poor, implicitly vindicated the ruined female victim by pleading indirectly that her foul client was also a pathetic loser and that she, the innocent sufferer, might even turn out to have been "the less deceived." He by no means omitted to picture the raw, latent violence of her own trauma. ("All the unhurried day / Your mind lay open like a drawer of knives.") Gem hard, it is also an immediately striking piece of imaginative sympathy. Reviewing it, D. J. Enright gave Larkin a rare moment of (almost) unmixed pleasure by saying, as he proudly reported to Monica, that "I persuade words into poetry & don't bully them." A critic could not have approached more nearly to the core of Larkin's gift.

It is inescapable that we should wonder how and why poetry manages to transmute the dross of existence into magic or gold, and the contrast in Larkin's case is a specially acute one. Having quit Belfast he removed himself forever to Hull, a rugged coastal city facing toward Scandinavia which may once have been represented in Parliament by Andrew Marvell but which in point of warmth and amenity runs Belfast pretty close. Here he brooded biliously and even spitefully on lack of privacy, the success of his happier friends

Amis and Conquest, the decline of standards at the university he served, the general bloodiness of pub lunches and academic sherry-parties, the frumpy manipulativeness of womenfolk, and the petrifying imminence of death. (Might one say that Hull was other people?) He may have taken a sidelong swipe at the daffodils, but he did evolve his own sour strain and syncopation of Wordsworth's "still, sad music of humanity." And without that synthesis of gloom and *angst* we could never have had his *Aubade*, a waking meditation on extinction that unstrenuously contrives a tense, brilliant counterpoise between the stoic philosophy of Lucretius and David Hume, and his own frank terror of oblivion. Many of Larkin's expeditions to churches were in fact an excuse to visit cemeteries or memorials in spite of his repudiation of the fantasy of immortality, and with another of the finest poetic results of these—*An Arundel Tomb*—it turns out he had taken Monica as a companion and later accepted some of her thoughtful proposals concerning its final form. We might agree to find it heartening that, in consequence of a dead-average Middle-England Sunday stroll, as the other half of an almost passionless relationship, Philip Larkin should notice the awkwardly conjoined couple on an ancient stone coffin-lid and, without forcing let alone bullying the language, still tentatively be able to find:

> Our almost-instinct almost true:
> What will survive of us is love.

(*The Atlantic*, May 2011)

Stephen Spender: A Nice Bloody Fool

ONE OF THE EARLY POEMS with which Stephen Spender made his name opens like this: "My parents kept me from children who were rough."

In 1957, in *The Sense of Movement*, Thom Gunn proclaimed: "I praise the overdogs from Alexander / To those who would not play with Stephen Spender."

Not long afterward two distinguished Englishmen of letters decided that "Stephen" had earned his very own limerick, and wrote,

> Then up spake the bold Stephen Spender
> "You may think my *conscience* is tender.
> You might think my *heart*
> Was my sensitive part—
> But you should see my poor old *pudenda*."

In a long life Spender never quite succeeded in overcoming the widespread impression (which he may have privately shared) that there was something vaguely preposterous about him. His official biographer, John

---

Review of *Stephen Spender: The Authorized Biography*, by John Sutherland.

Sutherland, perhaps unwittingly and certainly unwillingly, provides armfuls of ammunition for this view. He does not cite either of the cracks I have just mentioned, but he does give the passage below, taken from Spender's memoir *World Within World*. In 1930 T. S. Eliot had decided to publish four of the young man's poems in the *Criterion*, and furthermore invited him to lunch.

> At our first luncheon he asked me what I wanted to do. I said: "Be a poet." "I can understand you wanting to write poems, but I don't quite know what you mean by 'being a poet,'" he objected.

I think this is quite funny on its own, but additionally so because it inverts what ought to be the proper Jamesian scenario—the stuffy English don admonishing the brash young American student. Be that as it may, Stephen Spender was to pass a great deal more of his life "being a poet" than he ever did writing poetry.

The thought lay about him in his infancy (which was marked by an awful father, a frightful elder brother, and a hideous torment of a boarding school education—so far, "on track" for English writing). At the age of nine he went to the Lake District on a family holiday and was exposed to "the simple ballad poems of Wordsworth," which, as he further phrased it, "dropped into my mind like cool pebbles, so shining and so pure, and they brought with them the atmosphere of rain and sunsets, and a sense of the sacred cloaked vocation of the poet." He was already, in other words, what Byron witheringly called "a Laker." An early school poem sustains the same note of moist wonderment about the weather, yearning for the spring in Devonshire but opening, "The rain drops from the mist endless and slow / The trees are bare and black..."

This culminates in the line "O God!... would I were there." Sutherland misses a trick, I think, in failing to point out the obvious debt to Rupert Brooke and his *Grantchester*, inspiration of drooping and sensitive versifiers at that time and since. (Ten years later Geoffrey Grigson was dryly to say, in reviewing Spender's book *The Destructive Element*, "Stephen Spender is the Rupert Brooke of the Depression.")

Indeed, it was above all the sense of an epoch, and of a decade, that allowed Spender to get away with "being a poet." Crucial to this image were his friendships from Oxford days with W. H. Auden, Louis MacNeice,

Christopher Isherwood, and Cecil Day-Lewis. This cabal provoked Roy Campbell's joke about the "MacSpaunday" school: a joke that was a source of embarrassment (and rage, given Campbell's open sympathy for fascism) while simultaneously furnishing a near guarantee of immortality.

Among this book's assembly of sometimes very striking unpublished photographs is a shot of Spender, Auden, and Isherwood on the beach at Fire Island in 1947. Spender stands commandingly erect in the center, with his arms around the shoulders of his two much shorter comrades. There would be no doubt in the mind of the untutored as to which of them was the senior (the photo is presumably from Spender's private trove). And yet, as Sutherland shows very skillfully, it was Auden who was the literary boss from the beginning, and Isherwood (sometimes with Auden, and sometimes without) who was the sexually tougher and more resourceful one. Auden demonstrated his mastery from the very first, demanding to know of Spender how often he wrote poetry.

> Without reflecting, I replied that I wrote about four poems a day. He was astonished and exclaimed: "What energy!" I asked him how often he wrote a poem. He replied: "I write about one in three weeks." After this I started writing only one poem in three weeks.

So silly. Up until then, of course, Spender had been so impressed at attending the same Oxford college as Shelley that he had felt compelled to adopt yet another poetic pose: that of the agonized and alienated young dreamer.

Anyone who has seen *Cabaret* can read several of the succeeding chapters at speed. The three men pursued boys of various sorts and conditions (usually proletarian) all over Berlin and over much of Germany and Austria as well. (Auden ended up with a painful rectal fissure, which led him to write his wince-makingly titled *Letter to a Wound.*) They seem to have done most of it on borrowed money or on tiny publishing advances. Orwell's vicious remark, about the "nancy poets" who spent on sodomy what they had gained by sponging, was barely a match for the amazing narcissism revealed in these pages. However (and as Orwell was later to ruefully admit), there was a core of principle involved. Spender could feel fascism coming on, and was appalled by the premonitory symptoms of it. He may have made a complete fool of himself by going briefly to Spain. (The leader of the British Communist Party, the cynical Harry Pollitt, probably did say that he thought Spender's only usefulness would be to die the death of a Byronic martyr: another potential poetic "character" for him to have adopted, had he been less prudent than he was.) Spender may have written a fatuous book titled *Forward from Liberalism*, which among other things defended Stalin's show trials. But beneath all this playacting and conceit and gullibility was a pith of seriousness.

We can reconstruct this, not from *Goodbye to Berlin* but from the words of Isaiah. Dr. Berlin, whatever his many drawbacks, was an excellent judge of character. What he saw in Spender was an open-faced, vulnerable, rather captivating readiness to take chances. Most bullied English public school boys with oppressive fathers would soon have learned how to wear a protective carapace of some sort; Spender remained a naïf in the best sense of that term, even as he remained something of an adolescent in matters of the pudendum. (The reason I don't name the authors of the above limerick, written by contemporaries of his, is that even now they regard it as accurate but unkind.)

The hinge moment, if I read Sutherland correctly, came with the outbreak of the Second World War. Spender had become an admirer of America, but it would not have occurred to him to take ship and leave England at that moment, as Auden and Isherwood both famously did. In the course of an earlier quarrel Spender had exclaimed to Isherwood, "If we're going to part, at least let's part like men." Isherwood had won that round, replying bitchily, "But Stephen, we *aren't* men." In some fashion or manner brittleness of that sort was to become *de trop* after Dunkirk. Spender "stayed on," tried to enlist and was rejected on health grounds (which ranged from tapeworm to varicose veins), joined the London Fire Brigade (not a soft option at that time), and also became a husband and father. Sutherland rightly doesn't speculate about this, but there appears to me to have been a latent connection between the advent of war and the triumph of Spender's heterosexual side. His disastrous earlier, "open" marriage, to the bohemian hell-minx Inez Pearn, had been a failure partly because of his reluctance to break things off with his lover Tony Hyndman, here depicted as sponger and sodomite on a majestic scale. By falling for Natasha Litvin, a gifted musician and a considerable beauty, Spender found himself not only able to hold on to a serious woman for the first time but also—and perhaps not without its own significance that year—to confirm and affirm the slightly suppressed Jewish element in his family background. (His mother, Violet Schuster, was from a long line of converted and assimilated English Jews originating in Frankfurt.)

The war also improved his poetry. In the thirties Spender had had to contend with the criticism—obviously wounding to an aspiring writer and poet—that he didn't write very well at all. Eliot noticed it. Auden noticed it. Cyril Connolly noticed it. To Connolly, Spender wrote in that disarming manner that Isaiah Berlin so adored: "You are quite right about the bad writing. I am very sorry. It disturbs me very much." Hilarious. Even his most famous poem, "I Think Continually of Those Who Were Truly Great," with its closing line, "And left the vivid air signed with their honor," had to be retouched by Isherwood before it "sang." Spender's readers often had to put up with things like *Hampstead Autumn* (1932), yet another rumination on the seasons: "In the fat autumn evening street / Hands from my childhood stretch out / And ring muffin bells."

Possibly. But in 1943 he published *Exercises/Explorations*, the third "exercise" of which read,

> Since we are what we are, what shall we be
> But what we are? We are, we have
> Six feet and seventy years, to see
> The light, and then release it for the grave.
> We are not worlds, no, nor infinity,
> We have no claims on stone, except to prove
> In the invention of the city
> Our hearts, our intellect, our love.

This is very fine, and Sutherland is not stretching too far in comparing it, with its "mortuary sonorousness," to Donne's *Holy Sonnets*.

Spender was more than six feet tall and lived on to be well over seventy. He easily outlived all his more famous contemporaries, and became in a sense their living witness as well as their official obituarist. I heard him give a rather beautiful address at Auden's memorial in Oxford in the fall of 1973. His long, spare frame and his nimbus of white hair had by then become familiar at dozens of international conferences and seminars. Sutherland speaks of him as a pioneer version of what we now call "the public intellectual." But Noël Annan went a bit further in terming him a "cultural statesman": a concept with a trapdoor of absurdity built right into it. This trapdoor was soon to fall open with a dismaying bang.

Having stayed in wartime England while keeping lines open to America, Spender was ideally positioned after 1945 to become a figure in the Anglo-U.S. "special relationship" and in one of its aspects, the cultural Cold War. The flagship symbol of both was the magazine *Encounter*, published in London but financed from across the Atlantic. Spender was a distinguished member of the team of anti-communist liberals (Isaiah Berlin, Richard Wollheim) and not-so-liberals (Irving Kristol, Melvin Lasky) who characterized the magazine. His wife, Natasha, came up with the name.

Square miles of print have now been devoted to the scandal that occurred in the late 1960s when Conor Cruise O'Brien flatly accused *Encounter* of being a self- or at least semi-conscious organ of the Central Intelligence Agency. That it had long been receiving a thick-envelope CIA subvention was quickly established. But who among the editors had known all along? Lasky certainly had, and Berlin (in my opinion) equally certainly. Spender staked, and nearly lost, his reputation on the stubborn assertion that he had had absolutely *no idea*. It will be quickly seen that he was making it certain that he would look a fool. The English subdivide this title into categories, starting with plain fool, moving through damn fool to bloody fool, and ending with fucking fool—for which one has to be sinister as well as silly. By throwing wine over William Empson for even suggesting anything covert about *Encounter*'s finances, Spender qualified as at least a bloody fool. But a nice kind of fool for all that: the sort who could write, as he had in Germany many years before, "On the whole though I've decided that the best thing is to stick through thick and thin to the best one can find in one's fellow creatures, even though one is humiliated by having one's weakness and lack of pride exposed by one's dependence on them."

In the end, after dodging much collapsing scenery at *Encounter*, Spender announced that one was frightfully hurt to find that one's colleagues had been deceiving one. I don't doubt that this was largely genuine. But Sutherland provides a detail that was hitherto unknown to me. It seems that Spender had been unable to recruit the support of T. S. Eliot for the enterprise. The conservative sage of Faber had from the first been "chronically suspicious of the 'American auspices' of the magazine." Well then, how could Spender really maintain that the thought had never even occurred to him?

He managed, with that providence that sometimes protects the terminally innocent, to escape into a third act of his life. This period might be described as "Backward to Liberalism." There was always a threat of the farcical or the undignified in the interest Spender took in the young, but Sutherland makes a convincing case that he was kept young, in a sense, by the growth of his gifted children, Matthew and Lizzie. Thus his book about the events of 1968, with the potentially embarrassing title *Year of the Young Rebels*, did not go over the abyss into a glassy admiration of student revolt. And he became one of the first to see the moral importance of the dissident movement in the Soviet Union, with its synthesis of literary and ideological opposition. Having been an early defender of Boris Pasternak, he became an equally early patron of the exiled Joseph Brodsky and a vigorous organizer of petitions and support groups. This sympathy took institutional shape in the 1970s, with the imaginative inauguration of the magazine *Index on Censorship*. Devoted to the battle against repressive governments on all continents, this journal was and remains highly worthwhile. So over the long term Spender had had a part in launching *Horizon*, which for all Cyril Connolly's idiosyncrasies was indispensable to keeping alive a literary pulse in England during the war. Despite being despised by the true editor of *Encounter* and being kept on only as a "useful idiot" by the surreptitious moneymen, he ran a more than respectable "back half" of books pages for the magazine. This is a not altogether shabby record.

Attempts were made to smirch it all the same. Spender rather trustingly indulged a young opportunist named Hugh David, who then produced a scabrous "biography" titled *Spender: A Portrait With Background*. This gave infinite pain, both in its numerous falsifications and in its pitiless exposure of the old boy's days as a gay boy. The same trope was exploited without scruple by the forgettable American "gay writer" David Leavitt, who in 1993 extruded a novel called *While England Sleeps* and simply annexed some passages of *World Within World* in order to do so. Yet none of this seems to have prevented Spender from continuing to form friendships with writers younger than himself, of the generation of Peter Ackroyd and James Fenton (two rather acute choices). If his lifelong vice was that he could not stop himself from RSVPing to any old card of invitation, it can still be said of Spender that he continued to take the cheery chance of new encounters.

It may be that Sutherland felt a need to compensate for previous injustices in the writing of this biography, but one sometimes has the sense that his dutifulness became a chore to him. The word "idyllic" is employed so many times, even for scenes of relatively ordinary satisfaction at the seaside or in the countryside, that after a while I stopped circling it. Nothing excuses the use of "prevaricate" for "procrastinate," or "refute" for "repudiate." And Spender may well have been discharged from the Fire Brigade on June 13, 1944, but it is an abuse of a crucial word to say "Ironically, it was the same day that the first of the V-1 buzz bombs fell on London." That barely rises to the level of coincidence. An author has furthermore become far too close to his subject if he can write—this time unironically, and of a domestic row in the ski resort of Gstaad—that "the upheaval dwarfed the Suez crisis."

Still, by the time of his much mourned death, in 1995 (which occurred just after his unprecedented last-minute decision to decline a social invitation from the Holroyd/Drabble household), Spender had managed to outlive the sorts of taunt and nickname ("Stainless Splendor," "Stephen Savage") that his parents had feared when they first forbade him—pointlessly, as it was to turn out—the company of "rough" boys.

(*The Atlantic*, January/February 2005)

Edward Upward: The Captive Mind

EARLY IN THE 1930s, when he was managing the Hogarth Press for Leonard and Virginia Woolf and preparing the anthology—*New Signatures*—that would be received as a species of generational manifesto, John Lehmann wrote that he had

> heard with the tremor of excitement that an entomologist feels at the news of an unknown butterfly sighted in the depths of the forest, that behind Auden and Spender and Isherwood stood the even more legendary figure of... Edward Upward.

In that reference to the literary-political celebrities of the thirties, Upward received his due. In a once-famous attempt to get the whole set into one portmanteau term, which was Roy Campbell's coinage of *MacSpaunday* to comprehend the names of Louis MacNeice, Stephen Spender, W. H. Auden, and Cecil Day-Lewis, Upward was omitted altogether (as was his friend and closest collaborator, Christopher Isherwood). On the eve of Valentine's Day this year, at the age of 105, the last British author to have been born in the Edwardian epoch died. If Upward is not better known than perhaps he ought to be, it is probably because he helped instill the Communist faith in his more notorious friends, and then not only outlived them and their various apostasies but continued to practice a version of that faith himself. (For purposes of comparison, MacNeice died in 1963, Day-Lewis in 1972, Auden in 1973, Isherwood in 1986, and Spender in 1995, so with Upward's death, the last link to that era is truly snapped.)

His traces and spoor and fingerprints are to be found all over the work of those whom he so strongly mentored. Auden dedicated "The Exiles"—one of the Odes in *The Orators*—to Upward, and made him an executor of his will when he set off to take part in the Spanish Civil War. Upward also makes an appearance as a character in Auden's charade, *Paid on Both Sides*, published in T. S. Eliot's *Criterion* in 1930. In the same year, Auden sent Upward a copy of his *Poems* and wrote, "I shall never know how much in these poems is filched from you via Christopher." With Isherwood, who fictionalized him in *Lions and Shadows* under the name of Allen Chalmers, Upward coinvented the weird dystopia of Mortmere, and co-authored the fantastic gothic tales—*surreal medievalism* was Upward's term for the genre—that became grouped under that name. Isherwood dedicated *All the Conspirators* to him. Spender, in his 1935 study, *The Destructive Element*, presented Upward as an English Kafka. In 1938, the Hogarth Press published Upward's novel *Journey to the Border*, which was thought of by many as the only English effort at Marxist fiction that was likely to outlast the era in which it was written. And then... silence. There was some rumor of a "nervous breakdown." Nothing was heard from Upward until the early 1960s, when he abruptly produced a trilogy of didactic and autobiographical novels, each illustrating in different ways what a commitment to a Communist life could do to an aspiring author. (When I read them, I was put in mind of something Doris Lessing once said to me about the Communist Party's "Writers' Group," of which she had once been a member: Everybody liked to talk about the "problems" of being a writer, and most of the "problems" came from being in the Communist Party in the first place.)

A decade or so ago, becoming aware that Upward was still alive and still writing—and bethinking myself that if I wanted to interview this soon-to-be centenarian and last survivor of his generation, I had better hurry up—I made a voyage to the Isle of Wight, that little diamond-shaped island off the southern coast of England that helps form the natural harbors of Portsmouth and Southampton. In this almost parodic picture-postcard miniature of deep England, Upward had chosen to literally "isolate" himself. The Isle of

Wight is where Tennyson came to write *Crossing the Bar*. It is where Queen Victoria kept her favorite home, Osborne House, and it is where she died in 1901, two years before Upward was born.

In a vicarage-style house not far from the railway station in the small town of Sandown, Upward received me and led me to a side room. He explained without loss of time that the main rooms of the little home were out of bounds because his wife, Hilda, was in the process of dying there. "I shall miss Hilda," he said with the brisk matter-of-factness of the materialist, "but I have promised her that I shall go on writing." Attired in gray flannel trousers, a corduroy jacket, and a V-neck jersey, he reminded me of something so obvious that I didn't immediately recognize it. On a table lay the *Morning Star*, the daily newspaper of the Stalinist rump organization that survived the British Communist Party's decision to dissolve itself after the implosion of the Soviet Union. It is entirely possible that Upward was the paper's sole subscriber on this islet of thatched cottages and stained glass and theme-park rural Englishness. Seeing me notice the old rag, he said, rather defensively, "Yes I still take it, though there doesn't seem much hope these days." When I asked him if there was anyone on the left he still admired, he cited Arthur Scargill, the coal miners' thuggish leader, who was known to connoisseurs as the most *ouvriériste* and sectarian and demagogic of the anti-Blair forces in the Labour movement. Yet to this alarming opinion he appended the shy and disarming news that the last review he had had in the *Morning Star* had been a good one, precisely because it stressed that not all his work was strictly political. "It particularly mentioned my story 'The White-Pinafored Black Cat.'" I inquired if he was working on a story at that moment. "Yes I am." "And may one know the title?" "It's to be called 'The World Revolution.'" At this point and in this context, I began to find the word *surreal* recurring to my mind.

As so often, this feeling was prompted by a banal detail. Upward, in his flannels and corduroy and jersey, looked exactly like what he was: a retired schoolteacher. And yet, of all the figures detested by his set in the thirties, the schoolmaster was perhaps the most reviled. Auden in particular wrote that he understood fascism because he had experienced an English public school, and in his letters home from Hitler's Germany he described the place as being run "by a mixture of gangsters and the sort of school prefect who is good at [Cadet] Corps." But Upward had volunteered for a lifetime of schoolmastering, and of activism in the teachers union. It was as if he had determined to turn away from the magic realism of Mortmere, and concentrate on the quotidian. Confirming this, and sounding very much the schoolteacher, he said to me, "Writing is not a pleasure. It's a *discipline*."

The beauty of *Mortmere* as a name is its evocation both of dead and stagnant water and of a slightly macabre name for a bucolic setting. (That it also evokes "dead mother" did not occur to me until I read Katherine Bucknell's brilliant introduction to the most recent edition.) The Mortmere stories are fascinating because they take the classic English village and people it with psychopaths, revealed in titles like "The Leviathan of the Urinals." The vicar is a sicko. The choirboy is far from innocent. And as for the squire in the moated country house, or the headmaster...It seems to me that Upward took a conscious decision to rid himself of this hedonism and to become a fiction writer with a mission. In his contribution to Cecil Day-Lewis's anthology *The Mind in Chains*, published in 1937, he wrote sternly:

> A modern fantasy cannot tell the truth, cannot give a picture of life which will survive the test of experience; since fantasy implies in practice a retreat from the real world into the world of imagination.

This repudiation is expressed with equal severity in the trilogy of novels on which Upward worked after he dropped from view, before the Second World War. Collectively titled *The Spiral Ascent*, and individually titled *In the Thirties, The Rotten Elements*, and *No Home but the Struggle*, the novels tell of the distraught life of a Communist schoolteacher named Alan Sebrill, who discovers to his horror that the Communist Party has become insufficiently revolutionary. To give you an idea of how far away we are from the playfulness of Mortmere, the bleak, admonitory subtitle of the second volume is *A Novel of Fact*.

But Alan Sebrill has a secret. In addition to being a good Communist, he desires to be a good poet. (Upward had won a prize for poetry while at Cambridge University, but when Auden advised him to give up, he did so without demur.) There is even a desperate hope that Sebrill can fuse the two ambitions. Of the party, he tells himself:

> It was the enemy of his enemies: it aimed at the overthrow of a society which was dominated by poshocrats and public school snobs and which had no use for the living poets. It demanded that its converts should believe not in the supernatural nor in anti-scientific myths but in man. *If he joined the Communist Party he might be able to write poetry again.* [Emphasis mine.]

Yes, well of course you know what's going to happen, but Sebrill doesn't, and I am not even sure that Upward did. In his memorial poem for Yeats, Auden famously wrote, "Poetry makes nothing happen." In the world created by Upward for Sebrill, *nothing makes poetry happen*. And so fantasy keeps on breaking in again, in an unintended way, as the wretched protagonist suffers from hallucinations, nightmares, paranoia, thoughts of suicide, and despair. If Upward had himself hoped to be Maxim Gorky, he ended up vindicating Spender's comparison of him to Kafka.

In one respect of "realism," though, Upward deserves great praise. It is a deplorable fact that the English literature of the 1930s contains scarcely a mention of the phenomenon of fascism. Anthony Powell's long excursion through the upper crust doesn't turn up a single Blackshirt (something of a shortcoming in point of verisimilitude, as he might have phrased it). Evelyn Waugh avoids the subject. Graham Greene's fascists are not English. But for Upward, especially in his first volume of *The Spiral Ascent*, the miasma of fascism is in the very air that his characters breathe, and a direct clash with the Blackshirts conveys the intense and local reality that this force sometimes possessed in Britain. Upward at least faced what many shied away from.

I am not sure that this will excuse the *langue de bois* in which Sebrill's crisis of Communism is set down. I collect the dates and occasions on which various writers and intellectuals decided to "break" with "the Party," and these range from the Hitler-Stalin Pact of 1939 to the suppression of the Hungarian Revolution of 1956. There are some specialized ones as well, such as Eric Hobsbawm's decision not to renew his party card after 1989. In these annals, Upward stands alone for resigning his membership in 1948, on the grounds that the British Communists were insufficiently Stalinist! It makes him quite a collector's item. The experience was evidently a shock to his system, as it was to that of his main character:

> He found he could stop his trembling by thinking of Stalin and by speaking the name of Stalin, repeatedly but not quite aloud, much as a religious believer might have called on the name of God. Yet though this was an effective method of suppressing the physical symptoms of his anxiety it did not help him in the least with his writing.

Understandably. Upward may have been many things, but he was never an ironist.

Our conversation on politics was likewise arid, but things invariably improved when he discussed his relations with his departed comrades. He had, for instance, recently had a visit from Isherwood's longtime lover, Don Bachardy ("Yes, I keep in touch with Don"), and at first I had difficulty picturing a friendship between this austere provincial Englishman and a gay bohemian painter in Santa Monica. But then, Upward had been the first to spot Isherwood's quirky genius ("even though I didn't know or realize that he was homosexual"). With the others, the contacts (and eventual reconciliations) were conducted through the medium of... fantasy. In a strange little story called "An Unmentionable Man," Upward's rather self-pitying character encounters a former associate who is obviously Stephen Spender, and at first treats him with great bitterness:

> I may not have read every article you've written or television talk you've given about the 'thirties, but I have read and heard more than a few, and there wasn't one of them that didn't completely ignore me.

Yet after a few sharp exchanges with "this copiously white-haired broad-shouldered ruddy-faced man," he abruptly comes to view him as "someone he must not die unfriendly with." Upward's accommodation with Auden was, alas, posthumous: He could never forgive him for having called the thirties "a low, dishonest decade," but carried on a conversation with him in his head, and eventually conceded,

> I ought to have recognized that my indignation was less against the injuriousness of his opinions than against him for holding them. I could not dissociate him from himself as the young poet who for me and for other poets of his generation had been the only potential giant among us.

Our knowledge of the literary and ideological generation of the thirties is radically incomplete without some awareness of its founding father, or perhaps better say founding brother.

(*The Atlantic*, May 2009)

C. L. R. James: Mid Off, Not Right On

IN V.S. NAIPAUL'S 1994 novel, *A Way in the World*, the reader is introduced to a charismatic revolutionary intellectual named Lebrun, who has written a history of a forgotten rebellion in the Caribbean basin, and whose critical powers are able to produce the following admiring response in the part-autobiographical narrator:

> It was as though, from moving to ground level, where so much was obscured, I had been taken up some way, not only to be shown the pretty pattern of fields and roads and small settlements, but also, as an aspect of that high view, had been granted a vision of history speeded up, had seen as I might have seen the opening and dying of a flower, the destruction and shifting about of peoples, had seen all the strands that had gone into the creation of the agricultural colony, and had understood what simple purposes—after such activity—that colony served.

We rely not merely on internal evidence for the deduction that this is the fictionalized figure of Cyril Lionel Robert James, one of the few Marxist writers of the twentieth century whose work has survived it. In a

---

Review of *C. L. R. James: Cricket, the Caribbean and the World Revolution*, by Farrukh Dhondy.

personal reminiscence, Naipaul recalls meeting his fellow Trinidadian exile in London in 1962:

> It was all immensely intelligent and gripping. He talked about music and the influence on composers of the instruments of their time. He talked about military matters. I had met no one like that from our region, no one who had given so much time to reading and thought, no one who had organized so much information in this appetizing way...it was rhetoric, of course. And of course it was loaded in his favour. He couldn't be interrupted, like royalty, he raised all the topics; and he would have been a master of all the topics he raised.

Naipaul is not celebrated for his generosity to fellow authors, especially those hailing from the West Indies, and it is, of course, to be expected that he might take back with one hand what he offered with the other. I myself met C. L. R. James twice, once when I helped to organize a meeting for him at Ruskin College, Oxford, on the fiftieth anniversary of the Bolshevik Revolution, and once by visiting him in retirement at his home in Brixton, and would certify that Naipaul captures both his extraordinary polymathic range and the slightly cultish aura that later came to surround him.

On the platform, he had no equal for unscripted pure eloquence; without any demagogy, he spoke about the resistance of the Vietnamese and started hot tears of rage in his audience. In Brixton, he was attended in old age by a devoted group of admirers who seldom if ever argued with him and who treated him like a guru.

Farrukh Dhondy was himself a peripheral member of this circle, and his biography is in some part also a memoir. It is difficult to think of a better point of comparison and contrast than the one he offers between Naipaul and James. Both men left Trinidad in their youth, both men were magnetized by Britain and became masters of English prose. Naipaul showed little if any nostalgia for his roots, while James felt committed to the struggle for independence and was an early advocate of West Indian Federation. Naipaul evinced scant interest in the history of the region, while James's magnificent book *The Black Jacobins* (1938), a study of Toussaint L'Ouverture's slave republic, is still considered a founding document in the world of postcolonial studies. The chief resemblance between the two men lies (or lay—James died in 1989) in their shared suspicion of a self-pitying or "black power" or "Afrocentric" worldview. There is also a sense in which both managed to be *plus anglais que les Anglais.*

James had been formed in the striving Trinidadian world of the scholarship school and the cricket field. Before he ever saw England, he had developed an admiration for what might be called the public school or Arnoldian ethos. Dhondy has some fun with a moment in Manchester in 1956, when Aneurin Bevan and Michael Foot replied to the Labour leadership's charge of "not playing with the team." They did so by making sneering references to "straight bats" and "stiff upper lips." This seemed slightly profane to James, and his shocked reaction, in turn, seems somewhat quaint to Dhondy. However, it put me in mind of what Lionel Trilling once said about George Orwell—that "he must sometimes have wondered how it came about that he should be praising sportsmanship and gentlemanliness and dutifulness and physical courage. He seems to have thought, and very likely he was right, that they might come in handy as revolutionary virtues." (Orwell, incidentally, was a fan of James's and praised his 1937 book *World Revolution.*)

The two men also had in common an affiliation with the old Independent Labour Party. In James's case, this arose partly from his cricketing connection. Adopted as a ghostwriter by Sir Learie Constantine, he went to live with him in Lancashire, where the ILP was relatively strong, and soon became part of its Trotskyist wing. Adopted also by Neville Cardus, and composing cricket reports for the *Manchester Guardian* by day, he evolved into a semi-professional revolutionary by night. He campaigned for colonial freedom, for intervention against Mussolini in Ethiopia, and for workers' education. But the imperishable part of his writing in the 1930s and beyond concerns the struggle against Stalinism.

James had never had any illusions in the Communist Party to lose, and saw Stalin's Russia from the beginning as a grotesque new form of oppression and exploitation. He translated Boris Souvarine's seminal book *Stalin* from the French for Secker and Warburg, and in *World Revolution* showed how the Communist International had become a depraved apparatus in the service of a pitiless despot. The book reads rather creakily these days, because of its emphasis on Trotsky and the Left Opposition, but it contains the most wonderfully scornful review of the Webbs and their shameful *Soviet Communism: A new civilization?* (from the second edition of which the question mark was famously removed), and is both lucid and prescient about the famine and the treason trials. Again to suggest an Orwellian comparison, one notices time and again that James is moved to anger and contempt by the sheer ugliness and euphemism of the enemy's prose style. His training in English literature was as useful to him as his apprenticeship in dialectics.

He recrossed the Atlantic just before the outbreak of war, to visit Trotsky in Mexico and to make contact with his American epigones. This led to a long stay in the United States, a deep involvement with what was still called "the Negro question," and to more than one passionate attachment. (The tall and handsome James went through white women like an avenging flame, but there was none of the macho vulgarity that one finds described in Naipaul's narratives of black-white sex, and his former lovers are still loyal to him.) By the end of this deep engagement in sectarian politics, he had decided that the entire concept of a "vanguard party" was at fault, no matter who proclaimed it. The pamphlets and polemics of this period are still collector's items, though the most closely wrought of his political texts, *Mariners, Renegades and Castaways*, is actually an allegorical study of Herman Melville, written while awaiting deportation from the United States in 1953.

Indeed, Trotskyism's gain was in many respects literature's loss. James's only novel, *Minty Alley*, is a rather naive account of shanty-town or "barrack-yard" life in Trinidad, but can bear comparison with some early Naipaul (both V. S. and Shiva). His literary capacity was immense; he knew Thackeray's *Vanity Fair* almost by heart and later in life prepared a masterly series of lectures on Shakespeare. At all times he upheld the great tradition and was famous for his denunciations of those callow scholars who referred to English literature as "Eurocentric." (Dhondy has some very telling anecdotes here, of James tossing and goring those young apostles of negritude who came to pay homage to the old revolutionary without troubling to register his attachment to high culture, or his conviction that the "Third World" had much to learn from the "First.")

None of this inhibited him from taking an active part in the battle for decolonization—one of his first essays was a dignified refutation of J. A. Froude's quasi-eugenic defense of white rule—or from seeing the American civil rights revolution as a vindication of his own prophecies. Naipaul's Lebrun is eventually disappointed by the pettiness and infighting of the anti-colonial forces, and James, too, was to become disillusioned by the place-seeking and frequent viciousness of his former comrades in Ghana, Trinidad, and Grenada. (He was especially offended when the thugs who seized power in Grenada in 1983 claimed to be Jamesians.) Visiting at about that time, I was deeply impressed by the way that every little village appeared to be fielding a game of cricket, played in immaculate white kit. James is a part of the folklore of this pastime, and has an audience quite distinct from the following he attracted as a Marxist. (He appears, as the character K. C. Lewis, in Ian Buruma's splendid cricketing novel *Playing the Game.*) For him, cricket was not a sport so much as an art form, and also a reflection of social organization. It can be compared at once to a ballet, and to the Olympic ethic of Classical Greece. It is also, both as a game and as an entertainment, inherently democratic. And it teaches the values of equality and fairness. *Beyond a Boundary* (1963), his partly autobiographical study of the subject, is a lyrical account of both the aesthetics of batsmanship and the bonding and exemplary role played by cricket in the development of the West Indies. Astonishingly, it was rejected for publication by John Arlott, but soon found a home at Hutchinson's, and was warmly reviewed by V. S. Naipaul in *Encounter* in 1961. Dhondy barely exaggerates when he says that this book is for cricket what *Death in the Afternoon* is for the bullfight.

In 1948, in his *Notes on Dialectics,* James claimed to have evolved a "Hegelian algebra" with which to understand the historical process. This rash boast was the final break between himself and the little world of post-orthodox Trotskyists. One might, though, borrow a Hegelian phrase—"the cunning of history"—to describe the way in which the "dialectic" played out. In the early 1980s, James was one of those who unequivocally welcomed the flowering of the Polish Solidarity movement, both as a workers' movement in its own right and as the fulfilment of his prophecy about the end of Communism. As with Martin Luther King's movement in the United States, a real revolution was to be the creation of conscious and self-determined people, not professionalized cadres. CLR, as many called him, did not live to see the full promise of the year 1989, and the complete vindication of his dream. He died at the end of May, surrounded by his piles of beloved classics, in his modest Brixton flat, on the corner of Railton Road and Shakespeare Road.

(*Times Literary Supplement*, January 18, 2002)

J. G. Ballard: The Catastrophist

IN THE SPRING OF 2006, at the Hay-on-Wye book festival, I was introduced at dinner to Sir Martin Rees, who is the professor of cosmology and astrophysics at Cambridge University and also holds the pleasingly archaic title of Astronomer Royal. He was to give a lecture that was later reprinted with the title "Dark Materials," in honor of the late professor Joseph Rotblat. In the course of this astonishing talk, he voiced the following thought:

> Most educated people are aware that we are the outcome of nearly 4 billion years of Darwinian selection, but many tend to think that humans are somehow the culmination. Our sun, however, is less than halfway through its lifespan. It will not be humans who watch the sun's demise, 6 billion years from now. Any creatures that then exist will be as different from us as we are from bacteria or amoebae.

Among the several questions that jostled for the uppermost in my mind was this: Where is the fiction that can rise to the level of this stupefying reality? (Only one novelist, Julian Barnes, was sufficiently struck to include Rees's passage in a book, but that was in his extended nonfiction memoir about death, *Nothing to Be Frightened Of.*) I quite soon came to realize that there was indeed a writer who could have heard or read those words with

---

Review of *The Complete Stories of J. G. Ballard.*

equanimity, even satisfaction, and that this was J. G. Ballard. For him, the possibility of any mutation or metamorphosis was to be taken for granted, if not indeed welcomed, as was the contingency that, dead sun or no dead sun, the terrestrial globe could very readily be imagined after we're gone.

As one who has always disliked and distrusted so-called science fiction (the votaries of this cult disagreeing pointlessly about whether to refer to it as "SF" or "sci-fi"), I was prepared to be unimpressed even after Kingsley Amis praised Ballard as "the most imaginative of H. G. Wells's successors." The natural universe is far too complex and frightening and impressive on its own to require the puerile add-ons of space aliens and super-weapons: The interplanetary genre made even C. S. Lewis write more falsely than he normally did. Hearing me drone on in this vein about thirty years ago, Amis fils (who contributes a highly lucid introduction to this collection) wordlessly handed me *The Drowned World, The Day of Forever*, and, for a shift in pace and rhythm, *Crash*. Any one of these would have done the trick.

For all that, Ballard is arguably best-known to a wide audience because of his relatively "straight" novel, *Empire of the Sun*, and the resulting movie by Steven Spielberg. Some of his devotees were depressed by the literalness of the subject matter, which is a quasi-autobiographical account of being thirteen years old and an inmate in a Japanese internment camp in Shanghai. It's not possible to read that book, however, and fail to see the germinal effect that experience had on Ballard the man. To see a once-thriving city reduced to beggary and emptiness, to live one day at a time in point of food and medicine, to see an old European order brutally and efficiently overturned, to notice the utterly casual way in which human life can be snuffed out, and to see war machines wheeling and diving in the overcast sky: such an education! Don't forget, either, that young Ballard was ecstatic at the news of the atomic obliteration of Hiroshima and Nagasaki, an emotion that makes him practically unique among postwar literati. Included in this collection is a very strong 1977 story, "The Dead Time," a sort of curtain-raiser to *Empire*—Ballard's own preferred name for his book—in which a young man released from Japanese captivity drives a truckload of cadavers across a stricken landscape and ends up feeding a scrap of his own torn flesh to a ravenous child.

Readers of Ballard's memoir, *Miracles of Life* (a book with a slightly but not entirely misleading title), will soon enough discern that he built on his wartime Shanghai traumas in three related ways. As a teenager in postwar England he came across first Freud, and second the surrealists. He describes the two encounters as devastating in that they taught him what he already knew: Religion is abject nonsense, human beings positively enjoy inflicting cruelty, and our species is prone to, and can coexist with, the most grotesque absurdities. What could have been more natural, then, than that Ballard the student should devote himself to classes in anatomy, spending quality time with corpses, some of whom, in life, had been dedicated professors in the department. An astonishing number of his shorter works follow the inspiration of *Crash*, also filmed, this time by David Cronenberg, in morbid and almost loving accounts of "wound profiles," gashes, fractures, and other inflictions on the flesh and bones. Fascinated by the possibility of death in traffic, and rather riveted by the murder of John Kennedy, Ballard produced a themed series titled *The Atrocity Exhibition*, here partially collected, where collisions and ejaculations and celebrities are brought together in a vigorously stirred mix of Eros and Thanatos. His antic use of this never-failing formula got him briefly disowned by his American publisher and was claimed by Ballard as "pornographic science fiction," but if you can read "The Assassination of John Fitzgerald Kennedy Considered As a Downhill Motor Race" or "Why I Want to Fuck Ronald Reagan" in search of sexual gratification, you must be jaded by disorders undreamed-of by this reviewer. Both stories, however, succeed in being deadpan funny.

Another early story (though not represented here: The claim of this volume to be "complete" is somewhat deceptive) in something of the same style, "Plan for the Assassination of Jacqueline Kennedy," ignited a ridiculous fuss in the very news rags whose ghoulish coverage of her life Ballard was intending to satirize. Randolph Churchill led the charge, demanding punishment for the tiny magazine that printed it. This "modest proposal" furnishes one of many clues to a spring of Ballard's inspiration, which is fairly obviously the work of Jonathan Swift. In 1964 he even wrote an ultra-macabre story, "The Drowned Giant," which tells of what happens when the corpse of a beautiful but gigantic man washes ashore on a beach "five miles to the northwest of the city." The local Lilliputians find cheap but inventive ways of desecrating and disfiguring the body before cutting it up for souvenirs and finally rendering it down in big vats. One might characterize this as the microcosmically ideal Ballard fantasy, in that it partakes of the surreal—the "Gulliver" being represented as a huge flesh statue based on the work of Praxiteles—as well as of the Freudian: "as if the mutilation of this motionless colossus had released a sudden flood of repressed spite." In the pattern of many other stories, the narrator adopts the tone of a pathologist dictating a detached report of gross anatomy. A single phrase, *colossal wreck*, is a borrowing from Shelley's "Ozymandias," which may be the closest that Ballard ever came to a concession to the Romantic school.

Another and nearer literary source is provided by the name—Traven—of the solitary character in "The Terminal Beach." This is one of two tales—the other being "One Afternoon at Utah Beach"—in which Ballard makes an imaginarium out of the ruined scapes of the Second World War. Like his modern but vacant cities full of ghostly tower blocks (he is obsessed with towers of all sorts) and abandoned swimming pools, the Pacific and Atlantic beaches, still covered by concrete blocks and bunkers, furnish the ideal setting for a Ballardian wasteland. The beach in the first story has the additional advantage of having been the site of an annihilating nuclear test. The revenant shapes of long-dead Japanese and Germans are allowed a pitiless flicker before their extinction.

Ballard is not the most quotable of authors, because he takes quite a long time to set a scene and because his use of dialogue is more efficient than it is anything else. But he can produce arresting phrases and images. He is especially observant about eyes. On succeeding pages of "The Cloud-Sculptors of Coral D," we find that "memories, caravels without sails, crossed the shadowy deserts of her burned-out eyes" and that the dwarf, Petit Manuel, regards this same woman "with eyes like crushed flowers." This entire story is infused with an eerie beauty, as the wings of gliders carve marvels out of the cumulus, and one aesthetic pilot "soared around the cloud, cutting away its tissues. The soft fleece fell toward us in a cool rain." The cruel capricious beauty who becomes the wealthy patron of this art is careless of the human cost it may entail: "In her face the diagram of bones formed a geometry of murder."

Ballard wrote his heart out, especially after the random death of his beloved wife left him to raise three children, so I don't especially like to say that he wrote too much. (This book has almost 1,200 pages.) But some of the stories are in want of polish and finish. In "The Last World of Mr. Goddard," a department-store supervisor keeps a microcosm of his town, complete with live-action human figures, in a box in his safe at home. Each evening, he can watch what everybody is doing and use the knowledge the next day. At first I was surprised that he never exploited this advantage to observe anybody having sex, and then I noticed that Ballard had oddly deprived his minutely supervised miniatures of the power to be overheard, so that Mr. Goddard actually had no idea what was going on. Like a movie that is only part talkie, this scenario is leached of its initial power. In compensation, several of the stories are pure *jeu d'esprit*, where the charm of the conceit hardly requires any suggestion of the sinister or the doomed. Despite the menacing title of "Prima Belladonna," the first of the collection, one is immediately bewitched by the very idea of a flower shop where the gorgeously different blooms are all live stand-ins for musicians and opera singers (such as a "delicate soprano mimosa") and where the owner of this hard-to-manage "chloro florist" establishment eventually confronts "an audio-vegetative armageddon."

If this innocuous environment could not deflect Ballard from his insistence on apocalypse in familiar surroundings, it is hardly startling to find that his penultimate tale is titled "The Secret Autobiography of J. G. B." For most of his life, our great specialist in catastrophe made his home in the almost laughably tranquil London suburb of Shepperton, the sheltered home of the British movie studios. He obviously relished the idea of waking one day to find himself the only human being on the planet, to explore a deserted London and cross a traffic-free Thames, to pillage gas stations and supermarkets and then to drive contentedly home. "B was ready to begin his true work."

(*The Atlantic*, January/February 2010)

Fraser's Flashman: Scoundrel Time

IN THE LAST but one of his twelve novelistic gallops through history and imagination, *Flashman and the Tiger*, George MacDonald Fraser does something at least as daring as anything that his poltroonish hero has ever ventured. He inserts his main character smack-dab into the middle of a failed assassination attempt. Colonel John Sebastian Moran, a pitiless killer and big-game hunter, is drawing a bead from a window in London at a silhouette across the ghostly street. And just as old Flashy is drawing his own bead on Moran, there is a wild commotion when an austere, gaunt private detective, a bluff old physician, and a squad of bobbies come piling into the room.

Some of you will have seen this coming: It is the climactic moment of "The Adventure of the Empty House," the momentous story in which Sir Arthur Conan Doyle recalled Sherlock Holmes from the dead and then saved him from the bullet of Professor Moriarty's vile associate. In other words, Fraser has succeeded not just in making his creation the familiar Zelig of high-Victorian imperial history, but in giving him a cameo part in late-Victorian fiction as well. Flashman is everywhere. And why should this not be so? Tourists visit Baker Street every day to see where Sherlock Holmes "actually" lived and pondered, shooting cocaine and sharing rooms with a chap. (That was in 221B, which never existed.) George MacDonald Fraser has never claimed to be anything but the editor of the "Flashman papers," discovered by luck during an auction at an English country house. When the first "packet" of papers was published, in 1969, several well-gulled reviewers genuinely hailed it as a grand literary discovery (one of them going as far as to say that there had been nothing like it since the unearthing of Boswell's diaries). It is the deftest borrowing since Tom Stoppard helped himself to the walk-on parts of Rosencrantz and Guildenstern.

George MacDonald Fraser was eighty on his last birthday ("same day as Charlemagne, Casanova, Hans Christian Andersen, and Kenneth Tynan," as he tells me) and is celebrating the publication of a round dozen of edited Flashman papers. I dip my colors in a solemn salute. It makes me whistle when I think how I grabbed the first of his published efforts right off the bat in 1969. Even now I can tell a fellow addict at ten paces. Those of us who have tried to cover the new "Great Game" as it has unfolded on the Pakistan-Afghanistan border have forgathered in Flashman's Hotel, situated in the Pakistani Army's post-colonial garrison town of Rawalpindi, and in the Flashman Restaurant of the Gandamack Lodge, in Kabul (Gandamack Lodge being old Flashy's ill-gotten mansion in rural Leicestershire). These are places where the borders are "porous," as the newspapers like to say, but where the boundary between fact and fiction is the most porous of all. It is Fraser's huge achievement to have smuggled his main man across that frontier, in both directions.

Victorian empire ("the greatest thing that ever happened to an undeserving world," Fraser asserts) was largely dedicated to Lord Macaulay's belief in progress and improvement: a civilizing mission that would gradually spread light into the dark places of the earth. It involved the Whig theory of history and was supposed to operate according to a near-providential plan. Well, that's all balls for a start, as Flashman stoutly observes: "In my experience the course of history is as often settled by someone's having a belly-ache, or not sleeping well, or a sailor getting drunk, or some aristocratic harlot waggling her backside."

In a way—and there's no shame in this—Fraser works according to a formula. There is, in every Flashman story, a horrific villain, a brush with an unthinkably agonizing death, and a bodacious female. Pure Ian Fleming, you might murmur, and indeed Fraser himself was a screenwriter for *Octopussy*. Why read the James Bond series if not for the certainty of being transported into a reliable parallel universe where there is no Goldfinger without a corresponding

Pussy Galore? Ah, but the men Flashman vanquishes, and the women he tumbles, are for the most part "real." And so are the events depicted. Fleming on his best day would never have dared match James Bond with the modern equivalent of Otto von Bismarck or send him into the sack with Queen Ranavalona of Madagascar, let alone have succeeded in making it so believable that some readers still do truly believe it. (When Flashman sees Oscar Wilde at the theater, in the course of his authored but unauthorized invasion of that Sherlock Holmes story, and marvelously describes the poet of decadence as resembling "an overfed trout in a toupe," we can hear his crusty, clubland grunt.)

But, on the other hand, James Bond did have a license to kill, and a thirst to employ it, whereas Flashman is a cowering impostor who prefers whoring and bullying to any risking of his skin on the thin red line. Thus, every novel must begin with a mise-en-scène that shows not just history as a chapter of screwups and screwings but also Flashman's own participation as an unlucky accident. The anti-hero doesn't begin by calling coolly on "M" to be briefed on his latest lethal assignment. He begins by running away in the wrong direction. So, to the drama of Bond, Fraser brilliantly adds the absurdity of Bertie Wooster. When Fraser first ushered his Homeric duffer onto the stage, P. G. Wodehouse was tempted into a rare comment, saying, "If ever there was a time when I felt that 'watcher-of-the-skies-when-a-new-planet' stuff, it was when I read the first Flashman."

Well, just as Wodehouse could have quoted the whole of that Keats poem with ease, one imagines that Flashman (or his creator) knows better in the twelfth and latest novel, *Flashman on the March*, when he remarks that the British government is caught "between Scylla and t'other thing." This is Wooster to the life, half remembering something from the schoolroom until corrected by Jeeves. As Bertie ruefully phrases it, never learning from his mistakes, it is just when you are stepping high and confident that Fate waits behind the door with a stuffed eelskin. And here goes old Flashy:

> My spirits were rising as we set off down the bank, the birds were carolling, there was a perfumed breeze blowing from the water, we were within a few miles of journey's end, I was absolutely humming "Drink, Puppy, Drink," the larks and snails were no doubt on their respective wings and thorns, God was in his heaven, and on the

verge of the jungle, not twenty yards away, a white-robed helmeted lancer was sitting his horse, watching us.

Or as Bertie inquires in *The Code of the Woosters*:

> "But the larks, Jeeves? The snails? I'm pretty sure larks and snails entered into it."
>
> "I am coming to the larks and snails, sir. 'The lark's on the wing, the snail's on the thorn—' "
>
> "Now you're talking. And the tab line?"
>
> " 'God's in His heaven, all's right with the world.' "
>
> "That's it in a nutshell. I couldn't have put it better myself."

Instead of Aunt Agatha, Fraser has placed a sinister and armed horseman at the terminus of his idyll, but then, Raymond Chandler (an old schoolmate of Wodehouse's at Dulwich College) made it a maxim that when action was flagging you could always have a man enter the room carrying a gun.

To say that Fraser can so easily juggle Conan Doyle and Holmes, Fleming and Bond, Wodehouse and Wooster, and Chandler and Marlowe is, I hope, to offer reasonably high praise. But just to pile on the admiration for a bit, I know some eminent historians who have pored over Fraser's footnotes and appreciated details about, say, the Charge of the Light Brigade that are known to few. The battle scene at Balaklava is meticulously done, and if his own mad charge is started by Flashman himself, who panics his horse by farting so loudly with sheer hangover and pure fear, why then it's hardly less of a fiasco and a shambles than the real thing turned out to be.

I am not looking for faults after all this drooling on my part, but there is one problem that needs to be faced squarely. In the earlier stories, Flashman is a sadist and a brute as well as a rascally coward and goof-off. He takes positive, gleeful pleasure in the misfortunes of others, especially if he can turn those misfortunes to his own account. In the very first book, he tells us, within months of joining his first regiment, "Myself, I liked a good flogging, and used to have bets with Bryant, my particular crony, on whether the man would cry out before the tenth stroke, or when he would faint. It was better sport than most, anyway." Some volumes later, in *Flash for Freedom!*, he is on the Mississippi and running away with the beautiful slave girl Cassy, who has been his bedmate and his companion in adversity. The brutal slave-catchers corner them, and she is "quivering like a hunted beast." Our hearts are in our mouths as he ponders what to do.

> "Cassy!" I snapped. "Can you use a gun?"
>
> She nodded. "Take this, then," says I. "Cover them—and if one of them stirs a finger, shoot the swine in the stomach! There—catch hold. Good girl, good girl—I'll be back in an instant!"
>
> "What is it?" Her eyes were wild. "Where are you—"
>
> "Don't ask questions! Trust me!" And with that I slipped out of the door, pulled it to, and was off like a stung whippet. I'd make quarter of a mile, maybe more, before she would twig, or they overpowered her.

This gave new significance to the old phrase "self-preservation." All you needed, in order to anticipate old Flashy's moves, was to guess at the lowest possible motive. And then, unaccountably, our hero started to go soft. In *Flashman and the Dragon*, he is the captive of the sinuous Chinese courtesan Yehonala:

> When two of her eunuchs caught some crows and released them with firecrackers tied to their legs so that the birds were blown to bits in mid-air, Yehonala had the culprits' backsides cut to bloody pulp with bamboo whips, watching the infliction of the full hundred strokes with smiling enjoyment. You may say they deserved a drubbing, but you didn't see it.

The earlier Flashman would (a) not have thought the cruel eunuchs "deserved a drubbing" for their ingenuity, and (b) not have given a damn about their punishment. He would have relished both scenes. Deplorable signs of weakness were already evident in *Flashman's Lady*, where he burdened himself with a white woman while trying to escape the horrifying soldiers of Queen Ranavalona. On that occasion the inconvenient lady was also his wife, so conceivably an exception can be made. But by the time of *Flashman and the Tiger* the plain fact had to be faced: The old boy had gone positively mushy with emotion and was prepared to risk his own skin—his own skin, mark you—to save his granddaughter's honor. There was some muttering in the ranks of the fan base. One blushed to see the pitiful wreck of what had once been such an ignoble man. It is therefore a real pleasure to be able to record a corking return to form in the latest book. Flashman has been chivied all over Abyssinia and saved repeatedly by the exquisite Uliba, an African princess who has acted as his guide, protector, and lover. There comes the moment, however, when their canoe has been swamped, the deadly waterfall is just ahead, Flashman has contrived to catch hold of an overhanging bough, and she has managed to seize one of his legs. As he reflects,

> There was only one thing to be done, so I did it, drawing up my free leg and driving my foot down with all my force at Uliba's face staring up at me open-mouthed, half-submerged as she clung to my other knee. I missed, but caught her full on the shoulder, jarring her grip free, and away she went, canoe and all, the gunwale rasping against my legs as it was whirled downstream. One glimpse I had of the white water foaming over those long beautiful legs, and then she was gone.

Now, that, you will have to admit, is a damn sight more like it. "Yes," sighs Fraser, "a lot of readers thought he was going soft, or even getting braver. In fact, he can only display the courage of a cornered rat. And my daughter Caro—she's also a novelist—told me how delighted she was that this time he'd definitely turned nasty again."

Historians and critics will never stop arguing about the worthwhileness of it all: that amazing conquest and settlement of the known globe by the aristocrats and peasants of a rain-sodden archipelago in the North Sea. Fraser makes Flashman face it in all its squalor and grandeur: the British-owned slave ships, and the British vessels that put down the slave trade; the destruction of dens of tyranny in India and Abyssinia, and the hideous vandalizing of the Summer Palace in Peking; the serf armies and pirate navies that needed crushing, and the magnificent peoples—Zulus, Sikhs, Afghans—who the British had finally to admit were unconquerable. The empire on which the sun never set was also the empire on which the gore never dried. Only a few decades ago, when the Flashman papers were first unwrapped from their oilskin, all this seemed to have vanished like blood off a bayonet. But now British and American soldiers are back in Afghanistan and Mesopotamia, and George MacDonald Fraser, who is known as a curmudgeonly Tory war veteran and staunch hater of Tony Blair, is not best pleased. "Tony Blair," he snorts down the phone, "is not just the worst prime minister we've ever had, but by far the worst prime minister we've ever had. It makes my blood boil to think of the British soldiers who've died for that little liar." Even so, in *Flashman on the March*, he ends his footnotes on the Abyssinian campaign ambiguously by noting that, although the British overthrew a crazed despot and then withdrew, "if Britain had stayed, revisionist historians would certainly have condemned it as another act of selfish imperialism."

This is the morally fraught terrain, between the first sound of the bugle and the news of triumph or disgrace, which it takes a serious man to cover, whether saddled on a mettlesome charger or flourishing only a pen. And, since history is often recounted by the victors, why not have it related for once by one who is something worse than a loser? Imagine if King Hal had kept Falstaff on hand as his bosom chum until the eve of Agincourt and you have a sense of Flashy's imperishable achievement.

(*Vanity Fair*, March 2006)

Fleet Street's Finest: From Waugh to Frayn

JAMES BOND DOES NOT MAKE an appearance until Part Two of what is perhaps his most polished adventure, *From Russia with Love*. And when he has been briefed by "M" and outfitted by "Q," and told what is expected of him, he suffers a mild mid-life crisis. What, he asks as the plane takes him toward the Golden Horn, would his younger self think of the man now so "tarnished with years of treachery and ruthlessness and fear," sent off "to pimp for England"? Eventually dismissing this as an idle or feeble mood, he reflects further:

> What-might-have-been was a waste of time. Follow your fate and be satisfied with it, and be glad not to be a second-hand motor salesman, or a yellow-press journalist, pickled in gin and nicotine, or a cripple—or dead.

Yes, well, that seems to put the profession nicely in its place, and indeed in its context. I read those words when I was a schoolboy in Cambridge in the early 1960s and had already decided that only journalism would do.

Not long afterward, I was strolling along Tenison Road and saw, I swear, a wheezing second- or even third-hand motor belching toward me. Behind its wheel sat a man of impossibly fly-blown and lugubrious appearance; his skin sallow and wrinkled, an unfiltered cigarette in his mouth; his eyes like piss-holes in the snow. Only one detail was required to complete the scene, and at first my disordered senses almost refused to register it. Stuck in the corner of his windscreen was a faint and tattered card that read "PRESS." It was yellow all right. It might as well have been stuck in the band of his hat. Christ knows where he had been—perhaps to a bad day at the Newmarket races—but it took little imagination to see where he was bound. And this was not a Giles cartoon but a glimpse of the future I thought I wanted. I cheered up immensely. Clichés and caricatures are there to be overcome, after all. And I had my Orwell books to go back to.

Not much later, I came across Orwell's essay "Confessions of a Book Reviewer." It opens thus, in case you may have forgotten:

> In a cold but stuffy bed-sitting room littered with cigarette ends and half-empty cups of tea, a man in a moth-eaten dressing-gown sits at a rickety table, trying to find room for his typewriter among the piles of dusty papers that surround it. He cannot throw the papers away because the wastepaper basket is already overflowing, and besides, somewhere among the unanswered letters and unpaid bills it is possible that there is a cheque for two guineas which he is nearly certain he forgot to pay into the bank... He is a man of thirty-five, but looks fifty. He is bald, has varicose veins and wears spectacles, or would wear them if his only pair were not chronically lost. If things are normal with him he will be suffering from malnutrition, but if he has recently had a lucky streak he will be suffering from a hangover.

Orwell of course could be discouragingly pessimistic at times. But for light relief there was always Evelyn Waugh, who in his *Decline and Fall* had taught me that even original sin could have its lighter side. What could be funnier than the school sports-day at Dr. Fagan's awful Molesworth-like establishment at Llanabba? The arrangements are being made:

> Admirable! And then there is the Press. We must ring up the Flint and Denbigh Herald and get them to send a photographer. That means whisky. Will you see to that, Philbrick? I remember at one of our sports I omitted to offer whisky to the Press, and the result was a

> most unfortunate photograph. Boys do get into such indelicate positions during the obstacle race, don't they?

A picture appeared to be emerging here. In the opening pages of *Scoop*, as William Boot is still in the train from Somerset to London and as yet has no idea what awaits him at the offices of the *Daily Beast*, he recalls that:

> He had once seen in Taunton a barely intelligible film about newspaper life in New York where neurotic men in shirt-sleeves and eyeshades had rushed from telephone to tape-machines, insulting and betraying one another in circumstances of unredeemed squalor.

Could this squalor ever be redeemed? Perhaps not by one of my other favorite standbys, Graham Greene, who sent Hale of the *Daily Messenger* down to Brighton for the day, there to pass his time in hucksterism and fatuity, "drinking gins and tonics wherever his programme allowed":

> For he had to stick closely to a programme: from ten till eleven Queen's Road and Castle Square, from eleven till twelve the Aquarium and Palace Pier, twelve till one the front between the Old Ship and West Pier, back for lunch between one and two in any restaurant he chose round the Castle Square, and after that he had to make his way all down the parade to the West Pier and then to the station by the Hove streets. These were the limits of his absurd and well-advertised sentry-go.

(And so much of journalism is the "sentry go": the stake-out, the hand-out, the lobby correspondents attending on their "source" who knows as well as they do when the deadline is coming. Hale and the *Daily Messenger* are doomed to miss the only real story of the day, which is Hale murdered in broad daylight by having a stick of hard rock jammed down his throat: an apposite revenge upon the idle and the spoon-fed.)

Enough, perhaps, of the Catholic school of fiction. I graduated to the cool and elegant universe of Anthony Powell, in whose world the influence of the newspapers is relatively minimal. In fact, as it now seems to me, the absence of this influence is a limitation on his claim to have been describing English social reality. Surely Sir Magnus Donners, that tycoon of 1930s tycoons, should have been the ambitious and manipulative proprietor of at least one Fleet Street title? When Powell gets round to it, though, as he does in the tenth of his twelve-novel cycle, he does not stint. Here is the port-soaked "Books" Bagshaw, in *Books Do Furnish a Room*:

> He possessed that opportune facility for turning out several thousand words on any subject whatever at the shortest possible notice: politics: sport: books: finance: science: art: fashion—as he himself said, "War, Famine, Pestilence or Death on a Pale Horse." All were equal when it came to Bagshaw's typewriter. He would take on anything, and—to be fair—what he produced, even off the cuff, was no worse than what was to be read most of the time. You never wondered how on earth the stuff had ever managed to be printed.

Bagshaw's gift for non-specialization is further emphasized a little later on, when he hears a saloon-bar criticism of the Woman's Page from an irate X Trapnel:

> Don't breathe a word against the Woman's Page, Trappy. Many a time I've proffered advice on it myself under a female pseudonym.

And this only sent me back to Evelyn Waugh and *The Loved One*, in which the repulsive Jake Slump, wreathed in the fumes of a bar-fly and chain-smoker, is a veteran of the agony advice column "Aunt Lydia's Post Bag."

A few themes seem to be emerging from the way in which our novelists have treated our journalists: copious gin (or whisky, or port, or what you will), mediocrity, cynicism, sloth, and meanness of spirit. This is to say nothing of the greatest of all *les deformations professionelles*: shameless and indeed boastful fabrication. And I entirely forgot to mention the fiddling of expenses. All professions are deformed by this, of course, but only journalism has made a code out of it:

> Mr. Salter saw he was not making his point clear. "Take a single example," he said. "Supposing you want to have dinner. Well, you go to a restaurant and do yourself proud, best of everything. Bill perhaps may be two pounds. Well, you put down five pounds for

> entertainment on your expenses. You've had a slap-up dinner, you're three pounds to the good, and everyone is satisfied.
>
> (Evelyn Waugh: *Scoop*)

> Various members of the staff emerged from Hand and Ball Passage during the last dark hour of the morning, walked with an air of sober responsibility toward the main entrance, greeted the commissionaire and vanished upstairs in the lift to telephone their friends and draw their expenses before going out again to have lunch.
>
> (Michael Frayn: *Towards the End of the Morning*)

An absolutely brilliant deadpan account of the expenses racket is also given in Philip Norman's marvelous novel of the *Sunday Times* in the late sixties: *Everyone's Gone to the Moon*. This is the only rival to Frayn since Waugh.

Frayn's *Towards the End of the Morning*, first published in 1967, used to have the status of a cult book among the hacks (as we all agree to call ourselves). It does have more or less everything: the white-haired and burned-out old soak who can only reminisce about forgotten, bibulous trips with forgotten, bibulous stars of old Fleet Street; the bullying, self-loathing pictures editor who insists on how self-made he is; the dreamy assistant scribe who only wants to write book reviews for the *New Statesman* on the side (that dates it a bit: In those days the NS had a literary editor and was literate); the neurotic deputy editor who can't keep up the supply of pre-digested columns entitled "In Years Gone By," or hold his rural clergymen contributors to their deadlines. (In the latter respect, there is something of a lift from William Boot's "Lush Places" countryman column in *Scoop*.)

There was always, also, an interest in guessing whether Frayn had "set" it all at either the *Observer* or the *Guardian*, which in those days were separate institutions. (Malcolm Muggeridge's journalism novel *Picture Palace* had been too transparent in this regard, enraging his employers, the then–*Manchester Guardian* management, who obtained an injunction preventing its publication.) In the introduction to the new edition, Frayn says that it was a touch of both. The paper is never given a name, but it's in any case obviously not the *Observer* because it comes out every day. A possible clue, for addicts and cognoscenti, is contained on the very cover of the new edition which drops an entire word out of the title of the novel, and rather metaphysically offers it as *Towards the End of Morning*. The *Guardian* is no longer so celebrated for its misprints but there will always be those of us who are nostalgic for the days when it was, and when the opera critic Phillip Hope Wallace, for example, could wake up to find that he had reviewed last night's Covent Garden performance of *Doris Godunov*.

Admirers of Frayn's second novel are sneered at by those of us who are in the know, and who appreciate that it is his first novel about journalism that really demonstrates his genius. In *The Tin Men*, published in 1965, there are some boozers and louts and misfits, to be sure. But the brilliance of the thing lay in its attempt to reduce the business of hackery to an exact formula. At a demented research institute named for William Morris, eager eyes gaze at a computer that can handle UHL, or "Unit Headline Language." A survey is conducted, in which people are shown the random headlines:

ROW HOPE MOVE FLOP
LEAK DASH SHOCK
HATE BAN BID PROBE

A total of 86.4 percent of those responding say that they understand the headlines, though of this total a depressing number cannot quite say why. Thus the search must go on. Would people like to read about air-crashes with children's toys in the wreckage, or without children's toys in the wreckage? In the case of a murder of a woman, should the victim be naked or partially clad? Frayn re-summons the tones of old Fleet Street into this laboratory of shame, when the questing researcher Goldwasser is brusquely accosted by his vile assistant Nobbs: " 'Do you prefer a female corpse to be naked, or to be clad in underclothes?' he repeated to Goldwasser. 'That's what I call a good question, mate. That's what I call a good question.' "

How shall we know the cultural mayhem wrought by thinking in headlines? Philip Roth's Portnoy does it all the time, as he guiltily imagines how his foulness would be rendered on the front page. When a WASP girl will not administer him a blow-job for fear of suffocation, for example: JEW SMOTHERS DEB WITH COCK: Vassar Grad Georgetown Strangulation Victim; Mocky Lawyer Held.

The habit breaks out fairly mildly in *Scoop*, where all the genius goes into the reporter's cables that are now a thing of the past ("LOVELY SPRING WEATHER BUBONIC PLAGUE RAGING"). In *Decline and Fall*, a lazy journalist comes to interview the mad architect Dr. Silenus at Margot Beste-Chetwynde's country home, and "happily" visualizes as he talks: "Peer's Sister-in-Law Mansion Builder on Future of Architecture." In *Brideshead Revisited*, for that matter, debutantes shriek at the headline "Marquis's Son Unused to Wine."

In one movie version of Hecht and MacArthur's *The Front Page*, Walter Matthau sees the condemned man's distraught girlfriend launch herself from a window and barely breaks off to mutter: "Shady Lady Leaps for Love," thus anticipating the *New York Post*'s "Headless Body in Topless Bar" by some two decades. But in Frayn's *Tin Men* the examples are barely even satirical, or self-satirizing. "Child Told Dress Unsuitable by Teacher"; "Paralyzed Girl Determined to Dance Again." And since the demure days in which he was originally writing, further defenses against satire have been erected at the lower end of the business. (Just try adding "bonk" to the list of four-letter headline words listed earlier, and begin your computer simulation.)

Martin Amis's *Yellow Dog* does its level best at parody (as can be proven by the mild name of his fictional rag, the *Morning Lark*, which is far less grotesque than the *Daily Beast* or *Daily Brute* and could very easily be imagined on a newsstand right now). And yellow is the light in the newsroom, and in the eyes of the hacks, and in so many of the bodily fluids that they tirelessly seek to make their readers emit. The new modern skill is that of wildly overdone photo-caption-writing, where no groan-making multiple-entendre is off-limits, and again I wasn't absolutely sure that part of the yellowing Clint Smoker's effort, about royalty in a Chinese restaurant, couldn't have been at least partly stolen:

> But sweet turned to sour when photographers had the sauce to storm their private room. Wan tun a bit of privacy, the couple fled with the lads in hot pursuit—we'll cashew!

("That bit was good," said a hard-bitten old Fleet-Streeter of my acquaintance, "but the bit about how we discuss the readers at editorial meetings was bloody uncanny.") In Kingsley Amis's *Girl, 20*, which is the second-funniest of his novels and the only one I can call to mind that features journalism—though I suppose Jim Dixon in a low moment does briefly impersonate a newspaper reporter on the telephone—the description of the editor Harold Meers is so thoroughly and worryingly accurate that I have met people who are certain that they must know who the bastard was. ("'It's the way he keeps thinking up new ways of being a shit that you can't help taking your hat off to him for,' said Coates." Albert Coates, incidentally, exactly resembles Jake Slump in the tartarean depths of his smoker's cough—"Coates drew at his cigarette and coughed terribly. He seemed unaware of any link between these two actions"—while the hero of *Girl, 20* joins Slump, Boot, and the awful Reg Mounce of *Towards the End of the Morning*, in the notorious newspaper-industry bind of the hack who has been fired without knowing it.)

The Amises are the only ones of the authors I have mentioned who didn't serve time on a national newspaper. Fleming was a foreign editor for Kemsley when that family owned the *Sunday Times*, Waugh was a correspondent, and Greene had been a sub-editor as well. Powell toiled at the *Daily Telegraph*, and Frayn we all know about. They mostly did quite well out of it. Orwell never had a steady job, but he haunted Fleet Street in search of work and knew the argot. Yet they all unite in employing the figure of the journalist, or the setting of a newspaper, as the very pattern and mold of every type of squalor and venality. The sole exception I can call to mind is P. G. Wodehouse, who started out as a penny-a-liner on the *Globe* and seems to have found journalism to be innocent fun. Bertie Wooster never misses a chance to mention his article on "What the Well-Dressed Man Is Wearing," which appeared in his Aunt Dahlia's own magazine *Milady's Boudoir*, and to which he deprecatingly refers as "my 'piece,' as we journalists call it." Psmith, in *Psmith Journalist*, takes over a small magazine of domesticity in New York, named *Cosy Moments*, and transforms it briefly into a campaigning, reforming, and crime-fighting organ. His slogan when confronted by those who would intimidate him is: "*Cosy Moments* cannot be muzzled." This motto has been inscribed on the wall above my keyboard for many years.

Probably nothing is as boring as the reminiscences of an old Fleet Street hand, but I shall have to say that I pity those now in the trade who won't remember the atmosphere of that little enclave between Ludgate Circus and the Strand, with its byways and courts and alleys. Yes, the smell of printer's ink, the thunder of the presses like the engine-room of the *Titanic*. Yes, the lights blazing in the black-glass palace of the old *Daily Express*, and the vans swinging out on their way to catch the overnight trains with the first edition. Yes, the fog around Blackfriars Station. Yes, the exorbitant padding of the night-shift by printers with names like M Mouse.

Yes, the suicidal imbibing in the King and Keys, or the Punch, or El Vino. Yes, the demented whims of the latest proprietor. Yes, the overflowing ashtrays and the pounding of ancient upright typewriters. Yes, the callousness and gallows humor. ("Shumble, Whelper and Pigge knew Corker," as Waugh describes a hacks' reunion in *Scoop*. "They had loitered of old on many a doorstep and forced an entry into many a stricken home.") And yes, it's true that the most celebrated opening line of any Fleet Street war correspondent was that of the hack in the Congo who yelled: "Anyone here been raped and speaks English?"

The palm goes to Frayn, in the end, because well before it happened he could see that closing time was coming, to those pubs and those hot metal presses both. Hackery and Grub Street had of course been lampooned before, from Pope to Gissing, but the real "age" of newspapers begins roughly with the Northcliffe press—"written by office-boys for office-boys," as someone loftily said—and the era of mass literacy. In other words, it opened with the twentieth century and may have closed with it.

In Frayn's two novels in the sixth decade of that century, the lure of television is already beginning to exert its anti-magic. The mindlessness of the opinion poll and the reader-survey is coming to replace news and analysis. The reporters and editors are beginning to think about mortgages and pensions. The editor is a cipher. I do not think that there will again be a major novel, flattering or unflattering, in which a reporter is the protagonist. Or if there is, he or she will be a blogger or some other species of cyber-artist, working from home and conjuring the big story from the vastness of electronic space.

In any case, the literature of old Fleet Street was to a very considerable extent written by journalists and for journalists. Most reporters I know regard *Scoop* as a work of pitiless realism rather than antic fantasy. The cap fitted, and they wore it, and with a lopsided grin of pride, at that. Perhaps this assists us in answering the age-old question: Why does the profession of journalism have such a low reputation? The answer: Because it has such a bad press.

(*The Guardian* [London], December 3, 2005)

Saki: Where the Wild Things Are

AT THE AGE of fifteen, Noël Coward was staying in an English country house and found a copy of *Beasts and Super-Beasts* on a table: "I took it up to my bedroom, opened it casually and was unable to go to sleep until I had finished it." I had a similar experience at about the same age, and I agree with Coward that H. H. Munro—or "Saki," the author of the book in question—is among those few writers, inspirational when read at an early age, who definitely retain their magic when revisited decades later. I have the impression that Saki is not very much appreciated in the United States. Good. That means I can put into my debt many of you who are reading these words. Go and get an edition of this Edwardian master of the short story. Begin with, say, "Sredni Vashtar" or "The Lumber-Room" or "The Open Window." Then see whether you can put the book down.

The spellbinding quality of the stories is almost too easy to analyze and looks mawkish when set down in plain words, because Saki's great gift was being able to write about children and animals. But consider: How many authors have ever been able to pull off these most difficult of tricks? Kipling, for sure, but then, Kipling would not have been able to render the languid young princes of the drawing room, such as the exquisite Clovis Sangrail, with whom Saki peopled so many a scene. The character of these lethal

---

Review of *The Unbearable Saki*, by Sandie Byrne.

Narcissi is well netted in a phrase coined by Sandie Byrne, who refers to them as "feral ephebes."

If you want to incubate an author who will show lifelong sympathy for children and animals, it seems best to sequester him at an early age and then subject him to a long regime of domestic torture. This was the formula that worked so well for Kipling, as evidenced in his frightening autobiographical story, "Baa Baa, Black Sheep," and it is almost uncanny to see how closely Saki's early life followed the same course. Abandoned to the care of cold and neurotic aunts in England while his father performed colonial duties in India, he and his siblings had to learn how to do without affection, and how to resist and outpoint adult callousness and stupidity. But without those terrible women—and the villains in Saki's gem-like tales are almost always female—we might not have had the most-fearsome aunts in fiction, outdoing even Wodehouse's Aunt Agatha or Wilde's Lady Bracknell.

Wodehouse happily admitted to being influenced by Saki, and it would be interesting to know to what extent Saki was himself influenced by Wilde. There is a good deal of evidence to suggest that he was, because some of his epigrams ("Beauty is only sin deep") betray an obvious indebtedness, and one ("To lose an hotel and a cake of soap in one afternoon suggests willful carelessness") is an almost direct appropriation from *The Importance of Being Earnest*. But in that epoch, Wilde's name lay under a ban, and Saki would have been well advised to not challenge the unstated rules that underlay that prohibition. (I find the speculation about his own homosexuality pointless because there is nothing about which to speculate: He was self-evidently homosexual and, just as obviously, deeply repressed.)

As is by no means uncommon in such cases, Saki was of the extreme right, and even an admirer must concede that some of his witticisms were rather labored and contrived as a consequence. Several of his less amusing stories are devoted to ridicule of the women's suffrage movement, which was cresting during his heyday, while a persistent subtext of his work is a satirical teasing of his contemporary and bête noire, the ponderously socialistic Bernard Shaw ("Sherard Blaw, the dramatist who had discovered himself, and who had given so ungrudgingly of his discovery to the world"). And, like another of his great contemporaries, Arthur Balfour, future author of a famous Declaration, Saki harbored a suspicion of Jews. One of his feral ephebes, Reginald, tells a duchess while chatting at the theater that what she terms "the great Anglo-Saxon empire" is, in fact, "rapidly becoming a suburb of Jerusalem."

That same empire, and its survival, was at the center of the contradictions in Saki's personality. Byrne's insightful and sprightly book makes plain that his affectless poseurs and dandies may have reflected one half of the man, just as his repeated portrayals of lithe and lissome and amoral young men must have expressed his banked-down yearnings. But this other hemisphere of his character also admired wildness and risk and cruelty and warfare, and associated the concepts of empire and nation with manly virtue.

This point can be reinforced by some thoughts on his choice of nom de plume. I had not known, until I read Byrne's book, that there was any doubt about the provenance of this. She mentions almost casually that one of his obituarists claimed it was a shortened form of "Nagasaki," which seems unintelligible in more ways than one. Enormously more probable, given Munro's often expressed admiration for FitzGerald's version of Omar Khayyám, is that he saw himself in the cupbearer of the *Rubáiyát*:

> And fear not lest Existence closing your
> Account, and mine, should know the like no more;
> The Eternal Sáki from that Bowl has pour'd
> Millions of Bubbles like us, and will pour.
>
> When You and I behind the Veil are past,
> Oh, but the long, long while the World shall last,
> Which of our Coming and Departure heeds
> As the Sea's self should heed a pebblecast.

In a story called "The East Wing," a lazy young male creature named Lucien Wattleskeat expresses something of the same thought—not exempting the bubble metaphor—but with more focus on the paradoxical importance of his own ephemerality:

> I don't think I can risk my life to save someone I've never met or even heard about. You see, my life is not only wonderful and beautiful to myself, but if my life goes, nothing else really matters—to me. Eva might be snatched from the flames and live to be the grandmother

> of brilliant and charming men and women, but as far as I should be concerned she and they would no more exist than a vanished puff of cigarette smoke or a dissolved soda-water bubble.

I think this clears up any dispute about the source of the pseudonym (which often appeared on book jackets alongside his true name), and I pause to note that Lucien Wattleskeat is a poor register of Saki's generally brilliant and somewhat Wildean ability to devise memorable names. Like Wilde (and like Anthony Powell later on), he made good use of the atlas of Britain and Ireland to come up with surnames and titles that were at once believable and eccentric. Many of these were from his beloved West Country (Yeovil, Honiton, Cullompton), but he ranged far and wide in choosing names like Courtenay Youghal for a smoothly accomplished politician and, in a moment of sheer brilliance, Tobermory for one of his most outstanding characters, the house cat who learns to speak English (and also to eavesdrop). Of his selecting Clovis as the model par excellence of his breed of bored and elegant young men, I have heard it suggested that it was because he was so appallingly Frank.

Creatures that essentially can never be tamed—felines and wolves preeminently—were Saki's emotional favorites. In his best-known novella, *The Unbearable Bassington*, which contains in the figure of Comus Bassington one of the two most obviously homoerotic of his protagonists (the other being the boy-werewolf Gabriel-Ernest in the story of the same name), the hero is a man named Tom Keriway, whose daredevil nature is summed up in the echoing phrase "a man that wolves have sniffed at." But Keriway has become sickly and nearly destitute, and morosely recalls an observation about a crippled wild crane that became domesticated in a German park: "It was lame, that was why it was tame."

When he was in his early forties, Saki began to throw off some of the languor and ennui with which he had invested so many of his scenes and characters, and became extremely exercised about the empire that he had quite often lampooned. Perhaps as a result of his experiences in Russia and the Balkans as a correspondent for a High Tory newspaper, he emitted grave warnings about an imminent German invasion and even wrote an alarmist novel—*When William Came*—about how British life might feel under the Prussian heel of Kaiser Wilhelm. Its pages treat almost exclusively the outrage and dispossession that might be experienced by the humiliated gentry. (I can think of only one Saki tale that takes the side of egalitarianism or that views society from the perspective of the gutter rather than the balcony or the verandah, and that is the lovely and vindictive "Morlvera," in which a couple of proletarian children witness a delicious piece of malice and spite being inflicted on a grown-up by a hideous youngster of the upper crust.)

But in 1914, Saki surprised all his elite admirers. His reasons for insisting on signing up for the trenches, when he was easily old enough to evade that fate, were almost comically reactionary. Enraged by the anti-militarist left that thought socialism preferable to world war, he argued in effect that even world war was preferable to socialism. Yet he declined any offer of an officer's commission, insisted on serving in the ranks, appeared to forget all his previous affectations about hollandaise dressing and the loving preparations of wine and cheese, and was so reduced by front-line conditions of wounds and illness that he grew a mustache to conceal the loss of most of his top teeth. He carried on writing, though chiefly about the interesting survival of wildlife in the no-man's-land of the Western Front, and he repeatedly sought positions on the front line. In November 1916, near the village of Beaumont-Hamel on the river Somme, he found what it is quite thinkable that he had been looking for all along. On the verge of a crater, during an interval of combat, he was heard to shout "Put that bloody cigarette out!" before succumbing to the bullet of a German sniper who had been trained to look for such tell-tale signals. In that "vanished puff of cigarette smoke" or, if you prefer, his image of a dissolved bubble of effervescence, there died someone who had finally come to decide that other people were worth fighting for after all.

(*The Atlantic*, June 2008)

Harry Potter: The Boy Who Lived

IN MARCH 1940, in the "midnight of the century" that marked the depth of the Hitler-Stalin Pact (or in other words, at a time when civilization was menaced by an alliance between two Voldemorts or "You-Know-Whos"), George Orwell took the time to examine the state of affairs in fantasy fiction for young people. And what he found (in an essay called "Boys' Weeklies") was an extraordinary level of addiction to the form of story that was set in English boarding schools. Every week, boys (and girls) from the poorer quarters of industrial towns and from the outer edges of the English-speaking Empire would invest some part of their pocket-money to keep up with the adventures of Billy Bunter, Harry Wharton, Bob Cherry, Jack Blake, and the other blazer-wearing denizens of Greyfriars and St. Jim's. As he wrote:

> It is quite clear that there are tens and scores of thousands of people to whom every detail of life at a "posh" public school is wildly thrilling and romantic. They happen to be outside that mystic world of quadrangles and house-colors, but they can yearn after it, daydream about it, live mentally in it for hours at a stretch. The question is, Who are these people?

Review of *Harry Potter and the Deathly Hallows*, by J. K. Rowling.

I wish that the morose veteran of Eton and St. Cyprian's had been able to join me on the publication night of *Harry Potter and the Deathly Hallows,* when I went to a bookstore in Stanford, California, to collect my embargoed copy on behalf of the *New York Times Book Review.* Never mind the stall that said "Get Your House Colors Here" and was dealing with customers wise in the lore of Ravenclaw and Slytherin. On the floor of the shop, largely transformed into the Gryffindor common room for the occasion, sat dozens of small children listening raptly to a reading from a massively plausible Hagrid. Of the 2,000 or so people in the forecourt, perhaps one-third had taken the trouble to wear prefect gowns and other Hogwarts or quidditch impedimenta. Many wore a lightning-flash on their foreheads: Orwell would have recoiled at seeing the symbol of Sir Oswald Mosley's British Union of Fascists on otherwise unblemished brows, even if the emblem was tamed by its new white-magic associations. And this was a sideshow to the circus, all across the English-speaking and even non-English world, as the countdown to the witching hour began.

I would give a lot to understand this phenomenon better. Part of it must have to do with the extreme banality and conformity of school life as it is experienced today, with everything oriented toward safety on the one hand and correctness on the other. But this on its own would not explain my youngest daughter a few years ago, sitting for hours on end with her tiny elbow flattening the pages of a fat book, and occasionally laughing out loud at the appearance of Scabbers the rat. (One hears that not all children retain the affection for reading that the Harry Potter books have inculcated: This isn't true in my house at least.)

Scabbers turns out to mutate into something a bit worse than a rat, and the ancient charm of metamorphosis is one that J. K. Rowling has exploited to the uttermost. Another well-tested appeal, that of the orphan hero, has also been given an intensive workout with the Copperfield-like privations of the eponymous hero. For Orwell, the English school story from Tom Brown to Kipling's Stalky and Co. was intimately bound up with dreams of wealth and class and snobbery, yet Rowling has succeeded in unmooring it from these considerations and giving us a world of youthful democracy and diversity, in which the humble leading figure has a name that—though it was given to a Shakespearean martial hero and king—could as well belong to an English labor union official. Perhaps Anglophilia continues to play its part, but if I were one of the few surviving teachers of Anglo-Saxon I would rejoice at the way in which such terms as "muggle" and "Wizengamot," and such names as Godric, Wulfric, and Dumbledore, had become common currency. At this rate, the teaching of *Beowulf* could be revived. The many Latin incantations and imprecations could also help rekindle interest in the study of a "dead" language.

In other respects, too, one recognizes the school story formula. If a French or German or other "foreign" character appears in the Harry Potter novels, it is always as a cliché: Fleur and Krum both speak as if to be from "the Continent" is a joke in itself. The ban on sexual matters is also observed fairly pedantically, though as time has elapsed Rowling has probably acquired male readers who find themselves having vaguely impure thoughts about Hermione Granger (if not, because the thing seems somehow impossible, about Ginny Weasley). Most interesting of all, perhaps, and as noted by Orwell, "religion is also taboo." The schoolchildren appear to know nothing of Christianity; in this latest novel Harry and even Hermione are ignorant of two well-known biblical verses encountered in a churchyard. That the main characters nonetheless have a strong moral code and a solid ethical commitment will be a mystery to some—like His Holiness the Pope and other clerical authorities who have denounced the series—while seeming unexceptionable to many others. As Hermione phrases it, sounding convincingly Kantian or even Russellian about something called the Resurrection Stone:

> How can I possibly prove it doesn't exist? Do you expect me to get hold of—of all the pebbles in the world and test them? I mean, you could claim that anything's real if the only basis for believing in it is that nobody's proved it doesn't exist.

For all this apparently staunch secularism, it is ontology that ultimately slackens the tension that ought to have kept these tales vivid and alive. Theologians have never been able to answer the challenge that contrasts God's claims to simultaneous omnipotence and benevolence: Whence then cometh evil? The question is the same if inverted in a Manichean form: How can Voldemort and his wicked forces have such power and yet be unable to destroy a mild-mannered and rather disorganized schoolboy? In a short story this discrepancy might be handled and also swiftly resolved in favor of one outcome or another, but over the course of seven full-length books the mystery, at least for this reader, loses its ability to compel, and in this culminating episode the enterprise actually becomes tedious. Is there really no Death Eater or dementor who is able to grasp the simple advantage of surprise?

The repeated tactic of deus ex machina (without a deus) has a deplorable effect on both the plot and the dialogue. The need for Rowling to play catch-up with her many convolutions infects her characters as well. Here is Harry trying to straighten things out with a servile house-elf:

> "I don't understand you, Kreacher," he said finally. "Voldemort tried to kill you, Regulus died to bring Voldemort down, but you were still happy to betray Sirius to Voldemort? You were happy to go to Narcissa and Bellatrix, and pass information to Voldemort through them..."

Yes, well, one sees why he is confused. The exchange takes place during an abysmally long period during which the threesome of Harry, Hermione, and Ron are flung together, with weeks of time to spend camping invisibly and only a few inexplicable escapes from death to alleviate the narrative. The grand context of Hogwarts School is removed, at least until the closing scenes, and Rowling also keeps forgetting that things are either magical or they are not: Hermione's family surely can't be any safer from the Dark Lord by moving to Australia, and Hagrid's corporeal bulk cannot make any difference to his ability, or otherwise, to mount a broomstick. A boring subtext, about the wisdom or otherwise of actually uttering Voldemort's name, meanwhile robs the apotropaic device of its force.

For some time now the novels have been attempting a kind of secular dramatization of the battle between good and evil. The Ministry of Magic (one of Rowling's better inventions) has been seeking to impose a version of the Nuremberg Laws on England, classifying its subjects according to blood and maintaining its own Gestapo as well as its own Azkaban gulag. But again, over time and over many, many pages this scenario fails to chill: Most of the "muggle" population goes about its ordinary existence, and every time the secret police close in, our heroes are able to "disapparate"—a term that always makes me think of an attempt at English by George W. Bush. The prejudice against bank-monopoly goblins is modeled more or less on anti-Semitism and the foul treatment of elves is meant to put us in mind of slavery, but the overall effect of this is somewhat thin and derivative, and subject to diminishing returns.

In this final volume there is a good deal of loose-end gathering to be done. Which side was Snape really on? Can Neville Longbottom rise above himself? Are the Malfoys as black as they have been painted? Unfortunately—and with the solid exception of Neville, whose gallantry is well evoked—these resolutions prove to possess all the excitement of an old-style Perry Mason–type summing-up, prompted by a stock character who says, "There's just one thing I don't understand...." Most of all this is true of Voldemort himself, who becomes more tiresome than an Ian Fleming villain, or the vicious but verbose Nicolae Carpathia in the Left Behind series, as he offers boastful explanations that are at once grandiose and vacuous. This bad and pedantic habit persists until the final duel, which at least sees us back in the old school precincts once again. "We must not let in daylight upon magic," as Walter Bagehot remarked in another connection, and the wish to have everything clarified is eventually self-defeating in its own terms. In her correct determination to bring down the curtain decisively, Rowling has gone further than she should, and given us not so much a happy ending as an ending which suggests that evil has actually been defeated (you should forgive the expression) for good.

Greater authors—Arthur Conan Doyle most notably—have been in the same dilemma when seeking closure. And, like Conan Doyle, Rowling has won imperishable renown for giving us an identifiable hero and a fine caricature of a villain, and for making a fictional bit of King's Cross station as luminous as a certain address on nearby Baker Street. It is given to few authors to create a world apart, and to populate it as well as illustrate it in the mind. As one who actually did once go to boarding school by steam train, at eight, I enjoyed reading aloud to children and coming across Diagon Alley and Grimmauld Place, and also shuddering at the memory of the sarcastic schoolmasters (and Privet Drives) I have known.

The distinctly slushy close of the story may seem to hold out the faint promise of a sequel, but I honestly think and sincerely hope that this will not occur. The toys have been put firmly back in the box, the wand has been folded up, and the conjuror is discreetly accepting payment while the children clamor for fresh entertainments. (I recommend that they graduate to Philip Pullman, whose daemon scheme is finer than any patronus.) It's achievement enough that "19 years later," as the last chapter-heading has it, and quite probably for many decades after that, there will still be millions of adults who recall their initiation to literature as a little touch of Harry in the night.

(*The New York Times Book Review*, August 12, 2007)

Amusements, Annoyances, and Disappointments

Why Women Aren't Funny

BE YOUR GENDER WHAT IT MAY, you will certainly have heard the following from a female friend who is enumerating the charms of a new (male) squeeze: "He's really quite cute, and he's kind to my friends, and he knows all kinds of stuff, and he's so funny..." (If you yourself are a guy, and you know the man in question, you will often have said to yourself, "Funny? He wouldn't know a joke if it came served on a bed of lettuce with sauce bearnaise.") However, there is something that you absolutely never hear from a male friend who is hymning his latest (female) love interest: "She's a real honey, has a life of her own... (interlude for attributes that are none of your business)... and, man, does she ever make 'em laugh."

Now, why is this? Why is it the case?, I mean. Why are women, who have the whole male world at their mercy, not funny? Please do not pretend not to know what I am talking about. All right—try it the other way (as the bishop said to the barmaid). Why are men, taken on average and as a whole, funnier than women? Well, for one thing, they had damn well better be. The chief task in life that a man has to perform is that of impressing the opposite sex, and Mother Nature (as we laughingly call her) is not so kind to men. In fact, she equips many fellows with very little armament for the struggle. An average man has just one, outside chance: He had better be able to make the lady laugh. Making them laugh has been one of the crucial preoccupations of my life. If you can stimulate her to laughter—I am talking about that real, out-loud, head-back, mouth-open-to-expose-the-full-horseshoe-of-lovely-teeth, involuntary, full, and deep-throated mirth; the kind that is accompanied by a shocked surprise and a slight (no, make that a loud) peal of delight—well, then, you have at least caused her to loosen up and to change her expression. I shall not elaborate further.

Women have no corresponding need to appeal to men in this way. They already appeal to men, if you catch my drift. Indeed, we now have all the joy of a scientific study, which illuminates the difference. At the Stanford University School of Medicine (a place, as it happens, where I once underwent an absolutely hilarious procedure with a sigmoidoscope), the grim-faced researchers showed ten men and ten women a sample of seventy black-and-white cartoons and got them to rate the gags on a "funniness scale." To annex for a moment the fall-about language of the report as it was summarized in *Biotech Week*:

> The researchers found that men and women share much of the same humor-response system; both use to a similar degree the part of the brain responsible for semantic knowledge and juxtaposition and the part involved in language processing. But they also found that some brain regions were activated more in women. These included the left prefrontal cortex, suggesting a greater emphasis on language and executive processing in women, and the nucleus accumbens... which is part of the mesolimbic reward center.

This has all the charm and address of the learned Professor Scully's attempt to define a smile, as cited by Richard Usborne in his treatise on P. G. Wodehouse: "the drawing back and slight lifting of the corners of the mouth, which partially uncover the teeth; the curving of the naso-labial furrows..." But have no fear—it gets worse:

> "Women appeared to have less expectation of a reward, which in this case was the punch line of the cartoon," said the report's author, Dr. Allan Reiss. "So when they got to the joke's punch line, they were more pleased about it." The report also found that "women were quicker at identifying material they considered unfunny."

Slower to get it, more pleased when they do, and swift to locate the unfunny—for this we need the Stanford University School of Medicine? And remember, this is women when confronted with humor. Is it any wonder that they are backward in generating it?

This is not to say that women are humorless, or cannot make great wits and comedians. And if they did not operate on the humor wavelength, there would be scant point in half killing oneself in the attempt to make them writhe and scream (uproariously). Wit, after all, is the unfailing symptom of intelligence. Men will laugh at almost anything, often precisely because it is—or they are—extremely stupid. Women aren't like that. And the wits and comics among them are formidable beyond compare: Dorothy Parker, Nora Ephron, Fran Lebowitz, Ellen DeGeneres. (Though ask yourself, was Dorothy Parker ever really funny?) Greatly daring—or so I thought—I resolved to call up Ms. Lebowitz and Ms. Ephron to try out my theories. Fran responded: "The cultural values are male; for a woman to say a man is funny is the equivalent of a man saying that a woman is pretty. Also, humor is largely aggressive and pre-emptive, and what's more male than that?" Ms. Ephron did not disagree. She did, however, in what I thought was a slightly feline way, accuse me of plagiarizing a rant by Jerry Lewis that said much the same thing. (I have only once seen Lewis in action, in *The King of Comedy*, where it was really Sandra Bernhard who was funny.)

In any case, my argument doesn't say that there are no decent women comedians. There are more terrible female comedians than there are terrible male comedians, but there are some impressive ladies out there. Most of them, though, when you come to review the situation, are hefty or dykey or Jewish, or some combo of the three. When Roseanne stands up and tells biker jokes and invites people who don't dig her shtick to suck her dick—know what I am saying? And the Sapphic faction may have its own reasons for wanting what I want—the sweet surrender of female laughter. While Jewish humor, boiling as it is with angst and self-deprecation, is almost masculine by definition.

Substitute the term "self-defecation" (which I actually heard being used inadvertently once) and almost all men will laugh right away, if only to pass the time. Probe a little deeper, though, and you will see what Nietzsche meant when he described a witticism as an epitaph on the death of a feeling. Male humor prefers the laugh to be at someone's expense, and understands that life is quite possibly a joke to begin with—and often a joke in extremely poor taste. Humor is part of the armor-plate with which to resist what is already farcical enough. (Perhaps not by coincidence, battered as they are by motherfucking nature, men tend to refer to life itself as a bitch.) Whereas women, bless their tender hearts, would prefer that life be fair, and even sweet, rather than the sordid mess it actually is. Jokes about calamitous visits to the doctor or the shrink or the bathroom, or the venting of sexual frustration on furry domestic animals, are a male province. It must have been a man who originated the phrase "funny like a heart attack." In all the millions of cartoons that feature a patient listening glum-faced to a physician ("There's no cure. There isn't even a race for a cure"), do you remember even one where the patient is a woman? I thought as much.

Precisely because humor is a sign of intelligence (and many women believe, or were taught by their mothers, that they become threatening to men if they appear too bright), it could be that in some way men do not want women to be funny. They want them as an audience, not as rivals. And there is a huge, brimming reservoir of male unease, which it would be too easy for women to exploit. (Men can tell jokes about what happened to John Wayne Bobbitt, but they don't want women doing so.) Men have prostate glands, hysterically enough, and these have a tendency to give out, along with their hearts and, it has to be said, their dicks. This is funny only in male company. For some reason, women do not find their own physical decay and absurdity to be so riotously amusing, which is why we admire Lucille Ball and Helen Fielding, who do see the funny side of it. But this is so rare as to be like Dr. Johnson's comparison of a woman preaching to a dog walking on its hind legs: The surprise is that it is done at all.

The plain fact is that the physical structure of the human being is a joke in itself: a flat, crude, unanswerable disproof of any nonsense about "intelligent design." The reproductive and eliminating functions (the closeness of which is the origin of all obscenity) were obviously wired together in hell by some subcommittee that was giggling cruelly as it went about its work. ("Think they'd wear this? Well, they're gonna have to.") The resulting confusion is the source of perhaps 50 percent of all humor. Filth. That's what the customers want, as we occasional stand-up performers all know. Filth, and plenty of it. Filth in lavish, heaping quantities. And there's another principle that helps exclude the fair sex. "Men obviously like gross stuff," says

Fran Lebowitz. "Why? Because it's childish." Keep your eye on that last word. Women's appetite for talk about that fine product known as Depend is limited. So is their relish for gags about premature ejaculation. ("Premature for whom?" as a friend of mine indignantly demands to know.) But "child" is the key word. For women, reproduction is, if not the only thing, certainly the main thing. Apart from giving them a very different attitude to filth and embarrassment, it also imbues them with the kind of seriousness and solemnity at which men can only goggle. This womanly seriousness was well caught by Rudyard Kipling in his poem "The Female of the Species." After cleverly noticing that with the male "mirth obscene diverts his anger"—which is true of most work on that great masculine equivalent to childbirth, which is warfare—Kipling insists:

> But the Woman that God gave him,
> every fibre of her frame
> Proves her launched for one sole issue,
> armed and engined for the same,
> And to serve that single issue,
> lest the generations fail,
> The female of the species must be
> deadlier than the male.

The word "issue" there, which we so pathetically misuse, is restored to its proper meaning of childbirth. As Kipling continues:

> She who faces Death by torture for
> each life beneath her breast
> May not deal in doubt or pity—must
> not swerve for fact or jest.

Men are overawed, not to say terrified, by the ability of women to produce babies. (Asked by a lady intellectual to summarize the differences between the sexes, another bishop responded, "Madam, I cannot conceive.") It gives women an unchallengeable authority. And one of the earliest origins of humor that we know about is its role in the mockery of authority. Irony itself has been called "the glory of slaves." So you could argue that when men get together to be funny and do not expect women to be there, or in on the joke, they are really playing truant and implicitly conceding who is really the boss.

The ancient annual festivities of Saturnalia, where the slaves would play master, were a temporary release from bossdom. A whole tranche of subversive male humor likewise depends on the notion that women are not really the boss, but are mere objects and victims. Kipling saw through this:

> So it comes that Man, the coward,
> when he gathers to confer
> With his fellow-braves in council,
> dare not leave a place for her.

In other words, for women the question of funniness is essentially a secondary one. They are innately aware of a higher calling that is no laughing matter. Whereas with a man you may freely say of him that he is lousy in the sack, or a bad driver, or an inefficient worker, and still wound him less deeply than you would if you accused him of being deficient in the humor department.

If I am correct about this, which I am, then the explanation for the superior funniness of men is much the same as for the inferior funniness of women. Men have to pretend, to themselves as well as to women, that they are not the servants and supplicants. Women, cunning minxes that they are, have to affect not to be the potentates. This is the unspoken compromise H. L. Mencken described as "the greatest single discovery ever made by man" the realization "that babies have human fathers, and are not put into their mother's bodies by the gods." You may well wonder what people were thinking before that realization hit, but we do know of a society in Melanesia where the connection was not made until quite recently. I suppose that the reasoning went: Everybody does that thing the entire time, there being little else to do, but not every woman becomes pregnant. Anyway, after a certain stage women came to the conclusion that men were actually necessary, and the old form of matriarchy came to a close. (Mencken speculates that this is why the first kings ascended the throne clutching their batons or scepters as if holding on for grim death.) People in this precarious position do not enjoy being laughed at, and it would not have taken women long to work out that female humor would be the most upsetting of all.

Childbearing and rearing are the double root of all this, as Kipling guessed. As every father knows, the placenta is made up of brain cells, which migrate southward during pregnancy and take the sense of humor along with them. And when the bundle is finally delivered, the funny side is not always immediately back in view. Is there anything so utterly lacking in humor as a mother discussing her new child? She is unborable on the subject. Even the mothers of other fledglings have to drive their fingernails into their palms and wiggle their toes, just to prevent themselves from fainting dead away at the sheer tedium of it. And as the little ones burgeon and thrive, do you find that their mothers enjoy jests at their expense? I thought not.

Humor, if we are to be serious about it, arises from the ineluctable fact that we are all born into a losing struggle. Those who risk agony and death to bring children into this fiasco simply can't afford to be too frivolous. (And there just aren't that many episiotomy jokes, even in the male repertoire.) I am certain that this is also partly why, in all cultures, it is females who are the rank-and-file mainstay of religion, which in turn is the official enemy of all humor. One tiny snuffle that turns into a wheeze, one little cut that goes septic, one pathetically small coffin, and the woman's universe is left in ashes and ruin. Try being funny about that, if you like. Oscar Wilde was the only person ever to make a decent joke about the death of an infant, and that infant was fictional, and Wilde was (although twice a father) a queer. And because fear is the mother of superstition, and because they are partly ruled in any case by the moon and the tides, women also fall more heavily for dreams, for supposedly significant dates like birthdays and anniversaries, for romantic love, crystals and stones, lockets and relics, and other things that men know are fit mainly for mockery and limericks. Good grief! Is there anything less funny than hearing a woman relate a dream she's just had? ("And then Quentin was there somehow. And so were you, in a strange sort of way. And it was all so peaceful." Peaceful?)

For men, it is a tragedy that the two things they prize the most—women and humor—should be so antithetical. But without tragedy there could be no comedy. My beloved said to me, when I told her I was going to have to address this melancholy topic, that I should cheer up because "women get funnier as they get older."

Observation suggests to me that this might indeed be true, but, excuse me, isn't that rather a long time to have to wait?

(*Vanity Fair*, January 2007)

Stieg Larsson: The Author Who Played with Fire

I SUPPOSE IT'S JUSTIFIABLE TO DESCRIBE "best-selling" in quasi-tsunami terms because when it happens it's partly a wall and partly a tide: first you see a towering, glistening rampart of books in Costco and the nation's airports and then you are hit by a series of succeeding waves that deposit individual copies in the hands of people sitting right next to you. I was slightly wondering what might come crashing in after Hurricane Khaled. I didn't guess that the next great inundation would originate not in the exotic kite-running spaces at the roof of the world but from an epicenter made almost banal for us by Volvo, Absolut, Saab, and IKEA.

Yet it is from this society, of reassuring brand names and womb-to-tomb national health care, that Stieg Larsson conjured a detective double act so incongruous that it makes Holmes and Watson seem like siblings. I say "conjured" because Mr. Larsson also drew upon the bloody, haunted old Sweden of trolls and elves and ogres, and I put it in the past tense because, just as the first book in his "Millennium" trilogy, *The Girl with the Dragon Tattoo*, was about to make his fortune, he very suddenly became a dead person. In the Larsson universe the nasty trolls and hulking ogres are bent Swedish capitalists, cold-faced Baltic sex traffickers, blue-eyed Viking Aryan Nazis, and other Nordic riffraff who might have had their reasons to whack him. But if he now dwells in that Valhalla of the hack writer who posthumously beat all the odds, it's surely because of his elf. Picture a feral waif. All right, picture a four-foot-eleven-inch "doll" with Asperger's syndrome and generous breast implants. This is not Pippi Longstocking (to whom a few gestures are made in the narrative). This is Miss Goth, intermittently disguised as *la gamine*.

Forget Miss Smilla's sense of the snow and check out Lisbeth Salander's taste in pussy rings, tattoos, girls, boys, motorcycles, and, above all, computer keyboards. (Once you accept that George MacDonald Fraser's Flashman can pick up any known language in a few days, you have suspended enough disbelief to settle down and enjoy his adventures.) Miss Salander is so well accoutred with special features that she's almost over-equipped. She is awarded a photographic memory, a chess mind to rival Bobby Fischer's, a mathematical capacity that toys with Fermat's last theorem as a cat bats a mouse, and the ability to "hack"—I apologize for the repetition of that word—into the deep intestinal computers of all banks and police departments. At the end of *The Girl Who Played with Fire*, she is for good measure granted the ability to return from the grave.

With all these superheroine advantages, one wonders why she and her on-and-off sidekick, the lumbering but unstoppable reporter Mikael Blomkvist, don't defeat the forces of Swedish Fascism and imperialism more effortlessly. But the other reason that Lisbeth Salander is such a source of fascination is this: The pint-size minxoid with the dragon tattoo is also a traumatized victim and doesn't work or play well with others. She has been raped and tortured and otherwise abused ever since she could think, and her private phrase for her coming-of-age is "All the Evil": words that go unelucidated until near the end of *The Girl Who Played with Fire*. The actress Noomi Rapace has already played Salander in a Swedish film of the first novel, which enjoyed a worldwide release. (When Hollywood gets to the casting stage, I suppose Philip Seymour Hoffman will be offered the ursine Blomkvist role, and though the coloring is wrong I keep thinking of Winona Ryder for Lisbeth.) According to Larsson's father, the sympathy with which "the girl" is evoked is derived partly from the author's own beloved niece, Therese, who is tattooed and has suffered from anorexia and dyslexia but can fix your computer problems.

In life, Stieg Larsson described himself as, among other things, "a feminist," and his character surrogate, Mikael Blomkvist, takes an ostentatiously severe line against the male domination of society and indeed of his own profession. (The original grim and Swedish title of *The Girl with the Dragon Tattoo* is *Men Who Hate Women*, while the trilogy's third book bore the more fairy-tale-like name *The Castle in the Air That Blew Up:* The clever rebranding of the series with the word "girl" on every cover was obviously critical.) Blomkvist's moral righteousness comes in very useful for the action of the novels, because it allows the depiction of a great deal of cruelty to women, smuggled through customs under the disguise of a strong disapproval. Sweden used to be notorious, in the late 1960s, as the homeland of the film *I Am Curious (Yellow)*, which went all the way to the Supreme Court when distributed in the United States and gave Sweden a world reputation as a place of smiling nudity and guilt-free sex. What a world of nursery innocence that was, compared with the child slavery and exploitation that are evoked with perhaps slightly too much relish by the crusading Blomkvist.

His best excuse for his own prurience is that these serial killers and torture fanciers are practicing a form of capitalism and that their racket is protected by a pornographic alliance with a form of Fascism, its lower ranks made up of hideous bikers and meth runners. This is not just sex or crime—it's politics! Most of the time, Larsson hauls himself along with writing such as this:

> The murder investigation was like a broken mosaic in which he could make out some pieces while others were simply missing. Somewhere there was a pattern. He could sense it, but he could not figure it out. Too many pieces were missing.

No doubt they were, or there would be no book. (The plot of the first story is so heavily convoluted that it requires a page reproducing the Vanger dynasty's family tree—the first time I can remember encountering such a dramatis personae since I read *War and Peace*.) But when he comes to the villain of *The Girl with the Dragon Tattoo*, a many-tentacled tycoon named Wennerström, Larsson's prose is suddenly much more spirited. Wennerström had consecrated himself to "fraud that was so extensive it was no longer merely criminal—it was business." That's actually one of the best-turned lines in the whole thousand pages. If it sounds a bit like Bertolt Brecht on an average day, it's because Larsson's own views were old-shoe Communist.

His background involved the unique bonding that comes from tough

Red families and solid class loyalties. The hard-labor and factory and mining sector of Sweden is in the far and arduous North—this is also the home territory of most of the country's storytellers—and Grandpa was a proletarian Communist up toward the Arctic. This during the Second World War, when quite a few Swedes were volunteering to serve Hitler's New Order and join the SS. In a note the twenty-three-year-old Larsson wrote before setting out for Africa, he bequeathed everything to the Communist Party of his hometown, Umea. The ownership of the immense later fortune that he never saw went by law to his father and brother, leaving his partner of thirty years, Eva Gabrielsson, with no legal claim, only a moral one that asserts she alone is fit to manage Larsson's very lucrative legacy. And this is not the only murk that hangs around his death, at the age of fifty, in 2004.

To be exact, Stieg Larsson died on November 9, 2004, which I can't help noticing was the anniversary of Kristallnacht. Is it plausible that Sweden's most public anti-Nazi just chanced to expire from natural causes on such a date? Larsson's magazine, *Expo*, which has a fairly clear fictional cousinhood with "Millennium," was an unceasing annoyance to the extreme right. He himself was the public figure most identified with the unmasking of white-supremacist and neo-Nazi organizations, many of them with a hard-earned reputation for homicidal violence. The Swedes are not the pacific herbivores that many people imagine: In the footnotes to his second novel Larsson reminds us that Prime Minister Olof Palme was gunned down in the street in 1986 and that the foreign minister Anna Lindh was stabbed to death (in a Stockholm department store) in 2003. The first crime is still unsolved, and the verdict in the second case has by no means satisfied everybody.

A report in the mainstream newspaper *Aftonbladet* describes the findings of another anti-Nazi researcher, named Bosse Schön, who unraveled a plot to murder Stieg Larsson that included a Swedish SS veteran. Another scheme misfired because on the night in question, twenty years ago, he saw skinheads with bats waiting outside his office and left by the rear exit. Web sites are devoted to further speculation: One blog is preoccupied with the theory that Prime Minister Palme's uncaught assassin was behind the death of Larsson too. Larsson's name and other details were found when the Swedish police searched the apartment of a Fascist arrested for a political murder. Larsson's address, telephone number, and photograph, along with threats to people identified as "enemies of the white race," were published in a neo-Nazi magazine: The authorities took it seriously enough to prosecute the editor.

But Larsson died of an apparent coronary thrombosis, not from any mayhem. So he would have had to be poisoned, say, or somehow medically murdered. Such a hypothesis would point to some involvement "high up," and anyone who has read the novels will know that in Larsson's world the forces of law and order in Sweden are fetidly complicit with organized crime. So did he wind up, in effect, a character in one of his own tales? The people who might have the most interest in keeping the speculation alive—his publishers and publicists—choose not to believe it. "Sixty cigarettes a day, plus tremendous amounts of junk food and coffee and an enormous workload," said Christopher MacLehose, Larsson's literary discoverer in English and by a nice coincidence a publisher of *Flashman*, "would be the culprit. I gather he'd even had a warning heart murmur. Still, I have attended demonstrations by these Swedish right-wing thugs, and they are truly frightening. I also know someone with excellent contacts in the Swedish police and security world who assures me that everything described in the 'Millennium' novels *actually took place*. And, apparently, Larsson planned to write as many as ten in all. So you can see how people could think that he might not have died but been 'stopped.'"

He left behind him enough manuscript pages for three books, the last of which—due out in Europe this fall and in the U.S. next summer—is titled *The Girl Who Kicked the Hornet's Nest*, and the outlines and initial scribblings of a fourth. The market and appetite for them seems to be unappeasable, as does the demand for Henning Mankell's "Detective Wallander" thrillers, the work of Peter (*Smilla's Sense of Snow*) Høeg, and the stories of Arnaldur Indridason. These writers come from countries as diverse as Denmark and Iceland, but in Germany the genre already has a name: *Schwedenkrimi*, or "Swedish crime writing." Christopher MacLehose told me that he knows of bookstores that now have special sections for the Scandinavian phenomenon. "When Roger Straus and I first published Peter Høeg," he said, "we thought we were doing something of a favor for Danish literature, and then 'Miss Smilla' abruptly sold a million copies in both England and America. Look, in almost everyone there is a memory of the sagas and the Norse myths. A lot of our storytelling got started in those long, cold, dark nights."

Perhaps. But Larsson is very much of our own time, setting himself to confront questions such as immigration, "gender," white-collar crime, and, above all, the Internet. The plot of his first volume does involve a sort of excursion into antiquity—into the book of Leviticus, to be exact—but this is only for the purpose of encrypting a "Bible code." And he is quite deliberately unromantic, giving us shopping lists, street directions, menus, and other details—often with their Swedish names—in full. The villains are evil, all right, but very stupid and self-thwartingly prone to spend more time (this always irritates me) telling their victims what they will do to them than actually doing it. There is much sex but absolutely no love, a great deal of violence but zero heroism. Reciprocal gestures are generally indicated by cliché: If a Larsson character wants to show assent he or she will "nod"; if he or she wants to manifest distress, then it will usually be by biting the lower lip. The passionate world of the sagas and the myths is a very long way away. Bleakness is all. That could even be the secret—the emotionless efficiency of Swedish technology, paradoxically combined with the wicked allure of the pitiless elfin avenger, plus a dash of paranoia surrounding the author's demise. If Larsson had died as a brave martyr to a cause, it would have been strangely out of keeping; it's actually more satisfying that he succumbed to the natural causes that are symptoms of modern life.

(*Vanity Fair*, December 2009)

As American as Apple Pie

IS THERE ANYTHING more tragic than the last leave-taking between Humbert Humbert and Dolores Haze (his very own "Lolita, light of my life, fire of my loins")? They meet in the dreary shack where she has removed herself to become a ground-down baby machine for some prole. Not only does she tell Humbert that she will never see him again, but she also maddens him by describing the "weird, filthy, fancy things" to which she was exposed by his hated rival, Quilty. "What things exactly?" he asks, in a calm voice where the word "exactly" makes us hear his almost unutterably low growl of misery and rage: "Crazy things, filthy things. I said no, I'm just not going to (she used, in all insouciance really, a disgusting slang term which, in a literal French translation, would be *souffler*) your beastly boys..."

Souffler is the verb "to blow." In its past participle, it can describe a light but delicious dessert that, well, melts on the tongue. It has often been said, slightly suggestively, that "you cannot make a soufflé rise twice." Vladimir Nabokov spoke perfect Russian and French before he became the unrivaled master of English prose, and his 1955 masterpiece, *Lolita*, was considered the most transgressive book ever published. (It may still be.) Why, then, could he not bring himself to write the words "blow" or "blowjob"?

It's not as if Nabokov was squeamish. Try this, for example, when Humbert's stepdaughter is still within his power (and he is even more in hers):

> Knowing the magic and might of her own soft mouth, she managed—during one school year!—to raise the bonus price of a fancy embrace to three, and even four bucks. O Reader! Laugh not, as you imagine me, on the very rack of joy noisily emitting dimes and quarters, and great big silver dollars like some sonorous, jingly and wholly demented machine vomiting riches...

"The magic and might of her own soft mouth..." Erotic poets have hymned it down the ages, though often substituting the word "his." The menu of brothel offerings in ancient Pompeii, preserved through centuries of volcanic burial, features it in the frescoes. It was considered, as poor Humbert well knew, to be worth paying for. The temple carvings of India and the *Kamasutra* make rather a lavish point of it, and Sigmund Freud wondered if a passage in Leonardo da Vinci's notebooks might not betray an early attachment to that "which in respectable society is considered a loathsome perversion." Da Vinci may have chosen to write in "code" and Nabokov may have chosen to dissolve into French, as he usually did when touching on the risqué, but the well-known word "fellatio" comes from the Latin verb "to suck."

Well, which is it—blow or suck? (Old joke: "No, darling. *Suck* it. 'Blow' is a mere figure of speech." Imagine the stress that gave rise to that gag.) Moreover, why has the blowjob had a dual existence for so long, sometimes subterranean and sometimes flaunted, before bursting into plain view as the specifically American sex act? My friend David Aaronovitch, a columnist in London, wrote of his embarrassment at being in the same room as his young daughter when the TV blared the news that the president of the United States had received oral sex in an Oval Office vestibule. He felt crucially better, but still shy, when the little girl asked him, "Daddy, what's a vestibule?"

> Acey told me she was at a party and she said to a man, What do men really want from women, and he said, Blowjobs, and she said, You can get that from men.
>
> —From "Cocksucker Blues," Part 4 of *Underworld*, by Don DeLillo

I admire the capitalization there, don't you? But I think Acey (who in the novel is also somewhat Deecey) furnishes a clue. For a considerable time, the humble blowjob was considered something rather abject, especially as regards the donor but also as regards the recipient. Too passive, each way. Too grungy—especially in the time before dental and other kinds of hygiene. Too risky—what about the reminder of the dreaded *vagina dentata* (fully materialized by the rending bite-off scene in *The World According to Garp*)? And also too queer. Ancient Greeks and Romans knew what was going on, all right, but they are reported to have avoided the over-keen fellators for fear of their breath alone. And a man in search of this consolation might be suspected of being... unmanly. The crucial word "blowjob" doesn't come into the American idiom until the 1940s, when it was (a) part of the gay underworld and (b) possibly derived from the jazz scene and its oral instrumentation. But it has never lost its supposed Victorian origin, which was "below-job" (cognate, if you like, with the now archaic "going down"). This term from London's whoredom still has a faint whiff of contempt. On the other hand, it did have its advocates as the prototype of Erica Jong's "zipless fuck": at least in the sense of a quickie that need only involve the undoing of a few buttons. And then there's that nagging word, "job," which seems to hint at a play-for-pay task rather than a toothsome treat for all concerned.

Stay with me. I've been doing the hard thinking for you. The three-letter "job," with its can-do implications, also makes the term especially American. Perhaps forgotten as the London of Jack the Ripper receded into the past, the idea of an oral swiftie was re-exported to Europe and far beyond by a massive arrival of American soldiers. For these hearty guys, as many a French and English and German and Italian madam has testified, the blowjob was the beau ideal. It was a good and simple idea in itself. It was valued—not always correctly—as an insurance against the pox. And—this is my speculation—it put the occupied and the allied populations in their place. "*You* do some work for a change, sister. I've had a hard time getting here." Certainly by the time of the war in Vietnam, the war-correspondent David Leitch recorded reporters swapping notes: "When you get to Da Nang ask for Mickey Mouth—she does the best blow job in South-East Asia."

At some point, though, there must have been a crossover in which a largely forbidden act of slightly gay character was imported into the heterosexual mainstream. If I have been correct up until now, this is not too difficult to explain (and it fits with the dates, as well). The queer monopoly on blowjobs was the result of male anatomy, obviously, and also of the wish of many gays to have sex with heterosexual men. It was widely believed that only men really knew how to get the "job" done, since they were tormented hostages of the very same organ on a round-the-clock basis. (W. H. Auden's New York underground poem titled "The Platonic Blow"—even though there is absolutely nothing platonic about it, and it lovingly deploys the word "job"—is the classic example here.) This was therefore an inducement the gay man could offer to the straight, who could in turn accept it without feeling that he had done anything too faggoty. For many a straight man, life's long tragedy is first disclosed in early youth, when he discovers that he cannot perform this simple suction on himself. (In his stand-up routines, Bill Hicks used to speak often and movingly of this dilemma.) Cursing god, the boy then falls to the hectic abuse of any viscous surface within reach. One day, he dreams, someone else will be on hand to help take care of this. When drafted into the army and sent overseas, according to numberless witnesses from Gore Vidal to Kingsley Amis, he may even find that oral sex is available in the next hammock. And then the word is *out*. There might come a day, he slowly but inexorably reasons, when even women might be induced to do this.

Through the 1950s, then, the burgeoning secret of the blowjob was still contained, like a spark of Promethean fire, inside a secret reed. (In France and Greece, to my certain knowledge, the slang term used to involve "pipe smoking" or "cigar action." I don't mind the association with incandescence, but for Christ's sake, sweetie, don't be *smoking* it. I would even rather that you just blew.) If you got hold of Henry Miller's *Sexus* or Pauline Reage's *Story of O* (both published by Maurice Girodias, the same Parisian daredevil who printed *Lolita*), you could read about oral and other engagements, but that was France for you.

The comics of R. Crumb used to have fellatio in many graphic frames, but then, this was the counterculture. No, the big breakthrough occurs in the great year of nineteen *soixante-neuf*, when Mario Puzo publishes *The Godfather* and Philip Roth brings out *Portnoy's Complaint*. Puzo's book was a smash not just because of the horse's head and the Sicilian fish-wrap technique and the offer that couldn't be refused. It achieved a huge word-of-mouth success because of a famous scene about vagina-enhancing plastic surgery that became widely known as "the Godfather tuck" (sorry to stray from my subject) and because of passages like this, featuring the Mobbed-up crooner "Johnny Fontane":

> And the other guys were always talking about blow jobs, this and other variations, and he really didn't enjoy that stuff so much. He never liked a girl that much after they tried it that way, it just didn't satisfy him right. He and his second wife had finally not got along, because she preferred the old sixty-nine too much to a point where she didn't want anything else and he had to fight to stick it in. She began making fun of him and calling him a square and the word got around that he made love like a kid.

Earthquake! Sensation! Telephones trilled all over the English-speaking world. Never mind if Johnny Fontane likes it or not, what is that? And why on earth is it called a "blow job"? (The words were for some reason separate in those days: I like the way in which they have since eased more cozily together.) Most of all, notice that it is regular sex that has become obvious and childish, while oral sex is suddenly for real men. And here's Puzo again, describing the scene where the lady in need of a newly refreshed and elastic interior isn't quite ready to sleep with her persuasive doctor, and isn't quite inclined to gratify him any other way, either:

> "Oh that" she said.
>
> "Oh that" he mimicked her. "Nice girls don't do that, manly men don't do that. Even in the year 1948. Well, baby, I can take you to the house of a little old lady right here in Las Vegas who was the youngest madam of the most popular whorehouse in the wild west days. You know what she told me? That those gunslingers, those manly, virile, straight-shooting cowboys would always ask the girls for a 'French,' what we doctors call fellatio, what you call 'oh that.'"

Notice the date. Note also the cowboys, likewise deprived of female company for long stretches. Now that we know about Blowjob Mountain, or whatever the hell it's called, I think I can score one for my original theory.

Philip Roth took the same ball and ran with it, though he served up his guilt and angst with different seasonings. Imperishably associated with handjobs as his name will always be, his Alexander Portnoy fights like a wounded puma, throughout his boyhood, to find a girl, however hideous, who will get her laughing-tackle around his thing. When he finally persuades the woman he calls "The Monkey" ("a girl with a passion for The Banana") to do it right, his whole system explodes into a symphony of praise. "What cock know-how!" he yells to himself (thus rather confirming the nature and essence of the word "job"). On the other hand, his blonde WASP chick won't do it at any price, partly from disgust but also from a lively fear of asphyxiation. Portnoy resentfully ponders the social unfairness of this: She kills ducks in rustic settings but she won't fellate him. "To shoot a gun at a little quack-quack is fine, to suck my cock is beyond her." He also visualizes the awful headline if he presses things too far: JEW STRANGLES DEB WITH COCK... MOCKY LAWYER HELD.

Thus the sixties—the sixties!—ended with the blowjob still partly hyphenated and the whole subject still wreathed and muffled in husky whispers. The cast of *Hair* sang of "fellatio" under the list of things like "sodomy" that "sound so nasty," and oral sex was legally defined as sodomy by many states of the union until the Supreme Court struck down those laws only three years ago—Clarence Thomas dissenting. The colloquial expression in those intermediate days was in my opinion the crudest of all: "giving head." You can hear it in Leonard Cohen's droning paean to Janis Joplin in "Chelsea Hotel #2," and also in the lyrics of Lou Reed and David Bowie. It was a "knowing" and smirking term, but it managed somehow to fuse the mindless with the joyless. This state of affairs obviously could not last long, and the entire lid blew off in 1972, when some amateurs pulled together $25,000 for a movie that eventually posted grosses of $600 million. Is this a great country or what? This film, with performances by Harry Reems and Linda Lovelace, was one of the tawdriest and most unsatisfying screen gems ever made, but it changed the world and the culture for good, or at any rate forever. Interesting, too, that *Deep Throat* was financed and distributed by members of New York's Colombo crime family, who kept the exorbitant bulk of the dough. Mario Puzo, then, had been prescient after all, and without his deep insight the Sopranos might still be sucking only their own thumbs.

The recent and highly amusing documentary *Inside Deep Throat* shows—by re-creating the paradoxically Nixonian times that re-baptized *Deep Throat* to mean source rather than donor—how America grabbed the Olympic scepter of the blowjob and held on tight. In the film, there is the preserved figure of Helen Gurley Brown, den mother of *Cosmo*-style journalism for young ladies and author of *Sex and the Single Girl*, demonstrating her application technique as she tells us how she evolved from knowing nothing about oral sex to the realization that semen could be a terrific facial cream. ("It's full of babies," she squeals, unclear on the concept to the very last.) In closing, Dick Cavett declares that we have gone from looking at a marquee that read DEEP THROAT, and hoping it didn't mean what we thought it did, to "kids who don't even consider it sex." This would leave us with only one problem. Why do we still say, of something boring or obnoxious, that "it sucks"? Ought that not be a compliment?

There is another thinkable reason why this ancient form of lovemaking lost its association with the dubious and the low and became an American handshake and ideal. The United States is par excellence the country of beautiful dentistry. As one who was stretched on the grim rack of British "National Health" practice, with its gray-and-yellow fangs, its steely-wire "braces," its dark and crumbly fillings, and its shriveled and bleeding gums, I can remember barely daring to smile when I first set foot in the New World. Whereas when any sweet American girl smiled at me, I was at once bewitched and slain by the warm, moist cave of her mouth, lined with faultless white teeth and immaculate pink gums and organized around a tenderly coiled yet innocent tongue. Good grief! What else was there to think about? In order to stay respectable here, I shall just say that it's not always so enticing when the young ladies of Albania (say) shoot you a cheeky grin that puts you in mind of *Deliverance*.

The illusion of the tonsilized clitoris will probably never die (and gay men like to keep their tonsils for a reason that I would not dream of mentioning), but while the G-spot and other fantasies have dissipated, the iconic U.S. Prime blowjob is still on a throne, and is also kneeling at the foot of that throne. It has become, in the words of a book on its technique, *The Ultimate Kiss*. And such a kiss on the first date is not now considered all that "fast." America was not the land of birth for this lavish caress, but it is (if I may mix my anthems) white with foam from sea to shining sea. In other cultures, a girl will do "that" only when she gets to know and like you. In this one, she will offer it as a *baiser* as she is making up her mind. While this persists, and while America's gay manhood is still sucking away as if for oxygen itself, who dares to say that true global leadership is not still within our grasp?

(*Vanity Fair*, July 2006)

So Many Men's Rooms, So Little Time

I KNEW IT WAS all over for Senator Larry Craig when he appeared with his long-suffering wife to say that he wasn't gay. Such moments are now steppingstones on the way to apology, counseling, and rehab, and a case could be made for cutting out the spousal stage of the ritual altogether. Along with a string of votes to establish "don't ask, don't tell" and to prohibit homosexual marriage, Craig leaves as his political legacy the telling phrase "wide stance," which may or may not join "big tent" and "broad church" as an attempt to make the Republican Party seem more "inclusive" than it really is.

But there's actually a chance—a 38 percent chance, to be more precise—that the senator can cop a plea on the charge of hypocrisy. In his study of men who frequent public restrooms in search of sex, Laud Humphreys discovered that 54 percent were married and living with their wives, 38 percent did not consider themselves homosexual or bisexual, and only 14 percent identified themselves as openly gay. *Tearoom Trade: Impersonal Sex in Personal Places*, a doctoral thesis which was published in 1970, detailed exactly the pattern—of foot-tapping in code, hand-gestures, and other tactics—which has lately been garishly publicized at a Minneapolis–St. Paul airport men's room. The word *tearoom* seems to have become archaic, but in all other respects the fidelity to tradition is impressive.

The men interviewed by Humphreys wanted what many men want: a sexual encounter that was quick and easy and didn't involve any wining and dining. Some of the heterosexuals among them had also evolved a tactic for dealing with the cognitive dissonance that was involved. They compensated for their conduct by adopting extreme conservative postures in public. Humphreys, a former Episcopalian priest, came up with the phrase "breastplate of righteousness" to describe this mixture of repression and denial. So, it is quite thinkable that when Senator Craig claims not to be gay, he is telling what he honestly believes to be the truth.

However, this still leaves a slight mystery. In the 1960s, homosexuality was illegal in general, and gay men were forced to cruise in places where (if I can phrase it like this) every man and boy in the world has to come sometime. Today, anyone wanting a swift male caress can book it online or go to a discreet resort. Yet people still persist in haunting the tearoom, where they risk arrest not for their sexuality but for "disorderly conduct." Why should this be?

In my youth, I was a friend of a man named Tom Driberg, a British politician who set the bar very high in these matters. In his memoir, *Ruling Passions*, he described his "chronic, lifelong, love-hate relationship with lavatories." He could talk by the hour about the variety and marvel of these "public conveniences," as Victorian euphemism had dubbed them. In Britain, they were called "cottages" in gay argot, instead of "tearooms," and an experienced "cottager" knew all the ins and outs, if you will pardon the expression. There was the commodious underground loo in Leicester Square that specialized in those whose passion was for members of the armed forces. There was the one at the Institute of Contemporary Arts, much favored by aesthetes, where on the very foot of the partition, above the six-inch space, someone had scribbled "beware of limbo dancers." (The graffiti in cottages was all part of the fun: On the toilet wall at Paddington Station was written: "I am 9 inches long and two inches thick. Interested?" Underneath, in different handwriting: "Fascinated, dear, but how big is your dick?") On Clapham Common, the men's toilet had acquired such a lavish reputation for the variety of lurid actions performed within its precincts that, as I once heard it said: "If someone comes in there for a good honest shit, it's like a breath of fresh air."

Perhaps I digress. What Driberg told me was this. The thrills were twofold. First came the exhilaration of danger: the permanent risk of being caught and exposed. Second was the sense of superiority that a double life could give. What bliss it was to enter the House of Commons, bow to the speaker, and take your seat amid the trappings of lawmaking, having five minutes earlier fellated a guardsman (and on one unforgettable occasion, a policeman) in the crapper in St. James' Park. Assuming the story about the men's room in Union Station to be true, Senator Craig could have gone straight from that encounter to the Senate floor in about the same amount of time.

Driberg was a public campaigner for gay rights and carried on as such even after being elevated to the House of Lords (where I am pretty sure he told me there was more going on in the lavatory than most people would guess). But it was with a distinct hint of melancholy that he voted for the successful repeal of the laws criminalizing homosexuality. "I rather miss the old days," he would say wistfully. Well, the law legalized homosexual behavior only "in private," so he could (and did) continue to court danger in public places. The House of Lords actually debated the question of whether a stall in a public lavatory constituted "privacy," the reason being that in Britain you have to put money in a slot in order to enter such a place, and this could be held to constitute rent. *Private Eye* printed a poem about the learned exchange on this between two elderly peers of the realm: "Said Lord Arran to Lord Dilhorne, a penny / should entitle me to any / thing I may choose privately to do. Except you."

Thus, without overthinking it or attempting too much by way of amateur psychiatry, I think it's safe to assume that many tearoom traders have a need, which they only imperfectly understand, to get caught. And this may be truest of all of those who are armored with "the breastplate of righteousness." Next time you hear some particularly moralizing speech, set your watch. You won't have to wait long before the man who made it is found, crouched awkwardly yet ecstatically while the cistern drips and the roar of the flush maddens him like wine.

(*Slate*, September 1, 2007)

The New Commandments

WHAT DO WE SAY when we want to revisit a long-standing policy or scheme that no longer seems to be serving us or has ceased to produce useful results? We begin by saying tentatively, "Well, it's not exactly written in stone." (Sometimes this comes out as "not set in stone.")

By that, people mean that it's not one of the immutable Tablets of the Law. Thus, more recent fetishes such as the gold standard, or the supposedly holy laws of the free market, can be discarded as not being incised on granite or marble. But what if it is the original stone version that badly needs a re-write? Who will take up the revisionist chisel?

There is in fact a good biblical precedent for doing just that, since the giving of the divine Law by Moses appears in three or four wildly different scriptural versions. (When you hear people demanding that the Ten Commandments be displayed in courtrooms and schoolrooms, always be sure to ask which set. It works every time.) The first and most famous set comes in Exodus 20 but ends with Moses himself smashing the supposedly most sacred artifacts ever known to man: the original, God-dictated panels of Holy Writ. The second edition occurs in Exodus 34, where new but completely different tablets are presented after some heavenly re-write session and are for the first time called "the ten commandments." In the fifth chapter of Deuteronomy, Moses once more calls his audience together and recites the original Sinai speech with one highly significant alteration (the Sabbath commandment's justifications in each differ greatly). But plainly discontented with the effect of this, he musters the flock *again* twenty-two chapters further on, as the river Jordan is coming into view, and gives an additional set of orders—chiefly terse curses—which are also to be inscribed in stone. As with the gold plates on which Joseph Smith found the Book of Mormon in upstate New York, no trace of any of these original yet conflicting tablets survives.

Thus we are fully entitled to consider them as a work in progress. May there not be some old commandments that could be retired, as well as some new ones that might be adopted? Taking the most celebrated Top 10 in order, we find (I am using the King James, or "Authorized," version of the text):

I and II

These commandments are in fact a mixture of related injunctions. *I am the LORD thy God.... Thou shalt have no other gods before me.* This use of capitalization and upper- and lowercase carries the intriguing implication that there perhaps *are* some other gods but not equally deserving of respect or awe. (Scholars differ about the epoch during which the Jewish people decided on monotheism.) Then comes the prohibition of "graven images" or indeed "any likeness of anything that is in heaven above, or that is in the earth beneath, or that is in the water under the earth." This appears to forbid representational art, just as some Muslims interpret the Koran to forbid the depiction of any human form, let alone any sacred one. (It certainly seems to discourage Christian iconography, with its crucifixes, and statues of virgins and saints.) But the ban is obviously intended as a very emphatic one, since it comes with a reminder that *I the LORD thy God am a jealous God, visiting the iniquity of the fathers upon the children unto the third and fourth generation.* The collective punishment of future children, for the sin of *lèse-majesté*, may not strike everyone as an especially moral promise.

III

Thou shalt not take the name of the LORD thy God in vain, for the LORD will not hold him guiltless that taketh his name in vain. A slightly querulous and repetitive note is struck here, as if of injured vanity. Nobody knows how to obey this commandment, or how to avoid blasphemy or profanity. For example, I say "God alone knows" when I sincerely intend to say "Nobody knows." Is this ontologically dangerous? Ought not unalterable laws to be plain and unambiguous?

IV

Remember the sabbath day, to keep it holy. This ostensibly brief commandment goes on for a long time—for four verses in fact—and stresses the importance of a day dedicated to the LORD, during which neither one's children nor one's servants or animals should be allowed to perform any tasks. (Query: Why is it specifically addressed to people who are assumed to have staff?)

Nobody is opposed to a day of rest. The international Communist movement got its start by proclaiming a strike for an eight-hour day on May 1, 1886, against Christian employers who used child labor seven days a week. But in Exodus 20:8-11, the reason given for the day off is that "in six days the LORD made heaven and earth, the sea, and all that in them is, and rested the seventh day." Yet in Deuteronomy 5:15 a different reason for the Sabbath observance is offered: "Remember that thou wast a servant in the land of Egypt, and that the LORD thy God brought thee out thence through a mighty hand and by a stretched out arm: therefore the LORD thy God commanded thee to keep the sabbath day." Preferable though this may be, with its reminder of previous servitude, we again find mixed signals here. Why can't rest be recommended for its own sake? Also, why can't the infallible and omniscient and omnipotent one make up his mind what the real reason is?

V

Honor thy father and thy mother. Innocuous as this may seem, it is the only commandment that comes with an inducement instead of an implied threat. Both the Exodus and Deuteronomy versions urge it for the same reason: "that thy days may be long upon the land which the LORD thy God giveth thee." This perhaps has the slight suggestion of being respectful to Father and Mother in order to come into an inheritance—the Israelites have already been promised the Canaanite territory that is currently occupied by other people, so the prospective legacy pickings are rather rich. Again, why not propose filial piety as a nice thing in itself?

VI

Thou shalt not kill. This very celebrated commandment quite obviously cannot mean what it seems to say in English translation. In the original Hebrew it comes across as something more equivalent to "Thou shalt do no murder." We can be fairly sure that the "original intent" is not in any way pacifistic, because immediately after he breaks the original tablets in a fit of rage, Moses summons his Levite faction and says (Exodus 32:27-28):

> Thus saith the LORD God of Israel, put every man his sword by his side, and go in and out from gate to gate throughout the camp, and slay every man his brother, and every man his companion, and every man his neighbor. And the children of Levi did according to the word of Moses: and there fell of the people that day about three thousand men.

With its seven-word preface, that order, too, obviously constituted a "commandment" of some sort. The whole book of Exodus is a commandment-rich environment, littered with other fierce orders to slay people for numberless minor offenses (including violations of the Sabbath) and also includes the sinister, ominous verse "Thou shalt not suffer [permit] a witch to live," which was taken as a divine instruction by Christians until relatively recently in human history. Some work is obviously needed here: What is first-degree or third-degree killing and what isn't? Distinguishing killing from murder is not a job easily left to mortals: What are we to do if God himself can't tell the difference?

VII

Thou shalt not commit adultery. For some reason, "the seventh" is the only one of the commandments that is still widely known by its actual number.

Extramarital carnal knowledge was probably more of a threat to society when families and tribes were closer-knit, and more bound by stern codes of honor. Having provided the raw material for most of the plays and novels ever published in non–Middle Eastern languages, adultery continues to be a great source of misery and joy and fascination. Most criminal codes have long given up the attempt to make it a punishable offense in law: Its rewards and punishments are carefully administered by its practitioners and victims. It perhaps does not deserve to be classed with murder or theft or perjury, which brings us to:

VIII

Thou shalt not steal. Not much to query here. Those who have worked hard to acquire a bit of property are entitled to resent those who would rather steal than work, and when society evolves to the point where there is wealth that belongs to nobody—public or social property—those who plunder it for private gain are rightly regarded with hatred and contempt. Admittedly, the prosperity of some families and some states is also founded on original theft, but in that case the same principle of disapproval can apply.

IX

Thou shalt not bear false witness against thy neighbor. This is possibly the most sophisticated ruling in the whole Decalogue. Human society is inconceivable unless words are to some extent bonds, and in legal disputes we righteously demand the swearing of oaths that entail severe penalties for perjury. Until recently, much testimony before Congress was taken without witnesses being "sworn": This allowed a great deal of official lying. Nothing focuses the attention more than a reminder that one is speaking on oath. The word "witness" expresses one of our noblest concepts. "Bearing witness" is a high moral responsibility.

Note, also, how relatively flexible this commandment is. Its fulcrum is the word "against." If you are quite sure of somebody's innocence and you shade the truth a little in the witness-box, you are no doubt technically guilty of perjury and may be privately troubled. But if you consciously lie in order to indict someone who is *not* guilty, you have done something irretrievably foul.

X

Thou shalt not covet thy neighbor's house, thou shalt not covet thy neighbor's wife, nor his manservant, nor his maidservant, nor his ox, nor his ass, nor any thing that is thy neighbor's. There are several details that make this perhaps the most questionable of the commandments. Leaving aside the many jokes about whether or not it's okay. or kosher to covet thy neighbor's wife's ass, you are bound to notice once again that, like the Sabbath order, it's addressed to the servant-owning and property-owning class. Moreover, it lumps the wife in with the rest of the chattel (and in that epoch could have been rendered as "thy neighbor's wives," to boot).

Notice also that no specific *act* is being pronounced as either compulsory (the Sabbath) or forbidden (perjury). Instead, this is the first but not the last introduction in the Bible of the totalitarian concept of "*thought crime.*" You are being told, in effect, not even to think about it. (Jesus of Nazareth in the New Testament takes this a step further, announcing that those with lust in their heart have already committed the sin of adultery. In that case, you might as well be hung—or stoned—for a sheep as for a lamb, or for an ox or an ass if it cometh to that.) Wise lawmakers know that it is a mistake to promulgate legislation that is impossible to obey.

There are further objections to be made. From the "left" point of view, how is it moral to prohibit people from regarding the gains of the rich as ill-gotten, or from demanding a fairer distribution of wealth? From the "right" point of view, why is it wicked to be ambitious and acquisitive? And is not envy a great spur to emulation and competition? I once had a debate on these points with Rabbi Harold Kushner, author of that consoling text *When Bad Things Happen to Good People*, and he told me that there is a scholarly Talmudic argument, or *midrash*, maintaining that "neighbor" in this context really does mean immediate next-door neighbor. For that matter, there is persuasive textual argument that "neighbor" in much of the Bible means only "fellow Jew." But it seems rather a waste of a commandment to confine it to either the Joneses or the Semites.

What emerges from the first review is this: The Ten Commandments were derived from situational ethics. They show every symptom of having been man-made and improvised under pressure. They are addressed to a nomadic tribe whose main economy is primitive agriculture and whose wealth is sometimes counted in people as well as animals. They are also addressed to a group that has been promised the land and flocks of other people: the Amalekites and Midianites and others whom God orders them to kill, rape, enslave, or exterminate. And this, too, is important because at every step of their arduous journey the Israelites are reminded to keep to the laws, not because they are right but just because they will lead them to become conquerors (of, as it happens, almost the only part of the Middle East that has no oil).

So, then: how to prune and how to amend? Numbers One through Three can simply go, since they have nothing to do with morality and are no more than a long, rasping throat clearing by an admittedly touchy dictator. Mere fear of unseen authority is not a sound basis for ethics. The associated ban on sculpture and pictorial art should also be lifted. Number Four can possibly stay, though rest periods are not exactly an ethical imperative and are mandated by practicality as much as by heaven. At least, if shorn of its first and third and fourth redundant verses (none of which can possibly apply to non-Jews), Number Four does imply that there are rights as well as duties. For millions of people for thousands of years, the Sabbath was made a dreary burden of obligation and strict observance instead of a day of leisure or recreation. It also led to absurd hypocrisies that seem to treat God as a fool: He won't notice if we make the elevators stop on every floor so that no pious Jew needs to press a button. This is unwholesome and over-strenuous.

As for Number Five, by all means respect for the elders, but why is there nothing to forbid child abuse? (Insolence on the part of children is punishable by death, according to Leviticus 20:9, only a few verses before the stipulation of the death penalty for male homosexuals.) A cruel or rude child is a ghastly thing, but a cruel or brutal parent can do infinitely more harm. Yet even in a long and exhaustive list of prohibitions, parental sadism or neglect is never once condemned. Memo to Sinai: Rectify this omission.

Number Six: Note that mere human systems have done better subsequently in distinguishing different moral scales of homicide. Memo to Sinai:

Are you morally absolute or aren't you? If so, what about the poor massacred Midianites?

Number Seven: Fair enough if you must, but is polygamy adultery? Also, could not permanent monogamy have been made slightly more consonant with human nature? Why create people with lust in their hearts? Then again, what about rape? It seems to be very strongly recommended, along with genocide, slavery, and infanticide, in Numbers 31:1-18, and surely constitutes a rather extreme version of sex outside marriage.

Numbers Eight and Nine: Admirable. Also brief and to the point, with one rather useful nuance in the keyword "against."

Number Ten: Does wrong to women by making them property and also necessitates continual celestial wiretapping of private thoughts. Sinister and despotic in that it cannot be obeyed and thus makes sinners even of quite thoughtful people.

I am trying my best not to view things through a smug later prism. Only the Almighty can scan matters *sub specie aeternitatis:* from the viewpoint of eternity. One must also avoid cultural and historical relativism: There's no point in retroactively ordering the Children of Israel to develop a germ theory of disease (so as to avoid mistaking plagues for divine punishments) or to understand astronomy (so as not to make foolish predictions and boasts based on the planets and stars). Still, if we think of the evils that afflict humanity today and that are man-made and not inflicted by nature, we would be morally numb if we did not feel strongly about genocide, slavery, rape, child abuse, sexual repression, white-collar crime, the wanton destruction of the natural world, and people who yak on cell phones in restaurants. (Also, people who commit simultaneous suicide and murder while screaming "God is great": Is that taking the Lord's name in vain or is it not?)

It's difficult to take oneself with sufficient seriousness to begin any sentence with the words "Thou shalt not." But who cannot summon the confidence to say: *Do not* condemn people on the basis of their ethnicity or color. *Do not* ever use people as private property. Despise those who use violence or the threat of it in sexual relations. Hide your face and weep if you dare to harm a child. *Do not* condemn people for their inborn *nature*—why would God create so many homosexuals only in order to torture and destroy them?

Be aware that you too are an animal and dependent on the web of nature, and think and act accordingly. *Do not* imagine that you can escape judgment if you rob people with a false prospectus rather than with a knife. Turn off that fucking cell phone—you have no idea how *un*important your call is to us. Denounce all *jihad*-ists and crusaders for what they are: psychopathic criminals with ugly delusions. Be willing to renounce any god or any religion if any holy commandments should contradict any of the above. In short: Do not swallow your moral code in tablet form.

(*Vanity Fair*, April 2010)

In Your Face

THE FRENCH LEGISLATORS who seek to repudiate the wearing of the veil or the burka—whether the garment covers "only" the face or the entire female body—are often described as seeking to impose a "ban." To the contrary, they are attempting to lift a ban: a ban on the right of women to choose their own dress, a ban on the right of women to disagree with male and clerical authority, and a ban on the right of all citizens to look one another in the face. The proposed law is in the best traditions of the French republic, which declares all citizens equal before the law and—no less important—equal in the face of one another.

On the door of my bank in Washington, D.C., is a printed notice politely requesting me to remove any form of facial concealment before I enter the premises. The notice doesn't bore me or weary me by explaining its reasoning: A person barging through those doors with any sort of mask would incur the right and proper presumption of guilt. This presumption should operate in the rest of society. I would indignantly refuse to have any dealings with a nurse or doctor or teacher who hid his or her face, let alone a tax inspector or customs official. Where would we be without sayings like "What have you got to hide?" or "You dare not show your face?"

Ah, but the particular and special demand to consider the veil and the burka as an exemption applies only to women. And it also applies only to religious practice (and, unless we foolishly pretend otherwise, only to one religious practice). This at once tells you all you need to know: Society is being asked to abandon an immemorial tradition of equality and openness in order to gratify one faith, one faith that has a very questionable record in respect of females.

Let me ask a simple question to the pseudo-liberals who take a soft line on the veil and the burka. What about the Ku Klux Klan? Notorious for its hooded style and its reactionary history, this gang is and always was dedicated to upholding Protestant and Anglo-Saxon purity. I do not deny the right of the KKK to take this faith-based view, which is protected by the First Amendment to the U.S. Constitution. I might even go so far as to say that, at a rally protected by police, they could lawfully hide their nasty faces. But I am not going to have a hooded man or woman teach my children, or push their way into the bank ahead of me, or drive my taxi or bus, and there will never be a law that says I have to.

There are lesser objections to the covered face or the all-covering cloak. The latter has often been used by male criminals—not just religious terrorists but common thugs—to conceal themselves and make an escape. It has also been used to conceal horrible injuries inflicted on abused females. It is incompatible—because of its effect on peripheral vision—with activities such as driving a car or negotiating traffic. This removes it from the sphere of private decision-making and makes it a danger to others, as well as an offense to the ordinary democratic civility that depends on phrases like "Nice to see you."

It might be objected that in some Muslim societies women are not allowed to drive in the first place. But that would absolutely emphasize my second point. All the above criticisms would be valid if Muslim women were as passionately committed to wearing a burka as a male Klansman is committed to donning a pointy-headed white shroud. But, in fact, we have no assurance that Muslim women put on the burka or don the veil as a matter of their own choice. A huge amount of evidence goes the other way. Mothers, wives, and daughters have been threatened with acid in the face, or honor-killing, or vicious beating, if they do not adopt the humiliating outer clothing that is mandated by their menfolk. This is why, in many Muslim societies, such as Tunisia and Turkey, the shrouded look is illegal in government buildings, schools, and universities. Why should Europeans and Americans, seeking perhaps to accommodate Muslim immigrants, adopt the standard only of the most backward and primitive Muslim states? The burka and the veil, surely, are the most aggressive sign of a refusal to integrate or accommodate. Even in Iran there is only a requirement for the covering of hair, and I defy anybody to find any authority in the Koran for the concealment of the face.

Not that it would matter in the least if the Koran said otherwise. Religion is the worst possible excuse for any exception to the common law. Mormons may not have polygamous marriage, female circumcision is a federal crime in this country, and in some states Christian Scientists face prosecution if they neglect their children by denying them medical care. Do we dare lecture the French for declaring simply that all citizens and residents, whatever their confessional allegiance, must be able to recognize one another in the clearest sense of that universal term?

So it's really quite simple. My right to see your face is the beginning of it, as is your right to see mine. Next but not least comes the right of women to show their faces, which easily trumps the right of their male relatives or their male imams to decide otherwise. The law must be decisively on the side of transparency. The French are striking a blow not just for liberty and equality and fraternity, but for sorority too.

(*Slate*, May 10, 2010)

Wine Drinkers of the World, Unite

THE OTHER NIGHT, I was having dinner with some friends in a fairly decent restaurant and was at the very peak of my form as a wit and raconteur. But just as, with infinite and exquisite tantalizations, I was approaching my punch line, the most incredible thing happened. A waiter appeared from nowhere, leaned right over my shoulder and into the middle of the conversation, seized my knife and fork, and started to cut up my food for me. Not content with this bizarre behavior, and without so much as a by-your-leave, he proceeded to distribute pieces of my entree onto the plates of the other diners.

No, he didn't, actually. What he did instead was to interrupt the feast of reason and flow of soul that was our chat, lean across me, pick up the bottle of wine that was in the middle of the table, and pour it into everyone's glass. And what I want to know is this: How did such a barbaric custom get itself established, and why on earth do we put up with it?

There are two main ways in which a restaurant can inflict bad service on a customer. The first is to keep you hanging about and make it hard to catch the eye of the staff. ("Why are they called waiters?" inquired my son when he was about five. "It's we who are doing all the waiting.") The second way is to be too intrusive, with overlong recitations of the "specials" and too many oversolicitous inquiries. A cartoon in the *New Yorker* once showed a couple getting ready for bed, with the husband taking a call and keeping his hand over the receiver. "It's the maitre d' from the place we had dinner. He wants to know if everything is still all right."

The vile practice of butting in and pouring wine without being asked is the very height of the second kind of bad manners. Not only is it a breathtaking act of rudeness in itself, but it conveys a none-too-subtle and mercenary message: Hurry up and order another bottle. Indeed, so dulled have we become to the shame and disgrace of all this that I have actually seen waiters, having broken into the private conversation and emptied the flagon, ask insolently whether they should now bring another one. Again, imagine this same tactic being applied to the food.

Not everybody likes wine as much as I do. Many females, for example, confine themselves to one glass per meal or even half a glass. It pains me to see good wine being sloshed into the glasses of those who have not asked for it and may not want it and then be left standing there barely tasted when the dinner is over. Mr. Coleman, it was said, made his fortune not from the mustard that was consumed but from the mustard that was left on the plate. Restaurants ought not to inflict waste and extravagance on their patrons for the sake of padding out the bill. This, too, is a very extreme form of rudeness.

The expense of the thing, in other words, is only an aspect of the presumption of it. It completely usurps my prerogative if I am a host. ("Can I refill your glass? Try this wine—I think you may care for it.") It also tends to undermine me as a guest, since at any moment when I try to sing for my supper, I may find an unwanted person lunging carelessly into the middle of my sentence. If this person fills glasses unasked, he is a boor as described above. If he asks permission of each guest in turn—as he really ought to do, when you think about it—then he might as well pull up a chair and join the party. The nerve of it!

To return to the question of why we endure this: I think it must have something to do with the snobbery and insecurity that frequently accompany the wine business. A wine waiter is or can be a bit of a grandee, putting on considerable airs that may intimidate those who know little of the subject. If you go into a liquor store in a poor part of town, you will quite often notice that the wine is surprisingly expensive, because it is vaguely assumed that somehow it ought to cost more. And then there is simple force of custom and habit—people somehow grant restaurants the right to push their customers around in this outrageous way.

Well, all it takes is a bit of resistance. Until relatively recently in Washington, it was the custom at diplomatic and Georgetown dinners for the hostess to invite the ladies to withdraw, leaving the men to port and cigars and high matters of state. And then one evening in the 1970s, at the British Embassy, the late Katharine Graham refused to get up and go. There was nobody who felt like making her, and within a day, the news was all over town. Within a very short time, everybody had abandoned the silly practice. I am perfectly well aware that there are many graver problems facing civilization, and many grosser violations of human rights being perpetrated as we speak. But this is something that we can all change at a stroke. Next time anyone offers to interrupt your conversation and assist in the digestion of your meal and the inflation of your check, be very polite but very firm and say that you would really rather not.

(*Slate*, May 26, 2008)

Charles, Prince of Piffle

THIS IS WHAT YOU GET when you found a political system on the family values of Henry VIII. At a point in the not-too-remote future, the stout heart of Queen Elizabeth II will cease to beat. At that precise moment, her firstborn son will become head of state, head of the armed forces, and head of the Church of England. In strict constitutional terms, this ought not to matter much. The English monarchy, as has been said, reigns but does not rule. From the aesthetic point of view it will matter a bit, because the prospect of a morose bat-eared and chinless man, prematurely aged, and with the most abysmal taste in royal consorts, is a distinctly lowering one. And a king does have the ability to alter the atmosphere and to affect the ways in which important matters are discussed. (The queen herself proved that in subtle ways, by letting it be known that there were aspects of Margaret Thatcher's foreign policy that she did not view with unmixed delight.)

So the speech made by Prince Charles at Oxford last week might bear a little scrutiny. Discussing one of his favorite topics, the "environment," he announced that the main problem arose from a "deep, inner crisis of the soul" and that the "de-souling" of humanity probably went back as far as Galileo. In his view, materialism and consumerism represented an imbalance, "where mechanistic thinking is so predominant," and which "goes back at least to Galileo's assertion that there is nothing in nature but quantity and motion." He described the scientific worldview as an affront to all the world's "sacred traditions." Then for the climax:

> As a result, Nature has been completely objectified—She has become an it—and we are persuaded to concentrate on the material aspect of reality that fits within Galileo's scheme.

We have known for a long time that Prince Charles's empty sails are so rigged as to be swelled by any passing waft or breeze of crankiness and cant. He fell for the fake anthropologist Laurens van der Post. He was bowled over by the charms of homeopathic medicine. He has been believably reported as saying that plants do better if you talk to them in a soothing and encouraging way. But this latest departure promotes him from an advocate of harmless nonsense to positively sinister nonsense.

We owe a huge debt to Galileo for emancipating us all from the stupid belief in an Earth-centered or man-centered (let alone God-centered) system. He quite literally taught us our place and allowed us to go on to make extraordinary advances in knowledge. None of these liberating undertakings have required any sort of assumption about a soul. That belief is at best optional. (Incidentally, nature is no more or less "objectified" whether we give it a gender name or a neuter one. Merely calling it Mummy will not, alas, alter this salient fact.)

In the controversy that followed the prince's remarks, his most staunch defender was professor John Taylor, a scholar whose work I had last noticed when he gave good reviews to the psychokinetic (or whatever) capacities of the Israeli conjuror and fraud Uri Geller. The heir to the throne seems to possess the ability to surround himself—perhaps by some mysterious ultra-magnetic force?—with every moon-faced spoon-bender, shrub-flatterer, and water-diviner within range.

None of this might matter very much, until you notice the venue at which Charles delivered his farrago of nonsense. It was unleashed upon an audience at the Center for Islamic Studies at Oxford University, an institution of which he is the patron. Nor is this his only foray into Islamophilia. Together with the Saudi royal family, he supported the mosque in North London that acted as host and incubator to Richard "Shoe Bomber" Reid, the hook-handed Abu Hamza al-Masri, and several other unsavory customers. The prince's official job description as king will be "defender of the faith," which currently means the state-financed absurdity of the Anglican Church, but he has more than once said publicly that he wants to be anointed as defender of all faiths—another indication of the amazing conceit he has developed in six decades of performing the only job allowed him by the hereditary principle: that of waiting for his mother to expire.

A hereditary head of state, as Thomas Paine so crisply phrased it, is as absurd a proposition as a hereditary physician or a hereditary astronomer. To this innate absurdity, Prince Charles manages to bring fatuities that are entirely his own. And, as he paged his way through his dreary wad of babble, there must have been some wolfish smiles among his Muslim audience. I quote from a recent document published by the Islamic Forum of Europe, a group dedicated to the restoration of the Islamic caliphate and the imposition of *sharia*, which has been very active in London mosques and in the infiltration of local political parties. "The primary work" in the establishment of a future Muslim empire, it announces, "is in Europe, because it is this continent, despite all the furore about its achievements, which has a moral and spiritual vacuum."

So this is where all the vapid talk about the "soul" of the universe is actually headed. Once the hard-won principles of reason and science have been discredited, the world will not pass into the hands of credulous herbivores who keep crystals by their sides and swoon over the poems of Khalil Gibran. The "vacuum" will be invaded instead by determined fundamentalists of every stripe who already know the truth by means of revelation and who actually seek real and serious power in the here and now. One thinks of the painstaking, cloud-dispelling labor of British scientists from Isaac Newton to Joseph Priestley to Charles Darwin to Ernest Rutherford to Alan Turing and Francis Crick, much of it built upon the shoulders of Galileo and Copernicus, only to see it casually slandered by a moral and intellectual weakling from the usurping House of Hanover. An awful embarrassment awaits the British if they do not declare for a republic based on verifiable laws and principles, both political and scientific.

(*Slate*, June 14, 2010)

Offshore Accounts

Afghanistan's Dangerous Bet

I SPENT MY ENTIRE TIME in Afghanistan, from dawn until dusk and then beyond, utterly and completely obsessed with women. You may ask why I am telling you this. What about the land mines, the lurking Taliban, the warlords, the malaria and the dysentery, the battling tribes, the beating sun, and the forbidding landscape? These are all, I will happily concede, quite compelling in their way. But they pale, each of them and every time, when contrasted with the absolutely Himalayan question of Afghan womanhood. I could not get the subject out of my mind for an instant, waking or sleeping. (Violence and drugs featured, too, I must say, but only in second and third place. I'm seriously thinking of going back, quite soon. For one thing, the future of democracy may be at stake.)

"I gather," I said to the official of the National Democratic Institute in Kabul, "that you are holding a mock election?" Down the cell phone came his cautious, Canadian-accented response. "We are," he said, "as part of our training, conducting an election simulation." I silently reproached myself for my thoughtless flippancy, and managed to get myself invited along nevertheless.

Under the shade of a large, cool, open-sided tent, in the courtyard of one of the many NGO (or "non-governmental organization") buildings that now occupy so much of Afghanistan's battered and filthy capital, a sample electorate had been assembled. More than half were women, of whom all had donned some kind of head covering, while none wore the all-enclosing burka.

All, in other words, were showing the most ravishing part of the female form—the face—and almost all of them were displaying at least some of the second-most-hypnotizing feature—their hair. One had brought a daughter along and another a grandson (there are an awful lot of widows in Kabul). Good-humored, polite young men, most of them Afghan, were instructing them in how to cast a ballot. First, three "candidates" made ten-minute pitches for their hypothetical parties. Two of the candidates were women, and one an older man with a dark mustache that set off his whitening en brosse locks. Then the simulated electorate was invited to produce its voter-registration cards, to receive an indelible-ink stamp on the wrist, to show its punched voting paper to a man with Genghis Khan cheekbones, and to proceed into a curtained voting booth before emerging and modestly, proudly dropping the completed ballot into a locked box. The entire thing might have made a charming episode on Scandinavian public television: the blessings of universal suffrage, as brought by well-intentioned secular missionaries.

But three years ago, you could not look an Afghan woman or girl in the eye. Half the population was chattel or other property: invisible, enveloped, and voiceless. The male members of their families could literally give them away as bargaining chips, or prizes. Arbitrary and lascivious punishments, usually totted up in lashes but sometimes in lethal stones, were the enforcement of this slavery. You can still read, quite often, of young women who set themselves on fire to avoid forced marriage and other types of bondage. My sex obsession was nothing to that of the Taliban and their bin Ladenist "guests," who regarded the world of their mothers, sisters, wives, and daughters with plain contempt and even horror. (Of the men-only "martyrs" of this movement, the fascinating thing is not how many of them dreamed of virgins, but how many of them were virgins.) Yet, as I arrived in Kabul, the females of the country were in the process of astonishing all observers. Of those who had registered to vote, fully 41 percent were women. And this was in no mean turnout; there are even parts of the country where the number registered is higher than the supposed number of voters. President Hamid Karzai has joked publicly about this Chicago-like development, attributing it rather airily to an excess of democratic exuberance. But since estimates of Afghanistan's population fluctuate between 21 and 29 million, some allowance probably has to be made for its people's first-ever visit to the polls.

These people will not be casting their ballots in shaded tents in urban courtyards, before admiring international witnesses. They will be risking—and have already defied—acid in the face, mines on the road, bombs in the schools and even the mosques where voters gather, and every other imaginable kind of discouragement. The worst discouragement of all is the fear that the vote really will be "an election simulation," and that Afghanistan will continue to be run by gender-crazed old mullahs and bandits. A photo op from the twenty-first century can easily be negated by the terrible weight of the centuries that have gone before. As William Faulkner said about the Deep South, the past is never dead. Here, it's not even past.

The newspapers and television may have been telling you every day that the shrine of Imam Ali, cousin and son-in-law to the prophet Muhammad (peace be upon him), lies beneath the Golden Dome in Najaf, in southern Iraq. But no pious Afghan entirely believes this version. After his killing in A.D. 661, according to the local story, Ali's followers feared for the desecration of his corpse. They embalmed it, placed it on the back of a white female camel, and made the beast canter until it dropped. That spot would be the burial place. The camel gave up in northern Afghanistan, and the great imam is therefore interred in what is now the city of Mazar-i-Sharif, or "the tomb of the exalted one." The shrine is still there, even though its original was pretty thoroughly trampled by Genghis Khan. One of President Hamid Karzai's earlier actions, after the defeat and flight of the Taliban, was to journey to Mazar-i-Sharif and, in front of a huge *nawroz*, or "New Year," crowd, unfurl Ali's green flag. The Sunni Taliban had forbidden the pilgrimage because the origins of *nawroz* lie in Babylonian and Zoroastrian antiquity, and were considered—like the shell-blasted statues of the Buddhas in Bamiyan—pre-Islamic and therefore profane.

Then again, the early chroniclers among the Afghans claimed that it was they, and no others, who were the lost tribe of the Jews: descendants of King Saul and the true survivors of the Babylonian captivity. This claim was examined and disputed in 1815 by the Honorable Mountstuart Elphinstone of the East India Company (later to cut a sorry figure in the "memoirs" of Harry Flashman). But the idea resurfaced in the famous 11th edition of the *Encyclopaedia Britannica*, published in 1910, when imperial ethnography was at its zenith: "A respectable number of intelligent officers, well acquainted with the Afghans, have been strong in their belief of it; and though the customs alleged in proof will not bear the stress laid on them, undoubtedly a prevailing type of the Afghan physiognomy has a character strongly Jewish."

Perhaps we have been fighting over the wrong Holy Land all along? I personally began to find consolation in the small victories of the profane over the sacred. It's jolly to sit in "Flashman's" restaurant, sipping scotch and wine in the restored Gandamack Lodge, and know that this house used to be the sheltered enclave of one of Osama bin Laden's luckless wives. (No waitresses, yet, I had to notice: Only old men and young boys are trusted with the job.) It's a treat to get your glossy copy of *Afghan Scene* and read of the films and plays and photographic exhibitions that are on offer in town. It's heartening to see the female students at Kabul University, flaunting knockoffs of international fashion, and often earning enough as part-time translators to support their parents (and thus undermine patriarchal authority). It's cheering to see groups clustered around flickering TV sets, riveted to videos of swimsuit contests. It was a delight to sit with Wais in his pizza restaurant—more than 3.4 million Afghan refugees have come home since the fall of the Taliban—and hear his cut-with-a-knife New Jersey accent as he described how things had improved. "Night and day, man. Fuckin' night and day."

I think of my inspiring but sedate interview with Dr. Masuda Jalal, the only woman candidate for the presidency and the only female to have challenged Karzai's candidacy in the famous Loya Jirga, or Grand Council, which also prepared the new Afghan constitution. She's a well-known physician, who ran a clinic and a secret school during the Taliban years and was briefly detained. She lives, like a number of Kabul's educated middle class, in a hideous district of "People's Republic"–type apartment blocks, built by Soviet "advisers" on the outskirts of the capital. Indeed, I think her secret is that she's a former leftist, though of the pro-Chinese variety. Her rhetoric still bears traces of that "serve the people" idiom, and she speaks without embarrassment of a constituency of "progressive scholars, intellectuals, and democrats," not omitting a few, newer terms about "civil society." President Karzai, she says firmly, has "signed too many protocols" with warlords and mullahs. She herself would prefer a Cabinet of "technocrats," including the "cleaner" supporters of President Karzai, and even of Zahir Shah, the returned king who is recognized not quite as monarch of the country but as "father of his people."

In her anteroom, I met her three delightful daughters, ages nine, seven, and three, as well as her husband—a professor of law at the university—and her campaign manager, a grizzled old bear of a man from the border province of Khost, who looks like a retired chieftain. More men support the Masuda Jalal campaign than you might guess: They can at least be sure that they are not getting another warlord, possibly from the "wrong" ethnicity.

Before I said good-bye, my sex obsession got the better of me again. Throughout our conversation, Dr. Jalal had been toying with a headscarf that didn't seem all that comfortable. "How long," I made bold to inquire, "have you been wearing that? Have you always worn one?" Her downcast-eyed yet stirring reply was that, in her days as a medical student, she had worn what she liked. This was a nervous compromise. Even her revolutionary candidacy was, in a sense, being conducted with male permission.

You get the same sense, all the time, of a culture poised on a razor's edge. People mock President Karzai for being too compromising and for being "only the mayor of Kabul," but he's been brave enough to drop a militia leader as his running mate and, if he were to be assassinated, the effect would be felt way beyond the capital. In other words, this is a society which is still only one bullet away from chaos. (Cheer up: The same is probably true of neighboring Pakistan, with its reliable General Musharraf and its nuclear weapons.)

I had my own exposure to abrupt, vertiginous change when I journeyed to the provincial capital of Herat, in the far west of the country. Herat abuts the border with Iran, and its main flavor is Persian. It boasts a marvelous blue mosque and a still-standing cluster of antique minarets, from the times of Tamerlane, or "Timur the Lame." Its big-city boss was until recently a relatively jovial old warlord named Ismail Khan, who fought against the Red Army and the Taliban with equal gusto, but is said to be a bit twisted from his long imprisonment by the latter, and also a little distraught at the murder of his son last March. The killing was the result of a rivalry between Ismail and yet another local warlord, a representative of the Pashtun minority named Amanullah Khan. A few days before I arrived, Amanullah (or A.K.) had seized the old Russian-built airfield at Shindand, about sixty miles away, but this was thought to be mostly in the nature of a gesture. Herat itself continued to boom and bustle, prospering by the virtually open borders with Iran and Turkmenistan and from the trade in everything from opium to SUVs which results. Ismail Khan (I.K.) had been a political appointee of Karzai's and legally recognized as governor of Herat, but he didn't much relish passing on his portion of the revenues he raised. He preferred to distribute these locally, and thus be "a river to his people." Hence the well-kept streets, the humming bazaar, and the preservation—very rare in Afghanistan—of the groves and avenues of trees that would otherwise have gone to charcoal. (I passed an eating place called Shame Restaurant, but it was modestly closed.)

At about one o'clock one baking afternoon, as I was mincing happily through the fragrant and laden flower stalls, and noticing that, though burkas had become rarer, no woman was "manning" any shop, a definite pulse or tremor ran through the town. It was like watching a rumor take physical form: Suddenly there were clusters and clumps of people talking earnestly together, then the sound of shutters descending over windows, succeeded swiftly by the scamper of feet and then the arrival of pickup trucks, bearing bearded men with rocket-propelled grenades and Kalashnikov rifles. (Just what you don't want when taking in the local atmosphere in Afghanistan: to have your passport studied, unsmilingly and upside down, by some of these beauties.) In the course of the succeeding few hours, I was told by "the street" that A.K.'s men were at the edge of town, that A.K. and fifty of his followers had been killed by an American air strike, that the Americans were behind A.K. in an attempt to weaken I.K., and that the airport road had been closed. Only the last—and just possibly the second—of these stories turned out to be true. Kabul, about 600 miles distant by a road that was also closed, might as well have been on another planet: It suddenly began to seem to me like a shimmering metropolis.

"Street" opinion, as elsewhere in the region, is almost invariably deluded and distorted. And all the women, I noticed, were off the streets right away, which rather reduced the sample of viewpoints. But, during the hours of chaos, one could still get three strong and consistent impressions. The first is that the central government is not very highly regarded in the country's westernmost city. Hardly anyone had a good word for Karzai. The second is that pickup trucks with bearded gunmen are not popular, even when they seem to represent the winning side. (Applause from the sidewalk was perfunctory: Most people moved away and kept their counsel to themselves.) The third is that I.K. has a genuine following. "And he is a *jihadi*!" exclaimed one man as he finished reeling off a list of I.K.'s virtues. "Against whom?" I inquired. "You do not know what means 'jihad'?" "Well, yes I do, I think. That's why I asked, 'Against whom?'" I was still made to feel that I had asked a dumb question, which perhaps I had. Any war this guy fights is holy to some. An interlude of arduous phone-calling got me inside the "bubble" that is formed by the coalition forces, the United Nations teams, and the NGOs. I was able to spend a not-too-tense night inside the perimeter of the P.R.T., or Provisional Reconstruction Team: the system of decentralized mini-bases that some NATO contingents now wisely use to stay close to events. The HQ was right in the middle of town, and its compound contained several dozen armed Afghans. Many of them were awake and on guard while the bulk of the garrison was sleeping: a thing you would not see inside the equivalent American base in Iraq. ("Yeah, they're family," said a central-casting farm-boy soldier from Wisconsin. "Buddies for life.")

It was rather nice inside the bubble. I met some tough and smart guys, who had become good at collecting local intelligence and who mingle the job of collecting it with the job of distributing aid. One officer I met was carrying a briefcase with $150,000 in cash—"for schools," as he put it. I got a briefing or two, and found opinion divided on whether it was wise for the central government to try to undermine old Ismail Khan before the elections. I found it generally to be true that American soldiers—especially the ones this "far from the flagpole" and way out on the western frontier—felt less valued and less noticed since the invasion of Iraq. Eventually, I got a hitchhike from a Humvee, which took me to the airport, where I secured another hitchhike from a U.N. evacuation plane, flown by enormous bronzed South Africans. This international bubble, in theory, stretches protectively across the whole jagged country. But, boy, is it pulled thin and tight, and you don't want to be there when it punctures or leaks. Not many days after I had left, President Karzai did dismiss Ismail Khan as governor of Herat—which implied that perhaps the American Embassy had after all been behind the attacks on him—and at least nine of the bubble's offices were burned out.

What exactly *is* a warlord? The species clusters into two main groups: local pashas such as Ismail Khan, roughly content to harvest their own fiefdoms, and ethnic or confessional leaders with big ideas. Into the latter category would fall the grisly, sadistic figure of Gulbuddin Hekmatyar, once a favorite of Pakistan and the CIA but now a wanted man who combines

Taliban rhetoric with extreme corruption and opportunism. Yet we would also find the late Ahmed Shah Massoud, the brilliantly charismatic leader of the Northern Alliance, who was both a Tajik tribal commander and a devout Islamist. He it was who tried to warn the West that the Taliban were harboring Osama bin Laden, and he it was who was murdered by al-Qaeda suicide killers on September 9, 2001, to try to ensure that their upcoming assault on New York and Washington would be matched by the extinction of resistance within Afghanistan itself. I shall not forget those three days three years ago: It must have seemed to the fanatics that god was laughing along with them, and that everything was ordained in their favor. One must never again feel such defenseless shame.

Pictures of Massoud are now everywhere in Kabul, his brother is Karzai's vice-presidential pick, and a large monument is being built in his honor. But there is an older and surer definition of a warlord: He is someone who can control a piece of road and force you to pay a rent or a toll to pass along it. Roll a few rocks and oil drums onto the highway, place some gun-wielding desperadoes next to the barrier, and begin your extortion. It is the fear of this that keeps many Afghans ghettoized in their miserable villages, and that also keeps many humanitarians and diplomats penned up in the safety of the cities, or traveling only within the bubble. It is the same fear that Kipling called upon (you didn't think I was going to leave him out, did you?) in his extraordinary Afghan poem "Arithmetic on the Frontier":

A scrimmage in a Border Station—
A canter down some dark defile
Two thousand pounds of education
Drops to a ten-rupee *jezail*...
Strike hard who cares—shoot straight who can
The odds are on the cheaper man.

You can still see homemade *jezail* rifles, along with fearsome daggers, in the front of shops along Chicken Street and Flower Street in Kabul—placed there mainly to give the handful of tourists a cheap thrill. But it takes only an inexpensive improvised roadside or handheld weapon to put fright into the aid workers and election supervisors who have to leave the compounds or venture through the arid rural communities where 70 percent of Afghans still try to exist. In the town of Ghazni, for example, a young Frenchwoman named Bettina Goislard was cut down in broad daylight last November while working for the U.N. high commissioner for refugees. Not far away, a bomb exploded in a mosque—a mosque!—while voters were attempting to register the names they could barely write.

I will venture a prediction: The Taliban/al-Qaeda riffraff, as we know them, will never come back to power. They were able to seize Kabul in the first place only because the country had been reduced to "Year Zero" conditions by civil war, and they are now so much hated, and so heavily outgunned, that they can't expect to do any better than make life miserable in the more wretched areas of the South. Vicious though their tactics are, they don't show any sign of having a plan, or a coordinated leadership, or a directing brain. (If Osama bin Laden is still alive, he has a very faint and unconvincing way of demonstrating it. He doesn't even issue fiery sermons anymore. His deputy, Ayman al-Zawahiri, got the job of making the September-anniversary rant this year, and of issuing the false claim that Americans were cowering in their trenches in southern and eastern Afghanistan. And Osama used to be so voluble...)

I selected Ghazni just now for a reason: I paid it a visit just as the registration of voters was being completed. My expedition from Kabul was remarkably swift and easy, because the place lies along the new highway from the capital to Kandahar: the southern city that may well have been named for Iskandar, local name for Alexander the Great. The South is still in the danger zone; it abuts the near ungovernable Pakistani tribal areas, and even in Kandahar itself the female registration for the election is little more than half the national average. But two years ago that journey would have been an extremely rugged and hazardous undertaking that could consume at least a whole day. Now you can drive from Kabul to Kandahar in six hours. (Pedal to the metal, I hit eighty miles per hour on the straight and level, than which the car itself could do no more.) Roadblocks become redundant or archaic in these conditions. People sometimes sneer at the Kabul-Kandahar highway, saying that it's still unsafe and that, in order for it to be completed in time for President Bush to celebrate it in a speech, a couple of inches of blacktop had to be omitted from its surface. Well, I have now driven along a good bit of it, in daytime and darkness, and perhaps I was just lucky. It's patchy in places, but backup gravel and Tarmac are both being heaped lavishly on the roadside. Even more noticeable is that enterprise is beginning to rise up along the way—from gas stations to the outlines of factories and construction sites.

It is mainly a superstition from our own past that can absolutely ruin the hopes of those who wait on line in the sun and hope against hope that their votes will count. We can still get a failed state or a rogue state in Afghanistan, if we really work at it. Nothing is crazier, when you see it up close, than the stupid "war on drugs." Nobody believes in it for a second. The military specialists all think it is a waste of time, or at best (as the saying goes) a distraction from the hunt for al-Qaeda. The farmers all think it is an assault on their only viable crop. The warlords just can't believe their luck. There are whole areas of the country, recovered from Taliban control, where the "hearts and minds" battle is being lost every hour of every day, with dumb attempts to root out the only thing that grows, and the only thing that sells. After years of withering drought, and even more years of devastating crop burning and desolation, which would you plant: a vine that takes five years to grow to maturity—grapes used to be Afghanistan's main crop export—or a poppy that yields pods in six months? It has been calculated that as much as a fourth of the country's G.D.P. is opium-related, and that the crop gives a livelihood to millions in the countryside. Some of these are coerced into poppy farming, but until another economy has been created, or this one recognized, it's futile to be emulating the Untouchables. Thirty years of experience have not yet taught us that Westerners will buy the fruit of this poppy at almost any price, and that therefore Easterners and Southerners will stolidly continue to cultivate it. Many people think that the Taliban did a better job of drug "interdiction," which is a clue in itself to the madness of this calculus. In fact, the Taliban "banned" the trade in order to drive up the price of the existing tonnage that they held. The U.S. government actually grows opium in Turkey for our domestic painkiller market: Why not give Afghans a slice of the business?

Afghanistan is not in our past: Its astonishing inhabitants are our formerly abandoned and now half-adopted relations. And one can so easily fall for a place where everybody thinks about sex, where bombing has blasted a society out of the Stone Age, and where opium is the religion of the people.

(*Vanity Fair*, November 2004)

First, Silence the Whistle-Blower

IF THE TIME ever does come when we look back on our intervention in Afghanistan as a humiliating debacle, this past weekend may well be identified as one of the moments when the calamity became irreversible.

In the prelude to the 2004 elections in that country, I went around looking at the places where local people were being instructed in the principles as well as the mechanics of voting. It was like watching a very tightly furled bud beginning to burgeon and unfold. Officials of various international organizations had been hoping, for example, to attract a certain percentage of Afghan women to brave their former oppressors and come out to register; the facilities for this were overborne by the sheer number of women who spontaneously showed up. Minority groups that had been despised and butchered by the Taliban—such as the Hazara, a Shiite community with some cousinhood to Persia—were mobilizing to register. The press and television, entirely new to many Afghans, were showing some vivid scenes of democracy and some useful debates. On the actual day of voting, there was some complaint about the indelible ink for the fingertips being not so indelible as all that, but vast numbers of people braved the "night letters" from the Taliban and stood in line in the sun for the chance to cast a ballot. No procedural imperfection could quite destroy the impression that Afghans were acquiring the all-important idea of a free and competitive election.

The dreary, nasty farce of August 20 has almost eclipsed that memory. A ridiculous, banana-republic style shenanigan produced, in its first round, an outcome that did not survive even the most cursory scrutiny. On the very first inspection of the polling stations and the ballots, it was laughably easy to discover polling stations that never opened but that recorded vast turnouts and ballots that had gone straight from the printing press into the pockets of President Hamid Karzai and his associates—one of whom, Azizullah Lodin, doubles as the chairman of the absurdly named Independent Election Commission of Afghanistan.

That would be bad enough, were it not for the craven complicity of the U.N. mission in Kabul. Perhaps as much as $200 million of the international community's money was allotted to ensure that the Afghan people could vote, but when vast numbers of them did not or could not, and while many others of them managed to do so, in effect, five or six times, there was no alarm call from the responsible U.N. officers in Kabul. Or perhaps I should rephrase that: One officer did complain that there had been (a) widespread fraud, and (b) government collusion in same, and (c) U.N. indifference that amounted to complicity. This was Peter Galbraith, a senior American diplomat who was then the deputy special representative of the U.N. secretary-general, that scintillating figure known in song and story as Ban Ki-moon. Galbraith complained that Kai Eide, the Norwegian head of the U.N. mission, had been indifferent to the flagrant bias shown by the local Afghan officials who were in effect spending the United Nations' money to buy votes for their political boss. Eide in turn complained to Ban, who immediately obliged by firing Galbraith. Thus we cannot quite say that nobody involved in this fiasco and fiesta of corruption has yet lost his job—it would be almost true except that the main whistle-blower was fired as the first order of business.

It wouldn't now matter whether there was a runoff or not, or a "contested" election—there can't be any sentient Afghan who believes that the process is anything much more than a cynical fix. It is not as bad as the recent trampling on the voting rights of the people of neighboring Iran, but we are supposed to have a slightly more elevated standard than that (and the mere comparison, of course, goes to show how high the stakes are).

The Taliban, one imagines, can barely credit their luck. They are opposed to voting on principle, as something un-Islamic, and they are especially and viciously opposed to voting by women, but now they don't need to stress that. They can simply help swell the chorus of cynicism and contempt.

The panic measures proposed to redress this dreadful outcome have in some cases been as bad as the original disease. Admitting far too late and far too grudgingly that fraud had necessitated a second round, Kai Eide left us faced with a choice between a hasty second vote overseen by the same crooks or a postponement until after the brutal Afghan winter—another free gift to the forces of ruin and fanaticism. Some also proposed a ramshackle "interim" government or a face-saving cobble-up between Karzai and his main rival, Abdullah Abdullah (so nice they named him twice). All this represents an attempt to avoid facing the obvious fact that for months of this year, and with our money, the Afghan people were cheated and betrayed in their hour of most urgent need.

What will the big friends of the morally infallible United Nations say now, I wonder? And how will Congress and the president and the leaderships of the other donor and sponsor states account for what happened to the funding they authorized? I have written dozens of times about how none of the so-called parallels with Vietnam are any good (al-Qaeda a foreign import to Afghanistan; no Vietcong threat to American cities; you know the rest), but there is one thing that did disfigure South Vietnam and is essential to avoid in any case: the commitment of American forces to a government that contrives to be both enriched and bankrupt at the same time and makes its own people want to spit.

(*Slate*, November 2, 2009)

Believe Me, It's Torture

HERE IS THE MOST CHILLING WAY I can find of stating the matter. Until recently, "waterboarding" was something that Americans did to other Americans. It was inflicted, and endured, by those members of the Special Forces who underwent the advanced form of training known as SERE (Survival, Evasion, Resistance, Escape). In these harsh exercises, brave men and women were introduced to the sorts of barbarism that they might expect to meet at the hands of a lawless foe who disregarded the Geneva Conventions. But it was something that Americans were being trained to *resist*, not to *inflict*.

Exploring this narrow but deep distinction, on a gorgeous day last May I found myself deep in the hill country of western North Carolina, preparing to be surprised by a team of extremely hardened veterans who had confronted their country's enemies in highly arduous terrain all over the world. They knew about everything from unarmed combat to enhanced interrogation and, in exchange for anonymity, were going to show me as nearly as possible what real waterboarding might be like.

It goes without saying that I knew I could stop the process at any time, and that when it was all over I would be released into happy daylight rather than returned to a darkened cell. But it's been well said that cowards die many times before their deaths, and it was difficult for me to completely forget the clause in the contract of indemnification that I had signed. This document (written by one who knew) stated revealingly:

> "Water boarding" is a potentially dangerous activity in which the participant can receive serious and permanent (physical, emotional and psychological) injuries and even death, including injuries and death due to the respiratory and neurological systems of the body.

As the agreement went on to say, there would be safeguards provided "during the 'water boarding' process, however, these measures may fail and even if they work properly they may not prevent Hitchens from experiencing serious injury or death."

On the night before the encounter I got to sleep with what I thought was creditable ease, but woke early and knew at once that I wasn't going back to any sort of doze or snooze. The first specialist I had approached with the scheme had asked my age on the telephone and when told what it was (I am fifty-nine) had laughed out loud and told me to forget it. Waterboarding is for Green Berets in training, or wiry young *jihad*-ists whose teeth can bite through the gristle of an old goat. It's not for wheezing, paunchy scribblers. For my current "handlers" I had had to produce a doctor's certificate assuring them that I did not have asthma, but I wondered whether I should tell them about the 15,000 cigarettes I had inhaled every year for the last several decades. I was feeling apprehensive, in other words, and beginning to wish I hadn't given myself so long to think about it.

I have to be opaque about exactly where I was later that day, but there came a moment when, sitting on a porch outside a remote house at the end of a winding country road, I was very gently yet firmly grabbed from behind, pulled to my feet, pinioned by my wrists (which were then cuffed to a belt), and cut off from the sunlight by having a black hood pulled over my face. I was then turned around a few times, I presume to assist in disorienting me, and led over some crunchy gravel into a darkened room. Well, mainly darkened: There were some oddly spaced bright lights that came as pinpoints through my hood. And some weird music assaulted my ears. (I'm no judge of these things, but I wouldn't have expected former Special Forces types to be so fond of New Age techno-disco.) The outside world seemed very suddenly very distant indeed.

Arms already lost to me, I wasn't able to flail as I was pushed onto a sloping board and positioned with my head lower than my heart. (That's the main point: The angle can be slight or steep.) Then my legs were lashed together so that the board and I were one single and trussed unit. Not to bore you with my phobias, but if I don't have at least two pillows I wake up with acid reflux and mild sleep apnea, so even a merely supine position makes me uneasy. And, to tell you something I had been keeping from myself as well as from my new experimental friends, I do have a fear of drowning that comes from a bad childhood moment on the Isle of Wight, when I got out of my depth. As a boy reading the climactic torture scene of *Nineteen Eighty-four*, where what is in Room 101 is the worst thing in the world, I realize that somewhere in my version of that hideous chamber comes the moment when the wave washes over me. Not that that makes me special: I don't know anyone who *likes* the idea of drowning. As mammals we may have originated in the ocean, but water has many ways of reminding us that when we are in it we are out of our element. In brief, when it comes to breathing, give me good old air every time.

You may have read by now the official lie about this treatment, which is that it "simulates" the feeling of drowning. This is not the case. You feel that you are drowning because you *are* drowning—or, rather, being drowned, albeit slowly and under controlled conditions and at the mercy (or otherwise) of those who are applying the pressure. The "board" is the instrument, *not* the method. You are not being boarded. You are being watered. This was very rapidly brought home to me when, on top of the hood, which still admitted a few flashes of random and worrying strobe light to my vision, three layers of enveloping towel were added. In this pregnant darkness, head downward, I waited for a while until I abruptly felt a slow cascade of water going up my nose. Determined to resist if only for the honor of my navy ancestors who had so often been in peril on the sea, I held my breath for a while and then had to exhale and—as you might expect—inhale in turn. The inhalation brought the damp cloths tight against my nostrils, as if a huge, wet paw had been suddenly and annihilatingly clamped over my face. Unable to determine whether I was breathing in or out, and flooded more with sheer panic than with mere water, I triggered the pre-arranged signal and felt the unbelievable relief of being pulled upright and having the soaking and stifling layers pulled off me. I find I don't want to tell you how little time I lasted.

This is because I had read that Khalid Sheikh Mohammed, invariably referred to as the "mastermind" of the atrocities of September 11, 2001, had impressed his interrogators by holding out for upward of two minutes before cracking. (By the way, this story is not confirmed. My North Carolina friends jeered at it. "Hell," said one, "from what I heard they only washed his damn face before he babbled.") But, hell, I thought in my turn, no Hitchens is going to do worse than *that*. Well, okay, I admit I didn't outdo him. And so then I said, with slightly more bravado than was justified, that I'd like to try it one more time. There was a paramedic present who checked my racing pulse and warned me about adrenaline rush. An interval was ordered, and then I felt the mask come down again. Steeling myself to remember what it had been like last time, and to learn from the previous panic attack, I fought down the first, and some of the second, wave of nausea and terror but soon found that I was an abject prisoner of my gag reflex. The interrogators would hardly have had time to ask me any questions, and I knew that I would quite readily have agreed to supply any answer. I still feel ashamed when I think about it. Also, in case it's of interest, I have since woken up trying to push the bedcovers off my face, and if I do anything that makes me short of breath I find myself clawing at the air with a horrible sensation of smothering and claustrophobia. No doubt this will pass. As if detecting my misery and shame, one of my interrogators comfortingly said, "Any time is a long time when you're breathing water." I could have hugged him for saying so, and just then I was hit with a ghastly sense of the sadomasochistic dimension that underlies the relationship between the torturer and the tortured. I apply the Abraham Lincoln test for moral casuistry: "If slavery is not wrong, nothing is wrong." Well, then, if waterboarding does not constitute torture, then there is no such thing as torture.

I am somewhat proud of my ability to "keep my head," as the saying goes, and to maintain presence of mind under trying circumstances. I was completely convinced that, when the water pressure had become intolerable, I had firmly uttered the pre-determined code word that would cause it to cease. But my interrogator told me that, rather to his surprise, I had not spoken a word. I had activated the "dead man's handle" that signaled the onset of unconsciousness. So now I have to wonder about the role of false memory and delusion. What I do recall clearly, though, is a hard finger feeling for my solar plexus as the water was being poured. What was that for? "That's to find out if you are trying to cheat, and timing your breathing to the doses.

If you try that, we can outsmart you. We have all kinds of enhancements." I was briefly embarrassed that I hadn't earned or warranted these refinements, but it hit me yet again that this is certainly the *language* of torture.

Maybe I am being premature in phrasing it thus. Among the SERE veterans there are at least two views on all this, which means in practice that there are two opinions on whether or not "waterboarding" constitutes torture. I have had some extremely serious conversations on the topic, with two groups of highly decent and serious men, and I think that both cases have to be stated at their strongest.

The team who agreed to give me a hard time in the woods of North Carolina belong to a highly honorable group. This group regards itself as out on the front line in defense of a society that is too spoiled and too ungrateful to appreciate those solid, underpaid volunteers who guard us while we sleep. These heroes stay on the ramparts at all hours and in all weather, and if they make a mistake they may be arraigned in order to scratch some domestic political itch. Faced with appalling enemies who make horror videos of torture and beheadings, they feel that they are the ones who confront denunciation in our press, and possible prosecution. As they have just tried to demonstrate to me, a man who has been waterboarded may well emerge from the experience a bit shaky, but he is in a mood to surrender the relevant information and is unmarked and undamaged and indeed ready for another bout in quite a short time. When contrasted to actual torture, waterboarding is more like foreplay. No thumbscrew, no pincers, no electrodes, no rack. Can one say this of those who have been captured by the tormentors and murderers of (say) Daniel Pearl? On this analysis, any call to indict the United States for torture is therefore a lame and diseased attempt to arrive at a moral equivalence between those who defend civilization and those who exploit its freedoms to hollow it out, and ultimately to bring it down. I myself do not trust anybody who does not clearly understand this viewpoint.

Against it, however, I call as my main witness Mr. Malcolm Nance. Mr. Nance is not what you call a bleeding heart. In fact, speaking of the coronary area, he has said that, in battlefield conditions, he "would personally cut bin Laden's heart out with a plastic M.R.E. spoon." He was to the fore on September 11, 2001, dealing with the burning nightmare in the debris of the Pentagon. He has been involved with the SERE program since 1997.

He speaks Arabic and has been on al-Qaeda's tail since the early 1990s. His most recent book, *The Terrorists of Iraq*, is a highly potent analysis both of the *jihad*-ist threat in Mesopotamia and of the ways in which we have made its life easier. I passed one of the most dramatic evenings of my life listening to his cold but enraged denunciation of the adoption of waterboarding by the United States. The argument goes like this:

- Waterboarding is a deliberate torture technique and has been prosecuted as such by our judicial arm when perpetrated by others.
- If we allow it and justify it, we cannot complain if it is employed in the future by other regimes on captive U.S. citizens. It is a method of putting American prisoners in harm's way.
- It may be a means of extracting information, but it is also a means of extracting junk information. (Mr. Nance told me that he had heard of someone's being compelled to confess that he was a hermaphrodite. I later had an awful twinge while wondering if I myself could have been "dunked" this far.) To put it briefly, even the CIA sources for the *Washington Post* story on waterboarding conceded that the information they got out of Khalid Sheikh Mohammed was "not all of it reliable." Just put a pencil line under that last phrase, or commit it to memory.
- It opens a door that cannot be closed. Once you have posed the notorious "ticking bomb" question, and once you assume that you are in the right, what will you *not* do? Waterboarding not getting results fast enough? The terrorist's clock still ticking? Well, then, bring on the thumbscrews and the pincers and the electrodes and the rack.

Masked by these arguments, there lurks another very penetrating point. Nance doubts very much that Khalid Sheikh Mohammed lasted that long under the water treatment (and I am pathetically pleased to hear it). It's also quite thinkable, *if* he did, that he was trying to attain martyrdom at our hands. But even if he endured so long, and since the United States has in any case bragged that *in fact* he did, one of our worst enemies has now become one of the founders of something that will someday disturb your sleep as well as mine. To quote Nance:

> Torture advocates hide behind the argument that an open discussion about specific American interrogation techniques will aid the enemy. Yet, convicted al-Qaeda members and innocent captives who were released to their host nations have already debriefed the world through hundreds of interviews, movies and documentaries on exactly what methods they were subjected to and how they endured. Our own missteps have created a cadre of highly experienced lecturers for al-Qaeda's own virtual SERE school for terrorists.

Which returns us to my starting point, about the distinction between training *for* something and training to resist it. One used to be told—and surely with truth—that the lethal fanatics of al-Qaeda were schooled to lie, and instructed to claim that they had been tortured and maltreated whether they had been tortured and maltreated or not. Did we notice what a frontier we had crossed when we admitted and even proclaimed that their stories might in fact be true? I had only a very slight encounter on that frontier, but I still wish that my experience were the only way in which the words "waterboard" and "American" could be mentioned in the same (gasping and sobbing) breath.

(*Vanity Fair*, August 2008)

Iran's Waiting Game

DRIVING DOWN THROUGH THE DESERT, from Tehran to the holy city of Qom, I am following the path of so many who have made the pilgrimage before me. They either were seeking an audience with, or a glimpse of, Ayatollah Khomeini or, if they were journalistic pilgrims, were trying to test the temperature of Iran's clerical capital. As I arrive, darkness is gently settling over the domes and spires of the mosque and the Shia theological seminary, the latter of which is demarcated by a kind of empty moat which doubles as a market. But I am not headed for these centers of spiritual and temporal power. My objective is an ill-paved backstreet where, after one confirming cell-phone call, a black-turbaned cleric is waiting outside his modest quarters. This is Hossein Khomeini. The black turban proclaims him a sayyid, or descendant of the prophet Muhammad. But it's his more immediate ancestry that interests me. This man's grandfather once shook the whole world. He tore down the throne of Shah Mohammad Reza Pahlavi in 1979 and humiliated the United States. His supporters seized the American Embassy and kept fifty-two members of its staff prisoner for 444 days. The seismic repercussions of this event led to the fall of Carter, the rise of Reagan, the invasion of Iran by Saddam Hussein, and quite possibly the occupation of Afghanistan by the Red Army. It moved us from the age of the Red Menace to the epoch of Holy War. It was, at one and the same time, a genuine revolution and an authentic counterrevolution. I have become almost averse to shaking hands in Iran by now, because it isn't permitted for a man to shake a woman's hand in public in this nerve-racked country, and if you unlearn the conditioned reflex in one way, you unlearn it in another. But as I feel young Khomeini's polite grip, I fancifully experience a slight crackle from history.

Iranian hospitality is one of the most warming and embarrassing things it is possible to encounter. Before any conversation can begin on these grand questions, there must be fragrant tea, a plate of *sohan,* the addictive pistachio-and-saffron brittle that is the Qom specialty, and a pressing invitation to stay for dinner, and indeed for the night. The pressure is re-doubled on this occasion because the last time we met and talked I was the host.

Young Khomeini has been spending a good deal of his time in Iraq, where he has many friends among the Shia. He is a strong supporter of the United States intervention in that country, and takes a political line not dissimilar to that of Grand Ayatollah al-Sistani. In practice, this means the traditional Shia belief that clerics should not occupy posts of political power. In Iranian terms, what it means is that Khomeini (his father and elder brother died some years ago, so he is the most immediate descendant) favors the removal of the regime established by his grandfather. "I stand," he tells me calmly, "for the complete separation of religion and the state." In terms that would make the heart of a neocon soar like a hawk, he goes on to praise President Bush's State of the Union speech, to warn that the mullahs cannot be trusted with nuclear weapons, and to use the term "Free World" without irony: "Only the Free World, led by America, can bring democracy to Iran."

Anyone visiting Iran today will quickly become used to hearing this version of street opinion, but there is something striking about hearing it from the lips of a turbaned Khomeini. Changing the emphasis slightly, he asks my opinion of the referendum movement. This is an initiative, by Iranians inside the country and outside it, to gather signatures calling for a U.N.-supervised vote on a new Iranian Constitution. One of the recent overseas signatories is Reza Pahlavi, the son of the fallen Shah. Khomeini surprises me even more by speaking warmly of this young man. "I have heard well of him. I would be happy to meet him and to cooperate with him, but on one condition. He must abandon any claim to the throne."

(The opportunity of delivering a message from the grandson of Khomeini to the son of the Shah seemed irresistible, and the first thing I did upon my return to Washington was to seek out Reza Pahlavi, who lives in Maryland, and put the question to him. We actually met in a basement kitchen in the nation's capital, where he was being careful to be as unmonarchical as it is feasible to be. His line on the restoration of kingship is one of "Don't ask, don't tell." He doesn't claim the throne—though he did at one point in our chat refer bizarrely to his father as "my predecessor"—nor does he renounce it. All he will say, and he says it with admirable persistence, is that the next Iran must be both secular and democratic. So, even if they remain at arm's length, it can be said at last that a Khomeini and a Pahlavi agree.)

Iran today exists in a state of dual power and split personality. The huge billboards and murals proclaim it an Islamic republic, under the eternal guidance of the immortal memory of Ayatollah Khomeini. A large force of Revolutionary Guards and a pervasive religious police stand ready to make good on this grim pledge. But directly underneath these forbidding posters and right under the noses of the morals enforcers, Iranians are buying and selling videos, making and consuming alcohol, tuning in to satellite TV stations, producing subversive films and plays and books, and defying the dress code. All women are supposed to cover all their hair at all times, and to wear a long jacket, or manteau, that covers them from neck to knee. But it's amazing how enticing the compulsory scarf can be when worn practically on the back of the head and held in place only by hair spray. As for the obligatory manteau, any woman with any fashion sense can cut it to mold an enviable silhouette. I found a bootlegger on my arrival at Tehran airport and was offered alcohol on principle in every home I entered—Khomeini's excepted—even by people who did not drink. Almost every Iranian has a relative overseas and is in regular touch with foreign news and trends. The country is an "as if" society. People live as if they were free, as if they were in the West, as if they had the right to an opinion, or a private life. And they don't do too badly at it. I have now visited all three of the states that make up the so-called axis of evil. Rough as their regime can certainly be, the citizens of Iran live on a different planet from the wretched, frightened serfs of Saddam Hussein and Kim Jong-il.

Tehran is in fact more or less uncontrollable by anybody. It's the Mexico City or Calcutta of the region: a vast, unplanned, overpopulated nightmare of all-day traffic jams and eye-wringing pollution, tissue-paper building codes, and an earthquake coming like Christmas. It's also the original uptown-downtown city, built on the steep slopes of the snowy Elburz Mountains, which, on a good day, one can sometimes actually see. In the northern quarter, there are the discreet villas where the members of the upper crust keep their heads down and their wealth unostentatious. At the bottom of the hill, you can lose yourself in the vast bazaar, whose tough stall owners were the shock troops of the 1979 revolution. "Beware of north Tehran," one is invariably told. "Don't take its Westernized opinions at face value." So I didn't. Indeed, at one party, where the women by the interior swimming pool didn't have a scarf or a manteau among them, and where the butler handed me a card printed in English that advertised special caviar supplies, and where the bar went on for a furlong, I met a sleek banker who, full of loathing for the regime as he was, defended Iran's right to have nuclear weapons. In fact, his was the most vociferous defense that I heard. (Like all the others who ask so plaintively why Israel and Pakistan can have nukes and not Iran, he temporarily chose to forget that the mullahs keep denying that they have such weapons, or even seek them.)

Never mind Qom, which is an easy four-hour drive. I went as far from the north-Tehran suburbs as I could reasonably be expected to go. In the city of Mashhad, way up toward the Turkmenistan-Afghanistan border, the air is clearer and the traffic lighter. The place wears an aspect of prosperity and contentment, as befits the home of one of the most beautiful buildings in the world. This is the shrine of Imam Reza, the only one of the 12 Shia imams who is actually buried in Iran. The gold dome—not gold-leafed but gold—is at the center of a series of spacious courtyards and squares into which the Iraqi mosques of Karbala and Najaf could both easily fit. The main door is a continuously busy portal for groups of men bearing coffins either inward or outward, since all the devout dead must be taken as near as is feasible to the tomb of Imam Reza himself. I have to slightly muffle my next sentences, to protect some friends, but I had an introduction to a man who was a guardian of this holy place. Presenting myself, I was led wordlessly to what looked like a tapestry on an interior wall. This curtain was drawn aside to reveal an elevator door, and I was then, like some intruding raider of a lost ark, whisked upward. At the top level, I had a heart-stopping perspective on the gold dome: a view that I think few if any infidels have ever shared. I was as near as I could hope to be to an inner sanctum (to use the word properly for once) and also to something that I can only guess about: the pulsing and enduring and patient heart of Shiite Islam. Offered a cushion on the floor, and some tea and segmented oranges, I was, as usual, made more welcome than was easy for me. My host was a very serious man. Not by any means skipping the traditional questions about my health and my journey and my needs, he soon drove to the point. "Do you suppose," he inquired, "that the West will ever come to our aid? Or is it all hypocrisy?" I asked him in return how he would know, or how he would define, success. An invasion? He seemed to think it a fair question and gravely replied, "The minimum would be to have an American Embassy back in Tehran."

This answer might strike you as rather oblique. (Welcome to Iran, in that case.) But it was also admirably straightforward. In September 2002, an editor and columnist in Tehran named Abbas Abdi was among those who helped conduct a Gallup poll that had been commissioned by the foreign-affairs committee of the Iranian Parliament, or Majlis. The finding of the poll was that nearly 75 percent of all Iranians were in favor of "dialogue" at the very least with the United States. The chairman of the relevant Majlis committee was named Mohsen Mirdamadi. Abbas Abdi was imprisoned simply for publishing those findings. Mohsen Mirdamadi has since been disqualified by the mullahs from running again for elected office, and in December 2003 was beaten and clubbed by state-sponsored Hezbollah goons while giving a speech in the provincial city of Yazd. You may not know the names of A.A. or M.M., but you might like to know that both of them were among the student group that vandalized the American Embassy in November 1979 and violated the diplomatic immunity of its staff. And A.A. had probably marked himself for even more trouble with the authorities for having a reconciliation meeting, in Paris in 1998, with his former American hostage Barry Rosen. Both were acting "as if" a decent relationship between the two peoples were already extant.

The Islamic republic actually counts all of its subjects as infants, and all of its bosses as their parents. It is based, in theory and in practice, on a Muslim concept known as *velayat-e faqih*, or "guardianship of the jurist." In its original phrasing, this can mean that the clergy assumes responsibility for orphans, for the insane, and for (aha!) abandoned or untenanted property. Here is the reason Ayatollah Khomeini became world-famous: In a treatise written while he was in exile in Najaf, in Iraq, in 1970, he argued that the *velayat* could and should be extended to the whole of society. A supreme religious authority should act as proxy father for everyone. His own charisma and bravery later convinced many people that Khomeini was entitled to claim the role of supreme leader (*faqih*) for himself.

But the theory has an obvious and lethal flaw, built into itself like a trapdoor. What if some lamebrained mediocrity assumes or inherits the title of supreme leader, with its god-given mantle? You might as well accept the slobbering and gibbering firstborn of some hereditary monarch who claims divine right. For this reason, several ayatollahs in Najaf and Qom and other spiritual centers rejected the Khomeini interpretation as soon as it was proposed. Among other things, they doubted that any human was fit for the post of supreme leader or guardian, at least until the twelfth and last of the Shia imams reveals himself again and concludes the long period of mourning and grief that is everyday human life. And this division between mullahs, dear reader, is why you have to concentrate with breathless interest on the difference between an Iranian-born mullah who lives in Iraq (al-Sistani) and an Iranian mullah who went into exile in Iraq and came home (Khomeini). It is also the reason why several senior Iranian mullahs are in prison or have been in prison under what claims to be an Islamic republic. Get used to learning these names, too, while there is time. Grand Ayatollah Montazeri. Ayatollah Shabestari. These men, and their courageous disciples, say that Khomeini's version of the *velayat* has no Koranic justification. Hence my welcome in that small house in Qom. Hence, also, the present dictatorship by Ayatollah Khamenei: a semi-literate megalomaniac who presumes to regard his subjects as his pupils and his charges.

One almost wishes the "orphan" part of the theory were truer than it is. But Iran's problem is not a surplus of orphans. It is, rather, that the country is afflicted with a vast population of grieving parents and relatives, whose sons and daughters and nephews and nieces were thrown away in the ghastly eight-year war with Saddam Hussein, and who were forced to applaud the evil "human wave" tactics of shady clergymen who promised heaven to the credulous but never cared to risk martyrdom themselves.

The word "martyr," or *shahid*, is another expression that has become cheapened by overuse in Iran. Every ugly building and intersection seems to be named for one, and people are increasingly bored and sickened by the term. Still, I am bound to say that I was struck almost mute by the cemetery to the south of Tehran. I have made visits to the memorials of the Western Front, where headstones and arches bear the names of the unidentified dead of the First World War, and I have also been to the mass graves of Bosnia and Iraq. But this awful necropolis is of a different order. I don't think I met a family in Iran that didn't have a missing or "martyred" or mutilated relative from that era. The total butcher bill for the war was close to a million. Thus, even though the cemetery is placed right next to the hideous memorial to Ayatollah Khomeini (and "why the fuck," said the guard at the subway station when I asked directions, "would you want to go to that bastard's grave?"), I approached it with due respect. The Iranian expression for the war with Iraq is "the imposed war." The odd phrasing reflects the belief that Saddam Hussein was an ally of the West when he launched his aggression, and this time I knew that there was more truth than propaganda to the accusation. (Iranian physicians are the world's experts in treating those whose lungs have been corroded by poison gas, or whose skin has been agonizingly scalded by chemical bombardment. They have whole hospitals full of ruined patients.)

Despite the terrifying culling of its youth in the 1980s, Iran is once again a young country. Indeed, more than half of its population is under twenty-five. The mullahs, in an effort to make up the war deficit, provided large material incentives for women to bear great numbers of children. The consequence of this is a vast layer of frustrated young people who generally detest the clerics. You might call it a baby-boomerang. I am thinking of Jamshid, a clever young hustler whom I part-employed as a driver and fixer. Bright but only partially educated, energetic but effectively unemployed, he had been made to waste a lot of his time on compulsory military service and was continuing to waste time until he could think of a way of quitting the country. "When I was a baby, my mother took me to have my head patted by Khomeini. My fucking hair has been falling out ever since," he said. You want crack cocaine, hookers, pornography, hooch? This is the downside of the "as if" option. There are thousands of even younger Jamshids lining the polluted boulevards and intersections, trafficking in everything known to man and paying off the riffraff of the morals police. Everybody knows that the mullahs live in luxury, stash money overseas, deny themselves nothing, and indulge in the most blatant hypocrisy. Cynicism about the clergy is universal, but it is especially among the young that one encounters it. It's also among the young that one most often hears calls for American troops to arrive and bring goodies with them. Yet, after a while, this repeated note began to strike me as childish also. It's a confession of powerlessness, an avoidance of responsibility, a demand that change come from somewhere else.

A whole range of sincere Shia believers, from Grand Ayatollah Montazeri to the relatively lesser clerics such as the junior Khomeini, worry about this because they know that a whole generation is being alienated from religion. But I don't think the regime much cares that so many of its talented young people have left or are leaving. The Iranian diaspora now runs into millions, from California to Canada and all across Western Europe. Let the smart ones go: all the easier for us to run a stultified and stalled society. And every now and then they make a move to show who is in charge. Last August, in the city of Neka, a sixteen-year-old girl named Atefeh Rajabi was hauled into a court for having had sex with a man. She might possibly have gotten away with one of the lesser punishments for offenses against chastity, such as a hundred lashes with a whip. (That's what her partner received.) But from the dock she protested that she had been the object of advances from an older man, and she went as far as to tear off her *hijab*, or headscarf. The judge announced that she would hang for that, and that he would personally place the noose around her neck. And so, in the main square of Neka, after the Iranian Supreme Court had duly confirmed the ruling, poor Miss Rajabi was hanged from a crane for all to see.

Every now and then you can sit in on late-night discussions where young people wonder when the eruption will come. Perhaps the police or the Revolutionary Guards will make an irrevocable mistake and fire into a crowd? Perhaps, at a given hour, a million women will simply remove their *hijabs* and defy the authorities? (This discussion gets more intense every year as the summer approaches and women face the irritation and humiliation of wearing it in heat and dust.) But nobody wants to be the first to be blinded by acid, or to have their face lovingly slashed by some Hezbollah enthusiast. The student activists of the Tehran "spring" of 1999, and of the elections which seemed to bring a reformist promise, have been picked off one by one, their papers closed and their leadership jailed and beaten. What else to do, then, except tune in to the new Iranian underground "grunge" scene, or kick back in front of the Italian soft-porn channel or one of the sports and fashion and anti-clerical channels beamed in by satellite from exiles in Los Angeles? As if...

For what was Persian culture famous? For poetry, for philosophy, for backgammon, for chess, for architecture, for polo, for gardens, and for wine. (The southern city of Shiraz, once a vineyard town, may have a better claim to the invention of sherry than the Spanish city of Jerez.) The special figure of all this ancient civilization was Omar Khayyám, whose name means "maker of tents" but who flourished as a scholar and poet in the city of Neyshabur in the eleventh and twelth centuries. He is best known for his long, languorous poem *Rubáiyát*: a collection of quatrains, exquisitely rendered into English by Edward FitzGerald, among others. Khayyám was an astronomer and mathematician and was among those commissioned to reform the calendar. In his four-line stanzas, he praised wine, women, and song, found speculation on afterlife pointless, and ridiculed the mullahs of his day. He lived and wrote "as if" they didn't count. I made a special journey to Neyshabur to see the tomb of this man, who had somewhat cheered up my boyhood. The study of his poetry is not exactly encouraged by members of the theocracy, but they know better than to denounce anything that touches on national pride, and you can visit the site without hindrance. My escort, a quiet man who was slow to commit himself, could quote several quatrains in Farsi, and I was delighted to hear that they sounded exactly the same way as their rhythm fell on an English ear. As we compared notes and recitations, he began to melt a little and accepted a swig from my bootleg flask, and soon I was hearing a familiar story: no prospects, a depraved government, the school friends thrown away in hysterical warfare.

The museum of Omar Khayyám stands a little way from the tomb and contains some beautiful scientific instruments, including an intricate astrolabe, from medieval times. At last, a public place that was not dominated by black-draped and forbidding superstition, and that cared for learning and for reason. Deciding to make a stab at the visitors' book, I wrote out my favorite quatrain, from the Richard Le Gallienne translation, in which the poet speaks of the arrogance of the faithful:

And do you think that unto such as you
A maggot-minded, starved, fanatic crew
God gave a secret, and denied it me—
Well, well, what matters it? Believe that too.

A few visitors did look over my shoulder, but nobody seemed to mind.

Mashhad and Neyshabur are supremely worth seeing, and also well worth going to see, but nobody can claim to have tasted Iran without having seen Esfahan. It is well inland, so idle comparisons with Venice or Dubrovnik don't quite work. It is small and modest, so it is not Rome or Prague either. It is a thing unto itself: an imposing miniature and a miracle of proportion. Many fine bridges span its river, one with thirty-three arches in which slits have been carved through three walls. When you stand back and view them from the right angle, they give the perfect outline of a candle, while allowing you to see through to the other side. This miracle of perspective—such ingenuity for such a slight but pleasing effect—is seconded, if you like, by the tower which will convey the merest whisper from one stone corner to another. As for the symmetry of the azure Sheikh Lotfollah mosque on the grand but modest main square: The masons and decorators must have finished the job quite speechless with what they had achieved.

It is a few miles from this triumph of civilization and culture that the Islamic republic, hostile to every form of modernity except advanced weapons and surveillance techniques, has decided to dig a huge, ugly tunnel into a hillside, the better to conceal its ambitions to become a nuclear state. The tunnel, along with some other "facilities" at Natanz and Bushehr, has been laboriously exposed in the course of a long, dreary inspection that has caught the regime lying without conscience, and also lying without fear of reprisal. The Bushehr reactor was actually begun in the time of the Shah, and it's a good thing that he slightly outlived his mad kingly ambitions, because if he'd completed the work then the mullahs would have inherited a nuclear capacity ready-made.

And it is unlikely that sanctions will be lifted while the regime also continues to harbor so many wanted criminals, not just on its territory but among its leadership. Consider the repellent figure of Ali Fallahian, a former minister of "intelligence," who faces an arrest warrant from a court in

Berlin for sending a death squad to murder Iranian Kurds in the Mykonos restaurant in 1992. We also have the names of those Iranian officials who are wanted for blowing up a Jewish community center in Buenos Aires in 1994 and the Khobar Towers housing complex in Saudi Arabia in 1996.

All of these crimes were committed, without conscience and (so far) without reprisal, during the presidency of Ali Akbar Hashemi Rafsanjani, who was also the local star of the Iran-Contra arms-for-hostages racket, the last time that an Iranian connection threatened to bring down an American president.

On the first occasion when I managed to breathe the same air as Rafsanjani, he was addressing a conference of Iranian women, who were made to sit swaddled in heavy clothing while he took his sweet time making some tedious observations about females and the Koran. One of the women's magazines in Tehran is run by his daughter, but then, there is hardly an enterprise in the country, from the pistachio-nut monopoly to airlines and oil, in which Rafsanjani doesn't hold an interest. The second time I was able to drink in his words was at "Friday prayers" at the university, the weekly grandstand from which the mullahs address the masses.

On this occasion, Rafsanjani was bursting with sound and fury and insult about imperialist threats to Iran, and swelling like a turkey-cock. (He's a short guy, and is regularly lampooned on the street for his inability to grow a proper beard. In 2002, the last time he ran for election in Tehran, he came in below the bottom of the already fixed "list," and some deft work was required to show him registering in the poll at all.) Demagogy aside, everybody knows that if a deal is to be done with Europe and the Americans, then it will probably be Rafsanjani who brokers it. He's been on both sides of everything, all of his life, through war and revolution. He supported Khomeini in prolonging the war with Iraq, and then persuaded him to accept the U.N. resolution that ended it (and that may have killed the older man). He railed against the Great Satan, yet welcomed Reagan's shamed envoys when they brought the cake and the Bible and offered to deal arms for hostages. He's what our lazy press means when it describes some opportunist torturer and murderer as a "moderate," or a "survivor." I even met Iranians, completely sickened and disillusioned and ready to boycott any sham vote, who wearily said that Rafsanjani would be an improvement.

In Esfahan I met a woman, one of the few I saw who wore the whole black chador. She was devout, and she listened for a long time while the family who hosted me exhausted all its frustration and argued about the best way of overthrowing or outliving the mullahs. After a pause, she broke in softly, even wistfully. "Do you think," she inquired, "that the West could come here and remove the rulers but only stay for a week and then leave?" I put out my hand reflexively, not to take her palm but just to touch it, as if to reassure her that what she said was not childish or naïve. As if... And if only. And now I know that, until this is over, and until Iran recovers some of its Persian soul, I will never be able to see her, or Esfahan, again. Meanwhile, the trunk of the tree of the country simply rots, and millions of lives are being lived pointlessly while the state of suspended animation persists.

(*Vanity Fair*, July 2005)

Long Live Democratic Seismology

IN HIS DAYS on the staid old *London Times* of the 1930s, Claud Cockburn won an in-house competition for the most boring headline by coming up with "Small Earthquake in Chile: Not Many Dead." The shelf-life of this joke—which, I hasten to add, was at the expense of the *Times*, not the people of Chile—was so durable that when the anti-Allende and pro-Kissinger historian Alistair Horne came to write his book on the Unidad Popular government of the 1970s, he called it *Small Earthquake in Chile*. At approximately the same time, composing his memorable epitaph for Salvador Allende, Gabriel García Márquez spoke of the likable peculiarities of the Chileans and exaggerated his non-magical realism by only a few degrees when he said:

> Chile has an earth tremor on the average of once every two days and a devastating earthquake every presidential term. The least apocalyptic of geologists think of Chile not as a country of the mainland, but as a cornice of the Andes in a misty sea, and believe that the whole of its national territory is condemned to disappear in some future cataclysm.

Seismology in this decade is already emerging as the most important new department of socioeconomics and politics. The simple recognition that nature is master and that the crust of our planet is highly volatile has been thrown into some relief by the staggering 250,000 butcher's bill exacted from the people of Haiti by a single terrestrial spasm, and by the relative survival capacity of Chileans even when hit by a quake of superior magnitude. Gone are the boring-headlined stories about the magnitude of the quake and the likely epicenter. The effects of upheavals of the earth can now be quite expertly studied, and even predicted, along a series of intersecting graphs that measure them against demography, income level, and—this is a prediction on my part—the vitality of democratic institutions.

Professor Amartya Sen made a reputation some decades ago for pointing out that in the twentieth century no serious famine had occurred in an open or democratic society, however poor. In the classic case that he studied—that of Bengal under British colonial occupation in the 1940s—tens of thousands of people had starved to death in areas that had overflowing granaries. It was not a shortage of food, but of information and of proper administration, that had led to the disaster. The Ukrainian famine of the 1930s, as was pointed out by Robert Conquest in his book *The Harvest of Sorrow*, was the result of a dictatorial policy rather than any failure of the crops.

Taking this as an approximate analogy or metaphor, people are beginning to notice that the likelihood of perishing in an earthquake, or of being utterly dispossessed by it, is as much a function of the society in which one lives as it is of proximity to a fault. A most intriguing article in the *New York Times* of February 24, titled "Disaster Awaits Cities in Earthquake Zones," pointed out that millions of people now live in unplanned and jerry-built mega-cities—such as Istanbul, Turkey; Karachi, Pakistan; Katmandu, Nepal; and Lima, Peru—that are earthquake-prone and could easily become the sites of mass extermination. The instruments of this would be what Dr. Roger Bilham, a seismologist at the University of Colorado, calls "an unrecognized weapon of mass destruction: houses." Across the world, millions of people either live or work in structures that have been termed "rubble in waiting."

The article told the story of increasing efforts by Turkish and Chinese authorities to "proof" their cities against future disasters. Turkey and China, while by no means perfect examples of democracy and transparency, have become much more responsive to popular awareness and protest in the recent past. Chileans have long expected their government to be prepared for seismic events, while Haitians are so ground-down and immiserated by repression and corruption that a democratic demand for such protection would seem an almost ethereal prospect.

This general point was specified in a dramatic way by a sentence buried in the middle of the *Times* article: "In Tehran, Iran's capital, Dr. Bilham has calculated that *one million* people could die in a predicted quake similar in intensity to the one in Haiti." (Italics added.) Tehran is built in "a nest of surrounding geologic faults," and geologists there have long besought the government to consider moving the unprotected and crumbling capital, or at least some of its people, in anticipation of the inevitable disaster.

But the Iranian regime, as we know, has other priorities entirely, and it has worked very hard to insulate not its people from earthquakes, but itself from its people. I remember sitting in one of Tehran's epic traffic snarls a few years ago and thinking, "What if a big one was to hit now?" This horrible thought was succeeded by two even more disturbing ones: What if the giant shudder came at night, when citizens were packed tightly into unregulated and code-free apartment buildings? And what would happen to the secret nuclear facilities, both under the ground and above it? I know what the mullahs would say—that the will of Allah was immutable. But what would the survivors think when they looked around the (possibly irradiated) ruins and saw how disposable their leaders had considered them to be?

This outcome would be incomparably worse than the consequences of any intervention to arrest the Iranian nuclear program. I have droned on about this before, and I now drone on again. While the "negotiations" on Iran's weaponry are being artificially protracted by an irrational and corrupt regime, it should become part of our humanitarianism and our public diplomacy to warn the Iranian people of the man-made reasons that the results of a natural calamity would be hideously multiplied in their case. This, together with the offer of immediate help in earthquake-proofing, enhanced from our experiences in California, is nothing less than a moral responsibility. Together with the cross-border implications of an earthquake plus ill-maintained covert nuclear facilities, it also drives home the point that the future of Iran is not the "internal affair" of a regime that dreams luridly of one apocalypse while inviting a cataclysm of a quite different sort. Down with the earthquake deniers! Long live democratic seismology!

(*Slate*, March 1, 2010)

Benazir Bhutto: Daughter of Destiny

THE STERNEST CRITIC of Benazir Bhutto would not have been able to deny that she possessed an extraordinary degree of physical courage. When her father was lying in prison under sentence of death from Pakistan's military dictatorship in 1979, and other members of her family were trying to escape the country, she boldly flew back in. Her subsequent confrontation with the brutal General Zia-ul-Haq cost her five years of her life, spent in prison. She seemed merely to disdain the experience, as she did the vicious little man who had inflicted it upon her.

Benazir saw one of her brothers, Shahnawaz, die in mysterious circumstances in the south of France in 1985, and the other, Mir Murtaza, shot down outside the family home in Karachi by uniformed police in 1996. It was at that famous address—70 Clifton Road—that I went to meet her in November 1988, on the last night of the election campaign, and I found out firsthand how brave she was. Taking the wheel of a jeep and scorning all bodyguards, she set off with me on a hair-raising tour of the Karachi slums. Every now and then, she would get out, climb on the roof of the jeep with a bullhorn, and harangue the mob that pressed in close enough to turn the vehicle over. On the following day, her Pakistan Peoples Party won in a landslide, making her, at the age of thirty-five, the first woman to be elected the leader of a Muslim country.

Her tenure ended—as did her subsequent "comeback" tenure—in a sorry welter of corruption charges and political intrigue, and in a gilded exile in Dubai. But clearly she understood that exile would be its own form of political death. (She speaks well on this point in an excellent recent profile by Amy Wilentz in *More* magazine.) Like two other leading Asian politicians, Benigno Aquino of the Philippines and Kim Dae-jung of South Korea, she seems to have decided that it was essential to run the risk of returning home. And now she has gone, as she must have known she might, the way of Aquino.

Who knows who did this deed? It is grotesque, of course, that the murder should have occurred in Rawalpindi, the garrison town of the Pakistani military elite and the site of Flashman's Hotel. It is as if she had been slain on a visit to West Point or Quantico. But it's hard to construct any *cui bono*–analysis on which General Pervez Musharraf is the beneficiary of her death. The likeliest culprit is the al-Qaeda/Taliban axis, perhaps with some assistance from its many covert and not-so-covert sympathizers in the Pakistani Inter-Services Intelligence. These were the people at whom she had been pointing the finger since the huge bomb that devastated her welcome-home motorcade on October 18.

She would have been in a good position to know about this connection, because when she was prime minister, she pursued a very active pro-Taliban policy, designed to extend and entrench Pakistani control over Afghanistan and to give Pakistan strategic depth in its long confrontation with India over Kashmir. The fact of the matter is that Benazir's undoubted courage had a certain fanaticism to it. She had the largest Electra complex of any female politician in modern history, entirely consecrated to the memory of her executed father, the charming and unscrupulous Zulfikar Ali Bhutto, who had once boasted that the people of Pakistan would eat grass before they would give up the struggle to acquire a nuclear weapon. (He was rather prescient there—the country now does have nukes, and millions of its inhabitants can barely feed themselves.) A nominal socialist, Zulfikar Bhutto was an autocratic opportunist, and this family tradition was carried on by the PPP, a supposedly populist party that never had a genuine internal election and was in fact—like quite a lot else in Pakistan—Bhutto family property.

Daughter of Destiny is the title she gave to her autobiography. She always displayed the same unironic lack of embarrassment. How prettily she lied to me, I remember, and with such a level gaze from those topaz eyes, about how exclusively peaceful and civilian Pakistan's nuclear program was. How righteously indignant she always sounded when asked unwelcome questions about the vast corruption alleged against her and her playboy husband, Asif Ali Zardari. (The Swiss courts recently found against her in this matter; an excellent background piece was written by John Burns in the *New York Times* in 1998.) And now the two main legacies of Bhutto rule—the nukes and the empowered Islamists—have moved measurably closer together.

This is what makes her murder such a disaster. There is at least some reason to think that she had truly changed her mind, at least on the Taliban and al-Qaeda, and was willing to help lead a battle against them. She had, according to some reports, severed the connection with her rather questionable husband. She was attempting to make the connection between lack of democracy in Pakistan and the rise of mullah-manipulated fanaticism. Of those preparing to contest the highly dubious upcoming elections, she was the only candidate with anything approaching a mass appeal to set against the siren calls of the fundamentalists. And, right to the end, she carried on without the fetish of "security" and with lofty disregard for her own safety. This courage could sometimes have been worthy of a finer cause, and many of the problems she claimed to solve were partly of her own making. Nonetheless, she perhaps did have a hint of destiny about her.

(*Slate*, December 27, 2007)

From Abbottabad to Worse

SALMAN RUSHDIE'S UPSETTINGLY BRILLIANT psychoprofile of Pakistan, in his 1983 novel, *Shame,* rightly laid emphasis on the crucial part played by sexual repression in the Islamic republic. And that was *before* the Talibanization of Afghanistan, and of much of Pakistan, too. Let me try to summarize and update the situation like this: Here is a society where rape is not a crime. It is a *punishment.* Women can be *sentenced* to be raped, by tribal and religious kangaroo courts, if even a rumor of their immodesty brings shame on their menfolk. In such an obscenely distorted context, the counterpart term to shame—which is the noble word "honor"—becomes most commonly associated with the word "killing." Moral courage consists of the willingness to butcher your own daughter.

If the most elemental of human instincts becomes warped in this bizarre manner, other morbid symptoms will disclose themselves as well. Thus, President Asif Ali Zardari cringes daily in front of the forces who openly murdered his wife, Benazir Bhutto, and who then contemptuously ordered the crime scene cleansed with fire hoses, as if to spit even on the pretense of an investigation. A man so lacking in pride—indeed, lacking in manliness—will seek desperately to compensate in other ways. Swelling his puny chest even more, he promises to resist the mighty United States, and to defend Pakistan's holy "sovereignty." This puffery and posing might perhaps possess a rag of credibility if he and his fellow middlemen were not avidly ingesting $3 billion worth of American subsidies every year.

There's absolutely no mystery to the "Why do they hate us?" question, at least as it arises in Pakistan. They hate us because they owe us, and are dependent upon us. The two main symbols of Pakistan's pride—its army and its nuclear program—are wholly parasitic on American indulgence and patronage. But, as I wrote for *Vanity Fair* in late 2001, in a long report from this degraded country, that army and those nukes are intended to be reserved for war against the neighboring democracy of India. Our bought-and-paid-for pretense that they have any other true purpose has led to a rancid, resentful official hypocrisy, and to a state policy of revenge, large and petty, on the big, rich, dumb Americans who foot the bill. If Pakistan were a character, it would resemble the one described by Alexander Pope in his *Epistle to Dr. Arbuthnot:*

> Willing to wound, and yet afraid to strike.
> Just hint a fault, and hesitate dislike:
> Alike reserved to blame, or to commend,
> A timorous foe, and a suspicious friend...
> So well-bred Spaniels civilly delight
> In mumbling of the game they dare not bite.

There's an old cliché in client-state relations, about the tail wagging the dog, but have we really considered what it means when we actually are the *tail,* and the dog is our goddam lapdog? The lapdog's surreptitious revenge has consisted in the provision of kennels for attack dogs. Everybody knew that the Taliban was originally an instrument for Pakistani colonization of Afghanistan. Everybody knew that al-Qaeda forces were being sheltered in the Pakistani frontier town of Quetta, and that Khalid Sheikh Muhammed was found hiding in Rawalpindi, the headquarters of the Pakistani Army. Bernard-Henri Lévy once even produced a damning time line showing that every Pakistani "capture" of a wanted *jihad*-ist had occurred the week immediately preceding a vote in Congress on subventions to the government in Islamabad. But not even I was cynical enough to believe that Osama bin Laden himself would be given a villa in a Pakistani garrison town on Islamabad's periphery. I quote below from a letter written by my Pakistani friend Irfan Khawaja, a teacher of philosophy at Felician College, in New Jersey. He sent it to me in anguish just after bin Laden, who claimed to love death more than life, had met his presumably desired rendezvous:

> I find, however, that I can't quite share in the sense of jubilation. I never believed that bin Laden was living in some hideaway "in the tribal areas." But to learn that he was living in Abbottabad, after Khalid Sheikh Muhammed was discovered in Rawalpindi, is really too much for me. I don't feel jubilation. I feel a personal, ineradicable sense of betrayal. For ten years, I've watched members of my own family taking to the streets, protesting the U.S. military presence in northern Pakistan and the drone strikes etc. They stood there and prattled on and on about "Pakistan's sovereignty," and the supposed invasion of it by U.S. forces.
>
> Well, what fucking sovereignty? What fucking sovereignty were these people "protecting"? It's bad enough that the Pakistani army lacks sovereignty over the tribal area and can't control it when the country's own life depends upon it. But that bin Laden was living in the Pakistani equivalent of Annapolis, MD...

You will notice that Irfan is here registering genuine shame, in the sense of proper outrage and personal embarrassment, and not some vicarious parody of emotion where it is always others—usually powerless women—who are supposedly bringing the shame on you.

If the Pakistani authorities had admitted what they were doing, and claimed the right to offer safe haven to al-Qaeda and the Taliban on their own soil, then the boast of "sovereignty" might at least have had some grotesque validity to it. But they were too cowardly and duplicitous for that. And they also wanted to be paid, lavishly and regularly, for pretending to fight against those very forces. Has any state ever been, in the strict sense of the term, more shameless? Over the years, I have written many pages about the sick relationship between the United States and various Third World client regimes, many of which turned out to be false friends as well as highly discreditable ones. General Pinochet, of Chile, had the unbelievable nerve to explode a car bomb in rush-hour traffic in Washington, D.C., in 1976, murdering a political rival and his American colleague. The South Vietnamese military junta made a private deal to sabotage the Paris peace talks in 1968, in order to benefit the electoral chances of Richard Nixon. Dirty money from the Shah of Iran and the Greek dictatorship made its way at different times into our electoral process. Israeli religious extremists demand American protection and then denounce us for "interference" if we demur politely about colonization of the West Bank. But our blatant manipulation by Pakistan is the most diseased and rotten thing in which the United States has ever involved itself. And it is also, in the grossest way, a violation of our sovereignty. Pakistan routinely—by the dispatch of barely deniable death squads across its borders, to such locations as the Taj Hotel in Mumbai—injures the sovereignty of India as well as Afghanistan. But you might call that a traditional form of violation. In our case, Pakistan ingratiatingly and silkily invites young Americans to one of the vilest and most dangerous regions on earth, there to fight and die as its allies, all the while sharpening a blade for their backs. "The smiler with the knife under the cloak," as Chaucer phrased it so frigidly. (At our feet, and at our throat: Perfectly symbolic of the underhanded duality between the mercenary and the sycophant was the decision of the Pakistani intelligence services, in revenge for the Abbottabad raid, to disclose the name of the CIA station chief in Islamabad.)

This is well beyond humiliation. It makes us a prisoner of the shame, and co-responsible for it. The United States was shamed when it became the Cold War armorer of the Ayub Khan dictatorship in the 1950s and 1960s. It was shamed even more when it supported General Yahya Khan's mass murder in Bangladesh in 1971: a Muslim-on-Muslim genocide that crashingly demonstrated the utter failure of a state based on a single religion. We were then played for suckers by yet another military boss in the form of General Ziaul-Haq, who leveraged anti-Communism in Afghanistan into a free pass for the acquisition of nuclear weapons and the open mockery of the nonproliferation treaty. By the start of the millennium, Pakistan had become home to a Wal-Mart of fissile material, traded as far away as Libya and North Korea by the state-subsidized nuclear entrepreneur A. Q. Khan, the country's nearest approach (which in itself tells you something) to a national hero. Among the scientists working on the project were three named sympathizers of the Taliban. And that gigantic betrayal, too, was uncovered only by chance.

Again to quote myself from 2001, if Pakistan were a person, he (and it would have to be a he) would have to be completely humorless, paranoid, insecure, eager to take offense, and suffering from self-righteousness, self-pity, and self-hatred. That last triptych of vices is intimately connected. The self-righteousness comes from the claim to represent a religion: The very name "Pakistan" is an acronym of Punjab, Afghanistan, Kashmir, and so forth, the resulting word in the Urdu language meaning "Land of the Pure." The self-pity derives from the sad fact that the country has almost nothing else to be proud of: virtually barren of achievements and historically based on the amputation and mutilation of India in 1947 and its own self-mutilation in Bangladesh. The self-hatred is the consequence of being pathetically, permanently mendicant: an abject begging-bowl country that is nonetheless run by a super-rich and hyper-corrupt Punjabi elite. As for paranoia: This not so hypothetical Pakistani would also be a hardened anti-Semite, moaning with pleasure at the butchery of Daniel Pearl and addicted to blaming his self-inflicted woes on the all-powerful Jews.

This dreary story actually does have some bearing on the "sovereignty" issue. In the beginning, all that the Muslim League demanded from the British was "a state for Muslims." Pakistan's founder and first president, Muhammad Ali Jinnah, was a relatively secular man whose younger sister went around unveiled and whose second wife did not practice Islam at all. But there's a world of difference between a state for Muslims and a full-on Muslim state. Under the rule of General Zia there began to be imposition of sharia and increased persecution of non-Muslims as well as of Muslim minorities such as the Shiites, Ismailis, and Ahmadis. In recent years these theocratic tendencies have intensified with appalling speed, to the point where the state contains not one but two secret statelets within itself: the first an impenetrable enclave of covert nuclear command and control and the second a private nexus of power at the disposal of the military intelligence services and—until recently—Osama bin Laden himself. It's the sovereignty of *these* possessions that exercises General Ashfaq Kayani, head of the Pakistani Army, who five days after Abbottabad made the arrogant demand that the number of American forces in the country be reduced "to the minimum essential." He even said that any similar American action ought to warrant a "review" of the whole relationship between the two countries. How pitiful it is that a Pakistani and not an American should have been the first (and so far the only) leader to say those necessary things.

If we ever ceased to swallow our pride, so I am incessantly told in Washington, then the Pakistani oligarchy might behave even more abysmally than it already does, and the situation deteriorate even further. This stale and superficial argument ignores the awful historical fact that, each time the Pakistani leadership *did* get worse, or behave worse, it was handsomely rewarded by the United States. We have been the enablers of every stage of that wretched state's counter-evolution, to the point where it is a serious regional menace and an undisguised ally of our worst enemy, as well as the sworn enemy of some of our best allies. How could it be "worse" if we shifted our alliance and instead embraced India, our only rival in scale as a multi-ethnic and multi-religious democracy, and a nation that contains nearly as many Muslims as Pakistan? How could it be "worse" if we listened to the brave Afghans, like their former intelligence chief Amrullah Saleh, who have been telling us for years that we are fighting the war in the wrong country?

If we continue to deny or avoid this inescapable fact, then we really are dishonoring, as well as further endangering, our exemplary young volunteers. Why was the raid on Abbottabad so rightly called "daring"? Because it had to be conducted under the radar of the Pakistani Air Force, which "scrambled" its jets and would have brought the Black Hawks down if it could. That this is true is bad enough in all conscience. That we should still be submitting ourselves to lectures and admonitions from General Kayani is beyond shameful.

(*Vanity Fair*, July 2011)

The Perils of Partition

THE PUBLIC, or "political," poems of W. H. Auden, which stretch from his beautiful elegy for Spain and his imperishable reflections on September 1939 and conclude with a magnificent eight-line snarl about the Soviet assault on Czechoslovakia in 1968, are usually considered with only scant reference to his verses about the shameful end of empire in 1947. Edward Mendelson's otherwise meticulous and sensitive biography allots one sentence to Auden's "Partition."

> Unbiased at least he was when he arrived on his mission,
> Having never set eyes on this land he was called to partition
> Between two peoples fanatically at odds,
> With their different diets and incompatible gods.
> "Time," they had briefed him in London, "is short. It's too late
> For mutual reconciliation or rational debate:
> The only solution now lies in separation..."

Dutifully pulling open my *New York Times* one day last December, I saw that most of page three was given over to an article on a possible solution to the Cyprus "problem." The physical division of this tiny Mediterranean island has become a migraine simultaneously for the European Union (which cannot well allow the abridgment of free movement of people and capital within the borders of a potential member state), for NATO (which would look distinctly foolish if it underwent a huge expansion only to see two of its early members, Greece and Turkey, go to war), for the United Nations (whose own blue-helmeted soldiery has "mediated" the Cyprus dispute since 1964), and for the United States (which is the senior partner and chief armorer of Greece and Turkey, and which would prefer them to concentrate on other, more pressing regional matters).

Flipping through the rest of the press that day, I found the usual references to the Israeli-Palestinian quarrel, to the state of near war between India and Pakistan (and the state of actual if proxy war that obtains between them in the province of Kashmir), and to the febrile conditions that underlie the truce between Loyalists and Republicans—or "Protestants" and "Catholics"—in Northern Ireland. Casting aside the papers and switching on my e-mail, I received further bulletins from specialist Web sites that monitor the precarious state of affairs along the border between Iraq and Kuwait, between the hostile factions in Sri Lanka, and even among the citizens of Hong Kong, who were anxiously debating a further attempt by Beijing to bring the former colony under closer control.

There wasn't much happening that day to call a reader's attention to the Falkland Islands, to the resentment between Guatemala and Belize, to the internal quarrels and collapses in Somalia and Eritrea, or to the parlous state of the kingdom of Jordan. However, there was some news concerning the defiance of the citizens of Gibraltar, who had embarrassed their patron or parent British government by in effect refusing the very idea of negotiations with Spain on the future of their tiny and enclaved territory. I have saved the word "British" for as long as I decently can.

In the modern world the "fault lines" and "flash points" of journalistic shorthand are astonishingly often the consequence of frontiers created ad hoc by British imperialism. In her own 1959 poem Marya Mannes wrote,

> Borders are scratched across the hearts of men
> By strangers with a calm, judicial pen,
> And when the borders bleed we watch with dread
> The lines of ink across the map turn red.

Her somewhat trite sanguinary image is considerably modified when one remembers that most of the lines or gashes would not have been there if the map hadn't been colored red in the first place. No sooner had the wider world discovered the Pashtun question, after September 11, 2001, than it became both natural and urgent to inquire why the Pashtun people appeared to live half in Afghanistan and half in Pakistan. Sir Henry Mortimer Durand had decreed so in 1893 with an imperious gesture, and his arbitrary demarcation is still known as the Durand Line. Sir Mark Sykes (with his French counterpart, Georges Picot) in 1916 concocted an apportionment of the Middle East that would separate Lebanon from Syria and Palestine from Jordan. Sir Percy Cox in 1922 fatefully determined that a portion of what had hitherto been notionally Iraqi territory would henceforth be known as Kuwait. The English half spy and half archaeologist Gertrude Bell in her letters described walking through the desert sands after the First World War, tracing the new boundary of Iraq and Saudi Arabia with her walking stick. The congested, hypertense crossing point of the River Jordan, between Jordan "proper" and the Israeli-held West Bank, is to this day known as the Allenby Bridge, after T. E. Lawrence's commander. And it fell to Sir Cyril Radcliffe to fix the frontiers of India and Pakistan—or, rather, to carve a Pakistani state out of what had formerly been known as India. Auden again:

> The Viceroy thinks, as you will see from his letter,
> That the less you are seen in his company the better,
> So we've arranged to provide you with other accommodation.
> We can give you four judges, two Moslem and two Hindu,
> To consult with, but the final decision must rest with you.

Probably the best-known literary account of this grand historic irony is *Midnight's Children*, the panoptic novel that introduced Salman Rushdie to a global audience. One should never employ the word "irony" cheaply. But the subcontinent attained self-government, and also suffered a deep and lasting wound, at precisely the moment that separated August 14 and 15 of 1947. Rushdie's conceit—of a nation as a child simultaneously born, disputed, and sundered—has Solomonic roots. Parturition and partition become almost synonymous. Was partition the price of independence, or was independence the price of partition?

It is this question, I believe, that lends the issue its enduring and agonizing fascination. Many important nations achieved their liberation, if we agree to use the terminology of the post–Woodrow Wilson era (or their statehood, to put it more neutrally), on what one might call gunpoint conditions. Thus the Irish, who were the first since 1776 to break out of the British Empire, were told in 1921 that they could have an independent state or a united state but not both. A few years earlier Arthur Balfour had made a declaration concerning Palestine that in effect promised its territory to two competing nationalities. In 1960 the British government informed the people of Cyprus that they must accept a conditional post-colonial independence or face an outright division of their island between Greece and Turkey (not, it is worth emphasizing, between the indigenous Greek and Turkish Cypriots). They sullenly signed the treaty, handing over a chunk of Cyprus to permanent and sovereign British bases, which made it a potentially tripartite partition but also inscribed all the future intercommunal misery in one instrument: a treaty to which no party had acceded in good faith.

But it seemed to be enough, at the time, to cover an inglorious British retreat. And here another irony forces itself upon us. The whole ostensible plan behind empire was long-term, and centripetal. From the eighteenth to the twentieth century the British sent out lawyers, architects, designers, doctors, and civil servants, not merely to help collect the revenues of exploitation but to embark on nation-building. Yet at the moment of crux it was suddenly remembered that the proud and patient mother country had more urgent business at home. To complete the Auden version:

> Shut up in a lonely mansion, with police night and day
> Patrolling the gardens to keep the assassins away,
> He got down to work, to the task of settling the fate
> Of millions. The maps at his disposal were out of date
> And the Census Returns almost certainly incorrect,
> But there was no time to check them, no time to inspect.

The true term for this is "betrayal," as Auden so strongly suggests, because the only thinkable justification for the occupation of someone else's territory and the displacement of someone else's culture is the testable, honorable intention of applying an impartial justice, a disinterested administration, and an even hand as regards bandits and sectarians. In the absence of such ambitions, or the resolve to complete them, the British would have done better to stay on their fog-girt island and not make such high-toned claims for themselves. The peoples of India would have found their own way, without tutelage and on a different timetable. Yet Marx and Mill and Macaulay, in their different fashions, felt that the encounter between England and India was fertile and dynamic and revolutionary, and now we have an entire Anglo-Indian literature and cuisine and social fusion that seem to testify to the point. (Rushdie prefers the phrase "Indo-Anglian," to express the tremendous influence of the English language on Indian authorship, and who would want to argue? There may well be almost as many adult speakers of English in India as there are in the United Kingdom, and at the upper and even middle levels they seem to speak and write it rather better.)

The element of tragedy here is arguably implicit in the whole imperial project. Even since Rome conquered and partitioned Gaul, the best-known colonial precept has been *divide et impera*—"divide and rule." Yet after the initial subjugation the name of the task soon becomes the more soothing "civilizing mission," and a high value is placed on lofty, balanced, unifying administration. Later comes the point at which the colonized outgrow the rule of the remote and chilly exploiters, and then it will often be found convenient for the governor or the district commissioner to play upon the tribal or confessional differences among his subjects. From proclaiming that withdrawal, let alone partition, is the very last thing they will do, the colonial authorities move to ensure that these are the very last things they do do. The contradiction is perfectly captured in the memoir of the marvelously named Sir Penderel Moon, one of the last British administrators in India, who mordantly titled his book *Divide and Quit*.

The events he records occurred beyond half a century ago. But in the more immediate past it was Lords Carrington and Owen—both senior graduates of the British Foreign Office—who advanced the ethnic cantonization of Bosnia-Herzegovina. It was Lord Carrington who (just before Nelson

Mandela was released from prison) proposed that South Africa be split into a white Afrikaner reservation, a Zulu area, and a free-for-all among various other peoples. It was Sir Anthony Eden who helpfully suggested in 1954 that the United States might consider a division of Vietnam into "North" and "South" at the close of the French colonial fiasco. Cold War partitions or geopolitical partitions, such as those imposed in Germany, Vietnam, and Korea, are to be distinguished from those arising from the preconditions of empire. But there is a degree of overlap even here (especially in the case of Vietnam and also, later, of Cyprus). As a general rule it can be stated that all partitions except that of Germany have led to war or another partition or both. Or that they threaten to do so.

Pakistan had been an independent state for only a quarter century when its restive Bengali "east wing" broke away to become Bangladesh. And in the process of that separation a Muslim army put a Muslim people to the sword—rather discrediting and degrading the original concept of a "faith-based" nationality. Cyprus was attacked by Greece and invaded by Turkey within fourteen years of its quasi-partitioned independence, and a huge and costly international effort is now under way to redraw the resulting frontiers so that they bear some relation to local ethnic proportions. Every day brings tidings of a fresh effort to revise the 1947–1948 cease-fire lines in Palestine (sometimes known as the 1967 borders), which were originally the result of a clumsy partition of the initial British Mandate. In Northern Ireland the number of Catholic citizens now approaches the number of Protestant ones, so that the terms "minority" and "majority" will soon take on new meaning. When that time arrives, we can be sure that demands will be renewed for a redivision of the Six Counties, roughly east and west of the Bann River. As for Kashmir, where local politics have been almost petrified since the arbitrary 1947 decision to become India's only Muslim-majority state, it is openly suggested that the outcome will be a three-way split into the part of Kashmir already occupied by Pakistan, the non-Muslim regions dominated by India, and the central valley where most Kashmiris actually dwell. In all the above cases there has been continuous strife, often spreading to neighboring countries, of the sort that partition was supposedly designed to prevent or solve. Harry Coomer (Hari Kumar), the Anglo-Indian protagonist of Paul Scott's *Raj Quartet*, sees it all coming when he writes to an English friend in 1940,

> I think that there's no doubt that in the last twenty years—whether intentionally or not—the English have succeeded in dividing and ruling, and the kind of conversation I hear... makes me realize the extent to which the English now seem to depend upon the divisions in Indian political opinion perpetuating their own rule at least until after the war, if not for some time beyond it. They are saying openly that it is "no good leaving the bloody country because there's no Indian party representative to hand it over to." They prefer Muslims to Hindus (because of the closer affinity that exists between God and Allah than exists between God and the Brahma), are constitutionally predisposed to Indian princes, emotionally affected by the thought of untouchables, and mad keen about the peasants who look upon any Raj as God...

This is the fictional equivalent of Anita Inder Singh's diagnosis, in *The Origins of the Partition of India 1936–1947*:

> The Labour government's directive to the Cabinet Mission in March 1946 stressed that power would only be transferred to Indians if they agreed to a settlement which would safeguard British military and economic interests in India. But in February 1947, the Labour government announced that it would wind up the Raj by June 1948, even if no agreement had emerged. Less than four months later, Lord Mountbatten announced that the British would transfer power on 15 August 1947, suggesting that much happened before this interval which persuaded the British to bring forward the date for terminating the empire by almost one year. Also, the British have often claimed that they had to partition because the Indian parties failed to agree. But until the early 1940s the differences between them had been a pretext for the British to reject the Congress demand for independence...

Sigmund Freud once wrote an essay concerning "the narcissism of the minor differences." He pointed out that the most vicious and irreconcilable quarrels often arise between peoples who are to most outward appearances nearly identical. In Sri Lanka the distinction between Tamils and Sinhalese is barely noticeable to the visitor. But the Sinhalese can tell the difference, and the indigenous Tamils know as well the difference between themselves and the Tamils later imported from South India by the British to pick the tea. It is precisely the intimacy and inwardness of the partition impulse that makes it so tempting to demagogues and opportunists. The 1921 partition of Ireland was not just a division of the island but a division of the northeastern province of Ulster. Historically this province contained nine counties. But only four—Antrim, Armagh, Derry, and Down—had anything like a stable Protestant majority. Three others—Monaghan, Cavan, and Donegal—were overwhelmingly Catholic. The line of pro-British partition attempted to annex the maximum amount of territory with the minimum number of Catholic and nationalist voters. Two largely Catholic counties, Fermanagh and Tyrone, petitioned to be excluded from the "Unionist" project. But a mere four counties were thought to be incompatible with a separate state; so the partition of Ireland, into twenty-six counties versus six, was also the fracturing of Ulster.

In a similar manner, the partition of India involved the subdivision of the ancient territories of Punjab and Bengal. The peoples here spoke the same language, shared the same ancestry, and had long inhabited the same territory. But they were abruptly forced to choose between one side of a frontier and the other, on the basis of religion alone. And then, with this durable scar of division fully established between them, they could fall to quarreling further about religion among themselves. The infinite and punishing consequences of this can be seen to the present day, through the secession of Bangladesh, the Sunni-Shia fratricide in Pakistan, the intra-Pashtun rivalry, and the sinister and dangerous recent attempt to define India (which still has more Muslims on its soil than Pakistan does) as a Hindu state. To say nothing of Kashmir. This "solution," with its enormous military wastage and potentially catastrophic nuclear potential, must count as one of the great moral and political failures in recent human history. One of Paul Scott's most admirable minor characters is Lady Ethel Manners, the widow of a former British governor, who exclaims about the "midnight" of 1947,

> The creation of Pakistan is our crowning failure. I can't bear it... Our only justification for two hundred years of power was unification. But we've divided one composite nation into two and everyone

> at home goes round saying what a swell the new Viceroy is for getting it sorted out so quickly.

The year 1947 was obviously an unpropitious one for laying down your "confessional state" or "post-colonial partition" vintage. The Arabs of Palestine, who gave place to a half-promised British-sponsored state for Jews at the same time, are now subdivided into Israeli Arabs, West Bankers, Gazans, Jerusalemites, Jordanians, and the wider Palestinian-refugee diaspora. If at any moment a settlement looks possible between any one of these factions and the Israelis, the claims of another, more afflicted faction promptly arise to neutralize or negate the process. Anton Shammas and David Grossman have both written lucidly, from Arab-Israeli and Jewish-Israeli perspectives respectively, about this balkanization of a society that was fissile enough to begin with. And perhaps that splintering is why Osama bin Laden's fantasy of a restored caliphate—an undivided Muslim empire, organic and hierarchic and centralized—now exerts its appeal (as did the Nasserite and later the Baath Party dream of a single Arab nation in which the old borders would be subsumed by one glorious whole).

In the preface to his 1904 play *John Bull's Other Island*, George Bernard Shaw made highly vivid use of the metaphor of fracture or amputation.

> A healthy nation is as unconscious of its nationality as a healthy man of his bones. But if you break a nation's nationality it will think of nothing else but getting it set again. It will listen to no reformer, to no philosopher, to no preacher, until the demand of the Nationalist is granted. It will attend to no business, however vital, except the business of unification and liberation.

This, mark you, was seventeen years before the issue of Irish "liberation" was forcibly counterposed to that of "unification." "Unionist," in British terminology, means someone who favors the "union" of the Six Counties of Northern Ireland with the United Kingdom—in other words, someone who favors the disunion of Ireland. Among Greeks the word "unionist" is rendered as *enotist*—someone who supports *enosis*, or union, between Greece and John Bull's other European colony, Cyprus. (This is why the Ulster

Unionists in Parliament today are among the staunchest supporters of the ultra-nationalist Rauf Denktash's breakaway Turkish colony on the island.) And Shaw might have done well to add that preachers can indeed get attention for their views, while the national question is being debated, as long as they take decided and fervent nationalist positions. Even he would have been startled, if he visited any of these territories today, to find how right he was—and how people discuss their injuries as if they had been inflicted yesterday.

It is the admixture of religion with the national question that has made the problem of partition so toxic. Whether consciously or not, British colonial authorities usually preferred to define and categorize their subjects according to confession. The whole concept of British dominion in Ireland was based on a Protestant ascendancy. In the subcontinent the empire tended to classify people as Muslim or non-Muslim, partly because the Muslims had been the last conquerors of the region and also because—as Paul Scott cleverly noticed—it found Islam to be at least recognizable in Christian-missionary terms (as opposed to the heathenish polytheism of the Hindus). In Palestine and Cyprus, both of which it took over from the Ottomans, London wrote similar categories into law. As a partially intended consequence, any secular or nonsectarian politician was at a peculiar disadvantage. Many historians tend to forget that the stoutest supporters of Irish independence, at least after the rebellion of 1798, were Protestants or agnostics, from Edward FitzGerald and Wolfe Tone to Charles Stewart Parnell and James Connolly. The leadership of the Indian Congress Party was avowedly nonconfessional, and a prominent part in the struggle for independence was played by Marxist forces that repudiated any definition of nationality by religion. Likewise in Cyprus: The largest political party on the island was Communist, with integrated trade unions and municipalities, and most Turkish Cypriots were secular in temper. The availability of a religious "wedge," added to the innate or latent appeal of chauvinism and tribalism, was always a godsend to the masters of divide and rule. Among other things, it allowed the authorities to pose as overworked mediators between irreconcilable passions.

Indeed, part of the trouble with partition is that it relies for its implementation on local partitionists. It may also rely on an unspoken symbiosis between them—a covert handshake between apparent enemies. The grand mufti of Jerusalem, Haj Amin al-Husseini, was in many ways unrepresentative of the Palestinian peasantry of the 1930s and 1940s (and it does not do to forget that perhaps 20 percent of Palestinians are Christian). But his clerical authority made him a useful (if somewhat distasteful) "notable" from the viewpoint of the colonial power, and his virulent sectarianism was invaluable to the harder-line Zionists, who needed only to reprint his speeches. Many Indian Muslims refused their support to Mohammed Ali Jinnah, but once Britain became bent on partition, it automatically conferred authority on his Muslim League as being the "realistic" expression of the community. British policy also helped the emergence of Rauf Denktash, whose violence was principally directed at those Turkish Cypriots who did not want an apartheid solution. More recently, in Bosnia, the West (encouraged by Lords Carrington and Owen) made the fatal error of assuming that the hardest-line demagogues were the most authentic representatives of their communities. Thus men who could never win a truly democratic election—and have not won one since—were given the immense prestige of being invited as recognized delegates to the negotiating table. Interviewing the Serbian Orthodox fanatics who had proclaimed an artificial "Republica Srpska" on stolen and cleansed Bosnian soil, John Burns of the *New York Times* was surprised to find them citing the example of Denktash's separate state in Cyprus as a precedent. (The usual colloquial curse word for "Muslim," in Serb circles, is "Turk." But there is such a thing as brotherhood under the skin, and even xenophobes can practice their own perverse form of internationalism.) Most of these men are now either in prison or on the run, but they lasted long enough to see Bosnia-Herzegovina subjected to an almost terminal experience of partition and subpartition, splitting like an amoeba among Serb, Croat, and (in the Bihac enclave) Muslim bandits. Now, under the paternal wing of Lord Ashdown, the governorship of Bosnia is based on centripetal rather than centrifugal principles. But his stewardship as commissioner originates with the European Union.

The straight capitalist and socialist rationality of the EU—where "Union" means what it says and where frontiers are bad for business as well as a reproach to the old left-internationalist ideal—is in bizarre contrast to the lived experience of partition. The time-zone difference between India and Pakistan, for example, is half an hour. That's a nicely irrational and arbitrary slice out of daily life. In Cyprus, the difference between the clocks in the Greek and Turkish sectors is an hour—but it's the only in-country north-south time change that I am aware of, and it operates on two sides of the same capital city. In my "time," I have traversed the border post at the old Ledra Palace hotel in the center of Nicosia, where a whole stretch of the city is frozen at the precise moment of "cease-fire" in 1974, when everything went into suspended animation. I have been frisked at the Allenby Bridge and at the Gaza crossing between Israel and the "Palestinian authority." I have looked at the Korean DMZ from both sides, been ordered from a car by British soldiers on the Donegal border of Northern Ireland, been pushed around at Checkpoint Charlie on the old Berlin Wall, and been held up for bribes by soldiers at the Atari crossing on Kipling's old "Grand Trunk Road" between Lahore and Amritsar—the only stage at which the Indo-Pakistan frontier can be legally negotiated on land. In no case was it possible to lose a sense of the surreal, as if the border was actually carved into the air rather than the roadway. Rushdie succeeds in weaving magical realism out of this in *Midnight's Children*: "Mr. Kemal, who wanted nothing to do with Partition, was fond of saying, 'Here's proof of the folly of the scheme! Those [Muslim] Leaguers plan to abscond with a whole thirty minutes! Time Without Partitions,' Mr. Kemal cried, 'That's the ticket!' "

There is a good deal of easy analysis on offer these days, to the effect that Islam was the big loser from colonialism, and is entitled to a measure of self-pity in consequence. The evidence doesn't quite bear this out. In India the British were openly partial to the Muslim side, and helped to midwife the first modern state consecrated to Islam. In Cyprus they favored the Turks. In the Middle East the Muslim Hashemite and Saudi dynasties—rivals for the guardianship of the holy places—benefited as much as anyone from the imperial carve-up. Had there been a British partition of Eritrea after 1945, as was proposed, the Muslims would have been the beneficiaries of it. No, the Muslim claim is better stated as resentment over the loss of the Islamic empire: an entirely distinct grievance. There were Muslim losers in Palestine and elsewhere, mostly among the powerless and landless, but the big losers were those of all creeds and of none who believed in modernity and had transcended tribalism.

The largely secular Muslims of Bosnia and Kosovo were, however, the main victims of the cave-in to partition in the former Yugoslavia, and are now the chief beneficiaries of that policy's reversal. They were also among the first to test the improvised but increasingly systematic world order, in which rescue operations are undertaken from the developed world, assisted by a nexus of nongovernmental organizations, and then mutate into semi-permanent administrations. "Empire" is the word employed by some hubristic American intellectuals for this new dominion. A series of uncovenanted mandates, for failed states or former abattoir regimes, is more likely to be the real picture. And the relevant boundaries still descend from Sir Percy, Sir Henry, and Sir Cyril, who, as Auden phrased it, "quickly forgot the case, as a good lawyer must." However we confront this inheritance of responsibility (should it be called the global man's burden?), the British past is replete with lessons on how not to discharge it.

(*The Atlantic*, March 2003)

Algeria: A French Quarrel

IT WAS ARGUABLY FAIR, when André Maurois finished his *Histoire de la France*, to permit him a small allowance of *la gloire* and to agree with his conclusion that "the history of France, a permanent miracle, has the singular privilege of impassioning the peoples of the earth to the point where they all take part in French quarrels." And it was certainly true, when Alistair Horne began his long study of the Algerian war (or the Algerian Revolution), that no sentient person could fail to share his conviction that France in 1789, 1848, 1871 (the Paris Commune), 1916 (Verdun), and 1940 (the defeat and capitulation that led to Vichy) was in some sense both the mother and the daughter—and perhaps also the orphan—of modern history.

At all events, there is no doubt that the eight-year struggle for Algeria was momentous for *le monde entier* as well as for France herself. The intense and dramatic fighting marked the emergence of militant pan-Arab nationalism as well as, to some extent, the revival of Islam as a modern political force. It was one of the initial tests of the validity of the United Nations in bringing new states and countries to independence. It became an important early sideshow in the Cold War, with the United States this time attempting to play the role of an anti-colonial power. And it was a reprise, at some remove, of the fratricide between Gaullist and Vichyite forces that had ceased only a decade before the hostilities in Algeria broke out.

Review of *A Savage War of Peace: Algeria 1954–1962*, by Alistair Horne.

A history so intricately filiated will soon disclose the lineaments of tragedy, and Horne's achievement—in a book first published in 1977—was to speak with gruff respect of the might-have-beens without losing his concentration on the blunt and unavoidable facts. Had liberated France in 1945 begun to speak of the emancipation of its colonized peoples in the same tones that it demanded so peremptorily for itself (and had it realized that the world of European dominion was never coming back), the history of North Africa—and indeed, Indochina—might have been radically different. Horne's title is taken from Rudyard Kipling's poem "The White Man's Burden," which was originally addressed to Henry Cabot Lodge, Theodore Roosevelt, and other Americans who were pondering what to do with the Philippine Islands after shattering the Spanish Empire in 1898. But Algeria in 1945 was a province of a foredoomed French empire, so no invocation of the old *mission civilisatrice* had even a prayer of working.

Least of all did the impossible scheme of keeping Algeria as an actual *département* of France have such a chance. Relatively sober steps had been taken, especially under the prime ministership of Pierre Mendès-France, to bring independence to Tunisia and Morocco, and to end the long misery and shame of France's nostalgia for a renovated empire in Vietnam, which ended all in one day at the battle of Dien Bien Phu. When it came to Algeria, Mendès-France borrowed from an old plan, for modest autonomy, first evolved by his predecessor Léon Blum. It isn't exaggerating by much to say that both of these Jewish Frenchmen—products of the campaign to vindicate Captain Dreyfus—were viciously thwarted by a white-settler movement whose allegiance was to Pétain and Poujade, and in some cases to Charles Maurras and the Action Française. Every move to reform Algeria even slightly was vetoed by a *pied-noir* lobby that was addicted to overplaying its own hand.

This grandiose primitivism was not shared, as Horne brilliantly and movingly demonstrates, by the military men upon whom the *pieds-noirs* depended. Many of these soldiers had fought against Vichy and its Nazi backers (in French Africa, in the Middle East, or in France itself), and they had a concept of republican virtue, as well as an esprit de corps, that commands respect even at this distance. The same can be said of Jacques Soustelle, the brilliant, passionate proconsul who was, in the end, almost driven mad by the feeling of having been betrayed from Paris. When the *pied-noir* coup took place in Algiers, and was proclaimed from the balcony, it was announced—in a sort of perverse *hommage* to a degenerated Jacobinism—by a "Committee of Public Safety." In a comparable parody of anti-imperialism, the rightist mob in those days of May 1958 made one of its first acts the torching of the U.S. Cultural Center in Algiers.

By then, however, the curtain was already falling: The Anglo-French collusion in the 1956 invasion of Egypt, with its calamitous outcome, had not only written finis to European colonialism in the Arab world but impelled Washington to adopt a course that implicitly accepted independence as inevitable. Given the strong, if mainly rhetorical, support of the Soviet bloc for the Algerian Front de Libération Nationale (whose forerunner was founded on the day that Dien Bien Phu fell, and which had in its ranks hardened soldiers who had once fought under French colors in Indochina), all that was lacking was a French statesman who could see the need to disembarrass his country of those who ostensibly were the most devoted to it. The man who would perform this brilliant political—and rhetorical and emotional—feat had, as we know, been waiting for the call for a long time, and Horne does well to keep him offstage until almost halfway through this lengthy book. Charles de Gaulle could not be outshone by anybody who wished to speak of the destiny of France and the French, and his contempt for the Algerian right went back all the way to the Vichy regime, which it had supported. (His disdain for treason cut both ways: He could never bring himself to utter a good word about the quarter of a million or so *harkis*, those Algerian Muslims who took the side of France and paid a dreadful cost for it.)

Like the good historian he is, Horne leaves open the question of whether all this was as inevitable as it now appears. He tends to assume the long-run victory of colonial insurgencies and the near impossibility of defeating them—using the IRA of the 1970s as an example that now seems anachronistic—but he concedes that there were several moments when the FLN was nearly crushed, illuminates the deep divisions within its ranks that at several points were almost lethal to it, and reminds us almost casually that oil was not found in Algeria until 1958 and that even while it was negotiating with the rebels, France was exploding its first nuclear devices in the Sahara. Yes, indeed it might have been otherwise, as de Gaulle was forced to admit when, himself besieged by strikes and riots ten years after the Algerian coup had provoked his own seizure of power, he was obliged to fly secretly to Germany and beg for the loyalty of the mutinous generals he had exiled to NATO.

This is not the only way in which Algeria continued to haunt France, and continues to do so. There are now some 5 million people of Algerian provenance living in France, many of them strongly attracted to Islamic fundamentalist ideas. Their presence is rejected by a large and growing neofascist party led by a brutish veteran of the *Algérie française* movement named Jean-Marie Le Pen. During the civil war in Algeria in the 1990s, when the FLN and the army were able to repress an Islamist insurgency only by employing the most pitiless measures, an Air France plane was hijacked by militants who planned to crash it into the Eiffel Tower. (One wonders how different things might have been if *that* action had inaugurated our new age of transnational suicide-murder.)

In a much-too-brisk introduction to this new edition, Horne makes some rather facile comparisons with Iraq. The initial analogy does not hold at all: There is not a huge white-settler population in Mesopotamia; the United States does not consider Iraq to be a part of its metropole; the violence there is mainly *between* Arabs and Muslims, while the large Kurdish minority—loosely comparable perhaps to the Kabyle or Berber population of Algeria—fights stoutly on the American side. Moreover, it would be insulting to compare the forces of al-Qaeda and *revanchiste* Baathism to the FLN, which made consistent appeals to the discrepant ethnic groups in its country and which even asked for—and often got—support from the large Jewish community, whose members had suffered at the hands of the colonial right. Envoys from the al-Zarqawi school are furthermore unlikely to be received—as were the tough and often brilliant diplomats of the FLN—at the United Nations, whose headquarters and personnel in Baghdad they blew up. In Horne's bare and scrupulous account, it is the nihilistic tactics and propaganda of the colonialist Organisation de l'Armée Secrète that put one in mind of the bin-Ladenists. He emphasizes the problem of torture, which has indeed been allowed to work its poison on American policy in Iraq, but his own very exhaustive discussion of the way that this horror influenced Algeria makes it plain that official cruelty was a stern principle as well as a universal practice, and that this was not even denied, let alone punished. It would have been far more absorbing had he devoted his considerable expertise to answering the question, How was it that Algeria in the 1990s became the first country to defeat a full-scale *jihad* and *takfir* rebellion, which had at one point threatened to overwhelm the entire state and society? In other words, this is no longer a question of the world being privileged to observe French quarrels, and perhaps allowed to participate vicariously in them; it is more a matter of understanding one of the many origins of a current and permanent crisis.

Horne is a mild British Tory with a true feeling for France but a rather limited understanding of the "left." However, one of his recurrent tropes did stay in this reviewer's mind. He writes often about the honorable role of the secular and democratic forces, in both France and Algeria, that attempted to prevent and then to alleviate a war of mutilation versus torture, and of gruesome mutual reprisal. The world chooses to remember Albert Camus as the foremost personality among these, but Horne gives us many important reminiscences of Messali Hadj and Ferhat Abbas, and other brave Algerian figures (not "moderates," in the current patronizing argot) who might, if they could not have stopped the war entirely, have prevented it from taking a savage form that in some ways still persists. Must such people always lose? It is a question that this generation, too, will have to face—and have to answer.

(*The Atlantic*, November 2006)

The Case of Orientalism

OF WHAT BOOK and author was the following sentence written, and by whom?

> Rarely has an Oriental servant of a white-identified, imperial design managed to pack so many services to imperial hubris abroad and racist elitism at home—all in one act.

This was the quasi-articulate attack recently leveled, by a professor of comparative literature at Columbia University, on *Reading Lolita in Tehran*, Azar Nafisi's account of private seminars on Nabokov for young women in Iran. The professor described Nafisi's work as resembling "the most pestiferous colonial projects of the British in India," and its author as the moral equivalent of a sadistic torturer at Abu Ghraib. "To me there is no difference between Lynndie England and Azar Nafisi," Hamid Dabashi, who is himself of Iranian origin and believes that Nafisi's book is a conscious part of the softening-up for an American bombing campaign in Iran, has said.

I cannot imagine my late friend Edward Said, who was a professor of English and comparative literature at Columbia, either saying or believing anything so vulgar. And I know from experience that he was often dismayed by the views of people claiming to be his acolytes. But if there is a faction

Review of *Dangerous Knowledge: Orientalism and Its Discontents*, by Robert Irwin.

in the academy that now regards the acquisition of knowledge about "the East" as an essentially imperialist project, amounting to an "appropriation" and "subordination" of another culture, then it must be conceded that Said's 1978 book, *Orientalism*, was highly influential in forming this cast of mind.

Robert Irwin's new history of the field of Oriental studies is explicitly designed as a refutation of Said's thesis, and has an entire chapter devoted to a direct assault upon it. The author insists that he has no animus against Said personally or politically, that he tends to share his view of the injustice done to the people of Palestine, and that he regarded him as a man of taste and discernment. Irwin makes this disclaimer, perhaps, very slightly too fulsomely—at one point also recycling the discredited allegation that Said was not "really" a Palestinian from Jerusalem at all. But he is more lucid and reliable when he sets out to demonstrate the complexity and diversity of Orientalism, to defend his profession from the charge of being a conscious or unconscious accomplice of empire, and to decry the damage done by those whose reading even of *Orientalism* was probably superficial.

I still think that Said's book was useful if only in forcing people in "the West" to examine the assumptions that underlay their cosmology. If asked what I mean by that, I should cite Robert Hughes, who recalls how his parents' generation in Australia would refer to New Guinea or Indonesia, say, as "the Far East" when they were, in point of fact, their near North. The very term *Middle East*, I have recently learned from Michael Oren's absorbing history of American engagement in the region, was coined by Admiral Alfred Thayer Mahan, whose life's work was the creation of an American navy on the model of the British imperial fleet. I remember my own surprise when I realized, in New Delhi in the 1970s, that by the crisis in "Western Asia," the newspaper article I was reading meant to refer to the Israeli-Palestinian dispute. It can be said for Edward Said that he helped make us reconsider our perspectives a little.

"This book," writes Irwin in his agreeably breezy introduction to it, "contains many sketches of individual Orientalists—dabblers, obsessives, evangelists, freethinkers, madmen, charlatans, pedants, romantics. (Even so, perhaps still not enough of them.)" Indeed, its chief strength lies precisely in showing the vagary and variety of the subject, and thus obliquely convicting any single unified critique of it as essentially reductionist—a neat *tu quoque* against the Said school.

Among Irwin's initial points is one that should scarcely have needed to be made. The British proconsular class were for the most part not Orientalists at all. They were classicists. When they adapted old texts and languages to their task of dominion, they were looking to the grand precedents of Greece and Rome. And though it is true that the protracted Greek confrontation with the Persians created the first "East-West" division in the European mind, it is also true that the Greek word *barbaros*, with all its freight of later associations, was not a pejorative. It simply demarcated Greek-speaking from non-Greek-speaking peoples. So it was simplistic of Said to say that the roots of the problem lay with *The Iliad*: The Hellenes often looked down on uncouth northerners like the Scythians, while greatly admiring (and borrowing from) the Egyptians. As Irwin goes on to say:

> Lord Curzon, Sir Ronald Storrs, T. E. Lawrence and most of the rest of them were steeped in the Greek and Roman classics. Readings of Thucydides, Herodotus and Tacitus guided those who governed the British. Lord Cromer, the proconsul in Egypt, was obsessed with the Roman empire and its decline and fall. Sir Ronald Storrs used to read the *Odyssey* before breakfast. T. E. Lawrence read the Greek poets during his time as an archaeologist at Carcemish and later translated the *Odyssey*. Colonial administrators were much more likely to be familiar with the campaigns of Caesar than those of Muhammad and the Quraysh.

In contradistinction, or at any rate by contrast, those whose passion was for the Orient were very often numbered among the *anti*-imperialists. This was true not only of English scholars like Edward Granville Browne—author of *A Year Among the Persians*, who became a strenuous partisan of the struggle of Eastern peoples against British and Russian tutelage—but also of many of the French enthusiasts, from the wildly eccentric Louis Massignon, who campaigned for the independence of French North Africa and took his anti-Zionism to the point of Judeophobia, to Marxisant professors like Maxime Rodinson. Nor was it at all uncommon for Orientalist pioneers to "go native," if the expression can be allowed, and to adopt forms of Islam such as Sufism. This was not true of the Soviet and Nazi Orientalists, on whom Irwin gives us two tantalizingly brief sections; but the first group was concerned with negating and discrediting Islam, and the second was obsessed with bogus racist and pseudo-ethnological theories, which in their turn caused many of the finest German scholars to flee overseas and replant the discipline elsewhere. None of this makes a good "fit" with Said's over- and under-drawn picture of a discipline dedicated to the propagation of British and French imperial hegemony.

Though this book is an extraordinarily attractive short introduction to the different national schools of Orientalism, and to the various scholars who labored to make Eastern philology and philosophy more accessible, its chief interest to the lay reader lies in its consideration of Orientalism as a study of Islam. Irwin shows us the early Christian attempts to translate and understand the Koran, most of which were preoccupied with showing its heretical character. These make especially absorbing reading in the light of the pope's recent lecture at Regensburg University, and his revival of the medieval critique of the teachings of Muhammad. That tradition extends quite far into the modern epoch, with the consecrated work of Father Henri Lammens, a Belgian Jesuit who taught in Beirut in the early part of the twentieth century and made himself master of the suras and hadiths. Lammens's intention was to show that, to the extent that Muhammad could be said to have existed, the prophet was a sex-crazed brigand whose preachments were either plagiarized or falsified. The greatest Orientalist of them all, the Hungarian genius Ignaz Goldziher, asked ironically, "What would remain of the Gospels if [Lammens] applied to them the same methods he applies to the Qur'an?"

The same unwelcome implication of this excellent question may well have occurred to the Church itself: I can tell you that Lammens's books are now extremely hard to obtain. And though Irwin does not say so explicitly, the general academic reticence about Islam that he so much deplores may well have something to do with the potentially atheistic consequences of any unfettered inquiry. As he phrases it:

> Because of the possible offense to Muslim susceptibilities, Western scholars who specialize in the early history of Islam have to

> be extremely careful what they say, and some of them have developed subtle forms of double-speak when discussing contentious matters.

This is to say the very least: "Western scholars" and authors like Karen Armstrong and Bruce Lawrence have adopted the strategy of taking Islam's claims more or less at face value, while non-Western critics who do not believe in revealed religion at all, such as Ibn Warraq, are now operating on the very margin of what is considered tactful or permissible. Even a relatively generous treatment of the life of the Prophet Muhammad, such as that composed by Rodinson, is considered too controversial on many campuses in the West, and as involving readers or distributors in real physical danger if offered for discussion even in Cairo, let alone Baghdad or Beirut. The splendid nineteenth-century Oxford Orientalist David Margoliouth (described by Irwin as having "the kind of beautiful mind that could see patterns where none existed") was perhaps not so eccentric when he claimed to notice analogies "between the founder of Islam and Brigham Young, the founder of the Mormon faith." The usefulness of polygamy in forming and cementing alliances, as well as in satisfying other requirements, is something that was indeed noticed by Joseph Smith—the actual "founder of the Mormon faith"—who furthermore announced himself as the man who would do for North America what Muhammad had done for the Arabian Peninsula. Irwin might have done well to pursue this and other insights, rather than exhibiting a little of the very reluctance of which he claims to disapprove.

To return, then, to Said. It is, on reflection, a great mark against his book that it did not consider the work of Goldziher, whose preeminence Irwin has reasserted in a wonderfully readable thumbnail chapter that leaves one yearning for more. Even Said's friend Albert Hourani, who did so much to arouse interest in the neglected field of Arabic and Middle Eastern studies, could not pardon this omission. And Rodinson, that great Jewish foe of Zionism, felt constrained to remind his Palestinian comrade that it is a mistake to concentrate exclusively on the Arab world, since four-fifths of Muslims are not Arabs. Most of all, though, one must be ready to oppose any analysis that even slightly licenses the idea that "outsiders" are not welcome to study other cultures. So far from defending those cultures from depredation, such a stance actually permits them to fall under the dominance of stultified and conservative forces to whom everything depends on an affirmation of blind faith. This, and not the inquiry into its origins, might be described as the problem in the first place.

(*The Atlantic*, March 2007)

Edward Said: Where the Twain Should Have Met

I FIRST MET EDWARD SAID in the summer of 1976, in the capital city of Cyprus. We had come to Nicosia to take part in a conference on the rights of small nations. The obscene civil war in Lebanon was just beginning to consume the whole society and to destroy the cosmopolitanism of Beirut; it was still just possible in those days to imagine that a right "side" could be discerned through the smoke of confessional conflagration. Palestinian resistance to Israeli occupation was in its infancy (as was the messianic "settler" movement among Jews), and the occupation itself was less than a decade old. Egypt was still the Egypt of Anwar Sadat—a man who had placed most of his credit on the wager of "Westernization," however commercially conceived, and who was only two years away from the Camp David accords. It was becoming dimly apprehended in the West that the old narrative of "Israel" versus "the Arabs" was much too crude. The image of a frugal kibbutz state surrounded by a heaving ocean of ravening mullahs and demagogues was slowly yielding to a story of two peoples contesting a right to the same twice-promised land.

For all these "conjunctures," as we now tend to term them, Said was

Review of *Orientalism*, by Edward Said.

almost perfectly configured. He had come from an Anglican Palestinian family that divided its time and its property between Jerusalem and Cairo. He had spent years in the internationalist atmosphere of Beirut, and was as much at home in French and English as in Arabic. A favorite of Lionel Trilling's, he had won high distinction at Columbia University and was also up to concert standard as a pianist. Those Americans who subliminally associated the word "Palestinian" with swarthiness, bizarre headgear, and strange irredentist rhetoric were in for a shock that was long overdue. And this is to say little enough about his wit, his curiosity, his care for the opinions of others.

Within two years he had published *Orientalism*: a book that has exerted a galvanizing influence throughout the quarter century separating its first from its most recent edition. In these pages Said characterized Western scholarship about the East as a conscious handmaiden of power and subordination. Explorers, missionaries, archaeologists, linguists—all had been part of a colonial enterprise. To the extent that American academics now speak about the "appropriation" of other cultures, and seldom fail to put ordinary words such as "the Other" between portentous quotation marks, and contest the very notion of objective inquiry, they are paying what they imagine is a debt to Edward Said's work. It isn't unfair to the book, I hope, to say that it also received a tremendous charge from the near simultaneous revolution in Iran and the later assassination of Anwar Sadat. The alleged "Westernization" or "modernization" of two ancient civilizations, Persia and Egypt, had proved to be founded upon, well... sand. The word of the traditional policy intellectuals and Middle East "experts" turned out to be worth less than naught. Although this book said little on the subject of either Iran or Sadat, it burst on the knowledge-seeking general reader even as it threw down a challenge to the think tanks and professional institutes.

To be appraised properly, *Orientalism* ought to be read alongside three other books by Said: *Covering Islam* (1981), *Culture and Imperialism* (1993), and *Out of Place* (1999). The last of these is a memoir, which was the target of a number of scurrilous attacks essentially aimed at denying Said the right to call himself a Palestinian at all. The first is an assault on the generally lazy press coverage of the Iranian Revolution and of all matters concerned with Islam. *Culture and Imperialism* is a collection of essays showing that Said has a deep understanding, amounting at times to sympathy, for the work of writers such as Austen and Kipling and George Eliot, who—outward appearances notwithstanding—never did take "the Orient" for granted.

In scrutinizing instances of translation and interpretation, the inescapable question remains the same: Who is interpreting what and to whom? It is easy enough to say that Westerners had long been provided with an exotic, sumptuous, but largely misleading account of the Orient, whether supplied by Benjamin Disraeli's Suez Canal share purchases, the celluloid phantasms of Rudolph Valentino, or the torrid episodes in T. E. Lawrence's *Seven Pillars of Wisdom*. But it is also true that Arab, Indian, Malay, and Iranian societies can operate on a false if not indeed deluded view of "the West." This much became vividly evident very recently, with the circulation of bizarre libels about (say) a Jewish plot to destroy the World Trade Center. I, for one, do not speak or read Arabic, and have made only five, relatively short, visits to Iraq. But I am willing to bet that I know more about Mesopotamia than Saddam Hussein ever knew about England, France, or the United States. I also think that such knowledge as I have comes from more disinterested sources... And I would add that Saddam Hussein was better able to force himself on my attention than I ever was to force myself on his. As Adonis, the great Syrian-Lebanese poet, has warned us, there exists a danger in too wrong a counter-position between "East" and "West." The "West" has its intellectual and social troughs, just as the "East" has its pinnacles. Not only is this true now (Silicon Valley could hardly run without the work of highly skilled Indians, for example), but it was true when Arab scholars in Baghdad and Córdoba recovered the lost work of Aristotle for medieval "Christendom."

Cultural-political interaction, then, must be construed as dialectical. Edward Said was in a prime position to be a "negotiator" here. In retrospect, however, it can be argued that he chose a one-sided approach and employed rather a broad brush: "Without examining Orientalism as a discourse one cannot possibly understand the enormously systematic discipline by which European culture was able to manage—and even produce—the Orient politically, sociologically, militarily, ideologically, scientifically, and imaginatively during the post-Enlightenment period." ("Produce," as in "cultural production," has become one of the key words of the post-Foucault academy.) In this analysis every instance of European curiosity about the East, from Flaubert to Marx, was part of a grand design to exploit and remake what Westerners saw as a passive, rich, but ultimately contemptible "Oriental" sphere.

That there is undeniable truth to this it would be idle to dispute. Lord Macaulay, for example, was a near perfect illustration of the sentence (which occurs in Disraeli's novel *Tancred*) "The East is a career." He viewed the region both as a barbarous source of potential riches and as a huge tract in pressing need of civilization. But in that latter respect he rather echoed the feeling of his fellow Victorian Karl Marx, who thought that the British had brought modernity to India in the form of printing presses, railways, the telegraph, and steamship contact with other cultures. Marx didn't believe that they had done this out of the kindness of their hearts. "England, it is true, in causing a social revolution in Hindustan was actuated only by the vilest interests," he wrote, "...but that is not the question. The question is, can mankind fulfill its destiny without a fundamental revolution in the social state of Asia?" To the extent that empire licensed this, Marx reasoned, one was entitled to exclaim, with Goethe,

> Should this torture then torment us
> Since it brings us greater pleasure?
> Were not through the rule of Timur
> Souls devoured without measure?

Said spent a lot of time "puzzling" (his word) over Marx's ironies here: How could a man of professed human feeling justify conquest and exploitation? The evident answer—that conquest furnished an alternative to the terrifying serfdom and stagnation of antiquity, and that creation can take a destructive form—need have nothing to do with what Said calls "the old inequality between East and West." (The Roman invasion of Britain was also "progress," if the word has any meaning.) Moreover, Marxism in India has often been a strong force for secular government and "nation building," whereas Marxism in China has led by a bloody and contradictory route to a highly dynamic capitalist revolution. To discount all this, as Said did, as a "Romantic Orientalist vision" (and to simply omit the printing press, the railways, and the rest of it) is to miss the point in a near heroic way.

The lines from Goethe are taken from his *Westöstlicher Diwan*, one of the most meticulous and respectful considerations of the Orient we have. And Said's critics from the conservative side, notably his archenemy Bernard Lewis, have reproached him for leaving German Orientalism out of his account. This is a telling omission, they charge, because Oriental scholarship in Germany, although of an unexampled breadth and splendor, was not put to the service of empire and conquest and annexation. That being so, they argue, what remains of Said's general theory? His reply deals only with the academic aspect of the question: Goethe and Schlegel, he responds, relied on books and collections already made available by British and French imperial expeditions. It might be more exact to point out, as against both Lewis and Said, that Germany *did* have an imperial project. Kaiser Wilhelm II visited Damascus and paid for the restoration of the tomb of Saladin. A *Drang nach Osten* ("drive to the East") was proposed, involving the stupendous scheme of a Berlin-to-Baghdad railway. German imperial explorers and agents were to be found all over the region in the late nineteenth century and up to 1914 and beyond. But of course they were doing all this work in the service of another, allied empire—a Turkish and Islamic one. And that same empire was to issue a call for *jihad*, against Britain and on the side of Germany, in 1914. (The best literary evocation of this extraordinary moment is still *Greenmantle*, written by that veteran empire-builder John Buchan.) However, the inclusion of this important episode would tell against both Said, who doesn't really allow for Muslim or Turkish imperialism, and Lewis, who has always been rather an apologist for the Turks. Osama bin Laden, as we must always remember, began his *jihad* as an explicit attempt to restore the vanished caliphate that once ran the world of Islam from the shores of the Bosporus. As we often forget, Prussian militarism was his co-sufferer in this pang of loss.

Among Edward Said's considerable advantages are that he knows very well who John Buchan was and that he, Said, was educated at St. George's, an Anglican establishment in Jerusalem, and also at a colonial mock-English private school, Victoria College, in Cairo. (One of the head boys was Omar Sharif.) There were some undoubtedly penitential aspects to this, recounted with dry humor in his memoir, but they have helped him to be an "outsider" and an exile in several different countries and cultures, including the Palestine of his birth. When he addresses the general Arab audience, he makes admirable use of this duality or multiplicity. In his columns in the Egyptian paper *Al-Ahram* he is scornful and caustic about the failures and disgraces of Arab and Muslim society, and was being so before the celebrated recent United Nations Development Programme report on self-imposed barriers to Arab development, which was written by, among others, his friend Clovis Maksoud. Every year more books are translated and published in Athens than in all the Arab capitals combined. Where is there a decent Arab university? Where is there a "transparent" Arab election? Why does Arab propaganda resort to such ugliness and hysteria?

Much of secular Arab nationalism was led and developed by Europeanized Christians, often Greek Orthodox, whereas much of atavistic Islamic *jihad*-ism relies on anti-Jewish fabrications produced in the lower reaches of the Tsarist Russian Orthodox police state. Said has a fairly exact idea of the traffic between the two worlds, and of what is and is not of value. He is a source of stern admonition to the uncritical, insulated Arab elites and intelligentsia. But for some reason—conceivably connected to his status as an exile—he cannot allow that direct Western engagement in the region is legitimate.

This might be a narrowly defensible position if direct Islamist interference in Western life and society had not become such a factor. When *Orientalism* was first published, the Shah was still a gendarme for American capital in Iran, and his rule was so exorbitantly cruel and corrupt that millions of secularists were willing to make what they hoped was a temporary alliance with Khomeini in order to get rid of it. Today Iranian mullahs are enriching uranium and harboring fugitive bin Ladenists (the slaughterers of their Shia co-religionists in Afghanistan and Pakistan) while students in Tehran risk their lives to demonstrate with pro-American slogans.

How does Said, in his introduction to the new edition of *Orientalism*, deal with this altered and still protean reality? He begins by admitting the self-evident, which is that "neither the term Orient nor the concept of the West has any ontological stability; each is made up of human effort, partly affirmation, partly identification of the Other." Fair enough. He adds, "That these supreme fictions lend themselves easily to manipulation and the organization of collective passion has never been more evident than in our time, when the mobilizations of fear, hatred, disgust and resurgent self-pride and arrogance—much of it having to do with Islam and the Arabs on one side, 'we' Westerners on the other—are very large-scale enterprises."

This is composed with a certain obliqueness, which may be accidental, but I can't discover that it really means to say that there are delusions on "both" these ontologically nonexistent sides. A few sentences further on we read of "the events of September 11 and their aftermath in the wars against Afghanistan and Iraq." Again, if criticism of both sides is intended (and I presume that it is), it comes served in highly discrepant portions. There's no quarrel with the view that "events" occurred on September 11, 2001; but that the military interventions in Afghanistan and Iraq were wars "against" either country is subject to debate. A professor of English appreciates the distinction, does he not? Or does he, like some puerile recent "activists" (and some less youthful essayists, including Gore Vidal), think that the United States could not wait for a chance to invade Afghanistan in order to build a pipeline across it? American Orientalism doesn't seem that restless from where I sit; it asks only that Afghans leave it alone.

Misgivings on this point turn into serious doubts when one gets to the next paragraph: "In the U.S., the hardening of attitudes, the tightening of the grip of demeaning generalization and triumphalist cliché, the dominance of crude power allied with simplistic contempt for dissenters and 'others,' has found a fitting correlative in the looting, pillaging and destruction of Iraq's libraries and museums."

Here, for some reason, "other" is represented lowercase. But there can't be much doubt as to meaning. The American forces in Baghdad set themselves to annihilate Iraq's cultural patrimony. Can Said mean to say this? Well, he says it again a few lines further on, when he asserts that current Western policy amounts to "power acting through an expedient form of knowledge to assert that this is the Orient's nature, and we must deal with it accordingly."

> In the process the uncountable sediments of history, which include innumerable histories and a dizzying variety of peoples, languages, experiences, and cultures, all these are swept aside or ignored, relegated to the sand heap along with the treasures ground into meaningless fragments that were taken out of Baghdad's libraries and

> museums. My argument is that history is made by men and women, just as it can also be unmade and re-written, always with various silences and elisions, always with shapes imposed and disfigurements tolerated, so that "our" East, "our" Orient, becomes "ours" to possess and direct.

This passage is rescued from sheer vulgarity only by its incoherence. The sole testable proposition (or nontautology) is the fantastic allegation that American forces powdered the artifacts of the Iraq museum in order to show who was boss. And the essential emptiness of putting the "our" in quotation marks, with its related insistence on possession and appropriation, is nakedly revealed thereby. We can be empirically sure of four things: that by design the museums and libraries of Baghdad survived the earlier precision bombardment without a scratch or a splinter; that much of the looting and desecration occurred before coalition forces had complete control of the city; that no looting was committed by U.S. soldiers; and that the substantial reconstitution of the museum's collection has been undertaken by the occupation authorities, and their allies among Iraqi dissidents, with considerable care and scruple. This leaves only two arguable questions: How much more swiftly might the coalition troops have moved to protect the galleries and shelves? And how are we to divide the responsibility for desecration and theft between Iraqi officials and Iraqi mobs? The depravity of both is, to be sure, partly to be blamed on the Saddam regime; would it be too "Orientalist" to go any further?

I said earlier that I wondered whether Said was affected, in this direly excessive rhetoric, by his role as an exile. I am moved to ask again by his repeated and venomous attacks on Ahmed Chalabi and Kanan Makiya, Iraqi oppositionists denounced by him, in effect, for living in the West and being expatriates. Never mind that this is a tactical trope of which Said should obviously beware. The existence of such men suggests to me, in contrast, that there is every hope of cultural and political cross-pollination between the Levant, the Orient, the Near East, the Middle East, Western Asia (whatever name you may choose to give it), and the citizens of the Occident, the North, the metropole. In recent arguments in Washington about democracy and self-determination and pluralism, it seemed to me that the visiting Iraqi and Kurdish activists had a lot more to teach than to learn.

At that same far-off and long-ago conference in Cyprus, so near to the old Crusader fortresses of Farnagusta, Kantara, and St. Hilarion, I also had the good fortune to encounter Sir Steven Runciman, whose history of the Crusades is an imperishable work, because it demonstrates that medieval Christian fundamentalism not only constituted a menace to Islamic civilization but also directly resulted in the sack of Byzantium, the retardation of Europe, and the massacre of the Jews. It is desirable that the opponents of today's fanaticisms be as cool and objective in their recognition of a common enemy, and it is calamitous that one who had that opportunity should have chosen to miss it.

(*The Atlantic*, September 2003)

The Swastika and the Cedar

AS ARAB THOROUGHFARES GO, Hamra Street in the center of Beirut is probably the most chic of them all. International in flavor, cosmopolitan in character, it boasts the sort of smart little café where a Lebanese sophisticate can pause between water-skiing in the Mediterranean in the morning and snow-skiing in the mountains just above the city in the afternoon. "The Paris of the Middle East" used to be the cliché about Beirut: By that exacting standard, I suppose, Hamra Street would be the Boulevard Saint-Germain.

Not at all the sort of place you would expect to find a spinning red swastika on prominent display. Yet, as I strolled in company along Hamra on a sunny Valentine's Day last February, in search of a trinket for the beloved and perhaps some stout shoes for myself, a swastika was just what I ran into. I recognized it as the logo of the Syrian Social Nationalist Party, a Fascist organization (it would be more honest if it called itself "National Socialist") that yells for a "Greater Syria" comprising all of Lebanon, Israel/Palestine, Cyprus, Jordan, Kuwait, Iraq, and swaths of Iran, Saudi Arabia, Turkey, and Egypt. It's one of the suicide-bomber front organizations—the other one being Hezbollah, or "the party of god"—through which Syria's Baathist dictatorship exerts overt and covert influence on Lebanese affairs.

Well, call me old-fashioned if you will, but I have always taken the view that swastika symbols exist for one purpose only—to be defaced. Telling my two companions to hold on for a second, I flourish my trusty felt-tip and begin to write some offensive words on the offending poster. I say "begin" because I have barely gotten to the letter *k* in a well-known transitive verb when I am grabbed by my shirt collar by a venomous little thug, his face glittering with hysterical malice. With his other hand, he is speed-dialing for backup on his cell phone. As always with episodes of violence, things seem to slow down and quicken up at the same time: the eruption of mayhem in broad daylight happening with the speed of lightning yet somehow held in freeze-frame. It becomes evident, as the backup arrives, that this gang wants to take me away.

I am as determined as I can be that I am not going to be stuffed into the trunk of some car and borne off to a private dungeon (as has happened to friends of mine in Beirut in the past). With my two staunch comrades I approach a policeman whose indifference seems well-nigh perfect. We hail a cab and start to get in, but one of our assailants gets in also, and the driver seems to know intimidation only too well when he sees it. We retreat to a stretch of sidewalk outside a Costa café, and suddenly I am sprawled on the ground, having been hit from behind, and someone is putting the leather into my legs and flanks. At this point the crowd in the café begins to shout at the hoodlums, which unnerves them long enough for us to stop another cab and pull away. My shirt is spattered with blood, but I'm in no pain yet: The nastiest moment is just ahead of me. As the taxi accelerates, a face looms at the open window and a fist crashes through and connects with my cheekbone. The blow isn't so hard, but the contorted, glaring, fanatical face is a horror show, a vision from hell. It's like looking down a wobbling gun barrel, or into the eyes of a torturer. I can see it still.

And—though I suppose in a way that I did "ask for it"—this can happen on a sunny Saturday afternoon on the main avenue, on a block which I later learned has been living in fear of the S.S.N.P. for some time. In the morning, though, I had been given a look at a much more heartening version of "the Arab street." Valentine's Day was the fourth anniversary of the assassination, by a car bomb of military-industrial grade and strength, of the immensely popular former prime minister Rafik Hariri. A hero to millions of Lebanese for his astonishing rebuilding of the country (admittedly by his own construction consortium) after fifteen years of civil war, he became a hero twice over when he resisted Syrian manipulation of Lebanese politics. (The statistical connection between that political position and the probability of death by car bomb is something I'll come to.)

Martyrs' Square, the huge open space in downtown Beirut, dominated by the finest imaginable Virgin Megastore and by a brand-new sandstone mosque in the Turkish style commissioned by Rafik Hariri, was absolutely thronged by a crowd of hundreds of thousands. Although it was a commemorative event, there were no signs of the phenomena that the media have taught us to expect when death is the subject in the Middle East. That is to say, there were no hoarse calls for martyrdom and revenge, no ululating women or children wearing suicide-bomber shrouds, no firing into the air or coffins tossing on a sea of hysterical zealotry. As I made my way through the packed crowd I wondered why it seemed somehow familiar. It came to me that the atmosphere of my hometown of Washington on the day of Obama's inauguration had been a bit like this: a huge and unwieldy but good-natured celebration of democracy and civil society.

Lebanon is the most plural society in the region, and the "March 14" coalition, the group of parties that leads the current government, essentially represents the Sunnis, the Christians, the Druze (a tribe and creed unique to the region), and the Left. Hezbollah has a partial stranglehold on the Shiite community but by no means a monopoly, and one of the speakers at the rally was a Shiite member of Parliament, Bassem Sabaa, who argued very strongly that Arab grievances against Israel should not excuse Arab-on-Arab oppression. Almost nobody displayed any religious emblem, and even the few who did were usually careful to put it next to the ubiquitous cedar-symbol flag of Lebanon itself. Women with head covering were few; women with face covering were nowhere to be seen. Designer jeans were the predominant fashion theme. Eclectic musical choices came over the loudspeakers. The average age was low. Nobody had been bused in, at least not by the state. Nobody had been told to leave work and demonstrate his or her loyalty. You get my drift.

This is the way that Lebanon could be: a microcosm of the Middle East where ethnic and confessional differences are resolved by Federalism and by elections. But there is a dark, supervising power that keeps the process under surveillance, and then alters the odds by selecting some actors for abrupt removal. As Omar Khayyám unforgettably puts it in his *Rubáiyát:*

'Tis all a Checker-board of Nights and Days
Where Destiny with Men for Pieces plays:
Hither and thither moves, and mates, and slays,
And one by one back in the Closet lays.

If you want to replace the word "Destiny" with a more modern term, you might get a hint from a banner that was displayed after the murder of Rafik Hariri. SYRIAL KILLERS, it read, simply. The street reaction to the murder of Rafik Hariri was so intense that it led to the passage of a United Nations resolution mandating the withdrawal of the Syrian Army from Lebanon after almost three decades of occupation. However, it remains the case that those who inconvenience Syria by their criticisms are bad liabilities from the life-insurance point of view. Since somebody's car bomb killed Hariri and twenty-two others, somebody has killed Samir Kassir and Gibran Tueni, two of the bravest journalists and editors at the independent newspaper *An-Nahar* (The Day). Somebody has killed Pierre Gemayel, a leader of the country's Maronite Catholic community. Somebody has killed George Hawi, a former leader of the Lebanese Communist Party. Somebody has killed Captain Wissam Eid, a senior police intelligence officer in the investigation of the Hariri murder. The murders of these Lebanese patriots, and four others of nearly equal prominence, were all highly professional explosive-charge or hit-squad jobs, and their victims all had one, and only one, thing in common. In a highly unusual resolution, the United Nations has established a tribunal to inquire into the Hariri murder and its ramifications, four Lebanese former generals with ties to Syria have been arrested on suspicion, and an office in The Hague has already begun the preliminary proceedings. This investigation will condition the circumstances under which the next Middle East war—involving Israel, Syria, Iran, and Hezbollah—will take place on Lebanese soil.

Officially removed from that soil, Syria continues to manipulate by proxies and by surrogates. One of its projections of power is the S.S.N.P., the Christian Orthodox Fascist group with which I tangled (and which is thought to have provided the muscle in some of the above-mentioned assassinations). Another, which is also part of the shadow thrown on Lebanon by Iran, is Hezbollah. Two days after the anti-Syrian rally, I journeyed to the

Dahiyeh area of southern Beirut, where the "party of god" was commemorating its own martyrs. This is the distinctly less chic Shiite quarter of the city, rebuilt in part with Iranian money after Israel pounded it to rubble in the war of 2006, and it's the power base of Sheikh Hassan Nasrallah, the brilliant politician who is Hezbollah's leader.

The contrast between the two rallies could not have been greater. Try picturing a Shiite-Muslim megachurch in a huge downtown tent, with separate entrances for men and women and separate seating (with the women all covered in black). A huge poster of a nuclear mushroom cloud surmounts the scene, with the inscription OH ZIONISTS, IF YOU WANT THIS TYPE OF WAR THEN SO BE IT! During the warm-up, an onstage Muslim Milli Vanilli orchestra and choir lipsynchs badly to a repetitive, robotic music video that shows lurid scenes of martyrdom and warfare. There is keening and wailing, while the aisles are patrolled by gray-uniformed male stewards and black-chador'd crones. Key words keep repeating themselves with thumping effect: *shahid* (martyr), *jihad* (holy war), *yehud* (Jew). In the special section for guests there sits a group of uniformed and bemedaled officials representing the Islamic Republic of Iran. I remember what Walid Jumblatt, the leader of the Progressive Socialist Party and also the leader of the Druze community—some of my best friends are Druze—said to me a day or so previously: "Hezbollah is not just a party. It is a state within our state." It is also the projection of another state.

This glum, dark, regimented, organized event is in the boldest possible contrast to the color and informality and spontaneity of the Valentine's Day rally. On that occasion, all the speakers limited themselves to about 10 minutes each. No such luck for the attendees of the Hezbollah phalanx: When Sheikh Nasrallah eventually appears in his black turban (via video link) he allows himself an oration of Castroesque length, and was still visible and going strong on Hezbollah's TV station by the time I'd tired of him and gotten all the way back to my hotel.

"Lebanon is the template and the cockpit of the region," said Saad Hariri, his father's successor, at a dinner the night before I left. "Anyone who wants to deliver a message in the Middle East sends it first to Beirut." He was right. The new and dearly bought independence of the country is being ground between the upper and nether millstones of the Iran-Syria-Hamas-Hezbollah axis and the stubborn, intransigent southern frontier of the Israeli-Palestinian quarrel: the stark contours of the next Middle East combat. The whole place has an ominously pre-war feeling to it, as if the dress rehearsals are almost over. But we have a tendency to use the term "Arab street" as if it meant the same as anti-Western religious frenzy. (I think of the brutes who nearly abducted me, but I also remember those passersby who protested at the thuggery.) What I learned from my three street encounters in Beirut was that there is more than one version of that "street," and that the street itself is not by any means one-way.

(*Vanity Fair*, May 2009)

Holiday in Iraq

LAST SUMMER, you may have been among the astonished viewers of American television who were treated to a series of commercials from a group calling itself "Kurdistan—The Other Iraq." These rather touching and artless little spots (theotheriraq.com) urged you to consider investing in business, and even made you ponder taking your vacation, in the country's three northern provinces. Mr. Jon Stewart, of *The Daily Show*, could hardly believe his luck. To lampoon the ads, and to say, in effect, "Yeah, right—holiday in Iraq," was probably to summarize the reaction of much of the audience. Sure, baby, come to sunny Mesopotamia, and bring the family, and get your ass blown off while religious wack jobs ululate gleefully over your remains.

Well, as it happens, I decided to check this out, and did spend most of the Christmas holiday in Iraqi Kurdistan, bringing my son along with me, and had a perfectly swell time. We didn't make any investments, though I would say that the hotel and tourism and oil sectors are wide open for enterprise, but we did visit the ancient citadel in Erbil, where Alexander the Great defeated the Persians—my son is a Greek-speaking classicist—and we did sample the lovely mountains and lakes and rivers that used to make this region the resort area for all Iraqis. Air and road travel were easy (you can now fly direct from several airports in Europe to one of two efficient airports in Iraqi Kurdistan), and walking anywhere at night in any Kurdish town is safer than it is in many American cities. The police and soldiers are all friendly locals, there isn't a coalition soldier to be seen, and there hasn't been a suicide attack since May of 2005.

It wasn't my first trip. That took place in 1991, in the closing stages of the Gulf War. With a guerrilla escort, I crossed illegally into Iraq from Turkey and toured the shattered and burned and poisoned landscape on which Saddam Hussein had imprinted himself. In the town of Halabja, which has now earned its gruesome place in history, I met people whose hideous wounds from chemical bombardment were still suppurating. The city of Qala Diza had been thoroughly dynamited and bulldozed, and looked like an irretrievable wreck. Much of the area's lavish tree cover had been deforested: The bare plains were dotted with forbidding concrete barracks into which Kurds had been forcibly "relocated" or (a more accurate word) "concentrated." Nearly 200,000 people had been slaughtered, and millions more deported: huddling in ruins or packed into fetid camps on the Turkish and Iranian frontiers. To turn a spade was to risk uncovering a mass grave. All of Iraq suffered terribly during those years, but its Kurdish provinces were among the worst places in the entire world—a howling emptiness of misery where I could catch, for the first time in my life, the actual scent of evil as a real force on earth.

Thus, I confess to a slight lump in the throat at revisiting the area and seeing thriving, humming towns with multiplying construction sites, billboards for overseas companies, Internet cafés, and a choice of newspapers. It's even reassuring to see the knockoff "MaDonal," with pseudo-golden arches, in the eastern city of Sulaimaniya, soon to be the site of the American University of Iraq, which will be offering not only an M.B.A. course but also, in the words of Azzam Alwash, one of its directors, "the ideas of Locke, the ideas and writings of Paine and Madison." Everybody knows how to snigger when you mention Jeffersonian democracy and Iraq in the same breath; try sniggering when you meet someone who is trying to express these ideas in an atmosphere that only a few years ago was heavy with miasmic decay and the reek of poison gas.

While I am confessing, I may as well make a clean breast of it. Thanks to the reluctant decision of the first President Bush and Secretary of State James Baker, those fresh princes of "realism," the United States and Britain, placed an aerial umbrella over Iraqi Kurdistan in 1991 and detached it from the death grip of Saddam Hussein. Under the protective canopy of the no-fly zone—actually it was also called the "you-fly-you-die zone"—an embryonic free Iraq had a chance to grow. I was among those who thought and believed and argued that this example could, and should, be extended to the rest of the country; the cause became a consuming thing in my life. To describe the resulting shambles as a disappointment or a failure or even a defeat would be the weakest statement I could possibly make: It feels more like a sick, choking nightmare of betrayal from which there can be no awakening. Yet Kurdistan continues to demonstrate how things could have been different, and it isn't a place from which the West can simply walk away.

In my hometown of Washington, D.C., it's too easy to hear some expert hold forth about the essential character of any stricken or strategic country. (Larry McMurtry, in his novel *Cadillac Jack*, has a lovely pastiche of Joseph Alsop doing this very act about Yemen.) I had lived here for years and suffered through many Georgetown post-dinner orations until someone supplied me with the unfailing antidote to such punditry. It comes from Stephen Potter, the author of *Lifemanship, One-upmanship*, and other classics. Wait until the old bore has finished his exposition, advised Potter, then pounce forward and say in a plonking register, "Yes, but not in the South?" You will seldom if ever be wrong, and you will make the expert perspire. Different as matters certainly are in the South of Iraq, the thing to stress is how different, how very different, they are in the North.

In Kurdistan, to take a few salient examples, there is a memorial of gratitude being built for fallen American soldiers. "We are planning," said the region's prime minister, Nechirvan Barzani, in his smart new office in the Kurdish capital of Erbil, "to invite their relatives to the unveiling." Speaking of unveiling, you see women with headscarfs on the streets and in offices (and on the judicial bench and in Parliament, which reserves a quarter of the seats for women by law), but you never see a face or body enveloped in a burka. The majority of Kurds are Sunni, and the minority are Shiite, with large groups belonging to other sects and confessions, but there is no intercommunal mayhem. Liquor stores and bars are easy to find, sometimes operated by members of the large and unmolested Christian community. On the university campuses, you may easily meet Arab Iraqis who have gladly fled Baghdad and Basra for this safe haven. I know of more than one intrepid Western reporter who has done the same. The approaches from the south are patrolled by very effective and battle-hardened Kurdish militiamen, who still carry the proud title of their guerrilla days: the *peshmerga*, or, translated from the Kurdish language, "those who face death." These men have a very brusque way with al-Qaeda and its local supporters, and have not just kept them at a distance but subjected them to very hot pursuit. (It was Kurdish intelligence that first exposed the direct link between the psychopathic Abu Musab al-Zarqawi and Osama bin Laden.) Of the few divisions of the Iraqi Army that are considered even remotely reliable, the bulk are made up of tough Kurdish volunteers.

Pause over that latter point for a second. Within recent memory, the Kurdish population of Iraq was being subjected to genocidal cleansing. Given the chance to leave the failed state altogether, why would they not take it? Yet today, the president of Iraq, Jalal Talabani, is a Kurd: a former guerrilla leader so genial and humane that he personally opposed the execution of Saddam Hussein. Of the very few successful or effective ministries in Baghdad, such as the Foreign Ministry, it is usually true that a Kurd, such as Hoshyar Zebari, is at the head of it. The much-respected deputy prime minister (and moving spirit of the American University in Sulaimaniya), Dr. Barham Salih, is a Kurd. He put it to me very movingly when I flew down to Baghdad to talk to him: "We are willing to fight and sacrifice for a democratic Iraq. And we were the ones to suffer the most from the opposite case. If Iraq fails, it will not be our fault."

President Talabani might only be the "president of the Green Zone," as his friends sometimes teasingly say, but he disdains to live in that notorious enclave. He is now seventy-three years of age and has a rather Falstaffian appearance—everyone refers to him as "Mam Jalal" or "Uncle Jalal"—but this is nonetheless quite a presidential look, and he has spent much of his life on the run, or in exile, or in the mountains, and survived more dangerous times than these. You may choose to call today's suicide murderers and video beheaders and power-drill torturers by the name "insurgents," but he has the greater claim to have led an actual armed resistance that did not befoul itself by making war on civilians. In Baghdad, he invited me to an impressively heavy lunch in the house once occupied by Saddam Hussein's detested, late half-brother Barzan al-Tikriti, where I shared the table with grizzled Kurdish tribal leaders, and as the car bombs thumped across the city I realized how he could afford to look so assured and confident, and to flourish a Churchill-size postprandial cigar. To be chosen by the Iraqi Parliament as the country's first-ever elected president might be one thing, and perhaps a dubious blessing. But to be the first Kurd to be the head of an Arab state was quite another. When he was elected, spontaneous celebrations by Kurds in Iran and Syria broke out at once, and often had to be forcibly repressed by their respective dictators. To put it pungently, the Kurds have now stepped onto the stage of Middle Eastern history, and it will not be easy to push them off it again. You may easily murder a child, as the parties of god prove every single day, but you cannot make a living child grow smaller.

I got a whiff of this intoxicating "birth of a nation" emotion when I flew back with Talabani from Baghdad to his Kurdish home base of Sulaimaniya. Here, as in the other Kurdish center, in Erbil, the airport gives the impression of belonging to an independent state. There are protocol officers, official limousines, and all the appurtenances of autonomy. Iraq's constitution specifies that Kurdistan is entitled to its own regional administration, and the inhabitants never miss a chance to underline what they have achieved. (The Iraqi flag, for example, is not much flown in these latitudes. Instead, the golden Kurdish sunburst emblem sits at the center of a banner of red, white, and green.) Most inspiring of all, perhaps, is Kurdish Airlines, which can take a pilgrim to the hajj or fly home a returning refugee without landing at another Iraqi airport. Who would have believed, viewing the moonscape of Kurdistan in 1991, that these ground-down people would soon have their own airline?

The Kurds are the largest nationality in the world without a state of their own. The King of Bahrain has, in effect, his own seat at the United Nations, but the 25 million or so Kurds do not. This is partly because they are cursed by geography, with their ancestral lands located at the point where the frontiers of Iraq, Iran, Turkey, and Syria converge. It would be hard to imagine a less promising neighborhood for a political experiment. In Iraq, the more than four million Kurds make up just under a quarter of the population. The proportion in Turkey is more like 20 percent, in Iran 10 percent, and in Syria perhaps nine. For centuries, this people's existence was folkloric and marginal, and confined to what one anthropologist called "the Lands of Insolence": the inaccessible mountain ranges and high valleys that bred warriors and rebels. A fierce tribe named the Karduchoi makes an appearance in Xenophon's history of the events of 400 B.C. Then there is mainly silence until a brilliant Kurdish commander named Salah al-Din (Saladin to most) emerges in the twelfth century to unite the Muslim world against the Crusaders. He was born in Tikrit, later the hometown of Saddam Hussein. This is apt, because Saddam actually was the real father of Kurdish nationhood. By subjecting the Kurds to genocide he gave them a solidarity they had not known before, and compelled them to create a fierce and stubborn resistance, with its own discipline and army. By laying waste to their ancient villages and farms, furthermore, he forced them into urban slums and refugee centers where they became more integrated, close-knit, and socialized: historically always the most revolutionary point in the emergence of any nationalism.

"The state of Iraq is not sacred," remarked Dr. Mohammad Sadik as we drove through Erbil to his office at Salahaddin University, of which he is president. "It was not created by god. It was created by Winston Churchill." Cobbled together out of the post-1918 wreckage of the Ottoman Empire, Iraq as a state was always crippled by the fact that it contained a minority population that owed it little if any loyalty. And now this state has broken down, and is breaking up. The long but unstable and unjust post-Ottoman compromise has been irretrievably smashed by the American-led invasion. Of the three contending parties in Iraq, only the Kurds now have a serious Plan B. They had a head start, by escaping twelve years early from Saddam's festering prison state. They have done their utmost to be friendly brokers between the Sunni and Shiite Arabs, but if the country implodes, they can withdraw to their oil-rich enclave and muster under their own flag. There is no need to romanticize the Kurds: They have their own history of clan violence and cruelty. But this flag at present represents the closest approximation to democracy and secularism that the neighborhood can boast.

Americans have more responsibility here than most of us are aware of. It was President Woodrow Wilson, after the First World War, who inscribed the idea of self-determination for the Kurds in the 1920 Treaty of Sevres, a document that all Kurds can readily cite. Later machinations by Britain and France and Turkey, all of them greedy for the oil in the Kurdish provinces, cheated the Kurds of their birthright and shoehorned them into Iraq. More recently, the Ford-Kissinger administration encouraged the Kurds to rebel against Baghdad, offering blandishments of greater autonomy, and then cynically abandoned them in 1975, provoking yet another refugee crisis and a terrible campaign of reprisal by Saddam Hussein. In 1991, George Bush Sr. went to war partly in the name of Kurdish rights and then chose to forget his own high-toned rhetoric. This, too, is a story that every Kurd can tell you. However the fate of Iraq is to be decided, we cannot permit another chapter in this record of betrayal. Meanwhile, you should certainly go and see it for yourself, and also shed a tear for what might have been.

(*Vanity Fair*, April 2007)

Tunisia: At the Desert's Edge

IF WE ALL INDEED come from Africa, then the very idea of Africa itself comes from the antique northern coast of that great landmass, where the cosmology is subtly different and where the inhabitants look north to Europe and southward at the Sahara. Here was the mighty civilization known as Carthage, which came as close as possible to reversing what we think of as the course of "history" and conquering Europe from Africa instead of the other way around. With its elephants and armies, and under the brilliant generalship of Hannibal, it penetrated all the way through Spain and France and down over the Alps onto the smiling northern plains of Italy. Not even the later Muslim conquests, which surged out of the Arabian Desert and along northern Africa and across the Strait of Gibraltar, ever got so far. After Rome took its revenge and deleted Carthage from the historical page a hundred and forty-six years before Christ—as I was told by the Tunisian archaeologist Neguib Ben Lazuz as we sat in the shadow of the magnificent Roman amphitheater of El Djem—it cast around for a name to call its new colony.

The most imposing local people were the Afri, a Berber tribe in the northeastern quarter of what is now Tunisia. And the new province of "Africa," or "Ifriqiyyah," as its later, Muslim rulers were to call it, was sophisticated enough to give its title to a continent. There were Roman emperors—such as Septimius Severus—of African descent. In the eighth book of his *Natural History*, written in the first century A.D., Pliny the Elder made the observation, possibly borrowed from Aristotle, "*Ex Africa semper aliquid novi*" ("There is always something new out of Africa").

And so there is. If you look at the map now, you will see that Tunisia is like a little diamond-shaped keystone, its different facets constituting a front-line territory between Europe and Africa, North and South, East and West, the desert and the sea. It was from its gorgeous city of Kairouan—the oldest Muslim city in Africa—with its huge mosque built with the pillars of Roman and Carthaginian temples, that Islam was spread to the black sub-Saharan regions of Mali and Nigeria, and also northward to the Spanish region of Andalusia. And it is here that the crosscurrents between fundamentalism and cosmopolitanism, syncretism and puritanism, are being most acutely registered. From the northern tip of Tunisia on a clear day, you can see the shimmering Italian island of Pantelleria. Spanish and French and Italian coast guards regularly pick up Africans from as far south as Guinea who have traversed the interior to launch their craft across the Mediterranean. (One of these was picked up the other day, having attempted the perilous crossing with no more than an oil-drum raft and a G.P.S. navigation system. Give that man an entry permit! We require people with such initiative.)

On the other hand, so to speak, it was in Tunisia in April 2002 that an al-Qaeda suicide murderer drove a truckload of propane up to El Ghriba, the oldest synagogue in North Africa, a little gem of a building that has been the centerpiece of an ancient Jewish community—the largest in the Muslim world—that dates back two millennia. Nineteen people, mostly German tourists, were slaughtered.

I recently made my own visit to the place, which is on the island of Djerba, where Ulysses is said to have passed his time among the lotus-eaters. I was walking through the old ghetto, in which Arabs and Jews mix freely, when a series of bombs tore through cities in neighboring Morocco and Algeria, apparently to mark the fifth anniversary of this revolting crime. In January, there had been a firefight between Tunisian security forces and the newly named al-Qaeda in the Islamic Maghreb, a gang formerly known as the Salafist Group for Preaching and Combat, which joined the bin Ladenists and has apparently been granted the bearded one's franchise. This poses a fairly stark choice. Will the northern littoral of Africa become a zone of tension, uneasily demarcating a watery yet fiery line between Europe and the southern continent? Or will it evolve into a meeting place of cultures, trading freely and cross-fertilizing the civilizations, as it did once before?

Tunisian society contains some of the answers to these questions. On the face of it, the country is one of Africa's most outstanding success stories. In the 2006–7 World Economic Forum Global Competitiveness Report, it was ranked No. 1 in Africa for economic competitiveness, even, incidentally, outpacing three European states (Italy, Greece, and Portugal). Home ownership is 80 percent. Life expectancy, the highest on the continent, is 72. Less than 4 percent of the population is below the poverty line, and the alleviation of misery by a "solidarity fund" has been adopted by the United Nations as a model program. Nine out of ten households are connected to electricity and clean water. Tunisia is the first African state to have been accepted as an associate member of the European Union. Its Code of Personal Status was the first in the Arab world to abolish polygamy, and the veil and the burka are never seen. More than 40 percent of the judges and lawyers are female. The country makes delicious wine and even exports it to France. The Tunisian Jews make a potent grappa out of figs, which is available as a digestif in most restaurants. There were several moments, as I was loafing around the beautiful blue-and-white seaside towns or the exquisite classical museums and ruins, when the combination of stylish females, excellent food, clean streets, smart-looking traffic cops, and cheap and efficient taxis made me feel I was in a place more upscale than many European recreational resorts and spas. I remembered what my old friend the late Edward Said had told me: "You should go to Tunisia, Christopher. It's the gentlest country in Africa. Even the Islamists are highly civilized!"

But before I could be seduced into abject boosterism, I had a lengthy, not to say lavish, dinner with some of the country's academics and intellectuals and writers. The atmosphere in the restaurant was quasi–Left Bank Parisian, and I think I lulled them a bit by recounting some of the Davos statistics cited above. Then I added two more. Since its independence from France, in 1956, Tunisia has had exactly two presidents, the first of whom, Habib Bourguiba, became a "president for life" before being deposed for senility and megalomania. The current ruler, Zine El Abidine Ben Ali, will celebrate his twentieth year of uninterrupted power this November. At election times, he has been known to win more than 90 percent of the vote: a figure that never fails to make me nervous. I have not met the man, but within hours of landing in the country I could have passed an exam in what he looks like, because his portrait is rather widely displayed.

Well, you can say for Tunisia that people do not lower their voices or look over their shoulders (another thing that has made me nervous in my time) before discussing these questions. But the conversation still took on a slightly pained tone. Was the West—that's me—not judging the country by rather exacting standards? To the east lay the huge territory of Libya, underdeveloped and backward and Islamized even though floating on a lake of oil, and, furthermore, governed since 1969 by a flamboyantly violent nutcase. ("We are the same people as them," said my friend Hamid, "but they are so much *en retard*.") To the west lay the enormous country of Algeria, again artificially prosperous through oil and natural gas, but recently the scene of a heinous Islamist insurgency that—along with harsh and vigorous state repression—had killed perhaps 150,000 people. Looking farther away and to the south, Sudan's fanatical and genocidal militia, not content with what they had done in Darfur, were spreading their *jihad* into neighboring Chad, extending a belt of violent Islamism across the sub-Saharan zone. Increasingly, Africa was becoming the newest site of confrontation not just between Islam and other religions (as in the battle between Christian Ethiopia and Islamist Somalia, or between Islamists and Christians in Nigeria, or Islamists and Christians and animists in Sudan), but between competing versions of Islam itself. Why pick on mild Tunisia, where the coup in 1987 had been bloodless, where religious parties are forbidden, where the population grows evenly because of the availability of contraception, where you can see male and female students holding hands and wearing blue jeans, and where thousands of Americans and more than four million Europeans take their vacations every year?

When it's put like that, who wouldn't want the alternative of an African Titoism, or perhaps an African Gaullism, where presidential rule keeps a guiding but not tyrannical hand? A country where people discuss micro-credits for small business instead of "macro" schemes such as holy war? Mr. Ben Ali does not make lengthy speeches on TV every night, or appear in gorgeously barbaric uniforms, or live in a different palace for every day of the week. Tunisia has no grandiose armed forces, the curse of the rest of the continent, feeding parasitically off the national income and rewarding their own restlessness with the occasional coup. And the country is lucky in other ways as well. Its population is a smooth blend of black and Berber and Arab, and though it proudly defends its small minorities of Shiites, Christians (Saint Augustine spent time here), Baha'is, and Jews (there is a Jewish member of the Senate), it is otherwise uniformly Sunni. It has been spared the awful toxicity of ethnic and religious rivalry, which makes it very unusual in Africa. Its international airport is named Tunis-Carthage, evoking African roots without Afrocentric demagogy. I still could not shake the feeling that its system of government is fractionally less intelligent and risk-taking than the majority of its citizens.

However, it is not every day that you can go downtown to a university that is attached to a mosque—in this case the Zitouna, or "Olive Tree," mosque, with an old library housing thousands of ancient texts—and sit with a female professor of theology. Mongia Souaihi cheerfully explained to me the many reasons why the veil is not authorized by the Koran and why she is in danger for drawing this conclusion in print. "The fundamentalists from overseas have declared me to be *kuffar*—an unbeliever." This I know to be dangerous, because a Muslim who has once been declared to be an apostate is also a person who can be sentenced to death. "Which fundamentalists? And from where overseas?" "Rachid Ghannouchi, from London." Oh no, not again. If you saw my "Londonistan" essay, in the June *Vanity Fair*, you will know that fanatics who are unwelcome in Africa and Arabia are allowed an astonishing freedom in the United Kingdom. The leader of Ennahda, the outlawed Tunisian Islamist group, the aforesaid Mr. Ghannouchi, was until September 11, 2001, allowed to broadcast his hysterical incitements into Tunisia from a London station. "Almost everything we have worked for in this country among the young," I was told by Mounir Khelifa, a highly polished professor of English, "can be undermined by any one of a hundred satellite stations beamed into our society." I thought perhaps he was exaggerating, or perhaps feeling insecure. The Tunisian authorities sometimes give the same impression by hovering around in Internet cafés trying to invigilate what sites people are clicking on. In a society where satellite dishes are everywhere, this looks crude and old-fashioned.

So Tunisia's achievements, though real enough, are fragile. When the terrorists target tourists, they pick the economy's most vulnerable spot. (The Djerba atrocity had a real effect on that year's overall figures.) But, of course, they also isolate themselves, first by creating poverty and unemployment and second by violating the inflexible laws of Muslim hospitality. So this is the edge of uncertain awareness on which an outwardly happy and thriving society is poised. Some way to the south of that Roman amphitheater at El Djem, you begin to hit the Sahara. It was in this imposing dune landscape that *Star Wars*, *Raiders of the Lost Ark*, and *The English Patient* were filmed. It is also here that the desert ceaselessly, mindlessly, but somehow deliberately tries to move northward. Its rate of progress is uneven, and varies from country to country, and when you do see the Tunisian Army it is often helping in measures—of planting and irrigation—to stave off the remorseless encroachment. An enclave of development, Tunisia is menaced by the harsh extremists of a desert religion, and ultimately by the desert itself. As with everything else in Africa, this is not a contest we can view with indifference.

(*Vanity Fair*, July 2007)

What Happened to the Suicide Bombers of Jerusalem?

IT IS SOMETIMES IMPORTANT to write about the things that are not happening and the dogs that are not barking.

To do so, of course, can provide an easy hostage to fortune, which is why a lot of columnists prefer not to risk it. For all I know, some leering fanatic is preparing to make me look silly even as I write. But I ask anyway: Whatever happened to the suicide bombers of Jerusalem?

It's not that long since the combination of self-immolation and mass murder was a regular event on Israeli soil. Different people drew radically different conclusions from the campaign, which had a nerve-racking effect not just on Israeli Jews but on Israeli Arabs and Druze—who were often among the casualties—and on visiting tourists. It was widely said by liberals, including people as eminent as Tony Blair's wife, Cherie Blair, that the real cause of such a lurid and awful tactic was despair: the reaction of a people under occupation who had no other avenue of expression for their misery and frustration.

Well, surely nobody will be so callous as to say that there is less despair among Palestinians today—especially since the terrible events in the Gaza Strip and the return to power of the Israeli right wing as well as the expansion of Jewish-zealot settler activity. And yet there is no graph on which extra despair can be shown to have eventuated in more suicide. Indeed, if there is any correlation at all, it would seem to be in reverse. How can this be?

Of the various alternative explanations, one would be the success of the wall or "fence" that Israel has built or is building, approximating but not quite conforming to the "green line" of the 1967 frontier. Another would be the ruthless campaign of "targeted assassinations," whereby Israeli agents took out important leaders of Hamas and Islamic *Jihad*, the two organizations most committed to "martyrdom operations." A third might be the temporary truces or cease-fires to which Hamas (but not Islamic *Jihad*) have from time to time agreed.

But, actually, none of these would explain why the suicide campaign went into remission. Or, at least, they would not explain why it went into remission if the original cause was despair. If despair is your feeling, then nothing can stop you from blowing yourself up against the wall as a last gesture against Israeli colonial architecture. If despair dominates your psyche, then targeted assassinations of others are not going to stop you from donning the shroud and the belt and aiming yourself at paradise, even if only at a roadblock. If despair is what has invaded your mind, why on earth would you care about this or that short-term truce?

Even before the assault died away, there were good reasons to doubt that despair had been the motive or the explanation. For one thing, almost all the suicide attacks were directed at civilians in pre-1967 Israel "proper"—in other words, in the Jewish part of Jerusalem or in towns along the Israeli coastline (in one case, a hotel in Netanya on Passover). It can probably be said with some degree of confidence that nobody blows themselves up for a half-a-loaf compromise solution. These cold-blooded attacks did not just avoid well-defended West Bank settlements or Israeli army bases; they also vividly expressed the demand that all Jews leave Palestine or risk being killed. Despair cannot so easily be channeled so as to underline a strictly political/ideological objective.

Another possible reason for the slump in suicide is that those who were orchestrating it came to find that the tactic was becoming subject to diminishing returns. Despair must have meant a roughly constant stream of potential volunteers, but the immediate needs of Hamas and Islamic *Jihad* may not have always required the tap of despair to be left turned on. Indeed, there must have been some quite intense private discussions about how to turn it off. Not every despairing person can make, at home, the necessary belts, fuses, and lethal charges. These things require a godfather. And this, in turn, prompts the question: What will be said if or when the tap is ever turned back on? Surely it won't quite do to say that despair must have broken out all over again, though I can easily think of some fools who will be ready to say it.

There were children among the last wave of suicide-murderers, some of whom lost their nerve and surrendered at the last moment. There were also young women, some of whom, it seems, would otherwise have been killed for "honor" reasons and who were offered the relatively painless alternative of a martyr's fate. Nasty, vicious, fanatical old men, not human emotions, were making the decisions and deciding the days and the hours of death. And the hysterical ululating street celebrations when such a mission was successful did not signify despair at all but a creepy form of religious exaltation in which relatives were encouraged to make a feast out of the death of their own children as well as those of other people. To have added the promise of paradise to this pogrom is to have made spiritual and mental sickness complete; to have made it a sexual paradise is obscene into the bargain. (Women martyrs are obviously not offered the same level of bliss and promiscuity by the Koran.)

Meanwhile, the wall still stands and grows, ironically expressing the much more banal and worldly fact that there are two peoples in Palestine and that sooner or later there will be two states as well.

(*Slate*, July 13, 2009)

Childhood's End: An African Nightmare

IN WILLIAM FAULKNER'S STORY "Raid," set in Alabama and Mississippi in the closing years of the Civil War, a white family becomes aware of a sudden, vast, nighttime migration through the scorched countryside. They can hear it and even smell it before they can see it; it's the black population voting with its feet and heading, so it fervently believes, for the river Jordan: "We couldn't see them and they did not see us; maybe they didn't even look, just walking fast in the dark with that panting, hurrying murmuring, going on..."

Northern Uganda is centered on the headstreams of the Nile rather than the Jordan, and is a strange place for me to find myself put in mind of Faulkner, but every evening at dusk the main town of Gulu starts to be inundated by a mass of frightened humanity, panting, hurrying, and murmuring as it moves urgently through the crepuscular hours. Most of the "night commuters," as they are known locally, are children. They leave their outlying villages and walk as many as eight kilometers to huddle for safety in the towns. And then, in the morning, often without breakfast and often without shoes, they walk all the way back again to get to their schools and their families. That's if the former have not been burned and the latter have not been butchered. These children are not running toward Jordan and the Lord; they are running for their lives from the "Lord's Resistance Army" (L.R.A.). This grotesque, zombie-like militia, which has abducted, enslaved, and brainwashed more than 20,000 children, is a kind of Christian Khmer Rouge and has for the past nineteen years set a standard of cruelty and ruthlessness that—even in a region with a living memory of Idi Amin—has the power to strike the most vivid terror right into the heart and the other viscera.

Here's what happens to the children who can't run fast enough, or who take the risk of sleeping in their huts in the bush. I am sitting in a rehab center, talking to young James, who is eleven and looks about nine. When he actually was nine and sleeping at home with his four brothers, the L.R.A. stormed his village and took the boys away. They were roped at the waist and menaced with bayonets to persuade them to confess what they could not know—the whereabouts of the Ugandan Army's soldiers. On the subsequent forced march, James underwent the twin forms of initiation practiced by the L.R.A. He was first savagely flogged with a wire lash and then made to take part in the murder of those children who had become too exhausted to walk any farther. "First we had to watch," he says. "Then we had to join in the beatings until they died." He was spared from having to do this to a member of his family, which is the L.R.A.'s preferred method of what it calls "registration." And he was spared from being made into a concubine or a sex slave, because the L.R.A. doesn't tolerate that kind of thing for boys. It is, after all, "faith-based." Excuse me, but it does have its standards.

Talking to James about the unimaginable ruin of his childhood, I notice that when I am speaking he stays stock-still, with something a bit dead behind his eyes. But when it comes his turn to tell his story, he immediately starts twisting about in his chair, rubbing his eyes and making waving gestures with his arms. The leader of the L.R.A., a former Catholic acolyte in his forties named Joseph Kony, who now claims to be a spirit medium with a special mission to impose the Ten Commandments, knows what old Fagin knew: that little boys are nimble and malleable if you catch them young enough, and that they make good thieves and runners. Little James was marched all the way to Sudan, whose Muslim-extremist government offers shelter and aid—such an ecumenical spirit!—to the Christian fanatics. There he was put to work stealing food from neighboring villages, and digging and grinding cassava roots. Soon enough, he was given a submachine gun almost as big as himself. Had he not escaped during an ambush, he would have gotten big enough to be given a girl as well, to do with what he liked.

I drove out of Gulu—whose approach roads can be used only in the daytime—to a refugee camp nearer the Sudanese border. A few Ugandan shillings and a few packets of cigarettes procured me a Ugandan Army escort, who sat heavily armed in the back of the pickup truck. As I buckled my seat belt, the driver told me to unbuckle it in spite of the parlous condition of the road. "If you have to jump out," he said, "you will have to jump out very fast." That didn't make me feel much safer, but only days after I left, two Ugandan aid workers were murdered in daylight on these pitted, dusty highways. We bounced along until we hit Pabbo, where a collection of huts and shanties huddle together as if for protection. In this place are packed about 59,000 of the estimated 1.5 million "internally displaced persons" (I.D.P.'s) who have sought protection from the savagery of the L.R.A. Here, I had the slightly more awkward task of interviewing the female survivors of Joseph Kony's rolling Jonestown: a campaign of horror and superstition and indoctrination.

The women of Uganda are naturally modest and reserved, and it obviously involved an effort for them to tell their stories to a male European stranger. But they stood up as straight as spears and looked me right in the eye. Forced to carry heavy loads through the bush and viciously caned—up to 250 strokes—if they dropped anything. Given as gifts or prizes to men two or three times their age and compelled to bear children. Made to watch, and to join in, sessions of hideous punishment for those who tried to escape. Rose Atim, a young woman of bronze Nubian Nefertiti beauty, politely started her story by specifying her primary-school grade (grade five) at the time of her abduction. Her nostrils still flared with indignation when she spoke, whereas one of her fellow refugees, Jane Akello, a young lady with almost anthracite skin, was dull and dead-eyed and monotonous in her delivery. I was beginning to be able to distinguish symptoms. I felt a strong sense of indecency during these interviews, but this was mere squeamish self-indulgence on my part, since the women were anxious to relate the stories of their stolen and maimed childhoods. It was as if they had emerged from some harrowing voyage on the Underground Railroad.

Very few people, apart from his victims, have ever met or even seen the enslaving and child-stealing Joseph Kony, and the few pictures and films of him are amateur and indistinct. This very imprecision probably helps him to maintain his version of charisma. Here is what we know and (with the help of former captives and a Scotland Yard criminal profiler) what we speculate. Kony grew up in a Gulu Province village called Odek. He appointed himself the Lord's anointed prophet for the Acholi people of northern Uganda in 1987, and by the mid-nineties was receiving arms and cash from Sudan. He probably suffers from multiple-personality disorder, and he takes his dreams for prophecies. He goes into trances in which he speaks into a tape recorder and plays back the resulting words as commands. He has helped himself to about 50 captives as "wives," claiming Old Testament authority for this (King Solomon had 700 spouses), often insisting—partly for biblical reasons and partly for the more banal reason of AIDS dread—that they be virgins. He used to anoint his followers with a holy oil mashed from indigenous shea-butter nuts, and now uses "holy water," which he tells his little disciples will make them invulnerable to bullets. He has claimed to be able to turn stones into hand grenades, and many of his devotees say that they have seen him do it. He warns any child tempted to run away that the baptismal fluids are visible to him forever and thus they can always be found again. (He can also identify many of his "children" by the pattern of lashes that they earned while under his tender care.) Signs of his disapproval include the cutting off of lips, noses, and breasts in the villages he raids and, to deter informers, a padlock driven through the upper and lower lips. This is the sort of deranged gang—flagellant, hysterical, fanatical, lethal, under-age—that an unfortunate traveler might have encountered on the roads of Europe during the Thirty Years' War or the last Crusade. "Yes," says Michael Oruni, director of the Gulu Children of War Rehabilitation Center, who works on deprogramming these feral kids, "children who have known pain know how to inflict it." We were sitting in a yard that contained, as well as some unreformed youngsters, four random babies crawling about in the dust. These had been found lying next to their panga-slashed mothers or else left behind when their mothers were marched away.

In October, the Lord of the Flies was hit, in his medieval redoubt, by a message from the twenty-first century. Joseph Kony and four other leaders of the L.R.A. were named in the first arrest warrants ever issued by the new International Criminal Court (I.C.C.). If that sounds like progress to you, then consider this. The whereabouts of Kony are already known: He openly uses a satellite phone from a base across the Ugandan border in southern Sudan.

Like the United States, Sudan is not a signatory to the treaty that set up the I.C.C. And it has sponsored the L.R.A. because the Ugandan government—which is an I.C.C. signatory—has helped the people of southern Sudan fight against the theocracy in Khartoum, the same theocracy that has been sponsoring the genocide against Muslim black Africans in Darfur. Arrest warrants look pretty flimsy when set against ruthless cynicism of this depth and intensity. Kony has evidently made some kind of peace with his Sudanese Islamist patrons: In addition to his proclamation of the Ten Commandments, he once banned alcohol and announced that all pigs were unclean and that those who farm them, let alone eat them, were subject to death. So, unless he has undergone a conversion to Judaism in the wilderness, we can probably assume that he is repaying his murderous armorers and protectors.

I had a faintly nerve-racking drink with Francis Ongom, one of Kony's ex-officers, who defected only recently and who would not agree to be questioned about his own past crimes. "Kony has refused Sudan's request that he allow his soldiers to convert to Islam," said this hardened-looking man as he imbibed a Red Bull through a straw, "but he has found Bible justifications for killing witches, for killing pigs because of the story of the Gadarene swine, and for killing people because god did the same with Noah's flood and Sodom and Gomorrah." Nice to know that he is immersed in the Good Book.

The terrifying thing about such violence and cruelty is that only a few dedicated practitioners are required in order to paralyze everyone else with fear. I had a long meeting with Betty Bigombe, one of those staunch and beautiful women—it is so often the women—who have helped restore Uganda's pulse after decades of war and famine and tyranny and Ebola and West Nile fever and AIDS. She has been yelled at by Joseph Kony, humiliated by corrupt and hypocritical Sudanese "intermediaries," dissed by the Ugandan political elite, and shamefully ignored by the international "human rights" community. She still believes that an amnesty for Kony's unindicted commanders is possible, which will bring the L.R.A. children back from the bush, but she and thousands like her can always be outvoted by one brutalized schoolboy with a machete. We are being forced to watch yet another Darfur, in which the time supposedly set aside for negotiations is used by the killers and cleansers to complete their work.

The Acholi people of northern Uganda, who are the chief sufferers in all this, have to suffer everything twice. Their children are murdered or abducted and enslaved and then come back to murder and abduct and enslave even more children. Yet if the Ugandan Army were allowed to use extreme measures to destroy the L.R.A., the victims would be . . . Acholi children again. It must be nightmarish to know that any feral-child terrorist who is shot could be one of your own. "I and the public know," wrote W. H. Auden in perhaps his greatest poem, "September 1, 1939":

> What all schoolchildren learn,
> Those to whom evil is done
> Do evil in return.

And that's what makes it so affecting and so upsetting to watch the "night commuter" children when they come scuttling and scampering into town as the sun departs from the sky. These schoolchildren have not yet had evil done to them, nor are they ready to inflict any evil. It's not too late for them, in other words.

I sat in the deepening gloom for a while with one small boy, Jimmy Opioh, whose age was fourteen. He spoke with an appalling gravity and realism about his mother's inability to pay school fees for himself and his brother both, about the fatigue and time-wasting of being constantly afraid and famished and continually on the run. In that absurd way that one does, I asked him what he wanted to be when he grew up. His unhesitating answer was that he wanted to be a politician—he had his party, the Forum for Democratic Change, all picked out as well. I shamefacedly arranged, along with the admirable John Prendergast of the International Crisis Group, to get him the meager sum that would pay for his schooling, tried not to notice the hundreds of other eyes that were hungrily turned toward me in the darkness, wondered what the hell the actual politicians, here or there, were doing about his plight, and managed to get out of the night encampment just before the equatorial rains hit and washed most of the tents and groundsheets away.

(*Vanity Fair*, January 2006)

The Vietnam Syndrome

TO BE WRITING THESE WORDS IS, for me, to undergo the severest test of my core belief—that sentences can be more powerful than pictures. A writer can hope to do what a photographer cannot: convey how things smelled and sounded as well as how things looked. I seriously doubt my ability to perform this task on this occasion. Unless you see the landscape of ecocide, or meet the eyes of its victims, you will quite simply have no idea. I am content, just for once—and especially since it is the work of the brave and tough and undeterrable James Nachtwey—to be occupying the space between pictures.

The very title of our joint subject is, I must tell you, a sick joke to begin with. Perhaps you remember the jaunty names of the callous brutes in *Reservoir Dogs*: "Mr. Pink," "Mr. Blue," and so on? Well, the tradition of giving pretty names to ugly things is as old as warfare. In Vietnam, between 1961 and 1971, the high command of the United States decided that, since a guerrilla struggle was apparently being protected by tree cover, a useful first step might be to "defoliate" those same trees. Famous corporations such as Dow and Monsanto were given the task of attacking and withering the natural order of a country. The resulting chemical weaponry was euphemistically graded by color: Agent Pink, Agent Green (yes, it's true), Agent Purple, Agent Blue, Agent White, and—spoken often in whispers—Agent Orange. This shady gang, or gang of shades, all deferred to its ruthless chief, who proudly bore the color of hectic madness. The key constituent of Agent

Orange is dioxin: a horrifying chemical that makes total war not just on vegetation but also on the roots and essences of life itself. The orange, in other words, was clockwork from the start. If you wonder what the dioxin effect can look like, recall the ravaged features of Viktor Yushchenko—ironically, the leader of the Orange Revolution.

The full inventory of this historic atrocity is still being compiled: It's no exaggeration to say that about 12 million gallons of lethal toxin, in Orange form alone, were sprayed on Vietnam, on the Vietnamese, and on the American forces who were fighting in the same jungles. A prime use of the chemical was in the delta of the Mekong River, where the Swift Boats were vulnerable to attack from the luxuriant undergrowth at the water's edge. Very well, said Admiral Elmo Zumwalt Jr., we shall kill off this ambush-enabling greenery by poisoning it from the skies. Zumwalt believes his own son Elmo III, who was also serving in the delta, died from the effects of Agent Orange, leaving behind him a son with grave learning disabilities. The resulting three-generation memoir of the Zumwalt family—*My Father, My Son* (1986), written by the first and second Elmos about themselves and about the grandchild—is one of the most stoic and affecting family portraits in American history.

You have to go to Vietnam, though, to see such fallout at first hand. I had naïvely assumed that it would be relatively easy to speak to knowledgeable physicians and scientists, if only because a state that is still Communist (if only in name) would be eager to justify itself by the crimes of American imperialism. The contrary proved to be the case, and for two main reasons. The government is too poor to pay much compensation to victims, and prefers anyway to stress the heroic rather than the humiliating aspects of the war. And traditional Vietnamese culture has a tendency to frown on malformed children, whose existence is often attributed to the sins of a past life. Furthermore, Vietnamese in general set some store by pride and self-reliance, and do not like soliciting pity.

I am quite proud of what I did when I came to appreciate, in every sense of the word, these obstacles. The first time I ever gave blood was to a "Medical Aid for Vietnam" clinic, in 1967. That was also the moment when I discovered that I have a very rare blood type. So, decades later, seeing a small ad in a paper in Ho Chi Minh City (invariably still called Saigon in local conversation) that asked for blood donations for Agent Orange victims, I reported to the relevant address. I don't think they get many wheezing and perspiring Anglos at this joint, let alone wheezing and perspiring Anglos with such exclusive corpuscles; at any rate I was fussed over a good deal while two units were drawn off, was given a sustaining bowl of beef noodles and some sweet tea, and was then offered a tour of the facilities.

This privilege, after a while, I came almost to regret. In an earlier age the compassionate term for irredeemably deformed people was *lusus naturae*: "a sport of nature," or, if you prefer a more callous translation, a joke. It was bad enough, in that spare hospital, to meet the successful half of a Siamese-twin separation. This was a more or less functional human child, with some cognition and about half the usual complement of limbs and organs. But upstairs was the surplus half, which, I defy you not to have thought if you had been there, would have been more mercifully thrown away. It wasn't sufficient that this unsuccessful remnant had no real brain and was a thing of stumps and sutures. ("No ass!" murmured my stunned translator in that good-bad English that stays in your mind.) Extra torments had been thrown in. The little creature was not lying torpid and still. It was jerking and writhing in blinded, crippled, permanent epilepsy, tethered by one stump to the bedpost and given no release from endless, pointless, twitching misery. What nature indulges in such sport? What creator designs it?

But all evil thoughts about euthanasia dissolve as soon as you meet, first, the other children and, second, those who care for them. In the office of Dr. Nguyen Thi Phuong Tan, a wonderful lady who is in charge of the equally impossible idea of "rehabilitation," I was taking notes when a lively, pretty, but armless ten-year-old girl ran in and sprang with great agility onto the table. Pham Thi Thuy Linh's grandfather had been in the South Vietnamese Air Force, had helped to vent Agent Orange on his Communist foes, and had suddenly succumbed to leukemia at the age of forty-two. His curse has been transmitted down the generations, whether via the food chain or the chromosomes is unclear. While Pham Thi Thuy Linh deftly signed her name with her right foot—with which she also handled a biscuit from the fond nurses—I learned that she had been listed for some artificial arms, perhaps with modern synthetic flesh, from an organization in Japan. All this will take is a wait until she's fully grown, and some $300,000. Money well spent, I'd say. But there will be no "making whole" for these children—eerily combining complete innocence with the most sinister and frightening appearance, ridden and riddled with cleft palate and spina bifida. One should not run out of vocabulary to the point where one calls a child a monster, but the temptation is there. One sees, with an awful pang, why their terrified and shamed parents abandon them to this overworked clinic. One also realizes that it isn't nature, or a creator, that is to blame. If only. This was not a dreadful accident, or a tragedy. It was inflicted, on purpose, by sophisticated human beings.

I am not an epidemiologist. And there are professionals who will still tell you that there is no absolutely proven connection between the spraying of this poison and the incidence of terrifying illnesses in one generation, or the persistence of appalling birth defects in the next one or the next one. Let us submit this to the arbitration of evidence and reason: What else can possibly explain the systematic convergence? I left Ho Chi Minh City/Saigon and went down the road and along the river, by boat, to the delta town of Ben Tre. This is the very place where Peter Arnett heard the American soldier say in 1968 that "we had to destroy the town to save it." My ferry churned the big muddy waters that had once been cruised by the Swift Boats, and I stood out in the pre-monsoon rain to get a clear look at the riverbanks with vegetation that took so long to grow back. Ben Tre Province, then called Kien Hoa, was a kind of "ground zero" for this experiment on human beings and animals and trees.

Jungles can ostensibly rise again, but dioxin works its way down through the roots and into the soil and the water, where it can enter the food chain. The unforgivable truth is that nobody knew at the time they were spraying it how long it takes dioxin to leach out of the natural system. The muttered prayer of many Vietnamese villagers is that this generation will be the last to feel their grandparents' war in their bones and their blood and their epidermis, but the fact is that the town of Ben Tre is home to about 140,000 people, of whom, the Red Cross says, 58,000 are victims of Agent Orange. (I don't trust Vietnamese statistics, but these were supplied to me by a woman expert who is not uncritical of the Communist regime, and whose family had been subjected to forced "re-education" after the fall of Saigon.)

Once again, after a tour of some thatched hamlets and some local schools for the special cases, I experienced an urgent need to be elsewhere or alone.

How many times can one pretend to "interview" the parents of a child born with bright-yellow skin? The cleft palates, the deafness, the muteness, the pretzel limbs and lolling heads...and the terrible expressions on the faces of the parents, who believe that this horror can sometimes skip a generation. There is just enough knowledge for agony and remorse, in other words, but not enough for any "healing process." No answer, above all, to the inescapable question: When will it stop? A rain from hell began falling about forty years ago. Unto how many unborn generations? At a school full of children who made sign language to one another or who couldn't sit still (or who couldn't move much at all), or who couldn't see or couldn't hear, I took the tour of the workshops where trades such as fishnet weaving or car repair are taught, and was then asked if I would like to say a few words, through an interpreter, to the assembly. I quite like a captive audience, but I didn't trust myself to say a fucking thing. Several of the children in the front row were so wizened and shrunken that they looked as if they could be my seniors. I swear to you that Jim Nachtwey has taken photographs, as one of his few rivals, Philip Jones Griffiths, also took photographs, that simply cannot be printed in this magazine, because they would poison your sleep, as they have poisoned mine.

"After such knowledge," as T. S. Eliot asked in "Gerontion," "what forgiveness?" That's easy. The question of forgiveness just doesn't come up. The world had barely assimilated the new term "genocide," which was coined only in the 1940s, before the United States government added the fresh hell of "ecocide," or mass destruction of the web of nature that connects human and animal and herbal life. I think we may owe the word's distinction to my friend Orville Schell, who wrote a near-faultless essay of coolheaded and warmhearted prose in the old *Look* magazine in March 1971. At that time, even in a picture magazine, there weren't enough photographs of the crime, so his terse, mordant words had to suffice, which makes me faintly proud to be in the same profession. And at some points, being naturally scrupulous about the evidence, he could only speculate: "There are even reports of women giving birth to monsters, though most occurrences are not reported because of nonexistent procedures for compiling statistics."

Well, we know now, or at least we know better. Out of a population of perhaps 84 million Vietnamese, itself reduced by several million during the war, there are as many as one million cases of Agent Orange affliction still on the books. Of these, the hardest to look at are the monstrous births. But we agree to forgive ourselves for this, and to watch real monsters such as Robert McNamara and Henry Kissinger, who calmly gave the orders and the instructions, as they posture on chat shows and cash in with their "memoirs." But, hey, forget it. Forget it if you can.

No more Latin after this, I promise, but there is an old tag from the poet Horace that says, *Mutato nomine de te fabula narratur.* "Change only the name and this story is also about you." The Vietnam War came home, and so did many men who had been exposed to Agent Orange, either from handling it and loading it or from being underneath it. If you desire even a faint idea of the distance between justice and a Vietnamese peasant family, take a look at how long it took for the American victims of this evil substance to get a hearing. The chemical assault on Vietnam began in 1961, in the early days of the Kennedy administration, and it kept on in spite of many protests for another ten years. The first effective legal proceeding brought in any American court was in 1984, in New York. This class action, settled out of court, was so broadly defined, in point of American victims and their stricken children, that almost nobody got more than $5,000 out of it, and there was a sharp (or do I mean blunt?) cutoff point beyond which no claim could be asserted. Six million acres of Vietnam had been exposed to the deadly stuff, and, as is the way with protracted litigation, the statistics began to improve and harden. It was established that there was a "match" between those who had been exposed and those who were subject, or whose offspring were subject, to alarming disorders. Admiral Zumwalt, who had first used the phrase "wrong war, wrong place, wrong time" in connection with Vietnam, took a hand in forwarding the legal cause and might have added that his grandson should not be (or do I mean should be?) the last one to suffer for a mistake. More than a mistake. A crime.

Long after both senior male Zumwalts had died—or in 2003, to be precise—the Supreme Court ruled that the issue had not been completely put to rest by the 1984 settlement. The way now lies open for a full accounting of this nightmarish affair. A report, written by Professor Jeanne Stellman, of Columbia University, as part of a U.S. government study, has concluded that nearly two million more gallons of herbicide were disseminated than has yet been admitted, and that the dioxin content of each gallon was much higher than had been officially confessed. (It has been calculated from tests on some Vietnamese that their dioxin levels are 200 times higher than "normal.") The implications are extraordinary, because it is now possible that thousands of Americans may join a million of their former Vietnamese adversaries in having a standing to sue.

"Doesn't it ever end? When will Agent Orange become history?" These were the words of Kenneth Feinberg, who figured as the court's "special master" in the 1984 suit, and who has more recently run the Victim Compensation Fund for the families of those who died in the attacks of September 11, 2001. One should not leave him to answer his own question all by himself. Agent Orange will "become history" in a different way from the trauma of September 11. Of that event, it's fairly safe to say, there will be no lapse of memory at least until everybody who lived through it has died. Of this Vietnam syndrome, some of us have sworn, there will likewise be no forgetting, let alone forgiving, while we can still draw breath. But some of the victims of Agent Orange haven't even been born yet, and if that reflection doesn't shake you, then my words have been feeble and not even the photographs will do.

(*Vanity Fair*, August 2006)

Once Upon a Time in Germany

THE NUMBER OF COMMUNIST revolutionaries in the world has declined much faster than the number of gangsters and stickup artists, but at the movies it's still a fairly safe bet that such stories will be portrayed in such a way as to inspire at least a twinge of penis envy. You will know what I mean, even if you didn't actually bother to watch Benicio Del Toro playing Che, or Johnny Depp taking the part of John Dillinger. It's a trope that goes back at least as far as *Viva Zapata!*: the quasi-sexual charisma of the outlaw.

So don't miss the opportunity of seeing the year's best-made and most counter-romantic action thriller, *The Baader Meinhof Complex*. Unlike earlier depictions of the same events by German directors such as Volker Schlöndorff and Rainer Werner Fassbinder, Uli Edel's film interrogates and ultimately indicts (and convicts) the West German terrorists rather than the state and society which they sought to overthrow.

It does this in the most carefully objective way, by taking the young militants, at least in the first instance, at their own face value. It is Berlin on June 2, 1967, and the rather shabby and compromised authorities of the postwar Federal Republic are laying down a red carpet for the visiting Shah of Iran. A young journalist named Ulrike Meinhof has written a mordant essay, in the form of an open letter to the Shah's wife, about the misery and repression of the Iranian system. When students protest as the Shah's party arrives at the Berlin Opera, they are first attacked by hired Iranian goon squads and then savaged by paramilitary formations of brutish German cops. It's the best 1960s street-fighting footage ever staged, and the "police riot" element is done with electrifying skill. On the fringes of the unequal battle, a creepy-looking plainclothes pig named Karl-Heinz Kurras unholsters his revolver and shoots an unarmed student, named Benno Ohnesorg, in the head.

That is only the curtain-raiser, and the birth of "the Movement of 2 June." Not much later, the student leader Rudi Dutschke is also shot in the head, but in this instance by an unhinged neo-Nazi. Now the rioting begins in earnest as West German youth begin to see a pattern to events. The shaky postwar state built by their guilty parents is only a façade for the same old grim and evil faces; Germany has leased bases on its soil for another aggression, this time against the indomitable people of Vietnam; any genuine domestic dissent is met with ruthless violence. I can remember these events and these arguments and images in real time, and I can also remember some of those who slipped away from the edge of the demonstrations and went, as they liked to think of it, "underground." The title of the film announces it as an exploration of exactly that syndrome: the cult of the urban guerrilla.

There was a prevalent mystique in those days about the Cuban and Vietnamese and Mozambican Revolutions, as well as about various vague but supposedly glamorous groups such as the Tupamaros in Uruguay. In the United States, the brief resort to violence by the Black Panthers and then by the Weather Underground was always imagined as an extension of "Third World" struggles onto the territory of imperialist North America. Other spasmodic attempts to raise armed insurrection—the so-called Front for the Liberation of Quebec, the I.R.A., and the Basque E.T.A.—were confined to national or ethnic minorities. But there were three officially democratic countries where for several years an actual weaponized and organized group was able to issue a challenge, however garbled and inarticulate, to the very legitimacy of the state. The first such group was the Japanese Red Army, the second (named partly in honor of the first) was West Germany's Red Army Faction, led by Andreas Baader and Ulrike Meinhof, and the third was the Red Brigades in Italy.

You may notice that the three countries I have just mentioned were the very ones that made up the Axis during the Second World War. I am personally convinced that this is the main reason the phenomenon took the form it did: The propaganda of the terrorists, on the few occasions when they could be bothered to cobble together a manifesto, showed an almost neurotic need to "resist authority" in a way that their parents' generation had so terribly failed to do. And this was also a brilliant way of placing the authorities on the defensive and luring them into a moral trap. West Germany in the late 1960s and 1970s is not actually holding any political prisoners. Very well then, we will commit violent crimes for political reasons and go to prison for them, and then there will be a special wing of the prison for us, and then the campaign to free the political prisoners by violence can get under way. This will strip the mask from the pseudo-democratic state and reveal the Nazi skull beneath its skin. (In a rather witty move that implicitly phrases all this in reverse, the makers of *The Baader Meinhof Complex* have cast Bruno Ganz as the mild but efficient head of West German "homeland security," a man who tries to "understand" his opponents even as he weaves the net ever closer around them. It requires a conscious effort to remember Ganz's eerie rendition of the part of the Führer in *Downfall* five years back.)

It doesn't take long for the sinister ramifications of the "complex" to become plain. Consumerism is equated with Fascism so that the firebombing of department stores can be justified. Ecstatic violence and "action" become ends in themselves. One can perhaps picture Ulrike Meinhof as a "Red" resister of Nazism in the 1930s, but if the analogy to that decade is allowed, then it is very much easier to envisage her brutally handsome pal Andreas Baader as an enthusiastic member of the Brownshirts. (The gang bought its first consignment of weapons from a member of Germany's neo-Nazi underworld: no need to be choosy when you are so obviously in the right.) There is, as with all such movements, an uneasy relationship between sexuality and cruelty, and between casual or cynical attitudes to both. As if curtain-raising a drama of brutality that has long since eclipsed their own, the young but hedonistic West German toughs take themselves off to the Middle East in search of the real thing and the real training camps, and discover to their dismay that their Arab hosts are somewhat... puritanical.

This in turn raises another question, with its own therapeutic implications. Did it have to be the most extreme Palestinians to whom the Baader Meinhof gangsters gave their closest allegiance? Yes, it did, because the queasy postwar West German state had little choice but to be ostentatiously friendly with the new state of Israel, at whatever cost in hypocrisy, and this exposed a weakness on which any really cruel person could very easily play. You want to really, really taunt the grown-ups? Then say, when you have finished calling them Nazis, that their little Israeli friends are really Nazis, too. This always guarantees a hurt reaction and a lot of press.

Researching this in the late 1970s in Germany, I became convinced that the Baader Meinhof phenomenon actually *was* a form of psychosis. One of the main recruiting grounds for the gang was an institution at the University of Heidelberg called the Sozialistisches Patienten Kollektiv, or Socialist Patients Collective, an outfit that sought to persuade the pitifully insane that they needed no treatment save social revolution. (Such a reading of the work of R. D. Laing and others was one of the major "disorders" of the 1960s.) Among the star pupils of this cuckoo's nest was Ralf Reinders, who was arrested after several violent "actions" and who had once planned to destroy the Jewish House in Berlin—a restoration of the one gutted by the Brownshirts—"in order to get rid of this thing about the Jews that we've all had to have since the Nazi time." Yes, "had to have" is very good. Perhaps such a liberating act, had he brought it off, would have made some of the noises in his head go away.

The Baader Meinhof Complex, like the excellent book by Stefan Aust on which it is based, is highly acute in its portrayal of the way in which mania feeds upon itself and becomes hysterical. More arrests mean that more hostages must be taken, often in concert with international hijackers, so that ever more exorbitant "demands" can be made. This requires money, which in turn demands more robbery and extortion. If there are doubts or disagreements within the organization, these can always be attributed to betrayal or cowardice, resulting in mini-purges and micro-lynchings within the gang itself. (The bleakest sequence of the film shows Ulrike Meinhof and her once seductive comrade Gudrun Ensslin raving hatefully at each other in the women's maximum-security wing.) And lurking behind all this neurotic energy, and not always very far behind at that, is the wish for death and extinction. The last desperate act of the gang—a Götterdämmerung of splatter action, including a botched plane hijacking by sympathetic Palestinians and the murder of a senior German hostage—was the staging of a collective suicide in a Stuttgart jail, with a crude and malicious attempt (echoed by some crude and malicious intellectuals) to make it look as if the German authorities had killed the prisoners. In these sequences, the film is completely unsparing, just as it was in focusing the camera on official brutality in the opening scenes of more than ten years before.

Two real-world developments have made this movie even more relevant, and helped to vindicate the critical attitude that it manifests. Of the surviving members of the Baader Meinhof circle, one or two went the whole distance and actually became full-blown neo-Nazis. The gang's lawyer and co-conspirator, Horst Mahler, has been jailed again, this time for distributing CD-roms inciting violence against Jews. Contempt for German democracy can't be taken any further than that. And Ulrike Meinhof's daughter Bettina Röhl has published files from the archives of the East German secret police, or Stasi, showing that subsidies and other forms of support flowed regularly to the group from the other side of the Berlin Wall.

Most astonishing of all, perhaps, in May of this year it was revealed from the same files that Karl-Heinz Kurras, the twitchy cop who shot Benno Ohnesorg on June 2, 1967, thus igniting the whole train of events, was all along an informer for the Stasi and a card-carrying member of the East German Communist Party. (Herr Kurras, now eighty-one, was interviewed and made no bones about it.) This doesn't necessarily prove that the whole sequence of events was part of a Stasi provocation, but it does make those who yelled about the "Nazi" state look rather foolish in retrospect. (Rudi Dutschke, it now turns out, left a posthumous letter to his family stating his fear that "the East" was behind his own shooting. Dutschke's family has called for an investigation.) What this means in short is that the Baader Meinhof milieu, so far from providing a critique of German society, was actually a sort of petri dish in which bacilli for the two worst forms of dictatorship on German soil—the National Socialist and the Stalinist—were grown. It's high time that the movie business outgrew some of the illusions of "radical" terrorism, and this film makes an admirably unsentimental contribution to that task.

(*Vanity Fair* online, August 17, 2009)

Worse Than *Nineteen Eighty-four*

HOW EXTRAORDINARY IT IS, when you give it a moment's thought, that it was only last week that an American president officially spoke the obvious truth about North Korea. In point of fact, Mr. Bush rather understated matters when he said that Kim Jong-il's government runs concentration camps. It would be truer to say that the Democratic People's Republic of North Korea, as it calls itself, is a concentration camp. It would be even more accurate to say, in American idiom, that North Korea is a slave state.

This way of phrasing it would not have the legal implication that the use of the word "genocide" has. To call a set of actions genocidal, as in the case of Darfur, is to invoke legal consequences that are entailed by the U.N.'s genocide convention, to which we are signatories. However, to call a country a slave state is to set another process in motion: that strange business that we might call the working of the American conscience.

It was rhetorically possible, in past epochs of ideological confrontation, for politicians to shout about the slavery of Nazism and of communism, and indeed of nations that were themselves captive. The element of exaggeration was pardonable, in that both systems used forced labor and also the threat of forced labor to coerce or to terrify others. But not even in the lowest moments of the Third Reich, or of the Gulag, or of Mao's Great Leap Forward, was there a time when all the subjects of the system were actually enslaved.

In North Korea, every person is property and is owned by a small and mad family with hereditary power. Every minute of every day, as far as regimentation can assure the fact, is spent in absolute subjection and serfdom. The private life has been entirely abolished. One tries to avoid cliché, and I did my best on a visit to this terrifying country in the year 2000, but George Orwell's *Nineteen Eighty-four* was published at about the time that Kim Il Sung set up his system, and it really is as if he got hold of an early copy of the novel and used it as a blueprint. (Hmmm, good book. Let's see if we can make it work.)

Actually, North Korea is rather worse than Orwell's dystopia. There would be no way, in the capital city of Pyongyang, to wander off and get lost in the slums, let alone to rent an off-the-record love nest in a room over a shop. Everybody in the city has to be at home and in bed by curfew time, when all the lights go off (if they haven't already failed). A recent nighttime photograph of the Korean peninsula from outer space shows something that no free-world propaganda could invent: a blaze of electric light all over the southern half, stopping exactly at the demilitarized zone and becoming an area of darkness in the north.

Concealed in that pitch-black night is an imploding state where the only things that work are the police and the armed forces. The situation is actually slightly worse than indentured servitude. The slave owner historically promises, in effect, at least to keep his slaves fed. In North Korea, this compact has been broken. It is a famine state as well as a slave state. Partly because of the end of favorable trade relations with, and subsidies from, the former USSR, but mainly because of the lunacy of its command economy, North Korea broke down in the 1990s and lost an unguessable number of people to sheer starvation. The survivors, especially the children, have been stunted and malformed. Even on a tightly controlled tour of the place—"North Korea is almost as hard to visit as it is to leave"—my robotic guides couldn't prevent me from seeing people drinking from sewers and picking up individual grains of food from barren fields. (I was reduced to eating a dog, and I was a privileged guest.) Film shot from over the Chinese border shows whole towns ruined and abandoned, with their few factories idle and cannibalized. It seems that the mines in the north of the country have been flooded beyond repair.

In consequence of this, and for the first time since the founding of Kim Il Sung's state, large numbers of people have begun to take the appalling risk of running away. If they make it, they make it across the river into China, where there is a Korean-speaking area in the remote adjoining province. There they live under the constant threat of being forcibly repatriated. The fate of the fugitive slave is not pretty: North Korea does indeed operate a system of camps, most memorably described in a book, *The Aquariums of Pyongyang*, by Kang Chol-Hwan, that ought to be much more famous than it is. Given what everyday life in North Korea is like, I don't have sufficient imagination to guess what life in its prison system must be, but this book gives one a hint.

It seems to me imperative that the human rights movement, hitherto unpardonably tongue-tied about all this, should insistently take up the case of North Korea and demand that an underground railway, or perhaps even an overground one, be established. Any Korean slave who can get out should be welcomed, fed, protected, and assisted to move to South Korea. Other countries, including our own, should announce that they will take specified numbers of refugees, in case the current steady trickle should suddenly become an inundation. The Chinese obviously cannot be expected to take millions of North Koreans all at once, which is why they engage in their otherwise criminal policy of propping up Kim Jong-il, but if international guarantees for runaway slaves could be established, this problem could be anticipated.

Kim Jong-il and his fellow slave masters are trying to dictate the pace of events by setting a timetable of nuclearization, based on a crash program wrung from their human property. But why should it be assumed that their failed state and society are permanent? Another timeline, oriented to liberation and regime change, is what the dynasty most fears. It should start to fear it more. Bravo to President Bush, anyway, for his bluntness.

(*Slate*, May 2, 2005)

North Korea: A Nation of Racist Dwarves

VISITING NORTH KOREA some years ago, I was lucky to have a fairly genial "minder" whom I'll call Mr. Chae. He guided me patiently around the ruined and starving country, explaining things away by means of a sort of denial mechanism and never seeming to lose interest in the gargantuan monuments to the world's most hysterical and operatic leader-cult. One evening, as we tried to dine on some gristly bits of duck, he mentioned yet another reason why the day should not long be postponed when the whole peninsula was united under the beaming rule of the Dear Leader. The people of South Korea, he pointed out, were becoming mongrelized. They wedded foreigners—even black American soldiers, or so he'd heard to his evident disgust—and were losing their purity and distinction. Not for Mr. Chae the charm of the ethnic mosaic, but rather a rigid and unpolluted uniformity.

I was struck at the time by how matter-of-factly he said this, as if he took it for granted that I would find it uncontroversial. And I did briefly wonder whether this form of totalitarianism, too (because nothing is more "total" than racist nationalism), was part of the pitch made to its subjects by the North Korean state. But I was preoccupied, as are most of the country's few visitors, by the more imposing and exotic forms of totalitarianism on offer: by the giant mausoleums and parades that seemed to fuse classical Stalinism with a contorted form of the deferential, patriarchal Confucian ethos.

Karl Marx in his *Eighteenth Brumaire* wrote that those trying to master a new language always begin by translating it back into the tongue they already know. And I was limiting myself (and ill-serving my readers) in using the preexisting imagery of Stalinism and Eastern deference. I have recently donned the bifocals provided by B. R. Myers in his electrifying new book *The Cleanest Race: How North Koreans See Themselves and Why It Matters*, and I understand now that I got the picture either upside down or inside out. The whole idea of communism is dead in North Korea, and its most recent "Constitution," "ratified" last April, has dropped all mention of the word. The analogies to Confucianism are glib, and such parallels with it as can be drawn are intended by the regime only for the consumption of outsiders. Myers makes a persuasive case that we should instead regard the Kim Jong-il system as a phenomenon of the very extreme and pathological right. It is based on totalitarian "military first" mobilization, is maintained by slave labor, and instills an ideology of the most unapologetic racism and xenophobia.

These conclusions of his, in a finely argued and brilliantly written book, carry the worrisome implication that the propaganda of the regime may actually mean exactly what it says, which in turn would mean that peace and disarmament negotiations with it are a waste of time—and perhaps a dangerous waste at that.

Consider: Even in the days of communism, there were reports from Eastern Bloc and Cuban diplomats about the paranoid character of the system (which had no concept of deterrence and told its own people that it had signed the Non-Proliferation Treaty in bad faith) and also about its intense hatred of foreigners. A black Cuban diplomat was almost lynched when he tried to show his family the sights of Pyongyang. North Korean women who return pregnant from China—the regime's main ally and protector—are forced to submit to abortions. Wall posters and banners depicting all Japanese as barbarians are only equaled by the ways in which Americans are caricatured as hook-nosed monsters. (The illustrations in this book are an education in themselves.) The United States and its partners make up in aid for the huge shortfall in North Korea's food production, but there is not a hint of acknowledgment of this by the authorities, who tell their captive subjects that the bags of grain stenciled with the Stars and Stripes are tribute paid by a frightened America to the Dear Leader.

Myers also points out that many of the slogans employed and displayed by the North Korean state are borrowed directly—this really does count as some kind of irony—from the kamikaze ideology of Japanese imperialism. Every child is told every day of the wonderful possibility of death by immolation in the service of the motherland and taught not to fear the idea of war, not even a nuclear one.

The regime cannot rule by terror alone, and now all it has left is its race-based military ideology. Small wonder that each "negotiation" with it is more humiliating than the previous one. As Myers points out, we cannot expect it to bargain away its very *raison d'être*.

All of us who scrutinize North Korean affairs are preoccupied with one question. Do these slaves really love their chains? The conundrum has several obscene corollaries. The people of that tiny and nightmarish state are not, of course, allowed to make comparisons with the lives of others, and if they complain or offend, they are shunted off to camps that—to judge by the standard of care and nutrition in the "wider" society—must be a living hell excusable only by the brevity of its duration. But race arrogance and nationalist hysteria are powerful cements for the most odious systems, as Europeans and Americans have good reason to remember. Even in South Korea there are those who feel the Kim Jong-il regime, under which they themselves could not live for a single day, to be somehow more "authentically" Korean.

Here are the two most shattering facts about North Korea. First, when viewed by satellite photography at night, it is an area of unrelieved darkness. Barely a scintilla of light is visible even in the capital city. Second, a North Korean is on average six inches shorter than a South Korean. You may care to imagine how much surplus value has been wrung out of such a slave, and for how long, in order to feed and sustain the militarized crime family that completely owns both the country and its people.

But this is what proves Myers right. Unlike previous racist dictatorships, the North Korean one has actually succeeded in producing a sort of new species. Starving and stunted dwarves, living in the dark, kept in perpetual ignorance and fear, brainwashed into the hatred of others, regimented and coerced and inculcated with a death cult: This horror show is in our future, and is so ghastly that our own darling leaders dare not face it and can only peep through their fingers at what is coming.

(*Slate*, February 1, 2010)

The Eighteenth Brumaire of the Castro Dynasty

IF THERE HAD BEEN a military coup in any other Latin American or Caribbean country, even a fairly small or obscure one, I think it safe to say that it would have made the front page of the newspapers. But the military coup in Cuba—a nation linked to ours in many vital and historic ways—has not been reported at all. Indeed, in "Castro's Younger Brother Is Focus of Attention Now," by Anthony DePalma and James C. McKinley Jr., on page 8 of the *New York Times* of August 3, the very possibility of such an event was even denied:

> [O]ne of the most telling aspects of his career is that in the nearly five decades that Raúl Castro has led the Cuban armed forces, there has never been a coup attempt or an uprising of rank-and-file soldiers against their officers.

Thus did the newspaper of record digest the interesting novelty that the new head of government in Cuba was, in fact, the five-decade leader of the Cuban armed forces! In other words, an overt military takeover was the main evidence that these things don't happen in Havana. Perhaps Raúl Castro's accession doesn't count as a "coup attempt" (since it was successful), let alone a "rank-and-file" mutiny, but the plain fact remains that, for the first time in a Communist state since General Jaruzelski seized power in Poland in 1981, the army has replaced the party as the source of authority.

The even more grotesque fact that power has passed from one seventy-nine-year-old brother to a "younger" one who is only seventy-five may have assisted in obscuring the obvious. So may the fact that—continuous babble about his "charisma" notwithstanding—Fidel Castro has never taken off his uniform (except for the tailored suits he dons for appearances at international conferences) since the day he took power. Even my distinction between the army and the party may be a distinction without much of a difference. Cuba has been a garrison state run by a military caudillo for most of the past half-century. More than anything, the maximum leader always based his legitimacy on his status as commander in chief. The dynastic succession of his brother only formalizes the situation. As was once said of Prussia, Cuba is not a country that has an army but an army that has a country.

Nor does this army confine itself to the stern questions of political and military power. Under the stewardship of Raúl Castro, it has extended itself to become a large stakeholder in the few areas of the Cuban economy that actually make money. A military holding company known as "La Gaviota" oversees perhaps as much as 60 percent of Cuban tourist revenues. Large farms and resorts are operated by serving and retired officers reporting to Raúl, and according to the DePalma/McKinley story, he has also "sent officers to business schools in Europe to learn capitalist management techniques."

Awareness of all this makes it the more surprising that everyone seems to have forgotten the highly charged moment in 1989 when there did appear to be an important rift within the Cuban armed forces. On June 12 of that year, General Arnaldo Ochoa Sanchez was placed under arrest and accused of extreme corruption, dereliction of duty, and narcotics trafficking. Ochoa was no small fry. He had belonged to the original band of guerrillas in the Sierra Maestra, was a member of the 26th of July Movement that formed the inner core of the revolution, had been among those Cuban internationalists who tried to raise the flag of revolt in Venezuela and the Congo in the 1960s, and had headed the Cuban military missions to Angola, Ethiopia, and Nicaragua. (To mention something of which Cubans can be proud, I should add that he was prominent in the military defeat of South African forces at the

Battle of Cuito Cuanavale in 1987, which contributed handily to the independence of Namibia and the ultimate defeat of apartheid itself.) Perhaps he had seen too much of the outside world. Perhaps, in that year of 1989, he was one of many Cubans who saw promise in Mikhail Gorbachev's program of glasnost and perestroika. Or perhaps he was simply guilty as charged of colluding with the Colombian drug cartels in order to enrich himself and others. We shall never really know (or then again, we may be just on the verge of finding out), because the entire interval between his arrest and his death, and those of his associates, was a matter of four short weeks. His execution by firing squad was announced after a special court martial on July 13, 1989.

The man who made the long, rambling speech justifying the arrest and prejudging the verdict was Raúl Castro. Awarded the sort of TV time that was normally reserved for his brother, the head of the Cuban armed forces addressed the nation for two and a half hours instead of the allotted forty-five minutes (one hopes he does not now fall into the habit of doing this) and amazed many Cubans who had been brought up to think of Ochoa as "sea-green incorruptible."

The moment was a significant one, because, in general, Cuba had been able to avoid the spectacle of the Communist "show trial" that had been inaugurated by Stalin in Moscow in the 1930s and pursued in even more grotesque form in Prague, Budapest, and Sofia after the Second World War. The only arraignment of a "factional" group in Havana had been in the mid-1960s, and it was paradoxically directed at a bunch of Moscow-line Stalinists allegedly led by Aníbal Escalante. However, the show trial of Ochoa in 1989 was not a protracted ideological inquisition. It was a swift, ruthless business that produced immediate confessions, was conducted by a military "honor court," and concluded with an expeditious death sentence. All was decided within the framework of the military high command. Perhaps that should have been a warning of what was to come.

On the "new calendar" date of 18 Brumaire in 1799, Napoleon Bonaparte used his troops to seize power in Paris, proclaimed himself the nation's first consul, and soon after announced that the French Revolution had come to its end. (Karl Marx's celebrated essay on *The Eighteenth Brumaire of Louis Napoleon*, lampooning a much later and lesser French monarch than Bonaparte, gave us the overused jest about the relationship between tragedy and farce.)

Now the 26th of July Movement has arrived at its own belated historical terminus. The new pretender, once again, is much less flamboyant and impressive. If we cannot yet say that Castro is dead and we cannot decently say "long live" to the new-but-old Castro, we can certainly say that the Castro era is effectively finished and that a uniformed and secretive and highly commercial dictatorship is the final form that it will take.

(*Slate*, August 7, 2006)

Hugo Boss

RECENT ACCOUNTS of Hugo Chávez's politicized necrophilia may seem almost too lurid to believe, but I can testify from personal experience that they may well be an understatement. In the early hours of July 16—just at the midnight hour, to be precise—Venezuela's capo officiated at a grisly ceremony. This involved the exhumation of the mortal remains of Simón Bolívar, leader of Latin America's rebellion against Spain, who died in 1830. According to a vividly written article by Thor Halvorssen in the July 25 *Washington Post*, the skeleton was picked apart—even as Chávez tweeted the proceedings for his audience—and some teeth and bone fragments were taken away for testing. The residual pieces were placed in a coffin stamped with the Chávez government's seal. In one of the rather free-associating speeches for which he has become celebrated, Chávez appealed to Jesus Christ to restage the raising of Lazarus and reanimate Bolívar's constituent parts. He went on:

> I had some doubts, but after seeing his remains, my heart said, "Yes, it is me." Father, is that you, or who are you? The answer: "It is me, but I awaken every hundred years when the people awaken."

As if "channeling" this none-too-subtle identification of Chávez with the national hero, Venezuelan television was compelled to run images of Bolívar, followed by footage of the remains, and then pictures of the boss. The national anthem provided the soundtrack. Not since North Korean media declared Kim Jong-il to be the reincarnation of Kim Il Sung has there been such a blatant attempt to create a necrocracy, or perhaps mausolocracy, in which a living claimant assumes the fleshly mantle of the departed.

Simón Bolívar's cadaver is like any other cadaver, but his legacy is a great deal more worth stealing than that of Kim Il Sung. Gabriel García Márquez's novel *The General in His Labyrinth* is one place to begin, if you want to understand the combination of heroic and tragic qualities that keep his memory alive to this day. (In New York, his equestrian statue still dominates the intersection of the Avenue of the Americas and Central Park South.) The idea of a United States of South America will always be a tenuous dream, but in his bloody struggle for its realization, Bolívar cut a considerable figure, as he did in his other capacities as double-dealer, war criminal, and serial fornicator, also lovingly portrayed by Márquez.

In the fall of 2008, I went to Venezuela as a guest of Sean Penn's, whose friendship with Chávez is warm. The third member of our party was the excellent historian Douglas Brinkley, and we spent some quality time flying around the country on Chávez's presidential jet and bouncing with him from rally to rally at ground level, as well. The boss loves to talk and has clocked up speeches of Castro-like length. Bolívar is the theme of which he never tires. His early uniformed movement of mutineers—which failed to bring off a military coup in 1992—was named for Bolívar. Turning belatedly but successfully to electoral politics, he called his followers the Bolivarian Movement. Since he became president, the country's official name has been the Bolivarian Republic of Venezuela. (Chávez must sometimes wish that he had been born in Bolivia in the first place.) At Cabinet meetings, he has been known to leave an empty chair, in case the shade of Bolívar might choose to attend the otherwise rather Chávez-dominated proceedings.

It did not take long for this hero-obsession to disclose itself in bizarre forms. One evening, as we were jetting through the skies, Brinkley mildly asked whether Chávez's large purchases of Russian warships might not be interpreted by Washington as a violation of the Monroe Doctrine. The boss's response was impressively immediate. He did not know for sure, he said, but he very much hoped so. "The United States was born with an imperialist impulse. There has been a long confrontation between Monroe and Bolívar.... It is necessary that the Monroe Doctrine be broken." As his tirade against evil America mounted, Penn broke in to say that surely Chávez would be happy to see the arrest of Osama bin Laden.

I was hugely impressed by the way that the boss scorned this overture. He essentially doubted the existence of al-Qaeda, let alone reports of its attacks on the enemy to the north. "I don't know anything about Osama bin Laden that doesn't come to me through the filter of the West and its propaganda." To this, Penn replied that surely bin Laden had provided quite a number of his very own broadcasts and videos. I was again impressed by the way that Chávez rejected this proffered lucid-interval lifeline. All of this so-called evidence, too, was a mere product of imperialist television. After all, "there is film of the Americans landing on the moon," he scoffed. "Does that mean the moon shot really happened? In the film, the Yanqui flag is flying straight out. So, is there wind on the moon?" As Chávez beamed with triumph at this logic, an awkwardness descended on my comrades, and on the conversation.

Chávez, in other words, is very close to the climactic moment when he will announce that he is a poached egg and that he requires a very large piece of buttered toast so that he can lie down and take a soothing nap. Even his macabre foraging in the coffin of Simón Bolívar was initially prompted by his theory that an autopsy would prove that The Liberator had been poisoned—most probably by dastardly Colombians. This would perhaps provide a posthumous license for Venezuela's continuing hospitality to the narco-criminal gang FARC, a cross-border activity that does little to foster regional brotherhood.

Many people laughed when Chávez appeared at the podium of the United Nations in September 2006 and declared that he smelled sulfur from the devil himself because of the presence of George W. Bush. But the evidence is that he does have an idiotic weakness for spells and incantations, as well as many of the symptoms of paranoia and megalomania. After the failure of Bolívar's attempted Gran Colombia federation—which briefly united Venezuela, Colombia, Ecuador, and other nations—the U.S. minister in Bogotá, future president William Henry Harrison, said of him that "[u]nder the mask of patriotism and attachment to liberty, he has really been preparing the means of investing himself with arbitrary power." The first time was tragedy; this time is also tragedy but mixed with a strong element of farce.

(*Slate*, August 2, 2010)

Is the Euro Doomed?

SOMETIMES, sheer immodesty compels me to ask, of my long record of prescience, what did I know, and when and how did I know it? In the summer of 2005, *Foreign Policy* magazine asked its contributors to name one taken-for-granted thing that they thought was overrated or would not last. After a brief interval of reflection, I chose the euro.

I can be absolutely certain that I did not do this because I wanted to be right. On the contrary, I would much have preferred to be mistaken. When I still lived in Europe, I was one of the few on the left to advocate an enlargement of the community and to identify it with the progressive element in politics. This was mainly because I had seen the positive effect that Europeanism had exerted on the periphery of the continent, especially in Spain, Portugal, and Greece. Until the middle of the 1970s, these countries had been ruled by backward-looking dictatorships, generally religious and military in character and dependent on military aid from the more conservative circles in the United States. Because the European community allowed only parliamentary democracies to join, the exclusion from the continent's heartland gave a huge incentive to the middle class in these countries to support the overthrow of despotism.

The same attraction had a solvent effect on other countries, too. Once the Irish Republic became a member and was thus part of the same customs union as the United Kingdom, the border with Northern Ireland became an irrelevance, and it was only a matter of time before the sectarian war would begin to seem irrelevant. In Cyprus, the wish of both Greek and Turkish Cypriots to become European was a potent element in setting the stage for negotiations to end that post-colonial partition. The modernization and opening of Turkey, highly uneven as it is, has a great deal to do with the same pull toward a common European system. And it goes without saying that the people of Eastern Europe, even while the Berlin Wall still stood, measured their aspirations by how swiftly they, too, could meet the criteria for membership and escape the dreary, wasteful Comecon system that was the Soviet Union's own parody of a supranational agreement.

The logic of this seemed to necessitate a single currency, which in turn meant that a unified Germany, instead of dominating Europe, as the British and French reactionaries had always feared, would become a Europeanized Germany. The decision to give up the deutsche mark in 2002 must rank as one of the most mature and generous decisions ever taken by a modern state, full confirmation of the country's long transition from Nazism and Stalinism and partition, Europe's three great modern enemies.

As it happens, though, it was a German-speaking fascist who awoke my misgivings. I was interviewing Jörg Haider, the late leader of Austria's Freedom Party, just as the euro notes and coins were coming into circulation almost everywhere between Finland and Greece. With a disagreeable sneer, he asked me if I really liked "the new Esperanto money."

This was actually a rather clever psychological thrust. The old dream of a world language called Esperanto that would abolish the Babel of competing tongues is considered a quixotic one for obvious reasons. Nobody is going to learn a language that hardly anybody speaks. There is a further quixotry involved: The invention of Esperanto ended up doing no more than adding another minor language to the mix. Now consider the euro: What if it ends up being one European currency among many instead of the money equivalent of a lingua franca?

How tragic it is that the euro system has already, in effect, become a two-tier one and that the bottom tier is occupied by the very countries—Greece, Portugal, Spain, and Ireland—that benefited most from their accession to the European Union. The shady way in which Greece behaved in concealing its debts, and the drunken-sailor manner in which other smaller states managed their budgets, has, of course, offended the Germans. It is openly said in

Germany now that it would be better to bring back the deutsche mark than to be bailing out quasi-indigent and thriftless banana republics. Talk of that kind doesn't take long to evoke a biting response: Soon enough, Greek Foreign Minister Theodoros Pangalos was reminding nationalist audiences at home of the wartime German occupation of Greece and the carrying-off of the country's gold reserves. "Don't talk about the war" is a strong unspoken principle of European fraternity, and it didn't require very much strain to produce a major fraying of this etiquette. You can count on this atmosphere getting much worse as second-tier countries are requested by Berlin to haul in their waistlines and as Germans grumble about having to tighten their own belts to subsidize less efficient regimes.

The problem is endlessly reported as one of "bailout" terms and "packages" for "debt relief." These are all euphemisms, and they are also all short-term. The fact is that default has entered the European vocabulary on a national scale and therefore that this First World club has its own Third World to contend with. In any case, the great justification for the European Union was always political and not economic, and if the symbol of the second-order dimension becomes tarnished, then the first ideal will not escape great damage, either.

"PIGS" is the unlovely acronym for the nations—Portugal, Ireland, Greece and Spain—that constitute the shiftless out-group within the in-group. (Italy is sometimes included in the club.) It's very improbable that nations that haven't yet signed up to the euro—Britain and many Scandinavian states among them—will now do so. And that being the case, with the euro just another bill you have to exchange when moving around within Europe—then what becomes of the dream? I wish I could have ignored the croakings of an obscure Austrian fascist, but there's something about European history that makes this seem rash.

(*Slate*, April 26, 2010)

Overstating Jewish Power

IT'S SLIGHTLY HARD to understand the fuss generated by the article on the Israeli lobby produced by the joint labors of John Mearsheimer and Stephen Walt that was published in the *London Review of Books*. My guess is that the Harvard logo has something to do with it, but then I don't understand why the doings of that campus get so much media attention, either. The essay itself, mostly a very average "realist" and centrist critique of the influence of Israel, contains much that is true and a little that is original. But what is original is not true and what is true is not original.

Everybody knows that the American Israel Public Affairs Committee and other Jewish organizations exert a vast influence over Middle East policy, especially on Capitol Hill. The influence is not as total, perhaps, as that exerted by Cuban exiles over Cuba policy, but it is an impressive demonstration of strength by an ethnic minority. Almost everybody also concedes that the Israeli occupation has been a moral and political catastrophe and has implicated the United States in a sordid and costly morass. I would have gone further than Mearsheimer and Walt and pointed up the role of Israel in supporting apartheid in South Africa, in providing arms and training for dictators in Congo and Guatemala, and helping reactionary circles in America do their dirty work—most notably during the Iran-Contra assault on the Constitution and in the emergence of the alliance between Likud and the

Christian right. Counterarguments concerning Israel's help in the Cold War and in the region do not really outweigh these points.

However, Mearsheimer and Walt present the situation as one where the Jewish tail wags the American dog, and where the United States has gone to war in Iraq to gratify Ariel Sharon, and where the alliance between the two countries has brought down on us the wrath of Osama bin Laden. This is partly misleading and partly creepy. If the Jewish stranglehold on policy has been so absolute since the days of Harry Truman, then what was General Eisenhower thinking when, on the eve of an election fifty years ago, he peremptorily ordered Ben Gurion out of Sinai and Gaza on pain of canceling the sale of Israeli bonds? On the next occasion when Israel went to war with its neighbors, eleven years later, President Lyndon Johnson was much more lenient, but a strong motive of his policy (undetermined by Israel) was to win Jewish support for the war the "realists" were then waging in Vietnam. (He didn't get the support, except from Rabbi Meir Kahane.)

If it is Israel that decides on the deployment of American force, it seems odd that the first President Bush had to order them to stay out of the coalition to free Kuwait, and it is even more odd that the first order of neocon business has not been an attack on Iran, as Israeli hawks have been urging. Mearsheimer and Walt are especially weak on this point: They speak darkly about neocon and Israeli maneuvers in respect to Tehran today, but they entirely fail to explain why the main initiative against the mullahs has come from the European Union and the International Atomic Energy Agency, two organizations where the voice of the Jewish lobby is, to say the least, distinctly muted. Their theory does nothing to explain why it was French President Jacques Chirac who took the lead in isolating the death-squad regime of Assad's Syria (a government that Mearsheimer and Walt regard, for reasons of their own, as a force for stability).

As for the idea that Israel is the root cause of the emergence of al-Qaeda: Where have these two gentlemen been? Bin Laden's gang emerged from a whole series of tough and reactionary battles in Central and Eastern Asia, from the war for a separate Muslim state in the Philippines to the fighting in Kashmir, the Uighur territories in China, and of course Afghanistan. There are hardly any Palestinians in its ranks, and its communiqués have been notable for how little they say about the Palestinian struggle. Bin Laden does not favor a Palestinian state; he simply regards the whole area of the former British Mandate as a part of the future caliphate. The right of the Palestinians to a state is a just demand in its own right, but anyone who imagines that its emergence would appease—or would have appeased—the forces of *jihad* is quite simply a fool. Is al-Qaeda fomenting civil war in Nigeria or demanding the return of East Timor to Indonesia because its heart bleeds for the West Bank?

For purposes of contrast, let us look at two other regional allies of the United States. Both Turkey and Pakistan have been joined to the Pentagon hip since approximately the time of the emergence of the state of Israel, which coincided with the Truman Doctrine. Pakistan was, like Israel, cleaved from a former British territory. Since that time, both states have carried out appalling internal repression and even more appalling external aggression. Pakistan attempted a genocide in Bangladesh, with the support of Nixon and Kissinger, in 1971. It imposed the Taliban as its client in a quasi-occupation of Afghanistan. It continues to arm and train bin Ladenists to infiltrate Indian-held Kashmir, and its promiscuity with nuclear materials exceeds anything Israel has tried with its stockpile at Dimona. Turkey invaded Cyprus in 1974 and continues in illegal occupation of the northern third of the island, which has been forcibly cleansed of its Greek inhabitants. It continues to lie about its massacre of the Armenians. U.N. resolutions have had no impact on these instances of state terror and illegality in which the United States is also partially implicated.

But here's the thing: There is no Turkish or Pakistani ethnic "lobby" in America. And here's the other thing: There is no call for "disinvestment" in Turkey or Pakistan. We are not incessantly told that with these two friends we are partners in crime. Perhaps the Greek Cypriots and Indians are in error in refusing to fly civilian aircraft into skyscrapers. That might get the attention of the "realists." Or perhaps the affairs of two states, one secular Muslim and one created specifically in the name of Islam, do not possess the eternal fascination that attaches to the Jewish question.

There has been some disquiet expressed about Mearsheimer and Walt's over-fondness for Jewish name-dropping: their reiteration of the names Wolfowitz, Perle, Feith, etc., as the neocon inner circle. Well, it would be stupid not to notice that a group of high-energy Jews has been playing a role in our foreign-policy debate for some time. The first occasion on which it had any significant influence (because, despite its tentacular influence, it lost the argument over removing Saddam Hussein in 1991) was in pressing the Clinton administration to intervene in Bosnia and Kosovo. These are the territories of Europe's oldest and largest Muslim minorities; they are oil-free and they do not in the least involve the state interest of Israel. Indeed, Sharon publicly opposed the intervention. One could not explain any of this from Mearsheimer and Walt's rhetoric about "the lobby."

Mearsheimer and Walt belong to that vapid school that essentially wishes that the war with *jihad*-ism had never started. Their wish is father to the thought that there must be some way, short of a fight, to get around this confrontation. Wishfulness has led them to seriously mischaracterize the origins of the problem and to produce an article that is redeemed from complete dullness and mediocrity only by being slightly but unmistakably smelly.

(*Slate*, March 27, 2006)

The Case for Humanitarian Intervention

DEBATES AND DISCUSSIONS about humanitarian intervention tend (for good reasons) to be about American intervention. They also tend to share the assumption that the United States can afford, or at any rate has the power, to take or leave the option to get involved. On some occasions, there may seem to be overwhelming moral grounds to quit the sidelines and intervene. On others, the imperatives are less clear-cut. In all instances, nothing exceptional should be contemplated unless it has at least some congruence with the national interest. This interest can be interpreted widely: Is it not to the United States' advantage that, say, the charter of the United Nations be generally respected? Or the notion can be interpreted narrowly: If the United States had intervened in 1994 in the Francophone central African context of the genocide in Rwanda, then where would it not be asked to intervene?

In common with all such questions is the unspoken assumption that Washington can make all the difference if it chooses to do so and needs merely to be prudent and thoughtful before embarking on some redemptive project in another country. But, as I read Gary Bass's absorbing, well-researched, and frequently amusing book, I found myself rotating a seldom-asked question in

---

Review of *Freedom's Battle: The Origins of Humanitarian Intervention*, by Gary J. Bass.

my head: What about the days when the United States was the recipient, not the donor, of humanitarian solidarity?

When one places in context all those sapient presidential remarks about the danger of "entangling alliances" (Thomas Jefferson) or the reluctance to go abroad "in search of monsters to destroy" (John Quincy Adams), as Bass helps readers do, it becomes clear that they belonged to a time when America and Americans were in a poor position to conduct any intervention at all. It was no more than common sense to exercise restraint and concentrate on building up the homeland—while exploiting the quarrels between the British, French, and Spanish empires to do so. This constraint must have been felt very keenly at least until the closing third of the nineteenth century, after which it was possible to begin thinking of the United States as a global power.

But then remember what most people forget: how much international humanitarian intervention the United States had required in order to get that far. Not all of the aid to the fledgling thirteen colonies was entirely disinterested—the French monarchy's revenge for its earlier defeats in North America being an obvious motive. But the French did not overstay their welcome, and they did supply, in the form of Lafayette in particular, the model of the latter-day "international brigade" volunteer, often symbolized by Lord Byron or, more contentiously perhaps, those English literati who fought in defense of the Spanish republic between 1936 and 1939.

Many also forget that the international campaign in solidarity with the Union under the Lincoln presidency rallied at a time when it was entirely possible that the United Kingdom might have thrown its whole weight behind the Confederacy and even moved troops from Canada to hasten the partition of a country half slave and half free. This is often forgotten, I suggest, because the movement of solidarity was partly led by Karl Marx and his European allies (as was gratefully acknowledged by Henry Adams in his *Education*) and because the boycott of Confederate goods, the blocking of shipbuilding orders for the Confederate fleet, and other such actions were to some degree orchestrated by the founders of the communist movement—not the sort of thing that is taught in school when Abraham Lincoln is the patriotic subject. Marx and Friedrich Engels hugely admired Lincoln and felt that just as Russia was the great arsenal of backwardness, reaction, and superstition, the United States was the land of potential freedom and equality.

Now that all other examples of political revolution have become obsolete or have been discredited, the issue is whether the United States is indeed a different sort of country or nation, one that has a creed or an ethic that imposes special duties on it. One way I like to answer this question is by pointing out that if the United States had not been its host and patron in 1945, there would have been no United Nations. The original principles of the organization had to do almost entirely with war and peace, law and (through the International Monetary Fund and the World Bank) finance. But all its new members also found themselves invited to sign the Universal Declaration of Human Rights, originally drafted by Eleanor Roosevelt, and there is no question that U.S. influence lay behind this suggestion. By means of this and a number of other incremental steps, the United States has found itself becoming inexorably committed to upholding a certain standard of what its critics would call idealism.

The Rights of Men

Bass reaches a considerable distance into the past in order to demonstrate that this argument is not at all new and that idealism and realism are not as diametrically opposed as some would have one think; indeed, very often they complement each other. Bass opens by expending a lot of ink on the prototype of the "just cause" and of the Romantic movement: the struggle of the Greeks to be free of the Ottoman Empire. As an old philhellene myself (I have served on two active committees for the liberation of Cyprus and the return of the so-called Elgin Marbles), I thought I knew this subject well, but Bass provides a trove of fresh material, as well as fresh insight, concerning this exciting period of the early 1820s and the neglected topic of the United States' involvement in it. Let me try to do justice to his presentation.

First of all, and not merely judging with the benefit of hindsight, one should consider how likely it was that the Greeks would have continued as subjects of the Ottoman Empire—in other words, as a bastard form of Christian Turks. Not at all likely, really, which is to say that there was a prima facie case to be made that outsiders had a shrewd interest in supporting a cause that was probably going to be ultimately victorious. Second, if the Greeks did not win, then the Turks would, and this in turn would be a victory for the Turkophile Metternich-Castlereagh-Wellington forces in the rest of Europe. In other words, in this case, as in others, failing to help one side was the same thing, strategically as well as morally, as helping the other. (It is not as if famous American "realists" theoretically opposed to intervention have not also embroiled the United States in some grave foreign quarrels in their time, from Cambodia to Chile to, indeed, Cyprus.) Third, there were some "balance of power" questions that, even though they arose out of what the otherwise philhellenic Jefferson called "the broils of Europe," still had implications for the United States. Only the fear of entanglement in such "broils," Jefferson wrote to a Greek correspondent in 1823, "could restrain our generous youth from taking some part in this holy cause." James Madison was more affirmative, writing that year to President James Monroe and Jefferson that he favored an American declaration, in concert with other countries, such as the United Kingdom, in support of the Greeks. And the ethnologist, American diplomat, and former U.S. Treasury secretary Albert Gallatin proposed what Bass writes "would have been the United States' first humanitarian intervention." He did so in distinctly ironic tones, suggesting that Greece be aided by the United States' "naval force in the Mediterranean—one frigate, one corvette, and one schooner." This was even less of a navy than the Greek rebels could call on, but the point—not dwelled on by Bass, alas—is that only a few years previously, Jefferson had sent the navy, as well as the newly created U.S. Marine Corps, to shatter the Ottoman fleets that were both enslaving American crews and passengers and denying free trade through the Strait of Gibraltar. The move had led to a huge increase in American prestige as well as to vastly enhanced maritime commerce. Why should the two thoughts not occur again at the same time in the same minds?

In the end, then Secretary of State Adams carried the day (against that improbable champion of liberty: the slavery apologist John Calhoun, who was then secretary of war), and the United States did not go abroad in search of a chance to destroy the monster of Turkish imperialism. As if in compensation, however, the White House proclaimed the Monroe Doctrine, which denounced the "odious and criminal" slave trade, and freely issued warm expressions for the future of Greek statehood.

It is very often by these sorts of crabwise steps and political tradeoffs that the United States finds that it has—perhaps in a fit of absence of mind—avoided one humanitarian commitment by implicitly adopting other ones. These days, this happens every time someone who wants to leave, say, a Saddam Hussein alone is rash enough to wonder out loud what should be done about Darfur, Myanmar (also known as Burma), Tibet, or Zimbabwe. History has a way of adopting such taunts or at least of playing them back to their originators. And this, as Bass shows, is how the international community has gradually moved from double or multiple standards to something like a more intelligible and single one.

Sovereign Sovereignties

It is either unfortunate or significant—and probably both—that so many of Bass's early examples have to do with confrontations between a Christian (or liberal) West and a Muslim (or imperial) Turkey. In addition to the Greek case, there is the European powers' protracted intervention in Syria between 1841 and 1861 to underwrite and guarantee the lives and freedoms of the Christian minority there, which resulted in the country's partition—or, if one prefers, the emergence of a quasi-independent Lebanon. This was followed in depressingly swift succession by British prime minister William Gladstone's campaign for the cause of the martyred Bulgarians in the 1870s and U.S. ambassador Henry Morgenthau's extraordinary dispatches in the early months of the First World War about what Morgenthau called the "race murder" of the Armenians by the Ottomans. (Even though I do not really believe in the category of "race," I find this term more dramatic and urgent than the legal scholar Raphael Lemkin's "genocide.") At any rate, an amateur reader—or perhaps a resentful Muslim one—could be pardoned for taking away the idea that the West's views of human rights and humanitarian intervention were formed in opposition to the manifest cruelties and depredations of "the Turk," or, as he was sometimes called, "the Mussulman." In fact, the fight over Jerusalem and its status seems to have gone on for longer than most people know, the 1853–56 Crimean War that opposed the Russian Empire to the British, French, and Ottoman Empires being only one of many occasions when Christian states have fought one another for control over the holy sites of Palestine.

The argument over sovereignty and legitimacy, or the argument from the Peace of Westphalia, as it has come to be known by post-Metternichians such as Henry Kissinger, was very familiar in the mid-nineteenth century. In the United Kingdom, which was the fount of most of these claims and their transmitter to the United States, the difference between those who invoked sovereignty and those who scorned it as a cloak for despotism and aggression was very nearly a stand-in for the difference between Tory and Whig. There is not, in most of Europe, any equivalent of the American tradition of right-wing isolationists, from Charles Lindbergh to Pat Buchanan: Arthur Wellesley, Duke of Wellington, and British prime minister Benjamin Disraeli, who despised the philhellenes as poetry-sodden subversives, were robustly unhypocritical about wanting the Turks to win, and especially enthusiastic about this should it inconvenience the Russians. Not everyone was an Islamophobe.

Bass is most often but not always fair to those who do not share his view. In citing British prime minister Neville Chamberlain's notorious description of events in Czechoslovakia in 1938 as "a quarrel in a faraway country between people of whom we know nothing," Bass argues that Chamberlain "shrugged off" Hitler's invasion of the Sudetenland. In fact, Chamberlain was trying for a tragic note, saying how ghastly it was that Britons should be digging air-raid trenches for such an arcane reason. And this same man was later to issue a military guarantee to Poland that was much more quixotic than any stand taken on the Sudetenland might have been. Neither he nor any other Tory of the 1930s would have hesitated for a second to dispatch British troops to any part of Africa or Asia, however "faraway" or unknown, if doing so would have served the needs of empire. It is mainly the retrospective guilt of the Final Solution, and the shared failure of the Allied powers to do anything to prevent it, that invests arguments such as Bass's with the tension and anxiety that surround them today. I think that many rational people would applaud the defeat of German imperialism in 1945 on grounds more than merely humanitarian.

Yet here is the journalist Robert Kaplan, cited by Bass, in the immediate aftermath of the attacks of September 11, 2001: "Foreign policy must return to what it traditionally has been: the diplomatic aspect of national security rather than a branch of Holocaust studies." Kaplan was arguing, by means of this rather jarring contrast, that the humanitarian interventions in Bosnia and Kosovo had been "luxuries." But this runs the risk of making a distinction without much, if any, difference. Did the United States not have a national security interest, and NATO an interest of its own, in forcibly repressing the idea that ethnic cleansing, within sight of Hungary and Romania and Greece and Turkey and many other combustible local rivals, could be rewarded and that its perpetrators might go unpunished? Was not some valuable combat experience—and, indeed, nation-building experience—thereby gained? Were not some flaws and weaknesses in the post–Cold War international system, most notably those of the United Nations, rather usefully exposed? And then, a few years later, were the United States' hardheaded interests in Afghanistan not to be considered connected to the liberation of the Afghans themselves from medieval tyranny? These and other questions are not novel. They have a long and honorable pedigree, as Bass's book demonstrates.

Bass rightly points out that interventions are not invariably mere simulacra of, or surrogates for, superpower or imperial rivalries. (Thinking that they are is the mistake currently being made by the vulgar apologists for China, Iran, and Russia, three countries that opportunistically are seeking to ally themselves in the Shanghai Cooperation Organization but that denounce all human rights initiatives taken by others as colonial.) I wish Bass had found more space to debate the pros and cons of smaller-scale, nonsuperpower interventions: Tanzania's invasion of Idi Amin's Uganda, for instance, or the Vietnamese overthrow of the Khmer Rouge, both in 1979. But he does mention what he calls the role of the regional "middleweight" in more modern times, such as the part played by Australia in East Timor's transition to independence.

Regarding the Pain of Others

Bass has a considerable gift of phrase—even though one might not rush to adopt his term "atrocitarian" as a nickname for those revolted by acts of genocide. He also has a jaunty flair for recognizing such cynicism in others: It is not without relish that he cites Disraeli's dismissal of "merciless humanitarians." And he is no Mrs. Jellyby, fretting only about the miseries of Borrioboola-Gha while ignoring shrieks for mercy from under his own window. On the whole, he makes a sensible case that everyone has a self-interest in the strivings and sufferings of others because the borders between societies are necessarily porous and contingent and are, when one factors in considerations such as the velocity of modern travel, easy access to weaponry, and the spread of disease, becoming ever more so. Americans may not have known or cared about Rwanda in 1994, for instance, but the effect of its crisis on the Democratic Republic of the Congo could have been even more calamitous. Afghanistan's internal affairs are now the United States'—in fact, they were already so before Americans understood that. A failed state may not trouble Americans' sleep, but a rogue one can, and the transition from failed to rogue can be alarmingly abrupt.

Taking a Stand

The lines from which the title of Bass's book is taken are drawn from Byron:

> For Freedom's battle once begun,
> Bequeathed by bleeding Sire to Son,
> Though baffled oft is ever won.

These were posted by a militant of Solidarity in the Lenin Shipyard in Gdansk in 1980. Could the West's rational interest in defeating Soviet imperialism have been accomplished without the unquantifiable element represented by such gestures?

At the same time, I think that Bass occasionally says the right thing just because it sounds good. "The value of stability is that it saves lives," he writes, and quotes Woodrow Wilson in support: "Social reform can take place only when there is peace." Yet much of the evidence of his book shows that war and conflict are absolutely needful engines for progress and that arguments about human rights, humanitarian intervention, and the evolution of international laws and standards are all, in the last resort, part of a clash over what constitutes civilization, if not invariably a clash between civilizations.

Especially chilling to me, whether it is intentional or not, is the appearance of new foes in old forms. In 1831, after Tsarist Russia had crushed an independent Poland, the poet Aleksandr Pushkin wrote a minatory "Hands off!" verse, essentially warning the Western powers to stay out of eastern Europe. This thuggish literary effort was revived in 1999 by Russia's then foreign minister, Igor Ivanov, who loudly cited Pushkin as he cautioned NATO against intervening in Kosovo. Bass argues, I think rather dangerously, that the first occasion was a tragedy and the second one a farce—in other words, that there are times when despotisms are too strong to be stood up to and others when their bluff can be called. Surely, identifying the situation that is appropriate for intervention is both an art and a science, but history has taught us that tyranny often looks stronger than it really is, that it has unexpected vulnerabilities (very often to do with the blunt fact that tyranny, as such, is incapable of self-analysis), and that taking a stand on principle, even if not immediately rewarded with pragmatic results, can be an excellent dress rehearsal for the real thing.

(*Foreign Affairs*, September/October 2008)

Legacies of Totalitarianism

Victor Serge: Pictures from an Inquisition

IN *MIDDLEMARCH* the desiccated pedant Casaubon wastes his life, and the life of another, in a futile search for "the Key to all Mythologies." In *Bleak House* the wearisome and convoluted case of *Jarndyce* v. *Jarndyce* eventually exhausts all the resources of the contending parties in the sheer costs of the suit. In *The Case of Comrade Tulayev* a random political murder becomes the excuse for a gigantic, hysterical, all-enveloping bureaucratic investigation, and also the talisman for an ideological witch-hunt that intends to lay bare the most imposing of all conspiracies and convinces the last doubter of the existence of a grand design.

After Dostoyevsky and slightly before Arthur Koestler, but contemporary with Orwell and Kafka and somewhat anticipating Solzhenitsyn, there was Victor Serge. His novels and poems and memoirs, most of them directed at the exposure of Stalinism, were mainly composed in jail or on the run. Some of the manuscripts were confiscated or destroyed by the Soviet secret police; in the matter of poetry Serge was able to outwit them by rewriting from memory the verses he had composed in the Orenburg camp, deep in the Ural Mountain section of the Gulag Archipelago.

For many years Serge was almost lost to view. He was one of those

Review of *The Case of Comrade Tulayev* and *Memoirs of a Revolutionary*, by Victor Serge.

intellectual misfits (I intend no disrespect by the term) who were ground to powder between the upper and nether millstones of Stalin and Hitler. One of his novels was aptly titled *Midnight in the Century* (1939)—the phrase used by old "Left" oppositionists to sum up the nightmare years that culminated in the Hitler-Stalin Pact. He died in penurious exile in Mexico, in 1947. His scattered works were later reassembled and translated and kept alive by a small group of radical devotees, most notably Peter Sedgwick and Richard Greeman, whose work is both summarized and exceeded in *Victor Serge: The Course Is Set on Hope*, a tough-minded and well-written biography produced by Susan Weissman in 2001. Otherwise, Serge studies have been confined somewhere on the margins delineated by *Dissent* magazine and the now defunct *Partisan Review*. Not even Trotskyist sects were always willing to give this veteran revolutionary the respect that was his due: Serge had quarreled with "The Old Man," on matters of principle, several times.

So hunted and so cosmopolitan and so factional was Serge's life that it comes almost as a surprise that he was not Jewish. (When asked if he was—and he was asked fairly frequently—he would respond politely, "It happens that I am not." Among his many noms de guerre was Victor Klein.) He was born Victor Kibalchich in Belgium in 1890 to a family of commingled Russian, Polish, and Montenegrin ancestry, and a relative on his father's side had been hanged after the murder of Tsar Alexander II, in 1881. Young Victor soon gravitated to the world of proletarian rebellion, qualifying as a printer and a proofreader and living in the sort of mining village that might have been described by Zola. He took a leading part in denouncing the atrocious rule of King Leopold II of Belgium in the Congo. Impatient with gradualism, and obviously drawn in some way to the depths of society, he removed to Paris, became an anarchist militant with a vagabond streak, and was sentenced to a five-year stretch in solitary confinement in a French jail for his connection to the then-celebrated Bonnot gang. Interestingly, he drew this harsh penalty for refusing to testify against his former comrades. Released in 1917, he went to Barcelona to take part in a brief but intense anarchist revolt, was interned in a gruesome French camp after recrossing the Spanish border, and was exchanged for some French prisoners taken by the Bolsheviks as the First World War ground to its appalling conclusion. He thus involuntarily but not reluctantly made his way to Saint Petersburg, or Petrograd, where it looked as if the genuine article of revolution was at last on offer. By the time of his arrival, in 1919, he had begun to use the name Serge. So before he was thirty he had served some hard time behind bars and behind wire, had been on the losing side a good deal, had gotten to know insurgent Catalonia, and had made a good number of friends on the French intellectual left. All of this hard-won experience was to be pressed into service repeatedly in the even more testing years that lay ahead.

Serge had a gift for transferring experience to the page with graphic immediacy, and for doing so by rapid alternation between journalism and fiction. His jail time produced a novel titled *Men in Prison* (1930), and his presence in Barcelona another named *Birth of Our Power* (1931). His years in Saint Petersburg generated a freshet of on-the-spot reportage that is much superior to the more widely known work of John Reed. Serge was as convinced as Reed of the need for revolution, but he had fewer illusions. It can be claimed for him that he was the first person to recognize and comprehend the roots of the emerging Stalinist regime, or at least to do so from the inside.

It was perhaps a happy chance, if the phrase can be allowed, that the Bolsheviks put Serge in charge of the captured files of the Okhrana—the tsarist secret police. He gave minute attention to these papers, and published a pamphlet detailing the web of repression and surveillance and provocation that he thus uncovered. (It is to the Okhrana that we owe the creation and propagation of *The Protocols of the Elders of Zion*, sometimes mistakenly described as a "forgery"—a forgery, after all, must be of something original or authentic—but perhaps better defined as a cynical yet paranoid concoction: the key of keys to the greatest conspiracy theory of them all.) To have such a redaction supervised by a former prisoner, internee, and deportee was an intelligent move by the Party, but Serge, unlike others, did not thereby become a neresy hunter or an interrogator manqué. Where some might sniff for the presence of subversive or treasonous dissent, his nostrils were attuned to the stench of the secret policeman—a stench he regarded as far more indicative of decay.

One of the earliest actions of Leninism in power was the establishment of the CHEKA—first of the many, many police acronyms that would include GPU, NKVD, and KGB. Serge was a militant opponent of the Jew-baiting and homicidal White reactionaries, and fought against them with some physical bravery, but he saw at once that the permanence of such a secret apparatus on the Red side was a lethal menace of a different kind. His campaign against it, and against the death penalty (briefly abolished in the early years and then reinstated), marked the beginning of his losing battle against a more ruthless form of tyranny. Of the human type attracted to "CHEKIST" work he wrote in his memoirs, "Long-standing social inferiority-complexes and memories of humiliations and suffering in the Tsar's jails rendered them intractable, and since professional degeneration has rapid effects, the CHEKAs inevitably consisted of perverted men tending to see conspiracy everywhere and to live in the midst of perpetual conspiracy themselves."

For example, on the night of January 17, 1920, as the decree abolishing the death penalty was being printed, the CHEKA seized the opportunity to execute as many as 500 suspects—or, as Susan Weissman phrases it so caustically, to liquidate their stock. Serge had an instant intuitive understanding of what this portended. The death of the revolution, he was later to write, was a self-inflicted one.

Nonetheless, and fortunately for us if not for him, he resolved to stay on within the Party and to do what he could. Dispatched to Berlin to help with the Communist International, he discovered that Bolshevism was becoming as bureaucratic and intolerant beyond the borders of the USSR as it was within them. But he also learned about the mounting threat of the madness of fascism, and this produced in him a sort of dual consciousness: First, this new enemy needed to be defeated; second, it needed to be understood. The apparatchiks of communism, however, both underestimated the danger and helped to provoke it. Indeed, it could be said of fascism, as Serge was to write with an acuity that makes one almost dizzy, that "[this] new variety of counterrevolution had taken the Russian Revolution as its schoolmaster in matters of repression and mass-manipulation through propaganda... [and] had succeeded in recruiting a host of disillusioned, power-hungry ex-revolutionaries; consequently, its rule would last for years."

Attempting to synthesize these apparent opposites but latent collaborators,

Serge came up with the word "totalitarian." He believed that he had originated it himself; there are some rival claimants from the period of what was then called "war communism," but it is of interest that the term has its origins within the Marxist left, just as the term "Cold War" was first used by George Orwell in analyzing a then looming collision of super-powers in 1945. Incidentally, when Serge was later seeking to have his *Memoirs of a Revolutionary* (1951) published in English, it was to Orwell that he wrote asking for help.

Indeed (not that it did him much good), Serge had a knack for nosing out the right acquaintances. He met Antonio Gramsci and Georg Lukacs during his years outside Russia, and received a warning from Lukacs not to go back. He later not only escorted Nikos Kazantzakis and Panaït Istrati around the USSR but also was present when Istrati let fall the remark that made him famous: To the old saw "One can't make an omelet without breaking eggs," Istrati mordantly retorted, "All right, I can see the broken eggs. Where's this omelet of yours?" When the honest old Bolshevik diplomat Adolf Joffe committed suicide in 1927, to call attention to the "Thermidor" that was engulfing the revolution, Serge assisted in organizing a mass turnout for Joffe's funeral; he later realized that he had helped to lead the last legal anti-government protest to be held in Moscow. Within a short time he himself was in one of Stalin's prisons.

Released after some grueling experiences, he remained—despite his misgivings about the personality of Leon Trotsky—a partisan of the left opposition. Had he not been re-arrested in 1933 and deported to internal exile in Orenburg, he might well have been swept up and discarded forever in the period of even more hysterical persecution that followed the assassination of Sergei Kirov, on December 1, 1934. Kirov had been a popular leader of the Party in Leningrad; most historians now agree that his murder was the signal for the true frenzy of the purges to begin. It was the Soviet equivalent of the Reichstag fire.

Most historians also now agree on another important point: that the murder was organized by Stalin himself, either to remove a well-liked man who could have become a rival, or simply to help justify the political pogrom that he had long had in mind. (See in particular Robert Conquest's *Stalin and the Kirov Murder* [1989] and Amy Knight's *Who Killed Kirov?* [1999].) Some time before the assassination Serge had been overheard to say that what he most feared was the killing of some high Party satrap and the consequent licensing of a more comprehensive terror. Thus what is most interesting about his novel on the subject is that it begins by apparently exculpating Stalin from the main charge.

The Case of Comrade Tulayev (1948), which opens with the murder of a high Communist official by that name, makes an enormous sacrifice as a work of suspense by giving away the ostensible "plot" almost at once. We see a righteous and somewhat disturbed young man as he acquires a weapon by chance, takes to carrying it with him everywhere, and to his immense surprise runs into a senior "target of opportunity" on a darkened street. Pulling the trigger on impulse, to relieve his general feelings of alienation, he makes an easy escape, because there is absolutely nothing to connect him to the crime and he did nothing to prepare for it. But this apparently naive device actually imparts a considerable tensile strength to the ensuing chapters, as we see from the reaction of the Party and its leader that nothing in the Soviet Union can be admitted to happen by accident.

> The papers briefly announced "the premature death of Comrade Tulayev." The first secret investigation produced sixty-seven arrests in three days. Suspicion at first fell on Tulayev's secretary, who was also the mistress of a student who was not a Party member. Then it shifted to the chauffeur who had brought Tulayev to his door—a Security man with a good record, not a drinker, no questionable relations, a former soldier in the special troops, and a member of the Bureau of his garage cell. Why had he not waited until Tulayev had entered the house, before driving off? Why, instead of going in immediately, had Tulayev walked a few paces down the sidewalk?

(The subsequent fate of the chauffeur is more than you want to contemplate.) We all now understand that dictatorship depends to an unusual degree on sheer caprice rather than predictable or systematic enforcement, but it was Serge's early insight that those Marxists who had prided themselves above all on their cold and objective lucidity had become "fuddled with a theoretical intoxication bordering on delusion . . . enclosed within all the tricks and tomfooleries of servility." (This remark is from his *Memoirs*.)

The best novel of the postwar Stalinist purges—the ones that spread to Eastern Europe—is Eric Ambler's *Judgment on Deltchev* (1951). Here, the purge takes the form of isolating an inconvenient dissident (or potential dissident) and destroying his reputation before framing him. There's nothing of this glacial cynicism in Serge's novel. The post-1934 spy fever may have had a core of rationality when it began, or was inaugurated, but its special feature was the sheer mania and panic in which it engulfed society, becoming an exhausting, unstoppable thing in itself. At one point (Doris Lessing describes it somewhere in her account of abandoning communism) medieval instruments of torture were taken from Russian museums and deployed in the cellars and interrogation pits of Stalin's police. The image is perfect for evoking the choking medieval nightmare of plague-dread, xenophobia, and persecution that enveloped the Soviet Union and destroyed the last remnants of its internationalism. If the characters and automatons of *The Case of Comrade Tulayev* understand any one thing, it is the idea that the enemy is everywhere, and everyone. Poor old Makeyev, one of Serge's better-drawn minor characters, is a plebeian mediocrity with some physical courage who becomes a regional commissar by dint of brute force and sterling loyalty. He is the negation of the Bolshevik cosmopolitan—a figure from Chekhov. He at first feels himself "integrated into the dictatorship of the proletariat like a good steel screw set into its proper place in some admirable, supple, and complex machine." But Stalin—"the man of steel"—was at the helm of a locomotive determined to go off the rails, and who can redeem a Makeyev from a catastrophe like that?

As in the most intricate and sadistic courts of antique Oriental despotism, the thing to be feared almost as much as being "out of favor" was the special terror of sudden advancement. (Many later personal reminiscences of Stalin were to record that it was in genial mood that he was most to be feared.) I shall have to be forgiven for quoting at length here, since Serge captured this mental and moral atmosphere so faultlessly.

> Erchov, recalled from the Far East, where he had thought himself happily forgotten by the Personnel Service, had been offered an

> unparalleled promotion: High Commissar for Security in conjunction with Commissar of the People for Internal Affairs, which practically carried with it the rank of marshal—the sixth marshal—or was it the third, since three of the five had disappeared? "Comrade Erchov, the Party puts its confidence in you! I congratulate you!" The words were spoken, his hand shaken, the office (it was one of the Central Committee offices, on the same floor as the General Secretariat) was full of smiles. Unannounced, the Chief entered quickly, looked him up and down for a split second—a superior studying an inferior; then, so simply, so cordially, smiling like the others and perfectly at ease, the Chief shook Maxim Andreyevich Erchov's hand and looked into his eyes with perfect friendliness. "A heavy responsibility, Comrade Erchov. Bear it well." The press photographer flashed his magnesium lightning over all the smiles... Erchov had reached the pinnacle of his life, and he was afraid.

In the ensuing sentences, Serge transcends Gogol and anticipates *Nineteen Eighty-four*:

> Three thousand dossiers, of capital importance because they called for capital punishment, three thousand nests of hissing vipers, suddenly descended like an avalanche upon his life, to remain with him every instant. For a moment the greatness of the Chief reassured him. The Chief, addressing him as "Maxim Andreyevich" in a cordial tone, paternally advised him "to go easy with personnel, keeping the past in mind yet never failing in vigilance, to put a stop to abuses."—"Men have been executed whom I loved, whom I trusted, men precious to the Party and the State!" he exclaimed bitterly. "Yet the Political Bureau cannot possibly review every sentence! It is up to you," he concluded. "You have my entire confidence." The power that emanated from him was spontaneous, human, and perfectly simple; the kindly smile, in which the russet eyes and the bushy mustache joined, attested it; it made you love him.

Erchov, as you will have intuited from the above passage, doesn't last long in the job and is soon humiliated and purged in his turn. But by then he has helped to set in motion a machinery of inquisition, supported by a Borgesian labyrinth of bureaucratic incrimination, that assumes a horrific autonomy.

Men who were miles away at the time, or who had already been exiled or jailed, are put through the mill again and compelled to answer impossible questions. In faraway Spain, in the death throes of the republic and the last gasp of the Catalan Revolution, with Franco's and Hitler's forces at the very gates, random Trotskyists are kidnapped and forced to confess their part in the murder of Comrade Tulayev.

Or not to confess it. Serge was a friend to Andrés Nin, the leader of Catalonia's left-opposition POUM (and the translator of Dostoyevsky into Catalan), and he always had a special regard for the old revolutionaries who never "broke." In many ways, placed next to *Midnight in the Century*, this novel is their memorial. There's inevitable speculation about the influence exerted, by means of both title and subject matter, on Koestler's *Darkness at Noon*. It is certainly true that in *Tulayev* we meet the figure of Kiril Rublev, an old Bolshevik who is strenuously (and eloquently) pressed to admit to inconceivable offenses because he can perform a last service to the Party by abasing himself in this way. But unlike Koestler's Rubashov, many of Serge's characters stubbornly decline the logic of the grand inquisitor.

Serge himself was one of the few to refuse it, and this probably saved his life. There came a time when the agitation abroad in his behalf became too much to overlook, and when a campaign for his release—led by Romain Rolland—had embarrassed even the intellectual prostitutes of the French fellow-traveling classes. Stalin decided to examine the case in person, but before doing so he asked his police chiefs what crimes Serge had confessed to while in the Orenburg camp. He must have been somewhat startled to be told that the prisoner had confessed to nothing at all (a distinct rarity in those times), and this made it easier to release and deport Serge without too much loss of face.

Given this standard of fortitude, and given the contempt Serge always felt for Stalin's collaborators, a remarkable feature of *The Case of Comrade Tulayev* is its chiaroscuro. In one passage the monstrous figure of "The Chief" is represented as a prisoner of fate, only pretending to arbitrate the destiny of a sixth of the earth's surface and of every one of its inhabitants. That Serge intended no lenience here we may be sure, but we may likewise be sure that he would never have swallowed the later euphemisms and half-truths of Khrushchev, putting blame for all the enormities of an epoch on the evil of a single individual. One of the most despicable engineers of the Tulayev witch-hunt, a creepy old time-server named Popov who trades on a reputation for staunch service, is limned not like an Iago but like a modern Polonius, full of pathetic advice and mumbling rhetoric. And this old wreck has his Ophelia—a daughter in Paris whose spontaneity and generosity will not allow her to take part in the lie. The freshness and honesty of Xenia Popov are eventually suicidal, but deadly also to her father's sordid compromise with the usurper's court. In its remorseless emphasis on the ineluctable along with its insistence on the vitality of individual human nature, *The Case of Comrade Tulayev* is one of the most Marxist novels ever written—as it is also one of the least.

(*The Atlantic*, December 2002)

André Malraux: One Man's Fate

ISAIAH BERLIN once described someone whom I will not name as "that very rare thing: a perfect charlatan." Admit that this ostensibly lethal criticism contains a note of reluctant admiration, and you have the tone of Olivier Todd's newest biography, *Malraux: A Life* (which has been translated from the French by Joseph West). André Malraux was one of the most prolific self-inventors of the twentieth century, and it is "the Malrucian legend," as much as the life itself, that is Todd's subject.

This is perhaps a pity, since it causes Todd to devote more space to the succeeding stages of Malraux's dazzling metamorphoses—from marginal arriviste to major cultural impresario of Charles de Gaulle's Fifth Republic—than to the novels by which he is chiefly remembered. One might make that "the novel": *La Condition Humaine*, or *Man's Fate*. Published in 1933, it did for fiction what Harold Isaacs's *Tragedy of the Chinese Revolution* did for scholarship. It pointed up the increasing weight of Asia in world affairs; it described epic moments of suffering and upheaval, in Shanghai especially (it was nearly filmed by Sergei Eisenstein); and it demonstrated a huge respect for Communism and for Communists while simultaneously evoking the tragedy of a revolution betrayed by Moscow. Somewhat lushly Orientalist in its manner, the novel was ridiculed for its affectation by Vladimir Nabokov and hailed as prescient by Arthur Koestler.

Review of *Malraux: A Life*, by Olivier Todd.

For Todd, the author of several works, including a biography of Camus, all this is of less importance than the knowledge that Malraux had spent almost no time in China itself. Toward the end of this book, he hits on a near-perfect Left Bank encapsulation for his subject. Malraux was, we learn, "autonomous in relation to facts." That is to phrase it mildly. One of the characters in Flaubert's *Sentimental Education* is described as being so corrupt that he would happily have paid for the pleasure of selling himself. Malraux was such a fantasist that he would have paid handsomely for a forged narrative that was designed to deceive himself. He invented a relationship with Mao. He exaggerated his role in the Spanish Civil War. He fabricated a glorious past in the French Resistance.

Like all supreme con artists, he did possess the knack of being in the right place at the right time, and of scraping acquaintance with the great. As I turned the pages, I was put in mind of a Gallic version of Harry Flashman: fast-talking and protean, covered with unearned glory and full of embellished traveler's tales from many plundered colonies. (Malraux preferred to imagine himself as T. E. Lawrence. Either analogy would be imperfect in one respect: Malraux was a heterosexual but seems often to have preferred food and drink to sex.)

He was born in 1901 in Paris, the son of a small-time stockbroker. His first overseas adventure was the one that made him notorious: an expedition in 1923 to French-ruled Cambodia, during which he amputated priceless bits of sculpture and statuary from some ancient temples. Arrested and charged for this, he managed to induce quite a number of Parisian intellectuals and aesthetes, including André Gide and André Maurois, to take up his case as if it were an injustice being committed by the colonial authorities. Going even further than his fellow Andrés on behalf of another André, the Surrealist André Breton added, with magnificent condescension to the Cambodians, "Who in their homeland really cares about the preservation of these works of art?" The price for all this chutzpah was that Malraux then had to take up the cause of the colonial indigenes as if it really mattered to him. Moving to Saigon in the mid-1920s, he helped to produce a troublemaking newspaper, *L'Indochine*, which ventilated the many complaints of the Vietnamese about forced labor, land expropriation, and police brutality.

It was at this point, Todd dryly notes, that Malraux began to speak of his admiration for Gabriele D'Annunzio. As a model for emulation, this freebooting soldier and aviator might not seem so obvious. His freelance attack on Fiume at the end of the First World War was the inspiration for the thuggish Mussolini and his later march on Rome. Why or how should it have appealed to the sensitive Malraux, with his delicate features and his nervous facial tic—diagnosed by Todd as a symptom of Tourette's syndrome? But the later development of the Malraux myth makes it clear that D'Annunzio was in fact the near-perfect emblem for his vicariousness and ambition. Above all, he wished to be a hero, and the price in bombast and pretension and attitude-striking was one that he thought well worth paying. D'Annunzio was essentially a Nietzschean rhetorician who tried to dissolve the difference between word and deed. Malraux was to become a writer of fiction, and of quasi-fictional memoirs that he hoped would be taken literally.

One of those who stood aside from this division—Raymond Aron—regarded himself as prose and Malraux as poetry. In the meltdown and ferment of culture and civilization that succeeded the First World War, how banal it must have seemed to favor mere liberal democracy. But Aron's later judgment of Malraux ("one third genius, one third false, one third incomprehensible") would be remarkably useful in evaluating the novels with which Malraux made his reputation. These adaptations of his Asian travels, *Les Conquerants* (1928), *La Voie Royale* (1930), and *La Condition Humaine* (1993), amounted to a trilogy on the Chinese Revolution. In tone, they swung awkwardly between a sort of vulgar Marxism and a Bonapartist invocation of *la gloire*. Indeed, Malraux never lost his admiration for Napoleon, and produced a potboiling biography of him at the same time.

By this stage, Malraux had been compelled to confront the figure of Trotsky, who was a special synthesis of the cosmopolitan intellectual, man of action, and wielder of power. His expulsion from Stalin's Soviet Union in the late twenties had been partly the result of a furious debate on the future of the Chinese Revolution. (The first edition of Isaacs's *Tragedy of the Chinese Revolution* actually bore Trotsky's preface.) Todd devotes a brief chapter to Malraux's fascination with this epic figure. As ever, the Frenchman was torn between an admiration for a historic personality and a queasy consciousness that he himself had debts to pay and credit to keep in the Parisian leftist milieu. He did not waste all that much time in making up his mind. After an absurd, melodramatic proposal to mount a rescue team of intellectuals to snatch Trotsky from his place of exile in Alma-Ata, Malraux simmered down a bit and later read Trotsky's rather flattering critique of *Les Conquerants* in *La Nouvelle Revue Francaise.* When Trotsky's long exile wanderings brought him through France in the 1930s, Malraux went to call upon him and the two men discussed everything from Celine to cinema. But by then, the cultural ascendancy of the French Communist Party was making life distinctly tough for dissenters on the left, and Malraux seems to have decided that the old Bolshevik was just another loser. He began to pitch his tent with that most tiresome of the intellectual factions of the 1930s: the regulars at international conferences of writers and scholars.

Trotsky's own later verdict on this exhibition—"Malraux is organically incapable of moral independence; he was born biddable"—now appears quite restrained. Many Western intellectuals had to find their way through illusions about 1917, and make their own painful accommodations with the awful truths they discovered about Stalin. Malraux, who knew about the persecution and murder of Stalin's opponents well before most people had learned the facts, made a conscious decision to join what he must have thought was the winning side. Nothing else can explain his appalling, flatulent verbiage about the heroic continuity of 1789 and 1917, or his dogged attendance at sham events that were openly and cynically controlled by the Soviet cultural commissars.

But his chief excuse for this behavior became, paradoxically, his finest hour. General Franco's invasion of Republican Spain, as the surrogate of the Axis powers, provided our hero with the opportunity to become a sort of impresario of the left. Annexing some of the prestige of Antoine de Saint-Exupery, and trading on a very slight experience as an airman himself, Malraux flamboyantly decided to provide the Spanish Republic with air cover.

Todd is bent on puncturing most of the balloons that Malraux sent aloft in his long and boastful career, but even he cannot forbear to applaud once or twice in this account. Of course Malraux's flying circus was made up of aerial coffins, frequently piloted by unscrupulous mercenaries or crazed idealists. Of course Malraux himself claimed to have been on expeditions where he never flew, and to have sustained an honorable combat wound that was actually the result of an ignominious crash on takeoff. *Mais que voulez-vous*? A bit of dash, and an element of resistance, were added to the desperate struggle for the defense of Madrid. Yet Malraux was not quite the French Hemingway. He seconded all the falsehoods of Stalinism in Spain and excused all of its crimes and went back to Paris to try to persuade André Gide to bury or postpone his classic of anti-Soviet disillusionment: *Retour de I'URSS.* Todd himself, here, is somewhat hard to follow. He introduces the later French Resistance hero Jean Moulin as if we should already know who he was and what he was to become (which we doubtless should, but still), and he makes a confusion between the poet John Cornford and the philosopher Maurice Cornforth that, even given French disdain for the mere empiricism of British Marxists, shakes one's confidence in his grasp of the subject.

Malraux wrote, in *La Voie Royale,* that "every adventurer is born a mythomaniac." This could serve as a decoding of his next phase: the Nazi occupation of France. Most of the story is one long profile in prudence. Until well into 1944, he rebuffed all efforts to recruit him into the Resistance. Once again seeing a turn in the tide, he signed up just before the Allied landings in Normandy. His hero Napoleon used to ask, of any new general, "Is he lucky?" Malraux had the luck of the devil. He made some useful friends in British Intelligence and managed briefly to cut a figure during the siege of Strasbourg. Every single claim he subsequently made can be demonstrated as false by Todd, but there was a general need to pretend that the Resistance had been more epic than it really was. At the close of hostilities, Malraux was even approached by de Gaulle, who had heard garbled accounts of his record, and from then on Malraux was able to stick like a limpet to an authentic man of destiny.

It deserves to be said that he stuck through thick and thin, remaining at the general's side even during the years of political exile. He became the public intellectual of the R.P.F. (Rassemblement du Peuple Francais), the slightly shady populist projection of the Gaullist personality. His genius for publicity, and for the making of windy rhetorical presentations, served him well. When de Gaulle took power again in 1958, Malraux at first took charge of state broadcasting and information (in which capacity he told a number of cheerful lies about the collapsing French position in Algeria). But it wasn't long before he found himself in the position of inventing a Ministry of Culture for an otherwise rather prosaic government.

At this point, and given a certain recent *froideur* on the international front, some American readers may be thinking of Malraux as a typical French combination of pseudo-intellectual and *valet du pouvoir.* So it's of interest to note that he was always drawn to the United States. At the outbreak of the Second World War he had prophesied that America would be the decisive country in ending the conflict, and he was fond of saying that the United States was the first nation to rise to international pre-eminence without having sought the role. As minister of culture, he made tremendous overtures to the newly elected Kennedy administration, charming the former Miss Bouvier in particular and arranging to have the "Mona Lisa" brought for a special showing in Washington.

All his life, he was able to parlay one meeting or acquaintance into another, and to stay one jump ahead of his reputation. This, combined with his fascination for the superman, allowed him to bring off the following coup. As de Gaulle's minister, he was able to visit China in 1965 and to persuade the rather baffled Chinese authorities to grant him an audience with Mao. Todd's account of the interview is by turns hilarious—Malraux claimed to have led "peasant units" during the war against Germany—and revolting: Malraux's abject sycophancy tired even the ailing despot. The meeting was brief and platitudinous, but in later accounts, including his gloriously mendacious *Antimemoires,* Malraux turned it into a major summit of great minds. In consequence, and also because he had been seen so often with the Kennedys, he was invited to brief Richard Nixon and Henry Kissinger before they set off on their visit to Beijing. Malraux must have known he was on very thin ice here, and could have been exposed as an impostor at any moment, but he carried off the bluff with considerable aplomb. It is even possible that by this stage he had come to believe his own story.

Malraux's favorite symbol was the cat, and he would often inscribe his letters with an image of a feline. Todd admirably resists the temptation to make a cliché out of this metaphor, but I shall not. The man really did have nine lives, and he almost always landed on his feet. The upheaval in Paris in 1968, with which he may have felt a small sympathy, nonetheless allowed him to combat the street theater of the student revolutionaries with some histrionic gestures of his own, and he survived the eclipse of his hero de Gaulle with some credit still left.

The end was not glorious. Malraux's facial tic was accompanied by a black dog of depression, and he became dependent first on alcohol and then on a succession of medications. His family life deteriorated horribly. When the end came, in November 1976, two sprays of red flowers were delivered to the cemetery. One was from the French Communist Party, which he had fawned upon in the 1930s and turned upon in the 1940s. The other was from the restaurant Lasserre: grand scene of many of his dinner-table revolutions. On his bedside table, after his death, it was found that he had scrawled the words: "It should have been otherwise." A more apt, if lenient, epitaph might be located in *La Condition Humaine*: "*Ce n'etait ni vrai ni faux, c'etait vecu.*" "It was neither true nor false, but what was experienced."

(*The New York Times Book Review*, April 10, 2005)

Arthur Koestler: The Zealot

I CANNOT RECALL a book title that was less well-shaped to its subject. Far from being a "skeptic," Arthur Koestler was a man not merely convinced but actively enthused by practically any intellectual or political or mental scheme that came his way. When he was in the throes of an allegiance, he positively abhorred doubt, which he sometimes called "bellyaching." If he was ever dubious about anything, one could say in his defense, it was at least about himself. He was periodically paralyzed by self-reproach and insecurity, and once wrote a defensive third-person preface to one of his later novels (*The Age of Longing*) in which he described its style as modeled on that of a certain "A. Koestler," whose writing, "lacking in ornament and distinction, is easy to imitate." The author himself was written off as "a much afflicted scribe of his time, greedy for pleasure, haunted by guilt, who enjoyed a short vogue and was then forgotten, like the rest of them."

In fact, Koestler succeeded in achieving several things that transcended his own time and made him into what Danilo Kiš called the prototypical Central European intellectual. He was enabled to do them because he believed that the intellectual ought also to be a man of action. He took part in the anti-fascist struggles of the 1930s and '40s first as a true-believing Communist and then as an ex-Communist, and out of this synthesis he generated

---

Review of *Koestler: The Literary and Political Odyssey of a Twentieth-Century Skeptic*, by Michael Scammell.

at least one work of nonfiction (*Spanish Testament*) and one novel (*Darkness at Noon*), which between them helped redefine the essential struggle as the one against totalitarianism *tout court*. No other single individual, with the exception of George Orwell—upon whom Koestler had a marked influence—could claim as much. Second, he managed to register practically every phase, emotional and ideological, of diasporic engagement with Zionism. Third, he was able to demonstrate that an individual could make a difference in the battle of the behemoths that constituted the Cold War.

To be born Hungarian and Jewish and German-speaking is to start at a slightly odd angle to the world. For instance, Koestler was unusual in retaining what Michael Scammell calls "fond memories" of the 1919 Communist putsch in Hungary, a botched and bloody business that led many people to actually welcome the advent of the vengeful right as a deliverance. This right was organically hostile to Jewry, but not even that explains Koestler's nostalgia for Béla Kun, which in any case makes an odd fit with his decision, as a refugee and student in Vienna, to join a nationalist dueling-and-drinking club that effectively molded young Jews into ersatz Germans. Once more his formation and evolution were against the traditional grain: Most European Jews were drawn to Palestine by labor and socialist groups, but when Koestler set off for the Holy Land he did so as a consecrated follower of Vladimir Jabotinsky and the so-called Revisionists. Parlaying his fierce journalism from the Middle East into a job with a German newspaper syndicate in Berlin, Koestler was able to interview Einstein and begin a lifelong amateur engagement with science, while keeping up a keen interest in the subject of eugenics: a field that (in 1930s Germany, of all times and all places) he regarded as promising.

The word one might choose to describe this riot of enthusiasms and contradictions would be *promiscuous*. It would certainly sit very well with Koestler's private life, which was a hectic, alarming, and sometimes violent blend of alcoholism and satyriasis. Scammell holds retrospective psychology to a minimum but cannot escape noticing Koestler's flight from an overprotective mother or his keen awareness of his short stature. We have Koestler's own word for it—in *Arrow in the Blue*, which I think is the best of his volumes of memoirs—that he habitually felt awkward and uneasy and sometimes an impostor. This book provides persuasive evidence of acute manic depression, combated in one way by sex and booze and in another by devotion to a series of causes. Otto Katz once said to him, "We all have inferiority complexes of various sizes, but yours isn't a complex—it's a cathedral." Koestler liked this remark so much that he included it in his autobiography, thus attaining the status of one who could actually brag about his inferiority complex as if size mattered.

It was often believed in those days that absorption into the historic movement of the working class was the cure for the angst of the *petit bourgeois* and the deracinated intellectual. This could help explain the utterness of Koestler's surrender to Communism. Not even a visit to the famine-racked USSR—where he traveled around with a completely credulous Langston Hughes—was enough to unpersuade him. He set off for Spain and the civil war as a dedicated agent of the Comintern, and if the Spanish Fascists who arrested him had guessed his true identity, they would have shot him out of hand. Had they done so, they would have unknowingly dealt anti-Communism a frightful blow. Koestler's experience of Franco's cells in Málaga, with victims dragged to execution almost every night, helped furnish the stark raw material for *Darkness at Noon*: certainly the best jail book since Victor Serge's *Men in Prison* and almost as influential in combating Stalinism as *Nineteen Eighty-four*.

Koestler's decision to abandon Communism almost as soon as he had been freed from Spain—because of the hysterical faking of the Moscow purge trials in 1938—was expressed in such brilliantly diagnostic and dialectical terms that it bears quoting:

> It is a logical contradiction when with uncanny regularity the leadership sees itself obliged to undertake more and more bloody operations within the movement, and in the same breath insists that the movement is healthy. Such an accumulation of grave surgical interventions points with much greater likelihood to the existence of a much more serious illness.

To say that Koestler's zeal replicated itself in the anti-Communist cause would be to say the least of it. Scammell takes us once again through the story of the Congress for Cultural Freedom and the CIA, but spends time illustrating what few people understand even now: The CIA's hold on the financing of intellectual warfare was actually used as a *brake* on volunteers like Koestler, who were regarded as too vitriolically anti-Soviet and temperamentally hostile to compromise.

Having temporarily abandoned Zionism for Communism, he resumed his engagement by covering (and participating in) the violent birth of Israel, initially taking the side of the Menachem Begin ultra-nationalists but eventually becoming sickened by the violence of the Zionist right and finally worrying whether there should be a Jewish state at all. Scammell is not quite in his depth here: He conflates the Stern gang and the Irgun and gives superficial treatment (as he also does, bizarrely, to Koestler's part in producing *The God That Failed*) to a subsequent book, *The Thirteenth Tribe*. In this, his last semi-serious work, Koestler suggested that Ashkenazi Jews were actually descended from the lost people of Khazaria, who before vanishing from the northern Caucasus a thousand years ago had somehow opted to Judaize themselves. One implication of that theory was that no authentic Ashkenazi Jewish tie to Palestine could ever be established. "Arthur just rather enjoys betraying his former friends," I remember Patricia Cockburn snorting when this effort was published in the 1970s.

That might have been unfair—she remembered how her husband, Claud, had sweated to get Koestler out of jail in Spain, only to be rewarded with apostasy—but in his last two decades Koestler abandoned every kind of scruple and objectivity and became successively bewitched by "theories" of levitation, ESP, telepathy, and UFOs. He was enthralled by Timothy Leary and played for a sucker by the paranormal spoon-bender Uri Geller. The sleep of his reason did not even bring forth monsters: Poor Koestler simply gave a fair wind and his once-valued imprimatur to a succession of pathetic quacks and mountebanks.

In a noble if melodramatic way, Koestler had once held a sort of dress rehearsal for suicide with Walter Benjamin, as both contemplated being taken alive by the Gestapo. (He kept the pills Benjamin gave him, while the latter swallowed his on the Spanish border a few days later.) By comparison, his own suicide in 1983 was an affair very much lacking in grandeur. His mind and his body were certainly both giving way, but he seems to have allowed or perhaps encouraged his healthy wife, Cynthia, to join him in the extinction. An earlier study by David Cesarani was lurid to the point of sensationalism about Koestler's callousness toward his wives and other women (to say nothing of other people's wives). It has been plausibly alleged that in his compulsive seductions—of Simone de Beauvoir, for one—he did not always stop quite short of physical coercion. Scammell does his best to plead extenuation here, but is obviously uncomfortable. Just as many of the people who believe in numinous coincidence and supernatural intervention are secretly hoping to prove that it is they themselves who are the pet of the universe, so many of those who overcompensate for inferiority are possessed of titanic egos and regard other people as necessary but incidental. At least this case is a tragic one when considered as a life story, because it shows us what a noble mind was there o'erthrown.

(*The Atlantic*, December 2009)

Isabel Allende: Chile Redux

IT IS WHILE SPEAKING of the island of Crete, in Saki's story *The Jesting of Arlington Stringham*, that the eponymous character says that the place "produces more history than it can consume locally." We all know of certain distinctive countries on the map of which this seems to be true. For some reason, a lot of them also begin with the letter *C*: Czechoslovakia (which now exists only in memory), Cuba, Cyprus—and Chile. And there is also a literary surplus that often comes with these territories: Think only of Kafka, Kundera, Yglesias, and Neruda.

For people of a certain generation (my own, to be exact: those of us sometimes vulgarly described as the baby-boomers), the imagery and cosmology of Chile are a part of ourselves. A country shaped like a long, thin, jagged blade, forming the littoral of almost an entire continent, and poised to crumble into the ocean leaving only the Andes behind. A place of earthquakes and wine and poets, like some Antarctic Aegean. And a place of arms: the scene of the grand twentieth-century confrontation between Allende and Pinochet. The nation's territory includes the Atacama desert, an expanse of rain forest, a huge deposit of copper, a great valley full of vines, and the mysteriously-statued Polynesian outpost of Easter Island, known to the indigenous as *Rapanui*, or "the navel of the world." (The navel, or *omphalos*, was also the name given by the ancients to the oracular cave at Delphi.)

Introduction (2005) to *The House of the Spirits*, by Isabel Allende.

The voices and portents in *La Casa de los Espiritus* are also somewhat cryptic at times, as befits the school of "magical realism." This style, or manner, was actually pioneered somewhat earlier than most people think, by Jorge Luis Borges in neighboring Argentina. In 1926 he published an essay, "Tales of Turkestan," in which he hymned the sort of story where "the marvelous and the everyday are entwined... there are angels as there are trees." In 1931, in *The Postulation of Reality*, he announced that fiction was "an autonomous sphere of corroborations, omens and monuments," as bodied forth in the "predestined" *Ulysses* of James Joyce.

From the very beginning of Isabel Allende's narration, disbelief is suspensible in the most natural way, and (if you pay attention) the premonitions begin to register. Rather cleverly—and subversively—the action begins in a church. Bored by the blackmailing liturgy, and by the devotional decorations which make an everyday trade out of the officially supernatural, the Trueba family is preoccupied with the truly extraordinary developments within its own ranks. Effortlessly, we find ourselves conscripted into the truth of this tale; from green hair to the gift of prophecy and divination and the taken-for-granted ability to fly. Just off the center of the stage, in carefully placed hints and allusions to the Prussian goose-step, to the future burning of the books and to the Marxist gentleman referred to as "the candidate," we can also pick up the faint drum-taps of the far-off tragic denouement.

Children and animals are often the conveyors of the magical: innocence and experience being in their cases less immediately distinguishable. Clara and the dog Barrabás would make an almost cartoonish filmic double-act for anyone with the necessary entrepreneurial imagination: a sort of Scooby-Doo with the facts of life thrown in. Here it is Isabel Allende's brilliantly dead-pan and dry humor, concerning such things as the beast Barrabás's murderous penis, that draws us into the story and makes us surrender. In counterpoint to this highly bearable lightness, her notes of seriousness are correspondingly weighty. (Why does nobody ever believe Clara's prophecies? Because nobody ever believed Cassandra.) By the time we reach chapter five ("The Lovers") we are suddenly aware that we are watching a parody of *Animal Farm* in reverse, with a song about chickens organizing to defeat a fox heard by a wealthy landowner who wants to put a stop to such romantic nonsense.

The romance between the rich man's daughter and the penniless son of the peasant is such a folkloric cliché that one has to become wary for an instant, even with an author who has already won one's trust. However, *The House of the Spirits* depends for its ingenuity on the blending of the microcosmic with the macrocosmic: the little society of the family and the wider society of Chile. Lineage is important in the unfolding of this, and the Truebas all have one dynastic name, while the "Pedros"—like the nameless French serfs who were all called "Jacques"—mark their descent by numbers: Secundo, Tercero... just like monarchs in fact. Isabel Allende herself bears a great name that has become imperishable for nonhereditary reasons, and so it is rather generous of her, in the circumstances, to invert what is traditional and to make a hero out of what Marxism might normally prefer to cast as a villain. Esteban Trueba is a patriarch in every sense: a self-made man of property and a *seigneur* who haughtily insists on exercising every *droit*, libidinous or financial. His appetites are gigantic, and no peasant girl is safe from him, but he feels himself bound nonetheless by a *contrat social* and a sense of *noblesse oblige*. (If I lapse into French instead of Spanish at this point, it is because all metaphors of the *lutte de classe* are ultimately French ones.)

My own family is not the only one where there exists an extraordinary bond between grandfather and granddaughter. The emotional strength of this phenomenon has been noted many times (some people even joke that such alliances are so durable and intense because they are based upon a common enemy). At any rate, we know from the highly candid and affecting memoirs of Isabel Allende that her own grandfather, Agustin Llona, was in many ways the "main man" in her early life: the representative of the masculine virtues. Indeed, he is the *raison d'être* of this novel. One day, in exile from her martyred country, Isabel Allende heard the awful news:

> that my grandfather was dying, and that he had told the family he had decided to die. He had stopped eating and drinking, and he sat in his chair to wait for death. At that moment I wanted so badly to write and tell him that he was never going to die, that somehow he would always be present in my life, because he had a theory that death didn't exist, only forgetfulness did. He believed that if you can keep people in your memory, they will live forever. That's what he did with my grandmother. So I began to write him a long letter, elaborated from the awful thought that he was going to die.

Esteban Trueba, the fictional memorial of this grand old gentleman, is life-affirming. He builds a grand estate at *Tres Marías* out of his own unremitting struggle with adversity, and accepts the responsibility for his tenants even as he declines to listen to any whining or subversive back-chat from them. He also becomes a distinguished senator, and leads the charge against the party of Allende, even irritating the more conciliatory conservatives who dislike making a fuss:

> "The day we can't get our hands on the ballot boxes before the vote is counted we're done for," Trueba argued.
>
> "The Marxists haven't won by popular vote anywhere in the world," his confreres replied. "At the very least it takes a revolution, and that kind of thing doesn't happen in this country."
>
> "Until it happens!" Trueba answered furiously.
>
> "Relax, *hombre*. We're not going to let that happen," they consoled him. "Marxism doesn't stand a chance in Latin America. Don't you know it doesn't allow for the magical side of things?"

In the context, that's rather a clever question. And, in her grandpa's quoted opinion that forgetfulness is the equivalent of death, isn't there an echo of the author, much admired by Isabel Allende, who has most attempted to fuse Marxism with magic? Gabriel García Márquez, in his epic *One Hundred Years of Solitude*, describes a village which suffers an epidemic of insomnia. After an interval of chaotic and protracted wakefulness, the increasingly deranged inhabitants begin to forget the names of common objects. Their solution is to write labels and affix them to the said objects, which serves to keep the crisis at bay for a while. But then the insomnia mutates into radical amnesia, and they begin to forget what letters stand for, and how words are written or read.... Esteban Trueba's wife, Clara, the mistress of his other grand home in the capital city, experiences a similar difficulty, managing "to keep that immense covered wagon of a house rolling with its population of eccentrics, even though she had no domestic talent and disdained the basic operations of arithmetic to the point of forgetting how to add." By the way, in the same chapter we learn that "the presence of his granddaughter sweetened Esteban Trueba's character. The change was imperceptible, but Clara noticed it. Slight symptoms gave him away: the sparkle in his eyes when he saw the little girl, the expensive presents he bought her, the anguish he felt if he heard her cry. Still, it was not enough to bring him closer to Blanca. His relationship with his daughter had never been good..."

The class war is fought not just between the siblings of the Trueba dynasty and the humble Tercero family, but among them as well. Like many mighty patriarchs, Esteban Trueba is fated to be disappointed by his sons as well as his daughter. One of the boys, Nicolás, becomes somewhat futile and vapid, wasting his time on aeronautical fantasies and difficult women. Another, Jaime, becomes a conscience-stricken medical student who rejects his privileged upbringing in order to minister to the poor, or at least to make them the objects of his charity in the aptly-named Misericordia District. (Ever since Graham Greene, I sometimes think, the Socialist physician—Dr. Magiot, Dr. Czinner—has been an especially serious character. And of course, Salvador Allende himself was a doctor.)

In the discussions and encounters between the two young men—and during the acute crisis over Amanda's pregnancy and ghastly abortion—we are meeting people to whom the notion, at least, of cruelty and bloodshed is repugnant. But in Esteban García, the crafty youth who is also an illegitimate by-blow of old man Trueba, we are finally introduced to evil. Again spurning the ideal-types of radical romanticism, Isabel Allende portrays this cold, plebeian, ambitious type as the instrument of death foretold. Here is the sort of person, found in every society, who becomes a torturer and executioner when the state is taken over by sadists. By way of an ironic wrinkle in the genealogical plot, he gets his great opportunity from his unaware grandfather, who despises the surreptitious and whose combats have always been in the open. The patriarch wants the honest military gentlemen to seize power, to scatter the subversives, and to restore decency and tradition and order. But he wants them then to return to the barracks and supervise new elections. Esteban García, no aristocrat, desires the day when police rule will be permanent, and he himself can have endless official permission to humiliate his betters as well as his inferiors.

The House of the Spirits is, or rather retrospectively it became, the last of a trilogy that is comprised of itself, preceded by *Daughter of Fortune* and *Portrait in Sepia*. The "subject" is assuredly family life, which is also the tempestuous subtext of much of Isabel Allende's nonfiction. But the story is about Chile. For millions of people across the world, this very name took on the same resonance as had "Spain" forty years before. On one side, the landlords, the clerical hierarchy, the army, and the Fascists. On the other, "the people" in their various gnarled, exploited, neglected and semi-upright postures. Arbitrating and manipulating things were far-off superpowers and vested interests. My little summary does, admittedly, possess all the subtlety of a Brecht play put on in Berkeley. But sometimes things *are* quite simple, and even Brecht might have turned down the idea of multinational corporations instructing Richard Nixon and Henry Kissinger to use murderous force to protect their dividends. Given the starkness of this, as it appeared at the time, it is greatly to Señora Allende's credit that she contrived so much wit, grace, and *chiaroscuro*.

The Spanish Civil War is remembered today as having been a writers' and poets' war, among other things, and Chile in the 1970s exhibited some of that quality also. In these pages one can re-encounter at least a couple of the relevant figures. Pablo Neruda, one of the greatest love-poets of all time (and the hero of that gem of a movie *Il Postino*) appears as The Poet: someone almost too numinous and distinguished to be named. Victor Jara, the radical balladeer of Allende's *Unidad Popular* movement, is to be found in the strumming and singing of Pedro Tercero. Both real lives ended at the time of the military coup in 1973: Neruda died of natural causes—perhaps exacerbated by the violence of events—and his marvelous library was trashed by marauding soldiers. Victor Jara was dragged away in a roundup and murdered, but not before his sniggering captors had recognized him and gone to all the trouble of smashing his guitar-playing fingers. (Both of these men had dull and sometimes sinister Communist politics, and after all it is George Orwell whose writing on Spain survives the burblings and mendacities of the Popular Front, but the face of Fascism is still much the same whether it murders Lorca or pillages Neruda.)

So the last third of the novel is really a palimpsest for those who experienced those years, or who wish to profit by studying them. Sex and love and family drama persist, of course, as they have to (and sometimes ecstatically in the first case). But everything is enacted in the shadow thrown by the first pages of the book: the great confrontation that has long been doomed to occur within the Chilean family as a whole. These pages are, to the Chilean revolution and counterrevolution, what *A Tale of Two Cities* once was to their French equivalents.

They also capture—if I may be permitted this—the best of times and the worst of times. Again, it is Isabel Allende's nuance, combined with her fair-mindedness, that astonishes. We watch the festival of the oppressed as it takes place on the old feudal estate at *Tres Marías*, but we also see the element of riot and Saturnalia as the peasants up-end the vintage wine-bottles, eat the seed-corn, and slaughter the animals that were intended for husbandry. We meet the single-minded and zealous revolutionary Miguel but we also learn (and this through Jaime, who admires him too) that he could be "one of those fatal men possessed by a dangerous idealism and an intransigent purity that color everything they touch with disaster, especially the women who have the misfortune to fall in love with them." (This, by the way, is almost exactly what Komarovski says of Antipov in the Robert Bolt dramatization of *Doctor Zhivago*.) What I want to say is that, though I know that Isabel Allende was at the time heart and brain and soul a supporter of the Chilean Left, she does not present us with a politicized morality play. She understands how it came to be that many middling and even poor Chileans eventually welcomed the Pinochet moment, as a respite from disorder and dogma. Indeed, in her much later memoir *My Invented Country*, published thirty years after the coup, she freely says that the economic program adopted by her famous uncle was a calamitous one.

Nonetheless, there was a point at which family and honor and politics converged, in a kind of redemption of all the wreckage and intolerance. The leaders of the French Revolution, with the exception of Lafayette, went to the bad and consumed each other as well as many rivals. The leaders of the Russian Revolution—with the arguable exception of Leon Trotsky—went the same way. There are numerous other examples of Jacobin and Bolshevik cannibalism and fratricide, or the analogues of same. The Cuban Revolution, even as I write, is expiring in banana-republic futility (its most prescient chronicler having been the Chilean diplomat Jorge Edwards, posted by Allende to resume relations with Fidel Castro and subsequently expelled.) But Salvador Allende never murdered or tortured anyone, and faced his own death with unexampled fortitude, and that has made all the difference.

When I first met Isabel Allende, at the point when this novel was first published, she ended our conversation by recalling her uncle's last words, spoken over a hissing and howling static from an improvised radio-station, as the Western-supplied warplanes were wheeling and diving over the dignified old presidential palace of *La Moneda*: named for its former office as the Chilean mint. Here is what he said, as cited word-for-word in *The House of the Spirits*:

> I speak to all those who will be persecuted to tell you that I am not going to resign: I will repay the people's loyalty with my life. I will always be with you. I have faith in our nation and its destiny. Other men will prevail, and soon the great avenues will be open again, where free men will walk, to build a better society.

Our interview concluded with her saying that her ambition was to see this come true, and to one day walk those avenues herself, "along with everybody else." I recall saying rather feebly that I hoped I could join her. At the time, Chile was in a grip of adamantine rule, as I had seen for myself, and the prospect of any liberated stroll or saunter or *paseo* looked distinctly faint. I was too pessimistic.

On my next visit to Chile, in May 2002, a public statue of Salvador Allende had been restored. The former home of Pablo Neruda at Isla Negra had become a place of literary pilgrimage. I was given a tour of Santiago by the man, Pedro Alejandro Matta, who had helped turn the place of his own torture—the jauntily-named Villa Grimaldi—into a museum of the horrors of junta rule. In the public cemetery there was a plaque for Victor Jara and a whole section given over to the commemoration of the fallen members of *Unidad Popular*. An extremely conservative judge, Juan Guzman Tapia, had reopened an entire dossier about the death-squads and "the missing," and I was invited by him to testify about the complicity of Henry Kissinger in the coup and in its sickening aftermath. The judge's inquiry was only one aspect of a clarification that has now reached to the bottom of society and to the top of the state. On November 5, 2004, just as I was completing this little essay, the commander of the Chilean army, General Juan Emilio Cheyre, made a formal and public statement acknowledging "institutional" responsibility for "punishable and morally unacceptable acts in the past." An official commission, chaired by the bishop of Santiago, presented harrowing evidence of a republic of fear between 1973 and 1989. To have seen any of this was like seeing justice done, or in other words like watching water run uphill, or a fire burning underwater, as I slightly strained to say to Isabel Allende when I next saw her, in the lovely house she has now built in Marin County, California, and named *La Casa de los Espiritus.*

So that I suppose this is one of the very few "magical" fictions ever to have its wish come true. (I can only think of one other such case: Theodor Herzl's *Altneuland*, a utopian novel about a once-and-future Jewish state in Palestine, written by the founder of Zionism.) Herzl never lived to see his dream vindicated, and one rather wonders what he would make of the result as we know it today. But it was not only the veterans of the Chilean Left, emerging from torture-chambers and frigid far-off camps on island prisons in the South Atlantic, who celebrated when Ricardo Lagos was elected president of Chile at the turn of the twentieth century. It was understood by all who gathered for his inauguration—the first member of Allende's old party to be chosen by unhindered ballot since 1970—that he would have to leave the balcony of the palace, and walk down the "great avenues" without a bodyguard, to be among the people. And so he did, amid a great hush and also a great rejoicing.

Well, I thought, I have lived to see it. I have also lived to see General Pinochet arraigned in his own country, providing in his person one of the great individual benchmarks (Slobodan Milošević, Saddam Hussein) by which it is established that those who trample on law and justice will some day have to face a court. One trial cannot of course do duty for all the crimes and all the murders and "disappearances" and corruptions, but only those who believe in vicarious redemption and human sacrifice can expect all sins to be taken away in this manner, and though *The House of the Spirits* opens and closes with exactly the same sentence ("Barrabás came to us by sea"), it doesn't do to forget that this Barrabás was only a large and randy dog.

In a conversation of some years ago, Isabel Allende went back yet again to the subject of her magnificent and maddening maternal grandfather, and described her lifelong and posthumous connection to him as one of "enraged intimacy." One Balzac, as Karl Marx is supposed to have said, is worth a hundred Zolas, but this Zola fan can see that "enraged intimacy" is what makes the Balzacian narrative imperishable.

The Persian Version

IN *THE CAPTIVE MIND*, his brilliantly lucid reflection on totalitarianism and its temptations, Czeslaw Milosz devoted most of his essays to the problem of communism and the intellectuals. In one chapter, however, he turned aside to view another manifestation of tyranny, and also to examine the verbal and literary means by which it could be thwarted.

The essay is called "Ketman." The term was first introduced to the West by Arthur de Gobineau, a rather sinister ethnologist who in the mid-nineteenth century served two tours as a French diplomat in Tehran. It means the art and science of dissimulation, particularly in matters of religion. The ferocious orthodoxy of the Shia mullahs of Iran, Gobineau wrote, could be circumvented by, say, a heretical disciple of Avicenna, as long as the man was careful to make every outward show of conformity. With this done, he could begin to introduce all manner of subversive philosophy into his sermons and addresses:

> *Ketman* fills the man who practices it with pride. Thanks to it, a believer raises himself to a permanent state of superiority over the man he deceives, be he a minister of state or a powerful king: to him who uses *ketman*, the other is a miserable blind man whom one shuts off from the true path whose existence he does not suspect; while you, tattered and dying of hunger, trembling externally at the feet

---

Review of *Strange Times, My Dear: The PEN Anthology of Contemporary Iranian Literature*, edited by Nahid Mozaffari.

> of duped force, your eyes are filled with light, you walk in brightness before your enemies. It is an unintelligent being that you make sport of; it is a dangerous beast that you disarm. What a wealth of pleasures!

Milosz immediately saw the application of this to the double life that was being lived by so many writers and intellectuals under Stalin's imperium. The Soviet regime to some extent "needed" culture, but also needed to contain it. Milosz was not to foresee that this state of affairs—deemed "Absurdistan" by one Czech author—would one day satirize itself out of existence.

Today's Iran is also an Absurdistan in one sense, though the term should not be misused so as to mask the tragic element of the comic: Under the reign of the Shah, the country emulated almost everything Western except democracy; under the rule of the imams, it rejects almost every aspect of modernity except nuclearism. That this fate should have befallen such a sophisticated and energetic people is a catastrophe piled upon a disaster. Yet the clerics now ruling the country have fallen into the very error that their communist enemies used to commit. They claim to legislate for every aspect of life, and they claim the right to scrutinize everything that is said and even thought. In this they attempt the impossible. If they emulated the Taliban and simply forbade all forms of music and film and all forms of writing except the Koranic, they would fail. Instead, they try to permit these things while also controlling them. That will eventually fail even more miserably. This is because before there was any Iran or any Islam, there was a Persian civilization and a Persian language, neither of which the Turbaned Ones dare disown. Iranians may have been conquered and Islamized by Arabs, but they are proud of retaining their ancient tongue and their literary and cultural memories. And Persia was known for love poetry, for the anti-clerical satires of Omar Khayyam, for polo and for chess and for the wine of Shiraz. These ancient and lovely springs continue to bubble under the caked grime and muck of theocracy. Every March great numbers of Iranians laughingly celebrate the *nowruz*, or New Year holiday—a fire ceremony with dances long pre-dating Islam. The mullahs do not like the festival but do not feel strong enough to prohibit anything so old and so popular.

Milosz subdivided *ketman* under communism into various types—

"professional," "aesthetic," "skeptical," and "ethical." During a very enlightening visit to Iran last year, I found it was possible to distinguish some other individual forms of it. These range from the low to the sublime. An example of the low would be alcoholic *ketman*, whereby even those Iranians who do not touch the bottle make sure to have wine or liquor, often home-brewed, in their houses, for the benefit of guests—a small etiquette of defiance by the abstemious. More elevated is fashion *ketman*. The ayatollahs' law demands that all females in public must wear a *hijab* to cover the hair, and a long jacket to cover the area between the upper chest and the mid-thigh. (It's always useful to know what the pious are really thinking about.) In practice, there are not enough religious police to enforce this strictly. A woman without a *hijab* would certainly be beaten (and perhaps blinded or maimed with acid), but it is impressive to see the huge number who manage to conform to the letter of the law by sporting a colorful scarf, well back on the head and held in place by hair spray, as well as a coat so deftly cut as to make the very most of what it is intended to de-emphasize.

But Iranian culture and vivacity is kept going most of all by the country's writers and filmmakers (who are sometimes, like the director-poet Abbas Kiarostami, the same people). A continuous pressure leads to invention—to finding the cracks and gaps in the system, to testing its limits and transcending them. Once again, it must be remembered that when the Calibans of theocracy see their own faces in the glass, which they do not like to do, they are not always able to recognize their own features. (One thinks of the mirthless Bourbons when they first saw the faultless way that Goya had rendered them.) They dimly know that they are supposed to *have* a movie industry, publishing houses, newspapers, and such. An excerpt of a short story by Ghazi Rabihavi gives an account of what it's like to have to deal, after a thirteen-month wait, with the Ministry of Islamic Guidance:

> Unfortunately, your book has some small problems which cannot be corrected. I am certain you will agree with me. Take these first few sentences... nowhere in our noble culture will you find any woman who would allow herself to stand waiting for her husband to bring her a cup of coffee. OK? Well, the next problem is the image of the wind sliding over the naked arms, which is provocative and has sexual overtones. Finally, nowhere in any noble culture will you find

> a sunrise that is like a sunset. Maybe it is a misprint. Here you are then. Here is your book. I hope you will write another book soon. We support you. Support you.

This extract is taken from the recent *Strange Times, My Dear*, an admirable PEN anthology of Iranian fiction and poetry released in paperback this spring. (The title echoes the refrain with which Ahmad Shamlu ends every stanza of "In This Blind Alley," his famous poem about the revolution.) Anyone wanting to sample the range and depth of the country's contemporary writing would do well to begin here. The authors not only deal with every "transgressive" subject, from booze to sex, but also illustrate something that is often overlooked in the monochrome presentation of their country in the West: the diversity of Armenians, Jews, Zoroastrians, and Azeris that helps characterize Iranian society. (The collection is rather silent on the Kurds, a minority from whom we can expect to be hearing more, but it does contain a contribution from Roya Hakakian, whose molten yet tender memoir of growing up Jewish in the years of revolution, *Journey from the Land of No*, is itself one of the jewels of the exile literary renaissance.)

Some older readers of this essay will remember Reza Baraheni, whose 1977 book, *The Crowned Cannibals*, did much to alert the West to the sheer exorbitance and cruelty of the Pahlavi pseudo-dynasty. Baraheni is a Turkish speaker from Tabriz, and his poems, which lay a heavy emphasis on the material and the earthy, contain allusions to Ezra Pound, Walter Benjamin, and Charles Baudelaire. In one of the book's poems, "In The New Place, or Exile, A Simple Matter," he reminds us that Napoleon thought of mud as a fifth element. Baraheni's life experience is not unrepresentative: prison under the Shah, participation in the revolution of 1979, swift disillusionment with the rise of Khomeini's despotism, horror at the terrifying war subsequently unleashed by Saddam Hussein, a further spell in prison under the clerics, and then exile. A great number of Iran's best minds and voices are compelled to live at least partly in diaspora in Europe and North America, and although this is greatly to our benefit and pleasure (vide the work of Azar Nafisi on her Tehran Nabokoviennes), we cannot forget what a price it exacts from Iran itself. Meanwhile, for those who bear the heat and burden of the day in the country itself, we can guess the weight of the atmosphere from another line of Ahmad Shamlu's poem: "They smell your breath lest you have said: I love you."

Mention of Napoleon brings me to the work of Iraj Pezeshkzad. How is one to convey the extraordinary charm and power of this author? A little preface is needed. Iranian intellectuals are nostalgic (I do not think this use of the term is improper) for two moments in their nation's agonized history. The first is the 1906 constitutional revolution, when the liberal and cosmopolitan elements of the society, though eventually suppressed by Russian imperial gunnery, managed to establish a precedent for a modern and outward-looking system. The second is the atrocity of August 19, 1953, when the elected nationalist government of Mohammed Mossadegh was forcibly removed by an Anglo-American intrigue that instated the Shah as a dictator and returned the country's main natural resource to foreign control. These two external interventions gravely stultified Iran's development and had a retarding effect on the national psyche. It became almost customary and automatic, in a land that is so naturally internationalist, to attribute literally everything to the machinations of designing outsiders. (The Khomeinist regime, needless to add, exploits this plebeian tendency to this day. It also avails itself of the antique Shia concept of *taqqiya*, or the religious permission to dissemble in dealings with infidels. One might call this the top-down version of *ketman*.) As an Englishman I found it almost flattering to encounter the number of people in Tehran who—culturally rather despising Americans—believed that the British government determined absolutely all matters. Why, had they not even installed the mullahs in 1979 as a revenge for the way that the United States had taken the lion's share of oil after 1953? The British ambassador, whose official dominion includes two especially nice walled garden estates in upper and lower Tehran, confessed to me that he sometimes found this paranoia useful, since it meant that nobody would decline to meet him.

In 1973, Pezeshkzad published *My Uncle Napoleon*, a cheerful satire of this very mentality, and it became the best-loved work of fiction in Iran before it was banned by the clerics during the revolution. Likewise set in an enclosed garden house that contains several branches of an extended family, it could be summarized as a love story enfolded in a bildungsroman and wrapped in a conspiracy theory. Except that it cannot be summarized. Not even Azar Nafisi, who contributes a sparkling introduction to the new American edition, can accomplish that. Uncle Napoleon, the micro-megalomaniac who dominates the little world of the family, is convinced that the British imperialists really care about him and mean to get him by fair means or foul. A beautiful counterpoint to his fantastic solipsism is the appalling verbosity of his manservant, Mash Qasem. Some have claimed to see a Bertie-and-Jeeves duo in the setup; I think this is misleading, except with respect to the amazingly complex and farcical love affairs that form the subtext. Rabelais and Cervantes are in there somewhere as well. To return to my Caliban metaphor, we might remember that it was Swift who defined satire as a looking glass in which people discerned every face but their own. In the vanity and stupidity of Uncle Napoleon, the religious things of Qum must have glimpsed at least something but the joke is on them, because in today's widespread Iranian *samizdat* the book—and a now-banned television series that was once made of it—is a blockbuster.

Pezeshkzad also makes a contribution to *Strange Times, My Dear*, in the form of a gem-like story titled "Delayed Consequences of the Revolution." Now an exile himself, he makes gentle but deadly fun of those émigrés who forgather, like the White Russians of old, in a café society devoted to toasting the ancien régime. In this context—sometimes to be found in today's Los Angeles—old men forget, as well as remember, or remember "with advantages," what deeds they did. In what I like to think of as a homage to *ketman*, Pezeshkzad illuminates the private codes and allusions in which the participants convey discrepant meanings to one another, and also perpetuate the mythology of foreign conspiracy. ("If you want to explain something to your compatriot in your own language you can use five or six words and get the meaning across, but to explain the same thing to a foreigner in another language, you'll need to employ at least fifty or sixty words." This is offered as an account of the difficulty of elucidating simple property deals in the days of "His Highness the Shah.")

Half of Iran's citizens are regarded by the state as chattel, so it is not startling to find so many women writers in the most exposed positions of dissent.

Azadeh Moaveni's memoir, *Lipstick Jihad* (a perfect title for the practice of fashion *ketman* and the struggle for femininity, as well as feminism), was a salient effort in this regard, and it is good to see her helping to coauthor *Iran Awakening*, the autobiography of Shirin Ebadi, the country's most recent Nobel laureate. Ebadi was the first woman to be appointed a judge in Iran, in the waning days of the Shah, and she lost that job almost as soon as the revolution (which she supported) had taken place. She opens her book with a commonplace and uninteresting testimony to her enduring religious faith, the sincerity of which is impossible to gauge. If this is *ketman*—the apparent sharing of a belief with those who despise and oppress her—it is the price of her ticket. Without such protestations of faith she would almost certainly be dead. As it is, she was on a death-squad list drawn up by allegedly "rogue" elements in the Ministry of Intelligence, which debated only on the propriety of assassinating her before the end of the month of Ramadan. Her extraordinary fortitude in pressing on with her legal inquiry into the murders that had already taken place is not only a testimony in itself but also a window into the almost unrivaled sordidness and cynicism of the Islamic Republic. Here is a state that holds that a father *cannot* be convicted for murdering his own daughter; a state in which teenage girls are hanged in public for immorality, and virgins raped before execution because the Koran forbids the execution of virgins.

In *Persepolis*, Marjane Satrapi views matters from still another perspective: the special *ketman* of ironic cartooning. In smart and confident strokes she draws a history of the Khomeini revolution as seen by a girl who was nine when the old fanatic returned from exile. The whole chaotic world of parents and other adults, faced with crises that are wholly new and frightening to them, is affectionately and ironically caught by a girl who has a real talent for overhearing. Marxist relatives keep up false hopes that the people have not been fooled; Saddam Hussein's planes disgorge bombs over the city; veils are imposed on small children; the Jewish neighbors get into a spot of bother; and, yes, a young friend is legally raped by a Revolutionary Guard before being shot. Most stark are the growing girl's encounters with the *komiteh*, the brutish and depraved louts who are employed as the enforcers of morality and who take a special pleasure in the taunting and bullying of women. But there is low farce as well: The bastards who come looking for the homemade wine are actually seeking only a bribe, which becomes clear only after the precious fluid has been hastily poured away for nothing. The solidarity of the little family and its friends turns out to be less fragile than it looks. Yes, the bearded sadists do stop women in the street and harshly smell their breath for telltale traces of love, but, as in the resolution of Uncle Napoleon's madly hermetic domestic despotism, *amor vincit omnia*.

May it be so. The PEN anthology, as well as the work of Shirin Ebadi, was for a time treated as mere matter that could not be viewed by Americans. Reflecting a level of stupidity that would not disgrace the dumbest authoritarian state, the U.S. Treasury Department believed that unless Ebadi applied for a special license, the book's publication in this country would amount to trading with the enemy. A possible penalty of up to a million dollars or ten years imprisonment was mentioned. Prompt litigation held off the official notion that the words of Iranian writers can be forfeit as a "foreign asset." American readers have a special duty, in view of the distraught history between our two countries, to take an interest in this "asset." Whatever the outcome of the current confrontation, we have the right and the duty of engagement with a people and a culture very much imbricated with our own. How agreeable to be able to report that this is also a tremendous pleasure.

(*The Atlantic*, July/August 2006)

Martin Amis: Lightness at Midnight

IN HIS SUPERB MEMOIR, *Experience* (2000), Martin Amis almost casually expends a terrific line in a minor footnote. Batting away a critic he describes as "humorless," he adds, "And by calling him humorless I mean to impugn his seriousness, categorically: such a man must rig up his probity *ex nihilo*." A book in which such an observation can occur in passing is a very rich and dense one. Amis has won and held the attention of an audience eager for something very like this in reverse—a synthesis of astonishing wit and moral assiduity. Even the farcical episodes of his fiction are set on the bristling frontiers of love and death and sex. With his other hand, so to speak, he has raised the standard of essayistic reviewing, mounting guard over our muscular but vulnerable English language and registering fastidious pain whenever it is hurt or insulted. It is no accident, because he intuits the strong connection between linguistic and political atrocity, that he has also composed short but concentrated meditations on the three great collapses of twentieth-century modernism and civilization. With *Einstein's Monsters* (1987), and its accompanying flight of articles and polemics, he investigated the diseased relationship between suicide and genocide that is disclosed by the preparation of thermonuclear extinction. In *Time's Arrow* (1991) he made

Review of *Koba the Dread: Laughter and the Twenty Million*, by Martin Amis.

a very assured attempt to find a new literary mode for the subject of genocide *tout court*, and for the Nazi-generated race murder in particular. *Koba the Dread* aims to complete this triptych by interrogating the subject of Stalinism and the Great Terror.

Amis's two previous undertakings of this kind were reviewed ungenerously in some quarters, either because they seemed presumptuous in taking a familiar subject and presenting it as if for the first time, or because they relied a little too much on a senior source (Jonathan Schell in the first case, and Primo Levi in the second). To this I would respond rather as Winston Smith does when he has finished reading the occult "inner-party" book in *Nineteen Eighty-four*: "The best books... are those that tell you what you know already." Amis understands that cliché and banality constitute a menace to even the most apparently self-evident truths. "Holocaust" can become a tired synecdoche for war crimes in general. Before one knows it, one is employing terms like "nuclear exchange" and even "nuclear umbrella," and committing the mental and moral offense of euphemism. One must always seek for new means of keeping familiar subjects fresh, and raw.

Stalinism was, among other things, a triumph of the torturing of language. And, unlike Nazism or fascism or nuclear warfare, it secured at least the respect, and sometimes the admiration, of liberal intellectuals. Thus Amis's achievement in these pages is to make us wince again at things that we already "knew" while barely wasting a word or missing the implications of a phrase. Here is a short section titled "Rhythms of Thought":

> Stalin's two most memorable utterances are "Death solves all problems. No man, no problem" and (he was advising his interrogators on how best to elicit a particular confession) "Beat, beat and beat again."
>
> Both come in slightly different versions. "There is a man, there is a problem. No man, no problem." This is less epigrammatic, and more catechistic—more typical of Stalin's seminarian style (one thinks of his oration at Lenin's funeral and its liturgical back-and-forth).
>
> The variant on number two is: "Beat, beat, and, once again, beat." Another clear improvement, if we want a sense of Stalin's rhythms of thought.

To that second paragraph Amis appends a footnote, saying:

> If Stalin had been a modern American he would not have used the word "problem" but the less defeatist and judgmental "issue." Actually, when you consider what Stalin tended to do to his enemies' descendants, the substitution works well enough.

That is excellent: dry without being too detached. Next I would instance Amis's citations from the various cruelties and torments documented by Aleksandr Solzhenitsyn.

> This reader has endured none of them; and I will proceed with caution and unease. It feels necessary because torture, among its other applications, was part of Stalin's war against the truth. He tortured, not to force you to reveal a fact, but to force you to collude in a fiction.

Here is his close reading of the last paragraph of Trotsky's *History of the Russian Revolution*. Trotsky's closing stave reads,

> The language of the civilised nations has clearly marked off two epochs in the development of Russia. Where the aristocratic culture introduced into the world parlance such barbarisms as *tsar, pogrom, knout*, October has internationalized such words as *Bolshevik, soviet*, and *piatiletka*. This alone justifies the proletarian revolution, if you imagine that it needs justification.

Amis's first comment on this ensues directly. He adds to Trotsky's bombast the words "Which leaves you wondering if *piatiletka* is Russian for 'summary execution,' perhaps, or 'slave camp.' " There follows a footnote. (Like Gibbon, Amis seems to like to reserve the best for the footnotes.)

> I searched without success for *piatiletka* in five end-of-monograph glossaries. Its clinching "internationalisation," then, didn't last (although Hitler, and later Mao, took it up). *Piatiletka* means "five-year plan."

There is a very slight waste of words here, because the mordancy of Amis's second observation makes the first one seem merely taunting and sarcastic. But lapses of this kind are infrequent. When Amis summarizes a crux, it stays summarized. One doesn't have to have suffered torture and solitary confinement to get the point that is being made here:

> The confession was in any case merely part of a more or less inevitable process. When it was their turn to be purged, former interrogators (and all other Chekists) immediately called with a flourish for the pen and the dotted line.

One also wouldn't absolutely have to know which regime was under discussion: The potency of that *aperçu* derives from its disclosing of our animal nature. Indeed, and as in his other work on murder and tyranny, Amis has a better than approximate idea of what we as a species might get up to if given a chance. "*Arma virumque cano*, and Hitler-Stalin tells us this, among other things: given total power over another, the human being will find that his thoughts turn to torture."

This is an insight of extreme, frigid bleakness, amounting almost to despair, but it also involves a minor waste of words. We knew this, after all, before we knew of Hitler or Stalin. Again to cite Orwell, there is a tendency for all stories of cruelty and atrocity to resemble one another. For this reason some overfamiliar or recycled accounts provoke boredom or disbelief, and can be made to seem propagandistic. (The classic example is the way the British fabrication of German outrages during the First World War had the paradoxical effect of turning skeptics into cynics when they heard the initially incredible news of Nazi innovations in that terrible sphere.) Orwell was on guard against this blunting tendency. He thought it probable that given moral breakdown, the same hellish desires would replicate and repeat themselves. He also believed the worst about Stalin's system, and much earlier than most "enlightened" people, precisely because he found its public language so crude and brutal.

In a particularly luminous and funny passage on the correspondence between Vladimir Nabokov and Edmund Wilson, Amis puts his entire trust in Nabokov's ability to employ language with care and discrimination, and shows that Wilson's journeyman prose practically rigged itself to trap him, and others, into a more comforting "explanation" of the titanic misery and failure of the Stalin years. (Amis doesn't make as much as he might of the fact that Nabokov produced his diamond-hard phrases in English, whereas his first language was Russian, while Wilson offered in return some thoughts about Russia that were trudging even in English.)

Stalin was no fool when he said that the death of one person is a tragedy, whereas the death of a million people is a statistic. Marx and Engels had always shuddered at the gross, enormous crudity of the steppe and the taiga, the illimitable reserves of primeval backwardness that they contained; and European liberalism had long been mesmerized by the Asiatic horror of Russian autocracy. This howling wilderness and boundless hinterland were themselves factors of "historical materialism." So, "in the execution of the broad brushstrokes of his hate," as Amis phrases it, Stalin "had weapons that Hitler did not have":

> He had cold: the burning cold of the Arctic. "At Oimyakon [in the Kolyma] a temperature has been recorded of -97.8 F. In far lesser cold, steel splits, tires explode and larch trees shower sparks at the touch of an axe . . ."
>
> He had darkness: the Bolshevik sequestration, the shockingly bitter and unappeasable self-exclusion from the planet, with its fear of comparison, its fear of ridicule, its fear of truth.
>
> He had space: the great imperium with its eleven time zones, the distances that gave their blessing to exile and isolation...
>
> And, most crucially, Stalin had time.

In making the inescapable comparison with Hitler, who killed many fewer people (and even killed many fewer Communists) than Stalin, Amis is guided mostly by the view of Robert Conquest. He also relies, in varying degrees, on Martin Malia, Richard Pipes, and Aleksandr Solzhenitsyn. In Conquest's opinion, the visceral reaction to Nazism entails a verdict that it was morally worse than Stalinism, even if its eventual hecatomb was a less colossal one. This distinction rests on the sheer intentionality and obscenity of the *Shoah*, or Final Solution. Those who were killed in Ukraine, by a state-sponsored famine, were not killed as Ukrainians in quite the same way as the Ukrainian Jews of Babi Yar were later killed as Jews. The slave system of the Gulag did not have as its primary objective the turning of living people into corpses. The huge callousness of the system simply allowed vast numbers to be treated as expendable.

The distinction is certainly worth preserving. As Amis phrases it, "When I read about the Holocaust I experience something that I do not experience when I read about the Twenty Million: a sense of physical infestation. This is species shame." To this one might add that Germany was a literate, democratic, and advanced civilization before the Nazis got to it, whereas Russia at the time of the 1905 revolution was in a condition more like that of Turkey, or Iran, or even (in some areas) Afghanistan today. It did have a "Westernized" industrial and intellectual element, but it was from exactly this stratum that Marxism drew most of its followers. And many of them regarded the mass of the Russian people in much the way that a British official in early colonial Bengal might have viewed the benighted natives. Probably, if we look for explanations for the indulgence shown toward Stalinism by men like George Bernard Shaw and H. G. Wells, we will find part of the answer in the quasi-eugenic and quasi-anthropological approach they took to most questions. (Fabian socialism, in the same period, emphasized the progressive aspects of social engineering in the British Empire.) But Amis, who briefly mocks the gullibility of the Bloomsbury and *New Statesman* tradition, also forgets that the *grand prix* for prescience here belongs to the atheist, socialist, and anti-imperialist Bertrand Russell, whose *The Practice and Theory of Bolshevism* (1920) was the first and in many ways the most penetrating critique.

I don't know if it was at this point or a slightly later one that I realized that Amis was exhibiting a tendency to flail. There is certainly merit in restating Stalin's exorbitant and lustful criminality, which stands comparison to that of the most paranoid and sanguinary moments of antiquity as well as of modernity. (The title *Koba the Dread* is an amalgam of Stalin's nickname and the more straightforward Russian meaning of "the Terrible," as in Ivan.) But we have grown up reading Solzhenitsyn, Joseph Berger, Eugenia Ginzburg, Lev Kopelev, Roy Medvedev, and many other firsthand chroniclers of the nightmare. Names like Vorkuta and Kolyma are not as familiar to most people as Treblinka or Birkenau, but the word "Gulag" (one of the many hateful acronyms of the system) does duty for the whole, and is known to everybody. Amis appears to deny this when he says that a general recognition of the toll of Stalinist slavery and murder "hasn't happened," and that "in the general consciousness the Russian dead sleep on." He should have hesitated longer before taking the whole weight of responsibility for this memory, and our memory, on his shoulders.

The clue to this hubris comes in the second part of his title, with its allusion to mirth. Amis is acutely, vibrantly sensitive to the different registers of laughter. He knows that it can be the most affirming and uniquely human sound, and also the most sinister and animalistic one. He understands every note of every octave that separates the liberating shout of mirth from the cackle of a bully or the snigger of a sadist. (Nabokov's title *Laughter in the Dark* provides a perfect pitch here.) So he's in confident form when he describes the servile laughter that greeted Stalin when he was "forcibly" induced to take the stage at the Bolshoi Theater in 1937, and modestly agreed to be a candidate in the upcoming "election." Here is some of the transcript, according to Dmitri Volkogonov:

> Of course, I could have said something light about anything and everything. [laughter] . . . I understand there are masters of that sort of thing not just in the capitalist countries, but here, too, in our Soviet country. [laughter, applause]

Many surviving eyewitnesses of many tyrannical courts have told us that the most exacting and nerve-straining moments come when the despot is in a good mood. Stalin had perhaps the most depraved and limited humor of the lot. In addition to being a grand-opera widow-and-orphan manufacturer, and widow-and-orphan slayer, he was a sniggerer and a bad chuckler. Amis observes of the foul scene above:

> Ground zero of the Great Terror—and here was the Party, joined in a panic attack of collusion in yet another enormous lie. They clapped, they laughed. Did *he* laugh? Do we hear it—the "soft, dull, sly laugh," the "grim, dark laughter, which comes up from the depths"?

However, Amis also refers to laughter of a somewhat different sort, and here, having called attention to the splendors of this little book, I am compelled to say where I think it fails. And by "compelled" I suppose I must mean "obliged," since it appears on the author's own warrant that the book's shortcomings are mostly my fault. In the fall of 1999 Amis attended a meeting in London where I spoke from the platform. The hall was one of those venues (Cooper Union, in New York, might be an analogy) where the rafters had once echoed with the rhetoric of the left. I made an allusion to past evenings with old comrades, and the audience responded with what Amis at first generously terms "affectionate laughter." But then he gives way to the self-righteousness and superficiality that let him down.

> Why is it? Why is it? If Christopher had referred to his many evenings with many "an old blackshirt," the audience would have.... Well, with such an affiliation in his past, Christopher would not be Christopher—or anyone else of the slightest distinction whatsoever. Is *that* the difference between the little mustache and the big mustache, between Satan and Beelzebub? One elicits spontaneous fury, and the other elicits spontaneous laughter? And what kind of laughter is it? It is, of course, the laughter of universal fondness for that old, old idea about the perfect society. It is also the laughter of forgetting. It forgets the demonic energy unconsciously embedded in that hope. It forgets the Twenty Million.
>
> This isn't right:
>
> Everybody knows of Auschwitz and Belsen. Nobody knows of Vorkuta and Solovetsky.
>
> Everybody knows of Himmler and Eichmann. Nobody knows of Yezhov and Dzerdzhinsky.
>
> Everybody knows of the six million of the Holocaust. Nobody knows of the six million of the Terror-Famine.

George Orwell once remarked that certain terrible things in Spain had really happened, and "they did not happen any the less because the *Daily Telegraph* has suddenly found out about them when it is five years too late." Martin Amis can be excused for coming across some of the above names and numbers rather late in life, but he cannot hope to get away with accusing others of keeping these facts and names from him, or from themselves. He tells me that this fairly unimportant evening was what kick-started his book, and in an open letter to me on the preceding pages he contemptuously, even proudly, asserts his refusal even to glance at Isaac Deutscher's biographical trilogy on Leon Trotsky. Well, I have my own, large differences with Deutscher. But nobody who read his *Prophet Outcast*, which was published more than three decades ago, could possibly be uninstructed about Vorkuta or Yezhov. In other words, having demanded to know "Why is it?" in such an insistent tone, he doesn't stay to answer his own question, instead replacing it with a vaguely peevish and "shocked, shocked" version of "How long has this been going on?" The answer there is, longer than he thinks.

With infinitely more distress I have to add that Amis's newly acquired zeal forbids him to see a joke even when (as Bertie Wooster puts it) it is handed to him on a skewer with béarnaise sauce. The laughter in that hall was slightly shabby, I am quite prepared to agree. But it was the resigned laughter that "sees" a poor jest, and recognizes the fellow sufferer. In related anecdotes that are too obviously designed to place himself in a good light, Amis also recounts some aggressive questions allegedly put by him to me and to James Fenton in our (James's and my) Trotskyist years, when all three of us were colleagues at the *New Statesman*. The questions are so plainly wife-beating questions, and the answers so clearly intended to pacify the aggressor by offering a mocking agreement, that I have to set down a judgment I would once have thought unutterable. Amis's want of wit here, even about a feeble joke, compromises his seriousness.

I would be as solipsistic as he is if I persisted too long with this, so I redirect attention. In the excerpt above has he made up his mind about the moral equivalence between Stalin and Hitler? Or has he reserved the right to use the cudgel according to need? When he speaks of Ivan the Terrible and Joseph Stalin, does he mean to say that there was something comparable in their "Great Russian" ancestry? When he dilates upon torture and forced confessions, or upon the practice of eliminating even the families of opponents, is he suggesting that such terror was unknown to humanity before 1917? He states at one point, "Until I read *Man Is Wolf to Man: Surviving Stalin's Gulag* I had never heard of a prisoner, en route, lying crushed and ground on a section of rough wood and receiving a succession of monstrous splinters up and down his back." One would not need to refer him to the Nazi transports from

Salonika or Vichy. An allusion to the Middle Passage, or to the hell ships that populated Australia's "Fatal Shore," would be enough. Moral equivalence is not intended here. But moral uniqueness requires a bit more justification.

I do not mean these to sound like commissar questions, or wife-beating questions either. On the first and perhaps most important one posed by Amis, for example, I find that I never quite know what I think myself about this moral equivalence. Nor did I quite know when I was still a member of a Marxist/post-Trotskyist group, when such matters were debated from dawn until dusk, often with furious or thuggish Communists. However, I do know from that experience, which was both liberating and confining, that the crucial questions about the Gulag were being asked by left oppositionists, from Boris Souvarine to Victor Serge to C. L. R. James, in real time and at great peril. Those courageous and prescient heretics have been somewhat written out of history (they expected far worse than that, and often received it), but I can't bring myself to write as if they never existed, or to forgive anyone who slights them. If they seem too Marxist in tendency, one might also mention the more heterodox work of John Dewey, Sidney Hook, David Rousset, or Max Shachtman in exposing "Koba's" hideous visage. The "Nobody" at the beginning of Amis's sentences above is an insult, pure and simple, and an insult to history, too.

History is more of a tragedy than it is a morality tale. The will to power, the will to use human beings in social experiments, is to be distrusted at all times. The impulse to create, or even to propose, what Amis calls "the perfect society" is likewise to be suspected. At several points he states with near perfect simplicity that ideology is hostile to human nature, and implies that teleological socialism was uniquely or particularly so. I would no longer disagree with him about this. *Corruptio optimi pessima*: No greater cruelty will be devised than by those who are sure, or are assured, that they are doing good. However, one may come to such a conclusion by a complacent route or by what I would still dare to call a dialectical one. Does anybody believe that had the 1905 Russian Revolution succeeded, it would have led straight to the Gulag, and to forced collectivization? Obviously not. Such a revolution might even have forestalled the Balkan wars and the First World War. Yet that revolution's moving spirits were Lenin and Trotsky, defeated by the forces of autocracy, Orthodoxy, and militarism. Excuse me, but nobody can be bothered to argue much about whether fascism might have turned out better, given more propitious circumstances. And there were no dissidents in the Nazi Party, risking their lives on the proposition that the Führer had betrayed the true essence of National Socialism. As Amis half recognizes, in his *en passant* compliment to me, the question just doesn't come up.

Amis says he doesn't wish that the Second World War had gone the other way, which is good of him (though there were many Ukrainians and Russians who took their anti-Stalinism to the extent of enlistment on the Nazi side). However, it would be nice to know if he wishes that the Russian civil war, and the wars of intervention, had gone the other way. There are some reasons to think that had that been the case, the common word for fascism would have been a Russian one, not an Italian one. *The Protocols of the Elders of Zion* was brought to the West by the White emigration; even Boris Pasternak, in *Doctor Zhivago*, wrote with a shudder about life in the White-dominated regions. Major General William Graves, who commanded the American Expeditionary Force during the 1918 invasion of Siberia (an event thoroughly airbrushed from all American textbooks), wrote in his memoirs about the pervasive, lethal anti-Semitism that dominated the Russian right wing and added, "I doubt if history will show any country in the world during the last fifty years where murder could be committed so safely, and with less danger of punishment, than in Siberia during the reign of Admiral Kolchak." Thus "the collapse in the value of human life," as Amis describes the situation in post-revolutionary Russia, had begun some time before, perhaps in the marshes of Tannenberg, and was to make itself felt in other post–First World War societies as well.

Some confrontation with this line of thinking—I hesitate to use the word "context"—is essential if one is to avoid the merely one-dimensional or propagandistic. It might be concluded that upon reflection and analysis, the Bolshevik Revolution was the worst possible of the many available postwar outcomes, none of which (unlike Germany in 1933) included the prospect of parliamentary pluralism. It might also be concluded that Stalinism was the ineluctable and even the intended outcome of 1917, though this would involve some careful reasoning about whether things are or are not products of "historical inevitability." Yet Amis simply evades the question with a couple of sneers, saying that my argument "would have more weight behind it if

(a) there had been a similar collapse (i.e., total, and lasting thirty-five years) in any other combatant country, and if (b) a single Old Bolshevik had spent a single day at the front, or indeed in the army." Well, even the collapse of post-war Germany into the arms of first the *Freikorps* and then their successors doesn't seem to meet his first exacting condition, at least in point of duration (though the enforced shortening of the Nazi period did involve some fairly harsh decisions about the value of human life). As for the second sneer, is Amis telling us that he hasn't read, for example, Isaac Babel's *Red Cavalry*? Bolshevism was in some ways a product of the hard-line front fighters. Indeed, its very militarization was one of the several reasons for its ugliness.

Hard work is involved in the study of history. Hard moral work, too. We don't get much assistance in that task from mushy secondhand observations like this one:

> Accounting, as a Catholic, for his belief in evil as a living force, the novelist Anthony Burgess once said, "There is no A. J. P. Taylor-ish explanation for what happened in Eastern Europe during the war." Nor is there.

Oh, yes. And what might the Catholic explanation be? The Church is still trying to find new ways of apologizing for its role in these events, and for things like the Nazi puppet regime in Slovakia, which was actually headed by a priest. Of course, original sin would be just as persuasive a verdict as any other the Church might offer. But tautology is the enemy of historical inquiry: If we are all evil, then everything becomes a matter of degree. Amis for some reason has a special horror of Bolshevik anti-clericalism, and writes as if the Tsarist Russian Orthodox Church was some kind of relief organization run by nuns. If he would look even at the recent performance of state-sponsored militant Orthodoxy in Bosnia... Incidentally, do not the Churches also insist on trying to perfect the imperfectible, and on forcing the human shape into unnatural attitudes? Surely the "totalitarian" impulse has a common root with the proselytizing one. The "internal organs," as the CHEKA and the GPU and the KGB used to style themselves, were asked to police the mind for heresy as much as to torture *kulaks* to relinquish the food they withheld from the cities. If there turns out to be a connection between the utilitarian and the totalitarian, then we wretched mammals are in even worse straits than we suspect.

Amis might have profited from studying the novelistic gold standard here, which is Arthur Koestler's *Darkness at Noon*. Koestler's theory of Stalin's grim success, which was that some of his old Bolshevik victims half feared that "Koba" might be correct after all, is only partly superseded by the "beat, beat and beat again" account, which itself is an insufficient explanation for the actual capitulation of the defendants. (A handful of the old comrades, after all, never cracked.) But his theory allowed for a very illuminating fictional dramatization of the relationship of ideas to outcomes. And Koestler put such persuasive words into the mouth of the interrogator Gletkin—his version of the Grand Inquisitor—that some English and French readers (John Strachey most notably) were actually *persuaded* by them. That unintended consequence was obviously limited. But it points to an essential difference. Koestler exposed the ghastliness of Stalinism by means of a sophisticated deployment of historical irony, whereas Amis—and again I startle myself by saying this—has decided to dispense with irony altogether. (He mentions, with all the gravity of one returning from a voyage of discovery, that the sailors of Kronstadt fought against the Bolsheviks under red flags and with revolutionary slogans. He even italicizes the word "revolutionaries," as if this point were at the expense of the left opposition. As Daniel Bell pointed out decades ago, the only real argument among members of the old left was about the point at which their own personal "Kronstadt" had occurred. Bell was proud to say that Kronstadt itself had been his "Kronstadt.")

Writing toward the very end of his life, a life that had included surprising Stalin himself by a refusal to confess, and the authorship of a novel—*The Case of Comrade Tulayev*—that somewhat anticipated *Darkness at Noon*, Victor Serge could still speak a bit defensively about the bankruptcy of socialism in the "midnight of the century" represented by the Hitler-Stalin Pact. But he added,

> Have you forgotten the other bankruptcies? What was Christianity doing in the various catastrophes of society? What became of

> Liberalism? What has Conservatism produced, in either its enlightened or its reactionary form?...If we are indeed honestly to weigh out the bankruptcies of ideology, we shall have a long task ahead of us.

In the best sections of this book Amis makes the extraordinary demand that, in effect, the human species should give up on teleology and on all forms of "experiment" on fellow creatures. He is being much more revolutionary here than perhaps he appreciates. Had he allowed himself to ponder the implications, he might have engaged fruitfully with some of his own earlier work on fascism and on thermonuclear gamesmanship—two absolutist theories and practices that had in common the view that Leninism was the main enemy. If it matters, I now agree with him that perfectionism and messianism are the chief and most lethal of our foes. But I can't quite write as if a major twentieth-century tragedy had been enacted to prove that I was correct in the first place. And I don't say this just because I *wasn't* correct. After all, the most valiant of the historians and the resisters in our own time was undoubtedly Solzhenitsyn, who has now descended into a sort of "Great Russian" spiritual and political quackery, replete with nostrums about the national "soul" and euphemisms about pogroms and anti-Semitism. Amis should be self-aware enough to admit that this is an "ideology" too.

His is a short work, and one cannot ask for a complete theory of modern ideology and the various deathtraps it sets for the body and the mind. However, much of the space that could have been devoted to a little inquiry is instead given over to some rather odd reflections on Amis's family life, featuring some vignettes about his offspring and a meditation on the sadly short term that was set to the life of his younger sister. Few people could be more sympathetic to his children than I am (one of those children is my godson). But what is this doing? A baby daughter screams inconsolably one night and forces her father to summon the nanny.

> "The sounds she was making," I said unsmilingly to my wife on her return, "would not have been out of place in the deepest cellars of the Butyrki Prison in Moscow during the Great Terror. That's why I cracked and called Caterina."

From darkness at noon to...lightness at midnight. There's quite a lot more in the same vein. I find it inexplicable, partly because I can easily imagine the scorn with which Amis would write about anyone else who employed the Terror for purposes of relativism. His own purpose, presumably, is to refute Stalin's foul inhumanity by showing that an individual, too, can be a considerable "statistic." But the transition from macro- to micro-humanity is uneasy at its best.

Slightly easier to take is his letter to his late father, who was a believing Communist for many of the Stalin years, and whose irrational dogmatism is set down, probably rightly, to a series of emotional and attitudinal and familial complexes. In *Experience*, in contrast, we saw old Kingsley as he declined into a sort of choleric, empurpled Blimpishness, culminating in his denunciation of Nelson Mandela as a practitioner of Red Terror. The lessons here ought to have been plain: Be very choosy about what kind of anti-communist you are, and be careful not to confuse the state of the world with that of your family, or your own "internal organs."

(*The Atlantic*, September 2002)

Imagining Hitler

WHAT A PIECE OF WORK IS MAN!" says the Prince of Denmark. "How noble in reason! how infinite in faculty! in form and moving how express and admirable! in action how like an angel! in apprehension how like a god! the beauty of the world! the paragon of animals!" Well said, but where, as Ron Rosenbaum so intelligently asks in his recent book, *Explaining Hitler*, do all the Jeffrey Dahmers come from? This is sometimes put, by nervous theologians, as "the problem of evil." We often phrase it, colloquially, as the problem of Hitler. "His face in those early years," wrote Arthur Koestler in 1942, "an unshaped pudding with a black horizontal dot, came to life as the lights of obsession were switched on behind the eyeballs." And then those paragons of animals, those with the godlike and angelic faculties of reason and understanding, flung themselves down by the millions and groaned great noises of worship and adoration. And this in the country of Beethoven and Goethe, where, to continue with Koestler for a moment, "the features of it retained their crankish ridiculousness, with the black dot under the upturned nose and the second black dot pasted on the forefront, but it now assumed the grotesque horror of a totem-mask worn at ritual dances where human sacrifices are performed." A piece of work—no question about that.

I treasure one episode, in the clotted pages of *Mein Kampf*, above all others. As a young, resentful loser hanging around in the Austro-Hungarian

---

Review of *Hitler 1889–1936: Hubris,* by Ian Kershaw.

empire, Adolf Hitler was forced to seek employment on a construction site. He thought the labor beneath him, and he very much resented being pressed to join a union. The lunchtime chat of his fellows was even more repugnant to his nature: "Some of the men went into the nearest public house," while "I drank my bottle of milk and ate my piece of bread somewhere on the side." And when they talked politics,

> everything was rejected: the nation as an invention of the "capitalistic" classes—how often was I to hear just this word!—; the country as the instrument of the *bourgeoisie* for the exploitation of the workers; the authority of the law as a means of suppressing the proletariat; the school as an institution for bringing up slaves as well as slave-drivers; religion as a means for doping the people destined for exploitation; morality as a sign of sheepish patience, and so forth. Nothing remained that was not dragged down into the dirt and the filth of the lowest depths.

It was this, said the young Hitler, which first persuaded him to study "book after book, pamphlet after pamphlet," and to begin fighting back for race and nation and decency. "I argued till finally one day they applied the one means that wins the easiest victory over reason: terror and force. Some of the leaders of the other side gave me the choice of either leaving the job at once or of being thrown from the scaffold." He sloped wolfishly away, later to notice the beards and caftans of the Viennese Jews and to discover another source of lifelong resentment. (One has to admire, also, his early revulsion against "terror and force.")

The passage always sends me into a reverie. I think, first, of those solid Viennese workers who, by the ill luck of the draw, found themselves dealing with the staring eyes of Adolf Hitler at every lunch break. Austrian social democracy was not created by intimidation, so one imagines their patience being sorely tested before they finally told him he could either clear off or be dropped over the side. Then, in 1914, they and millions like them were dragooned into war by their Emperor and found—among others at the front—Corporal Adolf Hitler, the gung-ho enthusiast! All that having turned into a bloody nightmare for civilization, the few survivors got home and found... Adolf Hitler demanding revenge for the same war he had wanted in the first place! (He had meanwhile been exposed to poison gas, which I don't think can have brought out the best in him.) Then the annexation of Austria, the creation of a new, thousand-year Reich, and, after a mere twelve years of that, hardly one brick standing upon another from one end of Germany and Austria to the next. Plenty of opportunities for construction workers. Was there one, I wonder, who ever made the connection and sometimes thought of the chance he had missed, to send that little bastard over the edge and right onto the brick pile below?

A foe of political correctness in one way, Hitler was its friend in another. Recall the bottle of milk he swilled while the others were boozing? (The frightful mustache was grown partly to distract attention from his rotting fangs and suppurating gums.) In the same way, he abhorred smoking, was a fanatical vegetarian, and would never allow jokes about sex in his presence. His tedious hypochondria and health-cultishness found expression in hysteria about "bacilli" and "vermin," and were, eventually, something more than crankish. He was, like most of his gang leaders, morbidly pious about religion and the family.

Is it the insult to one's integrity and intelligence—the shame of having still to cringe at the thought of such a person—that partly accounts for our continued fascination with *der Führer*? The maddening thought that, in other circumstances, he could have been such an ordinary bore and nuisance? The man's opinions are trite and bigoted and deferential, and the prose in *Mein Kampf* is simply laughable in its pomposity. (When mutiny and rebellion broke out in Munich after the First World War, Hitler could not get over the shock. He burst into floods of tears, moaning in print that "the loyalty toward the honorable House of Wittelsbach [had] seemed to me to be stronger than the will of a few Jews.") Yet attempts to make him absurd by caricature and contempt are always, somehow, failures. Charlie Chaplin's 1940 farce, *The Great Dictator*, was in many ways a masterpiece, and Bertolt Brecht's 1941 play, *The Resistible Rise of Arturo Ui*, was a workmanlike attempt to cut Hitler down to size by depicting him as a cheap crook and a tool of the rackets. P. G. Wodehouse introduced one of his Mulliner stories, published in 1937, with a heated pub discussion about "the situation in Germany." Hitler must soon decide one way or another, says a thoughtful customer. There's no dodging the issue. "He'll have to let it grow or shave it off." But if this style of subversive or mocking wit could do the job, there wouldn't be a "problem of evil," or such a Hitler conundrum, in the first place.

It hurts and nags, above all, that we never got his mug in court. The British officer Airey Neave, an ex-prisoner of the Gestapo who was one of the military lawyers at Nuremberg, went from cell to cell and thought: We were frightened for years by *this?* This gaggle of sniggering, talentless, self-pitying picknoses? Hitler's foreign minister, the half-weeping Joachim von Ribbentrop, gave him, with shaking hands, a list of titled character witnesses, "chiefly members of the British aristocracy." Hitler's cashier, Walther Funk, on inspection, turned out to be a "depressing hypochondriac." Robert Ley, organizer of slave labor, was "a slobbering creature." Julius Streicher, purveyor of Jew-baiting pornography, was actually doing his second stretch in a Nuremberg jail. He'd been convicted of sadistic pederasty and resembled, as Rebecca West put it to Neave, the "sort of old man who gives trouble in parks." Yet Hitler was never reduced to "human" scale in such fashion; never had to hire a lawyer and try to cop a plea. He only affected to be fond of Wagner—his favorite film was the Disney version of *Snow White and the Seven Dwarfs,* his actress of choice was Shirley Temple, and in music he preferred the kitsch operetta—but he did arrange a *Götterdämmerung* ending to his rule. As a consequence, there is a recurrent fantasy of retrieving him, and of making him talk.

It's important to remember that many people, before the war, could look at Hitler and see a man with whom business could be done. Winston Churchill, in a 1935 essay from his book *Great Contemporaries,* had this to say:

> It is not possible to form a just judgment of a public figure who has attained the enormous dimensions of Adolf Hitler until his life work as a whole is before us. Although no subsequent political action can condone wrong deeds, history is replete with examples of men who have risen to power by employing stern, grim, and even frightful methods, but who, nevertheless, when their life is revealed as a

whole, have been regarded as great figures whose lives have enriched the story of mankind. So may it be with Hitler.

I've always thought that—coming as it did two years after Hitler's seizure of power—this was a bit lenient. Churchill raised his eyebrows all right at the maltreatment of the German Jews, and at the pace of German re-armament, but (as he had done earlier with Mussolini) could not withhold admiration for Hitler's *Kampf* itself: "The story of that struggle cannot be read without admiration for the courage, the perseverance, and the vital force which enabled him to challenge, defy, conciliate, or overcome all the authorities or resistances which barred his path."

Look up H. L. Mencken's review of *Mein Kampf*, as it appeared in *The American Mercury* of December 1933. Greatly to the distress of his old friend and publisher Alfred A. Knopf, among others, Mencken felt it his job to explain that the new *Führer* was potentially on to something good. Not only did he describe as "sensible enough" the idea that "Germany's first big task is to collar Austria and so consolidate the German people," but he went on to state that anti-Semitism was more or less to be expected. ("The disadvantage of the Jew is that, to simple men, he always seems a kind of foreigner.") Though he tried to soften the blow by comparing Hitler to fundamentalist Democrat William Jennings Bryan—harsh dispraise in the Mencken universe—he too found that there was a Jewish-Bolshevik threat to be combated: "The bloody Räterepublik at Munich—long forgotten elsewhere, but only too well remembered in Germany—had been set up and bossed by a Jew, and there were other Jews high in the councils of the Communist party, which proposed openly to repeat the Munich pillages and butcheries all over the country."

Munich, Munich, always Munich. It was there in 1919, just eighty years ago, that the essential catalyst was found. After all, had Hitler not redeemed Germany from the awful moment when, as Winston Churchill himself put it, "the pride and will-power of the Prussian race broke into surrender and revolution behind the fighting lines"? In his new book, *Hitler 1889–1936: Hubris*, Professor Ian Kershaw has hit upon the very moment that is suggested by the earlier passage in *Mein Kampf*, and the—let's be charitable—unintended compliments paid by Churchill and Mencken.

Do you recall the moment in *The Silence of the Lambs* when a moth chrysalis is discovered in the throat of a mutilated woman, and taken for examination? The entomologists at the Smithsonian lose no time in establishing that this sinister insect was present by design and had been carefully nurtured. "Somebody," says the man with the tweezers, "grew this guy. Fed him honey and nightshade. Kept him warm. Somebody loved him." The roach Hitler was just a drifter and a loser and a fantasist, but he was incubated all right, and shoved down the throats of the German people at the perfect psychological moment.

In Munich in late 1918 and 1919, Hitler's two greatest enemies made common cause. The Räterepublik, or "republic of councils," was a radical and improvised regime that deposed the monarchy and denounced the war. (Its leader, the Jewish journalist and leftist Kurt Eisner, published the secret documents that showed how the Kaiser had pushed Austria into making a bullying ultimatum after the Sarajevo incident in 1914.) What horror that in Bavaria, Jews and mechanics and longhairs should rule! And that they should expose the war guilt of Imperial Germany! Mencken is right that there was pillage and butchery as a result, but in fact the bloodbath began when Eisner was murdered by a fanatical right-wing officer, and it did not stop until hundreds of Jewish and other "suspect" elements had been lynched by the predecessors of the Brownshirts, and "order" had been restored. In the course of this sanguinary ferment, according to documents unearthed by Professor Kershaw, Hitler found his patrons. A cabal of extreme nationalist and conservative officers in the army hired him as a spy, gave him some walking-around money, and noticed his talent for demagoguery. The leader of this group, Captain Karl Mayr, wrote a year or so later to one of his Fascist-minded civilian friends: "I've set up very capable young people. A Herr Hitler, for example, has become a motive force, a popular speaker of the first rank."

"The drummer," his windup inventors called him. He was proud of the title. Later, it was the army that bought Hitler his first newspaper, the *Völkischer Beobachter*, on which he was to found a career as the first modern politician to enjoy absolute mastery of the mass media. The brass also gave him arms and uniforms on the side to set up the Brownshirts. *Somebody grew him.* You can chuck out your Alan Bullock and Joachim Fest and Hugh Trevor-Roper biographies, in my opinion, and read only one relatively short book: *The Meaning of Hitler*, by the brave, brilliant former German exile Sebastian Haffner. In one dense paragraph, written in 1978, before the Kershaw disclosures, he guessed correctly that Hitler's maniacal reaction to the Munich revolution in 1918–19 was the key that unlocked everything. Read it carefully, because it leaves nothing out:

> "There must never again be and there will never again be a November 1918 in Germany," was his first political *resolution* after a great many political ponderings and speculations. It was the first specific objective the young private politician set himself and incidentally the only one he truly accomplished. There was certainly no November 1918 in the Second World War—neither a timely termination of a lost war nor a revolution. Hitler prevented both.
>
> Let us be clear about what this "never again a November 1918" implied. It implied quite a lot. First of all the determination to make impossible any future revolution in a situation analogous to November 1918. Secondly—since otherwise the first point would be left in the air—the determination to bring about once more a similar situation. And this implied, thirdly, the resumption of the war that was lost or believed to be lost. Fourthly, the war had to be resumed on the basis of a domestic constitution in which there were no potentially revolutionary forces. From here it was not far to the fifth point, the abolition of all Left-wing parties, and indeed why not, while one was about it, of all parties. Since, however, one could not abolish the people behind the Left-wing parties, the workers, they would have to be politically won over to nationalism, and this implied, sixth, that one had to offer them socialism, or at least a kind of socialism, in fact National Socialism. Seventh, their former faith, Marxism, had to be uprooted and that meant—eighth—the physical annihilation of the Marxist politicians and intellectuals who, fortunately, included quite a lot of Jews so that—ninth, and Hitler's oldest wish—one could also, at the same time, exterminate all the Jews.

It becomes impossible to overstate the germinal importance of the 1918 collapse. The German army had fought, brilliantly and barbarously, against France, Britain, Russia, and later the United States. It had defeated Russia and, in the purely militarist sense, held the other Allies to a standoff. But it had, without noticing the fact, also ruined and beggared Germany. Either this calamity was the fault of the Imperial leadership (the view of the Marxist left) or it was the work of an "enemy within." The crazy, intoxicating one-word Nazi slogan for the latter was *Dolchstoss*, or the "stab in the back." Such a deluded fantasy required fantasists for its promotion.

The high intelligence of Haffner's analysis explains both Hitler's appeal to the lowest common denominator and the appeal of such a type to those who imagined *they* were using *him*. Hitler's inventors and backers, from the obscure Captain Mayr up to Field Marshal von Hindenburg (the dense military man) and Fritz Thyssen (the greedy and cynical tycoon) and Franz von Papen (the Establishment wheeler-dealer), could have been taken as caricatures from some Monopoly board game. They neither wanted nor needed an all-out war with Russia and Britain and America, with a Final Solution thrown in. They desired an insurance policy against Communism. But for that they needed Hitler. And Hitler *did* need all of the foregoing. But he didn't let on until it was too late. Professor Kershaw makes the same point in a different but equally chilling way. After the constitutional coup which brought Hitler to power in January 1933, the unscrupulous conservative von Papen, who had helped broker the deal, exclaimed, "We've hired him!" At the same moment, the senile President Hindenburg received a letter from his old comrade-in-arms Erich Ludendorff, who had led Germany's armies on the Western Front, had helped originate the myth of the "stab in the back," and had flirted often with Hitler in right-wing politics in Munich after 1919. "You have delivered up our holy German Fatherland to one of the greatest demagogues of all time," wrote the ultra-reactionary Ludendorff to his one-time commanding officer. "I solemnly prophesy that this accursed man will cast our Reich into the abyss and bring our nation to inconceivable misery. Future generations will damn you in your grave for what you have done."

This means that, as early as 1933, a brutish and conceited militarist was more farseeing than, say, Winston Churchill. (Actually, the only person in

Europe apart from Ludendorff who saw that there was something entirely new and completely hideous about Hitler was Russian revolutionary Leon Trotsky, about whom Churchill in his *Great Contemporaries* was much ruder than about Hitler himself. Trotsky also realized, unlike Ludendorff, that Hitlerism would be dire not just for the "holy German Fatherland." As he wrote, at the eleventh hour, "today, not only in peasant homes but also in the city sky-scrapers, there lives alongside the twentieth century the tenth or thirteenth. A hundred million people use electricity and still believe in the magic power of signs and exorcisms.... What inexhaustible reserves they possess of darkness, ignorance and savagery!")

Between Haffner's incisive analysis and Kershaw's meticulous historiography, it may be possible to give reason a small retrospective victory. Chroniclers of Hitlerism have tended to divide between those who stress the "subjective" personality, the man's ravings and delusions and sexual inversions, and those who emphasize the "objective" conditions, the resentment of millions of Germans at national humiliation and general penury. Some other scholars have simply pointed out, as if on a blackboard, that Hitler loudly proposed to "cure" the second condition by railing at an "enemy within," the Jews, and "an enemy without," the Bolsheviks, with their Jewish characteristics. But that's only to state the same problem in a different way. Obviously, there would have been nationalistic and anti-Semitic reaction to defeat on the battlefield, to the Communist threat, and to the Treaty of Versailles. W. H. Auden grasped this pathology, with a poet's insight, in his "September 1, 1939":

> Accurate scholarship can
> Unearth the whole offense
> From Luther until now
> That has driven a culture mad,
> Find what occurred at Linz,
> What huge imago made
> A psychopathic god...

So, what did occur at Linz, and in the other scenes of Hitler's enchanting boyhood? It's known that he had a brutal father and a doting mother, but as

Kershaw carefully shows, there is no serious foundation to the rumors of hidden Jewish ancestry, deformity of the genitals, the incompetence or greed of a Jewish doctor at his mother's deathbed, or any of the other whispers. His sex life managed to be both meager and distraught, but that just won't do as a theory. Nor is it possible, on the evidence, to believe that Hitler didn't really dislike the Jews and simply made a cynical, vote-getting "pitch" to those who did. (A surprising number of scholars have allowed themselves to think this.) For one thing—this is an observation of my own—*Mein Kampf* was published as an initially unsuccessful vote-getter in 1925, and at that time social democracy was very strong and popular, and the German Jews were still quite secure. To describe either as the work of Satan was to show what you really thought. ("There is no making pacts with Jews," he tells us he decided back in 1918 when he had recovered from his nervous collapse. "There can only be the hard either-or. I, however, resolved to become a politician.")

"To become a politician." Hitler got bad grades and spent several years mooching and brooding. He wanted to be an artist, and believed in his own distinctly slender genius as a painter. Aesthetic circles in Vienna boasted a strong Jewish presence, and envious mediocre bums throughout history have blamed their own lack of recognition on exclusion by such sophisticated cabals. Moreover, idle mediocre bums from the lower middle class have always detested trade unions and cosmopolitans in about equal measure. Young Adolf's prejudices were completely banal until, having identified his shriveled little self with the Kaiser and the Emperor and the army, he saw all his old foes exploiting the moment of defeat by trying to seize power and mock his values. That—and don't forget the gas with which he had been hit—drove him over the edge. (When he got power himself—*Führer* being the first actual job he had ever held—he at once shut down the unions and then viciously pillaged the galleries of a once civilized nation to hang most of the best modern paintings in Germany in a wildly philistine 1937 exhibition—in Munich—entitled "Degenerate Art.")

In those and other details, his military and business backers let him have his way. They really had overstated, for "opportunist" reasons, the Jewish and Marxist threat. But they thought they owned a marionette. I did not know until I read Kershaw that the proposal for all German soldiers to take their "oath of unconditional loyalty" to the *Führer* himself actually came from the High Command. They thought this clever move would detach him from the vulgar Nazi Party and confirm him as their creature. A mistake. Arguably a very big mistake. They helped nationalize the concept of the lowest common denominator.

Yet deep within himself, Haffner argues, Hitler did not trust the German people, or think them worthy of his leadership. With outright military catastrophe threatening in 1944, he ordered the arrest of 5,000 leading German politicians, from minister to mayor (including the highly conservative politician Konrad Adenauer, later to become the first West German chancellor), because he thought they might go soft, and even sue for peace, and perhaps allow another November 1918 defeat. He kept his Final Solution a state secret, to be conducted well away from German soil—a compliment to public opinion in its way—and, at the end, coldly decided that Germany itself should be laid waste as a punishment for its weakness.

But then what is one to say of his overseas "enablers"? Two decades after his Munich "incubation," Hitler must have giggled with incredulity in the fall of 1938 when the prime minister of Great Britain landed at the Munich airport and asked him if there was anything else, after Austria and the Rhineland, that he especially wanted. Hardly daring to hope, as we now know, Hitler replied in effect that Czechoslovakia would be nice. My own contribution to the anniversaries of 1919 and 1939, if I may mention it, is a foreword to a splendid book called *In Our Time: The Chamberlain-Hitler Collusion*, by Professors Clement Leibovitz and Alvin Finkel. This volume establishes conclusively that British prime minister Neville Chamberlain was no duped "appeaser," with a silly mustache of his own. He had made a cold calculation that Hitler should be re-armed, and be allowed—if not, indeed, encouraged—to expand his Reich. This was partly to keep his marauding hands off the British Empire, and partly to encourage his "tough-minded" solution to the Bolshevik problem in the East. Chamberlain and his foreign secretary, Lord Halifax, refused even to meet with senior German officers who belatedly implored their help, at the last available moment, in overthrowing the madman. The German people, said these brave men, had been partly duped by Hitler because he had apparently restored full employment and overturned the unpopular and humiliating Treaty of Versailles, without resorting to war. A credible threat of resistance by Britain would destroy this illusion, and there were several generals ready to move against their former protégé. Go away, said His Majesty's Government. (This story is also told in *The Unnecessary War: Whitehall and the German Resistance to Hitler*, by Patricia Meehan.) Hard to read about this, even now. Hard to remember, too, that in civilized France the reactionaries of 1936, appalled at the election of a Dreyfusard socialist Jew as premier, yelled "Better Hitler than Blum." M. Léon Blum was deported to Buchenwald.

Of the countless blood-freezing facts about Adolf Hitler that several historians have established independently, there is one that keeps me awake more than any other. Not only did he "time" everything in anticipation of his own early death (he had always had morbid fantasies of illness and suicide), but, at different moments, he actually told close associates that this was his explicit motive. *We must invade Russia now because I have not much time left to me... The transports to the East must begin because I am becoming frail and must see the task completed...* Even some of his most toughened and cretinous underlings went pale when they heard this and suddenly realized its staggering import. This howling nihilist didn't just need to destroy the Jews. He didn't care if *nobody* outlived him. In other words, there was no time at which a stiff political or diplomatic resistance, or an assassination backed by the High Command, or even the toe of an Austrian construction worker's cleated boot, might not have made all the difference. Any of these could have fucked him, and the apocalyptic horses he rode in on. He was a homicidal maniac in a hurry, and terribly afraid that he might not make it. Yet respectable circles in Germany, and in Britain and France (and, as we have recently learned from the files of Ford and General Motors, in these United States), decided that he was, on balance, a case of "the lesser evil." Indeed, that was the only use of the word "evil" that they ever permitted themselves.

(*Vanity Fair,* February 1999)

Victor Klemperer: Survivor

THE LITERATURE of twentieth-century totalitarianism, whether in prefiguring the epoch of Nazism and Stalinism or in drawing on it, often relied on *un homme moyen sensuel*—the luckless particle swept up in the process, or the worm from whose eye the titanic, forbidding edifice could be squintingly, even cringingly, scrutinized. Kafka's Joseph K was a prototype; Orwell's Winston Smith was given autonomy as a character only to have it very annihilatingly taken away from him. (Rubashov, in *Darkness at Noon*, was more of a Miltonian figure, flung from the heights of power yet still pitilessly judged by the standards of his former comrades.)

Almost a decade ago, in Germany, the diaries of Victor Klemperer were published. It became evident at once that this was a nonfiction event that quite eclipsed the journals of Anne Frank. Here was a middle-aged academic, converted from Judaism to Protestantism, who had decided in full maturity to keep a record of every feasible day (and some inconceivable ones) of the "thousand-year Reich": an enterprise that occupied him from 1933 to 1945 and filled two large volumes titled *I Will Bear Witness*. Superbly translated by Martin Chalmers, these appeared in English in 1998 and 1999, and gave rise to a very widespread critical and historical discussion about the Hitler period. Reading them, I noticed that at the end of the war—and after narrowly surviving the obliteration of Dresden—Klemperer had opted to stay in "East"

Review of *The Lesser Evil: Diaries 1945–1959*, by Victor Klemperer.

Germany, and to identify himself with what became the German Democratic Republic. Given the attachment to liberalism and skepticism that he had demonstrated throughout his diaries of the Nazi years, and given also his addiction to journal keeping, I felt sure that he would have kept up his solitary labor on the other side of the Iron Curtain, and that this work would one day surface. And now it has, in the form of *The Lesser Evil*, a fourteen-year personal journey through the academic bureaucracy and party-state institutions of the GDR. It ends a few months short of Klemperer's death, in 1960.

It is a disgrace that this book has not so far found a publisher in the United States, and I hope that readers will be able to bypass the bookstores and publishers and acquire copies by other means. (Phoenix Books is based in London; Trafalgar Square Books, of Vermont, is the U.S. distributor.) With this third volume we now have what is almost unique—a firsthand and intimate account by somebody who "survived" both versions of ideological dictatorship at close quarters, and who was in an unusually strong position to take, and to compare, notes. If American book publishers wish to give the impression that they cash in on Holocaust-related books before allowing their interest in Central Europe to lapse, then by this act of negligence they are well on their way to succeeding.

For all that, it is effectively impossible to begin a discussion of *The Lesser Evil* without reviewing some of the context and character of the preceding volumes. Klemperer was born in 1881, to the family of a rabbi in what was then Brandenburg and is now part of Poland. (To anticipate a question: The conductor Otto Klemperer was a cousin.) The father, an Orthodox Jew, switched allegiance to Reform Judaism when he moved to Berlin, and his sons "completed" this trajectory, it might be said, by converting to Protestantism. Victor took up the study of French Enlightenment literature, was an energetic literary journalist, married a Protestant musicologist named Eva Schlemmer, served in the German Army in the First World War with pride but without great distinction, and in 1920 secured a post teaching Romance languages and literature at Dresden Technical University. Thus when National Socialism came to power, in 1933, he had some reason to hope that his conversion, his academic position, his marriage, and his war record would give him a degree of immunity.

I should add, in all fairness and objectivity, that Klemperer also decided that nothing would induce him to emigrate: He would remain a German at any hazard. But the consuming interest of the hundreds of entries that he was later to set down is this: It took him quite awhile to appreciate just how futile this trust in partial immunity would prove. Not that he had any illusions about the nature of the Nazi Party, for whose propaganda and bombast he invariably expressed loathing and contempt. It was more that he had difficulty crediting the ghastly, inexorable fashion in which everything was taken from him, and from his wife. His marriage, position, and war record did, in fact, confer some rights on him: Even the Nuremberg "race" laws made some grudging exceptions for those married to "Aryans." But this postponement only made him feel more keenly the deep-seated and protracted sadism of the "cleansing" of Germany. One day it would be that he could not ride at the front of the tram or use the university library, the next a ban on Jewish ownership of typewriters or automobiles. Then it would be the imposition of the Yellow Star, or the forced use of "Israel" as a patronymic on official cards and papers. Then Jews were kicked off the tram altogether, and always there was fresh trouble about the shops that could be used or the rations that could be claimed. Eventually came expulsion from his university post and from his home, and a confinement in ghetto housing that became more and more obviously the anteroom to deportation; and then the only terminus of deportation. There is a horrid fascination in reading this day-by-day chronicle as it unfolds, along with each cuff on the head and gob of spittle, because we know what's coming, and he is only beginning to guess.

I'll select an ostensibly trivial instance that is somehow appallingly eloquent. The Klemperers were childless (thank heaven, one thinks—as they must sometimes have thought), and Victor and especially Eva had become devoted cat lovers. A time came when the magazine *The German Feline* began to publish articles exalting the authentic German cat over the suspect and degenerate "breeds" that had been allowed to creep in. Then Klemperer was informed that he could no longer make donations to the fund for the prevention of cruelty to German cats. Then all Jews in the Reich, and all those married to them, were told that they would have to surrender all pets, because dogs and cats and birds should live only in pure Aryan homes. Of this, in May of 1942, Klemperer minutes, about the couple's beloved tomcat, Muschel,

> I feel very bitter for Eva's sake. We have so often said to each other: The tomcat's raised tail is our flag, we shall not strike it... and at the victory celebrations Muschel will get a "schnitzel from Kamm's" (the fanciest butcher here)...
>
> Unless the regime collapsed by the very next morning, we would expose the cat to an even crueler death or put me in even greater danger. (Even having him killed today is a little dangerous for me.) I left the decision to Eva. She took the animal away in the familiar cardboard catbox, she was present when he was put to sleep by an anaesthetic.

Banish your sentimentality (and I have left out the most heart-touching passages): Is there not something fabulously grotesque about a regime that in the midst of total war will pedantically insist that Jews and their spouses either euthanize their own pets or surrender them to the state for extermination?

But even as the book is a bitter rebuke to all those who doubt or deny the methodical nature of the Nazi elimination policy, it is also a reproach to some of the more facile elements of the Goldhagen thesis, as put forth in *Hitler's Willing Executioners* (1996). Far from being made the object of hatred or violence by his fellow citizens, Klemperer is constantly being brought up short by astonishment at random—or even planned—acts of generosity or solidarity. Cuts of meat or fish are offered to him in rationed stores. Tram drivers abuse the Führer for his benefit. The man supposed to supervise the forced labor of elderly Jews gives repeated work breaks and takes every opportunity to express sympathy for the conscripts and disgust for the authorities. A worker passes by and says, "Chin up—the scoundrels will soon be finished." This persists even into the heavy Allied bombardments. Klemperer's friend Jacobi is invited into an air-raid shelter that's off limits to wearers of the Star with the words "Come on in, mate." When Jacobi says, "But you mustn't say that," the worker responds loudly, "We're all mates—and soon we'll be able to say it out loud again." If there is hope, it lies in the proles... Klemperer awards credit for this, and often mentions the exemplary behavior of communists and socialists, but nonetheless retains a certain reserve. Where are all the other Germans? Are they, as he suspects, in hiding somewhere?

Never much—or at all—interested in Marxism, he also manifests an abiding distrust of the Zionism to which so many of his fellows are drawn.

To him, the point is to maintain his right to be a liberal German. He abuses Theodor Herzl in the roundest of terms, as a mirror-image race theorist and nationalist who would deny this same right in another insidious way. And he shrinks, as a good Voltairean should, from Martin Buber's religiosity ("makes me downright ill"). There cannot have been many victims in 1942 who told their diaries that they planned an essay titled "Pro Germania, contra Zion from the contemporary standpoint of the German Jew."

Most arresting of all, however, is Klemperer's decision to compile a lexicon of what he calls *Lingua tertii imperii* ("the language of the Third Reich"), in which he notes and analyzes the rhetorical giveaways of the regime. This *LTI* notation becomes a subtext of the book, and puts one in mind even more forcibly of the diary kept by Winston Smith. As in *Nineteen Eighty-four*, it often involves noticing propaganda claims, about production at home or victories on far-off fronts, that are simply too loud and too immense to be believed. Then there is the Nazi habit of collectivizing races or nationalities, so that it's always "the Jew" or "the Englishman," with individuality doing duty for a mass. To say nothing of the use of words—"fanatical," for instance—as extra-strong positives. Klemperer develops a way of reading the newspapers so as to notice that when slightly tepid terms are employed, things must be going really badly for German armies in North Africa or Russia. (His guesses are usually correct.) With some satisfaction he examines the death notices in the press and counts up how many of them are accompanied by a swastika or some other Nazi rune, and how many simply announce a fallen son. After the war was over, Klemperer published his essays on *LTI* as a separate book, which had considerable success in both Germanys.

The Klemperer we come to know is a shrewd man, somewhat impatient with others and somewhat insecure, and fairly honest with and about himself. In one of his entries about the death of the cat, for example, he confesses that he resents his wife's giving a lavish piece of veal (the meat ration for some days) to the condemned Muschel as a farewell treat. By the time this third volume opens, we are accustomed to the sharp insights into motivation and character, and to the equally acute ear for falsity and pretension, that have helped him survive. We have also been introduced to an absolutely magnificent woman in Eva, herself a one-person refutation of the Goldhagen slur on the German character. It seems never even to have occurred to her that she could have saved herself by divorce; she had been condemned to join one of the last trains rumbling east toward the killing fields with her husband when the skies opened over Dresden, in 1945, and the Nazi authority went up in smoke. (She had loved the city, as had Victor, but said that her heart had hardened after the murder of little Muschel.)

In one of his diatribes against Herzl, Klemperer says that the man had an almost Bolshevik arrogance. From this and many other asides and observations it is quite clear that he was not in any sense a Communist; indeed, it's fairly plain that he was a relatively apolitical supporter of the old Social-Democratic Party. Yet his decision to take out a party card with the Communist Party (KPD) follows very shortly after the collapse of Hitler and the arrival of the Red Army. The Klemperers get their old house back, are offered compensation and many apologies (there are some mordant entries on the latter), and are able to have a tomcat again. But Party membership was not required for any of this.

A mixture of motives can be discerned. First, Klemperer feels that the most valiant anti-Nazis were the KPD and the Soviet Union. (That this conclusion involves some rewriting of history goes without saying.) And the VVN—the official association of victims of Nazi persecution, which he wishes to join—is quite clearly a Party front. But there is more to it than that. Deep down, and despite some memorable experiences to the contrary, he has ceased to trust the German people. In his mind, only a very strong regime will prevent the resurgence of anti-Jewish hatred that he regards as inevitable. This thought poisons even his better moments.

Historical context apart, Klemperer's journals can be read for their own sake as a gnawing meditation on the disappointments of life and the irrevocability of choices. He is intensely aware at all moments, perhaps because of his consciousness of being a "survivor," that death is only a breath away. He is one of the great kvetches of all time, endlessly recording aches and pains, bad dreams, shortages of food and medicine, snubs and humiliations. And, like everyone else, he wants everything both ways. In particular, he wants East Germany to be an open democracy with a real intellectual life, while insisting that all manifestations of reactionary and racist spirit be pitilessly crushed. This double-entry bookkeeping is something that he usually has the courage to confess ("between two stools" becomes his preferred cliché) even when he knows that the contradiction is not resolvable. Thus, while hailing the Red Army and the intransigent Party even in the earliest post-Nazi days, he is beginning to take notes for a successor study of lethal jargon, to be called *LQI*, or *The Language of the Fourth Reich*. Here's an example, from a commissar-type critique he receives of one of his books—which, he is informed, must, "taking account of all objectivity, of all devotion to scholarship, nevertheless above all be couched in such a way that it meets all the demands of our new democratic educational reform, which of course mutatis mutandis also applies to the universities." It continues, "Revolutionary times must on occasion make do with considerable abridgements in order to accentuate the political line more strongly." To that gem of what the French call *la langue du bois* Klemperer appends the single instinctive word "Revolting!" He adds that "class-consciousness" in this form is the counterpart to race-consciousness under the previous regime before reflecting, "Not quite as poisonous."

Oscar Wilde's objection to the socialism he professed—that it would take up far too many evenings—has never been better materialized than by Klemperer's record of soul-smashing monotony and conformity. He dares not refuse to attend meetings of the Kulturbund, because this deadening outfit is a meal ticket. But once you are on one committee... His acute sense of time wasted is intensified by his no-less-acute sense that he hasn't much time left.

The page-turning quality of the first two volumes isn't as urgent in *The Lesser Evil*, because although we know what is coming, we also know, at least, that it can and will be survived. When the workers of Berlin mount a revolt in 1953, Klemperer is only peripherally involved and gives the regime the benefit of the doubt while distrusting its propagandized explanation. One can feel the erection of the Wall coming on, even as one notices that Klemperer both does and does not want the segregation of Germany and the absorption of the east by the Soviet bloc. He died in February of 1960, just before that consummation of the Cold War forced so many of his compatriots to flee or go into internal opposition. It's doubtful that he could have nerved himself to do either thing; indeed, by then his nerve had gone. But toward the very last of the entries he says something that he hasn't said to himself before—namely, that the conduct of the East German security services is of a "Gestapo" type. For a childless man, also, he shows special insight in noticing how gruesome is regime propaganda when directed at infants. This is an *LQI* entry from May of 1959, taken from an East German newspaper interview, in which "Colleague Schubert, day nursery teacher at the 12th Primary School," said,

> With some groups in our nursery we have got to the point that the children are already working independently and *learning leadership*... From lunchtime, under the supervision of a nursery teacher, the children themselves take over. Thus we try to *teach leadership* to our worker and peasant children; because one day they will be in charge of the state.

Without pausing over the accidental absurdity of the second sentence, Klemperer simply notes that this is "purest Nazism, in *even* worse German!"

My Winston Smith analogy is obviously inexact in one way, in that during the Nazi period Klemperer was an axiomatically identified public enemy with no hope of concealing himself, and during the Communist years he was a man trying to convince himself not that the system was wrong but that it was right. His utter failure in this attempt is eloquent nonetheless, and amounts to a very strong and useful condemnation at a time when a movie of fatuous nostalgia for the GDR—*Good Bye, Lenin!*—can exert extensive box-office and critical appeal in the United States, and when former Stalinists and neo-Nazis are competing with each other to make a statist "One Nation" appeal in the eastern *Lander* of the Federal Republic.

In 1951 Eva Klemperer died; one is happy to know that she was to the last consoled by her new cat. Within a short time Victor had taken up with another woman, named Hadwig Kirchner, who likewise agreed to share his disappointments and struggles—and to put up with his evidently difficult personality—but whose deepest desire was that he agree to marry her within the Catholic Church and thus prevent her having to choose between him and holy communion. This he eventually agreed to do, so long as it could be arranged that nobody would know of it. One has the feeling that he would have made this a condition even in a state system that did not frown on religion. These journals are not the diary of a nobody, even though they were composed by a man who greatly feared that verdict. They are, rather, the life story of a man who in a time of diseased delusions tried—and failed—to live as if even comforting illusions were unnecessary.

(*The Atlantic*, December 2004)

A War Worth Fighting

IS THERE ANY ONE SHARED PRINCIPLE or assumption on which our political consensus rests, any value judgment on which we are all essentially agreed? Apart from abstractions such as a general belief in democracy, one would probably get the widest measure of agreement for the proposition that the Second World War was a "good war" and one well worth fighting. And if we possess one indelible image of political immorality and cowardice, it is surely the dismal tap-tap-tap of Neville Chamberlain's umbrella as he turned from signing the Czechs away to Adolf Hitler at Munich. He hoped by this humiliation to avert war, but he was fated to bring his countrymen war on top of humiliation. To the conventional wisdom add the titanic figure of Winston Churchill as the emblem of oratorical defiance and the Horatius who, until American power could be mobilized and deployed, alone barred the bridge to the forces of unalloyed evil. When those forces lay finally defeated, their ghastly handiwork was uncovered to a world that mistakenly thought it had already "supped full of horrors." The stark evidence of the Final Solution has ever since been enough to dispel most doubts about, say, the wisdom or morality of carpet-bombing German cities.

Historical scholarship has nevertheless offered various sorts of revisionist interpretation of all this. Niall Ferguson, for one, has proposed looking at the two World Wars as a single conflict, punctuated only by a long and ominous

---

Review of *Churchill, Hitler and the Unnecessary War*, by Pat Buchanan.

armistice. British conservative historians like Alan Clark and John Charmley have criticized Churchill for building his career on war, for ignoring openings to peace, and for eventually allowing the British Empire to be squandered and broken up. But Pat Buchanan, twice a candidate for the Republican nomination and in 2000 the standard-bearer for the Reform Party who ignited a memorable "chad" row in Florida, has now condensed all the anti-war arguments into one. His case, made in his recently released *Churchill, Hitler and the Unnecessary War*, is as follows:

- That Germany was faced with encirclement and injustice in both 1914 and 1939.
- Britain in both years ought to have stayed out of quarrels on the European mainland.
- That Winston Churchill was the principal British warmonger on both occasions.
- The United States was needlessly dragged into war on both occasions.
- That the principal beneficiaries of this were Joseph Stalin and Mao Zedong.
- That the Holocaust of European Jewry was as much the consequence of an avoidable war as it was of Nazi racism.

Buchanan does not need to close his book with an invocation of a dying West, as if to summarize this long recital of Spenglerian doomsaying. He's already opened with the statement, "All about us we can see clearly now that the West is passing away." The tropes are familiar—a loss of will and confidence, a collapse of the desire to reproduce with sufficient vigor, a preference for hedonism over the stern tasks of rulership and dominion and pre-eminence. It all sounds oddly...Churchillian. The old lion himself never tired of striking notes like these, and was quite unembarrassed by invocations of race and nation and blood. Yet he is the object of Buchanan's especial dislike and contempt, because he had a fondness for "wars of choice."

This term has enjoyed a recent vogue because of the opposition to the war in Iraq, an opposition in which Buchanan has played a vigorous role. Descending as he does from the tradition of Charles Lindbergh's America First movement, which looked for (and claimed to have found) a certain cosmopolitan lobby behind FDR's willingness to involve the United States in global war, Buchanan is the most trenchant critic of what he considers our fondest national illusion, and his book has the feel and stamp of a work that he has been readying all his life.

But he faces an insuperable difficulty, or rather difficulties. If you want to demonstrate that Germany was more the victim than the aggressor in 1914, then you must confine your account (as Buchanan does) to the very minor legal question of Belgian neutrality and of whether Britain absolutely had to go to war on the Belgian side. (For what it may be worth, I think that Britain wasn't obliged to do so and should not have done.) But the rest of the Kaiser's policy, most of it completely omitted by Buchanan, shows that Germany was looking for a chance for war all over the globe, and was increasingly the prisoner of a militaristic ruling caste at home. The Kaiser picked a fight with Britain by backing the white Dutch Afrikaner rebels in South Africa and by butchering the Ovambo people of what is now Namibia. He looked for trouble with the French by abruptly sending warships to Agadir in French Morocco, which nearly started the First World War in 1905, and with Russia by backing Austria-Hungary's insane ultimatum to the Serbs after the June 1914 assassinations in Sarajevo. Moreover, and never mentioned by Buchanan at all, the Kaiser visited Damascus and paid for the rebuilding of the tomb of Saladin, announced himself a sympathizer of Islam and a friend of *jihad*, commissioned a Berlin-to-Baghdad railroad for the projection of German arms into the Middle East and Asia, and generally ranged himself on the side of an aggressive Ottoman imperialism, which later declared a "holy war" against Britain. To suggest that he felt unjustly hemmed in by the Royal Navy's domination of the North Sea while he was conducting such statecraft is absurd.

And maybe a little worse than absurd, as when Buchanan writes: "From 1871 to 1914, the Germans under Bismarck and the Kaiser did not fight a single war. While Britain, Russia, Italy, Turkey, Japan, Spain, and the United States were all involved in wars, Germany and Austria had clean records." I am bound to say that I find this creepy. The start of the "clean record" has to be in 1871, because that's the year that Prussia humbled France in the hideous Franco-Prussian War that actually annexed two French provinces to Germany. In the intervening time until 1914, Germany was seizing colonies in Africa and the Pacific, cementing secret alliances with Austria and trying to build up a naval fleet that could take on the British one. No wonder the Kaiser wanted a breathing space.

Now, this is not to say that Buchanan doesn't make some sound points about the secret diplomacy of Old Europe that was so much to offend Woodrow Wilson. And he is excellent on the calamitous Treaty of Versailles that succeeded only—as was noted by John Maynard Keynes at the time—in creating the conditions for another world war, or for part two of the first one. He wears his isolationism proudly: "The Senate never did a better day's work than when it rejected the Treaty of Versailles and refused to enter a League of Nations where American soldiers would be required to give their lives enforcing the terms of so dishonorable and disastrous a peace."

Actually, no soldier of any nation ever lost so much as a fingernail in the service of the League, which was in any case doomed by American abstention, and it's exactly that consideration which invalidates the second half of Buchanan's argument, which is that a conflict with Hitler's Germany both could and should have been averted. (There is a third Buchanan subargument, mostly made by implication, which is that the democratic West should have allied itself with Hitler, at least passively, until he had destroyed the Soviet Union.) Again, in order to believe his thesis one has to be prepared to argue that Hitler was a rational actor with intelligible and negotiable demands, whose declared, demented ambitions in *Mein Kampf* were presumably to be disregarded as mere propaganda. In case after case Buchanan shows the abysmal bungling of British and French diplomacy—making promises to Czechoslovakia that could never have been kept and then, adding injury to insult, breaking those promises at the first opportunity. Or offering a guarantee to Poland (a country that had gleefully taken part in the dismemberment of Czechoslovakia) that Hitler well knew was not backed by any credible military force.

Buchanan is at his best here, often causing one to whistle at the sheer cynicism and stupidity of the British Tories. In the Anglo-German Naval Agreement of June 1935, for example, they astounded the French and Italians and Russians by unilaterally agreeing to permit Hitler to build a fleet one third the size of the Royal Navy and a submarine fleet of the same size as the British! Not only was this handing the Third Reich the weapon it would soon press to Britain's throat, it was convincing all Britain's potential allies that they would be much better off making their own bilateral deals with Berlin. Which is essentially what happened.

But Buchanan keeps forgetting that this criminal foolishness is exactly the sort of policy that he elsewhere recommends. In his view, after all, Germany had been terribly wronged by Versailles and it would have been correct to redraw the frontiers in Germany's favor and soothe its hurt feelings (which is what the word "appeasement" originally meant). Meanwhile we should have encouraged Hitler's hostility to Bolshevism and discreetly re-armed in case he should also need to be contained. This might perhaps have worked if Germany had been governed by a right-wing nationalist party that had won a democratic vote. However, in point of fact Germany was governed by an ultra-rightist, homicidal, paranoid maniac who had begun by demolishing democracy in Germany itself, who believed that his fellow countrymen were a superior race and who attributed all the evils in the world to a Jewish conspiracy. It is possible to read whole chapters of Buchanan's book without having to bear these salient points in mind. (I should say that I intend this observation as a criticism.) As with his discussion of pre-1914 Germany, he commits important sins of omission that can only be the outcome of an ideological bias. Barely mentioned except in passing is the Spanish Civil War, for example, where for three whole years between 1936 and 1939 Germany and Italy lent troops and weapons in a Fascist invasion of a sovereign European nation that had never threatened or "encircled" them in any way. Buchanan's own political past includes overt sympathy with General Franco, which makes this skating-over even less forgivable than it might otherwise be.

On the one occasion where Spain does get a serious mention, it illustrates the opposite point to the one Buchanan thinks he's making. The British ambassador in Berlin, Sir Neville Henderson, is explaining why Hitler didn't believe that Britain and France would fight over Prague: "[Hitler] argued as follows: Would the German nation willingly go to war for General Franco in Spain, if France intervened on the side of the Republican government? The answer that he gave himself is that it would not, and he was consequently convinced that no democratic French government would be strong enough to lead the French nation to war for the Czechs."

In this instance, it must be admitted, Hitler was being a rational actor.

And his admission—which Buchanan in his haste to indict Anglo-French policy completely fails to notice—is that if he himself had been resisted earlier and more determinedly, he would have been compelled to give ground. Thus the whole and complete lesson is not that the Second World War was an avoidable "war of choice." It is that the Nazis could and should have been confronted before they had fully re-armed and had begun to steal the factories and oilfields and coal mines and workers of neighboring countries. As General Douglas MacArthur once put it, all military defeats can be summarized in two words: "Too late." The same goes for political disasters.

As the book develops, Buchanan begins to unmask his true colors more and more. It is one thing to make the case that Germany was ill-used, and German minorities harshly maltreated, as a consequence of the 1914 war of which Germany's grim emperor was one of the prime instigators. It's quite another thing to say that the Nazi decision to embark on a Holocaust of European Jewry was "not a cause of the war but an awful consequence of the war." Not only is Buchanan claiming that Hitler's fanatical racism did not hugely increase the likelihood of war, but he is also making the insinuation that those who wanted to resist him are the ones who are equally if not indeed mainly responsible for the murder of the Jews! This absolutely will not do. He adduces several quotations from Hitler and Goebbels, starting only in 1939 and ending in 1942, screaming that any outbreak of war to counter Nazi ambitions would lead to a terrible vengeance on the Jews. He forgets—at least I hope it's only forgetfulness—that such murderous incitement began long, long before Hitler had even been a lunatic-fringe candidate in the 1920s. This "timeline" is as spurious, and as sinister, as the earlier dates, so carefully selected by Buchanan, that tried to make Prussian imperialism look like a victim rather than a bully.

One closing example will demonstrate the corruption and prejudice of Buchanan's historical "method." He repeatedly argues that Churchill did not appreciate Hitler's deep-seated and respectful Anglophilia, and he continually blames the war on several missed opportunities to take the Führer's genially outstretched hand. Indeed, he approvingly quotes several academic sources who agree with him that Hitler invaded the Soviet Union only in order to change Britain's mind. Suppose that Buchanan is in fact correct about this. Could we have a better definition of derangement and megalomania than the case of a dictator who overrules his own generals and invades Russia in wintertime, mainly to impress the British House of Commons? (Incidentally, or rather not incidentally, it was precisely that hysterical aggression that curtain-raised the organized deportation and slaughter of the Jews. But it's fatuous to suppose that, without that occasion, the Nazis would not have found another one.)

It is of course true that millions of other people lost their lives in this conflict, often in unprecedentedly horrible ways, and that new tyrannies were imposed on the countries—Poland, Czechoslovakia, and China most notably—that had been the pretexts for a war against fascism. But is this not to think in the short term? Unless or until Nazism had been vanquished, millions of people were most certainly going to be either massacred or enslaved in any case. Whereas today, all the way from Portugal to the Urals, the principle of human rights and popular sovereignty is at least the norm, and the ideas of racism and totalitarianism have been fairly conclusively and historically discredited. Would a frightened compromise with racist totalitarianism have produced a better result?

Winston Churchill may well have been on the wrong side about India, about the gold standard, about the rights of labor, and many other things, and he may have had a lust for war, but we may also be grateful that there was one politician in the 1930s who found it intolerable even to breathe the same air, or share the same continent or planet, as the Nazis. (Buchanan of course makes plain that he rather sympathizes with Churchill about the colonies, and quarrels only with his "finest hour." This is grotesque.) As he closes his argument, Buchanan again refuses to disguise his allegiance. "Though derided as isolationists," he writes, "the America First patriots kept the United States out of the war until six months after Hitler had invaded Russia." If you know anything at all about what happened to the population of those territories in those six months, it is rather hard to be proud that America was neutral. But this is a price that Buchanan is quite willing to pay.

I myself have written several criticisms of the cult of Churchill, and of the uncritical way that it has been used to stifle or cudgel those with misgivings. ("Adlai," said John F. Kennedy of his outstanding U.N. ambassador during the Bay of Pigs crisis, "wanted a Munich.") Yet the more the record is scrutinized and re-examined, the more creditable it seems that at least two Western statesmen, for widely different reasons, regarded coexistence with Nazism as undesirable as well as impossible. History may judge whether the undesirability or the impossibility was the more salient objection, but any attempt to separate the two considerations is likely to result in a book that stinks, as this one unmistakably does.

(*Newsweek*, June 23, 2008)

Just Give Peace a Chance?

THE VERY TITLE OF THIS BOOK, *Human Smoke,* is either very courageous or very tasteless (or conceivably both), and Nicholson Baker waits until his very last page to give us the origin of it. It is taken from the postwar interrogation of General Franz Halder, a mutinous German officer who was incarcerated in Dachau late in the war and "saw flakes of smoke blow into his cell. Human smoke, he called it." To use the ashes of Nazism's victims as the name of a polemic that says that the Second World War was not worth fighting takes a certain kind of nerve.

But of course if there had been no war it is at least thinkable that there would have been no Final Solution. It's not as if the treatment of European Jewry was in any sense part of the original *casus belli,* or even formed any part of the propaganda for the war while it was actually being fought. Instead, the opening of the camps has furnished a retrospective justification for the war: a conflict the outcome of which is probably one of the few elements of consensus still left to us.

Follow Baker's logic just a little further, and it becomes possible to imply that the war might actually have helped facilitate the Holocaust. This in turn would help make all participants in the Second World War into morally equivalent forces. And that in fact is Baker's view, as is the view not just that all wars are essentially the same, but that they are also all essentially part of

---

Review of *Human Smoke,* by Nicholson Baker.

the same war. What we call the Second World War was only an extension of the long struggle for mastery between the various European powers, all of which were all the time also wreaking indiscriminate cruelty on colonial peoples.

That there is some truth to all this is what gives pacifism its enduring appeal. Baker's narrative method is one that approximates collage. He builds up a heap of contemporary newspaper clippings, reports, and speeches, taking us at a brisk pace through the "First" World War and the volatile twenties and thirties and then slowing down as the great confrontation begins to unfold. He concludes the book on December 31, 1941, when the conflict has become truly global with Pearl Harbor, and when, as he rather tellingly puts it, "most of the people who died in the Second World War were at that moment still alive."

The ones who were to die at the hands of British and American bomber pilots are the ones who receive the greater part of Baker's compassion. If there is a villain in this book, it is certainly the Royal Air Force. Hardly a page goes by without Baker selecting a report of the British bombing of Iraq, or India, or Sudan in some colonial punitive expedition. And this, it becomes clear, is a curtain-raiser for the concept of "area bombing" and Hamburg and Dresden, with all restraint on the inflicting of civilian casualties thrown to the wind.

Some reviewers have expressed shock or even disbelief at evidence that Baker has adduced, from Winston Churchill's early anti-Semitism to the internment of anti-Nazi Jewish and German refugees in camps in Britain; from the cold decision to massacre German workers by concentrating bombs on their more closely packed housing to the open proclamation of imperialist British war aims. I myself, however, grew increasingly impatient with Baker's assumption of his own daring transgressiveness. I have mentioned all those above points in print myself, and attacked the Churchill cult from many angles, and defended the right of David Irving to publish his own revisionist screeds, but I still detect something smug and vacant in the superior attitudes struck by the peace-lover. By all means let us stipulate or concede (say) that Churchill was just as ruthless as Hitler about violating the neutrality of small European states and nations. The deformities of the anti-war faction are nonetheless threefold: They underestimate and understate the radical evil of Nazism and fascism, they forget that many "peace-loving" forces did the same at the time, and they are absolutist in their ahistoricism. A war is a war is a war, in their moral universe, and anyone engaging in one is as bad as anyone else.

Taking my above criticisms in reverse order, this would mean that if the warmonger Churchill had been in a position to intervene to save the Spanish Republic in 1936, perhaps exaggerating the threat of Franco to British interests in order to persuade Parliament and the press to endorse the use of force (as he would have had to do), he would be just as culpable. That in turn would involve regarding the old left slogan "Fascism Means War" as meaningless, either in the sense that fascism necessitated war or in the sense that fascism both desired and intended it. So I do hope that some current "anti-war" types don't find themselves tempted by Baker to abandon one of the left's finer traditions.

To the second point, Baker can't seem to get enough of the wisdom of Gandhi and cites at length an open letter he wrote to the British people on July 3, 1940. "Your soldiers are doing the same work of destruction as the Germans," wrote the Mahatma. "I want you to fight Nazism without arms." He went on to say: "Let them take possession of your beautiful island, with your many beautiful buildings. You will give all these, but neither your souls, nor your minds. If these gentlemen choose to occupy your homes, you will vacate them. If they do not give you free passage out, you will allow yourself, man, woman and child, to be slaughtered, but you will refuse to owe allegiance to them."

I must say that everything in me declines to be addressed in that tone of voice, but Baker contentedly adds the additional heart-warming observation that this very "method" of resistance, according to Gandhi, "had had considerable success in India." This is not the book's only reminder of how fatuous the pacifist position can sound, or indeed can be.

Finally one must mention the most damaging criticism of the peace-at-any-price view, which was the one noticed at the time by George Orwell. Behind all the "war never pays" rhetoric could often be detected the insinuation that the Nazis and fascists weren't really as bad as all that. On two pages to which I call your attention—pages 204 and 233—Nicholson Baker leaves the distinct impression that Hitler would have been content to ship all Europe's Jews to somewhere like Madagascar and would have done so were it not for Churchill's awful belligerence. You are perfectly free to believe this yourself, should you choose. As the book proceeds, the emollient and slightly sinister tone becomes more and more evident. A *New York Times* report of an Anglo-Soviet air raid on Berlin in late 1941, for example, is followed by Baker's comment: "These bombings immediately followed the endorsement of the peace-loving language of the Atlantic Charter." Oooh, the irony! But the Atlantic Charter—in many ways the founding document of the United Nations—was explicitly predicated on the idea that totalitarian fascism must first be destroyed.

Indeed, the little matter of democracy is entirely ignored by the self-satisfied Baker analysis. Not only are Britain and America discussed as if they were little if any better than the dictatorships of the time, but we are never even faced with the question of how much force would ever be justifiable in a war to the finish between the pluralist and the absolutist principle (in which the absolutist principle was, lest we forget, rather convincingly vanquished). In much the same way, London and Washington are reprobated for missing chances for negotiation before 1940 but Berlin doesn't draw the same standard of criticism for its decision to fight on (and to intensify genocide in the east as well as to prolong the misery of Germany) when all was obviously lost. Nor is Japanese imperialism pictured as anything much more than an island regime goaded into war by the exorbitant demands of Franklin Roosevelt. This will not do.

Baker and I share an admiration for the extraordinary courage of the German anti-war movement both civil and military, but he either doesn't know or completely forgets something that one is not entitled to overlook. When the envoys of the anti-Nazi officer corps visited London at the eleventh hour, they came to tell Chamberlain and Halifax that they could overthrow and imprison their demented Führer, *as long as Britain could be counted on to say, and to mean, that it could and would fight for Prague*. If you want to avoid a very big and very bad war later, be prepared to fight a small and principled war now. Who would not rather have removed Saddam Hussein from power in 1991, before the ruinous sanctions and during his genocide, and while he was red-handed with WMDs? Baker's book should have a contradictory effect on readers of leftist and/or anti-militarist bent: In hindsight it makes the white flag appear very dirty and the red flag look relatively clean.

(*New Statesman*, May 19, 2008)

W. G. Sebald: Requiem for Germany

THE NARRATOR of Thomas Mann's *Doctor Faustus* (1947) is relating his story against the clock, as the German homeland finds itself pulverized and encircled in the spring of 1945. He punctuates almost every chapter with contemporary tidings of apocalypse:

> This earth-shaking plummeting havoc has come breathtakingly close to my refuge several times now. The dreadful bombardment of the city of Dürer and Willibald Pirckheimer was no longer some distant event; and as the Last Judgment fell upon Munich as well, I sat here in my study, turning ashen, shaking like the walls, doors, and windowpanes of my house.

A little later comes Leipzig's turn:

> Its famous publishing district is, I sadly hear, only a heap of rubble and an immeasurable wealth of literary and educational material is now the spoil of destruction—a heavy loss not only for us Germans, but also for a whole world that cares about culture. That world, however, is apparently willing—whether blindly or correctly, I dare not decide—to take the loss into the bargain.

Review of *On the Natural History of Destruction*, by W. G. Sebald.

Almost a hundred pages later comes a thought to balance the preceding one:

> Granted, the destruction of our cities from the air has long since turned Germany into an arena of war; and yet we find it inconceivable, impermissible, to think that Germany could ever become such an arena in the true sense, and our propaganda has a curious way of warning the foe against incursion upon our soil, our sacred German soil, as if that would be some grisly atrocity... Our sacred German soil! As if anything were still sacred about it, as if it had not long ago been desecrated again and again by the immensity of our rape of justice and did not lie naked, both morally and in fact, before the power of divine judgment. Let it come!

Reeling nonetheless from the scarcely bearable consequences of his own wish, he trembles for his hometown once more:

> Awaiting our fate, beyond whose calamity no man can surmise, I have withdrawn into my hermit's cell in Freising and avoid the sight of our hideously battered Munich—the toppled statues, the façades that gaze from vacant eye sockets to disguise the yawning void behind, and yet seem inclined to reveal it, too, by supplying more of the rubble already strewn over the cobblestones.

By the opening of the penultimate chapter Mann has synthesized the two themes—first the crashing chords of *Götterdämmerung*, and second the awareness of nemesis:

> There is no stopping it: surrender on all sides, everyone scattering. Our shattered and devastated cities fall like ripe plums. Darmstadt, Würzburg, Frankfurt have succumbed. Mannheim and Kassel, even Münster, Leipzig—they all obey strangers now... Among the regime's great men, who wallowed in power, riches, and injustice, suicide rages, passing its sentence... *Whatever lived as German stands now as an abomination and the epitome of evil.* What will it be like to belong to a nation whose history bore this gruesome fiasco within it, a nation that has driven itself mad, gone psychologically bankrupt, that admittedly despairs of governing itself and thinks

> it best that it become a colony of foreign powers, a nation that will have to live in isolated confinement, like the Jews of the ghetto, because the dreadfully swollen hatred all around it will not permit it to step outside its borders—*a nation that cannot show its face*? [Italics added.]

The slightly glib analogy to Jewish ghetto life might have been forgiven by Victor Klemperer, who had been wearing a yellow star since the early 1940s in the doomed city of Dresden, and who had been gradually and humiliatingly stripped of his right to teach, to publish, to travel, to own a car, to own a *cat*, and to receive standard rations. On January 15, 1945, awaiting with dread the last roundup of Jews like himself, who had "Aryan" spouses, he heard of an anti-Nazi broadcast made by Thomas Mann from America. The fellow sufferer who described the broadcast, as they cowered together in a cellar, told Klemperer, "[It was] splendid—it gave my spirits such a lift!" Klemperer himself was more skeptical, admiring Mann as he always had, but suspecting him of having taken sides only when the outcome was clear. He also took some dry pleasure in informing his interlocutor that Mann was not a Jew, even though he was wed to one.

How to describe the experience of reading Klemperer's two-volume diary, *I Will Bear Witness* (1998 and 1999), and, so to speak, knowing what is going to happen before he does? He registered every premonition, both of the aerial destruction of Germany and of the simultaneous extirpation of the Jews, an extirpation that became more frenzied *and* more cold-blooded as the Hitler regime imploded. Klemperer clearly desired that the latter calamity might be forestalled—but without the necessity for the former. In a reckoning so ironic and fateful that even Faustus himself might have gasped at it, he and his wife were saved by the immolation of Dresden, on February 13 and 14, 1945, beginning just a few hours after they had been informed that all remaining Jewish spouses must report for deportation, which they both understood to be the end. The now overworked word "holocaust" means literally "destruction by fire": The old Klemperer couple escaped holocaust in one sense by passing through it in another. On the smoldering morrow they took advantage of the utter havoc, removed Victor's yellow star, and set off on foot toward survival and, ultimately, liberation.

Klemperer's journals have in common with Mann's writing an extraordinary and admirable quality: the blunt refusal to concede a particle of German pride to the gangrenous rabble of the Nazi Party. This is why both writers lend such emphasis to the magnificence of German civilization, whether expressed in architecture or painting or philosophy, and it is also why neither does so uncritically. Mann argued with himself in California, in what must have been exceedingly dark nights of the soul, by balancing his horror of a German defeat against his loathing for a German victory. Klemperer, for all his liberalism and all his rooted distrust for the similarity between Nazi slogans and Communist ones, eventually opted for East Germany as the inheritor of the "better" tradition. For those of us who never had to face such appalling choices, the question to be resolved at a distance and after a lengthy pause is, Can the survival of the Klemperers, weighed on a scale of ultimate judgment, balance or cancel the mass killing in Dresden? This is, without its being defined quite so strenuously, the question confronted by the author of *On the Natural History of Destruction*.

W. G. Sebald, whose premature death, in December of 2001, is still being mourned by all who love writing for its own sake, was quite willing to face the quasi-biblical implications that are involved here. And he could not avoid references to Teutonic antiquity and the ghastly, sanguinary struggles with Roman imperialism. Here is Sebald in *On the Natural History of Destruction*:

> And while [Fritz] Lang, in Babelsberg, turned Thea von Harbou's visions into images capable of reproduction for German cinema audiences, a decade before Hitler seized power the logisticians of the Wehrmacht were already working on their own Cheruscan fantasy, a truly terrifying script which provided for the annihilation of the French army on German soil, the devastation of whole areas of the country, and high losses among the civilian population. Even the originator and chief advocate of strategic extremism, General von Stülpnagel, could probably not have envisaged the ultimate outcome of this new battle of the Teutoburger Wald, which left great expanses of the German cities in ruins. Later, our vague feelings of shared guilt prevented anyone, including the writers whose task it

> was to keep the nation's collective memory alive, from being permitted to remind us of such humiliating images as the incident in the Altmarkt in Dresden, where 6,865 corpses were burned on pyres in February 1945 by an SS detachment which had gained its experience at Treblinka.

But even as Sebald underlines a very direct moral connection between the charnel house of Dresden and the revolting crimes of Nazism, he appears to be making his own subtle challenge to the official and unofficial "script." What is meant, for example, by "vague feelings of shared guilt"? Postwar Germans were approximately divided between those who indignantly disowned "guilt"—which ought surely to be placed on the active rather than the passive citizenry—and those who steadily accepted "responsibility." The crucial word here may be the rather weak and compromising "shared." Willy Brandt, who had worn the uniform of another army in combating Hitler (and who was never forgiven for it by the German right), proposed that although not all Germans could or should be held to collective guilt, there was nonetheless a general or collective responsibility. In stating this he was both brave and generous. But then look at Sebald's other weak qualifier. I certainly can't picture Herr Brandt describing this emotion or conviction as "vague." *Vague?* Remember what we are talking about. And Sebald isn't at all vague when he assigns to "writers" the "task" of keeping "the nation's collective memory alive." Suppose we agree that writers have national "tasks" in the first place, and that we further concede that a battle against amnesia forms a portion of such a task. Vagueness on certain points would then become an enemy to be contested with some vigor.

Quite by accident, the rather prosaic Chancellor Helmut Kohl came up with a sonorous phrase during the 1980s. Weathering one of the many periodic tempests that bring the terrible past to life in his country (it may well have been after his clumsy suggestion that Ronald Reagan lay a wreath at a cemetery where SS members had been interred ["*Ich bin ein Bitburger*"]), he ingenuously referred to himself as protected by "the grace of late birth." The element of luck, it might be said, was more conspicuous than that of grace.

But everybody knew what Kohl meant. As if to demonstrate the burden of history and the uneven distribution of its weight, a huge success has recently attended Antony Beevor's heart-freezing account (*The Fall of Berlin 1945*) of the rape and murder and humiliation that fell on Germans in the territory taken by the Soviet army in 1945. The book's publication in Germany provoked an uprush of repressed memory and shame that filled pages of newsprint: One of the girls battered and defiled by Stalin's soldiers had been, it turned out, Hannelore Kohl, the late wife of the ex-Chancellor. In common with a rather large number of German women and girls, she had evidently realized in the postwar period that nobody was likely to be very much moved by her story.

Not only was W. G. Sebald protected by "the grace of late birth"—he was born in 1944—but he chose to spend the greater part of his life in England. Indeed, he spent thirty years at the University of East Anglia, in the city of Norwich. The flatness of the East Anglian landscape, and its proximity to the North Sea, made it an ideal launching ground for the Royal Air Force during the war, as it does for the USAF today. As Sebald phrases it,

> Many of the more than seventy airfields from which the war of annihilation was waged against Germany were in the county of Norfolk. Some ten of them are still military bases, and a few others are now used by flying clubs, but most were abandoned after the war. Grass has grown over the runways, and the dilapidated control towers, bunkers, and corrugated iron huts stand in an often eerie landscape where you sense the dead souls of the men who never came back from their missions, and of those who perished in the vast fires. I live very close to Seething airfield. I sometimes walk my dog there, and imagine what the place was like when the aircraft took off with their heavy freight and flew out over the sea, making for Germany. Two years before these flights began, a Luftwaffe Dornier plane crashed in a field not far from my house during a raid on Norwich. One of the four crew members who lost their lives, Lieutenant Bollert, shared a birthday with me and was the same age as my father.
>
> So much for the few points at which my own life touches the history of the air war. Entirely insignificant in themselves, they have none the less haunted my mind, and finally impelled me to go at least a little way into the question of why German writers would not

> or could not describe the destruction of the German cities as millions experienced it.

I feel a tug of empathy when I read this melancholy account, complete with its Dickensian place-name of "Seething." I was born only five years after Sebald, and was brought up on and around British naval and air bases, and spent much time playing on disused airfields. The cities of my boyhood—most notably Portsmouth and Plymouth, but also Valletta, in Malta—still exhibited enormous scars from the Nazi blitzkrieg. Yet for me and for my cohort, all of this was a cause for pride, and excitement, and made us ready to listen to our fathers as they—with sometimes feigned reluctance—unfolded their war stories. What must it be like to have this in one's immediate past, yet with no cause for affirmation, let alone celebration? And why should my German contemporaries feel inhibited about discussing the erasure of great cities and churches and monuments in their country, to say nothing of the killing of numberless civilians? There are many British people who feel that needless harm was done, and cruelty inflicted; and the unveiling in London a decade ago of a statue to Air Chief Marshal Arthur "Bomber" Harris, the architect of the air campaign against Germany, was attended by some forceful protests in print and on the streets.

Looking over Sebald's evocative paragraphs, though, I find that I pause immediately at the terse way in which he says "war of annihilation." I also wince a bit at the way he mourns the Luftwaffe crew slightly more than he regrets the "raid" on Norwich. I don't do this, I trust, for any insular or tribal reason. In a letter left for his sons, the late Heinrich Böll told them that they would always be able to tell everything about another German by noticing whether this fellow citizen, in conversation, described April 1945 as "the defeat" or as "the liberation." Thomas Mann and Victor Klemperer were quite decided on this point, and they really did write about—and in the latter case endure—the very calamity that Sebald says is somehow unmentionable. (Böll's novel *The Silent Angel*, a book that unflinchingly discusses the ruins and the corpses, was written at the end of the 1940s but, as Sebald points out, not published until 1992.) Still, if one takes as one's standard the work and thought of the German oppositionists and dissidents, one is employing a measure that does nothing but give credit to German culture and tradition.

More recently another book, which seemingly seeks to reopen the same question in a different way, has been published in Germany. *Der Brand (The Fire)*, by the historian Jörg Friedrich, accuses Winston Churchill of a conscious policy of airborne terrorism against civilians. The right-wing mass-circulation tabloid *Das Bild* has called Churchill a war criminal in its editorial pages and, in serializing Friedrich's work, has demanded recognition of German suffering. The word "brand" in English, of course, carries a distinctly different vernacular meaning.

At times Sebald seems to want to have this both ways. He invites us to read the letters he received from German readers after he first broached this subject, in a series of public lectures in Zurich in 1997, and thus we discover that a certain combination of arrogance and self-pity, of the kind Christopher Isherwood noticed in his landlady in *Goodbye to Berlin*, is still around, and still tinged with anti-Semitism. Sebald stipulates what otherwise I would find myself pedantically pointing out: that the Nazi regime had its own plans for the destruction of other people's cities. (Even in 1945, when all was lost, the wretches amid the rubble of Germany were officially cheered up by the news that the Führer's ultimate "wonder-weapons"—the guided V1 and V2 missiles—were falling on London.) Indeed, it is possible to imagine that if anti-Jewish paranoia had not deprived the Third Reich of so many gifted physicists, the unthinkable might have occurred. Thus most people outside Germany itself still tend to shrug at the horror, if they agree to discuss it at all, as if to say, Well, what goes around comes around. And those non-Germans who have drawn attention to the promiscuously inflicted devastation are suspected of a covert sympathy for the other side.

This doesn't relieve the rest of us of some responsibility. After all, the fire-bombing of Dresden was so appallingly total that it might just as easily have killed Victor Klemperer (who was injured in the eye and for a while separated from his wife by the chaos) as rescued him. Few historians or strategists now argue that the bombing made much if any difference to the outcome of the war, and it may have been conducted partly to reassure Joseph Stalin, who always feared that the British and the Americans might conclude a separate peace. The opening of official papers long ago permitted us to read Lord

Cherwell's advice to Churchill that bombs should be concentrated on working-class housing, to maximize casualties; and one objects not just to the studied deliberation of this but also to the fact that these districts were the heart of anti-Nazi resistance in anti-Nazi cities like Hamburg. (So *that* was where all the "good Germans" went—into the firestorms of the RAF.)

Then one has to face the fact that Henry Morgenthau nearly achieved the adoption of his plan, which was to consummate the violent, dramatic depopulation of Germany and a subsequent reduction of its survivors to a servile or peasant status. The Churchill-Roosevelt papers tell the story of how, at the Quebec and Hyde Park conferences of 1944, Churchill accepted this idea (preferring to call it a "pastoral" solution to the German problem) after having initially described it as "unnatural, unChristian and unnecessary." He and Roosevelt then turned their attention to the deployment of nuclear weaponry, first directly against Japan and then—at least in Churchill's mind—as a means of impressing the Soviet Union. Thanks to Cordell Hull and Henry Stimson, the Morgenthau plan was not adopted in the postwar American and British zones, though the USSR did denude eastern Germany of much of its productive industrial capacity. And it might now be admitted that the Cold War's half acceptance of "two Germanys"—a policy that left a new generation of East Germans to grow up without any experience of democracy—was paradoxically conditioned by the same feeling of "woe to the conquered." (Interesting that we still employ the German word *Schadenfreude* when speaking of a cruel sense of satisfaction, as if nationalizing an emotion that is common to all.) However, it can be pointed out without too much defensiveness that American and British soldiers did not, upon their arrival in Germany, commit atrocities against civilians on the ground. This is much more than can be said for the legions of either Hitler or Stalin, and it must qualify any suggestion that the war against Nazism was allowed to become a war of "annihilation."

It is probably the creditably peaceful and democratic reunification of Germany that has impelled—or perhaps permitted—Sebald and other writers to revisit the half-buried past. Even Günter Grass, who opposed what he absurdly called the 1989 "Anschluss" with the eastern *lander*, and who could never utter a public word on local politics without emphasizing Auschwitz, has now published a novel (*Crabwalk*) about the suffering of German refugees in the closing moments of the war. I have already mentioned the terrible atrocities committed by the Red Army; the mass expulsion, dispossession, and killing of German-speaking minorities in the Czech lands and Hungary after 1945 has also recently become an issue that respectable people may mention without incurring suspicion. Sebald approaches this thicket very deftly, making good use of his long residence in England. He describes how in the 1980s he went to see Solly Zuckerman, who had been one of Churchill's circle of military-intellectual advisers on "area bombing." After the war Zuckerman had hastened to Cologne, to indulge his professional interest by viewing the results. He found that he was unable to summon any adequate words for what he saw. ("All that remained in his mind was the image of the blackened cathedral rising from the stony desert around it, and the memory of a severed finger that he had found on a heap of rubble.") It had been his intention, Zuckerman told Sebald, to compose an essay for Cyril Connolly's magazine *Horizon*. But he was unable to produce it. The working title of the never-written article was "On the Natural History of Destruction"...

In *Doctor Faustus*, Mann stated the problem that Sebald confronts: "It is not far from capitulation to pure abdication and the offer to let the victor go right ahead and govern the affairs of the fallen nation just as he pleases, since for its part that nation no longer knows up from down." Hans Magnus Enzensberger, the most astute and mordant of the German critics, phrased it more dialectically when he argued that this very docility was a source of strength. "The mysterious energy of the Germans" could not be understood, he wrote, "if we refuse to realize that they have made a virtue of their deficiencies. Insensibility was the condition of their success." The British liked to put this in an unworthily scornful tone. The Germans, one used to hear it said in my father's circles, are either at your throat or at your feet...But Sebald's well-chosen excerpts from Janet Flanner's reportage, and from the Swedish writer Stig Dagerman, suggest a missing element of German stoicism. Dagerman noticed that he could easily be identified as a foreigner on a train passing through the leveled city of Hamburg because he was the only one staring out the window.

With a part of themselves, thinking Germans obviously understood that their late Führer not only brought this devastation on them but actually wished it on them. He had preferred an immolated nation to a surrendered one. So the surrender was, in an admittedly less than glorious way, a double defeat for the madman. Even though no Western reporter worth his salt has since neglected any story, however trivial, that suggests a stirring of neo-Nazism, no German constituency worth its salt has ever shown any real interest in endorsing such a thing. In European discussions the most punctilious internationalists are the Germans, whose government even surrendered the special symbol of its deutsch mark to the idea of a Europeanized Germany. The large majority of refugees from the recent Balkan wars found hospitality on German soil. Nobody except the left-Green Joschka Fischer has really ever been able to commit or persuade Germans to send their troops overseas. Even the provincial-minded campaign run by Gerhard Schröder a few months ago illustrated this same point, in a different if less noble way.

In the past few years I have spent time with courageous Serbian dissidents, including veteran partisans for wartime Yugoslavia, who came to the point at which they welcomed and supported the NATO bombing of Belgrade and the military defeat of Milošević's "willing executioners." These days I have been talking to a number of Iraqi exiles and oppositionists who, with infinite pain but impressive honesty, have taken a similar position. These patriots do not want their country to humiliate or murder others, and neither do they wish their country to be humiliated or destroyed. (One has not just to hope but to demand that our war planners bear this in mind.) Germany suffered both those disgraces to the fullest possible extent, and Sebald registers that contradiction to the limit of his ability. His opening bid deserves criticism, as I hope I have shown. But how depressing it is to reflect that he did not live to take part in the discussion that his book ought still to inaugurate.

(*The Atlantic*, January/February 2003)

Words' Worth

When the King Saved God

AFTER SHE WAS elected the first female governor of Texas, in 1924, and got herself promptly embroiled in an argument about whether Spanish should be used in Lone Star schools, it is possible that Miriam A. "Ma" Ferguson did *not* say, "If the King's English was good enough for Jesus Christ, it's good enough for the children of Texas." I still rather hope that she did. But then, verification of quotations and sources is a tricky and sensitive thing. Abraham Lincoln lay dying in a room full of educated and literate men, in the age of the wireless telegraph, and not far from the offices of several newspapers, and we *still* do not know for sure, at the moment when his great pulse ceased to beat, whether his secretary of war, Edwin Stanton, said, "Now he belongs to the ages" or "Now he belongs to the angels."

Such questions of authenticity become even more fraught when they involve the word itself becoming flesh; the fulfillment of prophecy; the witnessing of miracles; the detection of the finger of God. Guesswork and approximation will not do: The resurrection cannot be half true or questionably attested. For the first 1,500 years of the Christian epoch, this problem of "authority," in both senses of that term, was solved by having the divine mandate wrapped up in languages that the majority of the congregation could not understand, and by having it presented to them by a special caste or class who alone possessed the mystery of celestial decoding.

Four hundred years ago, just as William Shakespeare was reaching the height of his powers and showing the new scope and variety of the English language, and just as "England" itself was becoming more of a nation-state and less an offshore dependency of Europe, an extraordinary committee of clergymen and scholars completed the task of rendering the Old and New Testaments into English, and claimed that the result was the "Authorized" or "King James" version. This was a fairly conservative attempt to stabilize the Crown and the kingdom, heal the breach between competing English and Scottish Christian sects, and bind the majesty of the King to his devout people. "The powers that be," it had Saint Paul saying in his Epistle to the Romans, "are ordained of God." This and other phrasings, not all of them so authoritarian and conformist, continue to echo in our language: "When I was a child, I spake as a child"; "Eat, drink, and be merry"; "From strength to strength"; "Grind the faces of the poor"; "salt of the earth"; "Our Father, which art in heaven." It's near impossible to imagine our idiom and vernacular, let alone our liturgy, without them. Not many committees in history have come up with such crystalline prose.

King James I, who brought the throne of Scotland along with him, was the son of Mary, Queen of Scots, and knew that his predecessor, Queen Elizabeth I, had been his mother's executioner. In Scotland, he had had to contend with extreme Puritans who were suspicious of monarchy and hated all Catholics. In England, he was faced with worldly bishops who were hostile to Puritans and jealous of their own privileges. Optimism, prosperity, and culture struck one note—Henry Hudson was setting off to the Northwest Passage, and Shakespeare's Globe Theatre was drawing thoughtful crowds to see those dramas of power and legitimacy *Othello, King Lear*, and *The Tempest*—but terror and insecurity kept pace. Guy Fawkes and his fellow plotters, believed to be in league with the Pope, nearly succeeded in blowing up Parliament in 1605. Much of London was stricken with visitations of the bubonic plague, which, as Bishop Lancelot Andrewes (head of the committee of translators) noted with unease, appeared to strike the godly quite as often as it smote the sinner. The need was for a tempered version of God's word that engendered compromise and a sense of protection.

Bishop Andrewes and his colleagues, a mixture of clergymen and classicists, were charged with revisiting the original Hebrew and Greek editions of the Old and New Testaments, along with the fragments of Aramaic that had found their way into the text. Understanding that their task was a patriotic and "nation-building" one (and impressed by the nascent idea of English Manifest Destiny, whereby the English people had replaced the Hebrews as God's chosen), whenever they could translate any ancient word for "people" or "tribe" as "nation," they elected to do so. The term appears 454 times in this confident form of "the King's English." Meeting in Oxford and Cambridge college libraries for the most part, they often kept their notes in Latin. Their conservative and consensual project was politically short-lived: In a few years the land was to be convulsed with civil war, and the Puritan and parliamentary forces under Oliver Cromwell would sweep the head of King Charles I from his shoulders. But the translators' legacy remains, and it is paradoxically a revolutionary one, as well as a giant step in the maturing of English literature.

Imagining the most extreme form of totalitarianism in his *Nineteen Eighty-four* dystopia, George Orwell depicted a secret class of occult power holders (the Inner Party clustered around Big Brother) that would cement its eternal authority by recasting the entire language. In the tongue of "Newspeak," certain concepts of liberty and conscience would be literally impossible to formulate. And only within the most restricted circles of the regime would certain heretical texts, like Emmanuel Goldstein's manifesto, still be legible and available. I believe that Orwell, a strong admirer of the Protestant Reformation and the poetry of its hero John Milton, was using as his original allegory the long struggle of English dissenters to have the Bible made available in a language that the people could read.

Until the early middle years of the sixteenth century, when King Henry VIII began to quarrel with Rome about the dialectics of divorce and decapitation, a short and swift route to torture and death was the attempt to print the Bible in English. It's a long and stirring story, and its crux is the head-to-head battle between Sir Thomas More and William Tyndale (whose name in early life, I am proud to say, was William Hychyns). Their combat fully merits the term "fundamental." Infuriating More, Tyndale whenever possible was loyal to the Protestant spirit by correctly translating the word *ecclesia* to mean "the congregation" as an autonomous body, rather than "the church" as a sacrosanct institution above human law. In English churches, state-selected priests would merely incant the liturgy. Upon hearing the words "Hoc" and "corpus" (in the "For this is my body" passage), newly literate and impatient artisans in the pews would mockingly whisper, "Hocus-pocus," finding a tough slang term for the religious obfuscation at which they were beginning to chafe. The cold and righteous More, backed by his "Big Brother" the Pope and leading an inner party of spies and inquisitors, watched the Channel ports for smugglers risking everything to import sheets produced by Tyndale, who was forced to do his translating and printing from exile. The rack and the rope were not stinted with dissenters, and eventually Tyndale himself was tracked down, strangled, and publicly burned. (Hilary Mantel's masterpiece historical novel, *Wolf Hall*, tells this exciting and gruesome story in such a way as to revise the shining image of "Saint" Thomas More, the "man for all seasons," almost out of existence. High time, in my view. The martyrdoms he inflicted upon others were more cruel and irrational than the one he sought and found for himself.)

Other translations into other languages, by Martin Luther himself, among others, slowly entered circulation. One of them, the so-called Geneva Bible, was a more Calvinist and Puritan English version than the book that King James commissioned, and was the edition which the Pilgrim Fathers, fleeing the cultural and religious war altogether, took with them to Plymouth Rock. Thus Governor Ma Ferguson was right in one respect: America was the first and only Christian society that could take an English Bible for granted, and never had to struggle for a popular translation of "the good book." The question, rather, became that of exactly *which* English version was to be accepted as the correct one. After many false starts and unsatisfactory printings, back in England, the Anglican conclave in 1611 adopted William Tyndale's beautiful rendering almost wholesale, and out of their zeal for compromise and stability ironically made a posthumous hero out of one of the greatest literary dissidents and subversives who ever lived.

Writing about his own fascination with cadence and rhythm in *Notes of a Native Son*, James Baldwin said, "I hazard that the King James Bible, the rhetoric of the store-front church, something ironic and violent and perpetually understated in Negro speech... have something to do with me today; but I wouldn't stake my life on it." As a child of the black pulpit and chronicler of the Bible's huge role in the American oral tradition, Baldwin probably was "understating" at that very moment. And, as he very well knew, there had been times when biblical verses *did* involve, quite literally, the staking of one's life. This is why the nuances and details of translation were (and still are) of such huge moment. For example, in Isaiah 7:14 it is stated that "behold, a virgin shall conceive, and bear a son, and shall call his name Immanuel." This is the scriptural warrant and prophecy for the impregnation of the Virgin Mary by the Holy Ghost. But the original Hebrew wording refers only to the pregnancy of an *almah*, or young woman. If the Hebrew language wants to identify virginity, it has other terms in which to do so. The implications are not merely textual. To translate is also to interpret; or, indeed, to lay down the law. (Incidentally, the American "Revised Standard Version" of 1952 replaced the word "virgin" with "young woman." It took the Fundamentalists until 1978 to restore the original misreading, in the now dominant "New International Version.")

Take an even more momentous example, cited by Adam Nicolson in his very fine book on the process, *God's Secretaries*. In the First Epistle to the Corinthians, Saint Paul reminds his readers of the fate that befell many backsliding pre-Christian Jews. He describes their dreadful punishments as having "happened unto them for ensamples," which in 1611 was a plain way of conveying the word "example" or "illustrative instance," or perhaps "lesson."

However, the original Greek term was *typoi*, which by contrast may be rendered as "types" or "archetypes" and suggests that Jews were to be eternally punished for their special traits. This had been Saint Augustine's harsh reading, followed by successive Roman Catholic editions. At least one of King James's translators wanted to impose that same collective punishment on the people of Moses, but was overruled. In the main existing text, the lenient word "ensamples" is given, with a marginal note in the original editions saying that "types" may also be meant. The English spirit of compromise at its best.

Then there are seemingly small but vital matters of emphasis, in which Tyndale did not win every round. Here is a famous verse which one might say was central to Christian teaching: "This is my Commandment, that you love one another, as I have loved you. / Greater love hath no man than this, that a man lay down his life for his friends." That's the King James version, which has echoed in the heads of many churchgoers until their last hour. Here is how the verse read when first translated by Tyndale: "This is my Commandment, that you love together as I have loved you. / Greater love than this hath no man, than that a man bestow his life for his friends."

I do not find that the "King's English" team improved much on the lovely simplicity of what they found. Tyndale has Jesus groping rather appealingly to make a general precept or principle out of a common bond, whereas the bishops and scholars are aiming to make an iron law out of love. In doing so they suggest strenuous martyrdom ("lay down," as if Jesus had been a sacrifice to his immediate circle only). Far more human and attractive, surely, is Tyndale's warm "bestow," which suggests that a life devoted to friendship is a noble thing in itself.

Tyndale, incidentally, was generally good on the love question. Take that same Epistle of Paul to the Corinthians, a few chapters later. For years, I would listen to it in chapel and wonder how an insipid, neuter word like "charity" could have gained such moral prestige. The King James version enjoins us that "now abideth faith, hope and charity, these three; but the greatest of these is charity." Tyndale had put "love" throughout, and even if your Greek is as poor as mine you will have to admit that it is a greatly superior capture of the meaning of that all-important original word *agape*. It was actually the frigid clerical bureaucrat Thomas More who had made this into one of the many disputations between himself and Tyndale, and in opting to accept his ruling it seems as if King James's committee also hoped to damp down the risky, ardent spontaneity of unconditional love and replace it with an idea of stern duty. Does not the notion of compulsory love, in any form, have something grotesque and fanatical about it?

Most recent English translations have finally dropped More and the King and gone with Tyndale on this central question, but often at the cost of making "love" appear too husky and sentimental. Thus the "Good News Bible" for American churches, first published in 1966: "Love never gives up; and its faith, hope and patience never fail." This doesn't read at all like the outcome of a struggle to discern the essential meaning of what is perhaps our most numinous word. It more resembles a smiley-face Dale Carnegie reassurance. And, as with everything else that's designed to be instant, modern, and "accessible," it goes out of date (and out of *time*) faster than Wisconsin cheddar.

Though I am sometimes reluctant to admit it, there really *is* something "timeless" in the Tyndale/King James synthesis. For generations, it provided a common stock of references and allusions, rivaled only by Shakespeare in this respect. It resounded in the minds and memories of literate people, as well as of those who acquired it only by listening. From the stricken beach of Dunkirk in 1940, faced with a devil's choice between annihilation and surrender, a British officer sent a cable back home. It contained the three words "but if not..." All of those who received it were at once aware of what it signified. In the Book of Daniel, the Babylonian tyrant Nebuchadnezzar tells the three Jewish heretics Shadrach, Meshach, and Abednego that if they refuse to bow to his sacred idol they will be flung into a "burning fiery furnace." They made him an answer: "If it be so, our god whom we serve is able to deliver us from the burning fiery furnace, and he will deliver us out of thy hand, O King. / *But if not*, be it known unto thee, o king, that we will not serve thy gods, nor worship the golden image which thou hast set up."

A culture that does not possess this common store of image and allegory will be a perilously thin one. To seek restlessly to update it or make it "relevant" is to miss the point, like yearning for a hip-hop Shakespeare. "Man is born unto trouble as the sparks fly upward," says the Book of Job. Want to try to improve that for Twitter? And so bleak and spare and fatalistic—almost non-religious—are the closing verses of Ecclesiastes that they were read at the Church of England funeral service the unbeliever George Orwell had requested in his will: "Also when they shall be afraid of that which is high, and fears shall be in the way, and the almond tree shall flourish, and the grasshopper shall be a burden, and desire shall fail: because man goeth to his long home.... Or ever the silver cord be loosed, or the golden bowl be broken, or the pitcher be broken at the fountain, or the wheel broken at the cistern. / Then shall the dust return to the earth as it was."

At my father's funeral I chose to read a similarly non-sermonizing part of the New Testament, this time an injunction from Saint Paul's Epistle to the Philippians: "Finally, brethren, whatsoever things are true, whatsoever things are honest, whatsoever things are just, whatsoever things are pure, whatsoever things are lovely, whatsoever things are of good report; if there be any virtue, and if there be any praise, think on these things."

As much philosophical as spiritual, with its conditional and speculative "ifs" and its closing advice—always italicized in my mind since first I heard it—to *think* and reflect on such matters: This passage was the labor of men who had wrought deeply with ideas and concepts. I now pluck down from my shelf the American Bible Society's "Contemporary English Version," which I picked up at an evangelical "Promise Keepers" rally on the Mall in Washington in 1997. Claiming to be faithful to the spirit of the King James translation, it keeps its promise in this way: "Finally, my friends, keep your minds on whatever is true, pure, right, holy, friendly and proper. Don't ever stop thinking about what is truly worthwhile and worthy of praise."

Pancake-flat: Suited perhaps to a basement meeting of A.A., these words could not hope to penetrate the torpid, resistant fog in the mind of a sixteen-year-old boy, as their original had done for me. There's perhaps a slightly ingratiating obeisance to gender neutrality in the substitution of "my friends" for "brethren," but to suggest that Saint Paul, of all people, was gender-neutral is to re-write the history as well as to rinse out the prose. When the Church of England effectively dropped King James, in the 1960s, and issued what would become the "New English Bible," T. S. Eliot commented that the result was astonishing "in its combination of the vulgar, the trivial and the pedantic." (Not surprising from the author of *For Lancelot Andrewes*.) This has been true of every other stilted, patronizing, literal-minded attempt to shift the translation's emphasis from plangent poetry to utilitarian prose.

T. S. Eliot left America (and his annoyingly colorless Unitarian family) to seek the traditionalist roots of liturgical and literary tradition in England. Coming in the opposite direction across the broad Atlantic, the King James Bible slowly overhauled and overtook the Geneva version, and, as the Pilgrim-type mini-theocracies of New England withered away, became one of the very few books from which almost any American could quote something. Paradoxically, this made it easy to counterfeit. When Joseph Smith began to fabricate his Book of Mormon, in the late 1820s, "translating" it from no known language, his copy of King James was never far from his side. He plagiarized 27,000 words more or less straight from the original, including several biblical stories lifted almost in their entirety, and the throat-clearing but vaguely impressive phrase "and it came to pass" is used at least 2,000 times. Such "borrowing" was a way of lending much-needed "tone" to the racket. Not long afterward, William Miller excited gigantic crowds with the news that the Second Coming of Jesus would occur in 1843. An associate followed up with an 1844 due date. These disappointed prophecies were worked out from marginal notes in Miller's copy of the King James edition, which he quarried for apocalyptic evidence. (There had always been those, from the earliest days, when it was being decided which parts of the Bible were divinely inspired and which were not, who had striven to leave out the Book of Revelation. Martin Luther himself declined to believe that it was the work of the Holy Spirit. But there Christianity still is, well and truly stuck with it.) So, of the many Christian heresies which were born in the New World and not imported from Europe, at least three—the Mormons, or Latter-Day Saints; the Millerites, or Seventh-Day Adventists; and their schismatic product the Jehovah's Witnesses—are indirectly mutated from a pious attempt to bring religious consensus to Jacobean England.

Not to over-prize consensus, it does possess certain advantages over randomness and chaos. Since the appearance of the so-called "Good News Bible," there have been no fewer than forty-eight English translations published in the United States. And the rate shows no sign of slackening. Indeed, the trend today is toward what the trade calls "niche Bibles." These include the "Couples Bible," "One Year New Testament for Busy Moms," "Extreme Teen Study Bible," "Policeman's Bible," and—somehow unavoidably—the "Celebrate Recovery Bible." (Give them credit for one thing: The biblical sales force knows how to "be fruitful and multiply.") In this cut-price spiritual cafeteria, interest groups and even individuals can have their own customized version of God's word. But there will no longer be a culture of the kind which instantly recognized what Lincoln meant when he spoke of "a house divided." The gradual eclipse of a single structure has led, not to a new clarity, but to a new Babel.

Those who opposed the translation of the Bible into the vernacular—rather like those Catholics who wish the Mass were still recited in Latin, or those Muslims who regard it as profane to render the Koran out of Arabic—were afraid that the mystic potency of incantation and ritual would be lost, and that daylight would be let in upon magic. They also feared that if God's word became too everyday and commonplace it would become less impressive, or less able to inspire awe. But the reverse turns out to have been the case, at least in this instance. The Tyndale/King James translation, even if all its copies were to be burned, would still live on in our language through its transmission by way of Shakespeare and Milton and Bunyan and Coleridge, and also by way of beloved popular idioms such as "fatted calf" and "pearls before swine." It turned out to be rather more than the sum of its ancient predecessors, as well as a repository and edifice of language which towers above its successors. Its abandonment by the Church of England establishment, which hoped to refill its churches and ended up denuding them, is yet another demonstration that religion is man-made, with inky human fingerprints all over its supposedly inspired and unalterable texts. Ma Ferguson was right in her way. She just didn't know how many Englishmen and how many Englishes, and how many Jesus stories and Jesuses, there were to choose from.

(*Vanity Fair*, May 2011)

Let Them Eat Pork Rinds

> And even in Atlantis
> of the legend
> The night the seas
> rushed in:
> The drowning men
> still bellowed
> for their slaves.

These lines are taken from Bertolt Brecht's magnificent poem "A Worker Reads History." These days, people associate Brecht with old Red cartoons in which men in shiny top hats spit on the poor while wielding truncheon-size cigars and flourishing gold watch chains across their distended bow-window waistcoats. And surely that epoch of ruling-class arrogance is in our past? Of course it is, but that doesn't mean that certain instincts and attitudes just evaporate. Here was the American president's mother, speaking grandly from Texas as the descendants of slaves took refuge in the Astrodome after the seas had rushed in upon their city:

> What I'm hearing, which is sort of scary, is they all want to stay in Texas. Everyone is so overwhelmed by the hospitality. And so many of the people in the arena here, you know, were underprivileged anyway, so this, this is working very well for them.

The White House was later to qualify these gorgeously phrased insults as "personal observation," which indeed they were. The unmediated personal observation, that is, of a very much overprivileged person. They made a good "fit" with the performance of her son on his visit to the submerged region. Meeting two sisters who had only the clothes on their backs, the president of the United States directed them to a Salvation Army shelter down the road. The shelter itself, as an embarrassed aide was quick to whisper, had been swept away. But the point was the same and contains the tone of the workhouse master down the ages: "You appear to be distinctly poor and fucked up. Do you not have a church basement to go to?" Even at such critical moments, the "faith-based initiative" takes priority. The poor we have always with us. And the rich we have always with us, too. Various benign arrangements will take care of the latter, while the former are better off on their knees and should pray as hard as they can. Perhaps a tract on "intelligent design" to go with that bowl of nourishing gruel?

The subconscious mentality of the uncontrollably well-off was deftly caught by the novelist Joyce Cary (a chap, despite his name), who evolved the phrase "tumbril remark" to catch the essence of polite upper-class incredulity at the sheer inconvenience of having to put up with other people. My preferred example of the remark was once given by the late British Tory politician Julian Amery, who described an acquaintance of his (was it Lady Diana Cooper?—there's an element of the apocryphal to some of these tales) as she waited under an umbrella outside the Dorchester hotel in the 1930s and tapped her foot with impatience as the Rolls was brought round to the front. Seizing his chance, a ragged man approached her without the courtesy of an introduction and announced that he had not eaten anything for three days. The outraged Lady Diana drew herself up. "Foolish man that you are," she instructed him. "You must try. If need be, you must force yourself."

Wilde's Lady Bracknell could hardly have bettered this. ("Fortunately in England, at any rate, education produces no effect whatsoever," she says. "If it did, it would prove a serious danger to the upper classes, and probably lead to acts of violence in Grosvenor Square.") Yet it's easy to cull non-apocryphal tumbrilisms. Let me introduce George Orwell, who was writing a wartime diary in 1940 as London braced for the Blitz. He noted:

> From a letter from Lady Oxford to the *Daily Telegraph*, on the subject of war economies:
>
> "Since most London houses are deserted there is little entertaining... In any case, most people have to part with their cooks and live in hotels."

Commenting on these perfectly wonderful uses of "most," Orwell noted, "Apparently nothing will ever teach these people that the other 99% of the population exists." Lady Oxford, by the way, was the title of the great socialite and memoirist Margot Asquith. And the decade then just closing—the 1930s—was the scene of some splendid tumbril stuff. The diaries of Sir Henry "Chips" Channon provide an especially rich seam, as he describes toddling off to Savile Row to spend a king's ransom on socks and scarves, before lunching at the German Embassy with the divine Herr and Frau Ribbentrop—the dessert consisting on one occasion of lobster ice cream. What a nuisance, though, to have to step over dirty and unwholesome people as one makes one's rounds.

"I see no point at all in being poor," the late Queen Mother is supposed to have said while being driven through some slum. "Mind you, that was a lot of money in those days," an English duke once told an interviewer known to me, while recalling the loss of some [GBP] 150 million by one of his ancestors in the goldfields of South Africa. These are the real thing: the failure of the upper crust and the cream of society to have the remotest glimmer of an idea of what life is like for others. (The "cream" was described by Samuel Beckett as "thick and rich," while nobody seems to know who defined the "upper crust" as "a lot of crumbs held together by dough.") Sometimes you can make an educated guess that the speaker is joking at his own expense. "I would not have *The Times*," remarked the late Duke of Devonshire in speaking of the decline of that newspaper, "in any of my houses." While making a documentary in Liverpool about how the other half lived, Auberon Waugh addressed a group of proles and breezily told them that his own manor in Somerset "probably costs more to heat than most of you people earn." Mark Boxer, that effortlessly superior and dandyish cartoonist, once drew a scene of two people in a restaurant during a coal miners' strike. "Do you mind the carafe wine?" says the host, looking up over a hugely ornate and tasseled menu. "I'm faintly unhappy when the bill gets too close to the miners' take-home pay." Mr. Humphry Berkeley, an Englishman whose ancestors came over with the Norman conquerors, left the Conservative Party partly in protest at its Africa policy and eventually ran for Parliament as a Labour candidate. Asked what was different about the experience, he replied with apparently perfect gravity that "I've been meeting the working class and I simply must say that it's absolutely the nicest class I've so far met."

But then there are old jokes—most of them also English for a reason that barely needs explaining—that are based more on *Schadenfreude*. Example: Two extremely rich men are sitting in companionable silence in their overstuffed armchairs in the upstairs window of the Carlton Club, in London. The silence is broken when the first man calls attention to the situation outside and says, "It's raining." "Good," replies the second man without looking up from his newspaper. "It'll wet the people."

Auberon Waugh's father, Evelyn, was a tremendous snob in many ways, but was generally rather careful to avoid such direct class combat. Indeed, in his masterpiece *Scoop* he gives a tumbril character to a radical type—Mr. Pappenhacker of the *Daily Twopence*, who is rude to waiters at a restaurant that must be the Savoy Grill. "He seems to be in a very bad temper," the shy William Boot observes of Pappenhacker to his host, Mr. Salter:

> Not really. He's always like that to waiters. You see he's a communist. Most of the staff at the Twopence are—they're University men, you see. Pappenhacker says that every time you are polite to a proletarian you are helping bolster up the capitalist system. He's very clever of course, but he gets rather unpopular.

In Kingsley Amis's *Girl, 20*, the radical-chic Sir Roy Vandervane tries for the same effect by plastering reactionary bumper stickers all over his limousine and driving as arrogantly as he can, honking the horn like Mr. Toad and seeking to create resentment among lesser drivers and humble pedestrians. That didn't work. A tumbril remark doesn't work if it's conscious or deliberate. (Indeed, one definition of a gentleman is that of someone who is never rude by accident.) But what does work is an unmistakable, revealing, unfakable reminder of how superiors really view inferiors. The wife of a British diplomat in Saigon in the 1960s, a certain Lady So-and-So, once considered the surrounding carnage and observed soothingly that it wasn't as bad as it might look, since one had to bear in mind that "Orientals" had a different attitude to death. My friend the poet and journalist James Fenton noted as calmly as he dared that from this you could tell one thing for certain—namely that Lady So-and-So had a different attitude toward the death of Asians.

For some reason, the Bush family excels at this kind of thing. I remember George senior, having come in third (after Pat Robertson, of all people) in a 1987 Iowa straw poll, being asked why his own supporters apparently hadn't bothered to turn out. Oh well, he replied, there was more to life than politics, and his sort of people "were at their daughters' coming-out parties, or teeing up at the golf course for that all-important last round." To be absolutely honest with you, I do not know to this day exactly what a "coming-out party" is, but it has a nice debutante, Marie Antoinette ring to it when uttered amid the corn-infested fields and pig-strewn farms of Iowa. (A bit like the distribution of free gateau to the masses, which somehow failed to occur in the inundated states of the Gulf of Mexico in September.) At a later stage, offended by the very idea that he lacked the common touch, George H. W. Bush put himself to the fatiguing effort of declaring in public his love for pork rinds and country music, and of guising himself in pleb-like clothing as if to the manner born. This is worse, in a way, because "slumming" on the part of the elite is a carefully graded insult—to the intelligence, among other things. (I knew that John Kerry was through when a friend of mine looked up from the *New York Times* and said, "Oh dear. He's gone goose hunting again.") Oddly enough, and for all the Versailles teasing that she herself had to endure, Nancy Reagan had more "class" when she turned up in rags to sing the parodic "Secondhand Clothes" at the Gridiron Club and "pre-empted" the media tumbrils that had been rumbling around the Pennsylvania Avenue district in the early 1980s.

"Because it turns on a sixpence, whatever that is." Thus remarked the Armenian tycoon Nubar Gulbenkian when asked why he modeled his custom town car on a London taxi. One can be reasonably certain that this is a rich man's joke. But "The levees broke? Who knew they could do that?" is not funny for one thing, and doesn't demonstrate any sense of noblesse oblige, either. It shows in a blinding flash what someone really thinks of you.

It is not self-satirizing, or deflecting. It is myopic, and arrogant. It reminds one that "levee" was the word used by King Louis XVI himself, in his royal bedchamber upon rising, for the reception of his courtiers. The word "tumbril" is in our language and in our minds because of the imperishable passage in *A Tale of Two Cities* where the carts full of those same, now fallen, haggard courtiers come grinding their way to the Place de la Revolution, and where Madame Defarge sits knitting with her fellow *tricoteuses*, coldly and contentedly marking each crashing slice of the blade. But, for me, the most chilling mention is the very first one, where Dickens recalls a particularly hideous torture-execution ordered by France's "Christian pastors" in defense of the old king's regime:

> It is likely enough that in the rough out-houses of some tillers of the heavy lands adjacent to Paris, there were sheltered from the weather that very day, rude carts, bespattered with rustic mire, snuffed about by pigs, and roosted in by poultry, which the Farmer, Death, had already set apart to be his tumbrils of the Revolution.

You can feel it coming... "like the stillness in the wind / 'Fore the hurricane begins." The reference to "mire," incidentally, isn't Dickens's only euphemism. A tumbril really means a cart for the carrying away of excrement. Don't tempt me...

Other expressions are in our language, also. We still use the adjectives "noble" as positive and "base" as negative: terms that derive their original meaning from the Anglo-French feudal order, where every person knew their divinely ordained position. We employ the word "chivalrous" to mean honorable and gallant, when all it denotes is a noble who owns a horse, or horses, and can thus ride over the unmounted—rather as if a specialist in Arabian equines was to be appointed the head of FEMA, and raise his eyebrows politely at the distasteful news that lesser breeds were sweltering in a dome. Another expression less "commonly" used—and there I go again with another instance of the same linguistic bias—is "below the salt." This refers to the long table in the baron's hall, when seating was by social gradation all the way to the bottom, where sat the greasiest serfs and scullions. The precious condiment could not be passed below a certain place about halfway down. How we smile now to think of such primitive social and class prejudices. And then there came a day in New Orleans, a town named for a scion of French feudalism, when the salt-water rose up and didn't just wet the people but drowned them, and nobody was above that salt except those who could fly over it and look down *de haut en bas*, while a lot of lowly people were suddenly well below it. Whatever is that distant rumble that I dimly hear?

(*Vanity Fair*, December 2005)

Stand Up for Denmark!

PUT THE CASE that we knew of a highly paranoid religious cult organization with a secretive leader. Now put the case that this cult, if criticized in the press, would take immediate revenge by kidnapping a child. Put the case that, if the secretive leader were also to be lampooned, two further children would be killed at random. Would the press be guilty of "self-censorship" if it declined to publish anything that would inflame the said cult? Well, yes it would be guilty, but very few people would insist on the full exertion of the First Amendment right. However, the consequences for the cult and its leader would be severe as well. All civilized people would regard it as hateful and dangerous, and steps would be taken to circumscribe its influence, and to ensure that no precedent was set.

The incredible thing about the ongoing *Kristallnacht* against Denmark (and in some places, against the embassies and citizens of any Scandinavian or even European Union nation) is that it has resulted in, not opprobrium for the religion that perpetrates and excuses it, but increased respectability! A small democratic country with an open society, a system of confessional pluralism, and a free press has been subjected to a fantastic, incredible, organized campaign of lies and hatred and violence, extending to one of the gravest imaginable breaches of international law and civility: the violation of diplomatic immunity. And nobody in authority can be found to state the obvious and the necessary: That we stand with the Danes against this defamation and blackmail and sabotage. Instead, all compassion and concern is apparently to be expended upon those who lit the powder trail, and who yell and scream for joy as the embassies of democracies are put to the torch in the capital cities of miserable, fly-blown dictatorships. Let's be sure we haven't hurt the vandals' feelings.

You wish to say that it was instead a small newspaper in Copenhagen that lit the trail? What abject masochism and nonsense. It was the arrogant Danish mullahs who patiently hawked those cartoons around the world (yes, don't worry, they are allowed to exhibit them as much as they like), until they finally provoked a vicious response against the economy and society of their host country. For good measure, they included a cartoon that had never been published in Denmark or anywhere else. It showed the Prophet Mohammed as a pig, and may or may not have been sent to a Danish mullah by an anonymous ill-wisher. The hypocrisy here is shameful, nauseating, unpardonable. The original proscription against any portrayal of the prophet, not that this appears to be absolute, was superficially praiseworthy because it was intended as a safeguard against idolatry and the worship of images. But now see how this principle is negated. A rumor of a cartoon in a faraway country is enough to turn the very name Mohammed into a fetish-object and an excuse for barbaric conduct. As I write this, the death toll is well over thirty and—guess what?—a mullah in Pakistan has offered $1 million and a car as a bribe for the murder of "the cartoonist." This incitement will go unpunished and most probably unrebuked.

Could things become any more sordid and cynical? By all means. In a mindless attempt at a *tu quoque*, various Islamist groups and regimes have dug deep into their sense of wit and irony and proposed a trade-off. You make fun of "our" prophet and we will deny "your" Holocaust. Even if there were any equivalence, and Jewish mobs were now engaged in trashing Muslim shops and embassies, it would feel degrading even to engage with such a low and cheap stunt. I suppose that one should be grateful that the Shoah is only to be denied rather than, as in some Islamist propaganda, enthusiastically affirmed and set out as a model for emulation. But only a moral cretin thinks that anti-Semitism is a threat only to Jews. The memory of the Third Reich is very vivid in Europe precisely because a racist German regime also succeeded in slaughtering millions of non-Jews, including countless Germans, under the demented pretext of extirpating a nonexistent Jewish conspiracy. As it happens, I am one of the few people to have publicly defended David Irving's right to publish, and I think it outrageous that he is in prison in Austria for expressing his opinions. But my attachment to free speech is at least absolute and consistent. Those who incite murder and arson, or who silkily justify it, are incapable of rising above the childish glee that culminates in the assertion that two wrongs make a right.

The silky ones may be more of a problem in the long term than the flagrantly vicious and crazy ones. Within a short while—this is a warning—the shady term "Islamophobia" is going to be smuggled through our customs. Anyone accused of it will be politely but firmly instructed to shut up, and to forfeit the constitutional right to criticize religion. By definition, anyone accused in this way will also be implicitly guilty. Thus the "soft" censorship will triumph, not from any merit in its argument, but from its association with the "hard" censorship that we have seen being imposed over the past weeks. A report in the *New York Times* of February 13 was as carefully neutral as could be but nonetheless conveyed the sense of menace. "American Muslim leaders," we were told, are more canny. They have "managed to build effective organizations and achieve greater integration, acceptance and economic success than their brethren in Europe have. They portray the cartoons as a part of a wave of global Islamophobia and have encouraged Muslim groups in Europe to use the same term." In other words, they are leveraging worldwide Islamic violence to drop a discreet message into the American discourse.

You may have noticed the recurrence of the term "One point two billion Muslims." A few years ago, I became used to the charge that in defending Salman Rushdie, say, I had "offended a billion Muslims." Evidently, the number has gone up since I first heard this ridiculous complaint. But observe the implied threat. There is not just safety in numbers, but danger in numbers. How many Danes or Jews or freethinkers are there? You can see what the "spokesmen" are insinuating by this tactic of mass psychology and mobbishness.

And not without immediate success, either. The preposterous person of Karen Hughes is quoted in the same *New York Times* article, under her risible title of "Under Secretary of State for Public Diplomacy." She tittered outside the store she was happily giving away: "The voices of Muslim Americans have more credibility in the Muslim world frankly than my voice as a government official, because they can speak the language of their faith and can share their experience of practicing their faith freely in the West, and they can help explain why the cartoons are so offensive." Well, let's concede that almost any voice in any world has more credibility on any subject than this braying Bush-crony ignoramus, but is the State Department now saying that we shall be represented in the Muslim world only by Muslims? I think we need a debate on that, and also a vote. Meanwhile, not a dollar of Wahhabi money should be allowed to be spent on opening madrassas in this country, or in distributing fundamentalist revisions of the Koran in our prison system. Not until, at the very least, churches and synagogues and free-thought libraries are permitted in every country whose ambassador has bullied the Danes. If we have to accept this sickly babble about "respect," we must at least demand that it is fully reciprocal.

And there remains the question of Denmark: a small democracy, which resisted Hitler bravely and protected its Jews as well as itself. Denmark is a fellow member of NATO and a country that sends its soldiers to help in the defense and reconstruction of Iraq and Afghanistan. And what is its reward from Washington? Not a word of solidarity, but instead some creepy words of apology to those who have attacked its freedom, its trade, its citizens, and its embassies. For shame. Surely here is a case that can be taken up by those who worry that America is too casual and arrogant with its allies. I feel terrible that I have taken so long to get around to this, but I wonder if anyone might feel like joining me in gathering outside the Danish Embassy in Washington, in a quiet and composed manner, to affirm some elementary friendship. Those who like the idea might contact me at christopher.hitchens@yahoo.com, and those who live in other cities with Danish consulates might wish to initiate a stand for decency on their own account.

Update, February 22: Thank you all who've written. Please be outside the Embassy of Denmark, 3200 Whitehaven Street (off Massachusetts Avenue) between noon and 1 p.m. this Friday, February 24. Quietness and calm are the necessities, plus cheerful conversation. Danish flags are good, or posters reading "Stand By Denmark" and any variation on this theme (such as "Buy Carlsberg/ Havarti/ Lego") The response has been astonishing and I know that the Danes are appreciative. But they are an embassy and thus do not of course endorse or comment on any demonstration. Let us hope, however, to set a precedent for other cities and countries. Please pass on this message to friends and colleagues.

(*Slate*, February 21, 2006)

Eschew the Taboo

ONE EFFECT of the witless racist tirade mounted by Michael Richards has been a call, made by Reverend Jesse Jackson and Representative Maxine Waters and endorsed by black comedian Paul Mooney, for a moratorium on the use of the word "nigger" by those in the entertainment industry. If successful, this might, I suppose, put an end to the pathetic complaint made by some white people that it's unfair that blacks can use the word while they cannot. In fact, no question of "double standards" arises here. If white people call black people niggers, they are doing their very best to hurt and insult them, as well as to remind them that their ancestors used to be property. If black people use the word, they are either uttering an obscenity or trying to detoxify a word and rob it of its power to wound them. Not quite the same thing.

There is a third category here, which is the use of the word in what I can only call an objective way. Thus, Professor Randall Kennedy not long ago became the second black American to publish a book called *Nigger*. (The first was Dick Gregory, who told his mother that henceforth whenever she heard the word, she could think of it as a promotion of her son's bestseller.) Kennedy's milder justification, with which I agreed, was that he was writing a history of the word's power and pathology, and it did not need a mealy-mouthed title.

However, in mentioning Kennedy's book in its treatment of the Richards affair, the article in the *Washington Post*'s "Style" section did not give its title at all, referring to it instead as "a controversial book about the word" and to the word itself as "the N-word." Indeed, the *Post* has a policy of not printing the word at all, as do many other media outlets.

I found this out myself recently, when I went on *Hardball with Chris Matthews*. It was just after John Kerry had (I thought unintentionally) given the impression that young people joining the armed forces were stupid. Chris asked me where liberals got the idea that conservatives were dumb. I said that it all went back to John Stuart Mill referring to the Tories as "the stupid party." After a while, the Tories themselves began to use this expression to describe themselves. I added that the word "Tory" was originally an insult. It means something like "brigand" in Gaelic, and it had also been adopted, by those at whom it was directed, as a badge of pride. In this respect, I went on to say, it anticipated other such appropriations—impressionist, suffragette—by which the target group inverted the taunt thrown at it and, by a kind of verbal jujitsu, turned it back on its originators. In more recent times, I finished with what I thought was a flourish, the words "nigger" and "queer" (and I may have added "faggot") had undergone some of the same transmutation.

Very suddenly, we went to a break, and the studio filled with unsmiling people who detached my microphone and announced that the segment was extremely over. My protests were futile. Should I have remembered to cover myself and say "the N-word" instead? It would have seemed somehow inauthentic. Did MSNBC think that anything I had uttered was inflected with the smallest tinge of bigotry? Presumably not. So, what we now have is a taboo, which is something quite different from an agreement on etiquette.

The next day, I was teaching a class on Mark Twain at the New School in New York, explaining why it was that there had always been attempts to ban *Huckleberry Finn*. In the old days, this was because of its rough manners and alleged lack of refinement and moral uplift. But now, as I went on to say, it is because of the name of the character for whom Huck is willing to risk going to hell. Excuse me, but I did not refer to this character as "N-word Jim." I have more respect for my graduate students than that. I suppose I could have just called him "Jim," but that would somehow have been untrue to the spirit and shade of Samuel Clemens. And I would have thought of myself as a coward.

I did, once, decide to be a coward anyway. It was while giving a speech in Washington, to a very international audience, about the British theft of the Elgin Marbles from the Parthenon. I described the attitude of the current British authorities as "niggardly." Nobody said anything, but I privately resolved—having felt the word hanging in the air a bit—to say "parsimonious" from then on. That's up to me, though.

Not long afterward, a senior member of the Washington, D.C., government used the word "niggardly" in a budget memo and was forced to resign, even though Mayor Anthony Williams said publicly that he knew the term was both harmless and precise. At this point, we see the effect of taboo. It got even worse a short while later, when a local teacher praised her class for being so "discriminating" and provoked floods of tears and much anguish. Now, the word "niggardly" can pass out of the language and leave us not much poorer. But the meaning of the verb "to discriminate" is of some importance and seems to me to be worth fighting over. It is odd, when you think about it, that we accuse racists of "discrimination." This is the very thing of which they are by definition incapable: They think all members of certain groups are the same. (The late Richard Pryor dropped the word "nigger" after he went to Africa, saying that he didn't meet anyone on that continent who answered to the description. Doubtless true, but when the Hutu militias in Rwanda referred to all Tutsis as "cockroaches," you can be sure they intended something more than a "stereotype.") Hatred will always find a way, and will certainly always be able to outpace linguistic correctness.

(*Slate*, December 4, 2006)

She's No Fundamentalist

W.H. AUDEN, WHOSE CENTENARY fell late last month, had an extraordinary capacity to summon despair but in such a way as to simultaneously inspire resistance to fatalism. His most beloved poem is probably "September 1, 1939," in which he sees Europe toppling into a chasm of darkness. Reflecting on how this catastrophe for civilization had come about, he wrote:

> Exiled Thucydides knew
> All that a speech can say
> About Democracy,
> And what dictators do,
> The elderly rubbish they talk
> To an apathetic grave;
> Analyzed all in his book,
> The enlightenment driven away,
> The habit-forming pain,
> Mismanagement and grief:
> We must suffer them all again.

"The enlightenment driven away..." This very strong and bitter line came back to me when I saw the hostile, sneaky reviews that have been dogging the success of Ayaan Hirsi Ali's bestseller *Infidel*, which describes the escape of a young Somali woman from sexual chattelhood to a new life in Holland

and then (after the slaying of her friend Theo van Gogh) to a fresh exile in the United States. Two of our leading intellectual commentators, Timothy Garton Ash (in the *New York Review of Books*) and Ian Buruma, described Hirsi Ali, or those who defend her, as "Enlightenment fundamentalist[s]." In Sunday's *New York Times Book Review*, Buruma made a further borrowing from the language of tyranny and intolerance and described her view as an "absolutist" one.

Now, I know both Garton Ash and Buruma, and I remember what fun they used to have, in the days of the Cold War, with people who proposed a spurious "moral equivalence" between the Soviet and American sides. Much of this critique involved attention to language. Buruma was very mordant about those German leftists who referred to the "consumer terrorism" of the federal republic. You can fill in your own preferred example here; the most egregious were (and, come to think of it, still are) those who would survey the U.S. prison system and compare it to the Gulag.

In her book, Ayaan Hirsi Ali says the following: "I left the world of faith, of genital cutting and forced marriage for the world of reason and sexual emancipation. After making this voyage I know that one of these two worlds is simply better than the other. Not for its gaudy gadgetry, but for its fundamental values." This is a fairly representative quotation. She has her criticisms of the West, but she prefers it to a society where women are subordinate, censorship is pervasive, and violence is officially preached against unbelievers. As an African victim of, and escapee from, this system, she feels she has acquired the right to say so. What is "fundamentalist" about that?

The February 26 edition of *Newsweek* takes up where Garton Ash and Buruma leave off and says, in an article by Lorraine Ali, that "it's ironic that this would-be 'infidel' often sounds as single-minded and reactionary as the zealots she's worked so hard to oppose." I would challenge the author to give her definition of irony and also to produce a single statement from Hirsi Ali that would come close to materializing that claim. Accompanying the article is a typically superficial *Newsweek* Q&A sidebar, which is almost unbelievably headed: "A Bombthrower's Life." The subject of this absurd headline is a woman who has been threatened with horrific violence, by Muslims varying from moderate to extreme, ever since she was a little girl. She has more recently had to see a Dutch friend butchered in the street, been told that she is next, and now has to live with bodyguards in Washington, D.C. She has never used or advocated violence. Yet to whom does *Newsweek* refer as the "Bombthrower"? It's always the same with these bogus equivalences: They start by pretending loftily to find no difference between aggressor and victim, and they end up by saying that it's the victim of violence who is "really" inciting it.

Garton Ash and Buruma would once have made short work of any apologist who accused the critics of the USSR or the People's Republic of China of "heating up the Cold War" if they made any points about human rights. Why, then, do they grant an exception to Islam, which is simultaneously the ideology of insurgent violence and of certain inflexible dictatorships? Is it because Islam is a "faith"? Or is it because it is the faith in Europe at least of some ethnic minorities? In neither case would any special protection from criticism be justified. Faith makes huge claims, including huge claims to temporal authority over the citizen, which therefore cannot be exempt from scrutiny. And within these "minorities," there are other minorities who want to escape from the control of their ghetto leaders. (This was also the position of the Dutch Jews in the time of Spinoza.) This is a very complex question, which will require a lot of ingenuity in its handling. The pathetic oversimplification, which describes skepticism, agnosticism, and atheism as equally "fundamentalist," is of no help here. And notice what happens when *Newsweek* takes up the cry: The enemy of fundamentalism is defined as someone on the fringe while, before you have had time to notice the sleight of hand, the aggrieved, self-pitying Muslim has become the uncontested tenant of the middle ground.

Let me give another example of linguistic slippage. In ACLU circles, we often refer to ourselves as "First Amendment absolutists." By this we mean, ironically enough, that we prefer to interpret the words of the Founders, if you insist, literally. The literal meaning in this case seems (to us) to be that Congress cannot inhibit any speech or establish any state religion. This means that we defend all expressions of opinion including those that revolt us, and that we say that nobody can be forced to practice, or forced to foreswear, any faith. I suppose I would say that this is an inflexible principle, or even a dogma, with me. But who dares to say that's the same as the belief that criticism of religion should be censored or the belief that faith should be imposed? To flirt with this equivalence is to give in to the demagogues and to hear, underneath their yells of triumph, the dismal moan of the *trahison des clercs* and "the enlightenment driven away." Perhaps, though, if I said that my principles were a matter of unalterable divine revelation and that I was prepared to use random violence in order to get "respect" for them, I could hope for a more sympathetic audience from some of our intellectuals.

(*Slate*, March 5, 2007)

Burned Out

FUEL. WHAT A NICE, reassuring word. Our remotest ancestors began to become civilized when they learned how to gather it from kindling wood and how to keep it burning. Cars and jets are powered, at one remove of refinement, from fossil fuels. Quite often in literature, it is used as a synonym for food or drink. Those who condescended to help the deserving poor at holiday times are often represented as donating winter fuel, in the form of a log or two, to the homes of the humble. Varying the metaphor a bit in his *Bright Lights, Big City,* Jay MacInerney described those who went to the men's room for a snort of Bolivian marching powder as having gone to the toilet to take on fuel. Further on the downside, a crisis of fuel would be a crisis of energy, or power.

This is "fuel" as a noun, if you like. As a verb, however, it has become a positive menace. Almost anything can be fueled by anything else, in a passive voice that bestows energy and power on anything you like, without any concomitant responsibility or attribution. "Fuel" is also a nice, handy, short word, which means that it can almost always be slotted into a headline.

This is the only possible excuse for a pull-quote that appeared in bold type inside the *New York Times* on March 2: "U.N. report could fuel American fears of weapons duplicity" (note that the Web version of the article does not include this quote). This was perhaps an attempt to clarify an overly complex sentence by Richard Bernstein concerning a report by the International Atomic Energy Agency, which provided clear evidence of Iranian concealment in the matter of inspections.

But the agency's report is virtually certain to be seized upon by the United States as further evidence of what Washington characterizes as Iranian duplicity in concealing what the United States believes to be a nuclear weapons program. The same report, on a news page and not bodyguarded by any news analysis warning, goes on to say that repeated discoveries of cheating and covert activity mean that the credibility of Iran has been harmed. Just look at the syntax. Plain and uncontroverted evidence is seized upon by those who characterize as true something that nobody has the nerve to deny. The slack and neutral language of the headline reinforces the pseudo-objectivity of the article, whereby things that are only latent or deductive (the fears, by no means all of them American, that Iran might be up to something nasty) are fueled by something that is real and measurable. Since the critical matter here happens to be the enrichment of uranium for fuel, one can see that words are becoming separated from their meaning with alarming speed. The same goes, as it happens, for the lame word "credibility." In this instance, it is assumed without any evasive or qualifying words that the Iranian mullahs do possess a stock of it and that this mysterious store of credibility could be harmed, presumably by such corrosive and toxic agents as mendacity. (Could undeniable mendacity fuel a perception of the entire absence of credibility? Not in any article on the subject that I have so far read.)

However, and on the opposite side of the page or ledger, it is repeatedly asserted that some things do indeed fuel a perception of other things or, sometimes, the thing itself as well as the perception of it. For example, I would like to have a dollar for every time I have read that the American presence in Iraq or Afghanistan fuels the insurgency. There must obviously be some self-evident truth to this proposition. If coalition forces were not present in these countries, then nobody would or could be shooting at them. Still, if this is self-evident one way then it must be self-evident in another. Islamic *jihad*-ism is also fueled by the disgrace and shame of the unveiled woman, or by the existence of Jews and Christians and Hindus and atheists, or by the publication of novels by apostates. The Syrian death squads must be fueled by the appearance of opposition politicians in Lebanon or indeed

Syria. The *janjaweed* militia (if we must call them a militia) in Sudan must be fueled by the inconvenience of African villagers who stand in their way.

This confusion between the active and the passive mode is an indicator of a wider and deeper reticence, not to say cowardice. I wrote last week about the way that the phrase "Arab Street" had been dropped, without any apology, when it ceased to apply in the phony way in which it had first been adopted. But extend this a little. Can you imagine reading that the American street had had its way last November? In all the discussion about the danger of offending religious and national sensibilities in the Muslim world, have you ever been invited to consider whether Iranians might be annoyed by Russian support for their dictators? Or whether Chinese cynicism about its North Korean protectorate is an interference in Korean internal affairs? There is a masochistic cultural cringe somewhere in our discourse, which was first evidenced by those who felt guilty at being assaulted in September 2001, or who felt ashamed by any countermeasures. Though it will take a much more profound discussion before all of this mental surrender is clarified and uprooted, a brisk war on the weasel word "fuel" is needed in any case.

(*Slate*, March 7, 2005)

Easter Charade

THE IMMEDIATE CRISIS has apparently passed. But all through Easter Sunday, one had to be alert to the possibility that, at any moment, the late and long-dead Terri Schiavo would receive the stigmata on both palms and both feet and be wafted across the Florida strait, borne up by wonder-working dolphins, to be united in eternal bliss with the man child Elián González.

I had sincerely intended to be the only scribbler in America who stayed out of this most stupid and degrading argument. I ought to have left that phone call from *Hardball* unreturned. Not a single toe should have been dipped into the water. But, once you engage for even an instant, you are drawn into a vortex of irrationality and nastiness that generates its own energy. A family lawyer appears before an American court and solemnly proposes that his client's client might have to spend extra time in Purgatory, or even in Hell, if the feeding-tube decision is adjudicated the wrong way. One Catholic fanatic, Patrick Buchanan, argues that federal marshals ought to burst in and preserve a corpse. Another Catholic fundamentalist, William Donahue, says that this would be unwise, but only because it might set a precedent for the rescue of living people on Death Row. Presiding from a distance is a nodding, senile pope whose church may possibly want to change the subject from its indulgence of the rape and torture of real-life children.

Wearying of this, I return to my e-mail and discover a letter from someone who signs himself as Dr. but who turns out to have a degree in something other than medicine. If I am correct in describing Terri Schiavo as dead, says this indignant correspondent, then how can I object to her receiving nourishment through a tube? It surely cannot do her any harm. I admit that I am caught out by this fallacy in my own position, and I briefly ponder the image of rows and rows of deceased Americans, all connected to life-support until the crack of doom. Dead? Yes, absolutely. But first do no harm. The mind reels.

My own bias is very strongly for the choose life position. I used to have horrible and exhausting arguments with supposedly pro-choice militants who only reluctantly conceded that the fetus was alive but who then demanded to know if this truly was a human life. I know casuistry when I see it, and I would respond by asking what other kind of life it could conceivably be. Down the years, there has been an unacknowledged evolution of the argument. Serious Catholics no longer insist that contraception is genocide, and pro-choice advocates have become quite squeamish about late-term abortions. Sensitive about consistency in the life ethic, the church has also moved to condemn if not to anathematize the death penalty. Things were improving slowly. Until now.

There is also a secular analogue of this debate. In the late eighteenth century, Jefferson and Madison had a serious argument about whether the earth belonged only to the living. Thomas Paine, proposing that man has no property in man, had condemned some traditional attitudes for, in effect, enfranchising the dead. Jefferson was inclined to agree, writing that past generations could be allowed no veto. Madison riposted that the deceased did have some rights and should be accorded some respect, since they had labored to create many of the benefits that the living actually enjoyed. But for this argument to be conducted reasonably, there had to be an agreement that the dead had actually died. Nothing can be done if the case is held in a permanent state of suspended animation.

If there was the least reason to believe that the late Terri Schiavo was not the ex-wife of her husband, I should say that he owed her a duty. But as it is—and here is my reply to the man who demanded that we ignore all responsible medical evidence yet still treat her as if she were alive—I think it is obscene that she is held in absentia to exert power from beyond the grave. As for the idea that this assumed power can be arrogantly ventriloquized by clerical demagogues and self-appointed witch doctors, one quivers at the sheer indecency of the thing. The end of the brain, or the replacement of the brain by a liquefied and shrunken void, is (to return to my earlier point) if not the absolute end of life, the unarguable conclusion of human life. It disqualifies the victim from any further say in human affairs. Tragic, perhaps, unless you believe in a better life to come (as, oddly enough, the parents of this now non-human entity claim that they do).

Meanwhile, the rest of us also have lives to live. And I hope and believe that we shall say, as politely and compassionately as we can, that we do not intend to pass our remaining days listening to any hysteria from the morbid and the superstitious. It is an abuse of our courts and our Constitution to have judges and congressmen and governors bullied by those who believe in resurrection but not in physical death. Which post-terminal patient could not now be employed, regardless of his or her expressed wish, to convene a midnight court or assemble a hasty nocturnal presidency? Not content with telling us that we once used to share the earth with dinosaurs and that we should grimly instruct our children in this falsehood, religious fanatics now present their cult of death as if it were a joyous celebration of the only life we have. They have gone too far, and they should be made to regret it most bitterly.

(*Slate*, March 28, 2005)

Don't Mince Words

WHY ON EARTH do people keep saying, "There but for the grace of God"? If matters had been very slightly different over the past weekend, the streets of London and the airport check-in area in Glasgow, Scotland, would have been strewn with charred body parts. And this would have been, according to the would-be perpetrators, because of the grace of God. Whatever our own private theology or theodicy, we might at least agree to take this vile belief seriously.

Instead, almost every other conceivable explanation was canvassed. The June 30 *New York Times* report managed to quote three people, one of whom attributed the aborted atrocity in London to Tony Blair's foreign policy; one of whom (a New Zealand diplomat, at that) felt "surprisingly all right about it"; and one of whom, described as "a Briton of Indian descent," was worried that "if I walk up that road, they're going to suspect me." The "they" there was clearly the British authorities, rather than the Muslim gangsters who have declared open season on all Hindus as well as all Jews, Christians, secularists, and other *kuffar*—or infidel—filth.

On the following day, July 1, the same newspaper informed us that Britain contained a "disenfranchised South Asian population." How this was true was never explained. There are several Muslim parliamentarians in both houses, often allowed to make the most absurdly inflammatory and euphemistic statements where acts of criminal violence are concerned, as well as several districts in which the Islamic vote keeps candidates of all parties uneasily aware of what may and may not be said. True, the Muslim extremist groups boycott elections and denounce democracy itself as profane, but this does not really count as disenfranchisement.

Only at the tail end of the coverage was it admitted that a car bomb might have been parked outside a club in Piccadilly because it was "ladies night" and that this explosion might have been designed to lure people into the street, the better to be burned and shredded by the succeeding explosion from the second car-borne cargo of gasoline and nails. Since we have known since 2004 that a near-identical attack on a club called the Ministry of Sound was proposed in just these terms, on the grounds that dead "slags" or "sluts" would be regretted by nobody, a certain amount of trouble might have been saved by assuming the obvious. The murderers did not just want body parts in general but female body parts in particular.

I suppose that some people might want to shy away from this conclusion for whatever reason, but they cannot have been among the viewers of British Channel 4's recent *Undercover Mosque*, or among those who watched Sunday's report from Christiane Amanpour on CNN's Special Investigations Unit. On these shows, the British Muslim fanatics came right out with their program. Straight into the camera, leading figures like Anjem Choudary spoke of their love for Osama bin Laden and their explicit rejection of any definition of Islam as a religion of peace. On tape or in person, mullahs in prominent British mosques called for the killing of Indians and Jews.

Liberal reluctance to confront this sheer horror is the result, I think, of a deep reticence about some furtive concept of "race." It is subconsciously assumed that a critique of political Islam is an attack on people with brown skins. One notes in passing that any such concession implicitly denies or negates Islam's claim to be a universal religion. Indeed, some of its own exponents certainly do speak as if they think of it as a tribal property. And, at any rate, in practice, so it is. The fascistic subculture that has taken root in Britain and that lives by violence and hatred is composed of two main elements. One is a refugee phenomenon, made up of shady exiles from the Middle East and Asia who are exploiting London's traditional hospitality, and one is the projection of an immigrant group that has its origins in a particularly backward and reactionary part of Pakistan.

To the shame-faced white-liberal refusal to confront these facts, one might counterpose a few observations. The first is that we were warned for years of the danger, by Britons also of Asian descent such as Hanif Kureishi, Monica Ali, and Salman Rushdie. They knew what the village mullahs looked like and sounded like, and they said as much. Not long ago, I was introduced to Nadeem Aslam, whose book *Maps for Lost Lovers* is highly recommended.

He understands the awful price of arranged marriages, dowry, veiling, and the other means by which the feudal arrangements of rural Pakistan have been transplanted to parts of London and Yorkshire. "In some families in my street," he writes to me, "the grandparents, parents, and the children are all first cousins—it's been going on for generations and so the effects of the inbreeding are quite pronounced by now." By his estimate and others, a minority of no more than 11 percent is responsible for more than 70 percent of the birth defects in Yorkshire. When a leading socialist member of Parliament, Ann Cryer, drew attention to this appalling state of affairs in her own constituency, she was promptly accused of—well, you can guess what she was accused of. The dumb word Islamophobia, uncritically employed by Christiane Amanpour in her otherwise powerful documentary, was the least of it. Meanwhile, an extreme self-destructive clannishness, which is itself "phobic" in respect to all outsiders, becomes the constituency for the preachings of a cult of death. I mention this because, if there is an "ethnic" dimension to the Islamist question, then in this case at least it is the responsibility of the Islamists themselves.

The most noticeable thing about all theocracies is their sexual repression and their directly related determination to exert absolute control over women. In Britain, in the twenty-first century, there are now honor killings, forced marriages, clerically mandated wife-beatings, incest in all but name, and the adoption of apparel for females that one cannot be sure is chosen by them but which is claimed as an issue of (of all things) free expression. This would be bad enough on its own and if it were confined to the Muslim "community" alone. But, of course, such a toxin cannot be confined, and the votaries of theocracy now claim the God-given right to slaughter females at random for nothing more than their perceived immodesty. The least we can do, confronted by such radical evil, is to look it in the eye (something it strives to avoid) and call it by its right name. For a start, it is the female victims of this tyranny who are "disenfranchised," while something rather worse than "disenfranchisement" awaits those who dare to disagree.

(*Slate*, July 2, 2007)

History and Mystery

WHEN THE *NEW YORK TIMES* scratches its head, get ready for total baldness as you tear out your hair. A doozy classic led the "Week in Review" section on Sunday. Portentously headed "The Mystery of the Insurgency," the article rubbed its eyes at the sheer lunacy and sadism of the Iraqi car bombers and random murderers. At a time when new mass graves are being filled, and old ones are still being dug up, writer James Bennet practically pleaded with the authors of both to come up with an intelligible (or defensible?) reason for his paper to go on calling them insurgents.

I don't think the *New York Times* ever referred to those who devastated its hometown's downtown as insurgents. But it does employ this title every day for the gang headed by Abu Musab al-Zarqawi. With pedantic exactitude, and unless anyone should miss the point, this man has named his organization al-Qaeda in Mesopotamia and sought (and apparently received) Osama bin Laden's permission for the franchise. Did al-Qaeda show interest in winning hearts and minds in building international legitimacy in articulating a governing program or even a unified ideology, or any of the other things plaintively mentioned as lacking by Mr. Bennet?

The answer, if we remember our ABC, is yes and no, with yes at least to the third part of the question. The bin Ladenists did have a sort of governing program, expressed in part by their Taliban allies and patrons. This in turn reflected a unified ideology. It can be quite easily summarized: the return of the Ottoman Empire under a caliphate and a return to the desert religious purity of the seventh century (not quite the same things, but that's not our fault). In the meantime, anyway, war to the end against Jews, Hindus, Christians, unbelievers, and Shiites. None of the experts quoted in the article appeared to have remembered these essentials of the al-Qaeda program, but had they done so, they might not be so astounded at the promiscuous way in which the Iraqi gangsters pump out toxic anti-Semitism, slaughter Nepalese and other Asian guest-workers on video and gloat over the death of Hindus, burn out and blow up the Iraqi Christian minority, kidnap any Westerner who catches their eye, and regularly inflict massacres and bombings on Shiite mosques, funerals, and assemblies.

A letter from Zarqawi to bin Laden more than a year ago, intercepted by Kurdish intelligence and since then well-authenticated, spoke of Shiism as a repulsive heresy and the ignition of a Sunni-Shiite civil war as the best and easiest way to thwart the Crusader-Zionist coalition. The actions since then have precisely followed the design, but the design has been forgotten by the journal of record. The bin Laden and Zarqawi organizations, and their co-thinkers in other countries, have gone to great pains to announce, on several occasions, that they will win because they love death, while their enemies are so soft and degenerate that they prefer life. Are we supposed to think that they were just boasting when they said this? Their actions demonstrate it every day, and there are burned-out school buses and clinics and hospitals to prove it, as well as mosques (the incineration of which one might think to be a better subject for Islamic protest than a possibly desecrated Koran, in a prison where every inmate is automatically issued with one).

Then we might find a little space for the small question of democracy. The Baath Party's opinion of this can be easily gauged, not just from its record in power but from the rancid prose of its founding fascist fathers. As for the bin Ladenists, they have taken extraordinary pains to say, through the direct statements of Osama and of Zarqawi, that democracy is a vile heresy, a Greek fabrication, and a source of profanity. For the last several weeks, however, the *Times* has been opining every day that the latest hysterical murder campaign is a result of the time it has taken the newly elected Iraqi Assembly to come up with a representative government. The corollary of this mush-headed coverage must be that, if a more representative government were available in these terrible conditions (conditions supplied by the gangsters themselves), the homicide and sabotage would thereby decline. Is there a serious person in the known world who can be brought to believe such self-evident rubbish?

On many occasions, the *jihad*-ists in Iraq have been very specific as well as very general. When they murdered Sergio Vieira de Mello, the brilliant and brave U.N. representative assigned to Baghdad by Kofi Annan, the terrorists' communiqué hailed the death of the man who had so criminally helped Christian East Timor to become independent of Muslim Indonesia. (This was also among the reasons given for the bombing of the bar in Bali.) I think I begin to sense the frustration of the insurgents. They keep telling us what they are like and what they want. But do we ever listen? Nah. For them, it must be like talking to the wall. Bennet even complains that it's difficult for reporters to get close to the insurgents: He forgets that his own paper has published a conversation with one of them, in which the man praises the invasion of Kuwait, supports the cleansing of the Kurds, and says that we cannot accept to live with infidels.

Ah, but why would the secular former Baathists join in such theocratic mayhem? Let me see if I can guess. Leaving aside the formation of another well-named group, "the Fedayeen Saddam," to perform state-sponsored *jihad* before the intervention, how did the Baath Party actually rule? Yes, it's coming back to me. By putting every Iraqi citizen in daily fear of his or her life, by random and capricious torture and murder, and by cynical divide-and-rule among Sunnis, Shiites, and Kurds. Does this remind you of anything?

That's not to say that the paper doesn't have a long memory. Having once read in high school that violence is produced by underlying social conditions, the author of this appalling article refers in lenient terms to the goal of ridding Iraq of an American presence, a goal that may find sympathy among Iraqis angry about poor electricity and water service and high unemployment. Bet you hadn't thought of that: The water and power are intermittent, so let's go and blow up the generating stations and the oil pipelines. No job? Shoot up the people waiting to register for employment. To the insult of flattering the psychopaths, Bennet adds his condescension to the suffering of ordinary Iraqis, who are murdered every day while trying to keep essential services running. (Baathism, by the way, comes in very handy in crippling these, because the secret police of the old regime know how things operate, as well as where everybody lives. Or perhaps you think that the attacks are so deadly because the bombers get lucky seven days a week?)

This campaign of horror began before Baghdad fell, with the execution and mutilation of those who dared to greet American and British troops. It continued with the looting of the Baghdad museum and other sites, long before there could have been any complaint about the failure to restore power or security. It is an attempt to put Iraqi Arabs and Kurds, many of them still traumatized by decades of well-founded fear, back under the heel of the Baath Party or under a home-grown Taliban, or the combination of both that would also have been the Odai/Qusai final solution. Half-conceding the usefulness of chaos and misery in bringing this about, Bennet in his closing paragraph compares *jihad*-ism to nineteenth-century anarchism, which shows that he hasn't read Proudhon or Bakunin or Kropotkin either.

In my ears, "insurgent" is a bit like "rebel" or even "revolutionary." There's nothing axiomatically pejorative about it, and some passages of history have made it a term of honor. At a minimum, though, it must mean rising up. These fascists and hirelings are not rising up, they are stamping back down. It's time for respectable outlets to drop the word, to call things by their right names (Baathist or bin Ladenist or *jihad*-ist would all do in this case), and to stop inventing mysteries where none exist.

(*Slate*, May 16, 2005)

Words Matter

ONE OF THE GREAT MOMENTS among many in Martin Scorsese's *Taxi Driver* is when we find the young Albert Brooks manning the phones in the campaign office of the man we know (and he does not) to be a double-dyed phony. On behalf of the empty and grinning Senator Palantine, he is complaining to a manufacturer of lapel buttons. "We asked for buttons that said, '*We* Are the People.' These say, 'We *Are* the People.'… Oh, you don't think there's a difference? Well, we will not pay for the buttons. We will throw the buttons away." Part of the joke here is that the joke itself is also at the expense of Brooks's character and his "candidate"—there really and truly isn't much, if any, difference. Fan of Jerry Brown as I had been, I still winced when he ran on his lame "We the People" slogan against Clinton as late as 1992.

Of course, in 1992, Clinton borrowed from an old slogan of John F. Kennedy's: "Change Is the Law of Life." Now, why did he annex that questionable truism, and why in that year? First of all, because he wanted to plagiarize the entire Kennedy effect for himself, and second, because he was the challenger and not the incumbent. When you are the incumbent, it is harder (but not impossible) to demand "change." Senator Hillary Clinton, who wants to run as the "change" candidate—because, well, because you can't so easily run as a status quo candidate—also wants to run as a stability-and-experience candidate. Hence the repeated alterations (or "changes") in her half-baked slogans. By the time the plagiarism row had been started by her very ill-advised advisers, she had run through: "Big Challenges, Real Solutions"; "Working for Change, Working for You"; "Ready for Change, Ready to Lead"; and "Solutions for America." Senator Obama, meanwhile, had picked the slightly less banal and more cryptic mantra "Change We Can Believe In," which I call cryptic only because at least it makes one ask what it can conceivably be intended to mean.

It is cliché, not plagiarism, that is the problem with our stilted, room-temperature political discourse. It used to be that thinking people would say, with at least a shred of pride, that their own convictions would not shrink to fit on a label or on a bumper sticker. But now it seems that the more vapid and vacuous the logo, the more charm (or should that be "charisma?") it exerts. Take "Yes We Can," for example. It's the sort of thing parents might chant encouragingly to a child slow on the potty-training uptake. As for "We Are the People We Have Been Waiting For" (in which case, one can only suppose that now that we have arrived, we can all go home), I didn't think much of it when Representative Dennis Kucinich used it at an anti-war rally in 2004 ("We Are the People We Are Waiting For" being his version) or when Thomas Friedman came across it at an MIT student event last December. He wrote, by the way, that just hearing it gave him—well, you guess what it gave him. Hope? That's exactly right.

Pretty soon, we should be able to get electoral politics down to a basic newspeak that contains perhaps ten keywords: Dream, Fear, Hope, New, People, We, Change, America, Future, Together. Fishing exclusively from this tiny and stagnant pool of stock expressions, it ought to be possible to drive all thinking people away from the arena and leave matters in the gnarled but capable hands of the professional wordsmiths and manipulators. In the new jargon, certain intelligible ideas would become inexpressible. (How could one state, for example, the famous Burkean principle that many sorts of change ought to be regarded with skepticism?) In a rather poor trade-off for this veto on complexity, many views that are expressible (and "We the People Together Dream of and Hope for New Change in America" would be really quite a long sentence in the latest junk language) will, in turn, be entirely and indeed almost beautifully unintelligible.

And it's not as if anybody is looking for coded language in which to say: "Health care—who needs it?" or "Special interests and lobbyists—give them a break," let alone "Dr. King's dream—what a snooze." It's more that the prevailing drivel assumes that every adult in the country is a completely illiterate jerk who would rather feel than think and who must furthermore be assumed, for a special season every four years, to imagine that everyone else "in America" or in "this country" is unemployed or starving or sleeping under a bridge. The next assumption made by the drivel is that only a new president (or perhaps a sitting president who is somehow eager to run against Washington and everything else in his hometown) can possibly cure all these ills. The non sequitur is breathtaking. The more I could be brought to believe in a stupid incantation such as "Washington Is Broken," the less inclined I would be to pay the moving expenses to bring a failed Mormon crowd-pleaser and flip-flopper to 1600 Pennsylvania Avenue. And this was the best that a supposed "full-spectrum conservative" could come up with by way of rhetoric. At this rate, Senator John McCain will have to campaign as a radical post-Castroite to deal with the perceptions that (a) he's too old and (b) the Republicans are too WASP-dominated.

How well I remember Sidney Blumenthal waking me up all those years ago to read me the speech by Senator Biden, which, by borrowing the biography as well as the words of another candidate's campaign, put an end to Biden's own. The same glee didn't work this time when he (it must have been he) came up with "Change You Can Xerox" as a riposte to Senator Obama's hand from Governor Deval Patrick. All that Obama had lifted from Patrick was the old-fashioned idea that "words matter," and all that one can say, reviewing the present empty landscape of slogan and cliché, is that one only wishes that this could once again be true.

(*Slate*, March 3, 2008)

This Was Not Looting

ONCE AGAIN, a major story gets top billing in a "mainstream paper"—and is printed upside down. "Looting at Weapons Plants Was Systematic, Iraqi Says." This was how the *New York Times* led its front page on Sunday. According to the supporting story, Dr. Sami al-Araji, the deputy minister of industry, says that after the fall of Baghdad in April 2003, "looters systematically dismantled and removed tons of machinery from Saddam Hussein's most important weapons installations, including some with high-precision equipment capable of making parts for nuclear arms."

As printed, the implication of the story was not dissimilar from the al-Qaeda disclosures, which featured so much in the closing days of the presidential election last fall. In that case, a huge stock of conventional high-explosives had been allowed to go missing and was presumably in the hands of those who were massacring Iraqi civilians and killing coalition troops. At least one comment from the Bush campaign surrogate appeared to blame this negligence on the troops themselves. Followed to one possible conclusion, the implication was clear: The invasion of Iraq had made the world a more dangerous place by randomly scattering all sorts of weaponry, including mass-destruction weaponry, to destinations unknown.

It was eye-rubbing to read of the scale of this potential new nightmare. There in cold print was the Al Hatteen "munitions production plant that international inspectors called a complete potential nuclear weapons laboratory." And what of the Al Adwan facility, which "produced equipment used for uranium enrichment, necessary to make some kinds of nuclear weapons"? The overall pattern of the plundered sites was summarized thus, by reporters James Glanz and William J. Broad:

> The kinds of machinery at the various sites included equipment that could be used to make missile parts, chemical weapons or centrifuges essential for enriching uranium for atom bombs.

My first question is this: How can it be that, on every page of every other edition for months now, the *New York Times* has been stating categorically that Iraq harbored no weapons of mass destruction? And there can hardly be a comedy-club third-rater or MoveOn.org activist in the entire country who hasn't stated with sarcastic certainty that the whole WMD fuss was a way of lying the American people into war. So now what? Maybe we should have taken Saddam's propaganda seriously, when his newspaper proudly described Iraq's physicists as "our nuclear mujahideen."

My second question is: What's all this about "looting"? The word is used throughout the long report, but here's what it's used to describe. "In four weeks from mid-April to mid-May of 2003... teams with flatbed trucks and other heavy equipment moved systematically from site to site. 'The first wave came for the machines,' Dr. Araji said. 'The second wave, cables and cranes.'" Perhaps hedging the bet, the *Times* authors at this point refer to "organized looting."

But obviously, what we are reading about is a carefully planned military operation. The participants were not panicked or greedy civilians helping themselves, which is the customary definition of a "looter," especially in wartime. They were mechanized and mobile and under orders, and acting in a concerted fashion. Thus, if the story is factually correct—which we have no reason at all to doubt—then Saddam's Iraq was a fairly highly evolved WMD state, with a contingency plan for further concealment and distribution of the weaponry in case of attack or discovery.

Before the war began, several of the administration's critics argued that an intervention would be too dangerous, either because Saddam Hussein would actually unleash his arsenal of WMD, or because he would divert it to third parties. That case at least had the merit of being serious (though I would want to argue that a regime capable of doing either thing was a regime that urgently needed to be removed). Since then, however, the scene has dissolved into one long taunt and jeer: "There were no WMD in Iraq. Liar, liar, pants on fire."

The U.N. inspectors, who are solemnly quoted by Glanz and Broad as having "monitored" the alarming developments at Al Hatteen and elsewhere, don't come out looking too professional, either. If by scanning satellite pictures now they can tell us that potentially thermonuclear stuff is on the loose, how come they couldn't come up with this important data when they were supposedly "on the ground"?

Even in the worst interpretation, it seems unlikely that the material is more dangerous now than it was two years ago. Some of the elements—centrifuges, for example, and chemical mixtures—require stable and controlled conditions for effectiveness. They can't simply be transferred to some kitchen or tent. They are less risky than they were in early 2003, in other words. If they went to a neighboring state, though.... Some chemical vats have apparently turned up on a scrap heap in Jordan, even if this does argue more for a panicky concealment than a plan of transfer. But anyway, this only returns us to the main point: If Saddam's people could have made such a transfer after his fall, then they could have made it much more easily during his reign. (We know, for example, that the Baathists were discussing the acquisition of long-range missiles from North Korea as late as March 2003, and at that time, the nuclear Wal-Mart of the A. Q. Khan network was still in business. Iraq would have had plenty to trade in this WMD underworld.)

Supporters of the overdue disarmament and liberation of Iraq, all the same, can't be complacent about this story. It seems flabbergasting that any of these sites were unsecured after the occupation, let alone for so long. Did the CIA yet again lack "human intelligence" as well as every other kind? The Bush administration staked the reputation of the United States on the matter. It won't do to say that "mistakes were made."

(*Slate*, March 15, 2005)

The *Other* L-Word

WHEN CAROLINE KENNEDY managed to say "you know" more than 200 times in an interview with the New York *Daily News*, and on 130 occasions while talking to the *New York Times* during her uninspired attempt to become a hereditary senator, she proved, among other things, that she was (a) middle-aged and (b) middle class. If she had been a generation younger and a bit more déclassé, she would have been saying "like." When asked if the Bush tax cuts should be repealed, she responded: "Well, you know, that's something, obviously, that, you know, in principle and in the campaign, you know, I think that, um, the tax cuts, you know, were expiring and needed to be repealed."

This is an example of "filler" words being used as props, to try to shore up a lame sentence. People who can't get along without "um" or "er" or "basically" (or, in England, "actually") or "et cetera et cetera" are of two types: the chronically modest and inarticulate, such as Ms. Kennedy, and the mildly authoritarian who want to make themselves un-interruptible. Saul Bellow's character Ravelstein is a good example of the latter: In order to deny any opening to a rival, he says "the-uh, the-uh" while searching for the noun or concept that is eluding him.

Many parents and teachers have become irritated to the point of distraction at the way the weed-style growth of "like" has spread through the idiom of the young. And it's true that in some cases the term has become simultaneously a crutch and a tic, driving out the rest of the vocabulary as candy expels vegetables. But it didn't start off that way, and might possibly be worth saving in a modified form.

Its antecedents are not as ignoble as those of "you know." It was used by the leader of the awesome Droogs in the 1962 novel *A Clockwork Orange,* by Anthony Burgess, who had possibly annexed it from the Beatnik Maynard G. Krebs, of *Dobie Gillis.* It was quasi-ironic in *Scooby Doo* by 1969, and self-satirizing by the time that Frank Zappa and Moon Unit deployed it ("Like, totally") in their "Valley Girl" song in the early 1980s. It was then a part of the Californianization of American youth-speak. In an analysis drawing upon the wonderfully named Sonoma College linguist Birch Moonwomon's findings, Penelope Eckert and Norma Mendoza-Denton phrase matters this way: "One of the innovative developments in the white English of Californians is the use of the discourse-marker 'I'm like' or 'she's like' to introduce quoted speech, as in 'I'm like, where have you been?' This quotative is particularly useful because it does not require the quote to be of actual speech (as 'she said' would, for instance). A shrug, a sigh, or any of a number of expressive sounds as well as speech can follow it."

So it can be of use to a natural raconteur. Ian McEwan rather surprised me when I asked him about "like," telling me that "it can be used as a pause or a colon: very handy for spinning out a mere anecdote into a playlet that's full of parody and speculation." And also of hyperbole, as in "She's been out with, like, a *million* guys."

Its other main use is principally social, and defensive. You will have noticed the way in which "uptalk" has also been spreading among the young. "Uptalk" can be defined as an ostensibly declarative sentence that is uttered on a rising note of apology and that ends with an implied question mark. An example: the statement "I go to Columbia University?" which seems to say, "If that's all right with you." Just as the humble, unassuming, assenting "Okay" has deposed the more affirmative "Yes," so the little cringe and hesitation and approximation of "like" are a help to young people who are struggling to negotiate the shoals and rapids of ethnic identity, the street, and general correctness. To report that "he was like, Yeah, whatever" is to struggle to say "He said" while minimizing the risk of commitment. (This could be why young black people don't seem to employ "like" quite as often, having more challenging vernaculars such as "Nome sane?"—which looks almost Latin.)

The actual grammatical battle was probably lost as far back as 1954, when Winston announced that its latest smoke "tasted good, like a cigarette should." Complaints from sticklers that this should have been "as a cigarette should" (or, in my view, "*as* a cigarette *ought* to do") were met by a second ad in which a gray-bunned schoolmarm type was taunted by cheery consumers asking, "What do you want, good grammar or good taste?" Usage of "like" has now almost completely replaced "as," except in the case of that other quite infectious youth expression "as if," which would now be in danger of being rendered "Like, as if."

How could one preserve what's useful about "like" without allowing it to reduce everyday vocabulary and without having it weaken the two strong senses of the word, which are: to be fond of something or somebody (*As You, Like, Like It*) or to resemble something or somebody ("Like, Like a Virgin")? Believe me when I say I have tried to combat it when teaching my class, and with some success (you have to talk well in order to write well, and you can't write while using "like" as punctuation). But I realize that it can't be expelled altogether. It can, however, be pruned and rationed, and made the object of mockery for those who have surrendered to it altogether. The restoration of the word "as," which isn't that hard a word to master, along with "such as," would also be a help in varying the national lingo. A speech idiosyncrasy, in the same way as an air quote, is really justifiable only if it's employed very sparingly and if the user consciously intends to be using it. Just to try to set an example—comparing "like" to "like," as you might say—I have managed to write all the above without using the word once, except in inverted commas. Why not try it? You might, like, like it.

(*Vanity Fair* online, January 13, 2010)

The You Decade

I SUPPOSE I STARTED to notice it about two or three years ago, when the salespeople at Rite-Aid began wearing dish-sized lapel buttons stating that "YOU are the most important customer I will serve today." It was all wrong, in the same way that a sign hung on a door saying "Back in five minutes" is out of time as soon as it is put in place. It was wrong in other ways, too, since it could be read from some distance (say, from ten spaces back in a slow-moving line) and thus became an irritant to anyone who could grasp that "they" or the "we" of this putative "you" were not really important at all. As in "Your call is important to us" but not important enough for us to supply enough operators to get you out of the holding pattern and the elevator or fasten-your-seat-belt music that comes with it.

The annoying lapel button was soon discontinued, and the bright consultant who came up with it was no doubt promoted to higher things, but "You" retained its centrality. A room-service menu, for example, now almost always offers "your choice" of oatmeal versus cornflakes or fruit juice as opposed to vegetable juice. Well, who else's choice could it be? Except perhaps that of the people who decide that this is the range of what the menu will feature. Fox TV famously and fatuously claims, "We report. You decide." Decide on what? On what Fox reports? Online polls promise to register what "you" think about the pressing issues of the moment, whereas what's being presented is an operation whereby someone says, "Let's give them the idea that they are a part of the decision-making process."

The next time you see an ad, the odds are increasingly high that it will put "you" in the driver's seat. "Ask your doctor if Prozac/Lipitor/Cialis is right for you" almost as if these medications could be custom made for each individual consumer. A lawyer or real-estate agent will promise you to address "your" concerns. Probably the most famous propaganda effort of the twentieth century, a recruiting poster with Lord Kitchener pointing directly outward and stating, "Your Country Needs YOU," was only rushed onto the billboards when it suddenly became plain that the country concerned needed several hundred thousand recruits in a big hurry and couldn't afford to be too choosy about who it was signing up.

Tourist posters are even more absurd. I saw one once for Cyprus, showing an empty beach with the slogan, "Keep It to Yourself." Probably at least a million of these were printed and distributed, with the result that the hotels on the island blocked out the sun on those unspoiled beaches. (Have you ever seen an inducement for a holiday that showed more than two people on the beach? Jamaica welcomes you but isn't dumb enough to show you alone on the sand without a girlfriend/boyfriend. It just omits all the other "you" targets who would otherwise mutate rather swiftly and disconcertingly into "them.")

I can clearly remember the first time I heard the expression "y'all," which was at a Greyhound bus stop in Georgia more than thirty years ago. A young black man, hearing my English accent but mistaking my age, told me with exquisite courtesy and solemnity that he greatly admired "the stand y'all"—he actually spun it out all the way to "you all"—"took in 1940." Stirred as I was then, I was stirred and baffled, later, when others in Dixie used "y'all" to mean just myself and not anything plural. But then I heard someone say "all of y'all," which restored the plural to its throne. And that's where I want it to be. As in "you fools," or "you lot," or "you the targets of our latest marketing campaign to make you think it's all about you."

I have just been sent a link to an Internet site that shows me delivering a speech some years ago. This is my quite unsolicited introduction to the now-inescapable phenomenon of YouTube. It comes with another link, enabling me to see other movies of myself all over the place. What's "You" about this? It's a MeTube, for me. And I can only suppose that, for my friends and foes alike, it's a HimTube. It reminds me of the exasperation I used to feel, years ago, when one could be accused of regarding others as "sex objects." Well, one can only really be a proper "subject" to oneself. A sentence that begins with I will be highly solipsistic if it ends only with me, and if the subject is sexual, then the object of the sentence will be an object. Would people rather be called "sex subjects"? (A good question for another time, perhaps.) Or "sex predicates"? Let us not go there.

Perhaps global-scale problems and mass-society populism somehow necessitate this unctuous appeal to the utter specialness of the supposed individual. What you can do to stop planetary warming. How the maximum leader is on your side. The ways in which the corporation has your needs in mind as it makes its dispositions. The candidate who wants to hear your views. Or, a little farther down the scale of flattery and hucksterism, come to our completely uniform and standardized food outlet and create your own salad and dessert, from our own pre-selected range of freshly prepared and tasteless ingredients!

So, whatever happened to the Me Decade? The answer is that nothing happened to it. It mutated quite easily and smoothly into a decade centered on another narcissistic pronoun. Which pronoun is that? You be the judge.

(*Slate*, April 9, 2007)

Suck It Up

WHEN PEOPLE IN AMERICA say "no man is an island," as Joan Didion once put it, they think they are quoting Ernest Hemingway. But when Hemingway annexed the seductive words from John Donne's *Devotions*, quoting the whole paragraph on his title page and borrowing from it one of the twentieth century's most resonant titles, he did not literally mean to say that all funerals are the same or that all deaths are to be regretted equally. He meant that if the Spanish republic went under to fascism, we should all be the losers. It was a matter both of solidarity and of self-interest: Stand by your friends now, or be shamed (and deserted in your turn) later on.

The grisly events at Virginia Tech involved no struggle, no sacrifice, no great principle. They were random and pointless. Those who died were not soldiers in any cause. They were not murdered by our enemies. They were not martyrs. But—just to take one example from the exhausting national sob fest of the past few days—here is how the bells were tolled for them at another national seat of learning. The president of Cornell University, David J. Skorton, ordered the chimes on his campus to be rung thirty-three times before addressing a memorial gathering. Thirty-three times? Yes. "We are here," announced the head of an institution of higher learning,

> for all of those who are gone, for all 33. We are here for the 32 who have passed from the immediate to another place, not by their own choice. We are also here for the one who has also passed. We are one.

For an academic president to have equated thirty-two of his fellow humans with their murderer in an orgy of "one-ness" was probably the stupidest thing that happened last week, but not by a very wide margin. Almost everybody in the country seems to have taken this non-event as permission to talk the starkest nonsense. And why not? Since the slaughter raised no real issues, it was a blank slate on which anyone could doodle. Try this, from the eighth straight day of breathless coverage in the *New York Times*. The person being quoted is the Reverend Susan Verbrugge of Blacksburg Presbyterian Church, addressing her congregation in an attempt, in the silly argot of the day, "to make sense of the senseless":

> Ms. Verbrugge recounted breaking through the previous week's numbness as she stopped on a morning walk and found herself yelling at the mountains and at God. Though her shouts were initially met with silence, she said, she soon was reassured by the simplest of things, the chirping of birds.
>
> "God was doing something about the world," she said. "Starting with my own heart, I could see good."

Yes, it's always about *you*, isn't it? (By the way, I'd watch that habit of yelling at mountains and God in the greater Blacksburg area if I were you. Some idiot might take it for a "warning sign.") When piffle like this gets respectful treatment from the media, we can guess that it's not because of the profundity of the emotion but rather because of its extreme shallowness. Those birds were singing just as loudly and just as sweetly when the bullets were finding their targets.

But the quest for greater "meaning" was unstoppable. Will Korean-Americans be "targeted"? (Thanks for putting the idea into the head of some nutcase, but really, what an insulting question!) Last week, I noticed from my window in Washington, D.C., that the Russian trade mission had lowered its flag. President Putin's commercial envoys, too, want to be a part of it all: surely proof in itself of how utterly painless all this vicarious "pain" really is. (And now, what are they going to do for Boris Yeltsin?)

On Saturday night, I watched disgustedly as the president of the United States declined to give his speech to the White House Correspondents' Dinner on the grounds that this was no time to be swapping jokes and satires. (What? No words of courage? No urging us to put on a brave face and go shopping or visit Disneyland?) Everyone in the room knew that this was a dismal cop-out, but then everyone in the room also knew that our own profession was co-responsible. If the president actually had performed his annual duty, there were people in the press corps who would have affected shock and accused him of "insensitivity." So, this was indeed a moment of unity—everyone united in mawkishness and sloppiness and false sentiment. From now on, any president who wants to duck the occasion need only employ a staffer on permanent weepy-watch. In any given week, there is sure to be some maimed orphan, or splattered home, or bus plunge, or bunch of pilgrims put to the sword. Best to be ready in advance to surrender all critical faculties and whip out the national hankie.

It was my friend Adolph Reed who first pointed out this tendency to what he called "vicarious identification." At the time of the murder of Lisa Steinberg in New York in 1987, he was struck by the tendency of crowds to show up for funerals of people they didn't know, often throwing teddy bears over the railings and in other ways showing that (as well as needing to get a life) they in some bizarre way seemed to need to get a death. The hysteria that followed a traffic accident in Paris involving a disco princess—surely the most hyped non-event of all time—seemed to suggest an even wider surrender to the overwhelming need to emote: The less at stake, the greater the grieving.

And *surrender* may be the keyword here. What, for instance, is this dismal rush to lower the national colors all the damned time? At times of real crisis and genuine emergency, such as the assault on our society that was mounted almost six years ago, some emotion could be pardoned. But even then, the signs of sickliness and foolishness were incipient (as in Billy Graham's disgusting sermon at the National Cathedral where he spoke of the victims being "called into eternity"). If we did this every time, the flag would spend its entire time drooping. One should express a decent sympathy for the families and friends of the murdered, a decent sympathy that ought to be accompanied by a decent reticence. Because Virginia Tech—alas for poor humanity—was a calamity with no implications beyond itself. In the meantime, and in expectation of rather stiffer challenges to our composure, we might practice nailing the colors to the mast rather than engaging in a permanent dress rehearsal for masochism and the lachrymose.

(*Slate*, April 26, 2007)

A Very, Very Dirty Word

THE FOLLOWING ANECDOTE appears in one of Niall Ferguson's absorbing studies of the British Empire. On the eve of independence for the colony of South Yemen, the last British governor hosted a dinner party attended by Denis Healey, then the minister for defense. Over the final sundown cocktail, as the flag was about to be lowered over the capital of Aden, the governor turned to Healey and said, "You know, Minister, I believe that in the long view of history, the British Empire will be remembered only for two things." What, Healey was interested to know, were these imperishable aspects? "The game of soccer. And the expression 'fuck off.' "

This prediction, made almost forty years ago, now looks alarmingly prescient. Soccer enthusiasm is sweeping the globe, and both Senator John Kerry and Vice President Dick Cheney have resorted to the "fuck" word in the recent past—Kerry to say "fucked up" in connection with postwar planning in Iraq and Cheney to recommend that Senator Patrick Leahy go and attempt an anatomical impossibility. The latter advice received the signal honor of being printed in full, without asterisks, in the *Washington Post*, thus provoking some ombudsmanlike soul-searching on its own account by the paper's editor, Len Downie.

At some media-pol event in Washington after the invasion of Afghanistan, I was told by an eyewitness that Al Franken attempted an ironic congratulation of Paul Wolfowitz, saying that Bush had won by using Clinton's armed forces. "Fuck off," was the considered riposte of the deputy defense secretary.

If things go on like this—which in a way I sometimes hope they do—we will reach the point where newspapers will report exchanges deadpan, like this:

> "'Fuck off,' he shot back."
> "'Fuck off,' he suggested."
> "'Fuck off,' he opined."
> "'Fuck off,' he advised."
> "'Fuck off,' he averred."
> "'Fuck off,' he joked."
> Or even, "'Fuck off,' he quipped."

The spreading of this tremendous rejoinder by means of the British Empire or its surrogates cannot be doubted. In London, older men of Greek Cypriot descent can be heard to say, as they rise from the card game or the restaurant table, "*Thakono* fuck off," by which they mean, "I shall now take my leave"; or, "It really is high time that I returned to the bosom of my family"; or perhaps, phrased more tersely and in the modern vernacular, "I am out of here."

A friend of mine was once a junior officer in Her Majesty's forces in the Egyptian Suez Canal Zone. One of his duties was the procuring of fresh fruit for those under his command. On a certain morning, an Egyptian merchant called upon him and announced that he could furnish a regular supply of bananas. "Just the thing," replied my friend, "that we are looking for." The man then spoiled the whole effect by stating, in poor but unmistakable English, that of course in the event of an agreement Captain Lewis could expect 5 percent on top. Peter—I call him this because it is his name—thereupon became incensed. He stated that such a suggestion was an unpardonable one and added that he was sure he could find another banana merchant and that, whatever the case might be, such a banana supplier would emphatically not be the man who had just made such an outrageous proposition to a British serving officer. Sensing his own lapse in taste, the Egyptian made a courteous bow and replied with perfect gravity: "Okay, *effendi*. I fuck off now." It was plain that he had acquired his basic English from loitering around the barracks gate.

Let us not forget, in other words, the implied etiquette of the term. If shouted at a follower or supporter of another soccer team, in a moment of heat, it may connote "please go away" or even "go away in any case." But if used of oneself—dare one say passively—it may simply express the settled determination to be elsewhere. (I once heard the late Sir Kingsley Amis, describing the end of an evening of revelry, saying, "So then—off I fucked.")

"Fuck you" or "Go fuck yourself"—the popular American form—lacks this transitive/intransitive element to some degree. At points, it even seems to confuse the act of sexual intercourse with an act of aggression: a regrettable overlap to be sure. Anglo-Americanism in Iraq may turn out to be the crucible of this difference. I know from experience that older Iraqis, who remember the British period with mingled affection and resentment, are aware of the full declensions of the "fuck" verb. But to judge by their gestures, some of the younger Iraqis are a bit coarser. "Fuck off," some of them seem to be yelling at coalition forces. A lot hinges on the appropriate military response. "Fuck you" might be risky. "Okay, off we fuck, then" might buy some valuable time.

(*Slate*, July 6, 2004)

Prisoner of Shelves

IN BRUCE CHATWIN'S NOVEL *UTZ*, the eponymous character becomes the captive of his porcelain collection—and eventually loses his life because he cannot move without it. From this book, I learned that a word actually exists—*Porzellankrankheit*—for the mania for porcelain acquisition. I also learned that the root of the word is the same as that for "pig," because poured trays of molten porcelain looked so pink and fat and shiny.

I'm pretty sure of my facts here. And if I could only put my hands on the book, I could be absolutely sure. But is it shelved under U for *Utz*, or perhaps under C for Chatwin? Or is it in that unsorted pile on top of the radiator? Or the heap of volumes that migrated from the living room to the dining room? I am certain that I didn't lend it to anyone: I am utterly miserly about letting any of my books out of my sight. Yet my books don't seem to reciprocate by remaining within view, let alone within easy reach.

I live in a fairly spacious apartment in Washington, D.C. True, the apartment is also my office (though that's no excuse for piling books on the stove). But for some reason, the available shelf space, which is considerable, continues to be outrun by the appearance of new books. It used to be such a pleasure to get one of those padded envelopes in the mail, containing a brand-new book with the publisher's compliments. Now, as I collect my daily heap of these packages from my building's concierge, I receive a pitying look.

It ought to be easy to deal with this excess, at least with the superfluous new arrivals: Give them away to friends or take them to a secondhand bookseller. But the thing is, you never know. Two new histories of the Crusades have appeared in the past year, for instance, and I already have several books on those momentous events. How often, really, do I need to mention the Crusades in a column or a review? Not that often—but then, it suddenly occurs to me, not that seldom either. Best be on the safe side. Should all these books sit on the same shelf? Or should they be indexed by author? ("Index" is good: It suggests that I have a system.) Currently, I pile the Crusades books near titles on the Middle East—an unsatisfactory arrangement, but I have no "History" section as such, because then I would have to decide whether to arrange it chronologically or geographically.

Bibliomania cripples my social life. In order to have a dinner party, I must clear all the so-far-unsorted books off the dining-room table. Either that, or invite half the originally planned number of people and just push the books temporarily down to one end of it. In the spring, my wife and I host the *Vanity Fair* party that follows the White House Correspondents' Dinner, and this means that I can get professional help with rearranging the furniture and the books. This past year, the magazine's omnicompetent social organizer, Sara Marks, gave me some ingenious vertical shelf units, allowing me to stack books on their sides. Alas, there wasn't time before the festivities to sort these useful display units by author or subject, so I've only been able to alter the shape of my problem, not solve it.

The units also make it easier to read the titles on the spines and thus to suffer reproach for their randomness. And let's say I did decide to organize these books: Should I start with A for Kingsley Amis? But wait, here's a nonfiction work by Amis, on language. Shouldn't it go on the reference shelf with the lexicons and dictionaries? And what about the new biography, and the correspondence between Kingsley and Philip Larkin?

Some kind friends argue for a cull, to create more space and to provide an incentive to organize. All right, but I can't throw out a book that has been with me for any length of time and thus acquired sentimental value, or that has been written by a friend, or that has been signed or inscribed by its author. I also can't part with one that might conceivably come in handy as a work of reference, however obscure. All of which provokes newfound sympathy for poor Kaspar Utz.

(*City Journal*, Winter 2008)

Acknowledgments

The thanking of friends and colleagues and co-conspirators ought to be the most enjoyable part of the completion of any work. However, the accumulation of decades of debt now forces a choice between the invidious and the ingratiating. To give their proper due to all whom I owe would now be impossible, resulting in one of those catalogs, so redolent of the name-drop and the back-scratch, that burden so many books these days. I am therefore restricting myself to those with whom work and life have become seamless: the close comrades who have become co-workers and vice versa.

In more than three decades of knowing Steve Wasserman, he has been my editor for publishing houses and for magazines, my closest reader, and now my agent. To have a literary intellect as my man of business is a privilege: Our work together has constituted truly unalienated labor.

It is twenty years since Graydon Carter asked me to join his enterprise at *Vanity Fair,* on the promise that I would try to find all topics interesting and, in return for much travel and instruction and variety, would agree to take on any subject. Managing only to exempt competitive sports, I have tried to be true to this. Every time an essay of mine has reached the office, it has passed through the meticulous care of Aimee Bell, Walter Owen, and Peter Devine, who conceive their task as putting the highest possible finish on my drafts. (In Aimee's case, I have to call the attention "loving," in the hope that she will notice, and perhaps blush.)

At the *Atlantic,* David Bradley, Benjamin Schwarz, and James Bennett give me the unique chance to take regular notice of serious new books, and a wide latitude in which to operate my choices. Again, and with further thanks to Yvonne Rolzhausen, there follows an effort to make the printed result the superior in tone of the original version.

It was a fair day that brought me close to Jake Weisberg, David Plotz, and June Thomas at *Slate* magazine, who suggested that the need to unburden a weekly polemic or *feuilleton* could be painlessly met by a column called "Fighting Words." Can there be any writer in America who has had three regular outlets as perfectly synchronous and complementary as these?

This book is the third of mine to be brought to you by Twelve: a house that exists to disprove rumors and alarms about the continued combination of serious publishing with flair and panache. The devoted individual attention received by each author and text is rightly the subject of widespread admiration and envy. Cary Goldstein, Colin Shepherd, and Bob Castillo have wrought invisible but palpable improvements in everything I have ever brought them.

Over a rather grueling past twelve months, those mentioned above have also been invaluable in helping me to stay alive, and to give me—it's not too much to say—persuasive reasons for doing so. This increases the bond, and makes it indissoluble. In that connection, while I cannot begin to thank everybody, I must mention Dr. Fred Smith of Bethesda, Maryland, Drs. James Cox and Jaffer Ajani of the M.D. Anderson Cancer Center in Houston (home of the world's most emancipating form of radiation); and Dr. Francis Collins of the National Institutes of Health. Without the persuasive powers of my exceptional wife, Carol Blue, I might well not have had the fortitude or the patience to enter some of these treatments, or to persist with them. That recognition and acknowledgment lies somewhere beyond gratitude: Any surrender to fatalism or despair would have been as rank a betrayal of what I hope to stand for as any capitulation to magical or wishful schemes would have been. Then not lastly but at last to my tough, smart, brave, humorous children—Alexander, Sophia, and Antonia—who are a living marvel in themselves but who also represent all I can ever hope to claim by way of futurity.

Index

Numerals in boldface indicate pages where the author and/or work is specifically the subject of a review or prose piece.

About the Author

Christopher Hitchens was born in 1949 in England and is a graduate of Balliol College at Oxford University. He is the father of three children and the author of more than twenty books and pamphlets, including collections of essays, criticism, and reportage. His book, *God Is Not Great: How Religion Poisons Everything*, was a finalist for the 2007 National Book Award and an international bestseller. His bestselling memoir, *Hitch-22*, was a finalist for the 2010 National Book Critics Circle Award for autobiography. A visiting professor of liberal studies at the New School in New York City, he has also been the I.F. Stone professor at the Graduate School of Journalism at the University of California, Berkeley. He has been a columnist, literary critic, and contributing editor at *Vanity Fair, The Atlantic, Slate, Times Literary Supplement, The Nation, New Statesman, World Affairs, Free Inquiry*, among other publications.

About TWELVE

TWELVE was established in August 2005 with the objective of publishing no more than one book per month. We strive to publish the singular book, by authors who have a unique perspective and compelling authority. Works that explain our culture; that illuminate, inspire, provoke, and entertain. We seek to establish communities of conversation surrounding our books. Talented authors deserve attention not only from publishers, but from readers as well. To sell the book is only the beginning of our mission. To build avid audiences of readers who are enriched by these works—that is our ultimate purpose.

For more information about forthcoming TWELVE books, please go to www.twelvebooks.com.